# REASON AND INSPIRATION IN ISLAM

# REASON AND INSPIRATION IN ISLAM

## THEOLOGY, PHILOSOPHY AND MYSTICISM IN MUSLIM THOUGHT

*Essays in Honour of Hermann Landolt*

*Edited by*

**TODD LAWSON**

For Mike + Betty
for everything

I.B.Tauris *Publishers*
LONDON • NEW YORK
*in association with*
The Institute of Ismaili Studies
LONDON

Published in 2005 by I.B.Tauris & Co Ltd
6 Salem Rd, London W2 4BU
175 Fifth Avenue, New York NY 10010
www.ibtauris.com

in association with The Institute of Ismaili Studies
42–44 Grosvenor Gardens, London SW1W 0EB
www.iis.ac.uk

In the United States of America and in Canada distributed by
St Martin's Press, 175 Fifth Avenue, New York NY 10010



ISBN 1 85043 470 0
EAN 978 1 85043 470 2

A full CIP record for this book is available from the British Library
A full CIP record for this book is available from the Library of Congress

Library of Congress catalog card: available

Typeset in Minion Tra for The Institute of Ismaili Studies

Printed and bound in Great Britain by MPG Books Ltd, Bodmin

# The Institute of Ismaili Studies

The Institute of Ismaili Studies was established in 1977 with the object of promoting scholarship and learning on Islam, in the historical as well as contemporary contexts, and a better understanding of its relationship with other societies and faiths.

The Institute's programmes encourage a perspective which is not confined to the theological and religious heritage of Islam, but seeks to explore the relationship of religious ideas to broader dimensions of society and culture. The programmes thus encourage an interdisciplinary approach to the materials of Islamic history and thought. Particular attention is also given to issues of modernity that arise as Muslims seek to relate their heritage to the contemporary situation.

Within the Islamic tradition, the Institute's programmes promote research on those areas which have, to date, received relatively little attention from scholars. These include the intellectual and literary expressions of Shiʿism in general, and Ismailism in particular.

In the context of Islamic societies, the Institute's programmes are informed by the full range and diversity of cultures in which Islam is practised today, from the Middle East, South and Central Asia, and Africa to the industrialised societies of the West, thus taking into consideration the variety of contexts which shape the ideals, beliefs and practices of the faith.

These objectives are realised through concrete programmes and activities organised and implemented by various departments of the Institute. The Institute also collaborates periodically, on a programme-specific basis, with other institutions of learning in the United Kingdom and abroad.

The Institute's academic publications fall into a number of interrelated categories:

1. Occasional papers or essays addressing broad themes of the relationship between religion and society, with special reference to Islam.
2. Monographs exploring specific aspects of Islamic faith and culture, or the contributions of individual Muslim thinkers or writers.
3. Editions or translations of significant primary or secondary texts.
4. Translations of poetic or literary texts which illustrate the rich heritage of spiritual, devotional and symbolic expressions in Muslim history.
5. Works on Ismaili history and thought, and the relationship of the Ismailis to other traditions, communities and schools of thought in Islam.
6. Proceedings of conferences and seminars sponsored by the Institute.
7. Bibliographical works and catalogues which document manuscripts, printed texts and other source materials.

This book falls into category two listed above.

In facilitating these and other publications, the Institute's sole aim is to encourage original research and analysis of relevant issues. While every effort is made to ensure that the publications are of a high academic standard, there is naturally bound to be a diversity of views, ideas and interpretations. As such, the opinions expressed in these publications must be understood as belonging to their authors alone.

# Contents

# Acknowledgements

I would first like to thank the contributors for the patience they have shown over the long gestation period needed for a volume of this kind. They, clearly, have the greatest role to play in this Festschrift and but for their cooperation and goodwill there would be no achievement. Annette Landolt deserves special praise for her enthusiasm and the assistance she has offered as undercover agent from the project's earliest days.

Dr Farhad Daftary's interest and encouragement have been most valuable. Several colleagues have been very helpful during the planning, collection and preparation of the volume. First and foremost is Professor Mohammad Ali Amir-Moezzi who generously offered encouragement, advice and assistance. I am also grateful to Dr Leonard Lewisohn of The Institute of Ismaili Studies and Dr Elizabeth Alexandrin of the University of Manitoba. Sincere thanks likewise go to Professor Parviz Morewedge whose and initiative inspired the original idea and to Dr Etin Anwar of Temple University for her initial editorial contribution. I would also like to express my gratitude and appreciation to the editors at The Institute of Ismaili Studies and I.B. Tauris who have spent many hours on the project. Without their interest, dedication, skill, patience and good humour there would be no Festschrift. It has been a pleasure working with them.

Professor B. Todd Lawson
Department of Near and Middle Eastern Civilizations
University of Toronto

# Note on the Transliteration and Abbreviations

The system of transliteration used in this book for the Arabic and Persian scripts is that of the new edition of *The Encyclopaedia of Islam*, with a few modifications, namely ch for č, j for dj, and q for ḳ; ligatures are also dispensed with. Diacritical marks are dispensed with for some of the dynastic and community names which occur frequently in the book and are treated as common English words in *The Concise Oxford Dictionary*. The most important of these are Abbasid for ʿAbbāsid, Fatimid for Fāṭimid, Ismaili for Ismāʿīlī, Sufi for Ṣūfī and Sunni for Sunnī. Certain articles, however, follow their own transliteration systems notably those by Mohammad Ali Amir-Moezzi and Bert Fragner.

The lunar years of the Islamic calendar are generally followed by the corresponding Gregorian solar years (for example, 11/632). The Islamic solar dates of the sources published in modern Iran are indicated by the suffix Sh., and are followed by the corresponding Christian years starting on 21 March.

The following abbreviations are used for certain periodicals and encyclopaedias cited frequently in the essay notes.

| | |
|---|---|
| *AS/EA* | *Asiatische Studien/Etudes Asiatiques* |
| *BCAI* | *Bulletin Critique des Annales Islamologiques* |
| *BSOAS* | *Bulletin of the School of Oriental and African Studies* |
| *EAL* | *The Encyclopedia of Arabic Literature*, ed. J. S. Meisami and P. Starkey. London, 1998 |
| *EI2* | *Encyclopaedia of Islam*, ed. H. A. R. Gibb et al., New Edition. Leiden, 1960–2004 |
| *EIr* | *Encyclopaedia Iranica*, ed. E. Yarshater. London and New York, 1982—. |

| | |
|---|---|
| *EJ* | *Eranos Jahrbuch* |
| *ER* | *Encyclopaedia of Religion*, ed. M. Eliade. New York and London, 1987 |
| *EU* | *Encyclopaedia Universalis: Le Grand Atlas des Religions*, ed. C. Baladier et al., 1988 |
| *GAL* | C. Brockelmann, *Geschichte der arabischen Literatur*, 2nd. ed. Leiden, 1943–1949 |
| *GALS* | C. Brockelmann, *Geschichte der arabischen Literatur*, Supplementbände. Leiden, 1937–1942 |
| *GAS* | F. Sezgin, *Geschichte des arabischen Schrifttums*. Leiden, 1967—. |
| IJMES | *International Journal of Middle Eastern Studies* |
| *JA* | *Journal Asiatique* |
| *JAAR* | *Journal of the American Academy of Religion* |
| *JAOS* | *Journal of the American Oriental Society* |
| *JIS* | *Journal of Islamic Studies* |
| *JNES* | *Journal of Near Eastern Studies* |
| *JRAS* | *Journal of the Royal Asiatic Society* |
| *JTS* | *Journal of Turkish Studies* |
| *MEJ* | *The Middle East Journal* |
| *MW* | *The Muslim World* |
| *RT* | *Religious Traditions* |
| *SI* | *Studia Islamica* |
| *SIr* | *Studia Iranica* |
| *ZDMG* | *Zeitschrift der Deutschen Morgenländischen Gesellschaft* |

# List of Contributors

| | |
|---|---|
| Todd Lawson | University of Toronto (Academic Editor) |
| Elizabeth Ross Alexandrin | McGill University, Montreal |
| Sajida S. Alvi | McGill University, Montreal |
| Mohammad Ali Amir-Moezzi | École Pratique des Hautes Études, Section de sciences religieuses (Sorbonne) |
| Etin Anwar | Temple Universiy, Philadelphia |
| William C. Chittick | State University of New York |
| Michel Chodkiewicz | École des Hautes Études en Sciences Sociales (Sorbonne) |
| L. Clarke | Concordia University, Montreal |
| Karim Douglas Crow | International Institute of Islamic Thought and Civilization, Kuala Lumpur |
| Farhad Daftary | The Institute of Ismaili Studies, London |
| Devin DeWeese | Indiana University |
| Bert G. Fragner | Karl Wilhelm Friedrich Universität, Bamberg |
| Soraya Mahdi Hajjajji-Jarrah | McGill University, Montreal |
| Peter Heath | American University of Beirut |
| F. M. Hunzai | The Institute of Ismaili Studies, London |
| Shigeru Kamada | University of Tokyo |
| Ahmet T. Karamustafa | Washington University, St. Louis |
| Leonard Lewisohn | The Institute of Ismaili Studies, London |
| Donald P. Little | McGill University, Montreal |
| Pierre Lory | École Pratique des Hautes Études, Section des sciences religieuses (Sorbonne) |

| | |
|---|---|
| Wilferd Madelung | University of Oxford and The Institute of Ismaili Studies, London |
| Roxanne Marcotte | University of Queensland |
| Richard J. A. McGregor | McGill University, Montreal |
| Mehdi Mohaghegh | University of Tehran |
| James Winston Morris | University of Exeter |
| Ahmad Kazemi Moussavi | International Institute of Islamic Thought and Civilization, Kuala Lumpur |
| Shin Nomoto | Keio University |
| Eric Ormsby | McGill University, Montreal |
| Fabienne Pironet | Université de Montréal |
| Nasrollah Pourjavady | University of Tehran |
| Bernd Radtke | University of Groningen |
| Bulbul Shah | The Institute of Ismaili Studies, London |
| Diana Steigerwald | California State University |
| Abdollah Vakily | McGill University, Montreal |
| Shafique Virani | Zayed University, UEA |
| John Walbridge | Indiana University |
| Paul E. Walker | University of Chicago |

# Introduction

*Todd Lawson*

The contributions collected here, and the art work which serves as the basis for the cover design, reflect the esteem, respect and affection in which Hermann Landolt, as Professor Emeritus of Islamic Thought at the Institute of Islamic Studies of McGill University is held by his peers and students around the world. The purpose of this Introduction must be to say a few words about the one who is the object of such attention. The facts are easy: Hermann Albert Landolt was born in 1935 in Basel Switzerland. His academic interests were, from his student days, anthropology, ethnology, philology, philosophy, Islamology and religious studies. He studied at the University of Basel under Alfred Bühler and Fritz Meier with whom he eventually wrote his Ph.D. dissertation. But before this research had been completed, *in medias res* as it were, Landolt – attracted to new scholarship in a slightly different key – left Basel for Paris to work with Henry Corbin. The research resulting from this would earn him a *diplôme* from the religious studies section of the Sorbonne's École Practique des Hautes Études. Landolt came to Canada in 1964 to teach at McGill's Institute of Islamic Studies. The Institute was, in those days, a relatively new entity. It had been founded ten years earlier by Wilfred Cantwell Smith, whose experience of the Islamic world had inspired with him a deep and abiding mission: to establish a place of study dedicated to bringing scholars from East and West together so that they might learn something of and from each other. In the pursuit of such a goal, the Institute had become a lively centre of Islamic studies, attracting such internationally-known scholars as Fazlur Rahman, Niyazi Berkes, and Toshihiko Izutsu, amongst many others. So when the then director, Charles Adams, needing a Persianist to round out the work of the Institute, asked Corbin for a recommendation, it was to such a unique milieu that Landolt would be welcomed for his first 'job' as a young scholar. Over a period of thirty-five years, he acquired a reputation as one of the Institute's leading scholars and, in the realm of student supervision, one of its more demanding taskmasters. From that day to this, his scholarly output has continued to be manifest in two distinct but profoundly related ways. The first is through his publications and the second is through his students. To some degree, his scholarship naturally reflects an ongoing conversation with both of his renowned teachers, Henry Corbin and Fritz Meier. But there are other traces as well.

The interests and activities of Landolt's professional life might best be represented by the triad: Philosophy, Sufism and Shiʿism. This life includes the position as Professor of Islamic Thought at McGill's Institute of Islamic Studies, Senior Research Fellow at The Institute of Ismaili Studies (where he was Head of Graduate Studies and Research in the early 1980s), or *Chercheur associé* with the Institut Français de Recherche en Iran and Guest Professor at the Sorbonne. But the triad does not tell the whole story. Landolt started academic life with an interest in ethnology and anthropology at Basel University where he also studied classical philology. This was during the 1950s, and Basel was home to scholars, such as the existentialists Karl Jaspers and Karl Barth, who had transferred from German universities, and Swiss scholars such as the above-mentioned Meier, or the ethnologist Alfred Bühler, who was the director of Landolt's Ph.D. thesis on the 'institution' of the prayer carpet in Sufism. Another influence at Basel was the anthropologist, Rudolph Gelpke, translator of, among other things, Niẓāmī's *Majnūn and Laylā*. The interest in anthropology and ethnology would eventually lead Landolt to spend his first year in Iran in 1960 as part of a Swiss-sponsored ethno-linguistic research project. But this interest would also lend a permanent and important dimension to his scholarly approach that went beyond mere philosophy.

As mentioned above, Landolt departed from the usual regime at Basel to embark upon a journey that would ultimately take him closer to an intellectual and spiritual home. His work with Henry Corbin has undoubtedly made by far the deepest impression of all of the influences on him. Yet, the 'Swiss approach' would never be abandoned. Ultimately, and reflecting what Islamic philosophical mysticism esteems as the hallmark of the human vocation, Landolt has successfully joined the two opposites in his own work. The proposition that the intellect is incapable of winning the prize of absolute certainty is, of course, held as an absolute certitude by classical Sufism. And, it is partly as a response to such paradoxes (or tautologies) that some of the ideas in Landolt's work have taken form. One of these is characterised by a theme that seems to run through Landolt's publications, namely the problems that arise in the relationship between prophetic religion and philosophy, or in terms used by Landolt, the dialogue between a static and dynamic ontology. His scholarship in depth, breadth and detail is remarkable for the insights it gives us into the individual particularity of the datum, whether it is an idea, or a motif, or an individual. The one orthodoxy he appears to follow is that of rigorous and careful scholarly praxis. Of course he would be the first to admit that even such a presumably transparent and benign orthodoxy will have its effect in the end. Ultimately, it is clear that with Hermann Landolt, such 'dogmatism' is adopted in the service of learning, and not in the service of itself.

His bibliography lists monographs on Iṣfarā'inī and Simnānī, detailed studies of the thought of Ibn 'Arabī's teachings, spiritual progeny ('Abd al-Razzāq Kāshānī) or influence (positive or negative) on such Persian Kubrā-influenced mystics as Sa'd al-Dīn Hamūya, Simnānī, 'Azīz Nasafī, and Ḥaydar Āmulī. In addition, he has published research on intricate and subtle problems in the works of Abū Ḥāmid al-Ghazālī, Suhrawardī's *al-Maqtūl*, Najm al-Dīn 'Daya' al-Rāzī, Naṣīr al-Dīn Ṭūsī and a translation of most of the important work by the early Ismaili philosopher, Abū Ya'qūb al-Sijistānī – the *Kashf al-maḥjūb*. Numerous encyclopedia articles such as '*Walāyah*' in the Eliade *Encyclopedia of Religion*, or '*Wudjūd*' in the *Encyclopaedia of Islam*, stand out as key summary contributions on the status of their respective questions. His many reviews in the *Bulletin critique* and other major journals over the years may be thought to give an insight into Landolt the teacher and director of student research, in addition to providing careful guidance to the reader about whatever publication might be under scrutiny at the time. In addition to these publications in German, French and English, there have been over the years numerous others in Persian books and periodicals, some as conscious contributions, and others as 'unauthorised' translations of articles or lectures.

In Landolt's scholarship there is perhaps a certain emphasis on the spiritual (a very unsatisfactory word here) phenomenon, but not to the exclusion of its context, what religious studies calls the *Sitz im Leben*. This means the pertinent history, political or otherwise, tragic or comic, that configures the circumstances in which the various thinkers that have attracted his interest worked and lived. It is not so much that the disciplines of history and/or historiography actually portray *what really happened* in some way. Rather, in Landolt's approach, they provide the setting and context for *what really happened* which was mostly the internal movements and articulations in the human mind – in contemplation and meditation and discursive thought. To strike an analogy from Qur'anic studies, history certainly does occur, but as *asbāb al-nuzūl*; Landolt is primarily concerned with the *tanzīl*. Although we frequently find the former technical term translated as the Causes of the Revelation, Islamic tradition would never see such causality in the Aristotelian sense; rather it prefers to translate the term *asbāb* as 'occasions' or *moyens*, in keeping with that most Islamic of convictions, that history and the world are theatres for the performance of the *āyāt* – 'signs' – in whatever garb they happen to choose in order to best point to the *haqā'iq* – 'divine realities'. It is obvious that our teacher, friend and colleague is mightily attracted to and by these realities.

At McGill, Professor Landolt was responsible for – in addition to Persian language studies – something called Islamic Thought. For Landolt, this was mainly philosophy and mysticism and his seminars typically were structured around a given thinker, such as Mullā Ṣadrā, al-Sijistānī, or Nāṣir-i Khusraw, or around problems in technical terminology. Usually it was during these seminars that students were introduced to his meticulous and painstaking approach to texts and his insistence upon absolute honesty (as distinct from 'objectivity') in scholarship, which would lead ultimately to independent thought. The remarkable number of Ph.D. dissertations and M.A. theses completed under his direct supervision indicate the degree to which such an approach was welcomed by students. (He directly supervised thirty-eight Master's theses and twenty Doctoral dissertations covering a wide variety of problems and themes.) Once the contract was signed, so to speak, a student could expect clear criticism, a willingness to spend generous amounts of time in consultation, reasonable judgements, a rare openness to the seriousness of the life of the mind and various scholarly approaches or methodologies – all with a characteristic (if uncommon) measure of fun and humour. This is called dedication.

Several of these dissertations went on to publication and, in some instances, have become classics of contemporary Islamic studies. One thinks here of the groundbreaking work on the Tustarī *tafsīr*, or the pioneering study of the Chishtī 'saint' Gisūdarāz (which, incidentally, had been an M.A. thesis). Other Ph.D. dissertations directed by Landolt cover such widely variegated topics as the life and work of Bāyazīd al-Bistāmī (also published), nineteenth-century jihad movements in West Africa, a structuralist study of 'poverty' in Sufism, the thought of Ḥamīd al-Dīn Kirmānī, Ottoman Sufism (published), the Qur'an commentary of the Bāb (published), the development in nineteenth-century Shiʿism of the office of *Marjaʿ-i taqlīd* (published), the theosophical Shiʿi milieu of thirteenth-century Bahrain, the twelfth-century scholar of religions, al-Shahrastānī (published), early Shiʿi doctrine, Hayy ibn Yaqzān in his various guises, the role of *ʿaql* in the Jaʿfar al-Ṣādiq corpus, contemporary Islamic political and religious thought, the thought of Abū Ḥātim al-Rāzī, al-Suhrawardī on Avicenna, *walāya* according to Muhammad and Ali Wafā, the influence of the Qādiriyya Naqshbandiyya on Indonesian education, and finally al-Muʾayyad fi'l-Dīn al-Shīrāzī.

We forbear listing each Master's thesis directed by Landolt; but it was well known that he required the same sort of rigour (from both student and teacher) regardless of the level of the particular project. Many of 'his' M.A.s are distinguished as original, in-depth explorations and soundings in Islamic Thought based on primary sources in Arabic and Persian.

In addition to the official teaching and supervision, and of course the usual administrative committees, reports, councils, and meetings that plague the contemporary university scene, Landolt also found the time and energy to provide what was truly an invaluable service to his students. Hermann, with his wife Annette (or 'Mrs Landolt' in this context), welcomed on a weekly basis into the warmth of their own home, the international and diverse assortment of persons who made up the student population at the Institute. These '*chai khāna*'s' were deeply appreciated by all, whether they hailed from the towering mountains of Hunza, the 'old world' culture of Europe, or the 'new world' culture of North America. Even if Montreal was not experienced as a foreign and inhospitable city, the Institute itself, with a faculty and curriculum entailing subjects, names and approaches frequently remote and aloof, was at times experienced as an isolated impenetrable fortress and a lonely place. The gatherings offered an opportunity for stimulating conversation, a relaxed sociability and a welcome respite from the anxieties and pressures academic life.

The essays and articles gathered here represent a significant contribution to our knowledge of Islamic thought. As such, they are published with the purpose of expressing our collective admiration for, gratitude and appreciation to and affection for Hermann Landolt: admiration for his unfailingly thorough and stimulating scholarship, gratitude for his guidance along the road of learning, appreciation for the knowledge he has either imparted or catalysed, for his publications and teaching, and affection he inspires as a practising human being.

The philosophy behind the selection process had less to do with conforming to some strict, and therefore exclusive, thematic guideline than with taking account of just who had worked under or with Landolt and those known to be scholars whom Landolt particularly esteems. Contributors were asked to conform to one stricture: their contribution should be made with a view as to how, in their own minds, they might honour our scholar. Hoping thus that the finished volume might reflect the rigorous openness of Landolt's own style and preoccupations, it was thought best to encourage invitees to specify their own topics for this Festschrift. Thus, we have a cornucopia, rather than a thematic volume as such. Many of the articles are concerned with philosophers and philosophical problems bearing the presence of Shi'i Islam – Ismaili or Ithnā'asharī – and many are concerned with Sufism.

The passage of time being one thing we can all agree on, the articles are arranged in chronological order. The contents are divided into five major periods according to the imprecise designations: Classical, Early Medieval, Later Medieval, Pre-Modern and Modern. The somewhat unscientific principle obtains: articles have been assigned to one of these categories based either on the date of death of the main subject in the case of persons or on the date of the texts involved. If there is a theme, then it is the very broad one of Islamicate Thought. But since Hodgson's perfectly sensible terminological suggestion of forty or so years ago has not been adopted by scholars – and we certainly do not wish to innovate – we have used the formulation, Islamic Thought. Thus, all the papers deal with matters theological, philosophical or mystical – or all three. One might object that the few papers here on history or historiography do not fall into this category. Contemporary tastes are disinclined to see historical problems in the light (or the shade) of spiritual concerns (how else could we possibly be objective after all?) But, history was hardly seen by the great representatives of the intellectual tradition treated here – beginning with the Qur'an itself – to be beyond the pale of religious or theological import and contemplation. Rather, in this tradition, what the vulgar called 'history' has always been seen as a religio-philosophical topic.

Ideally, the title of the volume *Reason and Inspiration* does identify two modes of thought and expression frequently problematised in Landolt's work. We hope he approves of the order of the two elements here. But then, one can easily imagine reversing this order and deriving sense from the reversal. We have a feeling that our scholar would consider this to be as it should be. The title also could have explicitly signalled another Islamic institution, that of friendship, *walāya* – a mode, theme, and topic frequently present in Landolt's distinctive scholarship and teaching (and certainly present in several of the papers collected here). After all, *walāya* is that which supplies the link between reason and inspiration. Perhaps it is also as it should be that this most important of topics remains only tacitly alluded to and invisible.

Todd Lawson
Montreal
July 2005

# Bibliography of the Works of Hermann Landolt

## 1958

***Review***

Mazahéry, Aly, *So lebten die Muselmanen im Mittelalter*, Stuttgart, 1957 (*Literaturblatt der Basler Nachrichten*, 111/11, 14 March 1958)

## 1960

'Kulturelle Beziehungen', *Sonntagsblatt der Basler Nachrichten*, 54. Jahrgang Nr. 29 - Beilage zu Nr. 310 (24 July 1960) [review-article of forum on a 'dialogue islamo-chrétien sur le plan théologique' with contributions by H. Laoust, H. Corbin, O. Yahya, et al., in *Monde non chrétien*, 51–52 (1960), pp. 79–151].

## 1962

***Translation***

'Henry Corbin: Mīr Dāmād und die Ispahaner Schule der Theologie im 17. Jahrhundert', *Antaios*, 3, 6 (1962), pp. 497–521 [German translation of 'Mîr Dâmâd et l'école théologique d'Ispahan au XVIIe siècle' published in *Études carmélitaines: Polarité du symbole*, 1960].

## 1963

***Translation***

'Henry Corbin: Über die philosophische Situation der Shî'itischen Religion', *Antaios* 5, 2 (1963), pp. 177–200 [German translation of 'De la situation philosophique du shî'isme' published in *Monde non chrétien*, 70 (1964), pp. 61–85].

'Henry Corbin: Über die prophetische Philosophie im shî'itischen Islam', *EJ*, 31 (1963), pp. 453–457 [German summary of 'De la philosophie prophétique en Islam shî'ite' in the same *Eranos* volume, pp. 49–116].

**1964**

'L'Epître sur le soufisme de Nûroddîn 'Abdorraḥmân-e Esfarâyenî intitulée *Kâshif al-Asrâr*', in *Annuaire de l'École Pratique des Hautes Études*, Section des Sciences Religieuses, 72 (1964–1965), pp. 150–155.

**1965**

'Gedanken zum islamischen Gebetsteppich. Eine vorläufige Skizze', in C. A. Schmitz, ed., *Festschrift Alfred Bühler*, Basler Beiträge zur Geographie und Ethnologie, Ethnologische Reihe, 2 (Basel, 1965), pp. 243–256.

**1971**

Editor with Mehdi Mohaghegh, *Collected Papers on Islamic Philosophy and Mysticism*. Wisdom of Persia Series, IV (Tehran, 1971).

'Simnânî on *Waḥdat al-Wujûd*', in M. Mohaghegh and H. Landolt, ed., *Collected Papers on Islamic Philosophy and Mysticism*. Wisdom of Persia Series, IV (Tehran, 1971), pp. 91–112.

**1972**

Editor of *Correspondance spirituelle échangée entre Nûroddîn Esfarâyenî (ob. 717/1317) et son disciple 'Alâ'oddawleh Semnânî (ob. 736/1336)*, Texte persan publié avec une introduction. Bibliothèque Iranienne, XXI (Tehran and Paris, 1972).

'Mystique iranienne: Suhrawardī *Shaykh al-Ishrāq* (549/1155–587/1191) et 'Ayn al-Quḍāt-i Hamadānī (429/1098–525/1131)', in C. J. Adams, ed., *Iranian Civilization and Culture. Essays in Honour of the 2500th Anniversary of the Founding of the Persian Empire* (Montreal, 1972), pp. 23–37.

**1973**

'Der Briefwechsel zwischen Kāšānī und Simnānī über *Waḥdat al-Wuǧūd*', *Der Islam*, 50 (1973), pp. 29–81.

**1974**

'Introduction', in M. R. Shafī'ī-Kadkanī, ed., *Marmūzāt-i Asadī dar Mazmūrāt-i Dāwūdī*. Wisdom of Persia Series, VI (Tehran, 1974; rpr. Tehran, 2002), pp. 1–30.

**1975**

***Review***

Nasr, Seyyed Hossein, *Sufi Essays*, Albany, 1973 (*Der Islam*, 52, 1975, pp. 152–153).

**1976**

(with Annette Landolt-Tüller), 'Qalamkar-Druck in Isfahan', in Beiträge zur Kenntnis traditioneller Textilfärbetechniken in Persien, *Verhandlungen der Naturforschenden Gesellschaft in Basel*, 87/88 (1976/1977), pp. 47–80.

**1977**

'Deux opuscules de Semnânî sur le moi théophanique', in S. H. Nasr, ed., *Mélanges offerts à Henry Corbin*. Wisdom of Persia Series, IX (Tehran, 1977), pp. 279–319.

'Khalwa', *EI2*, 1977.

'Sakralraum und mystischer Raum im Islam', *EJ*, 44 (1977), pp. 231–265.

'Two Types of Mystical Thought in Muslim Iran: An Essay' (English translation of 'Mystique iranienne'), *MW*, 68, 3 (1977), pp. 187–204.

**1980**

Editor of Nûruddîn ʿAbdurraḥmân-i Isfarâyinî (1242–1317), *Kâshif al-Asrâr*, Texte persan publié avec deux annexes, une traduction et une introduction. Wisdom of Persia Series, V (Tehran, 1980).

'Two Types of Mystical Thought in Muslim Iran: An Essay' (English translation of 'Mystique iranienne'), *MW*, 70 (1980), pp. 83–84.

**1981**

'Stufen der Gotteserkenntnis und das Lob der Torheit bei Najm-e Râzî (ob. 654/1256)', *EJ*, 46 (1981), pp. 175–204 [see below revised English translation, 'Stages of God-cognition...' in *SUFI*, Autumn 2000].

'Témoignage', in C. Jambet, ed., *Henry Corbin* (Paris, 1981), p. 304.

**1982**

***Reviews***

Akhavi, Shahrough, *Religion and Politics in Contemporary Iran: Clergy-State Relations in the Pahlavi Period*, Albany, NY, 1980 (*JAAR*, March, 1982, pp. 120–121).

Corbin, Henry, *The Man of Light in Iranian Sufism*, Translated from the French by Nancy Pearson, Boulder, CO, and London, 1978 (*JAOS*, 102, 1982, pp. 213–214) [This review also appeared in slightly modified form in *Sciences Religieuses/Studies in Religion*, 10/3 (1981), pp. 370–372].

Nasir-i Khusraw, *Forty Poems from the Divan*, tr. Peter Lamborn Wilson and Gholam Reza Aavani, Tehran, 1977 (*JAOS*, 102, 1982, pp. 214–216).

Nasr, Seyyed Hossein, ed., *Ismāʿīlī Contributions to Islamic Culture*, Tehran, 1977 (*JAOS*, 102, 1982, p. 213).

*The Precious Pearl: Al-Jāmī's* al-Durrah al-Fākhirah *together with his Glosses and the Commentary of ʿAbd al-Ghafūr al-Lārī*, tr. Nicholas Heer, Albany, NY, 1979 (*JNES*, 41, April 1982, p. 159).

Richard, Yann, *Le shî ʿisme en Iran: Imam et Révolution*, Paris, 1980 (*JAAR*, March, 1982, pp. 120–121).

**1983**

Editor of, Henry Corbin, *Cyclical Time and Ismaili Gnosis*, tr. R. Manheim and J. W. Morris. Islamic Texts and Contexts (London, 1983).

Preface to Syed Shah Khusro Hussaini, *Sayyid Muḥammad al-Ḥusaynī-i Gīsūdirāz (721/1321–825/1422): On Sufism* (Delhi, 1983), pp. xv–xvii.

'Abu'l-Ḥasan Kharaqānī', 'Abu'l-Wafā', *EIr*, 1983.

**1984**

'Ismāʿīlī and Ṣūfī Attitudes to Transmigration', in Y. Tatsuro, ed., *International Congress of Human Sciences in Asia and North Africa*, Proceedings of ICHSANA, vol. I (Tokyo, 1984), pp. 293–294 [abstract of paper].

(with T. Izutsu), 'Sufism, Mysticism, Structuralism – A Dialogue', *Religious Traditions*, 7–9 (1984–1986), pp. 1–24 [A Japanese translation of this English 'Dialogue' was first published in *Shisô*, 6 (1984), pp. 22–52. Indonesian translation in *Ulumul Qur'an*, 1 (1989), pp. 60–69].

**1986**

Editor of Nûruddîn Isfarâyinî, *Le Révélateur des mystères – Kâshif al-Asrâr*, Texte Persan publié avec deux annexes, traduction et étude préliminaire. Collection 'Islam spirituel' (Lagrasse, 1986) [2nd revised edition of *Kâshif al-Asrâr*].

**1987**

'Suhrawardī's Tales of Initiation (Review Article)', *JAOS*, 107 (1987), pp. 475–486.

'Walāyah', *ER*, 1987.

***Reviews***

Chodkiewicz, Michel, *Le Sceau des saints. Prophétie et sainteté dans la doctrine d'Ibn Arabî*, Paris, 1986 (*BCAI*, 4, 1987, pp. 83–85).

Freitag, Rainer, *Seelenwanderung in der islamischen Häresie*, Berlin, 1985 (*BCAI*, 4, 1987, pp. 58–61).

Marquet, Yves, *Poésie ésotérique ismaélienne. La* Tā'iyya *de 'Āmir b. 'Āmir al-Baṣrī*, Paris, 1985 (*BCAI*, 4, 1987, pp. 64–65).

*The Path of God's Bondsmen from Origin to Return...* Translated from the Persian by Hamid Algar, New York, 1982 (*JAOS*, 107, 1987, pp. 803–805).

**1988**

'La prière et la vie mystique (Islam)', *EU*, 1988.

***Review***

Shahrastani, *Livre des religions et des sectes*, *I*, tr. Daniel Gimaret and Guy Monnot, Louvain, 1986 (*BCAI*, 5, 1988, pp. 63–65).

**1989**

(with Fred A. Reed, et al.), 'Deciphering Babel: Translation and Communication', *CBC Ideas* (27 February/6 March 1989).

**1990**

***Reviews***

Addas, Claude, *Ibn 'Arabī ou la quête du soufre rouge*, Paris, 1989 (*BCAI*, 7, 1990, pp. 47–49).

Chittick, William C., *The Sufi Path of Knowledge: Ibn al-Arabi's Metaphysics of Imagination*, Albany, NY, 1989 (*MEJ*, 44, 1990, pp. 336–337).

*Das Sendschreiben al-Qušayrīs über das Sufitum*, eingeleitet, übersetzt und kommentiert von Richard Gramlich, Stuttgart, 1989 (*BCAI*, 7, 1990, pp. 39–41).

Sejestani, Abû Ya'qûb, *Le Dévoilement des choses cachées* (Kashf al-Mahjûb)*: Recherches de philosophie ismaélienne*, tr. Henry Corbin, Lagrasse, 1988 (*BCAI*, 7, 1990, p. 65).

**1991**

'Ghazālī and "Religionswissenschaft": Some Notes on the *Mishkāt al-Anwār* – For Professor Charles J. Adams', *AS/EA*, 45 (1991), pp. 19–72. [Persian translation in: *Muḥaqqiq-Nāma*, ed. B. Khurramshāhī (Tehran, 1380/2001), pp. 1020–1086; re-published in *Dar-Amadī bar Kashākash-i Ghazālī wa Ismāʿīliyān* ed. M. Karīmī-Zanjānī-Aṣl (Tehran, 1381/[2002]), vol. 2, pp. 463–543].

***Review***

Meier, Fritz, *Bahāʾ-i Walad. Grundzüge seines Lebens und seiner Mystik*, Leiden, 1989 (*BCAI*, 8, 1991, pp. 50–51).

**1994**

'Kurbin va Īzūtsū az Nigāh-i Landūlt', *Kiyān*, 17 (1372/[1994]), pp. 48–50.

***Reviews***

Ebn-e Monavvar, Mohammad, *The Secrets of God's Mystical Oneness or The Spiritual Stations of Shaikh Abū Saʿīd*, tr. John O'Kane, Costa Mesa, CA, and New York, 1992 (*BCAI*, 11, 1994, p. 85).

Hamadâni, ʿAyn Al-Quzât, *Les Tentations métaphysiques* (Tamhîdât). *Présentation, traduction...* par Christiane Tortel, Paris, 1992 (*BCAI*, 11, 1994, pp. 86–87).

Radtke, Bernd, ed., *Drei Schriften des Theosophen von Tirmiḏ: Das Buch vom Leben der Gottesfreunde; Ein Antwortschreiben nach Saraḫs; Ein Antwortschreiben nach Rayy*, Beirut and Stuttgart, 1991 (*JAOS*, 114, 1994, pp. 303–304).

Radtke, Bernd, ed., *Adab al-Mulūk: Ein Handbuch zur islamischen Mystik aus dem 4./10. Jahrhundert*, Beirut and Stuttgart, 1991 (*JAOS*, 114, 1994, pp. 457–459).

Walbridge, John, *The Science of Mystic Lights. Quṭb al-Dīn Shīrāzī and the Illuminationist Tradition in Islamic Philosophy*, Cambridge, MA, 1992 (*BCAI*, 11, 1994, pp. 123–125) [A Persian translation of this review was also published in *Iran-shenasi* (Chicago) vi (1995), pp. 873–876].

**1995**

(with R. Davari, N. Pourjavady, et al.), 'Forum on Islam and the West', [in Persian], *Nameh Farhang, A Quarterly Journal on Cultural and Social Research* (Tehran: Ministry of Culture and Islamic Guidance), 17 (Spring, 1995), pp. 4–8, 15–29.

'Saʿd al-Dīn al-Ḥammūʾī', *EI2*, 1995.

### 1996

Editor of Section on 'Muslim Mystics', in Howard M. Federspiel (general ed.), *An Anthology of Islamic Studies, Volume II* (Montreal, 1996)

'Prayer and the Mystical Life in Islam', in Howard M. Federspiel (general ed.), *An Anthology of Islamic Studies, Volume II* (Montreal, 1996), pp. 20–23 [= English version of 'La prière et la vie mystique (Islam)', see above 1988].

'The role of Sufism in the World of Islam', in Howard M. Federspiel (general ed.), *An Anthology of Islamic Studies, Volume II* (Montreal, 1996), pp. 109–111.

'La «double échelle» d'Ibn 'Arabī chez Simnānī', in M. A. Amir-Moezzi, ed., *Le voyage initiatique en terre d'Islam. Ascensions célestes et itinéraires spirituels*, Bibliothèque de l'École des Hautes Études, Section des Sciences Religieuses, tome 103/Institut Français de Recherche en Iran (Louvain and Paris, 1996), pp. 251–264.

'Le paradoxe de la "face de Dieu": 'Azîz-e Nasafî (VIIe/XIIIe siècle) et le "monisme ésotérique" de l'Islam', *SIr*, 25 (1996), pp. 163–192.

'Le soufisme à travers l'œuvre de 'Azîz-e Nasafî: Etude du *Ketâb-e Tanzîl*', in *Annuaire de l'École Pratique des Hautes Études*, Section des Sciences Religieuses, 103 (1994–1995) (Paris, 1996), pp. 227–229.

### 1997

*Preface* to Diane Steigerwald, *La pensée philosophique et théologique de Shahrastānī (m. 548/1153)* (Saint-Nicolas (Québec), 1997), pp. vii–viii.

### 1998

''Azīz-i Nasafī and the essence-existence debate', in Sayyid Jalāl al-Dīn Āshtiyānī et al., ed., *Consciousness and Reality: Studies in Memory of Toshihiko Izutsu* (Tokyo, 1998), pp. 387–395 [A Persian translation of this article was published in 'Special Issue dedicated to the commemoration of Professor Seyyed Jalâloddin Ashtiyani', *Faculty of Theology and Islamic Studies: A Research Journal*, 41–42 (Autumn–Winter, 1377/1998–1999), Ferdowsi University of Mashhad, pp. 407–417].

'Abū Ḥātim al-Rāzī', 'Abū Ya'qūb al-Sijzī', 'Ibn Sīnā', *EAL*, 1998.

***Reviews***

Elias, Jamal J., *The Throne Carrier of God: The Life and Thought of 'Alā' ad-Dawla as-Simnānī*, Albany, NY, 1995 (*IJMES*, 30, 1998, pp. 457–459).

Schubert, Gudrun, ed., *Annäherungen: Der mystisch-philosophische Briefwechsel zwischen Ṣadr ud-Dīn-i Qōnawī und Naṣīr ud-Dīn-i Ṭūsī, Edition und kommentierte*

*Inhaltsangabe* (Bibliotheca Islamica, 43), Beirut and Stuttgart, 1995 (*BSOAS*, 61, 1998, pp. 332–334).

**1999**

'Henry Corbin (1903–1978): Between Philosophy and Orientalism (Brief Communication)', *JAOS*, 119 (1999), pp. 484–490 [Paper originally read at 35th ICANAS conference, Budapest, July 1997].

**2000**

'Fritz Meier (1912–1998)', *SIr*, 29 (2000), pp. 143–146.

'Ḥaydar-i Āmulī et les deux *mi'rājs*', *SI*, 91 (2000), pp. 91–106 [Paper originally read at 4th SIE Conference, Paris, September 1999].

'Khwāja Naṣīr al-Dīn al-Ṭūsī (597/1201–672/1274), Ismā'īlism, and *Ishrāqī* Philosophy', in N. Pourjavady and Ž. Vesel, ed., *Naṣīr al-Dīn Ṭūsī: Philosophe et savant du XIII*e *siècle* (Actes du colloque tenu à l'Université de Téhéran 6–9 mars 1997) (Tehran, 2000), pp. 119–136.

'Nasafī and the *Bayān al-Tanzīl*', Introduction to Sayyid 'Alī Aḥghar Mīr-Bāqirī Fard, ed., *Bayān al-Tanzīl*, Anjuman-i Āthār u Mafākhir-i Farhangī, Series Nr. 225 (Tehran, 1379/2000), pp. 1–18.

'Stages of God-cognition and the Praise of Folly according to Najm-i Rāzī (d. 1256)', [revised English translation of 'Stufen der Gotteserkenntnis...'], *SUFI*, 47 (Autumn 2000), pp. 31–43.

***Reviews***

De Smet, Daniel, *La quiétude de l'Intellect: Néoplatonisme et gnose ismaélienne dans l'œuvre de Ḥamîd ad-Dîn al-Kirmânî (Xe/XIe s.)*. Orientalia Lovaniensia Analecta, 67, Leuven, 1995 (*ZDMG*, 150, 2000, pp. 639–642).

Nāṣir Khusraw, *Knowledge and Liberation: A Treatise on Philosophical Theology*. Edited and Translated by Faquir M. Hunzai, Introduced by Parviz Morewedge, London and New York, 1998 (*BCAI*, 16, 2000, p. 75).

Naṣīr al-Dīn Ṭūsī, *Contemplation and Action: The Spiritual Autobiography of a Muslim Scholar*. A New Edition and English Translation of *Sayr wa Sulūk* by S. J. Badakhshani, London and New York, 1998 (*BCAI*, 16, 2000, p. 84).

**2001**

Translator of 'Abū Ya'qūb Sijistānī, *Kashf al-maḥjūb* ('Unveiling of the Hidden') [translation of selections from the Persian text, with an introduction]', in Seyyed Hossein Nasr and Mehdi Aminrazavi, ed., *An Anthology of Philosophy in Persia*, vol. 2 (Oxford, 2001), pp. 71–124.

'Henry Corbin's Understanding of Mullā Ṣadrā' in *Islam-West Philosophical Dialogue: The Papers presented at the World Congress on Mulla Sadra (May, 1999, Tehran). Volume 1: Mulla Sadra and Transcendent Philosophy* (Tehran, 1380/2001), pp. 163–172. [Persian translation in: *Majmū'a-yi Maqālāt-i Hamāyish-i Jahānī-i Buzurgdāsht-i Ḥakīm Ṣadr al-Muta'allihīn (Sāl 1378). Jild-i awwal: Mullā Ṣadrā wa ḥikmat-i muta'āliya* (Tehran, 1380/2001), pp. 23–32. Another Persian translation of the same appeared in the Tehran periodical *Kīmiyā*, 5 (1382/2003), pp. 255–264].

'La transmigration de l'âme (*tanâsukh*) dans le shî'isme et le soufisme' in *Annuaire de l'École Pratique des Hautes Études*, Section des Sciences Religieuses, 108 (1999–2000), pp. 243–244.

'Remembering Toshihiko Izutsu', in *Biography and Academic Life of the Late Toshihiko Izutsu 1914–1993*. Tehran: Society for the Appreciation of Cultural Works and Dignitaries [Anjuman-i Āthār u Mafākhir-i Farhangī], March 2001, pp. 1–11 [English part].

'Gelpke, Rudolf', *EIr*, 2001.

'Ta'ammulī bar afkār va andīshashā-yi 'Aziz-i Nasafī', in *Āyīna-yi Mīrāth*, 4, 13 (1380/2001), pp. 19–24 [Unauthorised Persian translation of an unpublished paper presented at the occasion of the publication of the *Bayān al-Tanzīl*, at Anjuman-i Āthār u Mafākhīr-i Farhangī II, Tehran, 13 March 2001].

**2002**

*Preface* to Nasrollah Pourjavady, *Two Renewers of Faith: Studies on Muḥammad-i Ghazzālī and Fakhruddīn-i Rāzī* (Tehran, 1381/2002), pp. iii–vii.

'*Wudjūd* (section 2: mysticism)', *EI2*, 2002.

Untitled introductory note, in *Publications of the International Colloquium on Cordoba and Isfahan: Two Schools of Islamic Philosophy* – Isfahan, 27–29 April 2002, ed. Mehdi Mohaghegh (Tehran, 1381/2002), pp. 1–9.

**2003**

'Suhrawardī between Philosophy, Sufism and Ismailism: a Re-appraisal', *Dâneshnâmeh*, 1, Winter, pp. 13–29.

'Nasafī, 'Azīz b. Mo'ammad', *EIr*, 2003.

**2005**

'Introduction', in Jalal H. Badakhchani, ed. and tr., *Paradise of Submission; A Medieval Treatise on Ismaili Thought. A New Persian Edition and English Translation of Naṣīr al-Dīn Ṭūsī's* Rawḍa-yi taslīm (London/New York, 2005), pp. 1–11 and 244–247.

# Part One

# Classical Islam

# 3

# The 'Five Limbs' of the Soul: A Manichaean Motif in Muslim Garb?

*Karim Douglas Crow*

Manichaean dualism received much attention from Muslim thinkers in the first three centuries of Islam, and appears to have been one of the catalysts for the elaboration of theological teachings defending Islamic monotheism. A number of interesting thinkers may be seen to lie somewhere between *zandaqa* and the Shiʿa, although it is often difficult to distinguish a specifically Manichaean component in their ideas from a Zoroastrian or a Christian Gnostic one. The Manichaean ethical challenge was perhaps of even greater significance in provoking an Islamic response. At times, the Muslim rebuttal could take the form of assimilating certain elements of the Manichaean vision of man and the cosmos into an Islamic framework. For example, this process can certainly be glimpsed in the thought of the sixth Shiʿi Imam Jaʿfar al-Ṣādiq,[1] and, as we will discuss here, perhaps others, such al-Ḥakīm al-Tirmidhī and Jaʿfar b. al-Ḥasan Manṣūr al-Yaman.

## The 'Limbs of the Soul'

Mānī's religion drew upon Dayṣānī and Iranian dualism, where evil is opposed to good from the very beginning. Two Principles of Light and Darkness, Spirit and Matter, or God and Devil, stand opposed to one another as two 'natures' or 'substances', with their opposition replicated within man. Man's physical nature and his '*psyche*' (taken as sublimated matter) are engaged in a perpetual struggle against his '*soul*' (*pneuma*) whose substance is divine Light. Man's present condition is thus one of 'mixture' of the Two Principles and their associated natures. Divine activity intends to spiritualise matter, 'distilling the Light from Matter to which it is bound; … which also implies the separation of good from evil and the vanquishing of evil on an ethical level, ... particularly the forces of the psyche in its negative aspects'.[2]

In his cosmology, Mānī associated ethical and spiritual principles with the concepts of divine/good and demonic/evil substances. Originally these are opposed in duality, and then mixed in the unfolding cosmological drama which 'projects into cosmic dimensions a specific insight into the nature of man, his divine origin, his present plight, and his potential for attaining salvation'. [3] The divine world sends man the *Nous* ('mind') which teaches him *gnosis* or salvific knowledge of his original source and ultimate destination, namely the World of Light. The vivid mythological imagery of Manichaean teachings often portrayed the Two zones of Light and Darkness as opposing kingdoms made up of five elements or 'Areas' (with corresponding Trees), in contrast to the abstract conceptualisations developed by Greek philosophy and established in Western Christian thought.

An outstanding example of such imagery is the 'Five Limbs' or intellectual attributes of the Supreme Deity. These are five attributes of the Father of Light, or the five limbs of the Great *Nous* (Vahman): Reason, Mind, Intelligence, Thought and Understanding.[4] These five are forces in the body and are composed of divine Light (i.e. 'soul'), for the soul is a part of the divine Light and the very substance of the structure of the cosmos. The five basic aspects of God are figuratively called his 'limbs' or his 'dwellings', and correspond variously to five 'Areas' in the Realm of Light, as well as to the five Sons of the First Man (Ohrmazd) as five divine powers or Elements of Light (= Ether, Wind, Light, Water and Fire), which together comprise the 'Living Soul/Self' or sum of these five Elements.[5] The correspondences are extended to include the five classes of the Manichaean Church hierarchy. An interesting detail within the overlapping schemes of pentadic correspondences is that the first term may sum up all other members of the pentad. Thus in Western Manichaeism the first Limb of the soul, *bām* (*Nous*), encapsulates within itself the remaining Limbs and represents the whole soul.[6]

Manichaean thinking shares certain essential points with Zoroastrian tradition, such as 'the assumption that there is an identity of substance between the spiritual aspect of man and the spiritual world, represented in Manichaeism by the deities'.[7] Scholars have pointed out that the Iranian concept of multiple souls was typical of the Zoroastrian mode of thought, and was borrowed by Mānī. There is a solid Avestan tradition on the connections between man and the divine where human faculties are conceived as 'similar in structure to the *mēnōg* (spiritual) world of the deities, or more precisely to the organisation of the divine world'.[8] A series of speculative writings elaborated this tradition, and several schools of thought identified either four, five, or six spiritual entities in man,[9] even conceiving of Ohrmazd as keeping his 'limbs' within man.[10]

The Great *Nous* is closely connected with the figure of Jesus the Splendour, sharing the function of eschatological Judge; both are referred to as 'the God of the World of Wisdom'. Actually, the work of all great religious teachers including Zoroaster, Buddha, Jesus and Mānī, is that of the Great *Nous* ('Father of all Apostles'), who inspires them all. As Klimkeit summarises it: 'The five sons of the First Man ... are "clothed" by his "limbs", which are the limbs of God, so that they appear as and assume the function of the "limbs" of the soul. The *Nous* enters into the minds of those that open themselves to him, and he is instrumental in eradicating the seeds of evil in man .... It is the *Nous* that awakens the individual soul from its sleep of forgetfulness and imparts to it the knowledge of its divine origin ... .'[11] In this fashion is born the 'New Man' and his virtues, who prevails over the 'Old Man' and his vices.

The Manichaean sets of five spiritual constituents in man and God have been studied mainly in connection with earlier schemes of human mental faculties.[12] Little attention has been given to the possible prolongation of this notion of the 'Five Limbs of the Soul' in traditions which experienced creative interaction with Manichaean thought, such as Islam or Taoism. We now present textual data which suggest that these Manichaean teachings might have had a certain impact upon key spiritual exponents during the first three centuries of Islam.

## Imām Jaʿfar al-Ṣādiq (d. 148/765)

This revered spiritual leader and speculative teacher was active in Medina in the Hijaz, as well as in Kūfa in lower Iraq for short periods, during the first half of the second/eighth century. There are strong indications that his family preserved an inner teaching reaching back to the earliest Muslim community. More than anyone else, Jaʿfar and his father Muḥammad al-Bāqir (d. ca. 117/735) were responsible for the doctrinal and legal foundation of Shiʿi Islam. Furthermore, al-Ṣādiq elaborated a wisdom teaching on the role of human cognition (*al-ʿaql*) which had significant repercussions among later thinkers.

However, almost all of the voluminous materials assigned to his authority require careful scrutiny from various directions before their possible authenticity may be established. Here, we shall simply lay these issues aside, and select representative reports relevant to our topic.[13] Among these materials, certain reports found in the early literature appear to represent a body of teachings embraced by early Shiʿi thinkers working in the shadow of this Imam.

At the end of the opening chapter on 'Intelligence and Ignorance' in his *al-Kāfi*, al-Kulaynī (d. 329/940) includes a report treating the notion of the 'inspiration /strengthening' of the intelligence or cognitive faculty (*ta'yīd al-ʿaql*), related on the authority of his teacher Aḥmad al-Barqī '*mursalan*' al-Ṣādiq:[14]

> Man's chief support is intelligence, and from intelligence comes astuteness (*al-fiṭna*), comprehension (*al-fahm*), attentiveness or memory (*al-ḥifẓ*), and knowledge (*al-ʿilm*).

> By means of intelligence [man] becomes perfected, and it his guide, his illuminator … . If the 'inspiration' of his intelligence is through light, then he becomes knowing, attentive, mindful, sagacious and 'quick-of-Comprehension' (*kānā ʿālim*$^{an}$ *ḥāfiẓ*$^{an}$ *dhākir*$^{an}$ [*or dhakiyy*$^{an}$] *fāṭin*$^{an}$ *fahīm*$^{an}$).[15] Then he perceives (*ʿarafa*) [with these five faculties] the how, the why, the whence; and he perceives whomever sincerely counsels him and whomever deceives him. When he perceives [these things], then he perceives his proper course, what connects him and what separates him; and he is pure and clear in [confirming] Oneness of God and establishing obedience [to God].
>
> If he accomplishes that, he becomes a redresser of past defects and a recipient of what is yet to come, perceiving what he is about, and for what purpose he is here, and from where it reaches him, and to what end he is proceeding. All of this accrues [to him] from the inspiration of intelligence.

Al-Ṣādiq's statement represents an elaborately interiorised form of the widespread 'praise of intelligence' ubiquitous in Islamic wisdom teachings. The opening words echo early Muslim maxims about intelligence being man's chief guide or support (*diʿāma*, *dalīl*). Human intelligence or cognitive ability encompasses four or five primary perceptive faculties: knowledge, memory/attentiveness, mindfulness, astuteness and understanding or comprehension. These faculties, subsumed under intelligence, lead to man's acquisition of saving knowledge and true monotheist faith (Islam). The perfection of one's cognitive ability is accomplished through the illumination of intelligence when it is 'strengthened' through light (*mubṣiruhu*). Light is the source of perceptive faculties which collectively constitute the powers of intelligence. This is consonant with al-Ṣādiq's portrayal of the creation of *ʿaql* from divine Light (or Throne Light), the Heavenly *ʿaql* being the 'intelligence/wisdom' at the source of each individual's cognition.[16]

The five powers of intelligence, as well as *maʿrifa* (perception, 'deep cognition', 'cognisance') itself, should be viewed as divine aid or grace, not human. Here, *maʿrifa* may be construed as the mode of 'grasping/perceiving' one's course in the conduct of life and one's final goal. Meditation upon and cognition of the ultimate questions (e.g. whence?) permits man to attain pure monotheism and proper obedience to God.

Other passages assigned to al-Ṣādiq similarly mention intelligence as the faculty by which man perceives and understands, presenting the image of the higher part of the soul as 'a light strengthened through intelligence'.[17] Certain of these passages seem also to echo Hermetic teachings about the human person as a hierarchy of five enveloping substances (body, spirit, soul, reason, mind), with 'mind' (*Nous*) being ontologically the highest or innermost (cf. *Corpus Hermeticum* X. 13). Scholars have sought for Stoic ideas on material *pneuma*, or for Neoplatonic concepts that parallel this Hermetic doctrine. The motif of a pentad of elements for man's physical creation was common among Muslim thinkers in the late first/seventh and early second/eighth century. A typical scheme speaks of man's creation from fire, light, darkness, water and earth.[18] There may be a reason to link such pentads endowed with intellectual and ethical functions to the Manichaean and/or Christian Gnostic teachings diffused throughout early Islam.[19] However, such pentads detail physical components, not the constituents of the human soul.

Another report which partially parallels the previous statement by al-Ṣādiq may be quoted here. It comes from both Ibn Bābawayh and al-Ḥarrānī:[20]

> A man's knowledge of himself is that he know the self through four Natures [Constitutions], and four Supports, and four Elements [Principles]. His Constitutions are blood, bile, wind and phlegm. His four Supports are intelligence – and from intelligence comes acumen, comprehension, attentiveness (*ḥifaẓ/al-ḥifẓ* 'memory'), and knowledge. His Principles are Light, Fire, Spirit and Water. He sees, hears and understands (*'aqala*) by means of Light; he eats and drinks by means of Fire; he copulates and moves by means of Spirit; and he experiences the taste of ... food by means of water. This is the foundation of his [material] form.
>
> If the 'Inspiration' of his 'cognitive/aptitude' is through Light (*ta'yīd 'aqlihi min nūr*),[21] then he is knowing, attentive, intelligent, astute and discerning; and he perceives what he is about and from where things are coming to him ... .

This conception of four faculties or functions of *'aql* (the four supports (*da'ā'im*): astuteness, comprehension, attentiveness and knowledge, may be deemed a pentad if intelligence is taken as the all-encompassing cognitive aptitude of man, by means of which he receives divine inspiration or expanded cognition. The association of intelligence with divine Light as well as with Spirit (*rūḥ*) is certainly a definite feature of al-Ṣādiq's teaching. One might see in these Four Supports an echo of the Hermetic 'four faculties of thought, consciousness, memory and foresight (*animus, sensus, memoria, providentia*) by means of which he knows all things divine' (*Asclepius* #10–11).[22] Or one may prefer to view them as ultimately reaching back to platonising-neopythagorean teachings, e.g. Iamblichus identified four powers of the soul: intellect, science, opinion and sensation.[23] Another model may well be found in the Eastern Christian ascetic teaching of the five 'interior senses of the soul' (intellect/spirit, reason, spiritual perception, gnosis and knowledge);[24] the five outer senses can be trained to serve the spirit and intellect, promoting the growth of these interior senses. It is also possible that they reflect the Manichaean 'Five Limbs of the Soul'. Over a century after al-Ṣādiq, through channels upon which one may only speculate, one particular sage (*ḥakīm*) took up this pentad of cognitive powers subsumed under intelligence, in his remarkable esoteric system.

## Al-Ḥakīm al-Tirmidhī (d. ca. 295/907–310/922)

The Central Asian mystic Muḥammad b. ʿAlī al-Ḥakīm al-Tirmidhī produced a major corpus of writings exhibiting a profound appreciation of the essential sources of Islamic consciousness, the Qur'an and the *ḥadīth*. He seems to have been independent in his inclinations: a self-initiated mystic with no clear line of spiritual practice stemming from him. Most of his writings were composed during ten years of forced seclusion ending in 285/898. Among his published works, several make mention of five (or variously four, or six) powers of human spiritual cognition, referred to as 'troops of the Spirit (*junūd al-rūḥ*)', or 'troops of the heart (*junūd al-qalb*)', or the 'troops of cognitive/perception (*junūd al-maʿrifa*)'.[25] At times he makes a distinction and specifies certain powers or faculties as comprising the 'troops of *ʿaql*'.[26] Another writing entitled *Ghawr al-umūr* (*The Depth of the Issues*), is problematic, for its attribution to al-Ḥakīm has been questioned by the leading Western student of al-Tirmidhī's thought, Berndt Radtke.[27]

In his *Gnosis of the Saints*, al-Tirmidhī gives a profound dissertation on the 'science' of inner perception, including the crucial idea of 'knowledge within the heart'. His starting point is the Qur'anic teaching that God 'taught Adam all the names' (Qur'an 2 (*al-Baqara*): 31).[28] This notion is combined with the scheme given in a famous saying (often cast as a Prophetic *ḥadīth*) on the two types of knowledge: knowledge in the heart (*ʿilm fi'l-qalb*) = 'the profitable knowledge' and knowledge on the tongue (*ʿilm ʿalā 'l-lisān*) = 'God's decisive argument against humans' – respectively esoteric and exoteric knowledge.[29] While explaining these two types, al-Ḥakīm clarifies the relation of knowledge to cognisance (*ʿilm/maʿrifa*), linking both to the interplay of intellect/heart (*ʿaql/qalb*) and appetitive cravings/psyche (*shahwa/nafs*).

In effect, the 'knowledge of the heart' that truly profits one is 'the cognisance of God'; God inspires the gnostics (*al-ʿulamā' bi-llāhi*) with penetrating comprehension (*fahm*) and an abundance of intelligence and expands faith in their hearts. They are the executors of the decisive arguments (*al-ḥujaj*) in every time and place, endowed with the powers of explanation and proof (*bayān*). 'Knowledge on the tongue' is merely knowledge memorised or held in one's mind, not fixed permanently in the heart.

> *Hifẓ* is the consort of *ʿaql*, it is as if this knowledge is the repository of *ʿaql* and 'acute understanding' of (knowledge) is knowing the good from the morally repugnant ... ; thus the knowledge of the Mind (*al-dhihn*) shows you that which the eye of the head apprehends. Whereas the former knowledge is the repository of Cognisance and it is the knowledge of certainty, showing you what the eye of the heart apprehends.[30]

> A.[31] The Heart and the Psyche are two partners in this body; and the energy of the Heart comes from Cognisance and (from) Intelligence, Knowledge,

Comprehension, Mind (*dhihn*), Sagaciousness (*fiṭna*) and Attention [or Memory] (*ḥifẓ*); and (from) life for God, and from the joys of these things taking place within him, energising him and [being] a source of life for him.

B.[32] The servant needs to seek refuge in God and struggle with his self (cf. psyche) by means of the [6] forces he was given ...

C.[33] ... as for the 'goodly admonition' (*al-maw'iẓāt al-ḥasana*; cf., Qur'an 16 (*al-Naḥl*):37 and 125), the admonition is the 'impression' (*al-athāra*) ... the servant possesses a body in which has been mounted the Spirit (*al-rūḥ*), and the Mind, the Intelligence, Knowledge, Attentive Memory and Sagacity (*al-kays*); and these are the troops of the Spirit ... so the admonition awakens or enlivens these qualities.

D.[34] God created this Human (*ādamī*), and He created in his interior a piece of flesh, named Heart on account of its perturbations, and He made it the commander over the limbs (*amīr 'alā'l-jawārih*). God placed in the Heart Cognisance of Himself and the Knowledge of Himself. He entrusted the Heart with the preservation of the limbs, and He commissioned the worshipper with the preservation of [the Heart] and with restraining it; He did not entrust [the Heart] to anyone else ... .

And He entrusted [the servant] with Intelligence, and He placed within the Intelligence the Cognisance and the Knowledge of God. He made (the servant's) belly to be the source of appetitive cravings, and He placed in (the belly) the craving for things, entrusted it with Desire (*al-hawā*), and placed in Desire the gloom of the Ignorance of God (*al-jahl bi-llāhi*).

Thus, 'cognition' (*al-'aql*) of what is within [the person] of the Cognisance of God and Knowledge of Him, conveys [the] Heart towards God, whereas Desire invites [the] Psyche to passing appetites. Rather, these two are two spirits, in each of which is Life – one of them is celestial, the other earthly. The name of the former is 'Spirit' and of the latter 'Psyche'... [Spirit resides in the head, Psyche in the belly; both are dispersed throughout the entire corporeal body]... .

There occurs the battle between the Psyche and the Heart, so the Heart inclines toward the joys of God and love for him, while the Psyche is inclined to the joys of the appetitive cravings and love for them. So Intelligence, Knowledge, Cognisance, Comprehension, Astuteness, Sagaciousness and Mind are among the troops of the Heart; whereas desire for cravings and joys and adornment are the troops of the Psyche. Whoever loses the battle, the Psyche makes off with their Heart and imprisons it – then [the Heart] has no power to enjoin or forbid, and his interior becomes a town of the enemy camp. While whoever fights with his Heart until he imprisons the Psyche, then the sovereign authority belongs to the Heart... .

E.[35] Thanks be to God Who placed within you from among those things (*al-ashyā'*) that which He selected and upon which His blessings have alighted – the likes of Intelligence, Knowledge, Attentiveness, Mind, Comprehension, Sagacity. So He appointed them as the 'troops of Cognisance' within your Heart, which He invested with authority over your limbs. Then He gave leave to those things to emit it's (i.e. *ma'rifa*'s) benefits to your Heart so that the servant may bring forth from his limbs the goodly qualities of deeds and words … , and He shall reward (the servant) on the morrow for those goodly qualities – 'Gardens of Eternity, which the Gracious God has promised to His servants while (they are yet) hidden (from their sight). Surely, His promise must come to pass … .' Qur'an 19 (*Maryam*):61.

F.[36] God created the human being; then He bestowed benefits upon the folk from His Mercy; and He vivified their hearts; and appointed a Light for them; and opened the eyes of their Hearts to His light so that they draw upon Him and rely on Him (or: 'they draw upon the light and rely on it'). That light is made manifest from their bosoms through a 'word' possessed of letters, in each letter of which is a meaning – the 'word' is '*There is no divinity save The Divinity*!' (This 'word' has a beam and a flare which penetrates the celestial regions, reaches the Throne, rends the veils, and brings acceptance of good deeds and remission of sins … ;[37] and the more abundant one's share in being received and of forgiveness, then the more abundantly one is endowed with a share of the light in his bosom.) …

He placed this light within the bosom of this faithful one (*mu'min*), and appetitive craving in his 'interior', and desire below it within the two sides [of the corporeal body]; and the enemy is over the belly surrounded by cravings. So whenever something of worldly cravings occurs to the mind of the faithful one, his psyche is bestirred by the desire that is within it – by means of its heat and its authority, so that heat and desire flies to the bosom. And the Heart is the commander of the limbs. Thus, when this commander arises, and briskly sets to work to repel [that thing] if that thing was forbidden, and he gathers his troops of Intelligence, Knowledge, Mind, Attentiveness, Comprehension and Sagacity – and [the Heart] combats the Psyche and desire, then [the faithful one] is saved. If that was a thing not forbidden, he employs the Intelligence, Knowledge and all of these troops in pursuit of that thing until he performs it. Then he is possessed of Beauty and a goodly condition; thereby [his deed] ascends to God in advance of him, and God is content with him … .

G.[38] Cognisance and Knowledge and Intelligence and Comprehension and Mind and Attentive memory – they are *things* placed in the human being. Then when the [divine] authorisation comes, they all become actual deeds; and if the authorisation does not come, they remain in their condition … . With the (divine) authorisation, they pass by that which is inscribed on the Heart concerning the notification of faith[39] … .

Thus, when the servant works an act, then he acts by means of these things [thus they are 'limbs']. So his act and his Intelligence, his Mind, his Attentiveness, and his Comprehension ascend to God, and likewise the thing that he works … . Thus, in the same measure as a thing ascends to God, then the assistance (*al-madad*) from God is reaching those things that are there. …

H.[40] The 'epitome of worship' is that God Blessed and Exalted, created our bodies as 'moulded forms' in order to place in them that which the servant makes manifest by his motions through that life which is within his spirit and his Psyche. The spirit is celestial and life is within it, while the Psyche is earthly and life is within it, so both of them move the limbs. Then God placed cognisance in the heart, and the knowledge of cognisance in the bosom,[41] and the cognition of cognisance in the head, and decreed fate in the forehead. He made mind and comprehension and sagacity to be among the troops of intelligence. And He placed appetitive craving in the Psyche, and made desire to be its leader and driver. … Thus, the truly inspired fortunate person delves into cognisance and masters the science of cognisance, and cleaves to cognisance and occupies himself exclusively in all his affairs through his mind, his comprehension and his sagacity. His Heart clings to God until 'certainty' (*al-yaqīn*) comes to him – and it is the joy which he previously experienced from God (*al-faraḥ alladhī sabaqa la-hu min Allāh*) … .

I.[42] On the science of 'God-Mindfulness' (*'ilm al-taqwa*): the Heart is the treasury of God, He placed in it a rare substance of inestimable value – cognisance … . Thus, God the Exalted graciously favoured a great blessing upon the faithful by giving them the light of true guidance so that they declared His unity with 'There is no divinity save The Divinity'. He commanded them to be mindful of what He gave them: which is the light radiating in their hearts, and then from their Hearts to their bosoms … .

For cognisance is inspired (i.e. 'strengthened' *ayyada*) through intelligence, comprehension, attentive-memory, mind and remembrance, and these things are around it … . Thus, God the Exalted made 'mindfulness' incumbent on them by saying: 'O you who have faith, be mindful of God!' [Qur'an 8:29]; and so they comprehended of God Mighty and Majestic (*fahimu 'an Allah*) that 'Mindfulness' (*al-taqwā*) is binding on the seven [!] limbs [eye, tongue, ear, hand, foot, stomach, genitalia] … .

*Ghawr al-umūr* contains a gnostic-like creation myth about the clay of Adam,[43] followed by a chapter describing cognisance/*ma'rifa* and its garments, then one describing the creation of Adam's 'clay' (*ṭīna*).[44] Adam's clay is composed of earth kneaded with the water of mercy, into which the Light of Cognisance is placed as a yeast. Upon the thorough interpenetration of the Water with the Light making one light form, the 'Spirit of Life' is blown into it ('and the Light is the Spirit, and it is the "Spirit of Life"'). Then cognisance ('it is the source of the Light which had been placed into Adam a.s. when his clay was kneaded with it') is injected into the 'Spirit of Life'. The mutual mingling of this Light of cognisance with cognisance, which is the result of the act of the servant, illumines the Heart as these two cognisances recognise one another. Through this light or illumination in the Heart, a ray of light is cast up to the Throne and the Heart thereby perceives cognisance and the divine potency (*al-jalāl*). Thus the Heart *knew* its Lord and confessed true monotheism on the 'Day of *Alast*' … . The author expounds on the cognisance exercised by the worshipper:[45]

> Cognisance is due to the act of the servant, and is attributed to him … . But the cause through which the servant attains it is made up of five things; these things are not his, yet he is praised by his Lord for employing them and perceives his Lord by cognition. They are: comprehension, mental acuity, astuteness, attentive memory and knowledge – which is '*the remembrance of the fiṭra* [i.e. the "Day of *Alast*"]'. They are from God to his servant, and there is nothing owing to the servant from their part; for he is praised when he employs them and blamed when he forsakes them. As for the Light of cognisance, it is from his Lord; the servant is not responsible for it in any way.

Placed in the clay of Adam was this most elevated thing (*shay'*), namely the Light of cognisance, which is filled with the Light of divine potency and uniqueness. The author then expounds in more detail on the five 'things' (*ashyā'*):[46]

> Through mental acuity one penetrates into all that is hidden from him; and through comprehension one perceives the Unseen; penetrating intelligence is that by which the concealed is extracted through realisation; and through attentiveness he fully comprehends; as for knowledge – by means of it he recalls what elapsed. Thus, through employing [these five things], they acknowledged their Lord, and by means of them they understand thanks to their Lord.

These five (variously six) perceptive powers play an important role in al-Tirmidhī's understanding of human cognition. It is correct to depict them as central to his concept of the all important notion of cognisance as the 'energy of the heart'.[47] Yet the same may be true to some extent for his notion of intelligence, in so far as both are involved in the 'science of the heart'. The heart is the site where both cognisance and knowledge of God himself are found (see D and H above), as well as 'mindfulness'. In terms of the powers of cognition, clearly *ma'rifa*/cognisance is superior to *'aql*/intelligence and is depicted as the leader of the other troops (see A and G above). Cognisance is described as the 'peak of knowledge', which is none other than knowledge of God himself.[48] Yet at times we find intelligence apparently leading these troops, or at least placed first, at the head of five or six powers (see D and E above).

Recall the distinction drawn between the interior perception of the heart and the exoteric knowledge 'on the tongue'. Al-Ḥakīm specifies in this regard the functions of attention and memory leading to vision:[49]

> As for the science of the heart – its apparatus is the retentive mind (*dhihn*) and attentive memory (*ḥifẓ*). The retentive mind receives what the attentive memory consigns until it brings it forth when it is needed .... So when the eye of the heart 'images' in the bosom, the heart is empowered by what is imaged – producing an illuminating knowledge [even while there remains weakness and obscurity in the heart] then when the covering of gloom and desire is lifted and knowledge is present ... the vision of the heart alights on the image .... .

What he is concerned with here is the knowledge of certainty (*'ilm al-yaqīn*) that induces comprehension producing vision (*ru'ya*). The basic anthropology of this is rooted in early Islamic normative piety, with the opposition of *'aql* and *ruḥ* to the *nafs* and *hawā*. He comments: 'We find that desire incites cravings, while intelligence incites knowledge and cognisance.'[50] Interestingly, appetitive cravings are taken as a neutral force inherent in the human constitution, whose leanings or impulses may be positive or negative (see F above): [51]

> Desire and cravings come to the Psyche and occupy the Heart, surrounding the cognisance; then the strength of the cognisance departs and becomes suspended by a hair, and the bosom becomes the kingdom of the enemy [*Iblis*] ... ; and the intelligence is drunk, and the authority of desire and its power appear. Thus, intelligence becomes latent, and comprehension is blocked, and the mind becomes stupid, and memory is sealed, and knowledge becomes buried, and cognisance dissolves and ignorance unfurls [its banner] .... .

The theatre of operations is within the interior arena of awareness, the bosom. The heart must exercise authority over the limbs, and upon the impulses of desire, so as to allow the operation of cognisance to take place. This is an obvious difference between Manichaean imagery, where the 'limbs' are interior faculties of soul, and Islamic traditions in which the image of 'limbs' usually refers to the corporeal components of the person. In an esoteric linguistic exegesis of the Qur'anic term *ulā'l-nuhā* 'possessors of understanding', al-Ḥakīm points out that the word is a form of *nuhya* 'mind-understanding': '*al-nuhya* is the "pool" (*al-ghadīr*) where water terminates and stagnates; it is denominated "*ghadīr*" because water remains and subsists in it and is left behind; thus it is said, "*ulā'l-nuhā*", because there collects together in the bosom *al-'aql*, *al-'ilm*, *al-dhihn*, *al-fahm* and *al-fiṭna*; and all of these are *nuhya*: mind-cognition.'[52]

Although the materials from al-Ṣādiq are tantalising, their placement with the Imam is uncertain, and they could well reflect Hellenic and/or Eastern Christian concepts. When considering al-Ḥakīm al-Tirmidhī, the important details on these powers termed the 'troops of the spirit/the heart/cognisance /intelligence' are striking. One might argue al-Ḥakīm was the author of *Ghawr al-umūr* partly on the basis of their occurrence (although the style of this work differs from his authenticated writings). Of more relevance would be detecting functional relations between Manichaean notions and the idea of 'five powers of human [ap]prehension' as developed by al-Ḥakīm. Here, indeed, one could make links, and see parallels between these two spiritual practices. But to argue for a conscious impact of Manichaean thought on the Sage from Tirmidh requires a very fertile imagination indeed.

### Jaʿfar b. al-Ḥasan Manṣūr al-Yaman (d. ca. 380/990)

Finally, we point to another possible occurrence of this notion of 'five powers' constituting spiritual perception. This is found in a work by the Ismaili missionary Jaʿfar b. al-Ḥasan Manṣūr al-Yaman, *Sarāʾir wa-asrār al-nuṭaqāʾ*.[53] In his version of the early Ismaili gnostic myth of the creation of Adam, there is a description of the three 'hypostases' of the creation drama: *Jadd*, *Fatḥ*, *Khayāl*. These three levels in the cosmic hierarchy are also given angelic names: *Jibrāʾīl*, *Mikhāʾīl*, *Isrāfīl*.[54] 'Inspiration' (*taʾyīd*) reaches Adam by means of *ʿaql* (intellect, also termed *sābiq*) and the *nafs* (world soul, also termed *al-tālī*). Jaʿfar b. Manṣūr al-Yaman here effects a co-relation of these three 'hypostases' with *fikr*, *dhikr* and *ḥifẓ* (p. 27). Later, when portraying the five *ḥujaj* representing the spiritual *ḥudūd* operative at the epoch of the dispatching of the Prophet Muḥammad, he gives a suggestive co-relation (pp. 81–82):

| | | | | |
|---|---|---|---|---|
| Abū Ṭālib | Khadīja | Zayd b. ʿAmr | ʿAmr b. Nufayl | Maysara |
| *Sābiq* | *Tālī* | *Jadd* | *Fatḥ* | *Khayāl* |
| *ʿAql* | *Nafs* | *Dhikr* | *Dhihn* | *Fikr* |

Whether this scheme is to be linked with the above materials associated with Imām al-Ṣādiq is a pertinent question. One truth is evident from all the Islamic material examined here: the primary issue involving *ʿaql* and *maʿrifa*, or the process of higher human cognition, has to do with a synergy of forces exchanged between the human and the divine: the 'strengthening' of the cognitive function (*taʾyid al-ʿaql*). We refrain from pursuing the question beyond this point, hoping that the interested reader will take the materials presented here and ponder the questions raised. Such an exercise may make a fitting gift for my inspired teacher and friend, Professor Hermann Landolt.

## Notes

1. See our dissertation 'The Role of *al-ʿAql* in Early Islamic Wisdom', chapter 5 (McGill University, 1996), where the Manichaean ethical challenge is seen to provoke some features of al-Ṣādiq's myth of the creation of *ʿAql* and *Jahl.*

2. H. J. Klimkeit, *Gnosis on the Silk Road: Gnostic Parables, Hymns and Prayers from Central Asia* (New York, 1993), p. 6.

3. Klimkeit, *Gnosis on the Silk Road*, p. 7.

4. Mary Boyce, *A Reader in Manichaean Middle Persian and Parthian* (Leiden, 1975), p. 10. We rely on Klimkeit's lucid summary (pp. 8–17) of the complex drama of Manichaean cosmology and soteriology with its three 'moments' or movements of creation.

5. The powers of Darkness devoured the five Elements of Light, or Sons of First Man, offered up as bait by the First Man to forestall the attack of Darkness. Demons or Archons later used the Light they had devoured to fashion man's soul as the divine and living element in him. This captured Light is cumulatively termed 'the Living Soul/Self', captured in the bodies of the Archons in their semen. Out of fear of losing all the Light it had devoured, Matter sought to check the divine process of salvation by the creation of man, imprisoning the Light it had seized within his body as his soul. Through carnal reproduction the soul would be perpetually enthralled by the body and remain under the power of Matter.

6. Unlike in Iranian texts, where the second Limb of the Soul, *manohmēd* (Mind), assumes the role of the *Nous* or saving function; see Klimkeit, *Gnosis*, p. 17.

7. Shaul Shaked, *Dualism in Transformation; Varieties of Religion in Sasanian Iran* (London, 1994), p. 58.

8. Shaked, *Dualism*, p. 53.

9. In particular chapter 218 of the Pahlavi writing *Denkard III*, on the composition of man. See Shaked, *Dualism*, pp. 56–60, 143–144 and 150–160; and H. W. Bailey, *Zoroastrian Problems in the Ninth-century Books* (Oxford, 1943; repr. 1971), pp. 78 f., 98 f., 102, 184 f., 205–209. Further, J. P. de Menasce, *Le troisième livre du Dēnkart* (Paris, 1973), pp. 126 f. and 230 f.

10. Shaked, *Dualism*, pp. 54 + n. 6 and 63 n. 36 (= *GBd* 196) where each limb of men belongs to a *mēnōg*, e.g. the *jān* or vital soul and its luminosity, intelligence, and consciousness belong to Ohrmazd.

11. Klimkeit, *Gnosis*, pp. 16 and 17.

12. See H. J. Polotsky, *'Manichäismus', in Pauly Wissowa, Realencyclopädie*, Suppl. VI (1935), pp. 240–271, on 248 f.; Ernst Waldschmidt and Wolfgang Lentz, *Manichäische Dogmatik aus chinesischen und iranischen Texten* (Berlin, 1933), pp. 572 f.; J. P. de Menasce, *Une apologétique mazdéenne de IXe siècle, Škand-gumānīk vicār, La Solution décisive des doutes* (Freibourg, 1945), pp. 75 f.; and Shaked, *Dualism*, pp. 53–70 *passim.*

13. We intend to publish a more detailed study of these and related materials, in a forthcoming work entitled ʿAql *in Early Islamic Wisdom.*

14. Abū Yaʿqūb al-Kulaynī, *al-Uṣūl min al-kāfī*, ed. ʿAlī Akbar al-Ghaffārī (3rd ed., Tehran, 1388/1968), vol. 1, p. 25, no. 23. This *isnād* is weak, indicating a practice that earned al-Barqī a poor reputation among Twelver Shiʿi tradition experts.

15. Al-Kulaynī's text reads *dhākiran*; yet parallel pieces reported in slightly later works by Ibn Bābawayh in *ʿIlal al-sharāʾiʿ*, ed. M. S. Baḥr al-ʿUlūm (Najaf, 1386/1966), *bāb* 91, p. 103 #2,

and *bāb* 96, pp. 108–109, no. 6, Ibn Shuʿba al-Ḥarrānī, *Tuḥaf al-ʿuqūl*, ed. M. H. al-Aʿlamī (Beirut, 1969; repr. 1974), p. 260, read *dhakiyyan* (see below). This latter reading finds support in the treatment of a similar pentad of perceptive powers in a work ascribed to al-Ḥakīm al-Tirmidhī; see *Ghawr/al-Aʿda'*, pp. 111–113; see below n. 47.

16. See Crow, 'The Role of *'Aql* in Early Islamic Wisdom', chap. 5.

17. E.g. the report on al-Ṣādiq found in *'Ilal*, *bāb* 96, pp. 107–108 no. 5, *Tuḥaf*, pp. 260–261; see also variants in Ibn Bābawayh, *al-Khiṣāl*, ed. M. M. H. al-Kharsān (Najaf, 1971), p. 207; Muḥammad b. al-Nuʿmān al-Mufīd, *al-Ikhtiṣāṣ*, ed. A. A. al-Ghaffārī (Tehran, 1379/1959), *bāb al-qiyās*, p. 109. It begins: 'What pertains to the soul of the man of faith is a light "strengthened" through *al-ʿaql* (*mu'ayyadun bi'l-ʿaql*), and what pertains to the soul of the unfaithful is a fire aided by the vile part belonging to him ... .'

18. Attributed to Sufyān al-Thawrī (d. 160/776); *Tafsīr Sufyān al-Thawrī*, ed. Imtiyāz ʿAlī ʿArshī (Rampur, 1965), p. 236 no. 889 on Qur'an 45 (*al-Jathiya*), p. 13

19. See G. Vajda, 'Le Témoignage d'al-Māturīdī sur la doctrine des Manichéens, des Dayṣānites et des Marcionites', *Arabica*, 11 (1964), pp. 1–38 and 113–128, on 14–18. In particular, the five *ajnās* given by Abū 'Isa al-Warraq (G. Vajda, 'Le Témoignage', p. 17), quoted by al-Shahrastānī, *al-Milal wa'l-niḥal*, ed. M. Fatḥ Allāh Badrān (2nd ed., Cairo, 1956), vol. 1, p. 622, offers a close correspondence to that of al-Ṣādiq in note 20 above.

20. *'Ilal*, *bāb* 96, pp. 108–109, no. 6 (via ... al-Ḥasan b. Maḥbūb 'one of our associates' al-Ṣādiq) and *Tuḥaf*, p. 260 (without *isnād*).

21. Following the text of *Tuḥaf*, a phrase absent from *'Ilal*.

22. Translation by B. P. Copenhaver, *Hermetica* (Cambridge, 1992), p. 225. Compare *Corpus Hermeticum*, XIII, pp. 7–12 (on the Eighth and the Ninth); and for this aspect of the Hermetic theory of the microcosm, cf. A. S. Ferguson in W. Scott, *Hermetica* (London, 1924–1936), vol. 4, *Testimonia*, pp. 402–403.

23. See Dominic J. O'Meara, *Pythagoras Revived: Mathematics and Philosophy in Late Antiquity* (Oxford, 1989), Appendix I, pp. 218–229 = 'The Excerpts from Iamblichus' *On Pythagoreanism*, V–VII in Psellus, text p. 224; tr. p. 225.

24. As with the 11th-century Byzantine monk Nicetas Stethatos in his *Centuries*.

25. E.g. his *al-Masā'il al-maknūna*, ed. M. Ibrāhīm al-Juyūshī (Cairo, 1980), pp. 50, 61 and 65.

26. *Al-Masā'il al-maknūna*, p. 120.

27. B. Radtke and J. O'Kane, *The Concept of Sainthood in Early Islamic Mysticism* (Richmond, Surrey, 1996), p. 5.

28. *'Ilm al-awliya'*, ed. Sāmī Naṣr Lufī (Cairo, 1981), pp. 114 f.

29. Ibid., pp. 136–137 and pp. 160–161.

30. Ibid., pp. 160–161.

31. *Jawāb ... Ahl Sarakhs*, ed. B. Radtke, in *Drei Schriften Des Theosophen Von Tirmiḏ* (Beirut and Stuttgart, 1992), vol. 1, p. 139, lines 5–6.

32. *Jawāb ... Ahl Sarakhs*, ed. B. Radtke, in *Drei Schriften*, p. 168, lines 4–5.

33. *Al-Masā'il al-maknūna*, no. 3, p. 50.

34. Ibid., no. 10, pp. 58 f.

35. Ibid., no. 12, p. 65.

36. Ibid., no. 57, pp. 125–126.

37. See on the *kalima* of 'There is no divinity...': *'Ilm al-awliya'*, pp. 133–135.

38. *Al-Masā'il al-maknūna*, no. 39, p. 95.

39. Ibid., p. 95; I am not sure of having captured his meaning here, or whether textual emendation is required.

40. Ibid., no. 52, p. 120.

41. For the significance of al-Ḥakīm al-Tirmidhī's employment of *al-ṣadr*, see his work *Bayān al-farq bayna al-ṣadr wa'l-qalb wa'l-fū'ad wa'l-lubb*, ed. Nicola Heer (Cairo, 1958).

42. *'Ilm al-awliyā'*, p. 141.

43. *Ghawr al-umūr* or *al-A'dā' wa'l-nafs*, ed. Aḥmad 'Abd al-Raḥīm al-Sā'iḥ (Cairo, 1993), pp. 94–106, depicting Adam and his rival Iblīs' empowerment and granting of mastery over Adam.

44. Ibid., pp. 109–111, 'Chapter on the cognisance of "Cognisance" and the cognisance of its substantial essence'.

45. Ibid., p. 111.

46. Ibid., p. 112; on p. 116, there is mention of the employment of *dhihn*, *fahm* and *ḥifẓ*. In the listing of one hundred troops of *al-'aql*, the 'five things' occur in the following order: *'ilm*, *fahm*, *ḥifẓ*, *dhihn*, *dhakawa*; see *Ghawr/al-A'dā'*, pp. 152–154. The following faculties are included by al-Ḥakīm among the 46 parts of prophecy: *'aql*, *fahm*, *fina* and *dhakā'*; see his *Ma'rifat al-asrār*, ed. M. I. al-Juyūshī (Cairo, 1977), p. 68.

47. A significant portrait of *ma'rifa*, its training and conditions for its increase, is found in *al-Masā'il al-maknūna*, no. 59, pp. 133–136.

48. *'Ilm al-awliya'*, p. 126.

49. Ibid., p. 137.

50. *Al-Masā'il al-maknūna*, no. 11, p. 65.

51. *'Ilm al-awliya'*, p. 147.

52. *Al-Masā'il al-maknūna*, no. 43, p. 101; in the midst of his *ta'wīl* of Qur'an 53 (*al-Najm)*:42.

53. Ed. M. Ghālib (Beirut, 1984): in the section on the 'Tale of Adam', pp. 27–53, and 81–82.

56. 'Tale of Adam', pp. 24–26.

# 4

# Narrative Themes and Devices in al-Wāqidī's *Kitāb al-maghāzī*

*Donald P. Little*

Although Ibn Isḥāq's *Sīrat al-nabī* is generally regarded as the chief, earliest, source for the biography of the Prophet Muḥammad,[1] al-Wāqidī's *Kitāb al-maghāzī* has received considerable scholarly attention as a later, and therefore, ancillary source.[2] The question which first exercised scholars regarding the originality of al-Wāqidī and the nature and degree of his indebtedness to Ibn Isḥāq is still being debated. Until recently Marsden Jones was thought to have said the last word on this subject. By detailed comparison of a specific episode, Jones refutes the Wellhausen-Horowitz claim of al-Wāqidī's plagiarism, arguing that the two authors drew upon a common fund of materials, consisting of traditions and popular stories, to construct their own versions of events;[3] Patricia Crone concurs in her analysis of the sources in *Meccan Trade and the Rise of Islam*.[4] But in a painstaking study of the sources used by the two authors for the famous 'Ā'isha scandal, focusing on the *isnāds* that introduced the various *ḥadīths* and *khabars*, Gregor Schoeler insists that 'al-Wāqidī actually plagiarised Ibn Isḥāq' and went so far as to change the latter's *isnāds*.[5] In Schoeler's view, to be sure, Ibn Isḥāq was only one of al-Wāqidī's three main sources. Nevertheless, al-Wāqidī may have sporadically used still other sources, and 'some may have originated in his own imagination.'[6] Oddly enough, Schoeler gives only scant notice to Michael Lecker's article, 'The Death of the Prophet Muḥammad's Father: Did al-Wāqidī Invent Some of the Evidence?', published the previous year, where it is argued that, on the contrary, al-Wāqidī invented nothing but rather selected and redacted materials from the same or different sources.[7] Another scholar, G. H. A. Juynboll, anticipated Schoeler's opinion that al-Wāqidī's *isnāds* for the most part 'sprouted from al-Wāqidī's imagination.'[8] As ingenious as these detailed, sometimes tortured, studies of *isnāds* may be, they are in the last analysis speculative. Indeed, although Juynboll argues 'for the historical acceptability of most of its [the 'Ā'isha scandal's] constituent features,' he concedes that 'the question of whether or not the story, and the Qur'anic verse [associated with it], both stem from one and the same historical situation can then justly be reduced to one to be sorted out by faith, with or without a measure of rationalism, or by rationalism alone.'[9] Ella Landau-Tasseron has argued on the basis of comparative analysis of another specific episode that al-Wāqidī unintentionally conflated and confused two *riwāyas*, whereas Ibn Isḥāq retained their discreteness and thus was more faithful to the original material.[10] Lecker demonstrates the same tendency in al-Wāqidī, attributing its cause to the author's use of 'combined reports' rather than single *isnāds*.[11] In a more general comparative study using 'form criticism,' John Wansbrough argues, again using the example of the 'Ā'isha episode, that al-Wāqidī occupies an intermediate position between Ibn Isḥāq and al-Bukhārī, *Kitāb al-maghāzī* being a refined version of the *Sīra narratio* but without the reductive 'normative preoccupations' of al-Bukhārī's *exemplum*.[12] More conventionally, Rizwi S. Faizer has used comparative analysis of Muḥammad's conflicts with the Jews of Medina to claim that al-Wāqidī 'had a unique interpretation of the Prophet's life,' without, however, explaining what this interpretation is other than to suggest that al-Wāqidī had greater recourse to certain rhetorical devices, mainly repetition, than did Ibn Isḥāq.[13] Finally, and most recently, Fred M. Donner, following the path blazed by Albrecht Noth, has studied the themes, or *topoi*, of early Islamic historiography.[14] Focusing on al-Ṭabarī rather than Ibn Isḥāq or al-Wāqidī, Donner's discussion of the *nubuwwa* and *umma* themes in the life of the Prophet is nevertheless applicable to our two writers, and his approach has influenced my own work.[15]

Building on this body of research, I will examine still another episode in the Prophet's biography, an integral part of the 'Ā'isha scandal that has been neglected even by those scholars who discuss this story at length. All these scholars restrict their attention to the scandal as an isolated, discrete episode that occurred after the raid against the Banu'l-Muṣṭaliq, without scrutinising the accounts of the raid itself, despite the fact that these two aspects form one continuous narrative, bound together chronologically and, especially in al-Wāqidī, thematically. Although my main objective is to illustrate al-Wāqidī's use of motifs and other narrative devices, I will also refer to the relationship of his version to Ibn Isḥāq's. In the process I suggest that the scandal, when placed in its narrative and thematic context, takes on resonance.

We will begin with Ibn Isḥāq's short and simple account of the raid as a basis of comparison. (G 490–493) In Sha'bān of the year 6, according to a combined report, the Prophet marched against the Banu'l-Muṣṭaliq, who he had heard 'were gathering together against him'. (G 490) The Muslims defeated them and took their women, children, and property as booty. No details of the fighting are given other than the fact that some of the Banu'l-Muṣṭaliq fled and others were killed, including two men slain by ʿAlī, and another in error. Instead of the raid itself, Ibn Isḥāq focuses on five associated incidents:

1. A melee that broke out between the Muhājirun and the Anṣār at a watering place belonging to the Banu'l-Muṣṭaliq, in which the leader and would-be king of the Khazraj, ʿAbd Allāh b. Ubayy, threatened to drive the 'vagabonds of Quraysh' out of Medina. (G 491) A young boy, Zayd b. Arqam, reported this threat to the Prophet, but Ibn Ubayy denied having uttered it. In order to prevent further communal strife, Muḥammad rejected 'Umar's advice to execute Ibn Ubayy as well as the offer of the latter's own son to kill him lest someone else might do so and start thereby a blood feud. On the march back to Medina, Ibn Isḥāq says, 'The *sūra* came down in which God mentioned the disaffected with Ibn Ubayy and those like-minded with him', but he does not quote the actual words of the famous verse of the *Munāfiqūn*. Zayd's claim of Ibn Ubayy's treachery, Ibn Isḥāq implies, was confirmed by this revelation. (G 491–492)
2. When the troops reached a watering place in the Ḥijāz, they were alarmed by a violent wind. The Prophet calmed them by interpreting it as a harbinger of 'the death of one of the greatest of the unbelievers', who turned out to be an influential Jewish leader in Medina. (G 491)
3. Vengeance of the brother of the Muslim killed in error. Despite the fact that the Prophet agreed to pay him bloodwit, the man killed his brother's slayer and then apostasised. He commemorated this act with verses glorifying himself and his tribe. (G 492)
4. Muḥammad's marriage to Juwayriyya, daughter of the chief of the Banu'l-Muṣṭaliq. Interestingly enough, this incident is related on the authority of ʿĀ'isha, who accompanied the Prophet on the raid. Whether or not her report is authentic, it is certainly psychologically sound, and colourful, reflecting as it does ʿĀ'isha's resentment of the beautiful Juwayriyya: 'She captivated every man who saw her .... As soon as I saw her at the door of my room I took a dislike to her, for I knew that he [the Prophet] would see her as I saw her.' (G 493) Despite her jealous pique, ʿĀ'isha was forced to concede the salutary effect of the marriage when the one hundred Banu'l-Muṣṭaliq families that Muḥammad released from captivity converted to Islam.
5. Revelation of verse 49:6 regarding the evil done by false messengers. The Prophet's envoy to the converts falsely reported that they had refused to pay the poor tax and had threatened to kill him. When the converts denied this, God revealed the verse. (G 493)

With only two exceptions al-Wāqidī covers, and greatly amplifies, all of this material. (W I, 404–413; II, 415–426) The exceptions are the verses mentioned in (3) and the whole of (5). As we shall see he adds episodes that are not found in Ibn Isḥāq. I do not intend to rehash here the whole issue of *isnād*s except to repeat that al-Wāqidī does frequently use combined *isnāds* (as does Ibn Isḥāq) and does not use *isnāds* quoted by Ibn Isḥāq, even for the same or similar material. Nor, as is well known, does he ever mention the latter's name, despite evidence of plagiarism. The most that can be said is that there are sometimes striking instances of nearly identical phrasing. An example will suffice. In the *Sīra* of Ibn Isḥāq, ʿAbd Allāh b. Ubayy delivers the following words regarding the Anṣār in Medina:

> *fa-qāla wa-qad faʿalūhā qad nāfarūnā wa-kātharūnā fī bilādinā wallāhi mā aʿudduhā wa-jalābīb quraysh illā kamā qālaʾl-awwal sammin kalbak yaʾkulka ammā wallāhi laʾin rajaʿnā ilā al-madīna la-yukhrijanna al-aʿazz minhā al-adhall*
>
> (He said: 'Have they actually done this? They dispute our priority, they outnumber us in our own country, and nothing so fits us and the vagabonds of Quraysh as the ancient saying "Feed a dog and it will devour you." By Allāh, when we return to Medina the stronger will drive out the weaker.') (S I:2, 726; G 491)

With only a few minor changes and the addition of a sentence, al-Wāqidī quotes virtually the same words:

> *qad faʿalūhā qad nāfarūnā wa-kātharūnā fī baladinā wa-ankarū minnatanā wallāhi mā ṣirnā wa-jalābīb quraysh hadhihi illā kamā qāla al-qāʾil sammin kalbak yaʾkulka wallāhi la-qad ẓanantu annī sa-amūt qabla an asmaʿ hātif yahtif bimā hatafa bihi jahja wa-anā ḥāḍir lā yakūn li-dhālik minī ghiyar wallāhi laʾin rajaʿnā ilā al-madīna la-yukhrijanna al-aʿazz minhā al-adhall*
>
> (They have done this. They dispute our priority, they outnumber us in our own town, and they deny our benevolence so that we and these vagabonds of the Quraysh have become fit for the saying 'Feed a dog and it will devour you'. By Allāh, I thought I would die before hearing someone shouting what Jahja did while I was present, without taking offence at that. By Allāh, when we return to Medina the stronger will drive out the weaker.) (W II, 416)

There are other instances of close parallelism so that it is easy to see why some scholars have concluded that al-Wāqidī borrowed from Ibn Isḥāq and embellished his language without acknowledgment and even changed his *isnāds* in order to conceal his indebtedness. And yet, if it be accepted that both were drawing upon common sources, there is room for the possibility that these sources contained variants which each author may have edited for his own purposes.

But if indeed (as it would seem) the problem of plagiarism is insoluble, the nature and intentions of al-Wāqidī's full and detailed elaboration of the story can be glimpsed. First of all is evident a desire for precision, specificity, and explicitness. For example, as is often the case, al-Wāqidī assigns a specific date to the raid different from Ibn Isḥāq's: Monday 28 Shaʿbān, year 5, as opposed to Ibn Isḥāq's Shaʿbān, year 6. Al-Wāqidī provides no explanation for choosing a date a year earlier, just as he gives no reason for omitting material – verses and a whole episode – included by Ibn Isḥāq. Conceivably the sequence of events that took place before and after the raid could have influenced al-Wāqidī's choice of the date, but, then again, he may have merely opted for the reliability of his unnamed source. It should also be noted that al-Wāqidī breaks Ibn Isḥāq's chronological narration by discussing the melee between the Muhājirūn and Anṣār at the watering hole in a separate section entitled 'The Affair of Ibn Ubayy' (W II, 415–426) following the section entitled 'The Raid on al-Muraysī''. (W I, 404–413) Concern for specificity is evident chiefly in unique details provided by al-Wāqidī: the length of the campaign (twenty-eight days' absence from Medina); the tribal affiliations and location of the Banu'l-Muṣṭaliq, their preparations for attacking the Prophet; the names of eight of twenty-three eminent participants in the expeditionary force, comprising eight Muhājirūn and fifteen Anṣār, plus a large group of Munāfiqūn who had never participated in such a raid). Later, al-Wāqidī provides the names of eight of these hypocrites associated with 'Abd Allāh b. Ubayy whereas Ibn Isḥāq is content with a general reference to a '*rahṭ min qawmihi*' ('a group of his people/tribe'). (W II, 416; G 491) In addition to enumerating and naming the participants, al-Wāqidī relates that the expeditionary force had 'thirty horses, ten for the Muhājirūn, twenty for the Anṣār, plus two for the Prophet.' (W I, 405) In *al-Maghāzī* we find a wealth of concrete detail, some of which is important, if not essential, to al-Wāqidī's characterisation of the nature and significance of the raid, while others are of purely incidental, narrative interest. An example of the former is the fact, missing in the *Sīra*, that before attacking the Banu'l-Muṣṭaliq, the Prophet ordered 'Umar to call upon them to convert to Islam in order to protect their lives and property. Indeed, with a typically realistic narrative touch, 'Umar's actual words are reproduced: '*Qūlū lā ilāh illā Allāh tamna'ū bihā anfusakum wa-amwālakum*' ('Say there is no god but Allāh, protecting thereby yourselves and your property!'). (W I, 407) In the same vein al-Wāqidī provides a concrete reason for launching the raid with a report of how a scout was able to confirm by deceit the Banu'l-Muṣṭaliq's evil intentions. Surely there could be no reason other than a storyteller's love of immediacy and realistic detail for al-Wāqidī to tell us that the Prophet was resting under a tree, having his back rubbed by a little black slave, because he had hurt it when he fell from his camel during the night? Interestingly enough, this vignette is attributed to none other than 'Umar in order to set the scene for his offer to assassinate 'Abd Allāh b. Ubayy. (W II, 418)

Beyond matters of detail, al-Wāqidī narrates several significant reports left unmentioned by Ibn Isḥāq. Some of these serve as examples of, or possible precedents for, Muslim beliefs and practices. Among these I have already mentioned the Prophet's invitation, through 'Umar, to the Banu'l-Muṣṭaliq to avoid an attack by converting to Islam, which is, of course, a foreshadowing of the juristic 'necessity of invitation' as a preliminary to fighting pagan unbelievers.[16] Another anecdote with similar import concerns a spy for the Banu'l-Muṣṭaliq who, when captured, refuses to disclose any information about the activities of his fellow tribesmen, whereupon Muḥammad invites him to convert. He refuses until such time, he says, as the Muṣṭaliq make a joint decision in this regard. Decapitation is his reward, carried out by 'Umar with the Prophet's sanction. (W I, 406) Another instance of exemplary conversion occurs on the march to the camp of the Banu'l-Muṣṭaliq when a man of the 'Abd al-Qays presents himself to the Prophet to bear witness that 'I believe in you, and testify that you have brought the truth, and to fight with you against your enemy'. (W I, 406) The Prophet takes this encounter as an occasion to instruct the convert on 'God's favourite acts', namely the prompt performance of the prescribed daily prayers, which at this time were three. (W I, 406) Al-Wāqidī reinforces the theme of conversion during the expedition with two more instances: (1) after the battle the Prophet awarded a freedman who claimed to have induced the 'Abd al-Qaysī to convert, with a generous portion of the booty, since 'his conversion to Islam at your hands is the best thing that could happen to you between the rising and setting of the sun'. (W I, 409) In a typical narrative embellishment of this episode, al-Wāqidī claims that the tribesman declined the Prophet's original offer of sheep and camels for his service in favour of camels alone, to the Prophet's bemusement, and that he enjoyed the benefit of the camels for the rest of his life. (2) Juwayriyya's declaration to the Prophet, after the division of spoils that 'I am a Muslim woman, testifying that there is no god but God and that you are His Prophet!' (W I, 411) Ibn Isḥāq makes no mention at all of Juwayriyya's conversion, though his editor, Ibn Hishām, does claim that 'she became an excellent Muslim' after her converted father, al-Ḥārith, handed her over to the Prophet. (G 768) The rewards of conversion in the form of camels on the one hand and marriage to the Prophet on the other are obvious. In addition it should be noted that both al-Wāqidī and Ibn Isḥāq mention an example of the obverse of conversion, apostasy, when the brother of the Muslim slain in error abandoned Islam even though he was compensated by the Prophet for his brother's death. (W I, 408; G 492) Finally it should be mentioned that Ibn Isḥāq narrates one exemplary anecdote involving conversion that al-Wāqidī does not mention at all, namely the incident involving the false messenger to the Banu'l-Muṣṭaliq converts, which became the occasion for a Qur'anic revelation. (G 493)

Al-Wāqidī gives three more examples of Muḥammad's precedents for Muslim practices. Two of these, neither of which is mentioned by Ibn Isḥāq, relate to the Muṣṭaliq women taken as booty. While the Muslims who were awarded the captive women desired to get the ransom which would be paid for them, they also lusted after them because the celibacy imposed on them by the raid 'bore heavily upon them'. (W I, 413) Accordingly they asked for and received the Prophet's permission to practice *coitus interruptus* (*'azl*) until the women were ransomed or sold. In the same vein, when this practice was [labelled] as '*al-maw'ūda al-ṣughrā*' (the lesser coitus) by a Jewish vendor in Medina, the Prophet denounced the Jews as liars. (W

I, 413) Finally al-Wāqidī is much more expansive than Ibn Isḥāq on the subject of the booty in general taken on the raid. In contrast to the latter, who states merely that 'God gave the apostle their wives, children, and property as booty', (G 490) al-Wāqidī explains in detail how the Muslims' fifth was separated into alms (*ṣadaqa*) and booty (*fay'*) and distributed by an individual assigned this task by Muḥammad, the former being given to 'orphans, poor persons, and the weak.' (W I, 410–411) Interestingly enough, according to al-Wāqidī, orphans who had reached the age of puberty were given a share of the booty rather than alms, provided that they accept the obligation of jihad. But if they refused the obligation, they received nothing at all. (W I, 410) The remaining four-fifths of the booty was also distributed in an orderly manner under the supervision of Muslims appointed by the Prophet.

Other episodes developed more fully by al-Wāqidī do not function so overtly as Muhammadan precedents or examples but seem to serve other purposes in the author's presentation of the *Sīra*. One such purpose, I believe, was al-Wāqidī's desire to emphasise the role and significance of specific individuals or groups. In this respect, considerable attention is drawn to 'Umar b. al-Khaṭṭāb representing the Prophet's staunch defender and supporter; to 'Abd Allāh b. Ubayy b. Salūl as a hypocrite; and to the Muhājirūn and the Anṣār as a source of dissension and disunity in the Muslim community. 'Umar, it is true, does figure in Ibn Isḥāq's narrative, primarily as the one who impulsively but unsuccessfully advised the Prophet to have 'Abd Allāh b. Ubayy executed for his denunciation of the 'vagabond' Quraysh Emigrants in the melee before the battle. When Muḥammad later reminded 'Umar of the unsoundness of his advice, 'Umar contritely acknowledged that 'the apostle's order is more blessed than mine'. (G 492) In al-Wāqidī's version, 'Umar plays a more active role. Although his deferral to the Prophet's priority is not cited, he is credited, it will be recalled, with executing the recalcitrant unbeliever who refused to convert and with publicly inviting the Banu'l-Muṣṭaliq to convert to Islam as an alternative to war. (W I, 406, 407) More importantly, perhaps, 'Umar is the eyewitness quoted in two of al-Wāqidī's *isnād*s, as the authoritative source, in other words, of some of what transpired during the raid and its aftermath. (W I, 413; II, 418) One of these, on the authority of Isḥāq b. Yaḥyā from al-Zuhrī, from Mālik b. Aws b. al-Ḥadathān gives only the interesting report that the Prophet treated Juwayriyya, the Muṣṭaliq beauty whom he married, like all his other wives, i.e. he 'used to distribute (booty) to her in the same way as he did with his (other) wives, and he imposed the veil (*al-ḥijāb*) upon her'. (W I, 413) In the other he offered to kill 'Abd Allāh b. Ubayy. (W II, 418)

In contrast to the loyalty of 'Umar the role of the hypocrisy of 'Abd Allāh b. Ubayy is also more fully developed by al-Wāqidī than by Ibn Isḥāq. In the development of this theme al-Wāqidī focuses on 'Abd Allāh b. Ubayy but takes pains to stress that the entire raid was marred and threatened by the presence of dissident hypocrites – many of whom are identified by name (W II, 416) – who joined the expedition 'with no desire for jihad except the profits of this world that they would gain'. (W I, 405) Upon comparing the different treatments of this motif, it is striking that Ibn Isḥāq goes out of his way to present 'Abd Allāh in a sympathetic light by offering rationalisations of his conduct. Thus, Ibn Isḥāq says, the Anṣār told the Prophet 'that the boy, Zayd b. Arqam, may have misheard or misunderstood 'Abd Allāh's threat to drive the Quraysh from Medina, "sympathising with Ibn Ubayy and protecting him"'. (G 491) Even stronger support is offered by Usayd b. Ḥuḍayr, who advises the Prophet to 'treat him ['Abd Allāh b. Ubayy] kindly, for Allāh brought you to us when his people were stringing beads to make him a crown, and he thinks that you have deprived him of a kingdom'. (G 491, 278) Al-Wāqidī, on the other hand, says nothing about 'Abd Allāh's kingly ambitions and transforms the Anṣār's attempt to impeach Zayd's report into an opportunity to dramatise the boy's vehement insistence that he had heard and quoted 'Abd Allāh correctly: 'The Prophet disliked his report, so that his faced changed colour, and he said, "Boy, perhaps you were angry at him?" "No," Zayd said, "I heard this from him!" The Prophet said, "Perhaps your hearing was faulty?" "No, O Prophet of God!" The Prophet then said, "Perhaps it was obscure to you?" Zayd said, "No, by God! I did hear it from him, O Messenger of God!"' (W II, 420)

Zayd voiced similar protestations when some of the Anṣār rebuked him for slandering 'the leader of his people (*sayyid qawmika*) and breaking the ties of kinship'. '"By God," Zayd said, "I did hear that from him! By God, there is not one man of the Khazraj who is dearer to me than 'Abd Allāh b. Ubayy! Even, by God, if I heard these words from my father I would convey them to the Prophet! I hope that God the Exalted will send down a revelation to his Prophet in confirmation of my words!"' (W II, 417) Here appears another motif to which al-Wāqidī gives greater emphasis than Ibn Isḥāq, namely the desire, and its fulfilment, for a revelation confirming the integrity of a Muslim doubted by other Muslims, including the Prophet himself. The revelation does indeed come, complete with sweat and signs of pain on the Prophet's face. (W II, 418) But before it does, 'Abd Allāh b. Ubayy insists on his innocence to the Prophet himself and even after the revelation refuses to retract his slander or to repent. (W II, 420)

The motif of confirmatory revelation appears again in al-Wāqidī's version, again in the context of the theme of the opposition of hypocrites, when, on the rapid march back to Medina from the raid, one of Muḥammad's camels goes astray and cannot be found. On this occasion one Zayd b. al-Luṣayt, a hypocrite and an affiliate of some of the Anṣār, taunts the Muslims about God's failure to reveal to their prophet so trivial a thing as the whereabouts of his camel! Sure enough, a revelation soon comes down with the needed information, and Zayd, with this confirmation of Muḥammad's prophethood along with reproaches from loyal Muslims, professes his rebirth as a Muslim. But al-Wāqidī gives the conversion theme still another twist when he suggests that Zayd remained a false convert until his death and repeated his duplicitous behaviour on the raid against Tabūk. (W II, 423–425) No mention of this episode is found in Ibn Isḥāq's *Sīra*.

Another prominent theme of the raid in both accounts is the Prophet's ransom of and marriage to Juwayriyya, the daughter of the chief of Banu'l-Muṣṭaliq. In the *Sīra* Ibn Isḥāq tells us merely, on the authority of the jealous 'Ā'isha, that when the Prophet, impressed by her beauty, agreed to pay her ransom to the Muslim to whom she had been assigned as booty and then married her, the Muslims released a hundred families of her tribe, 'now that the Banu'l-Muṣṭaliq were the Prophet's relations by marriage'. (G 493) Al-Wāqidī recounts this story and repeats, along with Ibn Isḥāq, 'Ā'isha's words that 'I do not know of a woman who was greater blessing to her people than she'. (G 493; W I, 410) Later, he states his preference for 'Ā'isha's account to one which claimed that it was Juwayriyya's father, rather than the Prophet, who ransomed her and, moreover, gave his permission to Muḥammad to marry her. (W I, 412) In this respect it should be noted parenthetically that on no less than four occasions in his narration of the raid al-Wāqidī declares his preference for one *ḥadīth* over another, suggesting, perhaps, that he was not so cavalier in his citations of sources as some scholars have claimed. (W I, 407, 412; II, 419) Juwayriyya appears in other narrative and didactic guises in *al-Maghāzī*. To her are ascribed reports and portents of the fate that awaited her tribe as Muḥammad and his followers approached their territory. After she converted, al-Wāqidī states, she used to say that when news reached the Banu'l-Muṣṭaliq that 'Umar had executed the spy who refused to convert, fear filled her father and his followers, so that the Bedouin Arabs who had joined them quickly deserted. (W I, 406) She also had a vision, before the arrival of the Muslim raider, of the moon alighting in her lap from Medina; although this was an obvious portent of what was to occur she did not reveal it to her fellow tribesmen. (W I, 412) The significance of this vision was bound up with the issue of her conversion and marriage and, more importantly, the subsequent ransoming and freeing of her captive tribesmen and women. Her vision, she claimed, had nothing to do with later events since she never spoke to the Prophet about her tribe after he had freed and married her. Other reports state that the Prophet agreed to free all or some of the Banu'l-Muṣṭaliq prisoners as her bride price. But the soundest report in al-Wāqidī's view (*wa-hādhā'l-thabāt*) was that all the Banu'l-Muṣṭaliq women who had been taken prisoner were ransomed once they were taken to Medina. (W I, 412) Finally, in another instance of the vision motif Juwayriyya used to say after her conversion and marriage that before the attack the Muslims and their horses appeared innumerable which proved to be an illusory 'fear that God the Exalted had cast into the hearts of the Unbelievers'. (W I, 408–409)

Enough has been said, I think, to establish the originality of *Kitāb al-maghāzī* as a source and to demonstrate some of the means al-Wāqidī used to tell his own story in his own way. First, it is obvious that his version of the raid is much longer than Ibn Isḥāq's. Events recorded by both are amplified by al-Wāqidī with greater specificity and narrative detail, including direct quotations from the participants in the raid. Both, it is true, recount episodes omitted by the other, but al-Wāqidī clearly outstrips Ibn Isḥāq in this regard. However, most significant in my opinion, is al-Wāqidī's selection of anecdotes which illustrate specific motifs, in an attempt, I believe, to give his expanded narration of events some degree of thematic unity. Among those that we have cited is the dissension between the loyal Muslims and the Munāfiqūn. Although this theme also appears in the *Sīra*, al-Wāqidī as we have seen reinforces and individualises the drama by the increased attention he gives to individuals such as ʿUmar and ʿAbd Allāh b. Ubayy. Juwayriyya also receives greater attention as a part of al-Wāqidī's desire to emphasise the role of women on the raid in particular and in Muḥammad's life in general, focusing here on the roles of two of his wives. In this respect, the conversion of Juwayriyya is important as a variation on the several permutations of this theme, most of which stress the rewards of conversion and the penalty for refusing it. Who can have been better rewarded than Juwayriyya with her marriage to the Prophet and the freedom of her kinsfolk? Who could have been more grievously punished than the unrepentant spy with the loss of his life? The motif of confirmatory revelation apparent in the story of Zayd b. Arqam's suspect veracity is reinforced by al-Wāqidī when Muḥammad found his lost camel only through divine intervention. Minor motifs are also repeated by al-Wāqidī: signs and portents, for example, such as Zayd's recognition of the physical change in Muḥammad when he was receiving the revelation and those premonitions received by Juwayriyya regarding the threat posed by the Muslim raiders, echoed by the violent wind (mentioned by both authors) portending the death of a prominent Jew in Medina.

Finally it should be recognised that several of these themes and motifs of the raid recur in its aftermath, the story of the slander of ʿĀ'isha, in which the role of women is again stressed by both authors but for which al-Wāqidī has given better preparation by his greater attention to Juwayriyya, regarded by ʿĀ'isha as a rival for the Prophet's affections. Revelation confirming ʿĀ'isha's innocence has been prefigured by the one confirming Zayd's, again more fully elaborated by al-Wāqidī. Another case in point is the subversive role played by ʿAbd Allāh b. Ubayy in both the raid and the slander. Al-Wāqidī's greater attention to exemplary events can be seen in this unique report on the Prophet's condoning *coitus interruptus* on the raid and the substitution of sand for water in ablutions during the slander story. (W II, 427) Other minor motifs which I have not mentioned but which, with hindsight, might serve as unifying narrative elements include the races that al-Wāqidī alone says Muḥammad used to run with ʿĀ'isha, prefigured in the raid by mention of camel and horse races that the Muslims organised on their way back from the raid. (W II, 427, 426) Surely both these competitions serve only narrative – almost comic – relief? Camels, in fact, as trivial as they may seem, appear prominently in al-Wāqidī's raid – the lost camel and the convert's preference for camels to sheep have already been mentioned, perhaps as precursors to the camel bearing 'Ā'isha's litter and Ṣafwān b. al-Mu'aṭṭal's beast which bore her back in disgrace to Medina. Lost objects, Muḥammad's camel and 'Ā'isha's necklace, also constitute a unifying device for al-Wāqidī, as does water, or the scarcity of it. (W II, 415, 425, 427)

In conclusion, a couple of caveats: although I have been suggesting that al-Wāqidī can be seen on the basis of one episode as a better, fuller, storyteller than Ibn Isḥāq, with closer attention to detail and specifics, exemplary anecdotes and recurring motifs, it may well be that analysis of other episodes might yield different results, so that it would be foolhardy to make generalisations on the basis of this particular raid. Secondly, the whole basis of comparison is skewed by the assumption that Ibn Hishām's edition of Ibn Isḥāq's *Sīra* is a faithful one, disregarding the substantial additions made by Ibn Hishām, some of which turn up in al-Wāqidī. The need for a full comparison of the two – three, if we count Ibn Hishām's edition separately – works, with full attention to the use of *isnād*s, and, I might add, citations of Qur'anic revelations, is apparent. Finally, I would suggest that insufficient attention has been given by scholars to al-Ṭabarī's biography of the Prophet, given the fact that he used both Ibn Isḥāq and al-Wāqidī, complete with citations, as sources.

## Notes

1. References to this work will be to A. Guillaume's translation, *The Life of Muḥammad: A Translation of Sīrat Rasūl Allāh* (London, 1955), abbreviated as G in the text, and to the Arabic, *Das Leben Muhammed's nach Ibn Ishāq bearbeitet von Abd el-Malik Ibn Hischām*, ed. Ferdinand Wüstenfeld (Göttingen, 1858–1860), 3 vols., abbreviated as S.

2. References to this work will be to *The Kitāb al-Maghāzī of al-Wāqidī*, ed. Marsden Jones (London, 1966), 3 vols., abbreviated in the text as W.

3. Marsden-Jones, 'Ibn Isḥāq and al-Wāqidī: The Dream of 'Ātiqa and the Raid to Nakhla in Relation to the Charge of Plagiarism', *BSOAS*, 22 (1959), pp. 41–51.

4. Patricia Crone, *Meccan Trade and the Rise of Islam* (Princeton, NJ, 1987), p. 225.

5. Gregor Schoeler, *Charakter und Authentie der muslimischen Überlieferung über das Leben Mohammeds* (Berlin, 1996), p. 138.

6. Schoeler, *Charakter und Authentie*, p. 140.

7. Michael Lecker, 'The Death of the Prophet Muḥammad's Father: Did al-Wāqidī Invent some of the Evidence?', *ZDMG*, 145 (1995), p. 12.

8. G. H. A. Juynboll, 'Early Islamic Society as Reflected in Its Use of *Isnāds*', *Museon*, 107 (1994), p. 152.

9. Juynboll, 'Early Islamic Society', p. 183.

10. Ella Landau-Tasseron, 'Process of Redaction: The Case of the Tamimite Delegation to the Prophet Muḥammad', *BSOAS*, 49 (1986), pp. 253–270.

11. Michael Lecker, 'Wāqidī's Account on the Status of the Jews of Medina: A Study of a Combined Report', *JNES*, 54 (1995), pp. 15–32.

12. John Wansbrough, *The Sectarian Milieu: Content and Composition of Islamic Salvation History* (Oxford, 1978), p. 78.

13. Rizwi S. Faizer, 'Muḥammad and the Medinan Jews. A Comparison of the Texts of Ibn Ishaq's *Kitāb Sīrat Allāh* with al-Waqidi's *Kitāb al-Maghāzī*', *IJMES*, 28 (1996), p. 482.

14. Fred M. Donner, *Narratives of Islamic Origins: The Beginnings of Islamic Historical Writing* (Princeton, NJ, 1998); Albrecht Noth, *The Early Arabic Historical Tradition: A Source-Critical Study*, in collaboration with Lawrence I. Conrad, tr. Michael Bonner (2nd ed. Princeton, NJ, 1994).

15. Donner, *Narratives*, pp. 147–173.

16. See Majid Khadduri, *War and Peace in the Law of Islam* (Baltimore, MD, 1955), pp. 96–98.

5

# The Rise and Decline of *Taqiyya* in Twelver Shiʿism

*L. Clarke*

> The secret … the hiding of realities by negative or positive means, is one of man's greatest achievements. The secret produces an immense enlargement of life: numerous contents of life cannot even emerge in the presence of full publicity. The secret offers … the possibility of a second world alongside the manifest world.
>
> *Georg Simmel*[1]

*Taqiyya* (synonym *kitmān*) means among the Twelver Shiʿa either 'precautionary dissimulation of belief' or 'esoteric silence'. The first is the legal *taqiyya*, meant to guarantee, when necessary, the safety of the individual or community. The second (which is, I believe, quite distinct from the first) refers to the permanent guarding of a secret doctrine – essentially, that is, to esotericism. According to numerous *ḥadīth*s handed down from the Imams, the purpose of this second type is to protect the Truth from those not worthy of it. Such dicta, however, are only the seal of a wider esoteric complex with many functions and meanings. And this esoteric complex – aptly characterised by Henry Corbin as 'la discipline de l'arcane'[2] – does indeed facilitate 'numerous contents' of the Shiʿi worldview.

The first part of this essay demonstrates how esoteric *taqiyya* (to which the term *taqiyya* unless otherwise specified, henceforth refers) originally formed a necessary and integral part of Twelver Shiʿism. Without it, basic articles of early Shiʿism do not make sense and the system loses coherence. This proposition is illustrated through three central premises presented in the Traditions: first, the election of the Shiʿi community; second, the existence of a body of privileged Knowledge (*ʿilm*) belonging to the Imams; and third, quietism. The texts are sayings attributed to the Imams in books of Tradition collected before – or, in the case of Nuʿmānī's *Kitāb al-ghayba*, shortly after – the Occultation of the last,

Twelfth Imam in the mid tenth century.[3] I thus present an image of *taqiyya* in the early Imāmī community.

Many Twelver Shiʿa today[4] nevertheless deny *taqiyya* any special significance in their religion. The second part of the essay traces briefly some of the history behind this development. The evolution of *taqiyya* in Shiʿism is of interest not only for its own sake, but for the light it sheds on certain tensions within the tradition as a whole. A consideration of these brings the essay to a close.

## I

According to the dicta of the Imams, the Shiʿa are an elect community, superior to and apart from the others; this is a central proposition of the Tradition. Election is initially explained by several parallel myths of origin. It is said, for instance, that the only true believers are the Shiʿa because it was they who concluded the Covenant (*mīthāq*) with God in the primordial age by accepting the central tenet of loyalty (*walāya*) to the Imams.[5] And since the Shiʿa were created of a special substance – of pure clay and sweet water – akin to that of the Imams, no one can become a Shiʿi who was not created a Shiʿa, nor can a Shiʿi become a non-Shiʿi (for those 'rabble' were created of brackish water and inferior clay).[6] Thus love for the family of the Prophet and the Imams is the privilege of the created Shiʿa only. Others may wish to love them, but if they are among those who refused the *walāya* before they were created, they cannot. Similarly, as much as those who are numbered among the believers may try to disbelieve, they cannot: 'If a Shiʿi tries to abandon the right opinion, God shall return him to it by force!'[7]

*Taqiyya* plays a very important role in justifying and maintaining the central concept of election. God, we are told, has granted the Imams a special, occult knowledge (*ʿilm*). This knowledge is so extraordinary as to be oppressive; 'Our words (*ḥadīth*)', the Imams say in the Traditions, 'are difficult (*ṣaʿb*), such that none can bear them save an angel (*muqarrab*), a prophet sent with a message (*murassal*), or the servant whose heart God has tested for faith.'[8] When the Imams were commanded by God to propagate the 'secret' (*sirr*) and the knowledge (*ʿilm*) he gave them, they found no one to deposit it with except the Shiʿa.[9] As with loyalty, *ʿilm* can belong only to them; even if knowledge is revealed to a non-Shiʿi, he cannot really obtain it, since he is sure to misunderstand it. Possession of the secret confirms that the Shiʿa are an elite.

That the Shiʿa are elected to uniquely bear secret knowledge also makes them similar to the Imams, for the rare knowledge that they preserve through *taqiyya* from the unworthy is like the occult knowledge of the Imams. *Taqiyya* thus not only gives the Shiʿa a sense of superiority and solidarity against the majority; it also associates them in action with their sacred figures, the Imams. *Taqiyya* is the Shiʿi *Imitatio* of the Imams.

In order to understand the importance of *taqiyya* in relation to the *ʿilm* of the Imams (the second 'central premise' to be tested), it is necessary to focus on the form rather than supposed content of the secret. Prohibition against revealing knowledge serves to increase its value. This is the principle of the secret; human imagination enlarges that which it does not – and even more that which it cannot – know. In fact, it could be said that without *taqiyya*, there is no *ʿilm*; or, to borrow a phrase, '*taqiyya* is the message'. For, quite often (and I believe this to be largely true also for the Imāmī Shiʿa), the actual contents of the 'secret' of a sect or organisation are either not very significant in themselves, or not, in reality, hidden.[10] As the sociologist Simmel puts it, the allure of a secret exists separate from the 'momentary content' of what is concealed; the secret is instead primarily 'a *discursive strategy* that transforms a given piece of knowledge into a scarce and precious resource, a valuable commodity the possession of which bestows status, prestige, or symbolic capital on its owner'.[11] This is the function of statements attributed to the Imams asserting that, for instance, the divine mystery is 'a secret veiled in a secret';[12] or 'God likes to be worshipped in secret'.[13] It is also at least a part of the function of the strict prohibition against *idhāʿa*, the antonym of *taqiyya* denoting deliberate 'divulging' of supposed secrets to non-Shiʿis.

The largest number of pronouncements on *taqiyya*, however, speaks of the need to keep secrets from many or most *inside* the community. What could the function of these Traditions be? Would they not have undone the work of election by undermining feelings of community solidarity and intimacy with the Imams? Before attempting to answer this question, let us look at a few of the texts concerned.

The Traditions tell us that even the number of Shiʿa able to bear the full truth is small. The Sixth Imam, Jaʿfar al-Ṣādiq, reports that he brought up the subject of *taqiyya* one day in the presence of his grandfather the Fourth Imam, who was moved to declare:

> By God, if Abū Dharr had known what was in the heart of Salmān [al-Fārisī], he would have killed him – and the Prophet had made them 'brothers'! What then do you think would happen to the rest of the people [if the truth were revealed to them]? The knowledge possessed by learned men seems difficult, and is indeed so; none can bear it except a prophet sent with a message [and so on as in the similar Tradition cited above].[14]

*Taqiyya* applies, it is claimed, in different degrees to different kinds of knowledge. Some the Imams keep entirely to themselves, either because it was never meant to be revealed to humankind before the coming of the Mahdī, because they fear the consequences for themselves and their followers if their unconventional doctrine should come to the notice of the non-Shiʿa who would misunderstand it, or because they expect that their own followers would commit unbelief (*kufr*) by rejecting what they have to say.[15] For instance, the Eighth Imam, al-Riḍā, upon being asked about the sensitive issue of the vision of God (*ruʾyā*), simply refused to answer, saying only: 'If we were to give to you everything you wanted, it would be harmful for you, and "The Master of this Affair" [that is the Imam, meaning himself] would be seized by his neck!'[16] Another portion of the knowledge of the Imams may be disclosed to a select few, and a certain part may be revealed to the multitude:

> Some of our words we relate freely from the pulpit, and they are an adornment for us and put our enemies to shame. Others we speak of only to our Shiʿa, and they in turn speak of them only when they gather by themselves or visit one another. Then there are those of our words we relate only to one person or two persons – certainly not as many as three. And finally there are the words we entrust only to high fortresses, to secure hearts, firm minds, and unshakeable intellects .... [17]

If a Shiʿi relates a saying of the Imam to one who cannot bear it and is not fit to hear it, he deserves to be cursed and the Imam does *barāʾa* of him, that is he disassociates himself from him entirely;[18] that he had transmitted the narrative accurately does not help him.[19]

The function of Traditions such as these is to further accentuate the value of the exclusive Truth possessed by the community. For a Truth that is accessible to all or a substantial number of persons *even within the group* itself is still a lesser truth. The members of the group should feel that whatever learning they possess is valuable and unique; but they should not feel that there is nothing more to be had. Such a possibility would cancel a large part of the attraction of esoteric religion. Inaccessibility also sustains the ambition of the believers to attain higher levels of knowledge; it sustains, that is, their wonder and devotion.[20] To put it another way, the knowledge of the Imams becomes valuable to their followers not primarily as knowledge, but as mystery and charisma that can never be compassed, while it is, at the same time, a constant focus of aspiration. The mere idea or form of a secret has created for the Shiʿa 'a second world alongside the manifest world'.

Thus the value of the statement that the secret knowledge concealed by the heavy veil of *taqiyya* is 'unbearable' to most of humankind, that it is fully known only by 'less than three' persons and not even by the closest companions of the Imams, is that it keeps the secret always just out of reach. The language of such Traditions seems designed to build up 'symbolic capital'. They are not real statements about the distribution of knowledge, and there is no reason to suppose an actual secret kept from insiders or even outsiders. Similarly, the function of the Tradition that declares that the full meaning (*taʾwīl*) of the Qurʾan is known only by the Imams and will be finally revealed only at the end of time[21] is to underscore the mystery and inexhaustible potential of the revelation. The prohibition against naming the Mahdī is another example of the coining of symbolic capital. This is really sacred magic – of the order, perhaps, of refusing to pronounce the Name of God. It could have done nothing outside the logic of magic to actually 'conceal and protect' the Mahdī.[22] The existence of the whole recorded literature of the Traditions is itself, of course, evidence that *taqiyya* was often a discursive strategy rather than a real practice, since written communication is inherently opposed to secrecy.[23]

*Taqiyya*, then, does not simply guard Knowledge. It has, in effect, *created* the Knowledge on which so much of the prestige of the Imams and of the community depends. Without *taqiyya*, there is no *ʿilm*. Some of the Traditions quoted above, as well as in the first part of the section on quietism below, may in fact be read as protests or assurances that the famous Knowledge, despite its unavailability, does actually exist somewhere under the cover of *taqiyya*.

Finally, as for the importance of *taqiyya* to quietism: the necessity of *taqiyya* explains both why the Imams do not reveal all their knowledge – which would then trigger a final struggle with their enemies – and why they do not immediately rise up to defeat them, despite being the rightful rulers appointed by God. The 'discursive strategy' of *taqiyya* serves, in other words, as a check on messianic expectation.

The consequences of messianic fulfilment for a religious tradition are unsettling. Fulfilment or imminent fulfilment raises anticipation of a new age, which the Tradition has already painted in dramatic colours. The time of fulfilment, if it is ever felt to be near, is thus an 'open' one, in which the guardians of the Tradition must demonstrate their claims to authority and during which new claims may emerge. The degree to which expectation had been raised, in at least some Shiʿi circles, of a truly new and revolutionary order to be instituted by the returning Twelfth Imam can be seen in a group of traditions published in Nuʿmānī's late tenth-century *Kitāb al-ghayba* ('Book of the Occultation'). Here, the Fifth Imam Muḥammad al-Bāqir is reported as saying that the Mahdī when he comes would 'destroy that which came before him, just as the Messenger of God destroyed the order of pre-Islamic times – and then shall Islam begin anew'.[24] The Mahdī, say the Traditions in the *Kitāb al-ghayba*, shall come with 'a new book' (apparently meaning a new order and dispensation, rather than a book to replace the Qur'an) and 'new Sunna', 'a new rule' (*amr*, political order) and 'new judgement' (*qaḍāʾ*, a new legal order).[25]

The authoritative texts of a messianic tradition postpone the moment of fulfilment by locating it in an ever-receding future. In other words, in order to survive, the messianic tradition must both sustain and suspend the premise it is built on. Imposition of *taqiyya*, as we shall now see, accomplishes just that.

*Taqiyya*, it is said, is a 'trial', one of many which the Shiʿa undergo in this world to prove their faith, as in the words of Jaʿfar al-Ṣādiq: 'Our Shiʿa are tested … by their keeping of our secrets.'[26] But the Shiʿa have failed the trial. Thus the Imams do not reveal all their knowledge, because their followers cannot keep it from others. The Imams were ready, but the community was careless. This theme is addressed in the Traditions in the sharpest terms. Jaʿfar al-Ṣādiq witnessed the behaviour of his Shiʿa as they divulged his statements and remarked in disgust: 'These people claim that I am their Imam. By God, I am not any such thing! May God curse them; whenever I keep a secret, they violate it.'[27] Muḥammad al-Bāqir, in a similar mood, declared: 'God confided His secret to Gabriel, who confided it to Muḥammad, who confided it to 'Alī, who then passed it on to those whom he wished, one after the other [that is to the Imams in succession] – and now you talk about it on the streets!'[28]

If, say the Traditions, the Imams could have relied on their secret being kept, they would have revealed much more. The Fifth Imam says: 'By God, if your mouths were tied with thongs [if you were so reluctant to speak that one might think your mouths were bound – a phrase common in the Tradition], I would have told every man among you what was in store for him ... !'[29] The Fifth Imam sought only three men together to whom he could divulge his *ʿilm*, and if he had found these, he would, he claimed, have told them everything about the *ḥalāl* (permitted) and *ḥarām* (forbidden) until the coming of the Twelfth Imam.[30] If the Imams, furthermore, could have trusted their followers to say exactly as they said and no more, they would have acknowledged them as Companions. Do not Abū Ḥanīfa and Ḥasan al-Baṣrī have Companions (*aṣḥāb*)? Should not then the Imams, who know all that is in the universe, have their own companions? (yet they do not, since there are no reliable persons to be found).[31] The message of these texts is that messianic fulfilment is postponed because of the failings of the believers themselves – specifically, their failure to keep *taqiyya* – and not because the leadership or tradition has failed (which could not, of course, be admitted).

The Imams 'Alī and Ḥusayn did, of course, rise up and that, say that the traditions, is because their followers did, for a time, keep *taqiyya*. The companion Abū Baṣīr was told by Jaʿfar al-Ṣādiq that the 'door' to the Knowledge of the Imams had been opened to the companions of Ḥusayn for a time during his reign, for in that period 'there were thongs on their mouths', that is they behaved as if their mouths were bound and could be trusted to keep a secret.[32] But the age of knowledge came to an end because the followers of subsequent Imams could no longer be relied on to keep *taqiyya*. According to Jaʿfar al-Ṣādiq, the realisation of the 'affair', or *amr*, of the Imams was first put off because of the martyrdom of Ḥusayn – and then finally because people noised it about.[33] In another tradition, the Sixth Imam suggests that the *taqiyya* was first broken with the advent of the Abbasids: 'Our secret was well kept (*maktūm*) until it got into the hands of the Kaysanīs and they talked about it on the streets and in the villages of Iraq (*al-sawād*).'[34] Abū Baṣīr asked Jaʿfar: 'Is there no one to tell us about what is in the future, as 'Alī used to do for his Companions [i.e. will you not reveal to us the same knowledge]? 'By God, yes!' the Imam replied, 'But can you give me an example of one tradition I have related to you which you have kept secret?' Abū Baṣīr recalled: 'By God, I could not think of one!'[35] Because of these failings, *taqiyya* shall end only when the Mahdī returns.[36]

The Imams – or those who put into circulation the sayings attributed to them – go so far as to make *taqiyya* the ruling force of history. According to Shiʿi Tradition, there have always been two alternating *dawla*s – 'cycles' or 'reigns' – on the earth, one belonging to Satan, and one to God.[37] But there is, of course, no *dawla* that is not from God; rather it is God Himself who gives a cycle to Satan and a cycle to Adam.[38] What this implies is that it is not allowed to resist the cycle of Satan when it is ascendant. Thus the Fifth Imam is said to have remarked concerning the Umayyads (in whose time he lived) that they have a reign that people cannot shake; but when their time comes, those who are righteous and possess the truth (*ahl al-ḥaqq*) shall rule instead.[39] The Abbasids, similarly, have a *dawla* that is fixed.[40] Even if the whole world were to rebel against the Abbasids, the rebels would only be 'drenched in their own blood', if they rose before the proper signs of the coming of the Mahdī.[41]

Those who rise up before the appointed time are attempting to 'hasten' (*ʿ-j-l*) God's calendar.[42] The 'hasteners', as they are called, commit the sin of relying on their own will rather than the Will of God. Nuʿmānī comments:

> This sorrow [the Occultation] must exist and must also be lifted through the Will of God – not by the Will of His creatures and through their schemes .... The ones who will be destroyed during it are those who [attempt to] choose for themselves and are not content with the choice of their Lord, who attempt to hasten forward God's plan and are not patient.[43]

The Occultation, in other words, is a period in history to be characterised by complete and profound *taqiyya*. Messianic fulfilment is now out of the question.

It is characteristic of the believer that he views his whole life as rendered meaningful by his belief, and thus every adversity must also be shown to have meaning. In the face of the political necessity of quietism, it was for the Shiʿa the idea of *taqiyya* that supplied that meaning. It is for this reason that we find statements in the Tradition to the effect that patient faith and worship during the cycle of Satan, while maintaining *taqiyya* and awaiting the 'cycle of truth' (*dawlat al-ḥaqq*), are more praiseworthy than open worship after the appearance of the Mahdī. Worship in the former, says the Tradition, is always to be in secret and worship in the latter always public, and those who observe this rule – which has been, in fact, the rule of all prophets and believing communities in all ages[44] – shall go to Paradise.[45] Jaʿfar al-Ṣādiq was asked: 'Which is better: worship in secret while the Imam is hidden during the reign of falsehood, or worship while Truth and its reign are manifest, and the Imam is apparent?' 'By God,' the Imam replied, 'Your faithfulness in secret is better than your faithfulness in the open, and your worship in the reign of falsehood (*bāṭil*) while your Imam is hidden and you are fearful of the enemy and there is a truce [between us and them] is better than worship when the truth is manifest.' Jaʿfar then went on to describe the greater reward to be gained for each act of worship performed in secret, by those who 'adhere to *taqiyya* with regard to their religion, their Imam, and themselves, and who hold their tongues'.[46] Any distress the Shiʿa suffer is simply a condition of that cycle of history,[47] and actually better for them than the ease their enemies enjoy. When the Mahdī comes with 'the reign of the friend of God', the enemies of the Shiʿa will pay for their enjoyment with terrible punishment – while the Shiʿa will be well compensated for their suffering.[48]

Shiʿism has had to reconcile the reality of defeat, compounded by everyday integration into the community of the 'enemy',[49] with thoroughgoing triumphalism. As Momen puts it, there is a 'strange paradox' in Shiʿism's 'two contradictory attitudes of . . . patient endurance in suffering . . . [and] not submitting to tyranny and rising up and fighting even in the face of overwhelming odds and the certainty of martyrdom'.[50] Such a thoroughly reversed world, a world in which quietism – or better, forbearance in expectation of revenge – is superior to action could only be maintained in the hidden space created by *taqiyya*. Thus while the community appears to lose, it is victorious and knows so; while the Imams appear powerless, they foresee both the defeats they will suffer[51] and their final victory, and therefore, knowing God's plan, are in control of history; while the Shiʿa appear to suffer, they cannot ever really be harmed[52] and are in fact gathering blessings, while their enemies store up torment. ʿAlī is reported to have told a group of select followers in the month of Ramadan in which he was killed: 'Adhere [henceforth] to silence (*sukūt*), for they shall not be able to annihilate you while you maintain your own religion, and the enemy covets [what you have] and is envious.'[53]

*Taqiyya* also served to demonstrate to the followers of the Imams the error of their rivals, the most activist branch of the ʿAlids, the Hasanids. There is enough preoccupation in the Tradition with the Hasanids to make one think that some of the elements of the doctrines of *ʿilm* and *taqiyya* were formulated specifically in response to this group: that the Imam, knowing the future, knows also who shall rule; that history is governed by *dawla*s; and that the Imams keep hidden with them special books containing secret knowledge, along with the sword and other regalia of the Prophet.

The Hasanids, descendants of the Second Imam Ḥasan b. ʿAlī, would not accept Abbasid rule. The first and most significant uprisings were theirs. Their ambition was to lead the ʿAlids, and they asserted, like another rival activist branch, the Zaydīs, that the mark of the true Imam was that he would 'rise up' to establish his own rule. Neither did the Hasanids believe in the prescient and universal knowledge of the Imams, and in this too, they resembled the Zaydīs. This suggests an association between the idea of hidden knowledge and quietism; the connection, in fact, is a close one, as will shortly become clear.

Tradition reports that Jaʿfar al-Ṣādiq was informed of the Hasanid Muḥammad b. ʿAbd Allāh b. al-Ḥasan's claim to possess the scabbard of the Messenger of God. We know from history that ʿAbd Allāh b. al-Ḥasan, better known as al-Nafs al-Zakiyya or 'The Pure Soul', had indeed revived the military practices of the Prophet in Medina where his rebellion was staged, and that he claimed to use the Prophet's sword. Jaʿfar, however, denied that ʿAbd Allāh had the sword – that is he denied that the Hasanid was authorised to rise up in the name of the descendants of the Prophet.[54] Another Tradition relates how Jaʿfar al-Ṣādiq, asked when the 'relief' (*faraj*, i.e. the coming of the Mahdī) of his Shiʿa would come, stated that this would be after 'the Hasanid' had 'hastened' – that is before the proper time – to come out and fight. The Hasanid would, Jaʿfar said, be defeated and his head sent to Damascus – as was, in fact, done with the head of the unfortunate 'Pure Soul'.[55] The Sixth Imam, hearing that Muḥammad b. ʿAbd Allāh had asserted that he (Jaʿfar) did not have the knowledge (*al-ʿilm*), replied that indeed, he had, and that he also possessed the Prophet's sword and armour – ready to be used, it is implied, at the proper time known exclusively to him through *ʿilm* – whereas Muḥammad b. ʿAbd Allāh had neither one nor the other.[56]

Yaḥyā b. ʿAbd Allāh b. al-Ḥasan, the brother of al-Nafs al-Zakiyya, is also reported by Shiʿi Tradition to have reproached the Sixth and Seventh Imams for not rising up. Yaḥyā asserted that this was a sign that they were not worthy of the Imamate. The Seventh Imam, Mūsā al-Kāẓim, is supposed to have replied by writing to Yaḥyā, demanding that he prove his claims by answering two difficult questions about human anatomy (Yaḥyā, we are meant to understand, could not answer because he did not have the *ʿilm* a true Imam would have had). Al-Kāẓim predicted that Yaḥyā would be killed and advised him to seek clemency from the Abbasid caliph, Hārūn al-Rashīd. The Tradition goes on to relate how the caliph intercepted the letter and, reading it, remarked: 'People are trying to turn me against Mūsā the son of Jaʿfar, but he is innocent of that of which they accuse him!'[57] Ḥusayn b. ʿAlī, the Hasanid who rose up in the mid eighth century against the caliph al-Hādī, is reported in a Tradition to have asked the Seventh Imam, Mūsā al-Kāẓim, to swear fealty (*bayʿa*) to him. The Imam refused and stated that the Hasanid's uprising would be defeated and he himself killed – all of which came about exactly as he had predicted.[58]

The Hasanids rise up tragically unaware that they are acting contrary to God's plan but the Imams, in the meantime, fortified by the perfect occult Knowledge (convincingly embodied in the secret books they own) that opens up to them the long view of history, remain quiet and keep the arms of the Prophet, the exclusive sign of legitimate uprising, hidden. (In the Tradition, the secret books of *ʿilm* and the arms are often mentioned together as the warrant of the Imams, again highlighting the close relation between hidden knowledge and quietism.) The relations of the Twelver Imams with their Hasanid and Zaydī cousins are not portrayed in the Traditions as unfriendly. Rather, they feel pity for them and try to warn them.[59] This tone skilfully communicates the essence of their position – they feel pity rather than rivalry because their privileged knowledge of the certain course of events makes them utterly confident of their own position. Tradition reports that after al-Nafs al-Zakiyya once visited Jaʿfar al-Ṣādiq, the Imam's eyes filled with tears. His follower, curious, remarked: 'I see you doing on his account what you have never done for anyone before.' Jaʿfar explained: 'I pity him because he claims a thing [lit. 'an affair', also meaning legitimate rule] that does not belong to him. [Looking into] the [occult] Book of ʿAlī, I find him neither among the successors of this community, nor among its kings.'[60]

## II

In the first section, I presented a picture of *taqiyya* from the world of early Imāmī Shiʿism. The heritage of that world is still carried by the Twelvers in the Traditions. Nevertheless, the dominant (though not exclusive) trend among Twelver Shiʿa in our time is to minimise *taqiyya*; as Walker has observed, there is 'almost always' present in modern Shiʿism 'a tendency to claim that the nobler course is to abstain from practising it, if at all possible'.[61] How did this change come about?

A full historical study of the development of Twelver *taqiyya* might reveal an ebb and flow, rather than the linear progress sketched below.[62] A detailed survey of current tendencies would also likely reveal nuances in the landscape of modern Shiʿism. For the purposes of this study, however, I have limited myself to a preliminary review.

The first outstanding figure to be noticed after the early Traditions is Ibn Bābawayh (d. 413/991). Ibn Bābawayh's writings highlight the moderate face of Tradition, bridging the Traditionists who preceded him and the jurisprudents who came after. Nevertheless, in his 'Articles of Faith' (*iʿtiqādāt*), he says straightforwardly of *taqiyya* that it is 'obligatory' (*wājiba*). He who abandons (*t-r-k*, the word used for abandonment of a positive duty) *taqiyya*, warns Ibn Bābawayh, is like one who abandons prayer. 'It is not permitted to lift one's *taqiyya* until such time as "He Who Shall Arise" [the Twelfth Imam] emerges; and he who does so before places himself outside God's religion and the religion of the Imāmīs.'[63] Like Nuʿmānī, the author of the *Kitāb al-ghayba*, Ibn Bābawayh imposes the 'deep *taqiyya*' of the Occultation.

An important shift – in my view, the crucial shift – in the exposition of *taqiyya* then occurs with the rationalist theologian Shaykh al-Mufīd's (d. 413/1022) revision of Ibn Bābawayh's 'Articles of Faith', in his equally famous 'Correction of the Creed Through Just Critique' (*Taṣḥīḥ al-iʿtiqād fī ṣawāb al-intiqād*). According to al-Mufīd, *taqiyya* consists of nothing more than

> … concealing one's beliefs concerning the Truth and refraining from conversing openly about them with those opposed to oneself, both in regard to religion and

worldly affairs, as necessity dictates. *Taqiyya* becomes obligatory if there is known to exist or if it may be reasonably supposed that there exists a 'dire necessity'. But if there is no certain or likely harm in publishing the Truth, the duty of *taqiyya* does not apply.

It is true, admits al-Mufīd, that the Imams had advised some of their Shiʿa to practise *taqiyya* because it was in their own best interests; but they also used to urge others for whom it was not dangerous to openly engage with their opponents. Thus, the shaykh concludes, *taqiyya* is obligatory in some circumstances, but void as a duty in others; and if Ibn Bābawayh had taken care to make a qualified instead of an absolute statement, he would not have found himself tangled in the contradiction of prescribing *taqiyya* while making Shiʿi belief known, 'to the ends of the earth', through his own writings and public pronouncements.[64]

What al-Mufīd has done is to shift the focus from the *taqiyya* of esotericism to *taqiyya* as a legal subject. He has cast off the first, and limited himself to arguing about the second. This is highlighted by his dense use of legal language: 'duty' (*farḍ*), the 'voiding' or 'becoming null' (*s-q-ṭ*) of a duty, 'abandoning an obligation' (*tark al-wājib*), and 'absolute' (*ṭ-l-q*) and 'restricted' (*q-y-d*), as in the wording of a command or prohibition. The crucial legal term, however, is 'dire necessity' (*ḍarūra*). Here is the clearest indication that al-Mufīd is speaking not of a permanent duty or belief (as in Ibn Bābawayh's parallel between *taqiyya* and prayer), but something that is almost the direct opposite, since it takes effect only when forced by circumstances – that is the practical, necessitous, legal *taqiyya*. Ibn Bābawayh, on the other hand, consistent with the aims of a Creed, is speaking about *taqiyya* as a sacred belief – that is about esotericism. He recommends the *form* of a secret, a 'discursive strategy'; and there is no contradiction between open publication of his beliefs and advocacy of this *taqiyya*, as long as he continues to assert that a 'secret' does nevertheless exist, that there is still more to be known. Al-Mufīd, I think, knew the distinction between the two; but he was, after all, engaging in polemics, and his tactic serves the useful purpose of allowing him to sidestep the (for him) difficult question of esotericism.

Another attraction away from *taqiyya* for the Shiʿa has been the prospect of rapprochement with the majority Sunni community. The two attractions were, in fact, twins, since ratio-legalism once did provide (even if it does no longer today) a grounds for rapprochement.[65]

The move away from *taqiyya* – and then, following in consequence, even from legal, necessitous *taqiyya* – was thus accelerated by Sunni polemic. The favourite tactic of this polemic, not only in the case of *taqiyya* but also other controversial Shiʿi positions, was and still is to 'put the Shiʿa in their place' as heretics by bringing up Traditionalist beliefs – and sometimes also extremist *ghulāt* beliefs – that most of the community had already shed. The Ḥanbalī reformer Ibn Taymiyya's (728/1328) characterisation of *taqiyya* in his *Minhāj al-sunna fī naqḍ kalām al-shīʿa*

('Refutation of Shiʿi Doctrine by Way of the Sunna') is the mother of subsequent anti-Shiʿi polemic on this subject. According to Ibn Taymiyya, *taqiyya* is a Shiʿi 'principle of religion', that is an article of the Shiʿi creed. *Taqiyya* is lying and 'hypocrisy' – for what is hypocrisy other than that a man speak what he does not hold in his heart? The Shiʿa even go so far as to put in the mouth of Jaʿfar al-Ṣādiq the words: '*Taqiyya* is my religion and the religion of my fathers' – whereas (says Ibn Taymiyya) these were in reality the most truthful of men.[66]

The further path along which the Shiʿa presentation of *taqiyya* was driven as it was pursued by Sunni polemics can be seen in an exchange between the philosopher-theologian and exegete Fakhr al-Dīn al-Rāzī (d. 606/1209) and Twelver philosopher-theologian Naṣīr al-Dīn al-Ṭūsī (d. 672/1274). In his *Muḥaṣṣal*, al-Rāzī characterises, rather offhandedly, 'permissibility' of *taqiyya* as one of the 'rules' (*qāʿida*) of the Shiʿa. This essentially accurate mention elicits from al-Ṭūsī a disproportionately strong reaction. *Taqiyya*, he rejoins, 'is *not* permitted by the Shiʿa, except if someone were to fear harm against himself or those associated with him, such that an injury or corruption (*fasād*, a strong word) would inevitably befall a vital aspect (*amr aẓīm*) of religion'; but if such a condition does not obtain (al-Ṭūsī repeats for emphasis) the Shiʿa do not allow it.[67] Here al-Ṭūsī, while unable to claim that *taqiyya* is foreign to Shiʿism altogether, (something he might have liked to do), again limits it to the legal, necessitous kind – and then severely restricts even that.

More recently, modern politics has brought about a further downgrading of both esoteric and necessitous *taqiyya*. The problem is essentially this: both forms of *taqiyya* imply a quietism incompatible with the activism of the politicised religion that Shiʿism has become for many people. Objections by Sunnis against the perceived heretical colouring of *taqiyya* are also detrimental to the hope many of the Shiʿa currently cherish of rapprochement between themselves and other Muslims so that they can take a leading role in the Muslim world. The declaration of Ayatollah Khomeini during unrest in Iran in the early 1960s that non-involvement in politics under cover of *taqiyya* is illicit was one significant result of this.[68] Minimisation of *taqiyya* has not, however, resulted in a significant increase in messianic expectation; for the reason, I think, that the eternal hope has been replaced by expectations of political-economic restoration – what I would call 'political messianism'.

The present-day standard Shiʿi apologetic concerning *taqiyya* now typically combines a severe restriction upon it, as a defence against Ibn Taymiyya-like attacks, with the political argument. The 'Origin and Principles of the Shiʿa' or *Aṣl al-shīʿa wa-uṣūluhā* of Shaykh Muḥammad Ḥusayn Kāshif al-Ghiṭā' (d. 1954) is one widely read example. *Taqiyya*, Kāshif al-Ghiṭā' argues, applies only 'when necessary', while the martyrdom of Shiʿis in the past demonstrates that, far from being secretive or fearful, Shiʿism actively propagates the truth.[69] The phrase 'when necessary' alludes to a Tradition, obviously aimed at the practical, legal *taqiyya*, that describes it as applying to 'instances in which it is necessary'. This legal text is the one now popularly cited by the Shi'a in defence of their position; it is taken, apparently, to mean only instances in which it is absolutely necessary, as in threat to life.[70] Consequently, according to many and possibly a majority of modern believers, Shi'ism is active and open. *Taqiyya* is reduced to, at the most, something like the legal *taqiyya* found in Sunnism, the concept in both traditions being based on the incident in which a revelation relieved the Companion of the Prophet, 'Ammār ibn Yāsir, of blame for having outwardly denied his faith under torture.[71]

Thus the 'second world' of the Twelvers created by *taqiyya* and the propositions it once sheltered appear to have collapsed together. Not only quietism, but also election (which had already begun to be moderated by the time of the collection of al-Kulaynī's *Kāfī*, that is by the tenth century)[72] are no longer central tenets of Twelver Shi'ism. In fact, the Traditions that support election, as far as they are known at all, are regarded by the Shi'a as strange and repugnant. Most Twelvers seem to prefer the proposition that Muslims are one community and that, as far as the Shi'i way is superior, that can be demonstrated to any person through open argument. The symbolic strategy of *taqiyya* is of no use to this attitude.

As for the knowledge of the Imams, that was displaced in the tenth or eleventh century by *'iṣma*, divine 'protection' from error. That is to say, whereas the most important claim of the Imams in the Traditional literature is to knowledge, in subsequent systematic and rationalist arguments, the lynchpin of their pre-eminence is protection. Protection is still a mysterious quality, but not one that has to be adorned by secrecy. There is also increased focus in the present day on the *moral* qualities of the Imams, which can be understood and imitated by ordinary people;[73] the impenetrable mystique of *taqiyya* is not relevant to this view. The idea of privileged occult knowledge *within* the group has also lost its appeal, since the ambitions of believers are presently focused on acquired and discussable kinds of knowledge – for instance, ordinary religious learning such as sectarian history and ethics.

As for the secret as an inter-group strategy, sociologists have tended, apparently following Simmel's lead, to emphasise the fascination of secrecy and the secret as 'adornment'. But secrecy can also, of course, draw suspicion and hostility and be a liability. As we have just seen, prominent Twelver scholars decided fairly early on that the advantages of esoteric *taqiyya* for the community such as solidarity and self-esteem were far outweighed by just those disadvantages.

Why, one wonders, did the Twelver faction of Shi'ism move away from esotericism, while others such as the Ismailis and Druze remained drawn towards it? The answer is to be found, perhaps, in an accumulation of historical and social circumstances. The Imāmīs gained enough strength to be able to establish open communities even under non-Shi'i regimes; and they had at times both the chance to rule, and the gratifying experience of being acknowledged by Sunnis as a force – as, for instance, in the episode with the caliph al-Maʿmūn. There was the critical mass, that is, to begin to pull them toward the centre; and as the scholars responded with their own initiatives, such as the construction of a system of law parallel to that of the Sunni majority and moderation of Extremist doctrines, that momentum was generally sustained. Ironically, the first step in the process that would eventually whittle down Twelver esotericism was the preservation and growth of the community under shelter of quietism – which depended, ultimately, on the idea of *taqiyya*.

## Notes

1. Kurt H. Wolff, tr. and ed., *The Sociology of Georg Simmel* (New York, 1950), p. 330.

2. *En Islam iranien. Aspects spirituels et philosophiques* (Paris, 1971), 4 vols., vol. 1 (*Le Shîʿisme duodécimain*), and in other places (see Index).

3. *Kitāb al-aṣl* of Sulaym b. Qays al-Hilālī (d. between 65/694 and 95/714), also known as *Kitāb Sulaym*: *Kitāb Sulaym ibn Qays* (Najaf, n.d.), authenticity in doubt; for a summary of arguments for and against, see Khūʾī, *Muʿjam al-rijāl*, s.v. 'Sulaym bin Qays'; a recent, relatively optimistic Western assessment in Maria Dakake, 'Loyalty, Love, and Faith: Defining the Boundaries of the Early Shiʿite Community' (Ph.D., Princeton University, 2000). A manuscript of *Sulaym*, in any case, survives from the early 4th/10th century, and thus is within the time period covered here (see *GAL*, vol. 1, 199; *GAS*, vol. 2, 525–526; Āghā Buzurg Ṭihrānī, *Dharīʿa*, vol. 2, p. 157; W. Madelung, 'Die Šīʿa', in Helmut Gätje, ed., *Grundriss der Arabischen Philologie. Band II. Literaturwissenschaft*, Wiesbaden, 1987, p. 263); A collection of sixteen 'notebooks' (*aṣl*, that is traditions written down by persons who heard directly from the Imams): *al-Uṣūl al-sitt ʿashar*, ed. Ḥasan Muṣṭafawī (n.p., 1371/1951); Abū Jaʿfar Aḥmad b. Muḥammad al-Barqī (d. 274/887), *Kitāb al-Maḥāsin*, ed. Jalāl al-Dīn al-Ḥusaynī (Qumm, 1371/1951); Abū Ṣaffār al-Aʿraj al-Ṣaffār al-Qummī (d. 290/903), *Baṣāʾir al-darajāt fī ʿulūm Āl Muḥammad*, ed. Mīrzā Ḥasan Kūcha-bāghī (Tabrīz, 1380/1960); Abu al-ʿAbbās ʿAbd Allāh b. Jaʿfar al-Ḥimyarī (d. 290/903), *Qurb al-isnād*, ed. ʿAbd al-Mawlā al-Ṭurayḥī (Najaf, 1369/1950); Furāt b. Ibrāhīm al-Kūfī (d. 300/912), *Tafsīr Furāt al-Kūfī* (Najaf, n.d.); al-Naḍr (or Abu al-Naḍr) Muḥammad b. Masʿūd al-Sulamī, al-ʿAyyāshī (d. last part of the 3rd/9th century), *Kitāb al-tafsīr*, ed. Hāshim al-Rasūlī al-Maḥallātī (Tehran, n.d.), 2 vols.; Abu al-Ḥasan ʿAlī b. Ibrāhīm al-Qummī (d. early 4th/10th century), *Tafsīr al-Qummī*, ed. Ṭayyib al-Mūsawī al-Jazāʾirī (Najaf, 1387/1967–1968), 2 vols.; Abu al-Qāsim Saʿd b. ʿAbd Allāh al-Khalaf al-Ashʿarī al-Qummī (d. 301/914), *Mukhtaṣar baṣāʾir al-darajāt* [but unrelated to the work of the same name by al-Ṣaffār al-Qummī] (Najaf, 1370/1950) (This is in fact an abridgement of al-Ashʿarī al-Qummī's original work, by al-Ḥasan b. Sulaymān al-Ḥillī, d. early 10th/15th century, and contains a small number of *ḥadīth*s gathered by al-Ḥillī from other sources; see *GAS*, II, p. 538; *Dharīʿa*, vol. 2, p. 124 and vol. 20, p. 182); Abū Jaʿfar Muḥammad b. Yaʿqūb al-Kulaynī al-Rāzī (d. 329/941), *al-Uṣūl al-Kāfī*, ed. Jawād Muṣṭafawī (Tehran, n.d.), 4 vols.; Muḥammad b. Ibrāhīm al-Nuʿmān (fl. ca. mid 4th/mid 10th century), *Kitāb al-ghayba* (Beirut, 1403/1983); Abu al-Ḥasan ʿAlī b. al-Ḥusayn al-Masʿūdī (d. 345/956) or pseudo-Masʿūdī (see *EI2*, s.v. 'al-Masʿūdī', by Ch. Pellat), *Ithbāt al-waṣiya li'l-imām Abī Ṭālib* (Qumm, n.d.).

4. I refer throughout to Uṣūlī Twelvers; the Akhbārīs, who remain closer to the Shiʿism of the Traditions, are a different case.

5. E.g. al-ʿAyyāshī, *Tafsīr*, vol. 2, pp. 218–220, 126; al-Barqī, *Maḥāsin*, p. 136; al-Ashʿarī, *Baṣāʾir*, pp. 168 and 169; al-Qummī, *Tafsīr*, vol. 2, p. 271; Furāt, *Tafsīr*, pp. 88 and 161.

6. See for examples al-Kulaynī, *al-Kāfī*, vol. 3, p. 3; al-Barqī, *Maḥāsin*, pp. 133, 282; Ṣaffār, *Baṣāʾir*, p. 14, and this chapter in general); Ṣaffār, *Baṣāʾir*, pp. 80–81; Furāt, *Tafsīr*, p. 8.

7. *Uṣūl*, p. 103; al-Barqī, *Maḥāsin*, p. 200. From the Sixth Imam. See also al-Barqī, *Maḥāsin*, p. 280.

8. This formula is repeated many times, on the authority of different Imams. See for example Ṣaffār, *Baṣāʾir*, pp. 20–28 and al-Kulaynī, *al-Kāfī*, vol. 2, pp. 253–257.

9. Al-Kulaynī, *al-Kāfī*, vol. 2, pp. 255–257. From the Sixth Imam.

10. See Jan N. Bremmer, 'Religious Secrets and Secrecy in Classical Greece', in Hans G. Kippenberg and Gedaliahu G. Stroumsa, ed., *Secrecy and Concealment: Studies in the History of Mediterranean and Near Eastern Religions* (Leiden and New York, 1995), p. 72 and Hugh Urban, 'The Torment of Secrecy: Ethical and Epistemological Problems in the Study of Esoteric Traditions', *History of Religions*, 37 (1998), pp. 211–248; see esp. pp. 235 ff.

11. Wolff, *Simmel*, p. 332. Emphasis added.

12. Ṣaffār, *Baṣāʾir*, pp. 28–29, *passim*; al-Ashʿarī, *Baṣāʾir*, pp. 126 and 127.

13. Al-Kulaynī, *al-Kāfī*, vol. 3, pp. 309, 317; al-Ashʿarī, *Baṣāʾir*, pp. 101, 105 and 106.

14. Ṣaffār, *Baṣāʾir*, p. 25; al-Kulaynī, *al-Kāfī*, vol. 2, p. 254; al-Ashʿarī, *Baṣāʾir*, pp. 124–125. Abū Dharr and Salmān were declared 'brothers' by the Prophet in Medina, during the 'brothering' of the Emigrants and Helpers.

15. Thus Jaʿfar al-Ṣādiq declared that he would only relate a portion of the 'rights of a believer over another believer' because he feared that 'it could not be borne' by his questioner! (Al-Kulaynī, *al-Kāfī*, vol. 3, pp. 252–253, 274–275)

16. Al-Kulaynī, *al-Kāfī*, vol. 3, pp. 318, 274–275.

17. Furāt, *Tafsīr*, p. 132. From ʿAbd Allāh b. Muḥammad, the militant Hasanid! For this reason Jaʿfar al-Ṣādiq told one of his Companions to gather at different times with people of different degrees of understanding, rather than keep his rarest knowledge completely to himself. (Al-Ashʿarī, *Baṣāʾir*, pp. 102–103)

18. *Barāʾa* is the opposite of *walāya*; it is a kind of formal disavowal. See E. Kohlberg, 'Bara'a in Shīʿī Doctrine', *Jerusalem Studies in Arabic and Islam*, 7 (1986), pp. 139–175.

19. Nuʿmānī, *Ghayba*, p. 23. From the Sixth Imam, with the comment of the author. See also al-Kulaynī, *al-Kāfī*, vol. 4, p. 78.

20. These points are not, I believe, noticed by Simmel or his successors.

21. Al-Ḥimyarī, *Qurb*, p. 70.

22. Cf. Mohammad Ali Amir-Moezzi's *Le guide divin dans le shiisme originel: aux sources de l'esoterisme en Islam* (Lagrasse, 1992), tr. by David Streight as *The Divine Guide in Early Shiʿism* (Albany, NY, 1994) (with revisions). Amir-Moezzi regards the concealing of the Mahdī's identity as a strategy on the part of 'Imamate logic' to 'save the life of the Mahdī' (pp. 103–104). I, on the other hand, would regard exhortations to conceal the number of Imams and name the Mahdī only by epithets, separated letters, and so on, as attempts to enlarge his legend. Amir-Moezzi appears in general to view *taqiyya* as real, socio-political action; but I find that he comes closer to seizing the essence of *taqiyya* when he describes it as a 'sacred duty' (p. 81; see also p. 129).

23. Wolff, *Simmel*, p. 340.

24. Nuʿmānī, *Ghayba*, p. 152; see also *Kitāb Sulaym*, p. 110 and *Ghayba*, p. 164.

25. Nuʿmānī, *Ghayba*, pp. 128, 154, 155, 171, 175; see also pp. 220–221.

26. Al-Ḥimyarī, *Qurb*, p. 52.

27. Nuʿmānī, *Ghayba*, p. 23; see also al-Ashʿarī, *Baṣāʾir*, p. 102.

28. Nuʿmānī, *Ghayba*, p. 32; al-Ashʿarī, *Baṣāʾir*, pp. 104–105; al-Kulaynī, *al-Kāfī*, vol. 3, p. 318.

29. Al-Barqī, *Maḥāsin*, p. 258; Ṣaffār, *Baṣāʾir*, p. 104; al-Kulaynī, *al-Kāfī*, vol. 1, p. 394; Nuʿmānī, *Ghayba*, p. 23. For a similar statement by ʿAlī, see Ṣaffār, *Baṣāʾir*, p. 305 and Ashʿarī, *Baṣāʾir*, p. 105.

30. *Uṣūl*, p. 91; al-Ashʿarī, *Baṣāʾir*, pp. 98, 99 and 106. See also al-Kulaynī, *al-Kāfī*, vol. 3, p. 340.

31. Al-Kulaynī, *al-Kāfī*, vol. 3, p. 316; al-Ashʿarī, *Baṣāʾir*, p. 101.

32. *Ṣaffār, Baṣāʾir*, pp. 260–261. See also al-Kulaynī, *al-Kāfī*, vol. 1, p. 395.

33. Al-Ashʿarī, *Baṣāʾir*, p. 102.

34. Al-Kulaynī, *al-Kāfī*, vol. 3, p. 316. The Kaysanīs were a movement in favour of the Imamate and rule of Muḥammad b. al-Ḥanafiyya, another of the sons of ʿAlī. The group rose up and seized Kūfa in the years 66–67/685–687, but was soon defeated.

35. Ṣaffār, *Baṣāʾir*, pp. 258, 261, 262.

36. Ibid., pp. 28, 21.

37. ʿAyyāshī, *Tafsīr*, vol. 1, p. 199; al-Masʿūdī, *Ithbāt al-waṣiya*, p. 14.

38. ʿAyyāshī, *Tafsīr*, vol. 2, p. 106.

39. Nuʿmānī, *Ghayba*, p. 129.

40. Ibid., p. 167.

41. Ibid., p. 205.

42. The Fifth Imam al-Bāqir says to his brother Zayd: 'Do not hasten, for God will not hasten because of the haste of His servants'. (Al-Kulaynī, *al-Kāfī*, vol. 2, pp. 171–172)

43. Nuʿmānī, *Ghayba*, p. 128. See also Furāt, *Tafsīr*, p. 6.

44. A subject treated extensively in the *ḥadīths*, in accord with the Shiʿi belief that the lives of the Imams and community re-enact those of the past prophets and their communities. Thus, according to the Eighth Imam, al-Riḍā, the keeping of *taqiyya* is in fact the *Sunna* or custom of God which humankind was obliged to take upon itself (al-Kulaynī, *al-Kāfī*, vol. 3, p. 339). Because God 'refused to be worshipped except in secret until the proper time should come for His religion to be manifested', Muḥammad and his wife Khadīja concealed their faith until God ordered it to be announced, and ʿAlī also did not make his *islām* public until the appointed time. (al-Kulaynī, vol. 1, pp. 364–365, from the Fifth Imam)

45. Al-Masʿūdī, *Ithbāt al-waṣiya*, p. 14. See also *Uṣūl*, p. 52.

46. Al-Kulaynī, *al-Kāfī*, vol. 2, pp. 128–129.

47. *Uṣūl*, pp. 4–5; see also Ashʿarī, *Baṣāʾir*, p. 112.

48. God has put 'fear and calamity' into the cycle of the enemies of the Imams, but that is a 'delight' to them. (*Uṣūl*, p. 16)

49. From this last circumstance there grew up an ideal of exclusive association (*ṣuḥba*, *jalsa*) with one's own community. The Fifth Imam says: 'When God, Exalted and Glorified be He, is angry with His community, He forbids us to associate with them.' (Al-Kulaynī, *al-Kāfī*, vol. 2, p. 145)

50. Moojan Momen, *An Introduction to Shīʿī Islam* (New Haven, CT, 1985), p. 236.

51. ʿAlī knew that he would be defeated at the Battle of Ṣiffīn, and the Prophet Muḥammad knew that the Umayyads would prevail, and he passed on that knowledge to ʿAlī and the Imams. (al-Qummī, *Tafsīr*, vol. 2, pp. 60–61)

52. E.g. the Fifth Imam said: 'Any affliction suffered in this world by one whom God has honoured with being one of our Shiʿa – even if he cannot find anything to eat other than grass – will not harm him.' (*Uṣūl*, p. 61)

53. Al-Ashʿarī, Baṣā'ir, p. 104.

54. Ṣaffār, *Baṣā'ir*, pp. 177, 184, also pp. 168–169.

55. Nuʿmānī, *Ghayba*, pp. 180–181. The Imams often warn their followers not to 'come out [and fight]', *kharaja* being a term in Islam in general for activism.

56. Ṣaffār, *Baṣā'ir*, p. 153.

57. Al-Kulaynī, *al-Kāfī*, vol. 2, pp. 188–189. The title of the chapter is: 'That by which true claims to the imamate are distinguished from false claims.'

58. Al-Kulaynī, *al-Kāfī*, vol. 2, p. 187.

59. E.g. Ibid., vol. 2, pp. 173 ff. and vol. 3, pp. 226–227.

60. That is neither among the legitimate successors of the Prophet, nor even among those possessing purely temporal rule. (Ṣaffār, *Baṣā'ir*, pp. 168–169.)

61. John Esposito, ed., *Oxford Encyclopedia of the Modern Islamic World*, s.v. 'Taqīya', by Paul E. Walker.

62. Entry of '*taqiya*', '*taqiyya*' and '*takiyyah*' into the *Index Islamicus* brings up more than a dozen articles on the subject. The beginning point is Ignaz Goldziher's 'Das Prinzip der Takijja im Islam', *ZDMG*, 60 (1906), pp. 213–226, while Etan Kohlberg's 'Taqiyya in Shiʿi Theology and Religion', in Kippenberg, ed., *Secrecy and Concealment*, pp. 345–380, gathers much information; Diane Steigerwald's 'La dissimulation (*taqiyya*) de la foi dans le shiʿisme ismaelien', *Studies in Religion/Sciences religieuses*, 27 (1988), pp. 39–59 treats with the esoteric discipline in particular. Some of the development up to Shaykh Mufīd is covered in various parts of Martin J. McDermott, *The Theology of al-Shaikh al-Mufīd* (Beirut, 1978), see references in the index, as well as in Paul Sander, *Zwischen Charisma und Ratio. Entwicklungen in der frühen imāmitischen Theologie* (Berlin, 1994), see the 'Thematic Index' in the back.

63. *Iʿtiqādāt al-Ṣadūq*, together with Ibn al-Muṭahhar al-Ḥillī's *Sharḥ al-bāb al-ḥādī ʿashar*, in Arabic but under the Persian title *Sharḥ-i bāb-i ḥādī ʿashar* (Tehran, 1370/1950–1951), p. 104.

64. *Taṣḥīḥ al-iʿtiqād fī ṣawāb al-intiqād aw sharḥ ʿaqā'id al-ṣadūq* (Qumm, 1363 Sh./1984 or 5), pp. 115–116. An essentially similar but less pointed statement in Mufīd's *Awā'il al-maqālāt* is translated in McDermott, *Theology*, pp. 317 and 281.

65. See Ahmad Kazemi Moussavi, 'Sunnī-Shīʿī Rapprochement (*Taqrīb*)', in L. Clarke, ed. and tr., *Shiʿite Heritage: Essays on Classical and Modern Traditions* (Binghamton, NY, 2002), pp. 329–344, passim.

66. *Minhāj al-sunna fī naqḍ kalām al-Shiʿa*, 4 vols. (n.p., n.d.), vol. 1, pp. 159–160.

67. *Muḥaṣṣal afkār al-mutaqaddimīn wa'l-muta'akhkhirīn min al-ʿulamā' wa'l-ḥukamā' wa'l-mutakallimīn* (together with al-Ṭūsī's *Talkhīṣ al-Muḥaṣṣal*) (Cairo, 1323/1905), pp. 181–182.

68. See also his Treatise on *taqiyya* in his *Rasā'il*, ed. Mujtabā Ṭihrānī (Qumm, 1385/1965).

69. The book has been published many times and translated into several langauges. For an English translation, see *The Shiʿah, Origin and Faith*, published by 'Islamic Seminary' in 1982.

70. Al-Barqī, *Maḥāsin*, p. 259; al-Kulaynī, *al-Kāfī*, vol. 3, p. 313. I think, however, the reading is not the only one possible. It could just as well be read permissively, parallel, for instance, to the statement by the Fifth Imam Muḥammad al-Bāqir to the effect that the believer may resort to *taqiyya* in any time of need – and it is the one practising who will know best when his circumstances require it. (al-Kulaynī, *al-Kāfī*, vol. 3, p. 311)

71. The story of ʿAmmār b. Yāsir is attached to Qurʾan 16:106.

72. See L. Clarke, 'Faith and Unfaith in Pre-Occultation Shiism: A Study in Theology and Social History', *Islam and Christian-Muslim Relations*, 15 (2004), pp. 109–123.

73. This idea emerged from discussions with Ms. Linda Darwish, graduate student of the Department of Religion, Concordia University.

# 6

# *Walāya* According to al-Junayd (d. 298/910)

*Ahmet T. Karamustafa*

## Introduction

*Walāya*, 'friendship with God', is a central Sufi doctrine. Our understanding of the evolution and development of this concept has increased considerably with the recent publication of new studies on this topic by Chodkiewicz, Landolt, Radtke and O'Kane.[1] More particularly, we know more than we did a decade ago about the history of the idea that *walāya*, much like *nubuwwa*, 'prophethood', has a 'seal' or 'seals', (*khatm/khātam*). The line that connects the first surviving fully-fledged exposition of this idea in the *Kitāb Sīrat/Khatm al-awliyā'* of al-Tirmidhī (d. ca. 298/910) to the thought of Ibn al-'Arabī (d. 638/1240) has now been more finely drawn, even if its itinerary still remains obscure. Other aspects of the Sufi doctrine of *walāya*, however, still await attention. Questions about the identity, appointment, function and description of the *awliyā'*, 'friends of God', have not yet been systematically explored (one exception is Cornell 1990). Specifically, the study of the earliest phase in the history of *walāya* may be said to suffer from excessive concentration on the above-mentioned work of al-Tirmidhī. On balance, less attention has been paid to the approaches to this issue of other major figures of the 'classical' period, such as al-Tustarī (d. 283/896) and al-Kharrāz (d. probably 286/899) to this issue.[2] This paper is an attempt to redress the balance by reconstructing the views of al-Junayd (d. 298/910) on *walāya*.

Abu'l-Qāsim al-Junayd b. Muḥammad, a pivotal figure in early Sufism, was not a prolific writer. Only a limited number of mostly short treatises and letters by him are extant. A perusal of these works suggest that though al-Junayd was silent about the question of 'sealing', he had highly developed notions about *walāya*. His writings touch upon issues such as the selection and making of the *awliyā'*, their social and spiritual functions, as well as the proper signs or marks of being a *walī*.

The present paper extracts this information from al-Junayd's work and presents it in a systematic manner.[3]

## The Elect

It is commonly acknowledged that the doctrines of the covenant (*al-mīthāq*) and passing away (*fanā'*) form the pillars of al-Junayd's thought. While this is certainly an accurate characterisation, it is noteworthy for our purposes that al-Junayd clearly restricts the application of these key doctrines to a select group of individuals whom we can describe as the friends of God. Numerous passages in his writings leave no doubt that the doctrines of the covenant and passing away are applicable not to the generality of humankind, but only to the 'elect'. I quote, as an example, from the beginnings of 'The Book of the Covenant', *Kitāb al-mīthāq*:

> God has select ones among His worshippers and pure ones among His creatures. He has chosen them for friendship, selected them [for] His graciousness and [thus] set them aside for Himself. He has made their bodies to be of this world, their spirits of light, their ideas of spirit, their understanding of the throne of God, and their intellects of the veil.[4]

This passage and its continuation lead smoothly to the exposition of al-Junayd's understanding of the covenant, so that it becomes patently clear that only the elect were party to the pre-eternal covenant. Numerous other passages in al-Junayd's writings evince this same exclusive concern with the spiritual elect. In the more systematic tractates such as 'The Book of the Covenant', *Kitāb al-mīthāq*; 'The Book of Passing Away', *Kitāb al-fanā'* and 'On Divinity', *Fī ulūhiyya* these passages appear as explicit statements built into the general discussion, while in the letters he sent to fellow Sufis, they are normally incorporated into the opening invocations or the concluding blessings in the form of a supplication ('May God make us and you among His closest friends in station!').[5] In either case, there can be no doubt that in his attempts to give verbal expression to mystical experiences, al-Junayd focused on the collective experiences of the elect, of whom he considered himself a representative or typical member. In this respect, it is revealing that al-Junayd never describes these experiences as his own. Narrative in the first person is minimal, and his discussions are almost invariably cast in the third person. Moreover, he switches freely back and forth between the third person singular and the third person plural, which confirms the reader's initial impression that al-Junayd is really describing a stock of experiences common to the elect. In his letters, al-Junayd makes no bones about this conception of fellowship and his own connection with it. I quote from a letter to an anonymous 'fellow':

> You are one of my close companions, [one of] those who share in my longings. You are one of the distinguished ones of my fellowship and the friends of my heart

> with sincere devotion. Are you not one of the distinguished ones that remain of our brotherhood, one of our kind who has been singled out?[6]

It was, therefore, not a coincidence that much of al-Junayd's writing took the form of letters to fellow members of this spiritual club. One suspects that his other discourses preserved for us in the form of independent tractates were also originally directed to specific spiritual fellows. In short, it is hard to avoid the conclusion that al-Junayd viewed himself as one of the elect, and that he wrote exclusively *for* the elect.

## Election

Several features of al-Junayd's conception of spiritual election call for our attention at this point. To begin with, al-Junayd makes it clear that such election is the work of God alone. I quote from his letter to Yūsuf b. al-Ḥusayn al-Rāzī:

> May God uncover for you the truth of His revelations, and grant you the greatness of His favour and graciousness. May He contain you by His embrace in the fullness of His beneficences. These reach you by His raising you and exalting you. Then you will be where no other is a mediator between you and Him, in a relationship with God based on that which God had given you. He selects you by that which He chooses you from among the pure ones among the elect. He singles you out by rendering you among those on whom He bestowed his friendship. He chooses you by His choice of the great ones of His love. These are they whom He has marked out by his selection for the height of His companionship.[7]

Or, in another short passage:

> Know that you are veiled from him through yourself, and that you do not reach him through yourself but that you reach Him through Him.[8]

In these and other passages, al-Junayd seems to close the door to spiritual advancement through personal striving: the status of the elect is reserved only for those so designated by God. Furthermore, the spiritual elect appear, according to al-Junayd, to be perfectly cognisant of their own elite status. Indeed, not only is each friend of God conscious of being so chosen by God, he also seems to possess the power to identify all other friends of God. In this select company the individual identity of any given member is actually or potentially known to all other members, yet the collective identity of the elect as a group remains, on the whole, hidden from the public.

Interestingly, however, there is no sign in al-Junayd's writings of any hierarchical differentiation among the elect. While further spiritual progress always remains a distinct option for each friend of God, none is singled out as being superior to the others on any level. There is, as I have already indicated earlier, no question of 'sealing' in al-Junayd's conception of *walāya*, and al-Junayd himself certainly does not seem to have viewed himself as, for instance, the 'pole' of his time, to use an expression that is not found in al-Junayd's writing. Also noteworthy in this connection is the fact that al-Junayd does not care to clarify the relationship between the spiritual elect and the prophets. The connection between *nubuwwa* and *walāya* is, of course, a thorny issue, one that al-Junayd might simply have avoided altogether. Curiously, however, in this instance his silence on this front gives rise to the distinct impression that he may have seen too great a degree of overlap between prophethood and friendship with God than he could admit to in writing. Indeed, in one treatise of questionable authenticity (*Dawāʿ al-arwāḥ*), al-Junayd seems to move seamlessly back and forth from a discussion of prophetic revelation to an exposition of spiritual gnosis. Admittedly, it is possible to read this piece as a discourse on the prophetic experience of Muḥammad. It is, however, preferable to see it for what it is, namely a meditation on the elect's knowledge of God that revolves around the topic of revelation, *waḥy*. If this reading is warranted (and if the treatise really belongs to al-Junayd), then it would appear that al-Junayd may have come close to collapsing *nubuwwa* and *walāya* into a single phenomenon, at least from the perspective of the question of human knowledge of God. Relevant to all this is the question of terminology. It is evident to the careful reader that al-Junayd does not utilise specialised or standard terms when referring to the elect or to the process of election. The former are variously designated by such phrases as 'the choice of believers' (*ṣafwa min ʿibād*), 'the pure ones of his creation' (*khulaṣāʾ min khalq*), or simply 'our brethren' (*ikhwānunā*). Normally, al-Junayd simply uses the third person plural or resorts to longer descriptive expressions. I quote from 'The Book on the Distinction between Sincerity and Righteousness', *Kitāb fiʾl-farq bayn al-ikhlāṣ waʾl-ṣidq:*

> May He make your refuge near to Him, where He has made to abide the souls of His privileged ones – those to whom He has given His protection, whom naught can overtake and naught can hinder and whose devotion to God naught can disturb.[9]

This fluidity is also witnessed in the terms that al-Junayd uses to talk about God's appointment of the elect. *Intakhaba, iṣṭafā, iṣṭanaʿa, akhlaṣa* and *akhaṣṣa* are some of the verbs most often used in this connection, yet one does not see any attempt on al-Junayd's part to develop a specialised terminology of election, as it were. This absence of a technical language about the elect and their election not only confirms our view that al-Junayd addressed himself only to the elect, who, of course, did not stand in need of self-identification, but also indicates that al-Junayd was careful to preserve the anonymity and secrecy of the friends of God by equivocating on the question of their identity in his writings.

## Function

I have so far argued (1) that al-Junayd had a developed conception of what we can retrospectively call *walāya*; (2) that indeed, all of al-Junayd's writing was an internal affair confined to the circle of a select group of God's friends; (3) that al-Junayd did not elaborate on the identity or constitution of the elect; and tentatively, (4) that al-Junayd may have viewed the elect as an undifferentiated body inclusive of the prophets. With these observations it has been my intention to re-view al-Junayd not with an outlook based on the nature of mystical experience, but from one based on his doctrines of the covenant and passing away. If my approach is warranted, then there remains at least one other central question to be considered, and this is the issue of the function of the spiritual elect. Why does God appoint a select group of individuals as His privileged friends? Is this simply the divinely designed state of affairs that has to be accepted at face value (*bi-lā kayf*, so to speak), or do the elect serve a specific purpose? Al-Junayd seems to prefer the second option. In a short piece about *fanā'* and *baqā'*, al-Junayd describes how God's selection of His friends through *fanā'* eventually causes them to lose favour with the common people. Then, he continues:

> Surely, God has a design over him [that is, His friend who just achieved *baqā'* through the annihilation of *fanā'*] in returning him to the community. He returns him to them by manifesting His grace to him, so that the lights of His gifts in the return of his [human] traits scintillate in order to attract the community to him.[10]

A very similar passage ends:

> When he [the friend of God] has reached the zenith of spiritual achievement vouchsafed by God, he becomes a pattern for his fellow men.[11]

The friend of God has, then, the explicit function of acting as a role model (*iqtidā' bi-fi'lihi*) for the community of believers. Al-Junayd provides us with a more detailed coverage of his understanding of the function of the elect in his letter to 'Amr b. 'Uthman al-Makkī. This letter is cast in the form of a conversation between a wise sage (*ḥakīm*) and a scholar (*'ālim*). On the surface, it can be read as al-Junayd the Sage's advice to 'Amr b. 'Uthmān the Scholar. I think, however, that this long letter could be better understood as a discussion on certain knowledge based on experience versus discursive knowledge based on scholarship. Here, al-Junayd quite cleverly demonstrates how religious scholarship should go hand in hand with gnostic experience and further, how it is desirable, even imperative, to weld the two together. Al-Junayd's description of this ideal combination is lengthy; I quote only the following from it:

> God has made them unfurled flags of truth, lighthouses erected for guidance,

> made up paths for humanity. These are indeed the scholars among the Muslims, the truly trusting among the faithful, the noblest of those who are pious. They are those who guide in the crises of religion, and theirs is the light which leads in the darkness of ignorance, the brilliance of their knowledge shines through darkness. God has made them the symbol of His mercy for His creatures, and a blessing for whom He chooses. They are the instruments whereby He instructs the ignorant, reminds the negligent, guides the seeker aright .... They pass their lives in good and fine works and thus they leave behind them for their fellow men a praiseworthy memory and the brilliance of their light shines clearly for their fellow creatures. He who makes a choice from the brilliance of their light is illuminated thereby, he who follows in their footsteps is guided on the right path, he who follows their mode of life will be happy and never depressed.[12]

The elect, then, according to al-Junayd, are the instruments of God through whom God guides humanity to Himself and the springs with which He showers His mercy on His creatures. In a curious turn, the friends of God thus emerge as the friends of His creation. This is because the spiritual elect are the hinges that connect God to His creation; in al-Junayd's cryptic words, 'in God's manifesting them they are the hidden witnesses of God's concealment', *kānū fī ibdā'ihi shawāhid maknūn ikhfā'ihi*.[13]

All this leads us to the issue of the public identity of the elect. As I have indicated earlier, it is well known that al-Junayd was extremely cautious about making the discussions about the spiritual experiences of the elect available to the general public. To simplify matters for our purposes here, it can be said that he made a distinction between private discussion within the group – and all his writing belongs to this category – and public guidance. The former was an internal affair, which needed to be kept secret, while the latter was made possible not through the public revelation of gnostic truths but through the communal acceptance of the elect as pious role models. The friends of God, in other words, needed to have public recognition in order to fulfil their salvific function. Al-Junayd himself was a case in point, and if the judgement of posterity is a criterion, then he certainly lived up to the dictates of his own understanding of friendship with God: *raḥimahu'llāh*.

## Notes

1. M. Chodkiewicz, *Seal of the Saints: Prophethood and Sainthood in the Doctrine of Ibn 'Arabī*, tr. L. Sherrard (Cambridge, 1993), H. Landolt, 'Walāyah', in *ER*, vol. 15, B. Radtke, 'Tirmidiana Minora', *Oriens*, 34 (1994), pp. 242–298 and B. Radtke and J. O'Kane, *The Concept of Sainthood in Early Islamic Mysticism* (Richmond, Surrey, 1996).

2. A more comprehensive survey of *walāya* in early *taṣawwuf* might start with the following leads: al-Muḥāsibī's (d. 243/857) views are discussed in J. van Ess, *Die Gedankenwelt des Ḥārith al-Muḥāsibī* (Bonn, 1961), pp. 218–229. Al-Tustarī's ideas concerning *walāya* are

described in G. Böwering, *The Mystical Vision of Existence in Classical Islam: The Qur'ānic Hermeneutics of the Ṣūfī Sahl at-Tustarī (d. 283/869)* (Berlin and New York, 1980), pp. 233–241, also pp. 64–65 on Sahl's claim to be *Ḥujjat Allāh*; pp. 67 ff. on Sahl's view of himself as a *walī*; and p. 91 for a statement on the *awliyā'* by Muḥammad b. Sālim (a disciple of Tustarī). Al-Kharrāz's *Kitāb al-kashf wa'l-bayān*, a treatise on *walāya*, is discussed in P. Nwyia, *Exégèse coranique et langage mystique: nouvel essai sur le lexique technique des mystiques musulmans* (Beirut, 1970), pp. 237–242; also B. Radtke, 'The Concept of *Wilāya* in Early Sufism', in L. Lewisohn, ed., *The Heritage of Sufism, Vol. I, Classical Persian Sufism from its Origins to Rūmī* (London, 1993), pp. 484–486. 'Amr b. 'Uthmān al-Makkī (d. 291/903–904 or 297/909–910) also had things to say on the subject, see R. Gramlich, *Alte Vorbilder des Sufitums* (Wiesbaden, 1995), vol. 1, pp. 178–180. One should also check the index of this latter work under 'erwählt, Erwählung, Elite, Gottesfreund, Gottesfreundschaft'.

3. Detailed information on the life, times, and works of al-Junayd can be found in A. H. Abdel-Kader, *The Life, Personality and Writings of al-Junayd*, E. J. W. Gibb Memorial Series, New series (London, 1962) and S. Ateş, *Cüneyd-i Bağdadi: Hayati, Eserleri ve Mektuplari* (Istanbul, 1962). In what follows, I have used Abdel-Kader's English translation as a basis for my own rendering of al-Junayd's Arabic, with at times substantial revisions, unless otherwise noted.

4. Abdel-Kader, Arabic p. 40, English p. 160; Ateş, Arabic p. 43, Turkish p. 141.

5. Abdel-Kader, Arabic p. 2, English p. 123; Ateş, Arabic p. 2, Turkish p. 108.

6. Abdel-Kader, Arabic p. 6, English p. 127; Ateş, Arabic p. 6, Turkish p. 113.

7. Abdel-Kader, Arabic p. 27, English p. 147; Ateş, Arabic p. 29, Turkish p. 218.

8. Abdel-Kader, Arabic p. 54, English p. 175; Ateş, Arabic p. 57, Turkish p. 154.

9. Abdel-Kader, Arabic p. 47, English p. 167 [reproduced as is]; Ateş, Arabic p. 50, Turkish p. 108.

10. Abdel-Kader, Arabic p. 54, English p. 174; Ateş, Arabic p. 57, Turkish p. 153.

11. Abdel-Kader, Arabic p. 52, English p. 172 [retained]; Ateş, Arabic p. 55, Turkish p. 150.

12. Abdel-Kader, Arabic p. 23, English pp. 143–144 [reproduced with one revision]; Ateş, Arabic p. 25, Turkish p. 124.

13. Abdel-Kader, Arabic p. 45, English p. 166 (he translates: 'the elect ... are themselves the testimonies to the mysteries which He has concealed'); Ateş, Arabic p. 48, Turkish p. 146.

# 7

# L'importance du *Traité de l'harmonie* d'al-Fārābī: ses visées politiques

*Fabienne Pironet*

## Introduction

S'interroger sur l'importance et le rôle du *Traité de l'harmonie* d'al-Fārābī, c'est toucher plusieurs questions très importantes: ce traité est-il bien d'al-Fārābī? Si oui, quel est son statut et quelle importance faut-il lui accorder par rapport au reste de l'œuvre d'al-Fārābī et dans l'histoire de la philosophie en Islam de manière générale?

À une exception près, sur laquelle je reviendrai plus tard, l'authenticité de ce texte n'est pas remise en cause, et ce malgré les flagrantes différences de style et de doctrines qui apparaissent quand on compare ce texte aux autres ouvrages du même auteur. Ces particularités confèrent au *Traité de l'harmonie* un statut particulier qu'il convient de mieux cerner.

Il ne m'est pas possible de retracer ici toutes les controverses qui ont eu cours à ce sujet; le lecteur en trouvera un bon résumé dans le livre de Galston.[1] On peut cependant distinguer deux extrêmes parmi les interprétations: d'un côté, se trouvent ceux qui accordent une très grande importance au *Traité de l'harmonie*. Pour Madkour, par exemple, ce texte est l'expression la plus haute du syncrétisme philosophique, doctrine qu'il élève au rang de 'pierre angulaire de la philosophie musulmane' dans son ensemble.[2] De l'autre côté, Strauss et ses élèves pensent que le *Traité de l'harmonie* est une œuvre rhétorique, défensive et populaire à laquelle il ne faut pas accorder trop d'importance parce qu'al-Fārābī n'y a, volontairement, livré ni sa compréhension la plus profonde des philosophies de Platon et d'Aristote ni sa pensée réelle.[3]

N'étant tout à fait d'accord ni avec les uns ni avec les autres, je voudrais proposer une nouvelle interprétation du *Traité de l'harmonie* qui repose sur les thèses suivantes:

1. le *Traité de l'harmonie* est une œuvre authentique d'al-Fārābī;
2. le *Traité de l'harmonie* est une œuvre où al-Fārābī défend la philosophie contre les attaques des théologiens et contre les mauvaises opinions sur la philosophie que ceux-ci peuvent diffuser dans le peuple;
3. le *Traité de l'harmonie* est une œuvre exotérique ou populaire, au sens où al-Fārābī ne s'y adresse pas à un public de philosophes avertis et n'y a recours à des procédés rhétoriques et dialectiques;
4. le *Traité de l'harmonie* est une œuvre qui a pour but de réfuter les arguments de ceux qui pensent qu'il y a désaccord entre Platon et Aristote plutôt que d'établir effectivement un accord entre les thèses des deux sages;
5. le *Traité de l'harmonie* est une œuvre qui peut se lire à plusieurs niveaux;
6. le *Traité de l'harmonie* est une œuvre politique, non par le contenu mais par la visée, dans laquelle al-Fārābī expose les thèses les plus importantes de son propre système philosophique.

Les cinq premières thèses ne sont pas originales et sont aujourd'hui quasi unanimement acceptées; je me concentrerai donc sur la dernière. Mais avant d'argumenter en sa faveur, je voudrais faire deux remarques préliminaires, une sur le syncrétisme et une autre sur le recours à la dialectique.

## Remarques préliminaires

*1. Le syncrétisme*

À cause de ses nombreuses connotations péjoratives et de l'habitude qu'on a d'associer ce terme à la démarche particulière des néoplatoniciens de l'Ecole d'Alexandrie, je pense que, s'agissant de caractériser l'entreprise philosophique d'al-Fārābī, le terme 'syncrétisme' devrait être remplacé par le terme, avant tout musical, 'harmonisation'.[4] L'harmonie, en effet, s'oppose autant à l'unisson, qu'à la cacophonie; elle est composée de plusieurs notes différentes qui, mises ensemble, sonnent bien, c'est-à-dire sonnent agréablement à l'oreille. Transposant ces termes à la philosophie, on pourrait dire que construire un système philosophique qui se fonde sur l'harmonie entre les opinions de deux philosophes, ici Platon et Aristote, ne consiste ni à montrer la convergence de la substance matérielle de leurs vues, c'est-à-dire l'identité de leurs opinions, ni à juxtaposer de manière incohérente, et souvent en les déformant, des doctrines ou des éléments de doctrines incompatibles entre eux. Au contraire, un tel système est composé de plusieurs thèses qui, mises ensemble, forment un ensemble cohérent. L'harmonie étant ainsi définie, al-Fārābī, qui était aussi musicien, pourrait à juste titre être qualifié de 'philosophe de l'harmonie', non seulement parce que ce thème est au cœur de ses doctrines métaphysiques, politiques et cosmologiques, les trois étant d'ailleurs très intimement reliées, mais aussi, et surtout, parce que pour élaborer son système cohérent et harmonieux, al-Fārābī s'est inspiré à la fois de Platon et d'Aristote: recherchant la vérité, il a adopté certaines thèses de l'un et de l'autre et il n'est pas exagéré de dire que son système constitue en ce sens une harmonisation de la pensée des deux sages. Il me faudra montrer que l'harmonie que propose al-Fārābī dans le *Traité de l'harmonie* n'est pas d'un autre type que celle qu'il propose dans ses autres œuvres.

## 2. *Les utilités de la dialectique*

Il est évident que le *Traité de l'harmonie* se situe sur le terrain de la dialectique. Il est aussi évident qu'al-Fārābī, comme Aristote et Platon mais avec des accents qui lui sont propres, accorde à la dialectique une importance énorme tant du point de vue théorique que du point de vue politique: la dialectique est susceptible de mener à la science, et elle est un instrument d'éducation en même temps qu'un outil de protection pour le philosophe. L'extrait suivant de la paraphrase des *Topiques* illustre à souhait toutes les utilités qu'al-Fārābī reconnaît à la dialectique:

> Nous autres, philosophes, sommes politiques par nature. Il nous incombe de vivre en harmonie avec le vulgaire, de l'aimer et de préférer agir ainsi qu'il lui est profitable. Il nous revient d'améliorer sa condition, tout de même que la même chose lui incombe à notre égard. Nous devons l'associer à la jouissance des biens dont la garde nous est conférée, lui faire percevoir la vérité dans les opinions qui appartiennent à ses religions. Quand il s'associe à nous dans la vérité, il lui devient possible, dans la mesure de ses possibilités, de s'associer aux philosophes dans le bonheur de la philosophie. De même, il nous incombe de détourner le vulgaire des arguments, des opinions et des lois dans lesquelles nous voyons bien qu'il n'atteint pas la vérité.
>
> Tout cela, il n'est pas possible de le faire avec des démonstrations certaines, car celles-ci, il ne peut les comprendre; elles lui paraissent étranges et lui sont difficiles. Cela n'est possible qu'en utilisant les connaissances que nous partageons avec lui; c'est-à-dire en s'adressant à lui avec des arguments qui sont, chez lui, généralement acceptés, qu'il connaît bien et qu'il reçoit bien. De ce genre d'enseignement naît la philosophie répandue que l'on appelle la philosophie populaire et publique. Dans beaucoup de ses livres, Aristote dit qu'il a rédigé des livres sur la philosophie populaire, livres dans lesquels il cherche à instruire le vulgaire au moyen des choses généralement acceptées. Nous n'acquerrons la faculté de nous adonner à ce genre de philosophie que lorsque les choses généralement acceptées nous deviennent acquises et disponibles et cela ne nous arrive que par le moyen de la dialectique. Grâce à elle, le philosophe s'associe au vulgaire et devient bien protégé: il ne passe pas pour ennuyeux ni pour s'occuper de choses blâmables, puisqu'il entre dans les habitudes du vulgaire de trouver ennuyeux ce qui lui est étrange et de blâmer ce qu'il ne peut atteindre.[5]

Ce texte est, à mon avis, fondamental pour comprendre l'intention d'al-Fārābī dans le *Traité de l'harmonie*: recourant à toutes les armes de la dialectique, al-Fārābī y offre au vulgaire un exposé systématique de sa philosophie. Ainsi instruit sans être choqué ou perturbé dans ses croyances, le vulgaire pourra vivre en harmonie avec les philosophes et, qui sait, s'il en a les capacités, se convertir à la philosophie. Les théologiens seront obligés de constater que les philosophes ne soutiennent pas des thèses opposées à la religion et recourrent même à l'occasion à des types d'argument qu'ils utilisent eux-mêmes. Quant au philosophe averti, il saura reconnaître la vérité voilée sous les artifices rhétoriques et dialectiques. Sachant quel public est surtout visé par ce livre, il ne se choquera pas de ce qu'il pourrait juger être un manque de rigueur et prendra plutôt plaisir à dévoiler la vérité parfois si habilement énoncée et à décoder les nombreuses piques lancées aux théologiens. C'est en ce sens que le *Traité de l'harmonie* est susceptible d'une lecture à plusieurs niveaux selon le public ciblé (thèse 5).

*Preuve de la thèse 6*

Pour appuyer cette thèse, il me faut d'abord montrer que les doctrines exposées dans le *Traité de l'harmonie* correspondent bien aux doctrines exposées dans les autres œuvres d'al-Fārābī et que les contradictions habituellement relevées pour prouver que ce texte est de peu de valeur pour comprendre la pensée réelle d'al-Fārābī ne sont pas de réelles contradictions.

Il ne me sera pas possible ici de fournir une preuve exhaustive, je me limiterai donc à quelques thèmes et, particulièrement, à ceux que Lameer a mis de l'avant pour nier l'attribution de ce texte à al-Fārābī.[6]

Je ne m'étendrai pas sur les aspects formels de la discussion de Lameer:[7] il est assez habituel que les manuscrits ne portent pas tous la mention explicite de l'auteur du texte; il est clair par ailleurs que l'attribution à un auteur dans un ou même plusieurs manuscrits ne peut être le seul argument en faveur de l'authenticité d'un texte.

En ce qui concerne le style du *Traité de l'harmonie*, bien différent de celui que l'on retrouve dans les autres œuvres d'al-Fārābī, cela s'explique aisément par le recours à la rhétorique adopté dans ce texte, à cause de l'auditoire ciblé.

Les arguments sur lesquels insiste Lameer portent sur le contenu doctrinal: il y a sur plusieurs sujets importants contradiction entre les doctrines présentées dans le *Traité de l'harmonie* et les doctrines que l'on trouve dans les œuvres authentiques d'al-Fārābī; le *Traité de l'harmonie* ne peut donc être d'al-Fārābī lui-même. Ces contradictions sont les suivantes:

*1. La convergence des opinions*

L'auteur du *Traité de l'harmonie* prétend établir la convergence de la susbtance matérielle des vues des deux philosophes alors que dans ses œuvres authentiques, al-Fārābī ne fait part que d'une convergence des intentions des deux philosophes, ce qui n'est, certes, pas la même chose.[8]

Pour savoir ce que le *Traité de l'harmonie* cherche à établir, il faut nous référer d'abord à son introduction:

> Lorsque je vis la plupart des gens de notre époque se disputer et discuter à propos de la création du monde et de son éternité et prétendre qu'entre les deux principaux sages éminents il y a une opposition dans l'affirmation de l'existence du premier Créateur et dans l'existence des causes secondes à partir de lui puis à propos de l'âme et de l'intellect, à propos de la rémunération des actions, les bonnes et les mauvaises, et à propos de nombreuses questions politiques, morales et logiques, j'ai voulu, dans ce traité, *établir l'harmonie entre leurs opinions et exposer en termes clairs ce que signifie le contenu véritable de leurs discours, pour qu'apparaisse l'accord entre ce dont ils étaient convaincus*, que le doute et l'hésitation se dissipent dans le cœur de ceux qui étudient leurs livres et que s'éclairent les endroits de leurs traités qui laissent place aux incertitudes et aux doutes car c'est là, de ce qu'on se propose d'éclaircir, le plus important, et de ce qu'on souhaite expliquer et élucider, le plus utile.

Le *Traité de l'harmonie* s'adresse tout d'abord aux théologiens, la nature et l'ordre de présentation des thèmes de dispute ici évoqués en est un signe, mais aussi à tous ceux qui étudient les livres de Platon et d'Aristote et éprouvent quelque difficulté à les bien comprendre. Contre les théologiens qui *prétendent* qu'il y a opposition entre les deux sages et pour aider ceux qui doutent à propos de certains passages, al-Fārābī a donc trois objectifs:

1. établir l'harmonie' entre les opinions des deux sages: il est clair que pour défendre la philosophie face aux attaques des théologiens, première visée politique de cette œuvre, al-Fārābī doit montrer l'accord entre Platon et Aristote, d'une part, et entre la philosophie et la religion, d'autre part. Pour éduquer le vulgaire à la philosophie, seconde visée politique de cette œuvre, al-Fārābī doit montrer qu'il y a accord, ou à tout le moins absence de désaccord, entre Platon et Aristote, la philosophie et la religion. Mais l'expression 'établir l'harmonie' est ambiguë: comme je l'ai dit plus haut, établir l'harmonie, ou l'accord, entre deux choses n'est pas nécessairement établir que ces deux choses sont identiques (c'est toute la différence entre l'harmonie polyphonique et l'unisson). Seule l'étude du texte nous indiquera en quel sens il faut interpréter cette expression 'établir l'harmonie';
2. 'exposer en termes clairs ce que signifie le contenu véritable de leurs discours': il s'agit donc d'une entreprise herméneutique. À la différence de ce qu'il fait dans

*La philosophie de Platon et Aristote*,[9] al-Fārābī ne livrera pas ici un exposé des doctrines des deux philosophes, un relevé de ce qu'ils *ont dit*, mais présentera le contenu que lui-même considère véritable dans leurs œuvres, à savoir ce que selon lui ils *ont voulu dire*;

3. 'pour qu'apparaisse l'accord entre ce dont ils étaient convaincus': que le terme 'accord' soit pris ou non dans un sens qui implique l'identité d'opinion, je ne vois ici aucune contradiction avec d'autres œuvres d'al-Fārābī, car l'expression 'ce dont ils étaient convaincus' est suffisamment floue pour être interprétée en deux sens: elle peut aussi bien se référer à la convergence d'intention, qu'al-Fārābī ne nie pas entre Platon et Aristote, qu'à l'identité de leurs opinions. Ici encore, c'est l'étude du texte et non cette seule affirmation qui nous indiquera quelle interprétation adopter.

Quand on examine chacun des chapitres où al-Fārābī traite des aspects particuliers sur lesquels Platon et Aristote seraient en opposition, on constate que ce qu'il établit est l'absence de divergence d'opinion entre les deux philosophes, et que ses raisons pour arriver à cette conclusion sont d'un des types suivants:

- ce n'est pas une divergence d'opinion, mais une différence physique (§6[10])
- il y a une apparence opposée, mais que réunit une même intention (§7)
- il ne peut pas y avoir opposition, les jugements n'étant pas opposés sous le même rapport et en relation avec un but unique (§8, §10, §13)
- il n'y a d'opposition ni dans les principes ni dans les buts poursuivis (§9)
- l'apparente contradiction est due à la subtilité des concepts utilisés, que des commentateurs à l'esprit partisan ont d'ailleurs pu ou voulu déformer (§11, §14)
- l'apparente contradiction vient du fait qu'on s'en tient au sens littéral des énoncés sans les examiner séparément et sans considérer attentivement la place où se trouve l'énoncé, son rang et la science dont il est tiré (§12, §15, §16)
- il n'y a pas divergence d'opinion si on n'omet pas d'examiner des textes importants où ces opinions sont établies (§17).

Il apparaît donc évident que la première objection de Lameer n'est pas valable: ce qu'al-Fārābī cherche à établir dans le *Traité de l'harmonie* n'est pas la convergence de la substance matérielle des vues de Platon et Aristote.

## 2. *La définition de la philosophie*

Dans le *Traité de l'harmonie*, l'auteur prend la définition aristotélicienne de la métaphysique pour une définition de la philosophie en général alors que dans les œuvres authentiques d'al-Fārābī, la science qui étudie l'être en tant qu'être est la métaphysique et non la philosophie en général.[11]

Pour répondre à cette objection, il faut d'abord se rappeler l'objectif du *Traité de l'harmonie* et considérer qu'on ne s'embarrasse pas d'autant de nuances lorsqu'on s'adresse à des non-spécialistes.[12] Ensuite, il ne faut pas nécessairement voir là une contradiction, car donner comme définition de la philosophie la définition de sa branche la plus haute et la plus noble, la métaphysique, n'implique nullement contradiction. Enfin, il faut considérer l'aspect stratégique de cette définition de la philosophie et y voir une manière habile de poser à la fois sa suprématie et son exclusivité. En effet, si les autres disciplines comprises sous le terme 'philosophie', c'est-à-dire la physique, la logique, les mathématiques et la politique, peuvent être, sans trop de problèmes, revendiquées par les philosophes, la science de l'être en tant qu'être, Dieu étant l'être suprême, pourrait quant à elle être revendiquée par d'autres que les philosophes, à savoir les théologiens. Et si on se souvient que ce livre se veut, entre autres, une réponse aux théologiens hostiles à la philosophie …

### 3. *L'évidence et la certitude les plus solides*

Pour l'auteur du *Traité de l'harmonie*, l'évidence et la certitude les plus solides se fondent sur la convergence d'opinions du plus grand nombre, sur le consensus donc, alors que dans les œuvres authentiques d'al-Fārābī 'la certitude est considérée comme une conviction individuelle de la nécessité de la vérité d'une proposition mentale' et l'opinion des autres comme impertinente.[13]

Cette objection, qui porte sur le §4 du *Traité de l'harmonie*, peut paraître tout à fait fondée à première lecture, mais si on lit ce passage avec attention, on verra qu'al-Fārābī réussit ici un coup double. D'un côté, son discours est de nature à faire plaisir à ceux à qui il s'adresse, les théologiens et le vulgaire, pour qui le consensus est source d'évidence et de certitude. En conformité avec ce qu'il écrit dans sa *Paraphrase des Topiques*, al-Fārābī entre ici dans les habitudes du vulgaire et l'instruit au moyen des choses généralement acceptées. S'il parvient à montrer que de nombreuses intelligences, c'est-à-dire la plupart des gens qui ont une raison saine et un cœur pur, reconnaissent que Platon et Aristote sont de grands philosophes et leur accordent la prééminence, il emportera l'adhésion de son auditoire, théologien ou vulgaire. D'un autre côté, son discours n'est pas en contradiction avec ce qu'il dit dans d'autres traités, car après avoir dit que 'nous savons avec certitude qu'il n'est aucune preuve plus forte, plus persuasive ni plus sûre que quand les connaissances différentes témoignent d'une seule et même chose et que de *nombreuses intelligences* s'accordent à son sujet', il s'explique en ces termes:

> Car l'intelligence sert partout de preuve, mais comme celui qui est doué d'intelligence peut bien imaginer une chose comme différente de ce qu'elle est en réalité à cause de la ressemblance des signes auxquels on demande de faire con-

naître l'état de la chose, on a besoin que s'accordent de nombreuses intelligences différentes. Chaque fois qu'elles s'accordent, il n'est pas de preuve plus forte ni de certitude mieux établie.

Que l'existence d'un grand nombre de créatures dont les opinions sont erronées ne te trompe pas, car l'assemblée de ceux qui suivent aveuglément une seule opinion et se soumettent à un guide qui les commande et les dirige en cela sur quoi ils s'accordent occupe le même rang que l'intelligence unique et, ainsi que nous l'avons dit, l'intelligence unique peut bien errer à propos de la chose unique, surtout si elle n'a pas médité plusieurs fois, examiné à plusieurs reprises, avec ténacité et très attentivement l'opinion dont elle est convaincue. La seule bonne opinion que l'on a d'une chose et la négligence dans l'étude peuvent cacher, aveugler et égarer.

Quant aux intelligences différentes, si elles se sont accordées après qu'elles aient attentivement médité, considéré prudemment, recherché et examiné avec ténacité, tenu compte des objections et des opinions opposées, alors rien n'est plus juste que ce qu'elles jugent, dont elles témoignent et au sujet de quoi elles s'accordent.[14]

On remarquera d'abord que le sous-titre que Mallet a donné à ce chapitre ('Il n'est pas de preuve plus ferme que l'accord unanime des esprits') pourrait mal orienter la compréhension du lecteur, car al-Fārābī ne dit pas qu'il n'est pas de preuve plus ferme que l'accord unanime des *esprits*, mais qu'il n'est pas de preuve plus ferme que l'accord unanime des *intelligences*. Mais quelles sont les 'nombreuses intelligences' qui fondent une preuve ferme? S'agit-il de nombreuses personnes intelligentes qui sont d'accord sur une même chose? Dans ce cas, on pourrait peut-être reprocher à al-Fārābī de dire ici que c'est la convergence des opinions de plusieurs qui fonde la certitude la plus solide. S'agit-il de nombreuses intellections, faites par la même personne, qui s'accordent? Dans ce cas, on ne peut adresser le même reproche à al-Fārābī. Les deux alternatives sont possibles, mais la seconde me semble être, pour al-Fārābī, une condition nécessaire de la première, car le terme sur lequel il insiste est 'intelligence'. Et qui, selon al-Fārābī, mérite d'être appelé intelligent? Si on se reporte au *De intellectu*, dans lequel al-Fārābī définit et expose les différents sens du mot 'intellect', on voit qu'il opère une distinction entre l'intelligent selon le vulgaire, l'intelligent selon les théologiens et l'intelligent selon la philosophie. Est intelligent selon le vulgaire, celui qui est prudent, au sens aristotélicien du terme;[15] est intelligent selon les théologiens, ce qui apparaît reconnu au jugement de tous comme acceptable.[16] En ce qui concerne la philosophie, al-Fārābī enseigne que pour atteindre le plus haut degré d'intelligence, il faut avoir acquis tous les intelligibles, ou la majeure partie d'entre eux:[17]

Les formes pures ne peuvent être intelligées complètement qu'après que tous les intelligibles, ou la majeure partie d'entre eux, soient actualisés en tant qu'intelligibles en acte et que soit actualisé l'intellect acquis.[18]

Il apparaît donc que plus on intellige des choses différentes, plus on est intelligent[19] et, pour avoir une preuve forte et une certitude bien établie, on a besoin que ces intelligences ou intellections ou intelligibles s'accordent, c'est-à-dire permettent de former une proposition mentale dont on est convaincu qu'elle est nécessairement vraie.

Si une intelligence unique, c'est-à-dire un seul individu intelligent, a accès individuellement à une certitude ferme, plusieurs individus intelligents peuvent avoir accès à une certitude ferme, mais cela n'implique d'aucune manière que le nombre des individus ajoute quoi que ce soit au degré de certitude atteint par chacun. L'intelligence est donc bien une affaire personnelle, fondée sur un grand nombre de connaissances et qui requiert la méditation, la recherche attentive, la prudence et la persévérance.

On remarquera, en passant, que la note ironique d'al-Fārābī à l'égard des théologiens 'l'assemblée de ceux qui suivent aveuglément une seule opinion et se soumettent à un guide [*Imām*, terme qui est habituellement réservé au guide religieux]' reflète le peu d'intérêt qu'il accorde à la définition de l'intelligent selon les théologiens dans le *De intellectu*. Dans ce traité, le vulgaire est présenté comme ayant une opinion plus juste de ce qu'est l'intelligent, même s'il n'emploie pas le mot adéquat, que les théologiens qui, eux, 'font allusion à une chose tout en employant une autre'.[20]

## 4. *Les universaux*

Selon Lameer, les dires de l'auteur du *Traité de l'harmonie* à ce sujet ont deux implications:

1. que l'objet de la logique et de la physique est l'individuel;
2. que l'existence éternelle des Formes consiste en ceci que Dieu a en lui comme une partie de son essence des images de toutes les choses qu'il crée, tandis que dans les œuvres authentiques d'al-Fārābī, l'objet de la logique et de la physique, mais aussi des mathématiques, de la métaphysique, de l'éthique et de la politique n'est pas l'individuel, mais l'universel, et les universaux ne sont pas contenus en Dieu mais dans l'Intellect Agent qui est différent du Premier (Dieu); ils ne peuvent donc être une partie de l'essence de Dieu.[21]

À ce sujet, on pourrait dire qu'al-Fārābī procède à quelques simplifications: en gardant à l'esprit que son but est de convaincre un non-spécialiste en philosophie qu'il n'y a pas de contradiction fondamentale entre Platon et Aristote sur la question des universaux, adopter une telle distinction entre les champs disciplinaires permet à al-Fārābī d'évacuer le problème sans sacrifier sa propre doctrine. En effet, s'il ne résout pas véritablement le problème de l'opposition entre Platon et Aristote sur le statut ontologique des universaux, al-Fārābī fait cette réponse, habile, en deux temps:

1. en ce qui concerne la logique et la physique, les substances individuelles sont antérieures et supérieures aux universaux représentés. Il ne s'agit donc pas d'une priorité ontologique, mais d'une priorité épistémologique;[22]
2. du point de vue de la métaphysique, les universaux, c'est-à-dire les formes pures de toute matière et les intellects séparés, sont antérieurs et supérieurs aux substances individuelles. Il s'agit bien ici d'une priorité ontologique.

Cette réponse n'est pas du tout en désaccord avec la doctrine d'al-Fārābī sur les intelligibles telle qu'exposée, par exemple, dans le *De intellectu*: les intelligibles existent de manière permanente indivisibles dans l'Intellect Agent, mais il arrive qu'ils existent immanents à une matière et individualisés dans une matière. Alors, tout le travail de notre intellect, avec l'aide de l'Intellect Agent, est de les abstraire pour finalement les intelliger purs de toute matière.

On pourrait encore ajouter que l'on retrouve ici des éléments de la classification des sciences, chère à al-Fārābī, la logique, science auxiliaire par excellence, et la physique étant antérieures à la métaphysique ou science divine dans l'ordre de l'apprentissage, mais postérieures à celle-ci dans l'ordre de la noblesse. Au §9 du *Traité de l'harmonie*, al-Fārābī a recours à une métaphore que l'on pourrait aussi bien appliquer ici: si on considère les choses du point de vue épistémologique, on peut dire qu'on monte l'escalier de l'individuel à l'universel; si on considère les choses du point de vue ontologique, il faut descendre l'escalier de l'universel à l'individuel.

En ce qui concerne l'assimilation Dieu/Intellect Agent opérée dans le *Traité de l'harmonie*, il ne faut probablement y voir rien d'autre qu'une simplification stratégique qu'al-Fārābī consent pour ne pas paraître étrange au vulgaire ou impie aux théologiens.

### 5. *La Théologie d'Aristote*

Il y a dans le *Traité de l'harmonie* plusieurs références à la *Théologie* d'Aristote, alors que dans les œuvres authentiques d'al-Fārābī, aucune référence n'est faite à ce texte qui n'est de toute manière pas d'Aristote.[23]

Ce ne serait pas la seule fois dans ce texte qu'al-Fārābī détourne un texte d'Aristote; il faut y voir un artifice rhétorique, à mettre sur le même pied que la citation tronquée des *Seconds analytiques* I, 1, 71a1[24] au §13. Mais, dans un cas comme dans l'autre, les doctrines qu'al-Fārābī va présenter ne sont ni platoniciennes ni aristotéliciennes, mais farabiennes: doctrine de l'acquisition des connaissances (§13), d'un monde créé coéternel à son auteur (§14), de l'existence de formes immuables dans le monde divin – sans préciser ici s'il s'agit de Dieu ou de l'Intellect Agent (§15).

Al-Fārābī croyait-il sincèrement que la *Théologie* est une œuvre d'Aristote? Sans doute pas. Comme on le souligne généralement, il ne la mentionne nulle part ailleurs dans son œuvre. Les raisons pour lesquelles il a pu attribuer la *Théologie* à Aristote dans le *Traité de l'harmonie* sont cependant assez faciles à comprendre. Et si certains devaient considérer qu'al-Fārābī n'est pas excusable d'avoir eu recours à une telle supercherie, je leur répondrai en soulignant l'extrait suivant du §15, qui me paraît être le sommet de l'ironie d'al-Fārābī à l'égard des théologiens:

> Nous trouvons qu'Aristote, dans son livre sur la souveraineté intitulé la *Théologie*, affirme l'existence des formes spirituelles et dit clairement qu'elles existent dans le monde de la souveraineté. Si on les prend dans leur sens littéral, il en va nécessairement de ces propos[25] selon l'un de ces trois cas: ou bien ils se contredisent les uns les autres; ou bien les uns sont d'Aristote et les autres non; ou, enfin, ils ont des sens et des interprétations dont les significations profondes s'accordent au point que leur sens littéral en devient concordant. Que l'on croie qu'Aristote, malgré son mérite, sa grande vigilance et l'éminence qu'il reconnaît à ces concepts – je veux dire les formes spirituelles – se contredise lui-même dans une même science – à savoir, la science souveraine – est chose invraisemblable et inadmissible. Que certains de ces propos soient d'Aristote et d'autres non, est chose plus invraisemblable encore, puisque les livres qui les rapportent sont trop connus pour que l'on pense qu'il en est, parmi eux, d'apocryphes. Reste que ces discours aient des significations et des interprétations telles que le doute et l'embarras se dissipent quand on les découvre.[26]

Al-Fārābī applique ici aux textes d'Aristote, ou soi-disant d'Aristote, une des pratiques les plus communes en exégèse théologique: il est impossible qu'Aristote se contredise dans une même science, comme il est impossible que les textes sacrés se contredisent entre eux; en se basant sur la notoriété de la plupart des témoins (argument qui a force de preuve pour les théologiens, cf. *supra*), le texte ne peut pas être apocryphe; il faut donc interpréter ces textes en gardant à l'esprit 'que les significations divines que l'on exprime par ces mots sont d'une espèce plus noble et sont différents de ce que nous imaginons et nous représentons'.[27]

## Conclusion

Ayant répondu à toutes les objections de Lameer, beaucoup d'autres points mériteraient d'être développés pour appuyer encore plus la seconde partie de ma thèse 6, à savoir que le *Traité de l'harmonie* est un texte dans lequel al-Fārābī nous livre le fond sa pensée réelle. Je ne pourrai ici qu'en mentionner rapidement quelques-uns: la structure de l'ouvrage (les sujets sont traités selon un ordre qui va de l'inférieur, la force physique et la logique, au supérieur, les Idées, l'intellect et la rétribution des vices et des vertus dans l'au-delà); l'insistance constante du respect des méthodes et du vocabulaire particuliers à chaque discipline; le §11 sur l'explication de la vision et le §12 qui traite de la question de savoir si les caractères moraux sont habituels ou naturels, qui sont tous deux particulièrement intéressants, etc.

Tout ce qui précède me semble toutefois suffisant pour conclure que, même si le *Traité de l'harmonie* n'est pas une œuvre où al-Fārābī expose ses doctrines philosophiques de la manière la plus détaillée et la plus complète, rien n'interdit de considérer ce texte comme un des plus importants de son œuvre, non à cause de son 'syncrétisme', car al-Fārābī n'est pas plus 'syncrétiste' ici que dans ses autres œuvres, mais parce qu'on y voit le philosophe mettre en pratique sa propre doctrine politique. Conformément à ce qu'il dit dans la *Paraphrase des Topiques*, al-Fārābī, s'adressant ici aux non-philosophes en utilisant les connaissances qu'il partage avec eux et avec des arguments qu'ils connaissent bien et reçoivent bien, réalise ici une œuvre de philosophie répandue que l'on appelle philosophie populaire et publique, sans pour autant trahir sa pensée. Stratégique plutôt que sur la défensive - on a vu que les précautions prises à l'égard des théologiens n'empêchent pas les pointes d'ironie à propos de ceux qu'Averroès considérera plus tard comme le 'tiers inutile' de la société –, al-Fārābī propose à chacun d'accéder à la vérité selon ses moyens, condition nécessaire pour que tous vivent en harmonie. S'il n'est pas politique par son contenu, le *Traité de l'harmonie* d'al-Fārābī est donc éminemment politique par ses visées, à savoir la défense et la diffusion de la philosophie.

## Notes

1. Miriam Galston, *Politics and Excellence: The Political Philosophy of Alfarabi* (Princeton, NJ, 1990), introduction et chapitre 1, pp. 3–54.

2. I. Madkour, *La place d'al Fârâbî dans l'école philosophique musulmane* (Paris, 1934), p. 41. Avec moins d'emphase, de Libera insiste sur l'importance de la lecture concordataire entre Platon et Aristote dans le *Traité de l'harmonie* sur toute la tradition ultérieure - latine y compris, A. de Libera, *La philosophie médiévale* (Paris, 1993), p. 107.

3. L. Strauss, 'Farabi's Plato', in *Louis Ginzberg Jubilee Volume of the American Academy for Jewish Research* (New York, 1945), p. 358: 'It is however very doubtful whether al-Fārābī considered his *Concordance* as more than an exoteric treatise, and thus whether it would be wise of us to attach great importance to its explicit arguments.'

Sans être aussi explicite que l'extrait précédent, un court passage de l'*Histoire de la philosophie islamique* de Fakhry est très révélateur à ce sujet. Les premiers mots qui suivent le paragraphe dans lequel il décrit le traité intitulé *Conciliation des deux Sages* sont les suivants: M. Fakhry, 'La pensée réelle d'al-Fārābī' in M. Fakhry, *Histoire de la philosophie islamique*, tr. M. Nasr (Paris, 1989), p. 138.

4. À cet égard, le choix de traduction de Dominique Mallet pour le mot arabe *jamʿ*, qui ne semble pourtant pas être un terme technique musical, me paraît tout à fait judicieux.

5. Al-Fārābī, *Paraphrase des Topiques*, cité d'après Dominique Mallet, *Farabi. Deux traités philosophiques* (Damas, 1989), pp. 37–38.

6. J. Lameer, *al-Fârâbî and Aristotelian Syllogistics. Greek Theory and Islamic Practice* (Leiden, New York and Cologne, 1994), pp. 30–39.

7. En résumé, ses arguments sont les suivants: les attributions de ce texte à al-Fārābī dans plusieurs manuscrits ne suffisent pas à conclure qu'il est réellement de lui, tout ce qu'on peut conclure est que plusieurs personnes ont considéré le *Traité de l'harmonie* comme une œuvre attribuée à al-Fārābī (Lameer, 1994, p. 30).

8. Lameer, *al-Fârâbî and Aristotelian Syllogistics*, pp. 31–32.

9. M. Mahdi, *Alfarabi's Philosophy of Plato and Aristotle*, translation with an Introduction (New York, 1969).

10. Référence est faite aux chapitres tels qu'établis dans la traduction de Dominique Mallet, *Farabi. Deux traités philosophiques*.

11. Lameer, *al-Fârâbî and Aristotelian Syllogistics*, pp. 32–33.

12. Quiconque a enseigné, même au niveau universitaire, à des non-spécialistes sait qu'il est parfois nécessaire d'arrondir les angles sous peine de perdre son public (dans tous les sens de l'expression).

13. Lameer, *al-Fârâbî and Aristotelian Syllogistics*, pp. 33–34.

14. Tr. D. Mallet, *Farabi. Deux traités philosophiques*, pp. 60–61.

15. Al-Fārābī, *De intellectu (ʿAql. Risāla fi al-ʿAql)*, §§2–6 de l'édition arabe de Maurice Bouyges, S.J. (Beyrouth, 1938), trad. inédite Landolt-Pironet.

16. Al-Fārābī, *De intellectu*, §7 de l'édition Bouyges.

17. Il me faudra laisser ici de côté la différence que fait le philosophe entre le mode d'acquisition des connaissances théoriques et celui des connaissances pratiques, du moins en ce qui concerne leurs premiers principes respectifs.

18. Al-Fārābī, *De intellectu* §27 de l'édition Bouyges.

19. Dans le §13 du *Traité de l'harmonie*, al-Fārābī écrit encore ceci, qui correspond avec ce qu'il dit dans le *De intellectu*: 'Lorsque l'une de ces expériences [i.e. un universel] advient à l'âme, l'âme devient intelligente, puisque l'intellect n'est lui-même rien d'autre que ces expériences; *que ces expériences deviennent plus nombreuses et l'âme devient plus parfaite par l'intellect*', tr. D. Mallet, *Farabi. Deux traités philosophiques*, p. 82.

20. Al-Fārābī, *De intellectu*, §12 de l'édition Bouyges.

21. Lameer, *al-Fârâbî and Aristotelian Syllogistics*, pp. 34–35.

22. Il est évident que pour al-Fārābī les connaissances ne parviennent à l'âme que par la voie des sens, et l'objet des sens est individuel et non universel, ce qui lui confère une priorité épistémologique.

23. Lameer, *al-Fârâbî and Aristotelian Syllogistics*, p. 35.

24. Al-Fārābī écrit, 'Tout enseignement, donné ou reçu, ne peut résulter que d'une connaissance qui existait auparavant', là où Aristote écrit 'Tout enseignement donné ou reçu *par la voie du raisonnement* vient d'une connaissance préexistante', l'omission de l'expression 'par la voie du raisonnement' permet dès lors d'établir très facilement un pont entre Platon et Aristote sur la question de l'acquisition des connaissances.

25. Il s'agit de l'opposition entre ce que dit Aristote dans la *Métaphysique* où il critique la théorie platonicienne des Idées et ce qui est dit dans la *Théologie*.

26. Tr. D. Mallet, *Farabi. Deux traités philosophiques*, pp. 90–91.

27. Ibid., pp. 92–93.

# 8

# Philosophy of Religion in al-Fārābī, Ibn Sīnā and Ibn Ṭufayl

*Paul E. Walker*

## Introduction

A decade ago, in an essay on the origins of philosophy of religion, the eminent theologian, David Tracy, focused new attention on the founding of this discipline in the modern West. At the same time, he noted regretfully that the precursors (and alternatives) to this foundation have not been adequately investigated and therefore cannot be brought into a productive relationship with other disciplines in the study of religions.[1] Yet from an existing and relatively well-known Islamic interest in *religionswissenschaft*, Muslim philosophers, commencing with al-Fārābī, had long before turned to a new and largely unrelated field of inquiry that yielded for them a philosophy of religion. Modern students of this latter subject have, nevertheless, taken little notice of this early development. Surely, the desire expressed by David Tracy becomes an obligation for those conversant with the relevant material from Islamic philosophers to beginning to formulate a comprehensive understanding of this pre-modern origin for philosophy of religion.

Moreover, in contrast to the historical investigation of religious phenomena undertaken by other Muslim scholars, these philosophers came to the philosophical problem of religion purely from within philosophy itself, and from ideas indebted to Greek concepts of practical reasoning, mainly those of Aristotle, although mixed most conspicuously with the politics of Plato. The resulting attempt to comprehend religion philosophically was therefore a deductive enterprise and was thus not particular, or even partial, to Islam. While al-Fārābī was responsible for the theoretical base of this philosophy of religion, Ibn Sīnā carried out the detailed exploration of individual religious concepts and practices. Finally, others, notably Ibn Ṭufayl, through his account of Ḥayy Ibn Yaqẓān, brought these elements together, and coincidentally provided a vehicle for its possible later transmission to Europe. Because the Muslim philosophers' conception of religion had little influence on the development of Islam, this was, by and large, an area of minor consequence for Islam itself, or even for the history of Islamic thought in general. Nevertheless, it was of fairly great import for the eventual creation of philosophy of religion, perhaps even including that in the modern West. Thus, while the context for the discussion that follows is, therefore, somehow Islamic, as will become clear, the subject in question is not itself truly Islamic. In so far as philosophy entered the great Islamic debates, it and religion, having encountered each other most often as antagonists, separated and mutually exclusive, had few natural areas of overlap. One of these few however was prophecy, and an examination of it was also, most significantly, to be the area of the philosophers' most enduring contribution to the study of religion.

## The Origin of Philosophy of Religion in its Islamic Environment

Whether or not philosophy of religion exists in the absence of a fully developed, institutional concept of religion, the cultural tradition of Islam posed no such obstacle, especially not in its mature period, which began roughly at the end of the third/ninth or beginning of the fourth/tenth century. Three centuries of intense and often litigious elaboration, during which the concept of religion had become the subject of an enormous amount of scholarly speculation, preceded that era; an inventory of what religion included or might include was, by then, remarkably comprehensive. A sophisticated *religionswissenschaft* was thus already in place and Islamic scholars had created a fairly broad concept of what falls within the subject either of religion itself or of thinking about religion and religions.[2] As one example, in their attempt to comprehend and formulate a doctrine about God's attributes, scholars had become vitally concerned with a whole range of questions about language and semantics, including grammar, the origin of language, the role of metaphor, of names and the relationship between the name and the thing named. While a part of this interest was confined to an investigation of Arabic and of Islamic religious language, much of it was implicitly, if not explicitly, comparative, not so much in terms of the practical study of other languages and their scriptures – although some of that was done – but as a theoretical issue of the connection between religion and language itself. Another problem was how to account for the multitude of observable forms of faith while recognising that many once were and perhaps remained valid religions. Muslim scholars not only enumerated and explored the major religions they encountered but provided inventories of various factions within them as well. The literature of heresies, originally meant to explain deviation within the Islamic community, eventually expanded to encompass all the known religions. Al-Bīrūnī's famous study of

Indian religion, completed in 421/1030, is but one – albeit the most impressive – example of a tendency.[3]

However, although a vast number of interesting examples of Muslim exploration of religions and religious subjects in this period exist, they tend to be a part of the history of religions and not philosophy. They belong to an inductive, historical exploration of religious phenomena and are not deductive or theoretical enterprises. However, none of these confrontations so affected Islamic thinking as did its encounter with ancient Greek science and philosophy where obviously religion cannot have played the same part because the Muslims curiously took almost no notice of Greek religion.[4] Therefore, the question of religion was, by contrast, largely absent from the process of acquiring and assimilating Greek thought. Nonetheless, the influence on Islamic culture of various modes of Greek thinking, primarily in its connection with philosophy, was deep and profound. Elements of Stoicism pervaded Islamic debates about doctrine, particularly in law and dialectical theology; Plato, Plotinus and the Neoplatonists also left their mark on both mysticism and the early forms of rational thought. But of greater significance than these was the influence of Aristotle, who was to dominate Islamic philosophy from the middle of the fourth/tenth century onwards. Practically no Muslim writer subsequently avoided Aristotle, either by way of acceptance or explicit and conscious rejection.

Yet, if Islam was so completely overcome by an interest in and concern for religion, as asserted above, the paradox of willingly adopting non-religious knowledge from an (apparently) non-religious people was bound to perplex almost any Muslim. The answer to this dilemma provided in their own defence by the philosophers was never adequate for Muslims and therefore it was commonly rejected or ignored, leading ultimately to a radical separation between philosophy and *religionswissenschaft*. But the concern of these same philosophers for the philosophy of religion surely depended in part on this critical element in the Islamic background to their thinking. An interest in theories of religion may have been essential in the motivation for moving from philosophy into philosophy of religion even though the exact connection is ambiguous and difficult to prove. The critical question is to what degree does one religious understanding, as opposed to another, determine or lead to a philosophical inquiry. But it is clearly false to assert that the philosophers arrived at a philosophy of religion in a religious vacuum, even one self-imposed.

There is, moreover, an Islamic dimension to the philosophy written in this critical period, as will become apparent. One area points to the general dilemma confronting the early philosophers with the problem of how to reconcile reason, in the form of philosophical or scientific truth, with revelation, as the unique God-given message of Muḥammad. Without a resolution of these opposing positions no moral, ethical, political, and ultimately no religious philosophy, was for them conceivable. The conflict between reason and revelation, and consequently between

Islam and Greek philosophy, is only one of its major aspects. To be satisfactory (to even pretend to be so) philosophical theory must take account of, and provide for, an exclusive role for revelatory knowledge and, equally, the unique position of the prophet who possesses this knowledge in the shaping of human political associations. At the risk of oversimplification, the question is how a philosopher explains the role of the prophet (of Islam) in such a way that no other person, either historical or contemporary – least of all someone with only heightened intellectual capabilities – could have created Islam with all of the tremendous ethical and moral powers capable of uniting all men of every class in one common order and compelling them towards an ultimate good that is a spiritual and eternal happiness.

Despite this persisting requirement, it is best to begin by excluding all notions that the philosophy in question is essentially Islamic. The event here described belongs to the history of philosophy, not Islam, in spite of its context and the earlier suggestions about a link between *religionswissenschaft* and philosophy of religion. There was no 'Islamic' philosophy of religion and the philosophers to be discussed understood this point thoroughly. Even the term 'Islamic philosophy' is a contradiction, and it ought to be avoided even while admitting that it is almost impossible to do so. Islam should be taken as a particular historical religion – that of the Arabs and their Arabic-speaking prophet. Philosophy is, in contrast, universal and non-particular, of equal value for all nations and peoples. And this is most certainly the attitude of the philosophers in what follows.

## Al-Fārābī

The one philosopher who first raised the issues that brought about the inclusion of religion in philosophy proper was Abū Naṣr al-Fārābī (d. 339/950). Although for convenience he is called an Islamic philosopher, Islam had little or nothing to do directly with either his thinking or, more exactly, his writing. Thoroughly imbued with a concept of philosophy that he extracted from the logical works of Aristotle, al-Fārābī attempted in numerous treatises to establish demonstrative science as the canon of philosophical thought and in doing so he rejected ordinary standards of Arabic discourse in favour of a new, non-denominational style. All, or nearly all, references to Islamic terms, concepts and symbols disappear; al-Fārābī did not write about Islam, nor did he address his works to a Muslim audience.

His writings, needless to say, found a relatively small following and have therefore lived a rather obscure life until quite recently.[5] The edition, translation and serious analysis of them is hardly complete even now. This judgement also takes account of the faint reception al-Fārābī received in the Latin West. What might have suggested otherwise all along was an unbroken series of testimonies to his seminal position by such major classical figures as Ibn Sīnā, Ibn Rushd and Maimonides, who credit him with an achievement they accord no one else except

Aristotle. Al-Fārābī was a philosopher's philosopher; for them he was the 'Second Master' after Aristotle.

But one curiosity concerning the modern rediscovery of this thinker is that it occurred predominately among political philosophers, principally Leo Strauss and his students, or students of his students. Muhsin Mahdi, the most active of the modern scholars of al-Fārābī, was a student of Strauss and thus his intense probing of al-Fārābī is purposeful.[6] Significantly, the term 'political philosophy' here is the equivalent of 'philosophy of religion' and not 'religious philosophy'. It is thus no accident that the recovery of a 'philosophy of religion' follows closely the results of political philosophy.[7] For Strauss and the others, who have deep roots in Plato, there is great relevance in the fact that the political side of Plato disappeared from philosophy in Late Antiquity and that prior to Machiavelli the only major contributor to political philosophy is the early fourth/tenth century Muslim, al-Fārābī.

But what then is the significance of al-Fārābī's fairly sudden revival and the reinvigoration of such philosophy after centuries of neglect? This is a telling question; and in so far as religion is included with politics, the answer bears directly on the philosophy of both.

There is no doubt that al-Fārābī was then, and is now, a difficult person to read. He did not issue a single comprehensive account of his thought, but rather a confusing series of short, overlapping treatises, the content of each being determined by rigorous adherence to a narrow set of precise but unstated premises. Material not appropriate to those premises he considered in a separate treatise, while following a slightly different investigation based on a second set of premises. Because no one has managed to find a single focus for all of this material, all conclusions about it and about al-Fārābī are admittedly tentative. Nevertheless, two points about him are striking: first his careful, extremely knowledgeable devotion to Aristotle and the concept of demonstrative science which he saw as philosophy itself;[8] and yet, second, his responsibility for recovering from the Platonic legacy a political science or political philosophy. The theological side of Plato, as well as the falsely attributed *Theology of Aristotle*, he largely disregarded and possibly held in some contempt.[9]

Clearly, therefore, in his case the establishment of a philosophy of religion depended on his concept of political science – a point made fairly explicit by his use of the term 'religious community' (*milla*) in a treatise on religion at the exact point where he used the word 'city' (*madīna*) in a more political work.[10] In another context he states '*milla* and *dīn* (religion) are almost synonymous'.[11] And, accordingly, the connection between religion and politics is a key to al-Fārābī's philosophy of religion.

## The Connection between Practical Philosophy and Religion

Prior to embarking on either subject, however, al-Fārābī recognised the need to relate what he understood as philosophy – basically a theoretical perfection and a demonstrative certainty – with the variable particularity of voluntary things. His understanding is that philosophy is first of all a theoretical inquiry into being, in so far as it is existent being. This alone need not produce a requirement to investigate how it could be connected, if at all, to the knowledge of practical actions. However, in the effort to reach philosophy's theoretical goal – a realisation that man's true substantiality is tied to the acquisition of non-material intelligibles – a human being discovers that the use of theoretical knowledge has its real purpose in the attainment of an ultimate happiness.[12] If knowledge of ultimate truths constitutes perfection, theoretical virtues will constitute the sciences that aim to make beings and what they contain intelligible with certainty.[13] In seeking this ultimate perfection, however, two things happen: first, failure in attaining certainty in all problems, leading to confusion between which of them are certain and which yield belief and opinion as the only possibility; and second, the necessity of the realisation, implied by perfection itself, of having to bring it into being. Moreover, for al-Fārābī, to reach the fullest degree of perfection, humans must necessarily utilise other natural beings. To achieve the perfection possible for each individual, that person then must associate with others. Al-Fārābī concludes at this point,

> There emerges now another science and another inquiry that investigates these intellectual principles and the acts and states of character with which man labours toward this perfection.[14]

This then, broadly speaking, is the philosophy or science of politics. Theoretical perfection will provide knowledge of the things by which citizens attain supreme happiness. A further step is for these things to be realised and actually come to exist, while yet conforming to the account of them previously given in theoretical form only.[15]

While this highly condensed summary of al-Fārābī's entry into the philosophical problem of how to bring about the realisation of voluntary and variable conditions[16] in a way conducive to the attainment of ultimate happiness has yet to take him beyond classical Greek concepts, it implies an additional step that does. For him, the method of realisation, of instruction and of obtaining conviction, which is a part of practical reason and is what he calls a 'deliberative virtue', can be investigated philosophically. The comprehension of theoretical principles by demonstration is philosophy; *but* 'if they are known by imagining them through similitudes that imitate them, and assent to what is imagined of them is caused by persuasive methods', that is religion.[17] Religion is thus an imitation of philosophy, an idea al-Fārābī himself still attributes to the Ancients.[18]

> Both [religion and philosophy] comprise the same subjects and both give an account of the ultimate principles of the beings … an account of the ultimate end for the sake of which man is made. In everything of which philosophy gives an account based on intellectual perception or conception, religion gives an account based on imagination.[19]

Here he now begins to move more particularly into the domain of religion. An ability to receive the theoretical intelligibles either as they are or by imitating them is, according to al-Fārābī, revelation, or what might be called revelation, most particularly if such receptivity happens simultaneously in both the rational and the practical, or representative faculty, of the individual so endowed.[20] Other humans – the ordinary kind – who cannot comprehend these things as they are, solely as intelligibles, must therefore accept something that is merely an imitation of them. Although the intelligible is itself single and immutable, the methods of imitation, which are each grounded in the peculiarities of a given time and place, will inevitably be many. They will vary for each group or nation. Common people apprehend the abstract intelligibles according to symbols and images that differ for every nation and hence this will be true of every religion as well because, says al-Fārābī, 'religion is but the impressions of these things or the impressions of their images, imprinted in the [individual] soul'.[21]

This then, in essence, constitutes al-Fārābī's general theory of religion. The supreme 'instructor' is, in fact, for him a law giving philosopher-prophet, a person with the power to make particular instances of the virtues actually exist in nations and cities.[22] Another more complete statement of his general theory occurs in the following passage:

> Once the images representing the theoretical things demonstrated in the theoretical sciences are produced in the souls of the multitude and they are made to assent to their images, and once the practical things (together with the conditions of the possibility of their existence) take hold of their souls and dominate them so that they are unable to resolve to do anything else, then the theoretical and practical things are realised. Now these things are *philosophy* when they are in the soul of the legislator. They are *religion* when they are in the souls of the multitude. For when the legislator knows these things, they are evident to him by sure insight, whereas what is established in the souls of the multitude is through an image and a persuasive argument.[23]

This statement is by now well known as the classic account of the difference between philosophy and religion according to al-Fārābī. But it is important to perceive also from this same statement how for him religion and philosophy are connected, how philosophy, in fact, preserves a vital and essential interest in religion, and how a philosophy of religion must ultimately come into being in order to regulate the interaction of the two.

Whatever one thinks of what al-Fārābī said, whether it succeeds in defining a philosophy of religion, he did not back away from the confrontation with religious principles, as writers of philosophy before him had done, but rather instead faced them head on. Nothing specific in the statement deals with the religion of Muḥammad, for example, but more importantly there is also, at least on the surface, nothing against it either. This philosophy of religion does not force its proponent to choose between philosophy and revelation but rather incorporates both – though possibly granting the superior position to reason. But since religion is an imitation of philosophy, this is hardly a moot point. More interestingly, in philosophical terms, it seems to recognise the true rank of a supreme philosopher as someone who can be none other than a religious prophet, or at least this is one likely interpretation of what al-Fārābī says.[24] Most certainly this is one key element of his attempt to incorporate religion in philosophy and vice-versa.

Al-Fārābī, of course, did not escape the consequence that his supreme philosopher-prophet is a legislator, a law creator and lawgiver, and hence not merely a conduit though which God delivers messages.[25] Rather he is the agent, firstly, who translates theoretical intelligibles into similitudes and images and then, secondly, who is responsible for causing them to be accepted and used by the people he rules. Even were we to accept the idea that the primary revelation is one simply of the universal rational principles being transmitted whole to a philosopher-prophet as a special gift from the active intellect, the prophet's role in constructing the appropriate physical symbol with which to represent them to the masses is fraught with aspects of personal agency. The philosopher-prophet in al-Fārābī's scheme formulates laws and enforces them. Religion then is more than a simple imitation of philosophy; it is the perfection of a practical, deliberative virtue, requiring action. Philosophy of religion comprises a science of rhetorical and dialectic method, of the power to persuade, to instill virtue and to inculcate the means to achieve whatever portion of true happiness is possible for each citizen of every state.

## The Practice of Philosophy of Religion

The variance in al-Fārābī's theory of religion between his views which, on the one hand, seem to see religion simply as an imitation of philosophy but, on the other, indicate that it is specifically the activity, or the result of the activity, of the lawgiver raises interesting questions. In the first case, religion centres primarily on proper opinion about divine beings while, in the second, it revolves around the degree of conviction that the instruction of the lawgiver instilled in the community at large. An example of the former situation might occur where al-Fārābī attempts to 'demonstrate' religious – i.e. what might be called theological – principles.[26] According to him these are God, His attributes, the generation of things through or by God, their order, God's goodness and various refutations of false views about God. He does this, for example, by first showing the existence of a perfect first being which is one, existent and true. Then he says about it, 'It is that which ought to be believed God'.[27] He can prove the existence of a first being but not that that being is God as He is (or might be) understood religiously. The latter step is a matter of conviction and belief. Religion is, according to this, based on what is known demonstratively and is therefore what 'ought to be believed'. Belief presumably is the consequence of assent and conviction and these are the goals of religious, as well as philosophical discourse, although the methods of each differ.[28]

The connection between al-Fārābī's two concepts of religion was ultimately resolved by him 'historically'.[29] The best religion is based on the most complete philosophy; religion is thus subsequent to and generally dependent on philosophy. As philosophy itself proceeded historically through stages of, first, rhetorical, then dialectical methods of inquiry, before finally reaching perfection in the methods by which certainty is attained in demonstration, its practical component also follows this same progression. Religions have developed which correspond to each of these steps and their content in each instance betrays the strength and accuracy of the philosophy on which they were based. Those employing opinions grounded solely in rhetorical, dialectical or sophistical methods yield untruths; the imitations and similitudes in these religions will be false and generally misleading. Correct religion, therefore, can only exist after true philosophy; once the latter is available, the philosopher-lawgiver must still create the former.

Curiously, al-Fārābī insists here that this general theory applies only to a given nation and covers its internal development. He does recognise another situation, however, in which either religion or philosophy is transferred from one nation to another and in which case several potential results can occur. There might be a religion based on perfect philosophy but the fact is not known to its adherents. Its founder may have maintained silence about this fact and hence no one in that nation has realised that its symbols correspond to theoretical matter and that this can be verified by demonstration. Should philosophy be imported subsequently, its practitioners may or may not find themselves at odds with that religion. Another case is that of a religion based on corrupt philosophy where true philosophy arrives only later. The result is hostility, both between this religion and the new philosophy and between the old and the new philosophy. There can be no other outcome. A further situation is that of a proper religion that happens to be ignorant of its demonstrative base and which subsequently learns the methods of dialectic and sophistry. Religious belief must thereupon suffer because it has no defence against these forms of argument, which both prove and disprove it, and thus bring on doubts and confusion. Bad religion is a consequence of incomplete philosophy or an insufficient reliance on a properly trained philosophical elite who possess knowledge of the philosophy of religion.[30]

If law and religion are mere symbols, there will be a class of men who understand their true reality and meaning because they, too, receive instruction by demonstrative argument and thus comprehend abstract truth. When no lawgiver exists, these persons must be given the authority over the interpretation of an already established religion.[31] Others familiar only with dialectic methods must limit themselves merely to its defence, i.e. the defence of the existing faith, and not engage in its interpretation.[32] Interpretation, however, though not necessarily apparent in the literal form of the received text, does conform to theoretical knowledge. Al-Fārābī, on this issue, shows that he would clearly hold, in the end, that all 'religious' expression has an interpretation that accords with a theoretical knowledge that is of higher value, although some of the forms by which it is expressed adhere more closely to the theoretical than others. In other words all religions imitate philosophy but some do so better than others, and the quality of this relationship is subject to scrutiny and judgement.[33]

## Ibn Sīnā

If al-Fārābī had had no followers, not only would his notion of philosophy of religion probably have died with him, but its very meaning might now be much less clear. Even so there are serious questions about how far he went beyond merely stating a general theory. No treatises by him on this subject exist other than the ambiguous *Book of Religion* (*al-Milla*), which seems to support the political role of religion at the expense of any sense of its cognitive value as an imitation of philosophy. Fortunately, however, Ibn Sīnā did carry forward al-Fārābī's original concept and, in so doing, both confirmed the general theory and added his own exploration of its possible meanings in areas its founder was reluctant to touch.[34]

One direct consequence of Ibn Sīnā's willingness to expand and elaborate the philosophical examination of religion was a greater Muslim scholarly acceptance of it. Unlike his predecessor, Ibn Sīnā felt no hesitation in tackling explicitly religious subjects, such as prayer, the afterlife and pilgrimage – and in looking at them from a purely Muslim perspective.[35] He was responsible, therefore, for moving from the general theory into the philosophy of a particular religion and into the elucidation of actual religious concepts and practices.

One can easily cite interesting examples of, or areas which include, Ibn Sīnā's own contributions. There is his attempt to construct a purely metaphysical proof for the existence of God. Whether his famous notion of a being necessary-in-itself whose existence is proven because all other beings are in some way contingent on it is a valid proof is not the point. Ibn Sīnā believed that he was the first to prove this by philosophical, and not theological, means.[36] This was, in his eyes, a further development of al-Fārābī's philosophical agenda. Another area, already mentioned, is his exploration of the philosophical significance of the particular acts and states within religious practice. Here one might also include his interpretations of Qur'anic verses.[37]

Another fascinating addition by Ibn Sīnā was his personal involvement in the imaginative exposition of philosophical, and hence theoretical, knowledge. Al-Fārābī had indicated that a true philosopher should not only know intelligible things theoretically but also possess the means to recreate them in imaginative – that is, through religiously meaningful – similitudes. This he himself appears not to have done, unless a treatise like his *Opinions of the Citizens of the Virtuous City* was supposed to be exactly that.[38] If so, it hardly succeeded as its exposition is far too didactic and philosophical. In contrast, Ibn Sīnā embarked on a series of attempts, most notably in the *Recital of Ḥayy ibn Yaqẓān*, to write in a purely rhetorical style.[39] In his version of *Ḥayy* he employed a metaphorical, religious language, particularly that of Sufis and mystics, to illustrate imaginatively the universe, then thought to be what Aristotle had already described philosophically. He was consciously trying to express philosophy religiously by translating universal knowledge into a concrete set of imaginatively suggestive symbols. These works of Ibn Sīnā were, accordingly, experiments in religious discourse.

## Ibn Ṭufayl

A culmination of al-Fārābī's general theory of religion and of Ibn Sīnā's imaginative exploration of its discursive possibilities takes place in the highly unusual work of the sixth/twelfth century Spanish philosopher, Ibn Ṭufayl. Explicitly according recognition to both al-Fārābī and Ibn Sīnā and in particular the latter's *Ḥayy*, this writer offered a thoroughly revised account of *Ḥayy ibn Yaqẓān* in an attempt both to rectify and to incorporate his predecessors' general and specific philosophies of religion.[40]

The *Ḥayy* of Ibn Ṭufayl is set within a grand metaphor of a solitary human growing up alone on an otherwise uninhabited island. No longer is there any confusion between religion and politics; the protagonist of this story, Ḥayy, begins in isolation and thereafter discovers the principles of both philosophy and religion without human interaction. This account inductively reviews human experience and uncovers the abstract truths that explain it. Never mind that Ḥayy on his own also verifies exactly what Aristotle and the Aristotelians had described and that his philosophy conforms to that of al-Fārābī and Ibn Sīnā in all its details. The autodidact here analyses the particular experiences of acts and thoughts which are portrayed as if they are real, immediate and concrete examples of human interaction with the world; but the result is generic and is thus a philosophy of religion consistent with actual experience and does not depend merely on an imitation of deductive and theoretical intelligibles.

A final section of Ibn Ṭufayl's account has Ḥayy meet Asal, an ascetically inclined refugee from a neighbouring island on which there is a well-established prophetic religion.[41] Through the interaction of the two, as well as through a subsequent visit by Ḥayy to Asal's community, Ibn Ṭufayl proves that the religion of the self-taught Ḥayy agrees with that of the prophet. Whilst neither the religion of Ḥayy nor that on the other island are meant to be specific rather than generic, that of Ḥayy, of course, is presumably philosophically universal, whereas that on the other island is a largely modified form of it, adapted to the needs of ordinary human society and its non-scholarly, non-ascetic classes.

## European Knowledge of this Philosophy of Religion

The philosophical examination of religion, as just outlined, runs without break from its inception by al-Fārābī to Ibn Ṭufayl with interesting modifications along the way. In terms of assessing its further development in the Islamic world, there may be little more to add other than the details that support and explain its main development.[42] In the European West the situation may have been different. What is particularly intriguing for the moment is the reception of Ibn Ṭufayl's *Ḥayy*, not so much through the Hebrew translation and commentary of Moses Narbonesis in the early medieval period, but as a result of Edward Pococke's edition and Latin translation of 1671 (reissued 1700). Late seventeenth- and eighteenth-century Europe embraced it quickly and widely. Two English translations were published – one by G. Ashwell (1686) and one by the Quaker scholar George Keith (1674) – before Simon Ockley, Vicar of Swavesey, produced the most famous in 1708.[43] This last was reprinted in 1711 and again in 1731.[44] Although Ockley appended to his translation a refutation of what he called 'several things [in it] co-incident with the errors of some Enthusiasts of these present times', the publisher Edmond Powell offered in his Preface the following assessment,

> [The translator's] Design in publishing this Translation, was to give those who are as yet unacquainted with it, a Taste of the Acumen and Genius of the Arabian Philosophers, and to excite young Scholars to the reading of those Authors, which, through a groundless Conceit of their Impertinence and Ignorance, have been too long neglected.

Unfortunately, to the best of my knowledge, despite much recent scholarship on the study of Arabic and such works as this at that time in England,[45] no one has looked specifically into the possible influence of Ibn Ṭufayl, or of al-Fārābī and Ibn Sīnā,[46] on the development of philosophy of religion in Europe. For while the situation of Ḥayy and his self-taught religion certainly played a role in, and thus influenced, contemporary discussions of religion, without a detailed knowledge of al-Fārābī's theory as the precursor to and basis for Ibn Ṭufayl's romance, the tale of

Ḥayy would have lost much of the force of its original philosophical purpose. But perhaps that is an assumption still in need of testing.

## Notes

1. 'On the Origins of Philosophy of Religion: The Need for a New Narrative of Its Founding', in Frank Reynolds and David Tracy, ed., *Myth and Philosophy* (Albany, NY, 1990), p. 11.

2. There is, unfortunately, no complete account of this Islamic *religionswissenschaft*, although one is badly needed. An example of the richness of this field is illustrated by Hermann Landolt's 'Ghazali and "Religionswissenschaft"', *EA*, 45 (1991), pp. 19–72. Many other isolated studies of individual authors and works also exist.

3. Abu'l-Rayḥān al-Bīrūnī, *Kitāb al-Bīrūnī fī taḥqīq mā li'l-Hind*, revised text (Haydarabad, Deccan, 1958); English tr. *India* by E. C. Sachau (Delhi, 1964).

4. There is some curious evidence of such interest, albeit weak, in the *Rasā'il* of the Ikhwān al-Ṣafā' (Beirut edition, 1957; repr., 1974), vol. 4, pp. 263–268. They describe what they know to be the 'religious' practices of the Greek philosophers. On this and other occasions, Muslim authors reveal how poor their information was on Greek religion relative to other traditions.

5. A complete list of them, although not itself extensive, would serve no purpose here. The following items are those of special importance in this paper: M. Mahdi, ed., *Alfarabi's Book of Letters (Kitāb al-ḥurūf)* (Beirut, 1970); M. Mahdi, ed., *Alfarabi's Book of Religion and Related Texts (Kitāb al-milla wa-nuṣūṣ ukhrā)* (Beirut, 1968); R. Walzer, ed. with English trans., *al-Fārābī on the Perfect State: Abū Naṣr al-Fārābī's Mabādi' ārā' ahl al-madīna al-fāḍila* (Oxford, 1985); F. Najjar, ed., *Kitāb al-siyāsa al-madaniyya (The Political Regime)* (Beirut, 1964); partial English trans. of the same in Lerner and Mahdi, ed., *Medieval Political Philosophy: A Sourcebook* (New York, 1963); J. al-Yasin, ed., *Taḥṣīl al-sa'āda (The Attainment of Happiness)* (Beirut, 1981); English trans. by Mahdi in *The Philosophy of Plato and Aristotle* (Ithaca, 1969); F. Rosenthal and R. Walzer, ed., *Falsafat Aflāṭūn* (*The Philosophy of Plato*) (London, 1943); M. Mahdi, ed., *Falsafat Arisṭūṭālīs* (Beirut, 1961); English tr. of both by Mahdi in F. Dieterici, ed., *The Philosophy of Plato and Aristotle; Kitāb al-Jam' bayna ra'yat al-ḥakīmayn Aflāṭūn al-ilāhī wa-Arisṭūṭālīs* (Leiden, 1890); Gonzalez Palencia, ed., *Iḥṣā' al-'ulūm* (*The Enumeration of the Sciences*) (Madrid, 1953). For convenience in what follows, I will cite only the English translation where possible. This applies principally to the *Attainment*, the *Political Regime*, *al-Madīna al-fāḍila* (an alternate title for *Al-Fārābī on the Perfect State*), and the *Philosophy of Plato and Aristotle*.

6. See Strauss's 'Farabi's Plato', in *Louis Ginzberg, Jubilee Volume* (New York, 1945), pp. 357–393 and Mahdi's introductions to the revised edition of the *Philosophy of Plato and Aristotle* (Ithaca, NY, 1969), pp. xi–xxv and 3–10. See also Mahdi's study 'Alfarabi', in Strauss and Cropsey, ed., *History of Political Philosophy*, as well as the following articles by him: 'Al-Fārābī and the Foundation of Islamic Philosophy', in Parviz Morewedge, ed., *Islamic Philosophy and Mysticism* (Delmar, NY, 1981), pp. 3–21; 'Alfarabi on Philosophy and Religion', *Philosophical Forum*, 4 (1972), pp. 5–25; 'Remarks on Alfarabi's Attainment of Happiness', in

*Essays on Islamic Philosophy and Science* (Albany, NY, 1975), pp. 47–66; 'Science, Philosophy and Religion in Alfarabi's Enumeration of the Sciences', in *The Cultural Context of Medieval Learning* (Dordrecht, 1975), pp. 113–145; and 'Al-Fārābī's Imperfect State', *JAOS*, 110 (1990), pp. 691–726.

7. Mahdi has in fact suggested that al-Fārābī's achievement was the invention of the philosophy of 'revealed religion' ('Alfarabi's Enumeration', p. 143) which he calls 'the philosophic science of religion' (see pp. 143–145).

8. On this see M. Galston, 'Al-Fārābī on Aristotle's Theory of Demonstration', in *Islamic Philosophy and Mysticism* (Delmar, NY, 1981), pp. 23–34 as well as her *Politics and Excellence: The Political Philosophy of Alfarabi* (Princeton, NJ, 1990).

9. On this see Paul E. Walker, 'Platonisms in Islamic Philosophy', *SI* (1994), pp. 5–25.

10. In his introduction to al-Fārābī's 'Book of Religion' (*Kitāb al-milla*), Mahdi also notes, 'that al-Fārābī employs the term *al-milla* in *al-Fuṣūl* in many instances in which he uses the term *al-madīna* in the book on *al-Madīna al-fāḍila*'. (p. 30 of Arabic introduction)

11. See M. Mahdi, English trans. in *The Philosophy of Plato and Aristotle*, p. 141, n. 7.

12. 'Happiness means that the human soul reaches a degree of perfection in existence where it is in no need of matter for its support, since it becomes one of the incorporeal things ... and remains in that state continuously forever', *al-Madīna al-fāḍila*, pp. 205–207.

13. al-Fārābī, *Attainment*, pp. 13–14.

14. Ibid., pp. 22–23.

15. Ibid., p. 25.

16. What he calls 'voluntary intelligibles'. 'Things of this sort are not covered by the theoretical sciences, which cover only the intelligibles that do not vary at all. Therefore another faculty and another skill is required with which to discern the voluntary intelligibles, insofar as they possess these variable accidents: that is, the modes according to which they can be brought into actual existence by the will at a determined time, in a determined place, and when a determined event occurs. That is the deliberative virtue. It is the skill and the faculty by which one discovers and discerns the variable accidents of the intelligibles whose particular instances are made to exist by the will, when one attempts to bring them into actual existence', al-Fārābī, *Attainment*, pp. 27–28.

17. Ibid., p. 44.

18. Ibid.

19. Ibid. This passage in the *Attainment* in its entirety is one of the clearest statements of al-Fārābī's theoretical understanding of religion.

20. 'It is this man who receives divine revelation'; He is a 'visionary prophet'; 'This man holds the most perfect rank of humanity and has reached the highest degree of happiness', *al-Madīna al-fāḍila*, p. 145.

21. *Political Regime*, p. 41.

22. 'Once the conditions that render their actual existence possible are prescribed, the voluntary intelligibles are embodied in laws. Therefore the legislator is he who, by the excellence of his deliberation, has the capacity to find the conditions required for the actual existence of the voluntary intelligibles in such a way as to lead to the achievement of supreme happiness', al-Fārābī, *Attainment*, p. 45.

23. Ibid., p. 47.

24. See, for example, Galston, *Politics and Excellence*, p. 67.

25. Careful scrutiny of al-Fārābī's teaching reveals a series of problems depending on which understanding of Islam one starts with. From the orthodox and others there would be great reluctance to accept any notion of the Qur'anic legislation that established the agency in it of anyone other than God exclusively. If asked the question who is the lawgiver, the *shāriʿ*, the response must be God, not the prophet. The Holy Scripture is the word of God and all consequences of this statement follow necessarily and this militates against al-Fārābī's concept of a prophet who creates law through the manipulation of images and symbols. The Prophet Muḥammad was not in fact a legislator; he did not make law; no man does. Muḥammad received a divine law which he transmitted; other men merely attempt to discover what it is by trying to extract necessary meanings from the sacred text through conventional linguistic analysis. There are no hidden ideas, no realities, in it known by individuals or elites.

26. It is not at all clear that al-Fārābī intends his discussion of these principles to be actually 'demonstrative'. Unlike Ibn Sīnā, al-Fārābī was reticent, even ambiguous, concerning these issues.

27. *Enumeration*, 11th part, 4th chapter.

28. Note, in addition, al-Fārābī's sharp sense of the limitations of metaphysics. See the comments of Galston, *Politics and Excellence*, p. 75 and note 50.

29. This point is not clear except in his work called *Kitāb al-ḥurūf*, the 'Book of Letters' which is often taken as his commentary on Aristotle's metaphysics (whether it is or is not is a matter not yet resolved). See Mahdi's 'Alfarabi on Philosophy and Religion', *Philosophical Forum*, 4 (1972), pp. 5–25. This important article is the only analysis yet of the critical middle section of that treatise.

30. In other words a professional class of philosophers of religion. Their role is specified carefully in paragraph 47 (p. 40) of al-Fārābī's *Attainment*.

31. The notion that the religious scriptures are mere symbols of a different spiritual fact, something higher and something known by a special class using methods entirely independent of the text itself, is anathema to all kinds of Muslim thinkers. Nevertheless al-Fārābī says that the true, first philosopher-prophet provides for the preservation of his regime and law after his death by instructing in this task a class of men in a manner closer to the facts as they are in true reality – that is by demonstrative proof rather than either persuasion or representation. These for him are the philosophers who learn scientifically but who may not possess the complete range of skills of the supreme lawgiver.

32. This allows Ibn Rushd to conclude with his famous principle that there are two meanings in the scripture and the *sharīʿa*, one literal and the other allegorical, and it is only the former which can be taught to the masses. His argument is, in part, based on the Qur'anic pronouncement about itself,

> It is He who has sent down the Book to thee containing verses which are firm and are the Mother of the Book, and others which are ambiguous. Those in whose hearts there is perversity follow the ambiguous part seeking sedition and to misinterpret; but its interpretation no one knows except God and those firm in knowledge *(rāsikhūn fī'l-ʿilm)*. (Qur'an 3:7)

If the punctuation allows a full stop after the words 'those firm in knowledge', then at the minimum one must decide who are such people. It should be noted that the more widely accepted reading of this verse puts a stop after the word God – this is how Ibn Rushd would read it in public as well. Not only is the allegorical interpretation of the Qur'anic text unknown to any one other than God but the very notion that it symbolises something other than what it says is false and pernicious doctrine.

33. Al-Fārābī is interested in judging a particular religion against a standard set by philosophical or demonstrative knowledge and not, it would seem, in justifying any given religious practice or doctrine as being rational and therefore intellectually valid. As far as we know, he did not in fact engage in the examination of an historical religion as such, including his own – Islam. For another slightly different view of these issues, see Paul E. Walker, 'Alfarabi on Religion and Practical Reason', in Frank Reynolds and David Tracy, ed., *Religion and Practical Reason: New Essays in the Comparative Philosophy of Religion* (Albany, NY, 1994), pp. 89–120.

34. See Muhsin Mahdi's comments in his introduction to the entry on Ibn Sīnā in the *EIr*.

35. In general see, L. Gardet, *La Pensée religieuse d'Avicenna* (Paris, 1951). Some of Ibn Sīnā's specific treatises on religious forms are S. Dunya, ed., *Risāla 'adhawiyya fī 'amr al-ma'ād* ('On the Afterlife') (Cairo, 1949) (edition with Italian trans. by F. Lucchetta, Padua, 1969); *Risāla fī māhiyyat al-ṣalāt* ('Prayer') and *Fī ma'na al-ziyāra* ('Tomb Visitation') in A. F. Mehren, ed., *Traités mystiques*, vol. 3 (Leiden, 1889–1899).

36. Ibn Sīnā died in 1037 and thus precedes Anselm by more than half a century.

37. As for example in his *On the Proof of Prophecy* (*Fī ithbāt al-nubuwwa*), in *Tis' Rasā'il* (Cairo, 1908), pp. 125–132; English tr. by M. Marmura as *Medieval Political Philosophy*, pp. 116–121.

38. Much like his Plato had done in the *Timaeus*. See al-Fārābī's account of the *Philosophy of Plato* in the work of that name where he sets out Plato's purpose in the *Timaeus*, tr. M. Mahdi, p. 65 (para. #33). Note also especially *Attainment*, p. 45 (#55) which contains the most explicit reference to the *Timaeus* in this regard.

39. Henry Corbin, *Avicenna and the Visionary Recital* (New York, 1960) originally published as *Avicenne et le récit visionnaire* (Paris, 1954).

40. There are a number of modern editions and translations of this work.

41. On the name Asal/Absal, see Corbin, *Avicenna and the Visionary Recital*, p. 255 n.

42. This task alone involves numerous avenues of inquiry many of which are only hinted at in this presentation. This is especially true for Ibn Sīnā for whom – unlike either al-Fārābī or Ibn Ṭufayl – the philosophy of religion was a fully developed discipline.

43. *The Improvement of Human Reason, Exhibited in the Life of Hai Ebn Yokdhan: Written in Arabick above 500 Years ago, by Abu Jaafar Ebn Tophail. In Which it is demonstrated, By what Methods one may, by the meer Light of Nature, attain the Knowledg of things Natural and Supernatural; more particularly the Knowledg of God, and the Affairs of another Life* (London, 1708).

44. There was an early Dutch translation as well as one in German issued in 1782.

45. See, for example, G. A. Russell, ed., *The 'Arabick' Interest of the Natural Philosophers in Seventheenth-Century England* (Leiden, 1994), and G. J. Toomer, *Eastern Wisdome and Learning; The Study of Arabic in Seventeenth-Century England* (Oxford, 1996).

46. Ockley's footnote concerning al-Fārābī (Alpharabius) had certainly pointed in the right direction: 'Alpharabius, without Exception, the greatest of all the Mahometan Philoso-

phers, reckon'd by some very near equal to Aristotle himself. Maimonides … commends him highly; and tho' he allows Avicenna a share of Learning, and Acumen; yet he prefers Alpharabius before him.' (p. 13).

# 9

# Revisiting Religious Shiʿism and Early Sufism: The Fourth/Tenth-Century Dialogue of 'The Sage and the Young Disciple'

*James Winston Morris*

One major facet of Professor Landolt's work has been his ongoing interest in Ismaili and other Shiʿi traditions, an interest evidenced not only in his own writings and publications, but also in the ways he has helped to form and guide several generations of students and noted scholars from those Muslim communities. So it seems particularly fitting in this setting to introduce this remarkable work whose central theme is precisely the search for and transmission of religious 'knowing', especially given Professor Landolt's initial encouragement and assistance when we first undertook the critical edition of the Arabic text.[1]

Jaʿfar b. Manṣūr al-Yaman was born ca. 270/883 in the Yemen (where his father had helped found the first Ismaili community there, prior to the more lasting successes of the *daʿwa* in North Africa) and lived on to at least ca. 347/958, ending his career as a prolific Ismaili theologian and court companion of the earliest Fatimid caliphs (and the famous al-Qāḍī al-Nuʿmān) in Ifrīqiya. This particular dramatic dialogue – along with many of Jaʿfar's other Arabic writings – survived for centuries among the Mustaʿlī Ismailis of Yemen and Gujarat, where it continued to be used as an important text for spiritual teaching. Along with similar passages from Jaʿfar's even more dramatic account of his father's spiritual itinerary – the *Sīrat Ibn Ḥawshab* preserved by al-Qāḍī al-Nuʿmān and later Yemenī historians – this text is particularly remarkable, in the history of Arabic literature, for its unique literary form. For one finds here an accomplished, lengthy and yet coherent *dramatic dialogue* – evidently without any direct relation to Plato or other Hellenistic antecedents – which seems to have evolved directly out of creative meditation on diverse elements and forms of inspiration drawn from the Qur'an, much shorter episodes in the *Sīra*, *Ḥadīth* and Shiʿi tradition, theological disputations in the nascent *ʿilm al-kalām*, and possibly from speeches recorded by the early Arab historians.[2]

Within the history of Islamic thought and religious life and institutions, this dialogue is especially noteworthy for the new light it throws on two fundamental historical developments which – as so often happens in the history of religions – seem to appear mysteriously all over the Islamic world, with only fragmentary and problematic evidence as to how they actually came into being: (1) the formation of 'religious' Shiʿism[3] (as opposed to the better-attested, highly diverse political movements of the earliest Islamic centuries); and (2) the subsequent spread of institutionalised, *ṭarīqa* – Sufism, with its formalised relations between the *shaykh* and *murīd*, its elaborate systems of spiritual pedagogy and *adab*, its lineages and multiple branches of initiatic affiliation, and its complex depictions of the 'spiritual hierarchy' intimately interacting with the religious lives of initiates and devotees here on earth. What is most striking of all about the *Kitāb al-ʿālim wa'l-ghulām* – especially given what we know about the active spread of the Ismaili *daʿwa* from Sind and Central Asia through to Umayyad Spain during this same early period – is the way virtually all of those key institutional and ideological features of *ṭarīqa* Sufism are not only present but indeed central in the spiritual movement depicted here in Jaʿfar's work.[4] To be sure, one also finds here the exclusivist claims and messianic political expectations specifically typical of the Shiʿi milieu (and of Jaʿfar's own theological writings). But given the political disappointments and fragmentation of the following century, one can readily imagine the sorts of transitions that could easily, almost imperceptibly, lead from the distinctively Shiʿi religious forms described here to the familiar forms of Sufism that begin to appear in the immediately following centuries.

The limitations of this volume do not allow us to discuss each of these distinctive characteristics as they arise in this dramatic dialogue. For the sake of brevity, we have been obliged simply to illustrate them by quoting a few representative passages from the first half of the dialogue itself.

## The Book of the Sage and the Young Disciple
## In the Name of God, the Merciful, the Compassionate

[1] Now it has come down to us that a number of the truly faithful and a group among those who call (people) to the (true) religion once said to a Knower among them:

'You have liberated us by helping us to know an affair (*al-amr*) (of such great importance) that we are obligated to show our gratitude to you for three reasons: our thanks to you for having called us to that (religion); our thanks for the knowledge to which you directed us; and our thanks for the (religious) practice you ordered us to perform. So explain to us what one ought to do who wishes to show his thankfulness for that. Then inform us about the rights and duties that are obligatory for us among the ordinances of religion (*ḥudūd al-dīn*); and about what is obligatory for the seeker in his questioning, and for the person who is sought, in his responding to that. And let us know, as much as you can easily express (73:20), about the ways (*madhāhib*) of the righteous (*ṣaliḥūn*) and the proper behaviour (*adab*) of the seekers.'

[2] The Knower answered them:

'Now the affair to which I called you all is that (religion) God has bestowed as an honour for His servants, which He has perfected for them (5:3) and through which He honours whoever responds to Him. So for every beginning in it He has placed an end, and for each end in it a goal; and each goal has a limit whose full extent cannot be attained. These are the way-stations of the people of true understanding (2:269; 3:7, etc.): their keys are remembrance (of God), and their beginning is trials; their middle is right guidance; and their end is active mindfulness (of God: *taqwā*). So whoever has been seeking to know the foundation of all things and then discovers the ranks of the divinely-determined religion, that person has sought guidance from the right guideposts for the search and has set out upon it in the best possible way.

'As for showing thankfulness to the Knower (who guided you), that is through obedience to him. As for thankfulness for the knowledge (he gave you), that is through putting it into action and calling (others) to it. And as for thankfulness for the (right religious) practice (he taught you), that is through steadfastness in (continuing) it and in calling (people) to it.

[3] 'But as for (teaching you) the ways of the righteous and the proper behaviour of the seekers, (the following story) has come down to us concerning 'a man among the people of Persia'[5] who was among those subject to the trial of (spiritual) ignorance: although he had a rich heart and a brilliant intellect, and had acquired an agreeable culture and education, nonetheless ignorance outweighed (true) knowledge in him, because of his earlier experiences and the milieu in which he had grown up. So he was casting all about in the burning heat of his thirst, supposing that the glimmering of the mirage was the reflection of water, until, when he came to it, he found that it was nothing at all – but he found God there, and He paid him his account in full! (24:39). Then (God) honoured his abode (12:21) and removed from him his veil (50:22). He found him wandering astray, and He guided him; He found him in need, and He satisfied him (93:7–8) with (true) knowledge. So through the bestowing of (God's) grace, he became one of the Knowers of Sinai (19:52; 52:1, etc.) and the (angelic) dwellers in the well-populated temple (52:4).'

[4] Then, when his guidance had been completed and he had reached the goal of his aspiration, he (the Knower) was duty-bound to show thanks to his Maker and to exert himself for his Lord (84:6). For he used to hear his own (spiritual) father (*wālid*) repeat a proverb which for him was like his soul in relation to his body:

'The most excellent of good deeds is giving life to the dead' (5:30). So he thought to himself:

'I too used to be dead, and he gave me life; I was ignorant, and he gave me knowledge. I am not the first person to be ignorant, so that I attained knowledge before everyone else; nor am I the last one to be ignorant, so that the process of (spiritual) teaching will come to an end. Therefore it is only right for me, because of my gratitude for this blessing, to pass on this (divine) trust (4:58; 33:72, etc.) to those who come after me, just as those who preceded me have handed it down to me. For the beginning of this affair is from God, and it only reached me through its many intermediaries,[6] the first passing it on to the second, the second to the third, (and so on) until it descended from the heavenly host (37:8; 38:69) to the creatures of this lowly world.

'After that, did it tear asunder the veil (between God and humanity), and did the "gateways" (*abwāb*) pass it onward until it reached me, (only) so that I could be its goal and ultimate end? Not at all! For those who have transmitted it and handed on the trust in this way (before me) are more deserving of precedence and (spiritual) gains: what they have earned does not belong to me, so that I could rely on it. No, I am part of what they have earned through their actions (of teaching me). Nor does their precedence relieve me from having to act: so now I need to seek knowledge through (continuing right) action, just as (at first) I needed to seek knowledge.'

Thus he thought to himself, and he knew that, because of this, his obligation (to pass on his spiritual understanding to others) was now like the duty (of his own master) toward him, and that his duty in the end was like it had been in the beginning.

[5] So he left behind his people and his possessions, (travelling) toward his Lord and calling (people) to the good (3:104), so that he might come to deserve gratitude like that which was incumbent upon him (toward his own master). And he started to travel through the countries (9:2), passing among the non-Arabic peoples and the Arab tribes, scrutinising their faces (for signs of the right spiritual aptitude) and presenting the (religious) questions. But he did not find anyone responding, nor did he meet any seeker, until he ended up in the furthest part of the *Jazīra*. There he entered a city of that region while its people were unaware (28:15); and while he was recalling (God's) blessings (7:69) and searching their gatherings, he noticed a group of people from the town who were disputing about religion without any guidance (22:8; 31:20), recklessly following the inclinations of their passions. So he sat down in a nearby place, but out of sight of them, listening carefully to their discussion and scrutinising them closely (to see) which of them was closer to the (right) path.

[6] Then he said to himself: 'These people are more deserving of the life (of spiritual knowledge) for three reasons: first, because the (divine) argument (*al-ḥujja*) has reached them; secondly, because they belong to the people of (my own

Islamic) religious community (*al-milla*); and thirdly, because they are nearer to the right path (18:24), given their keen interest in religion and (the fact that) they are inquiring about it and discussing it together – for the person who is (already) seeking something is much closer to finding it.'

[7] [The narrator:] So when they had finished what they had been talking about, they turned to him and said: 'Who are you, and where are you from, O youth (*fatā*) (21:60, etc.)?'

[8] 'I am 'Abdullāh and I am among the residents of His sanctuary,'[7] he replied.

[9] 'Then what is your business (here) and what is your work?' they asked.

[10] 'My business is finished,' he replied, 'and as for my work, I am looking for it.'

[11] 'Well then,' they said, 'did you find anything in our discussion particularly striking?'

[12] 'All of it is striking for the person who finds it so,' he answered.

[13] 'But the word "striking" has two meanings,' they said, 'a commendable one and a reprehensible one... .'

[14] 'Of course I knew that,' he said, 'and likewise (all) speech can be commendable or reprehensible.'

[15] 'Then according to you,' they asked, 'just what is the commendable sort?'

[16] 'Speech that is correct,' he replied.

[17] 'And what kind is that?' they said.

[18] 'That whose origin comes from God and through which (people) are called to God,' he answered.

[19] 'Then what,' they asked, 'is the reprehensible sort of speech?'

[20] 'That which is based on passion,' he replied, 'and which is used to call (people) to something other than the right guidance.'

[21] 'You have spoken truly,' they said. 'So won't you let us hear something of your own words?'

[22] 'I have no words of my own,' he responded. 'For I am following the words (of another)!'

[23] 'Then let us hear you say something of your own that will tell us about your (particular religious) way,' they said. 'For you have made a good impression on us, and we were pleased by your brotherly concern, so now we ask you to be a gateway through which God may open up His loving kindness toward us.'

[24] 'All right,' he replied. So he stood up to speak, with the people listening attentively, and looked out at them.

[The 'Knower', the wandering Shi'i master, after speaking movingly to the larger group, goes on to discuss religion with the most receptive of his listeners, the 'young man' who is his future disciple, explaining to him the divine 'Argument' (*ḥujja*) concerning the need for the Imams and spiritual guides (*awliyā'*, the 'Friends of God') in general. In response the young man asks him to grant him this guidance, or to show him the way to someone who can.]

[61] 'O my dear son,' said the Knower, 'May God not estrange you (from the good), and there is no blame for you (12:92). What you've hoped for from me is coming to you. But it has limits you must not overstep and conditions you musn't forget to follow.'

[62] 'Set whatever limits you like and impose whatever conditions you think best,' declared the young man, 'for I hope that you will find me patient (18:69) and grateful for your kindness.'

[63] 'The first of these limits,' said the Knower, 'is to fulfil the outward aspect (*ẓāhir*) of the Book (2:2, etc.) and its revealed paths, acting upon that in accordance with what you know. For whoever acts for God's sake according to what they know, will be guided by God to that which they don't (yet) know.'

[64] 'But the (revealed) books are many,' the young man asked, 'and all of them are from what is with God (2:189). Each book among them has a large group of people adhering to it, so all of those people are agreed about upholding the books and worshipping in accordance with them.'

[65] 'But now we've returned to what we were saying before,' the Knower remarked, 'and we're obliging ourselves to argue in confirmation of what we don't (really) have to confirm!'

[66] 'And how is that?' asked the young man.

[67] 'Because of what you were saying about there being many books, all of them coming from God, and that each of them has its large group (of followers),' explained the Knower. 'So then do you imagine that God's words (6:34, 115; 66:12, etc.) and His books (2:285; 4:136) invalidate one another, or that the first of them denies the last, or that the last one denies the first?'

[68] 'No, I don't imagine that!' exclaimed the young man. 'But then what is the (true) argument concerning this?'

[69] 'If people acted according to what is in the first book,' replied the Knower, 'it would lead them toward the second. And if they acted in accordance with the second, that would lead them to the third, until in the end they came to act according to the latest of the books. For it is more deserving than what came before it – although all of them are from what is with God (2:189) – because the latest one is more recent in time and clearer in its way of proceeding, since it has replaced (2:106) what was before it, and nothing has come after it to replace it.'

[70] 'You've spoken truly,' said the young man, 'and you've made clear how we should acknowledge the truth and the signs of truthfulness. Now I will uphold those limits you've ordered me to keep, but what are your conditions for me?'

[71] 'My conditions for you are five,' replied the Knower. 'Don't neglect

anything I've entrusted you with (8:27; 2:283); don't conceal anything from me if I ask you about it (18:62); don't come looking for me to give you an answer (whenever you have a question); don't ask me about anything until I (18:70) bring it up with you; and don't speak about my concerns with your father.'

[72] 'I shall do everything that you have mentioned,' the young man declared. 'Indeed it seems easy for me, given all that I am hoping for from you. But why the subterfuge with my father? Surely that is the greatest test and the most painful trial for me! How about allowing me to go away from him?'

[73] 'Moving away from him,' explained the Knower, 'would be a sign for him pointing to someone else (i.e., the Knower and his mission). Instead you must stay with him, properly respect him, try to please him by being somewhat agreeable with him. And you must protect your innermost self and keep your (spiritual) concerns secret from him. For surely God will make up for (2:137) his hostility and that of other people.'

[74] [Then the narrator] said: So the Knower and the young man kept on occasionally meeting and then being apart for a period of time. And the young man was perplexed about his situation, not knowing anything other than what he had been assigned (to perform) from the *sharīʿa*. He didn't know the Knower's (permanent) place of residence (2:36, etc.), nor was he able to seek him out, because of the condition he had established for him. Until at last one night, when the young man's period (of initial testing) had grown long and his merit and his perseverance in (fulfilling) what had been prescribed for him had become clear to the Knower, the Knower was (able to be) alone with him undisturbed by the people and unheeded by (28:15) any would-be spies. So when their meeting was arranged, the young man sensed within himself that the moment (for fulfilling) his need was near. And as their being alone gave him the opportunity in relation to his master, he prostrated himself humbly (12:100; 32:15, etc.) before the Knower. Then when he raised his head, the Knower said to him …

[At this point the disciple performs the oath marking his formal allegiance to the Shiʿi 'call,' and the master begins a detailed description – the longest purely expository passage in the dialogue – of the basic structure of Qur'anic cosmology in its Shiʿi interpretation, and of the corresponding spiritual hierarchy (of prophets, Imams, etc.) linking God and humankind. This speech sets the stage for many illustrations of this general law of symbolic correspondences between the 'external' world, including the outward aspect (*ẓāhir*) of religions, and its inner, spiritual dimensions (*bāṭin*)]

[92] 'So it is through these intermediaries (*asbāb*) – that is, God's intermediaries whom I've just described for you – that God's argument has reached His creatures, and it is through them that His justice has become manifest, both outwardly and inwardly. For the inner aspect (*al-bāṭin*) is the religion of God (3:83; 110:2, etc.)

through which the friends of God (10:62, etc.) rightly worship Him, while the outer aspect (*al-ẓāhir*) is the revealed paths of religion and its symbols.[8] So religion is the soul and the (living) spirit of those revealed paths, and they are the body for religion and signs pointing to it. The body can only subsist through the spirit, because it is its life; and the spirit can only subsist through the body, because that is its covering.

'It is the same way with the outer aspects of the religious paths and (all) other things: they only subsist through the inner, spiritual religion (*dīn al-bāṭin*), because it is their light and their essential meaning (*maʿnā*). It is the spirit of life in them. Nor does the inner aspect subsist except through the outer aspect, because that is its covering and the sign pointing to it. Now the outer aspect is the distinctive mark of this lower world, which can only be seen through that; and the inner aspect is distinctive mark of the other world, which can only be seen through that. Hence there is not a single letter among the "letters" of the inner aspect,[9] nor any friend (*walī*) among the friends (of God), who does not have many visible signs in the outer aspect (of this world), because of the multiplicity of the symbols and the great extent of the revealed paths.

[93] 'Now our speaking about this could go on and be greatly expanded. But when one is speaking of wisdom, because of its preciousness and the purity of its substance, the longer one's reply is, the more the point becomes hidden; the later part makes you forget the beginning. For part of the light of wisdom can obscure another part, just as the light of the sun veils and weakens the light of the moon and the stars. That is how words of wisdom should embellish the tongue of the wise man.'

[The sage goes on to develop some examples of these symbolic correspondences between physical phenomena and the spiritual hierarchy.]

[105] 'So this lower world and all of its symbols,' continued the Knower, 'are the outer aspect of the other world (*ẓāhir al-ākhira*) and what it contains, while the other world is their spirit and their life. Therefore whoever strives in this lower world for this lower world, with no awareness of the other world – their striving is only aimless wandering, since their striving has no essential meaning and no ultimate result. But whoever strives in this lower world for the other world [with the right striving], while having faith (17:19) in the other world – their striving does have a meaning and an ultimate result, and their striving finds (God's) acceptance (17:19; 76:22).'

[The teacher and his disciple then go on to discuss a number of Qur'anic symbols referring to God and spiritual wisdom, until the young man begins to feel quite overwhelmed.]

[142] 'Now you've carried me into the depths of the seas of the loftiest assembly (37:8; 38:69)!' the young man remarked. 'But come back with me to the knowledge of this lower world and its symbols. Perhaps I'll be able to find help in that knowledge for my own situation and will be able to use it to uphold what is expected of me. For (just now) I became afraid for my soul and worried that my mind might have led me away toward something whose essence I am unable (to grasp).'

[143] 'You did climb high in your questioning,' the Knower replied, 'and my reply climbed with you to the very peak of the outward aspect of the spiritual meanings. Then your vision became lost and bewildered there and your mind was in perplexity about it. So how would it have been if I had begun to unveil for you their inner aspect? We would have been, you and I, like Moses and the knower (18:60–82)!'

[144] 'Then there is also an inner aspect to this inner dimension, even more inward (spiritual) than it is?' exclaimed the young man.

[145] 'By my life!' responded the Knower, 'there is indeed an inner aspect of this inner one: it is the very highest of (spiritual) stations, more extensive than this inner aspect in its power and more perfect than it as a guide. For it is the goal of all the signs pointing to the way of salvation.'

[146] 'Now I do see that there are three levels of knowledge here,' the young man answered. 'There is its outer aspect (*ẓāhir*), its inner aspect (*bāṭin*), and the inner (spiritual) dimension (*bāṭin al-bāṭin*) of that. So is there a sign pointing to this?'

[Here the master and disciple discuss a number of scriptural passages and other arguments pointing to these three levels of reality and insight; the master's presentation culminates with a reference to the three corresponding spiritual types, drawn from a famous speech attributed to Imām 'Alī and included in the *Nahj al-balāgha*.]

[157] 'Right you are,' said the Knower. 'So the pair of the outer aspect, which is the name, and the inner aspect, which is the distinctive characteristic, together point to God's knowledge and to God's religion – and that is the innermost dimension (*bāṭin al-bāṭin*).

'Likewise the creatures were created according to three levels: the first level was the creation of the angels; the second the creation of true humanity (*ādamiyyūn*);[10] and the third the creation of the brute beasts. So knowledge of the outer aspect (of this lower world) is the level of the brute beasts, and whoever knows it (alone), without its inner aspect, is at the level of those animals. And knowledge of the inner aspect is the knowledge of the (true) descendants of Adam and their distinctive level; whoever knows it has true faith and is at the level of humanity.

'But knowledge of the inner dimension of that inner aspect is the knowledge of the angels. So whoever knows that is spiritual in his knowledge and material with regard to his body. Such a person is a prophet sent (to humankind) (2:213), whom God places as His viceroy on His earth (2:30; 38:26; 24:55) and whom He makes His argument in regard to His creatures (6:83; 4:164–165). For (such a spiritual knower) is the veil of the angels, the exemplar of divine revelation and its interpreter for the children of Adam. He has the keys of the gardens (of Paradise), so that only those who willingly follow him may enter the gardens; and he has authority over Hell, such that only those who disobey him will enter there.

'So there are only two (types of) fully human beings among humanity: the "sanctified knower" (*rabbāniyyūn*) (5:44, 63), who already knows the goal of the divine sciences, and whose spirit is in direct contact with the spirit of certainty. That person is a knower through his knowledge, but he is sanctified through his actions.[11] And the other (type) is "those seeking knowledge along the path of salvation."

'For the rest of "humankind are riffraff and rabble" who don't (really) know anything, "the followers of every screaming voice" (of someone) who has become deluded in his error and has deluded them (28:63, etc.) through his own ignorance. Yet they suppose that they are doing good works (18:104)! But no, the exemplary (punishments) have already taken place before them (13:6), and God will never break His covenant (22:47), and surely the ungrateful ones will have their like (as punishments) (47:10).'

[The disciple goes on to ask whether he could possibly aspire to such a lofty rank – and if so, how he should go about it, whether perhaps the master could help him? His teacher replies that the outcome depends on the disciple's own efforts and God's grace, not anyone else's aid.]

[165] 'Now the farmer can fertilise the ground, and seed and water it,' the Knower responded, 'but he cannot make the plants and their flowers come forth.[12] And a man can sow his seed whenever he wants, but he is not able to create from it whatever he wishes. So it is painful for me, my son, that you should ask my help in something while I am unable to help you with it – May God open up your soul (6:125; 39:22) and illumine your heart with right guidance! Now it is obligatory for you to be mindful of God and to do what is good and beautiful, since God surely does not neglect the recompense of whoever is good and beautiful in their actions (9:120; 11:115; 12:90).

'For you are on the path of salvation and the highway of right guidance and the course of the people of God-mindfulness. So travel your path which you have just begun and hold tightly to your connection (to God) (2:256; 31:22) to whom you have been called, until you are guided by a connection from God [and from men] (3:112) to God's connection (3:103) – for that is the goal of all who are seeking.'

[166] 'But isn't God's connection the imam to whom you've been calling me?' asked the young man.

[167] 'He is an outward aspect of that,' replied the Knower, 'and he is your

connection and the firmest support (2:256; 31:22), your proof (*ḥujja*) and the gateway (*bāb*) to your imam.'

[168] 'But then, what is God's connection (3:103), and what is a connection from God (3:112)?' the young man continued.

[169] 'That (God's connection) is the goal of your guidance and the concluding degree of the (true) knowers,' the Knower answered

[After this climactic allusion to the true nature of the Imamate and the ultimate goal of the disciple's path, the dialogue turns toward a more accessible and sometimes humorous digression on the earlier questions of the proper relation of *ẓāhir* and *bāṭin*, this-worldly and spiritual concerns, on the planes of knowledge and action.]

[185] 'God did speak truly,' replied the Knower. 'He didn't say "Don't let this lower world deceive you." He only said: "Don't let the life of this lower world deceive you." Because "life" has four meanings: the outward life in this lower world and its ultimate outcome, (which is) passing away (55:26); and the life of the other world and its ultimate outcome, (which is eternally) lasting. Hence He said that you shouldn't act for this passing, transient life, but you should act for the lasting (eternal) life. For that (is the point of) His saying: "O would that I had prepared for my life!" (89:24) – which is to say, "If only I had prepared during this passing life for the lasting life." And the essential meaning of these two sorts of life is life through knowledge of its outward aspect, and life through knowledge of its inner (spiritual) aspect.

'For knowledge of the outward aspect is the life of this lower world (31:3, etc.), which is knowledge of what is lowest. But knowledge of the inner aspect is the life of the other world. Because of this He said: Don't let yourselves be deceived by the life of this lower world!' – that is, don't be deluded by the outward aspect of knowledge and by action according to that alone. For (the outcome of your actions) will only be accepted from you (at the Judgement) through the inner aspect and through your upholding and accomplishing that along with the outward aspect, since the outward aspect is not accepted without the inner.'

[186] 'What do you think,' asked the young man, 'about someone who knows the knowledge of the inner aspect, but who doesn't know the knowledge of the outer aspect and doesn't uphold that? What would their rank be, according to the people of religion?'

[187] 'What a terrible position!' the Knower replied. 'For in that case the inner aspect (of religion) couldn't subsist and be sound, since that person would have neglected something that has been commanded (by God) and has been established as a protection for the inner aspect, like the outer aspect of fruits: if their outer covering is peeled off before they're ripe, then they become rotten and are useless

after that. It is just like with the body: if its limbs are cut off, the spirit won't remain in it for even a moment. That is a likeness of the outward aspect of religion: if its basic obligations aren't carried out, then its inner aspect won't be realised for that person. But in fact, (such a person's) neglecting its outward aspect – without any permission from the one Who made it obligatory for them – can only be for one of two reasons. If they neglected it because of some incapacity, then they are even more incapable of (realising) the inner aspect. Or if they neglected the outward aspect intentionally, while being able (to uphold it), then they are wilfully disobedient to the one Who commanded them to uphold it. Now the disobedient person is an evildoer, and the evildoer cannot be a companion of the Friends of God. Indeed, the evildoer is the enemy of the friends of God (18:50), and they are his enemies, because of his cutting off what God has commanded should be joined (2:27; 13:25).'

[188] 'What about someone who knows the knowledge of the outward aspect and upholds it, but who doesn't know the inner aspect?' asked the young man. 'What is that person's rank, according to the people of religion?'

[189] 'The worst station of all,' the Knower responded, 'because they are like a body which has come into being without having the spirit (of life) breathed into it, so such a person is numbered among the dead bodies (2:28; 16:21). These corpses are the ranks of those who reject (God), and those who reject God's signs are the enemies of religion and of its people.'

[190] 'So I see,' said the young man, 'that the outward aspect can only be sound through its inner dimension, and that the inner aspect can only subsist through the outer. So this lower world can only be (religiously) licit for someone who truly knows the other world, which is its life and its inner aspect. Likewise religion is only complete for its people once they uphold both its outward and its inner aspects.'

[191] 'Yes,' the Knower answered, 'that is the true meaning (of religion), and that is the way (your own) actions should be, because upholding the totality of what God has commanded (2:27; etc.) leads you to deserve His satisfaction (3:162); but neglecting some of what God has commanded exposes you to His wrath (3:162).'

[192] 'Then isn't the person who knows the outer aspect through the inner dimension (of religion) and who upholds and accomplishes both of them the (genuine) person of faith (*mu'min*)?' asked the young man.

[Here the conversation continues for many more pages, taking up such questions as the reasons for the diversity of religions, the proper relation to one's guide, the role of the imam, and so forth. Eventually the disciple is invited to travel to the Knower's own 'spiritual father' and 'master' (*shaykh*) – described simply as 'the greatest Knower' (256) – where he receives his culminating initiation and spiritual teaching. Their final encounter falls at the exact centre of the dialogue.

After bidding farewell to the great master, the Knower and his disciple travel back to the young man's home town. There the Knower advises his disciple how to continue his own work in the 'Call', starting with his father, the wealthy and influential 'Shaykh al-Bukhtūrī'. After some initially angry discussions with his father, Ṣāliḥ – the name of the young man, which is only revealed at this point – eventually succeeds in converting him. When the news of this event reaches the learned religious scholars (*'ulamā'*) of the town, who are financially dependent on the support of Ṣāliḥ's father, they angrily turn for guidance to their most respected leader, a jurist-theologian[13] named Abū Mālik, 'father of the king'.

Ṣāliḥ, through a long and involved discussion with Abū Mālik, gradually leads him to understand that what he is really seeking is not to be found in yet another variation of his previous beliefs, but rather in the direct spiritual insight that is only accessible through the guidance provided by the 'Friends of God' and the living representatives of the spiritual hierarchy. Abū Mālik is led to see that they – and not the doctrines of theology or traditional reports – are the true gateways to discovering God's 'Unity and Justice', the keynotes of Abū Mālik's earlier Mu'tazilī beliefs. In the end, Abū Mālik and his friends among the religious scholars are ready to seek that guidance. Ṣāliḥ lets them go, and sets out to seek the advice of his own master.]

[555] Then the Knower said: 'You know your companions better (than I do), so if you recognise some good in them, then guide them rightly as you were guided. But if you are apprehensive about them, then don't let your desire for them lead you to approach them while putting yourself at risk. And test them by ignoring them, but not harshly. Order your father to treat them kindly and to be respectful toward them for a while. For the person who is truly seeking the good will not remain hidden. Surely God will not leave you behind and He will open up for you, from the light of His providential arrangement (of things), that through which He manages the affair (13:2; 32:5, etc.) of His creatures. And He will open up for you from the gateways of right guidance what will show you the (appropriate) actions of those who are rightly guided.'

[556] [The narrator] continued: So Abū Mālik and his companions continued to go through their different kinds of testing, until their affair was complete and they recognised their right guidance. And it was God's friend among them who took care of their guidance, and they thanked God for that. Then they returned to their people warning them (46:29), so that through them God guided a great many of His servants to His religion.

[557] Nor was this a made-up story, but rather the confirmation (12:111) of what God has commanded (2:27, etc.). For in it is the confirmation of the (divine) messengers, the signs of their trustees (the imams), and the proper behaviour of those who are seeking.

[558] So praise be to God, in the beginning and at the end! May God's blessings be upon His Messenger, our master Muḥammad, who was sent by Him to His creatures as a bearer of good news and as a warner (2:119). And (may His blessings be) upon his trustee, the imam of those who are mindful (of God), 'the best of the best,' the beloved of the Lord of the worlds; and upon the imams from the people of His house (11:73; 33:33) upon whom God has bestowed His favours (19:58) – may He take away from them (all) impurity and purify them totally (33:33). And God is sufficient for us, the best of trustees (3:173), the best of protectors and the best of supporters (8:40; 22:78). And there is no strength and no power except through God (18:39), the Exalted, the Tremendous (2:255; 42:4).

## Notes

1. When it was originally submitted (1998), this essay was intended as a 'preview' of our edition and translation of the *Kitāb al-ʿālim wa'l-ghulām* ('The Book of the Knower and the Young Man'), by Jaʿfar b. Manṣūr al-Yaman. That book has since been published as *The Master and the Disciple: An Early Islamic Spiritual Dialogue* (London, 2001), by J. W. Morris: numbers correspond to paragraphs of our critical edition of the Arabic text.

2. These and other major literary features of the work are discussed in detail in the Introduction to the edition and translation cited above.

3. In *all* of its varieties and manifestations: the absence in this and other early Ismaili texts of the themes of martyrdom and mourning/commemoration that were to become so central to Imāmī Shiʿi piety and devotional life already in Buyid times is particularly striking.

4. These historical dimensions of the significance of this book are now discussed in more detail in the Introduction to the translation and edition cited above.

5. The allusion is not to his nationality, but rather to the special rare spiritual aptitude indicated in a famous *ḥadīth* – also found in the major Sunni collections – in which the Prophet says of his close disciple Salmān the Persian, 'Even if true faith (*īmān*) were in the Pleiades, people like this [or in another version: 'people from among the Persians'] would reach it!'

6. *Asbāb*: literally, the celestial spiritual hierarchy of 'ladders' or (intermediate) 'causes' linking the ultimate Godhead and humankind, usually associated with the highest archangels or – as in the (Sunni) *ḥadīth* of the Miʿrāj – with the spiritual 'Realities'/archetypes of the prophets (or imams) inhabiting each of the seven (or more) spiritual heavens. By extension this term refers to the corresponding earthly, historical religious hierarchy (here associated with the Shiʿi *daʿwa*) responsible for transmitting that spiritual influence throughout humanity.

7. There is a double pun in his response: his readers understand him to be saying he is a man named ʿAbd Allāh from Mecca; but he actually means that he is 'a (true) servant of God' and, as an initiated follower of the imam, *spiritually* dwelling in the divine Presence. A similar, but more obvious pun is included in his following answer about his own 'business' and his 'work'.

8. *Sharāʾiʿ* (pl. of *sharīʿa*): literally, the 'paths' or everything 'set down' in the prophetic

messages, including both the scriptures themselves (e.g. Qur'an, Torah, Gospel) and, in the case of Islam, the wider body of prophetic traditions preserved in the *ḥadīth* literature. By the time of this work at the end of the 3rd century (AH), the term was often understood more broadly in reference to the various complex traditions of ritual and legal interpretation of the Qur'an and *Ḥadīth*.

9. Like the 'intermediaries' (*asbāb*) discussed in the note to paragraph 4 above, these 'Letters' are another common Shi'i technical term referring to the pleroma of divine messengers and vehicles of grace (imams, prophets, etc.); this technical usage is apparently derived from the frequent Qur'anic description of the prophets themselves (or their Messages) as divine '*Words*'.

10. *Adamiyyūn*: Adam and his descendants, the Qur'anic *insān* (theomorphic, spiritual humanity), in contrast to the mortal animal *bashar*.

11. The phrases given in double quotation marks throughout this paragraph indicate sections taken directly from the famous story of 'Alī's secret encounter with his close disciple Kumayl b. Ziyād, recorded in the *Nahj al-balāgha* and other works of the Shi'i tradition.

The meaning of the key Qur'anic term *rabbāniyyūn* (cf. Qur'an 5:44 and 63), translated vaguely here as 'sanctified', apparently is related both to the Arabic root referring to God as 'Lord' (*rabb*, hence 'divine' or 'god-like'), and to the aspect of that Arabic root referring to *teaching* and education in the broadest sense (*r-b-y*). The latter meaning is emphasised at Qur'an 3:79, which probably underlies the special usage here: 'Be *rabbāniyyūn* through your teaching the Book and through your studying (It)'.

12. Cf. the Qur'anic reference to 'the symbol of the sower in the Torah and the Gospel' at 48:29, which is further applied in numerous Qur'anic verses and themes involving water, vegetation, etc. Ismaili (and other Shi'i) writings generally take such Qur'anic passages to symbolise the activities and missions of the prophets, imams, and other religious and spiritual teachers.

13. The later discussion makes it clear that Abū Mālik follows the Mu'tazilī school of Islamic theology (*'ilm al-kalām*), which was fairly widespread and flourishing at the time this dialogue was written. In particular, Mu'tazilī thought was closely associated with the Zaydī Shi'i sect, which was actually competing for influence in the Yemen with the Ismaili teachings of the author of this dialogue (and his father) at the time this work was composed.

# 10

# Al-Qāḍī al-Nuʿmān and the Concept of *Bāṭin*

*Bulbul Shah*

The elaboration of the esoteric aspect of the Islamic revelation has remained one of the primary commitments of the Ismaili thinkers. They have consistently engaged themselves in the examination of the esoteric aspect throughout history. Here, an attempt will be made to examine the view of al-Qāḍī al-Nuʿmān (d. 363/974) in relation to the esoteric aspect, particularly the extent of its implications and the means of its manifestation.[1]

Let us, first, give the definitions of the terms that the Fatimid author employs during the analysis of the theme and that are pertinent in terms of forming the basis for the implications of the esoteric aspect and those of the means through which it becomes manifest.

According to al-Nuʿmān, everything has two aspects; one is exoteric and the other is esoteric. He defines the exoteric aspect (*ẓāhir*) as perceptible through the senses and the esoteric aspect (*bāṭin*) as comprehended by knowledge. In other words, *bāṭin* is the object of true knowledge.[2] The other terms which al-Nuʿmān employs with regard to the elaboration of the categories of the exoteric and esoteric aspects include *tanzīl* and *ta'wīl*, respectively. Although *bāṭin* and *ta'wīl* are identical in terms of conveying the inner aspect, al-Nuʿmān uses the former in a broad sense, applying it to both the Islamic revelation and creation. However, he uses the term *ta'wīl* relatively restrictively, emphasising the esoteric interpretation of the Qur'an.[3]

Before proceeding to the formulation of the categories of the exoteric and esoteric aspects it may, however, be mentioned that the Fatimid author makes the Qur'an, the tradition of the Prophet and the sayings of the Imams the sources of his information in providing us with the definitions of the terms and the elaboration of the theme under consideration.

## The Implications of the Categories of the Exoteric and Esoteric Aspects

Al-Nuʿmān formulates the categories of the exoteric and esoteric aspects applying them to both the Islamic revelation and creation, as regards their inter-relationship. Creation, in his opinion, corroborates the Islamic revelation and leads one ultimately to the acceptance of religious belief such as the Unity of God.[4] The inter-relationship in question, he suggests, can well be understood by concentrating on the categories of the exoteric and esoteric aspects. In elaborating the categories in question he refers to the Qur'an which states: 'And of everything have We created in pairs (*zawjayn*), that you may reflect.' (Qur'an 51:49)

The idea of *zawjān* is one of those bases which, according to al-Nuʿmān, not only determines that Islamic revelation and creation comprise the exoteric and the esoteric aspects, but also points to the Unity of God (*waḥda*), Who is far beyond being associated with any human attributes, including the idea of duality. Al-Nuʿmān suggests that the negation of the idea of *zawjān* and of *muzāwaja*, duality, would simply lead to anthropomorphism, which is inconceivable to him. Furnishing evidence for the presence of the *zawjān* in creation, he uses the example of the human being who is compounded of two entities: one is the body and the other is the soul. The body is evident and the soul is hidden. Each of these aspects contains two further dimensions: the human body has the characteristics of coldness and dryness and the soul is warm and wet. When the soul leaves the body, the latter becomes cold and dry, implying the inevitability of the coexistence of these aspects for survival in this world and also their multi-dimensional nature.[5]

Al-Nuʿmān provides further Qur'anic references for the concept of *zawjān*. These references are made in numerous contexts, reinforcing the two aspects. Among these references are the ones which describe the bounties which human beings receive and which the Qur'an emphatically declares to be of two sorts: seen and unseen bounties (Qur'an 31:20) and that, on the Day of Judgement, people will be asked about these bounties (Qur'an 102:8).[6]

The Fatimid writer finds that these verses compel one to have a comprehensive knowledge of these bounties, particularly the unseen bounties. Anyone who is ignorant of the unseen bounties, he states, would not be able to provide an answer when asked to do so, in spite of their awareness of accountability on that matter.[7] Therefore, the Ismaili thinker's view leads one to conclude that attaining knowledge of the esoteric aspect is indispensable in order to be able to discharge one's responsibility for providing the answer, ideally with regard to the bounties.[8]

Furthermore, al-Nuʿmān applies the principle of *ẓāhir* and *bāṭin* to sins. For him, the Qur'anic injunction 'Forsake open and secret sins (*dharū ẓāhira'l-ithmi wa-bāṭina*)' (Qur'an 6:120) provides evidence for the aspects in question. Accentuating the consequences of this Qur'anic injunction, he raises the issue that, if a person is ignorant of a secret sin, is it not feared that they might indulge in that sin?[9] The only remedy available for indulging in the sin, he would suggest, is to acquire knowledge of the *bāṭin*.

As already indicated, *tanzīl* and *ta'wīl* comprise another set of terms which the Fatimid writer applies to the meanings of the Qur'an.[10] He particularly examines the unique nature of *ta'wīl* by referring to the Qur'an. The verses he quotes describe *ta'wīl* as mysterious and arcane. Because of these particular characteristics, it remains beyond the comprehension of everybody except God and 'those well rooted in knowledge' (*al-rāsikhūna fi'l-ʿilm*), who, according to al-Nuʿmān, are the Prophet and the Imams descended from his progeny. This is the essential aspect of the theme which will be discussed afterwards. Our author evidently is aware of the contemporary controversy within the Muslim community as a whole surrounding the interpretation of the verse quoted, that is to say, as to the identity of 'those well rooted in knowledge' and whether they have knowledge of *ta'wīl*. He understandably advocates the Fatimid position. In doing so, he reads the verse under consideration in this manner. 'No one knows its *ta'wīl* except Allāh and those who are of sound instruction (*al-rāsikhūna fi'l-ʿilm*).'[11]

Al-Nuʿmān elaborates the theme further by considering the application of the esoteric aspect to the whole Qur'an. To corroborate this, he refers to a *ḥadīth* of the Prophet in which he is reported to have described the Qur'an as containing both exoteric and esoteric aspects. It appears from the statement of the Fatimid author that the interpretations of the *ḥadīth* given by Muslim writers varied though the *ḥadīth* itself was accepted and agreed upon not only by Ismaili writers but also by a number of other Muslim writers, including Ithnāʿashariyya and Sufis.[12]

The other classification which al-Nuʿmān relates to the meanings is that of the Qur'anic 'symbol/s' (*mathal /amthāl*),[13] implying that they are incomprehensible to an ordinary mind because of their complex implications and extraordinarily profound meanings. The verses of the Qur'an under consideration suggest that the symbols have distinctive characteristics and thus are subject to special treatment.

At this point it should be mentioned that the Fatimid author does not define the term 'symbol/s' *mathal/amthāl* in explicit terms in the relevant chapter of his *Asās al-ta'wīl*. However, in considering his discussion of the term in a wider context, it is clear that he also uses the term 'symbolised meaning/s' (*mamthūl /mamthūlāt*), to refer to the ultimate implications and aims of the symbols.[14]

Al-Nuʿmān examines these textual elements further from the perspective of language as the vehicle for the Divine revelation. He holds that the expressions 'the esoteric aspect' (*al-bāṭin*), 'the inner interpretation' (*al-ta'wīl*) and the symbols (*al-amthāl*) are not external to the Arabic language, but parts of it. However, he suggests that the Qur'anic language is unique and special by stating that it is the embodiment of the Divine revelation. Because of the synthesis of wonders and marvels of the revelation, he states, there is more than one meaning for the same thing, namely the exoteric and the esoteric aspects.[15]

## The Imams as the Inheritors of the Knowledge of the Revelation

On the basis of the divinely revealed traits of the Qur'an, al-Nu'mān states that the Prophet Muḥammad and the Imams are both the possessors and sources of its knowledge. He emphasises the functions of the Prophet and the Imams by attributing the exoteric aspect to the former and the esoteric aspect to the latter. The *ẓāhir*, he states is the miracle of the Prophet and the *bāṭin*, that of the Imams. The designated Imam, in his opinion, is the source and depository (*mustawdaʿ*) of the knowledge of the *bāṭin*.[16] The word '*mustawdaʿ*' connotes that the Imam receives the knowledge from the Prophet as an inheritance, a point to which we should now turn.

The knowledge of the *bāṭin*, as one of the hereditary characteristics, is an integral aspect of the concept of the Imāma. The Imams receive these characteristics as a result of designation based on the divine order.[17] The status of the Imams as the possessors of the knowledge under consideration is believed to be referred to in the Qur'an and to be interpreted by the Prophet and the Imams. For example, as it has been discussed already, the Qur'an makes references to its *ta'wīl* by considering it to be arcane and thus only fathomable by God and 'those of sound instruction' (*al-rāsikhūna fi'l-ʿilm*).[18]

'Alī was one of 'those of sound instruction' since the Prophet referred to him as responsible for the interpretation of the *ta'wīl*[19] and the gate of the city of knowledge (of revelation).[20] Al-Nu'mān holds that 'Alī's knowledge continued through the Imams. Among the proofs which al-Nu'mān furnishes with regard to the transmission of the knowledge is a statement made by 'Alī, who considers the knowledge of the Imams to be the same as that of the prophets. Thus, the knowledge that the Imams received from the last Prophet, according to 'Alī, was originally deposited with Adam and, on the basis of this, the prophets were divinely awarded preferential treatment.[21]

The concept of knowledge may further be elaborated upon in order to determine how this permeates through other aspects of inheritance in the Imāma. Amongst the inheritance-related characteristics of the Imam, the Qur'anic imperative 'restore deposits to their owners' (*tu'addu'l-amānāti ilā ahlihā*) (Qur'an 4:58) will be focused on presently.[22] Al-Nu'mān, on the authority of Imām Muḥammad al-Bāqir, propounds the Qur'anic command by concentrating on the components of the inheritance and their owners. The components of the inheritance, according to the Imam, are: the books (*al-kutub*), the knowledge (*al-ʿilm*) and the weapon (*al-silāḥ*).[23] 'The books' (*al-kutub*) and 'the knowledge' (*al-ʿilm*) refer to the knowledge of the Imams. The Imams possess the knowledge of the revealed books and particularly that of the Qur'an.[24]

We may now turn to the subject of 'the weapon' (*al-silāḥ*) as it relates to the question of knowledge. From the context it can evidently be understood that by weapon al-Nu'mān means the famous sword, Dhu'l-Fiqār, which was given to 'Alī by the Prophet and which is held to be inherited by the Imams.[25]

According to our author, the metaphorical significance of the sword, Dhū'l-Fiqār, lay in its symbolising the special knowledge of the Imams. To support this, al-Nuʿmān refers to Imām al-Muʿizz who holds that the Prophet gave the Dhu'l-Fiqār to ʿAlī to show his divinely granted qualities such as his nobility (*karāma*), his aptitude for furnishing evidence (*al-ḥujja*) and, above all, his knowledge.[26] In the realm of knowledge, other characteristics of the Imams are also emphasised. These characteristics include the status of the Imams as the bearers of the Divine illuminating substance (*nūr*), and the ones who receive Divine help (*ta'yīd*), and inspiration (*ilhām*).[27]

The traits of the Imams as discussed in the above paragraphs emphasise the divinely bestowed and inherited knowledge, on the basis of which they guide. The traits also denote that an Imam does not require any teacher other than the preceding Imam from whom he imbibes the particular knowledge. The preceding Imam entrusts the Imāma to him and thus teaches him.[28] On the basis of all this, al-Nuʿmān refers to the knowledge of the Imams as the real and true knowledge (*al-ʿilm al-ḥaqīqī*) and the one which is transmitted from one Imam to another Imam (*al-ʿilm al-ma'thūr*).[29]

## The Imams as the Interpreters of the *Bāṭin*

Examining the interpretative authority of the Imams, it can be seen that the unfolding of the esoteric aspect depends upon suitability. The Imams consider the various levels of the comprehension of the believers. A *bāṭinī* 'knowledge' that is appropriate for the one advanced in understanding is not to be revealed to the one whose understanding is inferior and who does not deserve it, which, in turn, indicates that the *bāṭin* itself has more than one level.[30]

Esoteric instruction is to be provided by the Imams for selected individuals in groups and also on a one-to-one basis. The availability of this particular instruction, as al-Nuʿmān implies, is subject to the required level of comprehension. The utmost grade of the *bāṭin*, that is the highest level of the stages of teachings, may well be understood by considering the overall Fatimid *daʿwa* instructional system.

According to al-Nuʿmān, Imām al-Muʿizz classified Ismaili teachings, dividing the corpus into three categories: (1) the exoteric aspect (the primary stage); (2) introduction to the esoteric aspect (the intermediary stage); (3) the pure esoteric aspect (the highest stage).[31]

Our author describes the different levels of Fatimid teachings somewhat in detail. The primary stage comprises the exoteric teachings as authorised and recommended by the Imams. Specifically, the authorised and recommended source for these teachings was the *Daʿā'im al-Islām* of al-Qāḍī al-Nuʿmān,[32] one of those books compiled under the direct supervision and guidance of the Imam. The reason for this insistence on the *Daʿā'im* may be visualised by taking into consideration the fact that even the exoteric aspect, particularly of Islamic teachings, as understood by various schools of thought within Islam, is not absolutely homogeneous. These schools of thought, for example, agree on the understanding and performance of some religious obligations while differing on those of others.

At any rate, the primary stage of instruction is followed by the intermediary stage which is referred to as 'the stage of spiritual infancy' (*ḥadd riḍāʿ al-bāṭin*). The Imam admitted into this level the ones whom he had selected from those at the primary stage. He introduced *taʾwīl* to the elevated ones. Although (esoteric) allusions were made frequently, sometimes clear (exoteric) indications were also given. Al-Nuʿmān considers his *Ḥudūd al-maʿrifa* to be the sort of collection of teachings suitable for this level. The training took two years.[33]

Afterwards, the Imam initiated those selected into 'the spiritual upbringing stage' (*ḥadd al-tarbiyya*). At this stage, it was recommended that the *Taʾwīl al-daʿāʾim* be taught. Those who fulfilled all the conditions of this level were considered to be spiritually mature adherents.[34]

Finally, we may briefly refer to the modes of the manifestation of the knowledge of the Imam in relation to the believers. According to al-Nuʿmān, as we have already said, the Imam is the divinely authorised interpreter of the revelation, the master of its *taʾwīl*. However, he provides guidance and *bāṭinī* instructions, either himself or by means of the hierarchical system which he sets up. The Fatimid hierarchy drew its authority from the Imam and was ultimately responsible to him regarding all matters relating to the believers.

Al-Nuʿmān substantiates the Imam's overall guiding relationship with the believers in ways both directly and also indirectly through his disciples, those who received religious instruction from him and became responsible for working for the *daʿwā*. For example, he cites a *ḥadīth* of the Prophet in which he is reported to have said: 'Obtain the knowledge from the learned of my progeny (*ʿālim ahl baytī*), namely the Imam, or from him who has obtained it from the learned of my progeny and you will be saved from Hell.'[35]

The prophetic tradition emerges as evidence for the Ismaili hierarchy; the phrase '... or from him who has obtained it from the learned of my progeny' must be read as an oblique reference to the hierarchy. Elucidating this, al-Nuʿmān describes the knowledge of the Imam as emanating from him to his *ḥujja* and thence to the lower ranks.[36]

However, the Fatimid author reiterates the supremacy of the Imam by examining the intrinsic nature of his knowledge. Accordingly, in his opinion, it is the Imams who are learned in the real sense (*al-ʿUlamāʾ biʾl-ḥaqīqa*). The hierarchy below him does not enjoy that status, as they lack the qualifications necessary for it, including inheritance. However, the hierarchy working under the Imam can be referred to as learned in a figurative sense (*al-ʿUlamāʾ biʾl-majāz*) since they receive knowledge from the Imam. The knowledge of the disciples, however, is subject to their obedience to, and love and reverence for the Imams. Al-Nuʿmān's view is based on the Qur'an. For example Ibrāhīm, one of the leading prophets, insisting on the role of obedience states: 'But whoso followeth me he verily is of me.' (Qur'an 14:36)[37]

## Conclusion

The concept of *bāṭin*, then, is a tenth-century Ismaili principle of interpretation of the Islamic revelation that is seen to coordinate the revelation with creation, including man. The aims of this study include creating and reinforcing the awareness of the truths underlying the Islamic revelation and creation, and reinforcing the need for identification and recognition of the ways and means of acquiring knowledge of them. In understanding the points underlined above (among other aspects of the formulation of the view of al-Nuʿmān) the sequence and organisation of the texts concerned, particularly that of the introduction to the *Asās al-ta'wīl*, are significant.

In his formulation, the Ismaili author proceeds from creation to the revelation, perhaps referring to the former as a stepping stone to the latter. The easiest method by which a human being may learn is from creation, and particularly from his or her own self. By concentrating on creation properly, the 'horizon' of one's understanding is widened which results in him or her being led to the belief system.

Qur'anic knowledge, and particularly of the *bāṭin/ta'wīl*, is the highest instructional level as envisaged and elaborated by al-Nuʿmān. This is the aspect of the revelation which is beyond the comprehension of an ordinary person. It therefore necessitates the presence of divinely designated guides after the Prophet, namely the Imams descended from his progeny, who inherit the knowledge from him.

In short, the Imam, al-Nuʿmān's analysis would suggest, is the final authority for Qur'anic knowledge and through his instrumentality one can take cognisance of the truths as necessary for spiritual advancement.

## Notes

1. References to various features of the life of al-Nuʿmān, including his works, have been made in several works. Some contemporary scholars have undertaken serious studies of him. See, for example: Wilferd Madelung. 'The Sources of Ismaʿīlī Law', *JNES*, 35 (1976), pp. 29–40; A. A. A. Fyzee, 'Al-Qāḍī al-Nuʿmān the Fāṭimid Jurist and Author', *JRAS* (1934), pp. 11–532.

2. Al-Qāḍī al-Nuʿmān, *Asās al-ta'wīl*, ed. ʿĀrif Tāmir (Beirut, 1960), p. 28.

3. Ibid., pp. 28–29, 31.

4. Al-Qāḍī al-Nuʿmān, *Ta'wīl al-daʿā'im*, ed. Muḥammad Ḥasan al-Aʿẓamī (Cairo, n.d.), vol. 1, pp. 48–49; also see *Asās al-ta'wīl*, pp. 43–49, 51–52.

5. Al-Nuʿmān, *Asās al-ta'wīl*, pp. 28–29.

6. Ibid., p. 29.

7. Ibid.

8. Ibid.

9. Al-Nuʿmān, *Asās al-ta'wīl*, pp. 29, 31.

10. Ibid., p. 29.

11. The vast majority of Shiʿi writers explicitly state that 'those of sound instruction' (*al-rāsikhūna fi'l-ʿilm*), namely, the Prophet and the Imams, possess the knowledge of the *ta'wīl* of the Qur'an. Therefore, the phrase '*al-rāsikhūna fi'l-ʿilm*' is to be connected with the name, *Allāh*. See: Al-Nuʿmān, *Asās al-ta'wīl*, p. 29; his *Daʿā'im al-Islām*, ed. A. A. A. Fyzee (Cairo, 1951–1960), vol. 1, pp. 28–29; al-Kulaynī, *al-Uṣūl min al-kāfī*, ed. ʿAlī Akbar al-Ghaffārī (4th ed., Beirut, 1401/1980–1981), vol. 1, p. 213; ʿAlī Ibrāhīm al-Qummī, *Tafsīr al-Qummī*, ed. al-Sayyid Ṭayyib al-Mūsawī (2nd ed., Najaf, 1388/1968), vol. 1, pp. 96–97; however, Abū Jaʿfar al-Ṭūsī, one of the Ithnāʿasharī commentators on the Qur'an totally neglects the Shiʿi position under consideration, while at the same time referring to some other views on the theme; these will be given below shortly. See: Muḥammad Ḥasan al-Ṭūsī, *al-Tibyān fī tafsīr al-Qur'an* (Najaf, 1383–1389/1964–1969), vol. 2, pp. 394–400. As for a few of the Sunni sources, according to al-Ṭabarī, the commentators on the Qur'an from the earlier generations hold different views as to whether 'those of sound instruction' (*al-rāsikhūna fi'l-ʿilm*) possess the knowledge of the *ta'wīl* of the Qur'an. ʿĀ'isha and Ibn ʿAbbās, for example, are said to have held that 'those of sound instruction' do not know the *ta'wīl*. Because in the opinion of these individuals, the phrase 'those of sound instruction' is not to be taken as connected with the name, *Allāh*. However, according to these individuals, 'those of sound instruction' reaffirm their belief in the revelation in its entirety.

On the other hand, the name of Ibn ʿAbbās is put in the list of names of those who are of the opinion that 'those of sound instruction' have the knowledge of the *ta'wīl*. On the basis of firmness in the knowledge, they reaffirm their belief in the revelation. See al-Ṭabarī, *Tafsīr* (Cairo, 1954), vol. 3, pp. 182–184.

The position of Ibn ʿAbbās on the knowledge of the *ta'wīl* needs further consideration, in view of the significance which the non-Shiʿi sources award to him and also to make an attempt to clarify the ambiguity surrounding the conflicting reports about his understanding of the knowledge of the *ta'wīl*. If the reports attributed to Ibn ʿAbbās are genuine, there can be two possible interpretations of them, either of which may represent the actual attitude of Ibn ʿAbbās towards *ta'wīl*. In the first place, Ibn ʿAbbās may have expressed a view similar to that of ʿĀ'isha and others who hold that only God knows the *ta'wīl*. Then he may have changed it to the other view. Alternatively, it cannot be ruled out that Ibn ʿAbbās expressed both views with different interpretations in mind. One may adhere to this assumption on the basis of the view of Ibn ʿAbbās that *ta'wīl* has more than one level. According to Ibn ʿAbbās, the Qur'anic interpretation (*tafsīr*) has four aspects or levels. The 'level one' interpretation can be known to anybody, as it relates to the basics. While the 'level two' interpretation is known to the Arabs. This is so because of the language skills involved. The third level interpretation is known to 'those of sound instruction'. However, the final level of interpretation is known to God alone. Nobody else can understand it. See: Ibn Kathīr, *Mukhtaṣar tafsīr Ibn Kathīr*, ed. Muḥammad ʿAlī al-Ṣābūnī (Beirut, 1981), vol. 1, p. 265. On the basis of this definition, one may hold the view that when Ibn ʿAbbās denies his involvement in the knowledge of the *ta'wīl*, he may be referring to the 'level four' interpretation. On the other hand, his claim of knowledge of the *ta'wīl* may be a reference to the 'level three' interpretation.

12. Al-Nuʿmān, *Asās al-taʾwīl*, p. 30; for some of the non-Ismaili interpretations of the categories of the exoteric and esoteric aspects see Muḥammad b. Khālid al-Barqī, *Kitāb al-Maḥāsin*, ed. Sayyid Muḥammad Ṣādiq (Najaf, 1383/1964), vol. 2, p. 243; Badr al-Dīn Muḥammad al-Zarkashī, *al-Burhān fī ʿulūm al-Qurʾān*, ed. Muḥammad Abu'l-Faḍl Ibrāhīm (Dār Iḥyāʿ Kutub al-ʿArabiyya, 1957–1958), vol. 2, p. 169; Abū Ṭālib al-Makkī, *Qūt al-qulūb* (Cairo, 1932), vol. 2, pp. 6–7; Ibn Taymiyya, 'al-Risāla fī'l-ʿilm al-bāṭin wa'l-ẓāhir', in *Majmūʿāt rasāʾil al-Munīriyya*, ed., Muḥammad Amīn Damaj (Beirut, 1970), vol. 1, p. 230; Gerhard Böwering, *The Mystical Vision of Existence in Classical Islam* (Berlin, 1980), pp. 138–142; al-Ḥabīb al-Faqī, *al-Taʾwīl: Ususuhu wa-maʿānīhi fī'l-madhhab al-Ismāʿīlī* (Tunis, n.d.), p. 45, n. 81. It should be born in mind that even some non-Shiʿi thinkers and writers insist on *bāṭin* or *taʾwīl* to be revealed only to those who are capable of comprehending it. Ibn Rushd appears to be vehemently advocating this view. He corroborates the secrecy by referring to ʿAlī who is reported to have said: 'Tell people what they can understand. (By telling them otherwise), do you want them to accuse God and His Prophet of lying?' Ibn Rushd thinks that the *bāṭin* relates to some parts of the Qur'an but not to others. See: Ibn Rushd, *Kitāb faṣl al-maqāl wa-taqrīr bayn al-sharīʿa wa'l-ḥikma mina'l-ittiṣāl*, ed. B. N. Nadir (5th ed., Beirut, 1986), pp. 38, 36; Muḥammad b. Ismāʿīl al-Bukhārī, *Ṣaḥīḥ al-Bukhārī*, ed. Muḥammad Muḥsin Khān (Beirut, n.d.), vol. 1, p. 95.

13. Al-Nuʿmān, *Asās al-taʾwīl*, pp. 30–31; see Qur'an 29:43, 2:26, 25:39, 39:27.

14. Al-Nuʿmān, *Asās al-taʾwīl*, pp. 61–62.

15. Ibid., p. 31.

16. Ibid., pp. 31–32.

17. See for al-Nuʿmān's elaboration of the designation and of inheritance in the *Imāma*: Bulbul Shah, 'The Imām as Interpreter of the Qur'an according to al-Qāḍī al-Nuʿmān' (MA, Institute of Islamic Studies, McGill University, 1984), pp. 23–25, 31–33; also see: S. M. H. Jafri, *The Origins and Early Development of Shīʿa Islam* (2nd ed., Qumm, 1409/1989), pp. 289–292.

18. See above notes 11 and 12.

19. Al-Nuʿmān, *Asās al-taʾwīl*, p. 200; Ibn al-Athīr, *Usd al-ghāba* (Cairo, n.d.), vol. 4, p. 32. According to some other sources, the Prophet addressed his Companions and said: 'There is a person among you who will fight for the sake of the *taʾwīl* of the Qur'an as I fought for the sake of its *tanzīl*.' Upon hearing this, Abū Bakr and ʿUmar stood up, thinking that the Prophet had referred to them. However, the Prophet said: 'No, it is the one who is mending the shoes.' At the time ʿAlī was mending the shoes. See: Aḥmad Ibn Ḥanbal, *Musnad* (Beirut, n.d.), vol. 3, pp. 33, 82; al-Ḥākim al-Nayshābūrī, *Mustadrak ʿalā al-ṣaḥiḥayn* (Deccan, 1341/1922–1923), vol. 3, pp. 132–133.

20. Al-Nuʿmān, *Asās al-taʾwīl*, p. 86; Ibn Ḥajar al-ʿAsqalānī, *Tahdhīb al-tahdhīb* (Deccan, 1326/1907–1908), vol. 7, p. 337; al-Ḥakīm, *Mustadrak*, pp. 133, 146–147.

21. Al-Nuʿmān, *Asās al-taʾwīl*, p. 61; this view was also expressed by Imām Jaʿfar al-Ṣādiq. See *al-Majālis wa'l-musāyarāt*, ed. al-Ḥabīb al-Faqī, Ibrāhīm Shabbūḥ and Muḥammad al-Yaʿlāwī (Tunis, 1978), p. 272; al-Kulaynī, *al-Kāfī*, vol. 1, p. 223. It is to be noted that Abu Ḥafṣ ʿUmar Shihāb al-Dīn al-Suhrawardī, one of the most respected authorities in Sufism, has expressed a similar view with regard to the Sufi shaykh. According to him, the saint is the heir of the Prophet. He substantiates this view with one of the *aḥādith* of the Prophet: 'The scholars are the heirs of the Prophet'. This being the case, according to Suhrawardī, the

knowledge of the saint is the continuation of the Divine knowledge deposited with Adam. See: Shihāb al-Dīn al-Suhrawardī, *'Awārif al-Ma'ārif* (Cairo, 1357/1939), pp. 62–63.

22. Al-Nu'mān, *Da'ā'im*, pp. 26–27; al-Kulaynī, *al-Kāfī*, vol. 1, p. 276.

23. Al-Nu'mān, *Da'ā'im*, pp. 26–27.

24. Ibid., p. 29, al-Nu'mān, *al-Majālis*, p. 379; al-Nu'mān, *Asās al-ta'wīl*, p. 61; al-Kulaynī, *al-Kāfī*, vol. 1, pp. 223–229 and 213–214.

25. Al-Nu'mān, *al-Majālis*, pp. 208–209; al-Kulayni, *al-Kāfī*, vol. 1, pp. 232–237.

26. Al-Nu'mān, *al-Majālis*, pp. 208–209.

27. Al-Nu'mān, *Kitāb al-himma fī ādab atbā' al-a'imma*, ed. Muḥammad Kāmil Ḥusayn (Cairo, n.d.), p. 128; *Iftitāḥ al-da'wa*, ed. F. Dashrāwī (Tunis, 1975), p. 338; some of Ithnā'asharī sources have made references to similar ideas. For a detailed study see Abd al-Karim (Douglas Sloan) Crow, 'The Teaching of Ja'far aṣ-Ṣādiq' (M.A., Institute of Islamic Studies, McGill University, Montreal, Canada, 1980), pp. 37–38, 143–145 and 148–149.

28. Al-Nu'mān, *Iftitāḥ*, p. 338.

29. Al-Nu'mān, *Asās al-ta'wīl*, p. 66; al-Nu'mān, *Iftitāḥ*, p. 338.

30. Al-Nu'mān, *Asās al-ta'wīl*, p. 32.

31. Al-Nu'mān, *Ta'wīl*, pp. 48–49.

32. Ibid., p. 48.

33. Al-Nu'mān, *Ta'wīl*, p. 49; al-Nu'mān, *Asās al-ta'wīl*, pp. 25–26.

34. Al-Nu'mān, *Ta'wīl*, p. 49.

35. Ibid., p. 71.

36. Ibid., p. 66; al-Nu'mān, *al-Majālis*, p. 94; al-Nu'mān, *Asās al-ta'wīl*, p. 85.

37. Al-Nu'mān, *Ta'wīl*, p. 66.

# 11

# The Concept of Knowledge According to al-Kirmānī (d. after 411/1021)

*Faquir Muhammad Hunzai*

## I. Introduction

The concept of knowledge is one of the best known and most debated topics in religion and other fields of human enquiry. Its prime importance lies in the fact that a clear understanding of a system of thought depends on a clear understanding of its concept of knowledge. The concept of knowledge has a particular relationship with Ismailism as one of the appellations given to Ismailis is *Taʿlīmiyya* or *Aṣḥāb al-taʿlīm*. Contradictory views have been expressed by critics about the Ismaili concept of knowledge, mainly based on non Ismaili hostile sources. This article is an attempt to present the Ismaili concept of knowledge based on Ismaili sources. To this end, we will focus on Ḥāmid al-Dīn Aḥmad b. ʿAbd Allāh al-Kirmānī, as an outstanding Ismaili *dāʿī* and thinker who lived in the fourth/tenth and fifth/eleventh centuries, a period extremely important for both philosophical and *daʿwa* activities, and whose important works are available, and in doing so it is hoped that it will be helpful in understanding an essential concept of Ismailism. This article mainly concentrates on the nature and source of knowledge according to al-Kirmānī, its relationship to the intellect and to authority.

In order to place al-Kirmānī's position into a proper perspective, it would be helpful to examine the classification of Muslim schools of thought by Abū Ḥāmid al-Ghazālī (d. 505/1111), a renowned figure in the history of Islamic thought, who claimed to have thoroughly studied all Islamic schools of thought, including Ismailism. Al-Ghazālī divided Muslims into five categories with respect to their attainment of true knowledge or truth: the *Muqallidūn*, the *Mutakallimūn*, the *Bāṭiniyya* or *Taʿlīmiyya*, i.e., Ismāʿīliyya, the *Falāsifa* and the *Ṣūfiyya*. Al-Ghazālī did not include the *Muqallidūn* among the seekers of knowledge but considered them servile conformists. He said: 'A prerequisite to being a *Muqallid* is that one does not know himself to be such.'[1]

Thus al-Ghazālī confined seekers of truth or knowledge to the remaining four categories:

1. The *Mutakallimūn* or Theologians who claim that they are the people of opinion (*ra'y*) and speculation (*naẓar*) and who attain true knowledge through such enquiry;
2. The *Baṭiniyya* or Esotericists who allege that they are the people of Teaching (*aṣḥāb al-ta'līm*) and that they acquire truth only from the infallible Imam;
3. The *Falāsifa* or Philosophers who allege that they are the people of logic (*manṭiq*) and demonstration (*burhān*) and who can reach true knowledge through this;
4. The *Ṣūfiyya* or Mystics who claim to be the privileged ones of the Divine presence and people of vision (*mushāhada*) and unveiling (*mukāshafa*) and thereby they can attain true knowledge through a beatific vision and unveiling.[2]

The key points of the schools that al-Ghazālī has described enable us to assess the Ismaili point of view in juxtaposition to the others.

Quite often, Ismailism is described by its critics in contradictory terms, as an anti-authoritarian philosophical movement,[3] or an anti-rationalistic authoritarian movement. Al-Ghazālī accuses them of the latter and says that the basis of their *madhhab* is the invalidation of the exercise of intellect and opinion because of their invitation to the *ta'līm* of the infallible Imam.[4]

Because al-Ghazālī occupies an important place among the critics of Ismailism and as he claimed to have a thorough knowledge of their doctrine, it is relevant to discuss his criticism of the doctrine of *ta'līm* for this enables us to assess the Ismaili point of view and the reliability of al-Ghazālī's information on Ismailism. Al-Ghazālī in his *al-Munqidh min al-ḍalāl* says regarding the Ismaili doctrine of *ta'līm*:

> There is no substance to their views and no force in their argument. Indeed, had it not been for the maladroit defence put forward by the ignorant friend of the truth, that innovation, given its weakness, would never have attained its present position. But intense fanaticism led the defenders of the truth to prolong the debate with them over the premises of their argument and to contradict them in everything they said. Thus they fought the Ta'līmites (*Ta'līmiyya*) over their claim that there must be authoritative teaching (*ta'līm*) and an authoritative teacher (*mu'allim*) and also their claim that not every teacher is suitable and that there must be an infallible teacher (*mu'allim ma'ṣūm*). Their argument proving the need for authoritative teaching and an authoritative teacher was lucid and clear and the counter arguments of their opponents were weak. Because of that, many were seduced into thinking that it was due to the strength of the Ta'līmites' doctrine and the weakness of their opponents' doctrine, not understanding that it was

> really due to the dim-wittedness of the defender of the truth and his ignorance of how to go about it. In fact, the right way to proceed is to acknowledge the need for an authoritative teacher who must also be infallible. But our infallible teacher is Muḥammad – God's blessing and peace be upon him! If they say: 'Our teacher has indeed taught his emissaries and scattered them throughout the countries and he expects them to return to consult him if they disagree on some point or encounter some difficulty', we say: 'Our teacher has taught his emissaries and scattered them through the countries, and he has perfected this teaching, since God Most High said: "Today I have perfected for you your religion and have accorded you My full favour" (Qur'an 5:3). And once the teaching has been perfected, the death of the teacher works no harm, just as his hiding works no harm.'[5]

Due to the inaccessibility of Ismaili literature, it has for a long time been extremely difficult for students of Ismailism to verify what has been said about it by its critics – al-Ghazālī and others like him. As a result, whatever has been said by them has been accepted at face value. However, the recent discovery and publication of Ismaili literature shows that – although there are particles of truth in what has been said – because it is not usual for polemicists to present their opponent's views accurately such views are presented in a way that makes them vulnerable to attack. Thus the way rationalism or authoritarianism is attributed to them shows that reason and authority are mutually exclusive and contradictory to each other. On the contrary, according to Ismailism, reason and authority together are necessary otherwise they are not useful. One of the eminent *dāʿīs*, al-Mu'ayyad (d. 470/1078) says:

> The Prophet is the lamp of insights (*baṣā'ir*) through which they understand, just as the sun is the lamp of eyesight(s) (*abṣār*) through which they see. The lamp is useless to the blind who has lost his eyesight and similarly the guidance of prophethood is useless to the one who is blind of intellect and insight. And just as the eye can see through the collectivity of the lamp and the sound eye, the intellect understands through the collectivity of the prophethood and the sound intellect.[6]

Further, the very necessity of an authority is based on the testimony of the intellect. As al-Sijistānī (d. after 361/971) says: 'The intellect attests to the existence of the most excellent and the best from every species according to its excellence and nobility.'[7] Thus in Ismailism, there is no incompatibility or mutual exclusiveness between authority and reason. In fact, the perfection of the intellect lies in following and obeying the authority, the latter being the actual and perfect Intellect and the former being the potential or imperfect intellect.[8]

As for al-Ghazālī's criticism that the basis of the *madhhab* of the *Taʿlīmiyya* is the invalidation of the exercise of intellect and opinion, it is true that they reject the exercise of personal opinion in matters of religion, on the basis of several Qur'anic verses such as: 'And who is more astray than one who follows his desire without guidance from God' (Qur'an 28:50) and 'They follow but a guess, and indeed, a guess never takes the place of the truth' (Qur'an 53:28).[9] However, as is clear from the above, to accuse them of not exercising the intellect does not accord with the way in which they view the intellect. It appears that al-Ghazālī attempts to depict Ismailis as *muqallids* or servile conformists, whom he treats with great contempt.

Al-Ghazālī's information about Ismaili belief in an infallible Imam is basically true but in order to attack this, he has added certain accretions, such as the notion of the hidden Imam, which bears no relation to the Ismaili doctrine of Imamate. Because the Ismaili concept of knowledge depends on the *taʿlīm* of the infallible Imam or Teacher, it is pertinent to provide a summary of their arguments on the necessity for an infallible Imam. Numerous works on the necessity of Imamate written by Ismaili *dāʿīs* are now available. A detailed description of the necessity for the continuity of Imamate after the Prophet and thereby to continue his mission to guide people according to God's command, is given in the *Kitāb al-wilāya/walāya* of the *Daʿāʾim al-Islām* by al-Qāḍī al-Nuʿmān. Al-Kirmānī himself has written an entire book on the establishment, necessity, infallibility and other aspects of Imamate, called *al-Maṣābīḥ fī ithbāt al-imāma*. Some of the arguments from *al-Iftikhār* of al-Sijistānī and from *al-Maṣābīḥ* of al-Kirmānī are offered here. Al-Sijistānī in his *al-Iftikhār*, referring to the Qur'anic verses: 'One day We shall summon all people with their Imam' (Qur'an 17:71), 'You are a warner only, and for every people is a guide' (Qur'an 13:7), 'And We appointed them Imams who guide by Our command' (Qur'an 21:73), says that by these verses, God makes it clear that there is an Imam in every age, who guides by the command of God to His religion and to His straight path. Therefore, it is necessary for there to be a guiding and guided Imam for people in every age, and the world is never devoid of such a guide. And the matter is not as ordinary people think, that God has neglected His creatures and left them without someone to invite, guide and command them.[10]

Al-Sijistānī further argues:

> By God sending Messengers to people and neglecting them after their departure without appointing ... an Imam lies the main part of corruption which leads to disorder and perdition. The proof of this is the differences which appeared in the *umma* which led to the shedding of blood ... and accusing each other of infidelity. The cause of this was nothing but diverting the Imamate from the one to whom God had granted it ... When God has sent a learned and wise Messenger to unite the people by the purity of his soul and the subtlety of his mind with the power of revelation conferred upon him, (and) a noble *sharīʿa* and a sound and perfect Book (*tanzīl*) and then He does not appoint someone to guard and protect them in the ages (to come), it would be a mockery, futility and weakness from Him, but He is free from and above such things.[11]

Al-Kirmānī in his *al-Maṣābīḥ* gives fourteen arguments on the establishment and necessity of an Imam after the Prophet, of which some are given here:

1. Because the Prophet had brought from God profound wisdom, it was incumbent upon him to convey it to those who were in his time and also to those who were yet to come until the Day of Resurrection. But those who were in his time were not capable of accepting the entirety of wisdom all at once, nor was it possible for those to come in future to be there in his time, nor was it ordained for the Prophet to remain in this world until the end of all people and so convey to them the trust of God, so it became necessary for him to appoint a successor to take his place and convey this trust and for his successor at the time of his own demise to designate someone else to continue to convey the trust of God to people.[12]
2. The Prophet brought the *tanzīl* and the *sharīʿa* in Arabic, a language in which a single word, by its being a parable or allegory can lead to diverse and manifold meanings. It is therefore possible to interpret every Qurʾanic verse and every Prophetic Tradition according to the desire of the interpreter. But this possibility is rejected by the intellect and we see in the Islamic community that each sect argues for the validity of its own sect, interpreting a Qurʾanic verse and a prophetic tradition, in a sense different from the senses held by the others. For example, in the verse: 'What hindered you from falling prostrate before that whom I have created with My two *yads*' (38:75), the Muʿtazila say that 'two *yads*' mean power (*qudra*) and strength (*quwwa*), others interpret them as bounty (*niʿma*) and favour (*minna*), and the *Mujbīra* interpret them as the two hands which form part of the body.

   All these interpretations are correct and cannot be rejected, for the word '*yad*' contains all these meanings. Therefore, either all these meanings which are the esoteric aspects that the word conveys are correct and therefore it is incumbent to know them all; or, only one or two are correct in which case it is necessary to know which ones so as to avoid the others; or, the meaning is other than any of these and the word is used as a simile or parable in which case it is necessary to know the object (*mamthūl*). If all the meanings of the word are correct, then wisdom necessitates that there should be someone in the community who knows the form of wisdom in all of them so that one is not left with only one meaning to the exclusion of the others. All this is necessary so that unity prevails in the community in the worship of God and any differences of opinion are resolved. If, however, only one or two of the meanings are correct, then wisdom necessitates for there to be someone to make such meanings known so that there is guidance and to prevent people from mistaken belief, for without a teacher one cannot distinguish which meaning is most worthy of belief. This, so that controversy and hatred vanishes and unity prevails in the worship of God. And if the purpose of the word is other than the apparent meaning and the word is a simile or symbol, then again wisdom necessitates that someone in the community explain the object (*mamthūl*) of it so that people do not go astray or believe in that which is not correct. Thus all three possibilities require the existence of someone in the community to guide and teach.[13]

3. God by the command 'If you have a dispute concerning any matter, refer it to God and the Messenger', (Qur'an 4:59) enjoins upon believers to have recourse to the Prophet in their disputes and indeed they did so on religious matters in his time. But as it was not possible nor was it ordained for the Prophet to remain in the midst of the community for all time so that people could continue to have recourse to him, it became necessary for someone to take his place to make such decisions so that the command of God would endure. He who stands in the place of the Prophet is the Imam.[14]
4. God by the command: 'O you who believe! Obey God, obey the Messenger and the *ulū al-amr* from among you', (Qur'an 4:59) has enjoined upon believers in one verse three acts of obedience, each linked with one another. It is obvious that obedience to the *ulū al-amr* is other than obedience to the Messenger and that obedience to the Messenger is other than obedience to God and that one is not accepted without the second nor the second without the third. The address in this verse is to the generality of believers, to those in the time of the Prophet and to those after him, without any distinction. It is absurd to believe that God would enjoin upon His servants obedience to someone whom He has joined in this verse with Him and the Prophet if He had not made him infallible like the Messenger. Thus, due to the fact that the address is to the generality of believers, the existence of someone to whom obedience is obligatory upon the community is necessary so that they may fulfil this duty.[15]

Keeping to the Ismaili argument of the necessity for an infallible Imam, it is interesting to juxtapose this to al-Ghazālī's argument. Al-Ghazālī, unlike his predecessors, realised the necessity for an infallible Imam and labelled his predecessors ignorant for their failure to realise this. However, his own arguments 'Our infallible teacher is Muḥammad(s)' or 'Your teacher is hidden (*ghā'ib*)' do not seem to refute in any way the necessity of the Imam. The Ismaili doctrine of the necessity of the Imam is based on the belief that the nature of human intellect is imperfect or potential and that it requires a perfect or actual Intellect to attain perfection or actuality. Further, al-Ghazālī cannot in any sense justify that Muḥammad(s) belongs only to him and his party, for the Ismailis too, as is clear from the above, claim that the perpetual necessity of an infallible Imam is to accomplish the Prophet's mission, which due to the spatial and temporal hindrances and limitations of human intellect, it was not possible to complete in the lifetime of the Prophet. Similarly, the concept of a hidden Imam is not an Ismaili concept, for as al-Sijistānī has pointed out, the Imam according to Ismailis is either manifest (*ẓāhir*) or is concealed (*mastūr*). However, *mastūr* does not mean that he is unavailable to his *dā'īs* but that he is concealed only from his enemies and ordinary members of the community to whom the *dāʿīs* convey the guidance of the living Imam.

The Ismaili interpretation of the completion of religion also differs from al-Ghazālī's in the sense that this verse was revealed after the appointment of the successor or the *waṣī* or *asās*[16] who through his progeny, continues the *ta'wīl* of the Qur'an by the command of God. If completion of religion is understood as the Prophet having completed the teaching of the Qur'an and the Sunna, then any attempt to solve problems using sources other than the Qur'an or Sunna would be futile and superfluous. Thus, according to Ismailis, religion is only complete with the Qur'an and the teacher of the Qur'an, the *ulū al-amr* (Qur'an 4:59), who has to be as infallible as the Prophet by virtue of his being linked in obedience to God and the Prophet.

It is due to such interaction that the different schools of thought have developed and expounded most of their concepts. The study of the concept of knowledge propounded by al-Kirmānī, an eminent exponent of Ismailism, will be examined in the context of such interaction.

## II. Definition of Knowledge and its Relation to Existence

Al-Kirmānī defined knowledge or *ʿilm* in both concise and elaborate expressions. In his epistle *al-Ḥāwiya*, he defines *ʿilm* as 'to find out things according to their form'.[17] In his *Rāḥa* he defines it as 'the conception of the Divine signs, which is the comprehension of what has preceded the human soul in existence, such as the archetypes of the *ibdāʿī* and *inbiʿāthi* intellects and the higher and lower bodies'.[18] It is obvious from al-Kirmānī's definition that it is closely linked with forms, archetypes or realities of things or existents, therefore in order to have a clear concept of knowledge, it is necessary first to have a clear understanding of the concept of existence in al-Kirmānī's schema of the existents.

In al-Kirmānī's schema of existence, there are many grades from the First Intellect as the first end to mankind as the second end. But basically he divides it into two categories: the physical and the non-physical. By the physical, he means this world with its heaven, earth, planets, stars, elements and generated beings and by non-physical, intellects, souls, Paradise, Hell, resurrection, reward, punishment, reckoning, and so on. The essential difference between the two is that the former kind of existents are *ẓāhir*, or manifest by their nature and are perceptible by the senses. In the perception of the perceptibles, there is no difference between participants with sound senses. That is to say that in the perception of such things there is no difference between a learned man and an illiterate person.[19]

The non-physical existents by their nature are *bāṭin*, or hidden, and they cannot be perceived by the senses, rather their knowledge is acquired through the intellect and therefore, they are intelligibles. Since their grasp or comprehension does not depend on perception which is common among people, but on the intellectual capacity of people in which they differ according to their individual acquisition of knowledge, therefore, there is a difference between people in their grasp of knowledge. Al-Kirmānī thus stresses that in the comprehension of the physical or external things, people are equal in their means, but in non-physical or internal things, they differ according to their acquisition.[20]

Al-Kirmānī, in order to illustrate this, uses the example of the utterance '*Bism Allāh al-Raḥmān al-Raḥīm*'. He says that when the uvulae and tongues are moved to pronounce it and the voice is raised, because the voice is perceptible, all those who have sound senses can participate equally in hearing it, but as for its meaning, i.e. the exegesis and *ta'wīl*, because it is imperceptible, it cannot be participated in equally by all those who have sound senses, since the comprehension of the meaning is the prerogative of those who have acquired knowledge or the hidden aspect of things.[21]

The preceding description of the nature of things leads to the conclusion that, just as there are two kinds of existents, with their distinctive characteristics of being *ẓāhir* and *bāṭin*, or perceptible and imperceptible, accordingly, there are two kinds of comprehension. Al-Kirmānī in keeping with the classification of existents, classifies knowledge into two kinds: the first knowledge and the second knowledge.

The first knowledge is related to the physical world and the world of nature and the protection of its bodies, which al-Kirmānī calls the first perfection. This kind of knowledge in nature can be seen in the mineral, vegetative and animal souls. An example of the knowledge of the mineral soul is that minerals mingle only with minerals which protect them and avoid those which harm them. For example, mercury mingles with gold but does not mingle with iron. An example of the knowledge of the vegetative soul is that roots of plants move in the direction of moisture, which protects them, but when they reach a stone or other obstruction, turn away. An example of the knowledge of the animal soul is that animals eat that which is useful for their bodies and avoid that which is harmful. Al-Kirmānī concludes that had this knowledge not been in minerals, plants and animals, they would not have been able to protect their bodies, and that therefore the Wise Creator has granted them the first knowledge to protect the first existence or the first perfection.

The second knowledge, according to al-Kirmānī, is the second perfection, of which the soul is initially devoid. Al-Kirmānī basing his argument on the verse: 'Surely, God brought you forth from the wombs of your mothers when you knew nothing' (Qur'an 16:78), says that in this verse by 'you knew nothing' is meant the second perfection which is the second knowledge, which is related to religions and beliefs by which the soul becomes perfect and turns into an intellect. Al-Kirmānī says that the nature of these two kinds of knowledge is different. The first is given to every soul innately and for this it does not require a teacher, while the second which is related to religions and beliefs can be obtained only from a teacher.[22]

It is obvious that since the first kind of knowledge is given to every soul innately, it is not necessary to seek this kind of knowledge. What is useful now is to investigate what al-Kirmānī says about the necessity of the second knowledge and its source, upon which depends the second perfection of the soul. We have seen al-Kirmānī's division of the existents into *ẓāhir* and *bāṭin* and how the second knowledge is related to the *bāṭin*. The establishment of the *bāṭin* and belief in it has been one of the most essential and important issues in Ismailism. We have also seen in al-Ghazālī's classification of Muslim schools of thought that one of the names given to Ismailis by their opponents is the Bāṭiniyya, due to their belief in the *bāṭin* of the Book and the *sharīʿa*. In fact, in al-Kirmānī's own time, Ismailis were attacked by the Zaydī Imam, who was asked for a *fatwā* about their belief in the *bāṭin* vis-à-vis the *ẓāhir* of all religious practices, such as *ṣalāt*, *zakāt*, etc. and about their belief that the *ẓāhir* cannot be complete without the knowledge of the *bāṭin*. Al-Kirmānī wrote his epistle *al-Kāfiya* in response to the Zaydī Imam on the establishment of the *bāṭin*. In addition, al-Kirmānī deals with the necessity of *bāṭin* or *ta'wīl* in *al-Maṣābīḥ*, *al-Waḍiyya fī maʿālim al-dīn*, *Tanbīh al-hādī wa'l-mustahdī* and particularly in the *Rāḥa*. He produced numerous proofs on the necessity of the *bāṭin* or *ta'wīl* some of which are presented here. Al-Kirmānī uses the words *bāṭin*, *ta'wīl*, *bayān*, *tafsīr*, *sharḥ*, *maʿnā*, and *ʿilm* interchangeably.

1. Intellects and souls have no way to recognise the Return (*maʿād*) and that which is imperceptible to the senses, except through perceptible examples drawn by the Messengers and the practices laid down by them. The Prophet taught perceptible examples, which are profound wisdom, and it became necessary that in order to accept these examples, wisdom should be implied in them. But the *ẓāhir* or exoteric aspect of the Qur'an and the *sharīʿa*, which the Prophet brought, conflicts with the rules of the intellect, such as the verse 'And when your Lord brought forth from the children of Adam, from their reins, their seed, and made them testify of themselves, (saying): Am I not your Lord? They said: Yes verily' (Qur'an 7:172). The impossibility of bringing forth the children of Adam as particles and to take covenant of His Lordship from them, has created difficulties explaining this for the people of the *ẓāhir*[23] for elsewhere He commands that one cannot accept the testimony of children, let alone babies or seed, because they are not yet of an age where they are obliged to observe the requirements of religion. Similarly, there is the Prophetic Tradition: 'Between my grave and my pulpit there is a garden from among the gardens of Paradise'. The absurdity of the exoteric aspect of this Tradition lies in the fact that at that particular place there is nothing that can remotely be described as a garden. But as the Prophet is a sage and free from ignorance, it becomes necessary to look beyond the exoteric aspect of what the Prophet has brought so that it is not devoid of meanings with

which the intellect can agree and the revelation can be established as true and full of wisdom. These meanings are called *ta'wīl*.[24]

2. According to the Divine command 'Invite unto the way of thy Lord with wisdom and good exhortation' (Qur'an 16:125), the Prophet invited people unto God with wisdom, and whoever does not believe this is an unbeliever. But according to the *ẓāhir*, he invited the people unto God and His worship with certain actions, which if they are repeated by a human being at a place other than where they have been commanded, would be considered madness or a joke, such as the strange actions and rites of pilgrimage. No wisdom is attached to the *ẓāhir* of such acts, such as conversations with stones, walking fast on tiptoe, abstinence from paring nails and shaving the hair on the head and pelting the *Jamra*s with pebbles. However, because the Prophet invited with wisdom, it is necessary for these actions not to be devoid of the meanings with which wisdom agrees and the intellect accepts as knowledge, for salvation lies in such behaviour. Those meanings are called the *ta'wīl*.[25]
3. According to Divine justice nobody will be punished for the sins of others, as God says: 'No bearer of burden bears the burden of another' (Qur'an 6:164). But it is in the law of the Prophet to punish the uncle for the sin of the nephew, when he kills someone by mistake. That is against God's justice and what He has commanded, and it is inconceivable that the Prophet can do something against His justice and mercy, or that he commands something which is contradictory to His command. It is therefore necessary that this and commands like this have certain meanings and wisdom compatible with His justice and mercy and which can be understood by the intellect. That meaning which is compatible with God's justice and mercy and understood as such by the intellect is the *ta'wīl*.[26]
4. It is absurd for a wise human being, let alone God, to talk to an inanimate thing which has no life, no reward, no punishment, nor is it possible for an organ to accept a command or prohibition and to respond to it. But the Prophet, by the verse 'Then He turned to the heaven when it was smoke and said unto it and the earth: Come both of you, willingly or unwillingly. They said: We come, obedient'. Qur'an 41:11 informs us that He spoke to the heaven and the earth, which are both inanimate and have no intellect, nor do they have any organs of speech. The absurdity of this conversation of God, the Wise, with the inanimate necessitates that His conversation with heaven and earth and their response, have a meaning which establishes the speech of God to be true and which the intellect accepts. That meaning is called *ta'wīl*.[27]
5. God says: 'When He made the slumber fall upon you as a reassurance from Him and sent down water from the sky upon you, and thereby He might purify you and remove from you the dirt of Satan, and make stronger your hearts and firm your feet thereby' (Qur'an 8:11). It is known that the dirt of Satan is disbelief, doubt, confusion, hypocrisy, ignorance, deviation, etc. which is in the hearts,

intellects and souls and as such it is unimaginable that they can be purified by the water which comes from the visible sky. Had the water mentioned in the verse been natural water than everyone, whether believer or unbeliever, would have been purified and accordingly it is necessary for water to have a different meaning without which it would have been absurd for God to say this. That meaning we call *ta'wīl*.[28]

6. God by His command says: 'He it is Who has revealed unto you (Muḥammad) the Book wherein are clear verses. They are the mother of the Book and others are allegorical. But those in whose heart is perversity, pursue the part thereof that is allegorical, seeking discord, and searching for its *ta'wīl*, but no one knows its *ta'wīl* except Allāh and those who are firmly grounded in knowledge (*al-rāsikhūn fi'l-'ilm*) saying: 'We believe in it (Book); the whole is from our Lord; but only men of understanding really heed.' (Qur'an 3:7). This verse has made the *ta'wīl* of what the Prophet has brought necessary. If someone raises an objection and says that the *ta'wīl* of it no one knows except God, and that *rāsikhun fi'l-'ilm* is the subject, not the predicate of the preceding sentence, his objection is absurd in the context of many examples in the Arabic idiom of brevity. For instance, '*Lā yusallimu 'alayka fulānun wa-fulānun ya'tadhir* (No one sends you greetings except so and so, and so and so apologies)'. That is, both of them send greetings and one of them apologises. Thus in addition to God the *rāsikhūn fi'l-'ilm* also know the *ta'wīl* and hence it is necessary.[29]
7. It is not possible to recognise the invisible and imperceptible things except by designating them by visible and perceptible things. Therefore the Prophet has informed us about the invisible things, such as Allāh, Paradise and its felicity, Hell and its torture, through visible and perceptible things. He informed us about Paradise, which is the next world and is invisible and imperceptible, by using such descriptions as gardens, trees, fruits and all kinds of physical bounties etc., and Hell by the fire and all kinds of physical tortures. Therefore it is necessary for whatever the Prophet has said, done and invited us to, about the life hereafter, to be like symbols and allegories (*amthāl*) of their true realities (*mumaththalāt*). The symbolised realities are called *ta'wīl*. Thus it is necessary for there to be the *ta'wīl* of what the Prophet has brought from God and what he has invited us to, such as the Book and the *sharī'a*.[30]

Al-Kirmānī in his *al-Kāfiya* cites as evidence and asserts that, not only do the allegorical teachings of the Prophets have *ta'wīl*, but also that everything that they have brought and that everything that they have commanded us to do has a *ta'wīl* and a knowledge which is other than the apparent and perceptible.[31] The core of his argument is that the purpose of religion cannot be achieved without the *ta'wīl*, which enables the human soul to attain the second perfection, become an intellect and return to its original abode, the world of intellects.

## III Source of Knowledge

The question of knowledge or *ta'wīl*, which is imperceptible, leads to the question of its source and whether it is available to all humans equally or whether it is a prerogative of a particular group. We have already seen that al-Kirmānī differentiates between perceptible cognisance and imperceptible knowledge, the former being related to those things which are perceptible by their nature and the latter to the things that are imperceptible by their nature. Al-Kirmānī emphasises the point that, with respect to the former, there is no distinction between human beings, but with respect to the latter, there are grades and differences among them. This means that true knowledge or *ta'wīl* is not equally available to or attainable by people, and accordingly there are different views about the possibility and attainability of it.

As far as these views are concerned, we have noticed in the sixth argument of al-Kirmānī the necessity of *ta'wīl* in Qur'an 3:7, and that there is a difference in the reading and punctuation of this verse. Those who maintain that the *ta'wīl* of the Qur'an and the *sharīʿa* is not possible, place a full stop (or *waqf lāẓim*) after 'Allāh' and confine the knowledge of *ta'wīl* to Allāh only and consider *al-rāsikhūn fi'l-ʿilm* a new subject. These are the Literalists or *ahl al-ẓāhir* who do not seek deeper meanings beyond the apparent wording of the parables and allegories of the Qur'an and the Prophetic Traditions.

There are others, such as Ibn Qutayba (213–276/828–889),[32] who argue that since God has mentioned the *rāsikhūn fi'l-ʿilm* in an honorific and distinctive sense, this honour lies in their knowledge of *ta'wīl* and in the light of this knowledge they say: 'We believe in it; the whole is from our Lord'. Had this knowledge not been possessed by them, then Ibn Qutayba says: 'They would have no superiority over the learners, or over all ignorant Muslims. For all of them say: "We believe in it; the whole is from our Lord."' Those who maintain that the *rāsikhūn fi'l-ʿilm* know the *ta'wīl* are also divided into two groups: those who allege to reach the truth by opinion and speculation, logic and demonstration or vision and unveiling. For them the status of the *rāsikhūn fi'l-ʿilm* is open to anyone who struggles through these means. For those who claim to attain the truth or *ta'wīl* from the infallible Imam or Teacher, for them the *rāsikhūn fi'l-ʿilm* are only the rightful Imams from the *ahl al-bayt* of the Prophet, i.e. Imām ʿAlī and his designated descendants to the office of Imamate. The former group includes the *Falāsifa*, the *Ṣūfiyya* and the *Mutakallimūn* as a whole, the latter group comprises Shiʿi Islam in general and Ismailis in particular who are known as the *Taʿlīmiyya*. Al-Kirmānī obviously belongs to the latter group and firmly adheres to the Ismaili doctrine of the source of *taʿlīm* and *ta'wīl*.

According to the Ismailis, *ta'wīl* and *tanzīl* are correlative. Thus they argue that just as the *tanzīl* cannot be attained by effort, neither can the *ta'wīl* which is the hidden meaning of *tanzīl*. They argue that as God had chosen the Prophets to convey the *tanzīl*, so He has appointed the Imams to impart the *ta'wīl* of it after the Prophets. Al-Qāḍī al-Nuʿmān says: 'God ... has made the *ẓāhir* (= *tanzīl*) of the Book, the miracle of the Prophet; and the *bāṭin* (= *taʾwīl*), the miracle of the Imams from his *ahl al-bayt* ... As nobody except Muḥammad, the Messenger of God, can bring the *ẓāhir* of the Book, so also, nobody except the Imams from his progeny, can bring the *bāṭin* of it.'

Al-Kirmānī, following the same line, asserts in his *al-Waḍiyya*, that it has been a Divine *Sunna* (law) to appoint an *asās* with every *nāṭiq*. Al-Kirmānī says that it has been a Divine *Sunna* to assign the *tanzīl* to the *nāṭiq*s and the *taʾwīl* to their *asās*es who continue the mission through their descendants. According to this *sunna*, Ādam, Nūḥ, Ibrāhīm, Mūsā and ʿĪsā appointed as their *asās*es or *waṣīs*, Shīth, Sām, Ismāʿīl, Hārūn and Shamʿūn al-Ṣafāʾ, respectively and that the Prophet received a Divine command to reveal the position of his *asās*: 'O Messenger! Convey that which has been revealed unto you from your Lord. If you did not, you would not have conveyed His message.' (Qurʾan 5:67) As a result of this the Prophet appointed Imām ʿAlī to continue the *taʾwīl* or *al-ʿibāda al-ʿilmiyya*. Al-Kirmānī commenting on 'If you did not, you would not have conveyed His message', says that by this God means that had there not been the one who establishes the *taʾwīl* or *al-ʿibāda al-ʿilmiyya* then *al-ʿibāda al-ʿamaliyya* would have been useless and futile. For one *ʿibāda* cannot be acceptable and complete without the other, and the form of the *ʿibāda* and the attainment of bliss is impossible except by knowledge and action, i.e. *taʾwīl* and *tanzīl* together. Thus, according to Ismailis the *rāsikhūn fīʾl-ʿilm* are the Prophet, his *asās* and the Imams from their progeny and hence that the *taʾwīl* is confined only to them. They further substantiate this doctrine by citing the Prophetic Traditions such as: '*Anā ṣāḥib al-tanzīl wa-ʿAliyyun ṣāḥib al-taʾwīl*' ('I am the master of the *tanzīl* and ʿAlī is the Master of the *taʾwīl*').[33]

Having established, according to al-Kirmānī, that true knowledge is the *taʾwīl* and its source is the *asās* of the *nāṭiq* and after him, the Imam of the time in his respective age, the question arises: What is the nature of the *taʾwīl* and how can it be obtained?

From al-Kirmānī's works and also from other Ismaili sources, it appears that the *taʾwīl* in the case of the Prophets and Imams, is not something acquired but is given or taught by God Himself. Hence this is perfect and complete knowledge, which comprises the knowledge of those that have passed away and of those who are to come or the events that have already taken place and those that are to take place in the future (*ʿilm al-awwalīn waʾl-ākhirīn*). However, since people do not have the capacity to accept this knowledge all at once, it gradually continues to be revealed through the chain of Imams, until the Day of Resurrection. It is because of this perfect and firm knowledge, that the Prophet and the Imams are called the *rāsikhun fīʾl-ʿilm*. In Qurʾanic language this is called the *taʾyīd biʾl-rūḥ al-qudus* or Divine help with the Holy Spirit. The Prophets and Imams – '*muʾayyad*' or 'Divinely assisted souls' – in the physical world are the actual Intellects, who make souls or the potential intellects actual.

As far as the non-*mu'ayyad* souls are concerned, they have to acquire this knowledge from the *mu'ayyad* souls or actual Intellects. As for its acquisition, it is not only through the speculative exercise of the mind, it also requires the element of action. That is to say that in order to attain this kind of knowledge, one has to obey the Prophet and the Imams, leading to the attainment of *ta'wīl*. In the case of the Prophets and Imams, because they are both in the position of the Single Soul (*nafs wāḥida*), it is the same thing. In the case of the *umma* or followers, because they have not attained the position of the Single Soul, their *ta'wīl* is on different levels. In the case of both the *ifāda*, giving of knowledge by the Prophets and the Imams and *istifāda* or the receiving of it, it depends on the capacity and receptivity of the followers. Al-Kirmānī says: 'It is possible for one *ta'wīl* to be clearer and more evident than another depending on the purity of the nature of the *mu'awwil* (one who does *ta'wīl*) and his power in knowledge and in deduction.'

Al-Kirmānī also implies that the meanings of *ta'wīl* cannot be confined to some expressions or words. They can be expressed in different words, provided that they do not elevate or degrade the position of the *ḥudūd*. Al-Kirmānī says: 'The words in conveying the meanings of the *ta'wīl* are different, but their meanings, despite the difference in words, are in agreement. Every *ta'wīl* is adequate and satisfactory so long as it does not raise a *ḥadd* above its limit or lower another below its rank.'

To sum up, knowledge according to al-Kirmānī, in its ultimate form is in the higher *ḥudūd* in the world of Intellect or in the First or Universal Intellect, which is reflected in the *nāṭiq*, *asās* and in the Imam of the time, in their respective ages and below them, through *ḥujja*s and *dā'ī*s until the *mustajīb*s for it descends through different stages and forms. It descends through the ladder of the *ḥudūd* and the *mustajīb*s ascend gradually up this ladder, according to their acquisition of this knowledge. This knowledge, which is granted by the Prophets and Imams on acceptance of their *da'wa*, leads to the spiritual life

## IV Conclusion

Al-Kirmānī's concept of knowledge is in line with the Ismaili doctrine of *ta'līm* from the infallible Imam or Teacher, the pre-requisite for which is to obey his commands and follow his guidance. This, however, does not mean not exercising one's own rational faculties. In fact, the very concept of the infallible Imam is based on the sound intellect in the sense that in the physical world the intellects are in a potential state and cannot be actualised except by an actual Intellect, namely the Prophet or the Imam of the time. Thus al-Kirmānī's concept of knowledge presents a balanced approach to the realities of the world of the intellect and helps to identify oneself with them to attain eternal bliss.

## Notes

1. Abū Ḥāmid al-Ghazālī, *al-Munqidh min al-ḍalāl* ('Freedom and Fulfilment'), tr. into English by R. J. McCarthy (Boston, MA, 1980), p. 67.
2. Ibid.
3. cf. Muḥammad b. Ḥasam al-Daylamī, *Bayān madhhab al-bāṭiniyya*, ed. R. Strothmann (Istanbul, 1939), pp. 3–25.
4. Abū Ḥāmid al-Ghazālī, *Faḍā'iḥ al-bāṭiniyya*, ed. A. Badawī (Cairo, 1964).
5. Al-Ghazālī *al-Munqidh*, pp. 83–84.
6. Al-Mu'ayyad fi'l-Dīn al-Shīrāzī, *al-Majālis al-Mu'ayyadiyya*, ed. M. Ghālib (Beirut, 1974), vol. 1, pp. 226–227.
7. Abū Ya'qūb al-Sijistānī, *Ithbāt al-nubuwwāt*, ed. Ā. Tāmir (Beirut, 1982), p. 50.
8. Ḥamīd al-Dīn al-Kirmānī, *Rāḥat al-'aql*, ed. M. K. Ḥusayn and M. Ḥilmī (Cairo, 1952), p. 84.
9. Al-Qāḍī al-Nu'mān, *Ikhtilāf uṣūl al-madhāhib*, ed. M. Ghālib (Beirut, 1973), p. 37.
10. Al-Sijistānī, *al-Iftikhār*, ed. M. Ghālib (Beirut, 1980), p. 70.
11. Ibid., p. 71.
12. Ḥamid al-Dīn al-Kirmānī, *al-Maṣābīḥ fī ithbāt al-imāma*, ed. M. Ghālib (Beirut, 1969), pp. 80–81.
13. Ibid., pp. 82–85.
14. Ibid., pp. 90–91.
15. Ibid., pp. 91–92.
16. Al-Qāḍī al-Nu'mān, *Da'ā'im al-Islām*, ed. A. A. A. Fyzee (Cairo, 1370–1379/1951–1960), vol. 1, p. 15.
17. Al-Kirmānī, *Majmū'at rasā'il al-Kirmānī*, ed. M. Ghālib (Beirut, 1983), p. 103.
18. Al-Kirmānī, *Rāḥat*, p. 15.
19. Ibid., p. 39; al-Kirmānī, *Majmū'a*, pp. 151–152.
20. Al-Kirmānī, *Majmū'a*, pp. 152–153.
21. Al-Kirmānī, *Rāḥat*, pp. 163–165.
22. Ibid., p. 165.
23. For the *ẓāhirī* interpretation, see: al-Ṭabarī, *Jāmi' al-bayān* (Cairo, 1954), vol. 7, pp. 110–118.
24. Al-Kirmānī, *al-Maṣābīḥ*, pp. 66–68.
25. Ibid., pp. 68–69.
26. Ibid., p. 69.
27. Ibid., pp. 69–70.
28. Ibid., pp. 70–71.
29. Ibid., pp. 71–72.
30. Ibid., pp. 71–72.
31. Al-Kirmānī, *Majmū'a*, p. 157.
32. Ibn Qutayba, *Ta'wīl mushkil al-Qur'ān*, ed. A. Saqr (Cairo, 1973), pp. 98–101.
33. Al-Kirmānī, *Majmū'a*, p. 156.

12

# An Early Ismaili View of Other Religions: A Chapter from the *Kitāb al-Iṣlāḥ* by Abū Ḥātim al-Rāzī (d. ca. 322/934)*

*Shin Nomoto*

## Introduction

At an early stage in its history, the Islamic religious tradition started to take a keen interest in other religions, especially those of 'the people of the book' (*ahl al-Kitāb*).[1] Later on, as cultural activities in Muslim-dominated areas began to reach a stage of maturation, as of the third/eighth century, knowledge of other religions was integrated by Muslim intellectuals into their writings, a phenomenon most often seen in those works which take the form of heresiography.[2] One can, to a greater or lesser degree, detect in such works a heresiographer's own religious identity, reflected in the way in which he describes the characteristics of other faiths.[3] In this paper we will consider how this applies in the case of early Ismailism in the Fatimid period. To this end, we will analyse the chapter on various religions from the *Kitāb al-iṣlāḥ* ('The Book of Correction')[4] by an influential and polemical thinker of the fourth/tenth century, Abū Ḥātim al-Rāzī (d. 322/934).[5]

In relation to the issue of 'Ismaili heresiography' of the Fatimid age, P. E. Walker, in conjunction W. Madelung, has recently published a section on certain Muslim sects from the *Kitāb al-shajara* by Abū Tammām, a fourth/tenth century *dā'ī* or missionary.[6] In his introduction to the part of the text in question (as well as in some earlier articles dealing with similar topics) Walker attempts to shed light on this example of an Ismaili view of dissension within the Islamic community, while at the same time trying to identify the text itself and its sources and sort out the new information that it provides on some 'sects'.[7] However, investigating the Ismaili view of faiths other than Islam is not within the scope of his study.

As for the chapter from *al-Iṣlāḥ* which is the focus of this paper, it was in fact already introduced into Western academic discussion by the late S. M. Stern who, in a posthumously published article, intensively analysed the reports on Iranian religions found therein.[8] Nevertheless, he makes only brief reference to the author's discussion of various non-Islamic religions and religious groups or 'sects' within Islam, leaving aside the specifically Ismaili view of these subjects.

Given the fact that these issues fall outside the scope of the studies by Walker and Stern, we propose to investigate in this paper al-Rāzī's evaluation, in the chapter in question, of non-Islamic religions such as Zoroastrianism and, for the sake of comparison, of certain groups within Islam as well. In so doing we hope to shed some light on the question of how al-Rāzī perceived his own Ismaili religious identity. Finally, we will also attempt to investigate the Ismaili intellectual basis for al-Rāzī's argument regarding various religions.

## The Chapter on Iranian Religions, Religious Communities and Groups from al-Rāzī's *Kitāb al-iṣlāḥ*

The *Kitāb al-iṣlāḥ* aims at a comprehensive refutation of *Kitāb al-maḥṣūl*, a work dealing with cosmology, anthropology and psychology (among other topics), written by one of the first Ismaili philosophers, Muḥammad al-Nasafī (d. 332/942).[9] Later, two prominent Ismaili thinkers added their voices to this doctrinal dispute, viz. Abū Yaʿqūb al-Sijistānī (fl. fourth/tenth century)[10] and Ḥamīd al-Dīn al-Kirmānī (d. after 441/1021).[11]

The extant text of *al-Iṣlāḥ*, insofar as we can tell, seems to have been transmitted to us in incomplete form. We are led to this conclusion for the following reasons: the text begins abruptly with a quotation from the Qur'an (24: 27–29), leaving out much of the usual introductory formulae (even the *basmala* in some manuscripts: see f. 1v./p. 5 of the printed edition);[12] the ending is likewise abrupt and, moreover, features two different versions among the manuscripts (see f. 168v.–f. 169r./f. 169r./ p. 331); and lastly the numbering/division of the parts (s. *juz'*) of the text differs between the manuscripts (see f. 115v., l. 11/f. 116v., l. 7/p. 229).[13]

The chapter in question is the second chapter from the third part (*al-juz' al-thālith*), entitled 'Chapter on the Statement [of al-Nasafī] on the Third Enunciator-Prophet' (*Bāb al-qawl fī thālith al-nuṭaqā'*, f. 72r., l. 11–f. 83r., l. 2/f. 71v., l. 3–f. 82v., l. 6/pp. 148–167). To summarise the contents of this chapter,[14] al-Rāzī begins his discussion by refuting al-Nasafī's opinion that Zoroastrians are the followers of the *Sharīʿa* of Abraham (Ibrāhīm), i.e. the third *nāṭiq* or enunciator-prophet: this term in Ismailism means a great prophet who starts a new cycle or era (*dawr*, pl. *adwār*) in sacred history, in most cases by bringing a new *sharīʿa* (sacred law).[15] According to al-Rāzī, Zoroastrians have no precepts which resemble certain of Abraham's such as circumcision (*khitān*) or the taboo against consanguineous marriage (f. 72r., l. 12–f. 73r., l. 10/f. 71v., l. 4–f. 72v., l. 2/pp. 149–150). He insists moreover that all doctrinal idiosyncrasies of that kind are novel deviations (*bidaʿ*) caused by the antagonists (*aḍdād*) (f. 73v., ll. 8–11/f. 73r., ll. 3–5/p. 150).[16]

As the next step in his refutation of al-Nasafī, al-Rāzī asserts his own view of Zoroastrians and their place in sacred history. According to a tradition from the 'forefathers' (*salaf*), al-Rāzī holds, the precepts which Zoroastrians follow came not from Abraham but from the *lawāḥiq* or lieutenants (s. *lāḥiq*, a *dāʿī* or missionary attached to superior leaders high in the missionary hierarchy [*daʿwa*] according to Ismaili terminology), who lived in the period of Moses, i.e. the fourth *nāṭiq* (f. 75r., ll. 5–8/f. 74v., ll. 1–3/p. 153).[17] One of these lieutenants was Zoroaster, whose authentic religious precepts were altered and distorted by those who came after him (f. 77r., ll. 6–14/f. 76v., ll. 1–11/p. 156).[18] This kind of deviation from the original, true teaching of the *sharīʿa*, al-Rāzī continues, has taken place many times in the past and in several different religious communities, right up to his own day. Among the deviations that he cites is that of dualism which was advocated by the founders of Iranian religions such as Mānī and Mazdak (f. 78v., ll. 9–16/f. 78r., ll. 6–15/p. 159).[19] Al-Rāzī also cites dualism, as a factor in the split between the Ṣābiʾan community and Christianity[20] (f. 77v., ll. 1–f. 78r., l. 2/f. 76v., l. 14–f. 77v., l. 16/pp. 157–158) and refers also to Bardesanes (Dayṣān or Ibn Dayṣān in Arabic), a Christian heresiarch with Gnostic tendencies[21] (f. 78v., l. 15–f. 79r., l. 8/f. 77v., l. 13–f. 78r., l. 6/pp. 159–160).

After discussing Iranian religions, al-Rāzī turns his attention to other non-Islamic religious communities, and to Muslim 'sects'. It is at this point we begin our own analysis. Here al-Rāzī lists four such religious communities that, according to him, 'God mentioned' in the Qurʾan, i.e. Jews, Christians, Zoroastrians and Ṣābiʾans. Of these communities, he maintains, the Ṣābiʾans should be included within the Christian community in its broader sense (f. 80r., l. 12–v., l. 1/f. 79v., ll. 12–16/pp. 162–163), since they originated as a dualist deviation from the latter. This effectively leaves three non-Islamic religious communities. These communities, according to al-Rāzī, can be compared to three Muslim groups or 'sects' on the basis of certain doctrinal similarities. This is already taught, al-Rāzī holds, by a Prophetic tradition, which he cites as follows: the Murjiʾa correspond to Jews in the Islamic Community; the Rāfiḍa (an appellation which was sometimes applied as a pejorative to the Imāmī Shiʿa) to Christians; and the Qadariyya to Zoroastrians (f. 80v., ll. 2–3/f. 79v., l. 17–f. 80r., l. 2/p. 163; also cf. f. 80v., l. 3–f. 81v., l. 16/f. 80r., l. 2–f. 81v., l. 1/pp. 163–165).[22]

The doctrinal similarities between non-Islamic communities and Muslim groups derive for the most part from the nature of the prophetic or divinely-guided figures that each of these religious communities and Muslim groups recognises. Thus, according to al-Rāzī:

> Just as the Jews recognise [the authority of] one of the two enunciator-prophets (*aḥad al-nāṭiqayn*), [that is,] Moses, but deny [that of] another one, who is Jesus, the Murji'a likewise recognise [the authority of] one of the two 'foundations' (*aḥad al-asāsān*) but deny [that of] another one. And just as the Christians recognise [the authority of] both of the enunciator-prophets, the Rāfiḍa likewise recognise [the authority of] both of the 'foundations'. (f. 81v., ll. 2–6/f. 81r., ll. 2–5/pp. 164 f.)

The *asāsān* or two 'foundations', referred to above, are the enunciator-prophet (*nāṭiq*), the bringer of *Sharīʿa* and the 'foundation' of the esoteric interpretation (*ta'wīl*) of *Sharīʿa*, who together represent the highest-ranking religious leaders in each cycle or era (*dawr*) according to the Ismailis of the Fatimid age: in the present cycle (both al-Rāzī's and our own) they are the Prophet Muḥammad and the *Amīr al-mu'minīn*, ʿAlī b. Abi Ṭālib.[23] Thus, while the Jews and Murji'a are related to each other because each recognises only the first and not the second of two prophets or *asāsān*, the Rāfiḍa and Christians are linked since they each recognise both leaders according to their respective faiths.

At this point al-Rāzī mentions the Ṣābi'ans a second time, adding them once again to the three religious communities. Then he does the same for the 'Māriqa' (the Khawārij)[24] with regard to the three Muslim groups or 'sects'. By so doing al-Rāzī reminds us of the origin of the Ṣābi'ans as defectors from the community of Jesus and compares them to the Māriqa who deserted from ʿAlī's camp.

The above-mentioned four religious communities, according to al-Rāzī, make up the 'reproachable religions' (*al-milla al-madhmūma*), since they do not accept the prophethood of Muḥammad (f. 81r., l. 2–v., l. 16/f. 80r., l. 17–f. 81r., l. 1/pp. 163–165). Beyond these four, al-Rāzī holds, there are the people of the fifth community (*ahl al-milla al-khāmisa*), namely, the Muslims, whom he calls the 'praiseworthy community' (*al-milla al-maḥmūda*) because of their recognition of the prophethood of Muḥammad. The following passage is al-Rāzī's summary evaluation of the five religious communities:

> [The] four religious communities of the cycles of the two enunciator-prophets (i.e. Moses and Jesus) did not recognise the Prophet Muḥammad – May God grant him and his family His grace! – in his cycle, thus becoming the hateful people. However, the people of the fifth community of Islam recognise him (i.e. the Prophet) and his prophethood, and recognise all the prophets [who came after him] and all sacred laws, from which all the religions branched … . (f. 82r., ll. 4–8/f. 81v., ll. 5–10/p. 165)

Corresponding to the fifth religious community, moreover, there is a fifth Muslim group. But whereas the other four Muslim groups are called the 'reproachable groups' (*al-firaq al-madhmūma*) (f. 81v., l. 14/f. 81r., ll. 15–16/p. 165), the fifth one is called the 'people of the pure religion' (*ahl al-dīn al-khāliṣ*), the 'people of reality' (*ahl al-ḥaqīqa*) and the 'Believers' (*al-mu'minūn*) (f. 82r., ll. 2–3/f. 81v., ll. 3–4/p. 165). That is, whereas the other four 'reproachable groups' recognise either only the Prophet Muḥammad or both Muḥammad and 'Alī b. Abi Ṭālib, those belonging to the fifth group, called the 'people of reality' (*ahl al-ḥaqīqa*), recognise not only the authority of both Muḥammad and 'Alī b. Abi Ṭālib as divinely-guided leaders, but also the rank (*ḥadd*, literally 'limit') and position (*manzila*) of the master of the coming cycle (*ṣāḥib al-dawr al-ātī*), namely, the Qā'im or the awaited Messiah (f. 82r., ll. 8–12/f. 81v., ll. 10–15/pp. 165–166), who will reveal all the esoteric meanings concealed in the sacred laws handed down in the past.[25] Thus, both the fifth religious community and the fifth Muslim group are valued much more highly than the others.

The above statement suggests the possibility that by the fifth group of people, whom he esteems more highly than any other Muslims, al-Rāzī meant his own group, i.e. the Ismailis. Next, we should also note that al-Rāzī classifies the Rāfiḍa as one of the reproachable groups, although they recognise both the Prophet Muḥammad and 'Alī, the Commander of the Believers. These facts suggest that al-Rāzī attempted to exclude some Shi'i groups from his ideal vision of Shi'ism, and even to distinguish his own group from others as being the genuine Shi'a.[26]

Yet we should refrain, at the moment, from drawing any conclusion on the issue of al-Rāzī's identification of this fifth group as his own. Although al-Rāzī esteems this group more highly than any other Muslim group, he never refers to it explicitly using the name that the Ismailis of the Fatimid period applied to themselves, i.e. the 'rightly-guiding mission' (*al-da'wa al-hādiya*).[27]

## The Realms of Nature and Religion in the Cosmos according to al-Rāzī

Towards the end of the chapter in question, al-Rāzī outlines the following argument regarding the fifth religious community (f. 82v., l. 9–f. 83r., l. 2/82r., l. 13 –v., l. 6/pp. 166–167): just as the form (*ṣūra*) of any composite being in the world of nature appears as a fifth entity only with the coalescing (*ijmā'*) of the four elements (*arba' al-ummahāt*), the fifth religious community, namely, the Muslims, and the fifth Muslim group emerged as the 'perfection of the religious communities' (*tamām al-milal*) with the genesis of the four religious communities and the four Muslim groups respectively. Here attention should be drawn to al-Rāzī's use of a concept taken from Hellenistic physics, the 'four elements'.

In addition the concept of a 'fifth being' in the form of a fifth religious community and a fifth Muslim group reminds us of the Hellenistic notion of the fifth element (*quinta essentia* or *pémptē ousia*) in addition to the four elements. This fifth element, also called 'ether', is of higher quality than the other four.[28] Since in his other work *A'lām al-nubuwwa* ('The Signs of Prophecy') al-Rāzī mentions a 'fifth body' (*jism khāmis*) as one of the cosmological principles cited by Aristotle, it is very possible that he utilises the concept of the fifth element as a theoretical basis for his argument.[29]

Al-Rāzī also utilises the term 'ether' in *al-Iṣlāḥ* to explain the mission that is to be accomplished by the Qā'im in sacred history.[30] Apparently using the terms 'ether' and 'fire' interchangeably, al-Rāzī holds that just as either 'ether' or 'fire' can fuse with the other three elements (*al-usṭuqussāt al-thalātha*), so can *ta'wīl* (or esoteric interpretation), which is the Qā'im's function, be applied to any of the six previous sacred laws to 'unveil' all the meanings hidden within them (f. 111r., l. 12–v., l. 2/f. 111v., l. 14–f. 112r., l. 2/p. 221). This work of 'unveiling', or *kashf*, of the 'final point of esoteric interpretation' (called *nihāyat al-ta'wīl* in the same passage), is the mission unique to the Qā'im.

A further example of al-Rāzī's utilisation of the language of Hellenistic physics is his reference to the concepts *in actu* (*bi'l-fi'l*) and *in potentia* (*bi'l-quwwa*), as shown in his discussion of the *ahl al-ḥaqīqa*: [31]

> They (i.e. the people of the reality) are the fifth group which is the form of the subtle world *in potentia* (*bi'l-quwwa*), and it (i.e. the form of the subtle world and the fifth group) will emerge *in actu* (*bi'l-fi'l*) at the time of the completion of the mission of the *awliyā'* (*'inda tamām amr al-awliyā'*) – the Peace of God be upon them and His mercy [as well]! (f. 82v., l. 14–f. 83r., l. 2/f. 82 v., ll. 2–6/p. 167)

The important role al-Rāzī here grants to the 'fifth group' in this development in sacred history parallels the role of the 'fifth element' or 'ether' in the physical world, according to his argument. The term *awliyā'*,[32] although not clearly explained in the passage, seems to be used in *al-Iṣlāḥ* to refer to all the believers in the Ismaili community.[33]

In addition, in the first chapter of the same part 3 of *al-Iṣlāḥ*, one can find a similar explanation of the development of religion in terms of the world of nature. There al-Rāzī begins by declaring that each product (*mawlid*, pl. *mawālid*), which means every being formed in the world of nature, emerges from the composition of all four elements (f. 70v., l. 13–f. 71r., l. 1/f. 70r., ll. 3–7/p. 146). After declaring this principle to hold true in the physical realm of the cosmos, al-Rāzī turns his attention to religion:

> Except with the coalescing of the four members all together' (*illā bi-ijtimā' al-arba'a kulli-hā*), the hidden birth (*al-wilāda al-mustajanna*) within them (i.e. sacred laws) does not appear. (f. 71r., ll. 15–16/f. 70v., ll. 7–8/p. 146)

By 'four members' here, al-Rāzī means the *ẓāhir* and *bāṭin*, i.e. the exoteric and esoteric aspects of *Sharī'a*, with in addition the enunciator-prophet and the 'foundation' who appear in each cycle of human history as the *asāsān* (dual of *asās*, the 'two foundations') (f. 71v., l. 15–v., l. 3/f. 70v., ll. 8–13/pp. 146–147).[34]

In another place al-Rāzī points out that the emergence of the sacred law and the missionary hierarchy (*daʿwa*) result from the conjunction of the two highest hypostases in heaven and their counterparts on earth: this conjunction is also compared to the coupling (*izdiwāj*) or union (*ijtimāʿ*) of male and female, which results in the birth of a child (f. 70r., ll. 4–12/f. 69r., ll. 6–15/p. 144).[35] These passages suggest that the above-mentioned 'hidden birth' could refer to the emergence of a new order of the religion or a new development in the order. In describing the birth as 'hidden' (*mustajanna*), however, al-Rāzī may be implying that this type of 'birth' means a further stage or new development coming after the establishment of the sacred law and the *daʿwa*. This is because the adjective 'hidden' implies the existence of the inner phase, or *bāṭin*, of religion, which is to be revealed after the *ẓāhir*, i.e. the precepts of the sacred law, is made public.

A new development in the religious order is also represented as the birth of the 'spiritual forms' *(al-ṣuwar al-rūḥāniyya)*, which can be interpreted as referring to the forms of human souls. It can be said that this birth takes place in a cycle after those of the sacred law and the *daʿwa*, as happened in the case of the first cycle that al-Rāzī cites (f. 64v., l. 15–f. 65r., l. 1/f. 63v., ll. 5–7/pp. 135–136); hence, the 'spiritual forms' are brought up and trained to the sacred law and, according to the result, will gain either punishment or reward in the hereafter (f. 31v., ll. 4–6/f. 31r., ll. 2–4, p. 64). Thus this form of birth is of a more spiritual or internal nature than those of the sacred law and the *daʿwa*, suggesting that the meaning of the birth of 'spiritual forms' can be similar to that of 'hidden birth', given our discussion above.

In addition, there is another expression that can be used to describe a new development in the sacred order, that is, the 'secret birth *in potentia*' (*wilāda khafiyya bi'l-quwwa*) of the 'spiritual form(s)' (*al-ṣūra* [or *al-ṣuwar*] *al-rūḥāniyya*) which seems to refer to the forms of human souls, as does the expression 'spiritual forms' (f. 70r., ll. 9–12/f. 69r., ll. 12–15/p. 144 and f. 71v., ll. 3–12/f. 70v., l. 11–f. 71r., l. 3/p. 147). Thus the 'secret birth *in potentia*' may hold the key to understanding what al-Rāzī means by 'hidden birth.' He goes on to describe the 'secret birth' as follows:

> We have said the birth (*al-wilāda*) occurs with the coalescing of the *asāsān*, for this is a secret birth *in potentia* (*wilāda khafiyya bi'l-quwwa*). This is because the simple form (*al-ṣūra al-basīṭa*)[36] is born through the establishment of the *daʿwa* and lives with the knowledge. And every *daʿwa* is a part of the world of this [simple] form. (f. 71v., ll. 3–5/f. 70v., ll. 11–15/p. 147)

This 'secret birth *in potentia*' presumably needs to achieve its full actualisation, i.e. *in actu* form. The following passage can be interpreted as suggesting that this process would take all the cycles up to the *parousia* of the Qā'im before being completed:

> Thus at that time (i.e. the termination of all the cycles) it (i.e. the simple form) will emerge with the form of this world affected in these cycles … . At that time

the form (*al-ṣūra*) will emerge with its completion (*bi-tamāmi-hā*, i.e. of the form of this world), because of the coalescing of its parts in the four *dāʿwas* (*al-daʿwāt al-arbaʿa*, sic) [borne] upon the three [pairs of] sacred laws (*al-sharāʾī al-thalāla*, sic)[37] at the time of the *parousia* of the master of the seventh cycle .... (f. 71v., ll. 8–11/f. 71r., ll. 1–3/p. 147)

Examining the passages concerning the 'hidden birth' or 'secret birth', we may recognise again al-Rāzī's belief that the emergence of new being or the coming of a new situation results from the coalescing of four members of a particular group, whether this be in the domain of religion or in nature, for example, the four religious communities, the four Muslim 'sects', and the four *daʿwas*. In brief, the same principle or law operates in the realms of religion and nature.

We can also infer that the coalescing of four members and the emergence of a new being has for al-Rāzī the status of an intellectual framework providing the theoretical basis for his own argument on various religions. Similar ideas can be recognised not only in al-Rāzī's *Kitāb al-iṣlāḥ*, but also, we would suggest, in works by other Ismaili thinkers such as al-Sijistānī[38] and al-Kirmānī. According al-Sijistānī, all existent beings in the world of composition (*ʿālam al-tarkīb*, the world of four elements) can be divided into two groups: those in a 'state of goodness' (*ḥāl al-ṣalāḥ*) and those in a 'state of wickedness' (*ḥāl al-fasād*).[39] Human beings can also be divided into these same two groups. Those in the 'state of goodness' include the apostles (*rusūl*, s. *rasūl*), who lead others to salvation, while on the other hand, among those in the 'state of wickedness' there are the 'fabricators' (*mukhtariʿūn*).[40]

Ḥamīd al-Dīn al-Kirmānī in his *Kitāb al-riyāḍ*[41] maintained that any being possessing a given quality moves from a state of potentiality (*biʾl-quwwa*) to that of actuality (*biʾl-fiʿl*), whereas a being which has the exact opposite quality moves in the reverse direction, i.e. from actuality to potentiality.[42] He cites pairs of opposing qualities, which occur alternately, such as coldness and heat, dryness and humidity, etc. This principle operates among humans: whenever knowledge (*ʿilm*) is in actuality, ignorance (*jahl*) is in potentiality, and vice versa. The process began with Adam[43] and will culminate in the advent of the awaited messiah, the Qāʾim.

To conclude, al-Rāzī's argument on various religions and Muslim groups, as well as views quoted above from his two co-religionists are based on the concept that the same principle underlies the realms of religion and nature. This idea also led al-Rāzī to establish his own ideal image of a religious community and a Muslim religious group.

## IV Discussion

Our analysis of al-Rāzī's text on various religions shows clearly that he relies for the most part on analogy as the pattern for his arguments.[44] According to this, since the same principle or 'laws' operate in several realms of the cosmos, a phenomenon that occurs in one realm will have its counterparts in the others. Analogy is one of the prevailing patterns in classical and medieval Islamic thought: a typical example of this is the principle of correspondence between macrocosm and microcosm.[45] By examining al-Rāzī's text and selected passages from other Ismaili thinkers, our study demonstrates that the analogical pattern of thinking exerted a strong influence on Ismaili philosophy especially.

Eschatology is another important element in the background to al-Rāzī's arguments here. As was seen in the second section above, al-Rāzī believed that recognition of the 'master of the coming cycle', the Qā'im, whose *parousia* is to take place with the approach of the *eschaton*, is an indispensable qualification of the most religiously authentic Muslim group. Through this doctrine of the Qā'im, al-Rāzī's argument on various religions and Muslim sects acquires an eschatological element.

Is this eschatological element however related to the idea of analogy or correspondence between the two realms of nature and religion in al-Rāzī's thought? The answer to this question lies in al-Rāzī's comparison of the Qā'im's function of esoteric interpretation which culminates in his mission of *kashf* respecting all the sacred laws, to the 'ether' or 'fire' which can fuse all the other three elements (f. 111r., l. 12–v., l. 2/f. 111v., l. 14–f. 112r., l. 2/p. 221). Here it is obvious that the messianic and eschatological figure of the Qā'im is discussed using analogy as a logical device.

We should also remind ourselves of al-Rāzī's explanation of the actualisation of the 'form of the subtle world' with the fifth Muslim group. In that passage al-Rāzī explains the coming of a new, higher religious order using notions borrowed from physics, such as '*in potentia*' and '*in actu*', and, possibly, the concept of the fifth element. This new sacred order would replace the present state of existence, which means the end of our present world. Because of this implication, al-Rāzī's argument can be interpreted as referring to the eschatological transformation of the cosmos. Thus it can safely be said that eschatology and the idea of analogy are connected to each other in al-Rāzī's thought.

In the above discussion on the connection between eschatology and the idea of analogy in al-Rāzī's view of religions one may recognise his idea of the new religious order expected to follow the *parousia* of the Qā'im, though it is only alluded to. Related to this, in another passage al-Rāzī compares a religious knowledge purified of all that is *ẓāhir*, which is to be conveyed by the Qā'im to faithful human souls, to the pure light (*al-nūr al-ṣāfī*) or purified fire (f. 113r., ll. 6–9/f. 113v., ll. 5–8/p. 224).[46] This image of purified fire seems grounded in the alchemical notion of the purification of each element directed towards acquiring the philosophers' stone.[47] Does al-Rāzī's utilisation of alchemical notions suggest that the situation brought by the Qā'im is entailed by the completion and perfection of the cosmos through the purification of matter? This question, though seemingly still open, forces us to reconsider the issue of how and to what extent early Ismaili eschatology as well as cosmology owes its content to alchemical thought.[48]

Our discussion of the background to al-Rāzī's views on various religions leads us back to the issue of the Qā'im and his role in bringing salvation to his community. For, ultimately, this lies at the heart of the problem. After all, why else would al-Rāzī and other early Ismaili missionary thinkers have fought so assiduously over eschatological issues and engaged in such bitter religio-political and intellectual battles?

## Notes

*The earlier versions of this paper are: 'Shoki Ismāʿīl Ha no Tashūkyō kan ni tuite no Shiron: Abū Ḥātim al-Rāzī (d. 322/934–935) no Teisei no Sho (Kitāb al-Iṣlāḥ) kara no Isshō ni itmotozuite', (in Japanese), *Reports of Keio Institute of Cultural and Linguistic Studies*, 25 (1993), pp. 121–143; 'An Early Ismāʿīlī View of Other Religions: Based on a Chapter from *Kitāb al-Iṣlāḥ* by Abū Ḥātim al-Rāzī (d. 322/934–5)', a paper read at the 28th annual meeting of the Middle East Studies Association of North America in Phoenix, Arizona, in November, 1994; §1 and §4 of chapter 5, 'Various Prophets and Religious Communities in Sacred History', in 'Early Ismāʿīlī Thought on Prophecy According to the *Kitāb al-Iṣlāḥ* by Abū Ḥātim al-Rāzī (d. ca. 322/934-5)', my Ph.D. dissertation submitted to McGill University, Montreal, in December 1999. On being incorporated into the present paper, however, the contents of these studies were, of course, extensively revised. I would like to take this opportunity to express my humble but very deep gratitude to Professor Hermann Landolt, my dissertation supervisor at The Institute of Islamic Studies, McGill University, for his painstakingly thorough guidance of my work.

1. For an overview of this issue, see the following studies: G. Vajda, 'Ahl al-Kitāb', *EI2*; J. Waardenburg, 'World Religions as Seen in the Light of Islam', in A. T. Welch and P. Cachia, ed., *Islam: Past Influence and Present Challenge* (Edinburgh, 1979), pp. 245–275; J. Waardenburg, ed., 'The Early Period: 610–650', and 'The Medieval Period: 650–1500', in *Muslim Perceptions of Other Religions: A Historical Survey* (New York and Oxford, 1999), pp. 3–17 and 18–69; A. T. Welch, 'Muḥammad's Understanding of Himself: The Koranic Data', in R. G. Hovanissian and S. Vryonis Jr., ed., *Islam's Understanding of Itself* (Malibu, CA, 1983), pp. 15–52.

2. See Waardenburg, 'World Religions', p. 245 and p. 270, n.1. Also cf. W. Madelung, 'Häresiographie', in *Grundriss der Arabischen Philologie*, vol. 2, *Literaturwissenschaft*, ed. H. Gätje (Wiesbaden, 1987), pp. 374–378.

3. Cf. Waardenburg, 'World Religions', pp. 245–247 and 'The Medieval Period', pp. 20–23; A. Welch, 'Muḥammad's Understanding', pp. 30 and pp. 47–50.

4. The important task of editing *al-Iṣlāḥ* was recently accomplished by Ḥ. Mīnūchihr and M. Mohaghegh and published as Abū Ḥātim Aḥmad b. Ḥamdān al-Rāzī, *Kitāb al-iṣlāḥ*, ed. Ḥ. Mīnūchihrī and M. Mohaghegh, English introduction by S. Nomoto (Tehran, 1377 Sh./1998). My deep thanks go to Professor Mehdi Mohaghegh for having generously sent me a copy. In this paper I also refer to the following manuscripts of *Kitāb al-iṣlāḥ:* Hamdani

Collection MS (Milwaukee) and Tübingen MS VI 327. With regard to the Hamdani MS, I would like to express my sincere gratitude to two of the leading scholars in Ismaili studies: to Professor Abbas Hamdani of the University of Wisconsin at Milwaukee for his kind permission to use the manuscript in his possession, and to Dr Paul E. Walker for graciously sending me a photocopy of it.

5. For Abū Ḥātim al-Rāzī's life and works, including *al-Iṣlāḥ*, see H. Halm, 'Abū Ḥātem Rāzī', *EIr*; H. Landolt, 'Abū Ḥātim al-Rāzī, Aḥmad ibn Ḥamdān (d. 322/933–934)', in J. S. Meisami and P. Starkey, ed., *Encyclopedia of Arabic Literature* (London and New York, 1998), vol. 1, p. 34; I. K. Poonawala, *Biobibliography of Ismāʿīlī Literature* (Malibu, CA, 1977), pp. 36–39; A. Shamsuddin Talbani, 'The Debate About Prophecy in 'Aʿlām al-Nubuwwa': An Analytical Study' (M.A., McGill University, 1989); S. M. Stern, 'Abū Ḥātim al-Rāzī', *EI2*. In his Sunni-inclined lexicography of religious terms, *Kitāb al-zīna*, al-Rāzī wrote a section which is similar in style to heresiography. This was edited by ʿA. S. al-Sāmmarā'ī in *al-Ghūlūw wa'l-firaq al-ghāliya fī al-ḥaḍāra al-islāmiyya* (Baghdad, 1396/1972), pp. 248–312 (whenever al-Rāzī's *al-Zīna* is cited in this paper, this will be referred to). On *al-Zīna* and its heresiographical part, see P. E. Walker, 'An Ismaʿili Version of the Heresiography of the Seventy-Two Erring Sects', in F. Daftary, ed., *Mediaeval Ismaʿili History and Thought* (Cambridge, 1995), p. 161.

6. W. Madelung and P. E. Walker, *An Ismaili Heresiography: The 'Bāb al-Shayṭān' from Abū Tammām's Kitāb al-Shajara* (Leiden, 1998).

7. See P. E. Walker, 'Abū Tammām and his *Kitāb al-Shajara*: A New Ismaili Treatise from Tenth-Century Khurasan', *JAOS*, 114 (1994), pp. 343–352 and 'An Ismaʿili Version of the Heresiography', pp. 161–177; Madelung and Walker, 'Introduction', in their *An Ismaili Heresiography.*

8. S. M. Stern, 'Abū Ḥātim al-Rāzī on Persian Religion', chapter in *Studies in Early Ismaʿilism* (Jerusalem and Leiden, 1983), pp. 30–49, hereafter referred to as Stern, 'Persian Religion'. See also: W. Ivanow, 'Early Controversy in Ismailism', chapter in his *Studies in Early Persian Ismailism* (2nd ed., Bombay, 1955), pp. 116–122, which provides a brief introduction to *al-Iṣlāḥ*.

9. For al-Nasafī's life and works including *al-Maḥṣūl*, see Poonawala, *Biobibliography*, pp. 40–43 and 'al-Nasafī, I. Abu'l-Ḥasan Muḥammad b. Aḥmad al-Bazdawī or al-Bazdahī', *EI2*. S. M. Stern regards al-Nasafī as the founder of Ismaili philosophy. See his 'The Early Ismāʿīlī Missionaries in North-West Persia and in Khurasan and Transoxiana', chapter in *Studies in Early Ismāʿīlism* (originally published in *BSOAS*, 23, 1960, pp. 50–90), pp. 219–220.

10. In support of al-Nasafī's view, al-Sijistānī wrote the now lost *Kitāb al-nuṣra*, some passages of which are preserved in quotations by al-Kirmānī in his *Kitāb al-riyāḍ*. This work was edited by ʿĀrif Tāmir (Beirut, 1960). For al-Sijistānī's life and work, see: H. Landolt, 'Abū Yaʿqūb al-Sijzī, Isḥāq ibn Aḥmad (fourth/tenth century)', in J. S. Meisami and P. Starkey, ed., *Encyclopedia of Arabic Literature* (London and New York, 1998), vol. 1, pp. 50 f.; Poonawala, *Biobibliography*, pp. 82–91; P. E. Walker, 'Abū Yaʿqūb al-Sejestānī', *EIr* and *Early Philosophical Shiism: The Ismaili Neoplatonism of Abū Yaʿqūb al-Sijistānī* (Cambridge, 1993), pp. 16–24.

11. For al-Kirmānī's life and works, see the following: J. T. P. de Bruijn, 'al-Kirmānī, Ḥamīd al-Dīn', *EI2*; D. de Smet, *La quiétude de l'intellect: Néoplatonisme et gnose ismaélienne dans l'œuvre de Ḥamīd al-Dīn al-Kirmānī (Xe/XIe s.)* (Leuven, 1995), pp. 3–23; Poonawala, *Biobibliography*, pp. 94–102. For an overview of this debate, see W. Ivanow, 'An Early Controversy', pp. 87–122; P. E. Walker, 'The Debate on the Mahsul', Chapter in 'Abū Yaʿqūb al-Sijistānī and

the Development of Isma'ili Neoplatonism' (Ph.D. University of Chicago, 1974), pp. 81–107 and 'Ismaili Predecessors', chapter in *Early Philosophical Shi'ism*, pp. 46–63.

12. Hereafter the pages of the Hamdani MS. are referred to first, followed by those of the Tübingen MS., and then by those of the printed edition by Ḥ. Mīnūchihrī and M. Mohaghegh. Also hereafter any line referred to in the two MSS or the printed edition is designated by the abbreviation l. (pl. ll.). The printed edition is based on three manuscripts called by its editors, *alif, bā'*, and *jīm* respectively, all of which presumably date back to the late 19th or early 20th century, and all of which were apparently copied in the Indian subcontinent. For details on these manuscripts, see M. Mohaghegh, 'Sar-āghāz', in the printed edition, p. xiv, and the note by the editors to l. 4 on p. 331 of the printed edition.

13. Cf. Ivanow, 'An Early Controversy'.

14. Since the details of al-Rāzī's views on Iranian religions have already been discussed by Stern, this paper follows only the outline of his argument, in order to avoid duplication.

15. On the *nāṭiq* or enunciator-prophet, see Halm, *Kosmologie und Heilslehre der frühen Ismā'īliyya* (Wiesbaden, 1978), pp. 18–37; Madelung, 'Aspects of Ismā'īlī Theology: The Prophetic Chain and the God Beyond Being', in S. H. Nasr, ed., *Ismā'īlī Contributions to Islamic Culture* (Tehran, 1977), pp. 54–55. Also cf. F. Daftary, *The Ismā'īlīs: Their History and Doctrines* (Cambridge, 1990), pp. 104–105.

16. Cf. Stern, 'Persian Religion', pp. 36–37.

17. Ibid., p. 39.

18. Ibid., pp. 38–40, especially p. 39.

19. On these religionists, see for example: C. E. Bosworth, 'Mānī', *EI2*; C. Colpe, 'Development of Religious Thought', in *The Cambridge History of Iran*, vol. 3 (2), *The Seleucid, Parthian and Sasanian Periods*, ed. E. Yarshater (Cambridge, 1983), pp. 819–865; M. Guidi [-M. Morony], 'Mazdak', *EI2*; E. Yarshater, 'Mazdakism', in *The Cambridge History of Iran*, vol. 3 (2), pp. 991–1024. Also concerning the issue of dualism in Iran we should point out Stern's high estimation of al-Rāzī's report on another important religionist and rebel leader in Iran, Bihāfarīd (fl. the 2nd/7th century). Stern, 'Persian Religion', pp. 43–44.

20. Cf. Stern, 'Persian Religion', pp. 33–36. With regard to the Ṣābi'ans, the Mu'tazilī theologian al-Zamakhsharī (d. 538/1144) also counts them as a Christian sect in his commentary on Qur'an 22:17; see his *al-Kashshāf 'an ḥaqā'iq al-tanzīl wa- 'uyūn al-aqāwil fī wujūh al-ta'wīl* (Beirut, n.d.), vol. 3, p. 28. Cf. the translation of al-Zamakhsharī's passage in H. Gätje, *The Qur'an and its Exegesis: Selected Texts with Classical and Modern Muslim Interpretations*, tr. and ed. A. T. Welch (London, 1976), p. 130. For the Ṣābi'ans, see the following studies: F. de Blois, 'The "Sabians" (Ṣābi'ūn) in pre-Islamic Arabia', *Acta Orientalia*, 56 (1995), pp. 39–61; T. Fahd, 'Ṣābi'a', *EI2*; S. Gündüz, *The Knowledge of Life: The Origins and Early History of the Mandeans and their Relation to the Sabians of the Qur'an and to the Harranians* (Oxford, 1994); J. D. McAuliffe, 'Exegetical ldentification of the Ṣābi'ūn', *MW*, 72 (1982), pp. 95–106.

21. On Bardasanes, see: A. Abel, 'Dayṣāniyyah', *EI2*; W. Madelung, 'Abū 'Īsā al-Warrāq über die Bardasaniten, Marchioniten und Kantaer', in *Studien zur Geschichte und Kultur des Vorderen Orients: Festschrift für Belthold Spuler zur siebzigsten Geburtstag*, ed. H. R. Roemer and A. Moth (Leiden, 1981), pp. 210–224.

22. For this *ḥadīth*, cf. *Concordance et indices de la tradition musulmane*, ed. A. J. Wensinck et al. (Leiden, 1936–1988), vol. 5, p. 318. In *al-Zīna*, al-Rāzī quotes a similar *ḥadīth*, but enumerates the five sects as the Shi'a, the Murji'a, the Rāfiḍa, the Qadariyya and the

Māriqa on the authority of the 'companions [of the Prophet]' (*al-Ṣāḥāba*) and 'the following generation' (*al-Ṭābiʿūn*), *al-Zīna*, p. 209.

23. For Ismaili terminology on the hierarchies in heaven and on earth we consulted for this article the following studies: H. Corbin, *Histoire de la philosophie islamique*, 2nd ed. (Paris, 1986), pp. 133–136; Halm, *Kosmologie und Heilslehre*, pp. 67–74; A. Hamdani, 'Evolution of the Organizational Structure of the Fāṭimī Daʿwah: The Yemenī and Persian Contribution', *Arabian Studies*, 3 (1976), pp. 85–114; P. E. Walker, 'Cosmic Hierarchies in Early Ismāʿīlī Thought: The View of Abū Yaʿqūb al-Sijistānī', *MW*, 66 (1976), pp. 14–28.

24. For the identification of the 'Māriqa' with the Khawārij, see al-Shahrastānī, *Kitāb al-milal wa'l-niḥal*, ed. M. F. Allāh Badrān (Cairo, 1910), vol. 1, pp. 18, 197–198 and 201–202. Cf. French translation of the text, *Livre des religions et des sectes*, tr. D. Gimaret and G. Monnot (Paris, 1986), vol. 1, pp. 124, 366 and 370.

25. For the early Ismaili notion of the Qā'im, see Halm, *Kosmologie und Heilslehre*, pp. 18–37; Madelung, 'Aspects of Ismāʿīlī Theology', pp. 54–55; Madelung, 'Qāʿim Āl Muḥammad', *EI2*, vol. 4, pp. 456–457.

26. In *al-Zīna*, al-Rāzī endeavours to explain etymologically the appellations of some Shiʿi groups (*alqāb firaq al-Shīʿa*), among whom he includes the 'Ismāʿīliyya' and their sub-'sect', the 'Mubārakiyya' (*al-Zīna*, pp. 287–89). In describing these groups, there is the possibility that he was covertly attacking non-Ismaili Imāmīs. However, this requires investigation.

27. On this term, see Hamdani, 'Evolution of the Organizational Structure', p. 86. Also cf. Daftary, *The Ismāʿīlīs*, p. 93.

28. On this important concept, see, for example, P. Moraux, 'quinta essentia', in G. Wissowa, W. Kroll and K. Mittelhaus, ed., *Paulys Realencyclopädie der classischen Altertumswissenschaft* (Stuttgart, 1963), Bd. 47, cols. 1171–1263, 1430–1432, and F. Solmsen, *Aristotle's System of the Physical World: A Comparison with his Predecessors* (Ithaca, NY, 1960), pp. 287–303 and 304–309. On the acceptance of this concept in the Islamic milieu, see, for example S. Diwald, *Arabische Philosophie und Wissenschaft der Enzyklopädie, Kitāb Ikhwān al-Ṣafā' (III), die Lehre von Seele und Intellekt* (Wiesbaden, 1975), pp. 110, 118 and 190; P. Kraus, *Jābir ibn Ḥayyān: Contribution à l'histoire des idées scientifiques dans l'Islam* (Cairo, 1942–1943), vol. 2, pp. 152–157.

29. See al-Rāzī, *Aʿlām al-nubuwwa*, ed. Ṣ. al-Ṣāwī and G. R. al-Aʿwānī (Tehran, 1977), p. 138.

30. Al-Rāzī refers to this 'fifth body' as 'ether' (*al-athīr*) and the 'most exalted matter' (*al-ʿunṣir al-aʿẓam*) in *Aʿlām*, p. 138.

31. We follow the reading of the printed edition, يجمعها (p. 167, l. 2). MS. Ham. Has بجميعها (lit. with the total of them) (f. 82v., l. 16), while MS. Tüb. has بجمعها (with a gathering of them) (f. 82v., l. 4).

32. As far as the word *awliyā'* is concerned, there is a verse (Qur'an 8: 72) which states that the true believers are *awliyā'* or 'friends' together, who struggle for the cause of God. Yet, according to another verse (Qur'an 8:73), unbelievers are also *awliyā'*. Thus, in the Qur'anic context, the term can refer to either. Cf. H. Landolt, 'Walāyah', in *ER*, vol. 15, pp. 319–322. There are likewise several references in Shiʿism to the *awliyā'* of God as the Imams of the people of the household (*ahl al-bayt*). See, for example, H. Corbin, *Histoire de la philosophie islamique* (2nd ed., Paris, 1986), pp. 53–55, 74–75 and 105–107 (English tr. by L. Sherrard with the assistance of P. Sherrard in *History of Islamic Philosophy* (London, 1993), pp. 26–28, 43–45

and 66–68) and P. E. Walker, 'Wilāya 2. In Shīʿism', *EI2*. On the Ismaili-Shiʿi understanding of the term *awliyāʾ Allāh* as referring to the Imams of the *ahl al-bayt*, see al-Qāḍī al-Nuʿmān, 'Kitāb al-Walāyah' in *Daʿāʾim al-Islām*, ed. A. A. A. Fyzee (Cairo, 1380/1951), vol. 1, pp. 14–98 cf. English tr. A. A. A. Fyzee, 'The Book of *Walāya*' in *The Pillars of Islam:* Daʿāʾim al-Islām *of al-Qāḍī al-Nuʿmān,* completely revised and annotated by I. K. Poonawala, vol. 1 (New Delhi and Oxford, 2002), pp. 18–22.

33. Comparing Uriel and David, and Noah and Jonah, al-Rāzī holds that each of the *awliyāʾ*, divinely-guided or not, is assigned his own status in accordance with his 'faithfulness' and inner sincerity but not with his effectiveness in running the *daʿwa*. David and Jonah attracted more people than Uriel and Noah: however this did not threaten the rank of these latter two. See f. 7v., ll. 1–6/f. 7v., l. 17–f. 8r., l. 6/p. 16 and f. 7v., ll. 7–16/f. 8r., ll. 6–17/pp. 16–17.

34. For the roles of these 'four members' of the hierarchies, we consulted the studies by P. E. Walker on al-Sijistānī entitled 'Cosmic Hierarchies', pp. 24–28 and *Early Philosophical Shiism*, pp. 18–19.

35. This argument comes in his refutation of al-Nasafī's claim that two enunciator-prophets, like a man and a woman, give birth (*wilāda*). According to al-Nasafī, this was the case with the first sacred law which was born from the union of Adam and Noah. In opposition, al-Rāzī states that the first sacred law is the product (*mutawallida*) of the junction of the first enunciator-prophet with the *ṣābiq* (another name for the universal intellect). See *al-Iṣlāḥ*, f. 64v., l. 2–f. 65r., l. 9/f. 63r., l. 7–v., l. 14/pp. 135–136. Here al-Rāzī as well as al-Nasafī used terms related to birth.

36. We adopt the reading of the printed edition (p. 147, ll. 1–2) and MS. Tüb. (f. 70v., l. 14), whereas MS. Ham. (f. 71v., l. 4) has الصور البسيطة that is, the plural form of the words. The reading of the printed edition and MS. Tüb. makes even more sense however, if we interpret it not as a simple singular but as a generic singular, as will be seen shortly.

37. These expressions 'three [pairs of] sacred laws' and 'four *daʿwas*' need some explanation. The phrase 'three [pairs of] sacred laws', in *al-Iṣlāḥ* means the sacred laws brought by the first three *nuṭaqāʾ* and renewed by the latter three. Thus, although these sacred laws are six, they are in reality three: the latter being renewed versions of the former. See f. 102r., l. 3–v., l. 15/f. 102v., l. 4–103v., l. 3/pp. 203–204. However, to emphasise the fact that the sacred laws were brought by the six *nuṭaqāʾ*, we translate the expression *al-sharāʾiʿ al-thalātha* as 'the three [pairs of] sacred laws'. Although al-Rāzī does not definitively explain the meaning of 'four *daʿwas*', we can assume that the expression refers to three *daʿwa*s which were directed by the three pairs of *nuṭaqāʾ* corresponding to the 'three [pairs of] sacred laws' and a fourth *daʿwa* to be initiated by the Qāʾim.

38. Al-Sijistānī, *Ithbāt al-nubuwwa*, ed. ʿĀrif Tāmir (Beirut, 1960), pp. 82–85.

39. Ibid., pp. 83–84.

40. Ibid., p. 84.

41. Al-Kirmānī, *al-Riyāḍ*, pp. 195–198. This is an excerpt from al-Kirmānī's attempt to reconcile al-Nasafī, al-Rāzī, and al-Sijistānī's views on the prophethood of Adam. For an overview of this debate, see, for example H. Halm, *Kosmologie und Heilslehre*, pp. 101–109; W. Madelung, 'Das Imamat in der frühen ismailitischen Lehre', *Der Islam*, 37 (1961), pp. 101–114.

42. W. Madelung has already mentioned this argument. But although he places it within

the development of doctrines of *imāma* and Qā'im, he does not investigate its intellectual basis. Madelung, 'Das Imamat', pp. 124–125.

43. Al-Kirmānī, *al-Riyāḍ*, pp. 197–198.

44. Walker has already pointed out a similar case in al-Sijistānī's cosmology, P. E. Walker, *Early Philosophical Shiism*, p. 69. Also see his 'Cosmic Hierarchies', p. 27.

45. For example, see A. al-'Azmeh, 'Metaphysical Foundations, 2: Relations of Creation, Sympathy and Analogy', chapter 2 in his *Arabic Thought and Islamic Societies* (London, 1986), pp. 55–105; J. C. Bürgel, *The Feather of Simurgh: The Licit Magic of the Arts in Medieval Islam* (New York, 1988), pp. 66–74; P. Heath, *Allegory and Philosophy in Avicenna (Ibn Sinā)* (Philadelphia, PA, 1992), pp. 179–182, 186–187, and 189 n. 26 and 27. For the principle of correspondence of macrocosm and microcosm in particular, see also the following classic study: S. H. Nasr, *An Introduction to Islamic Cosmological Doctrines* (rev. ed., London, 1978), pp. 66–74, 96–104.

46. The translation of this passage is:

> Their (i.e. the sacred laws') ] *ẓāhir* is mixed with their *bāṭin* like the mixture of the heat of the fire with its light. On the other hand they (i.e. the Ismailis) are [potentially] in conjunction with him (the Qā'im) and *in actu* at the time of the unveiling (*'indat al-kashf)* and surpass the mixture [of the *ẓāhir* of the sacred laws] with the esoteric interpretation, if (or when) it (i.e. the esoteric interpretation) is purified. Thus the simple forms affected in the sacred laws with esoteric interpretation (*al-ṣuwar al-basīṭa al-munfa'ila fī'l-sharā'i' bi'l-ta'wīl*) come into the pure light (*al-nūr al-ṣāfī).*

47. P. Lory, 'Introduction', in H. Corbin, *Alchimie comme art hiératique*, ed. P. Lory (Paris, 1986), pp. 13–14; see also S. Nomoto, 'Early Ismā'īlī Thought in Prophecy', pp. 327–329. See also the notion of the 'transmuted fire' (*feu transmué*), another appellation of the purified fire, in the homily attributed to Imām 'Alī b. Abī Ṭālib, commented upon by Aydamur Jaldakī (d. 750/1349–1350 or 761/1360–1361) and discussed in Corbin, 'Commentaire de la *khotbat al-bayān* par Jaldakī', in *Alchimie comme art hiératique*, pp. 31, 46–47. Also cf. the purification of four elements for the production of the elixir in P. Kraus, *Jābir ibn Ḥayyān*, vol. 2, pp. 8–9.

48. P. Kraus suggests an interaction between the alchemist Jābir b. Ḥayyān and the early Ismailis. See P. Kraus, 'Dschābir ibn Ḥajjān und die Ismā'īlījja', in *Der Zusammenbruch der Dschâbirlegende* (Berlin, 1930), pp. 23–42; 'Les dignitaires de la hiérarchie religieuse selon Jâbir ibn Ḥayyân', *Bulletin de l'Institut français d'archéologie orientale*, 41 (1942), pp. 83–97; and *Jābir ibn Ḥayyān*, vol. 1, pp. XLVIII–LIII. Among scholars who have recently questioned Kraus's position see S. N. Haq, *Names, Natures and Things: The Alchemist Jābir ibn Ḥayyān and his Kitāb al-Aḥjār ('Book of Stones')* (Dordrecht, 1994), pp. 21–24. The possible similarities between Jābir's thought and early Ismailism deserve re-examination in the light of recent scholarship and the above discussion.

# 13

# An Ismaili Interpretation of Ibn Sīnā's *Qaṣīdat al-Nafs*

*Wilferd Madelung*

Ibn Sīnā's *'Ayniyya* poem on the terrestrial exile of the human soul from its heavenly home has by its mystical and aesthetic qualities always appealed to a wider public than the circle of experts and students occupied with his philosophical thought. Its unusual contents and style as compared with his other works have even aroused doubts about its authenticity among a few modern scholars.[1] Over the centuries, however, Ibn Sīnā's authorship has not been questioned, and numerous commentaries, some by renowned mystics such as Ibn al-'Arabī and 'Afīf al-Dīn al-Tilimsānī, have been composed on it. They have been listed in the bibliographies of Ibn Sīnā's works by C. Brockelmann, G. Anawati, and Y. Mahdavi, but have not yet been seriously studied.[2] Entirely missing in their lists of commentaries is one composed by the fifth Ṭayyibī Ismaili *dā'ī muṭlaq* in the Yemen, Sayyidnā 'Alī b. Muḥammad b. al-Walīd (d. 612/1215), entitled *al-Risāla al-mufīda fī īḍāḥ mulghaz al-qaṣīda*. It has been registered in the bibliographies of Ismaili literature by W. Ivanow and I. Poonawala, and some excerpts from it have been published in the sixth *Risāla ramaḍāniyya* of Sayyidnā Ṭāhir Sayf al-Dīn, the fifty-first *dā'ī muṭlaq* of the Bohra community in India.[3] In Western scholarship, however, it has remained virtually unknown.

At the beginning of his treatise, Ibn al-Walīd states that one of the 'virtuous brethren', evidently a member of the Ismaili community, had come upon a *qaṣīda* ascribed to the Ra'īs Abū 'Alī b. Sīnā in which the latter obscured the meanings and hinted at esoteric mysteries (*asrār ḥaqīqiyya*). The author's purpose in doing so was, Ibn al-Walīd suggests, to reserve its noble concepts and subtle sciences for those whom God has blessed with seeking them from their owners (*arbāb*) and aiming for them through their gates (*abwāb*), while withholding them from the partisans of the satans and devils who claim the ranks they do not deserve.

By the owners and gates of the esoteric science, Ibn al-Walīd evidently means the Ismaili Imams. He is thus implying that Ibn Sīnā, or the author of the poem, was in fact a disciple of the Imams who veiled the spiritual truths so that the members of their community might discover them through the teaching hierarchy of the *daʿwa*. It may be recalled here that Ibn Sīnā's father and brother had, according to his own testimony, been attracted to Ismaili teaching by a Fatimid *dāʿī*. Ibn Sīnā himself, however, had repudiated it, and in his philosophical thought rather adhered to the Peripatetic tradition.[4] The Ismaili *daʿwa* did not count him as an initiate and in general ignored his philosophy and his writings. His theological views, it is true, had been radically criticised from an Ismaili perspective by Tāj al-Dīn al-Shahrastānī in his philosophical *Wrestling Match* (*Kitāb al-muṣāraʿa*). The latter, however, was, in the words of al-Samʿānī, associated with the 'people of the mountain fortresses (*ahl al-qilāʿ*)', the Nizārī Ismailis in Iran,[5] and Ibn al-Walīd in the Yemen most likely was not aware of his work. Ibn Sīnā's *qaṣīda* on the soul evidently was also unknown in the Ṭayyibī *daʿwa*, and Ibn al-Walīd's attention was drawn to it only because of its discovery by a member of the community. How then should he react to its message? Impressed by its affinity to Ismaili esoteric thought, he could not fail to recognise its author, whoever he was, as inspired by the spiritual wisdom of the Imams. The identity of the author presumably was of not much importance to him. He does not name Ibn Sīnā again in his commentary.

When requested by the 'virtuous brother' to elucidate the subtle secrets, enigmas, and noble truths which the author had deposited in his poem, Ibn al-Walīd felt obliged to comply, obeying the maxim of the Prophet: 'Do not give wisdom to others than those worthy of it lest you wrong it, nor withhold it from those worthy of it lest you wrong them.' Thus he came to compose his treatise, entitling it *The Instructive Epistle in Elucidation of the Enigmatic in the Qaṣīda* and seeking the assistance of God and the blessing of the one whose sphere encompassed him. He adds that he would not in his exposition go beyond indication, in order to protect wisdom from falling into the hands of the ignorant rabble who do not deserve it.

Ibn al-Walīd explains the fall of the 'ash-grey dove' (*warqāʾ*), as Ibn Sīnā depicts the human soul, from its lofty abode, stating that this refers to the laxness (*futūr*) that occurred in a part of the spiritual world of origination (*ʿālam al-ibdāʿ*) in its response to the divine summons, which led to its coarsening (*takaththuf*) and fall from the world of subtleness to the site of coarseness, from the space of the exalted lights to the centre of decaying bodies and the darkness of the world of generation and corruption and the abode of mixture. This statement distinctly alludes to the mythical events designated first by H. Corbin as the 'drama in heaven',[6] which had become characteristic of Ṭayyibī gnostic cosmology ever since it was described by the second *dāʿī muṭlaq* Ibrāhīm al-Ḥāmidī (d. 557/1141–1142) in his *Kanz al-walad*. According to it, the Third Intellect and Second Emanation, not identified here by Ibn al-Walīd, fell from its rank as it refused to recognise the priority of the Second

Intellect and so became the Tenth Intellect in rank, the demiurge (*mudabbir*) who governs the sublunar material world. The sublunar world was constituted by the spiritual forms, including the human souls, which had, together with the Third Intellect, repudiated the priority of the Second Intellect and remained in a state of disobedience.

Ibn al-Walīd goes on to explain that the dove's description as possessing pride and aloofness (*dhāt taʿazzuz wa-tamannuʿ*) is an allusion to the haughty refusal of the spiritual forms to submit to the one who preceded them in responding to the divine summons and their resistance to obey whomever they were ordered to obey. They became then divided into three groups, those who repented and asked for forgiveness after that had become difficult, those who doubted and remained in bewilderment and who in reality came to constitute the three elements, and those who persisted in their haughty refusal and became the centre of the earth.[7] The demiurge placed these three divisions in the proper place they deserved according to the rule of justice. The spheres and stars became the fathers (*ābāʾ*), the elements the mothers (*ummahāt*), in order that the realms of nature (*mawālīd*) would be borne by them. The first of these realms was that of the minerals, and their ultimate limit was the true man, who was the aim, the first thought and the last work. The demiurge arranged the macrocosm so that in the encompassing sphere, its highest, brightest, and most noble part, matter, would, because of its subtlety, almost become assimilated to its form, while in the earth, its lowest, coarsest, and darkest part, form, would almost be assimilated to matter. In between these extremities all revolving spheres and moving globes were placed higher in accordance with their subtlety and nobility or lower in accordance with their deficiency and coarseness.

Ibn al-Walīd then documents the pre-existence of the human soul from Ismaili religious literature, noting that the 'virtuous person, Author of the Epistles', that is the concealed Imam believed to have composed the *Rasāʾil Ikhwān al-Ṣafāʾ*, had hinted at it, or upheld it explicitly, in many places. As an example he quotes a passage from the *Risāla al-jāmiʿa*, where it is explained that when the sages speak of the 'partial souls', they mean the power that emanates from the Universal Soul and falls to the low centre, being driven into the world of nature. They have fallen short of accepting the spiritual outpouring and lagged behind in the glorification and sanctification in the abode of lights and have therefore been cast into the centre, where servitude and the hardship of obedience with physical instruments and in bodily shape was imposed on them. They had been of a kind which they are not now and to which they shall return when they have repented of their sin and sought forgiveness for their stumbling. For this reason the Universal Soul inclines in compassion towards them, and God sends His Messengers to warn them, aided by His close angels. If they repent they will return to blessed repose, but if they disobey and remain haughty, they will stay in bewilderment, ever more cut up into nations in the darkness of the lowest nether world.[8]

It may be noted that this description of the human souls as an emanation of the Universal Soul stands in contrast with Ṭayyibī cosmology, which, based upon the philosophical system of Ḥamīd al-Dīn al-Kirmānī, considers them as issuing from the Third Intellect, which is identified with Nature. In the present context, however, this difference hardly required a comment from the learned *dāʿī*. He next quotes another text of the Author of the Epistles, this time from the *Jāmiʿat al-jāmiʿa*, referring to an act of disobedience on the part of the Universal Adam in the world of the Soul from which the psychic power (*quwwa nafsāniyya*) flowed to the first human individual, the partial, rebellious Adam, who was forbidden to eat from the tree.[9]

The Commander of the Faithful ʿAlī b. Abī Ṭālib, Ibn al-Walīd notes, also hinted in some of his statements, in the *Nahj al-balāgha* and elsewhere, at the pre-existence of the human soul. Thus he said: 'Let one of you look out whether he is moving forward or turning back; for from the hereafter he has come and to it he will return.' Next Ibn al-Walīd adduces Qur'an 77:30–31 and 2:36 as evidence and concludes with the verse: 'Oh you trustful soul, return to your Lord, approving and approved'. (Qur'an 89:27–28) He observes that the order to return to a place in reasonable speech is only given to someone who was there before.

In the second line of the poem Ibn Sīnā describes the dove representing the soul as hidden from every eye, yet showing itself openly and not wearing a veil. Ibn al-Walīd explains that he meant by this the aforementioned life that has fallen and has been covered by the waves of perplexity and become mixed up with the bodies in blackest darkness. It is at times termed Nature, at other times the 'pervading life' (*ḥayāt sāriya*) or the 'originational leaven' (*khamīra ibdāʿiyya*) and is meant by the word of God: 'And He is the one who brings forth what is hidden (*al-khab'*) in the heavens and the earth'. (Qur'an 27:25) No part of the macrocosm and its realms is bare of it, nor is any corporeal being without it. Rather it is the substance (*jawhar*) that bears its accidents, leading them to their most excellent states and most perfect purposes. Ibn al-Walīd then quotes from the first *mashraʿ* of the fifth *sūr* of al-Kirmānī's *Rāḥat al-ʿaql*, where he discusses matter and form and explains that Nature is the more noble part of them and is termed form. It is, al-Kirmānī affirms, life *in actu*, emanating from the world of sanctity, but is not independent by itself in its existence. Rather it is carried by prime matter. Al-Kirmānī goes on to explain that life pervades everything in the heavens and on earth as its active part, endowing it with its first perfection (*kamāl awwal*) and moving it on.[10]

Ibn al-Walīd then describes in some detail the action of latent life as it moves from potentiality to actuality: the spheres govern; the Mothers (= elements) become parturient; minerals, plants, and animals emerge successively, until the human being is reached, who is the intended purpose. In the minerals, life remains mostly concealed, yet its actions may be witnessed in the magnetic stone and other phenomena. As it rises through the realms of nature, its actions become more and more varied, apparent and noble. In man it constitutes the faculty of imagination, memory, thought, recollection, intelligence, artisanship, discrimination, and reflection. It continues to rise through the ranks of humanity until it reaches its ultimate end in the rank of those receiving the divine support (*ta'yīd*), who are in touch with the close angels through the subtleness of their souls, not their coarse bodies. These manifest acts of life are what in reality the bodies alone are incapable of, and are what is meant by the poet's words: 'it shows itself openly and does not wear a veil.'

The third line of the poem depicts the soul as loath to join the body and then, paradoxically, as perhaps loath to depart from it, while in agony. Ibn al-Walīd explains that this refers to its fall into this world under compulsion, involuntarily as a result of its lagging behind in the affirmation of the priority of those preceding it and of its continued unbelief and haughtiness. Therefore the darknesses of the three dimensions enveloped the souls, and divine wisdom necessitated their removal. The demiurge in charge of them knew that they could not stay in that noble luminous world and sacred spiritual abode and that they would not be cured of the disease attaching to them but through the succession of times, the motion of the spheres, and the mixture of the elements. He arranged them therefore in accordance with the requirements of justice in this world, against their will and choice, leading them to their first physical perfection which consists in the shape of the human body. Ibn al-Walīd adds that this compulsion occurs in reality between two conditions of choice, a hardship between two states of ease, yet only the knowing understand this.

With regard to the souls being loath to leave the body and being in agony, Ibn al-Walīd observes that all souls, the good and the evil, hate death. The evil do so because as they become accustomed to the natural, animal world and absorbed in the sea of dark matter, forget the noble luminous world from which they departed, and their state, origin and destination are obscured to them, and so they wish to enjoy this terrestrial transitory life and choose to stay in these decaying bodies. They hate death out of ignorance of where they are going and out of fear of what they are approaching. In contrast, the good souls, the friends of God, as they realise into what affliction they have fallen, understand the mistake and sin which necessitated that, and repent of their shortcomings, they seek to take advantage of acquiring good qualities and deeds through the tool of their body as long as they remain in the abode of acquisition (*iktisāb*). For that reason they hate death. Ibn al-Walīd again refers to the 'virtuous person, the Author of the Epistles' for corroboration of his argument. This time he quotes from the 'Sessions of Purification by Cleanliness of the Souls' (*Majālis al-tanaẓẓuf bi ṭahārat al-nufūs*), a work so far unknown. The excerpt closely resembles the Epistles of the Sincere Brethren in style and analyses at considerable length the different motives of the friends of God as well as of His enemies for hating death.

The next line repeats, in different terms, the point that the soul at first disdains her coming to this world but after joining it becomes fond of 'the neighbourhood of the desolate ruin'. Ibn al-Walīd notes that the explanation of this has already been given in the previous section. Then he points out that the Author of the Epistles told a parable relating to this theme in which he alluded to the departure of the souls from the abode of simple spiritual beings, their joining with the composite corporeal shapes, and their becoming fond of them after initial aversion and disdain. He will summarise it here because of its pertinence and its clear intimations about origin and destination. From the *Epistle in Explanation of the Belief of the Sincere Brethren* he then quotes the story about the fortunate city located on a mountain top on an island whose inhabitants live in permanent peace, concord and prosperity. A group of them travel by sea and suffer shipwreck. They are cast ashore on a wretched island with rugged mountains, dark caves, murky water and wild beasts of prey, inhabited by a race of apes. A bird of powerful constitution dominates the island and every day carries off some of the apes to eat them. The castaways live a life of hardship and misery on the island. As the apes get accustomed to them, some of the men get attracted to their females, mingle with them and reproduce. Eventually they compete eagerly for the favour of the female apes, hate and fight each other, find enjoyment in this life and desire its perpetuity. Then one of them has a dream in which he returns to his home town. When the people there hear of his arrival they come out full of joy to receive and welcome him. They see that travel and life abroad have changed him and, loath for him to enter in this state, wash him in a spring at the gates of the city, shave his hair, cut his nails, dress him in new clothes and perfume him. Then they put him on a mount and enter the town with him. All gather around him, marvelling at him and at his safe return after his/their (?) despair, while he feels happy with them and that God has rescued him from his exile, the company of those apes, and that miserable life. As he awakes and finds himself among the apes he becomes sad and averse to remaining in that wretched place, thinking about how to return to his home. He tells his dream to one of his brethren who now also remembers their home town and their people and the bounty they used to enjoy. They decide to gather wood on the island so as to build a ship and to return to their home by sea. They remind others of their brethren who had come with them of their former abode of happiness, opening their eyes to the sordid state of their present abode, and everyone joins in the task of building the ship. Then one day the bird comes and snatches one of them, flying off to eat him. When the bird notices that he is a man, not an ape as he was accustomed to, he carries on flying until he reaches the island from which he (the man) had originally come and drops him on the very roof of his house. As the man recognises his town and home he simply wishes that the bird would snatch one of his brethren every day and return him to his home. The people on the wretched island, however, weep after the bird carries him away and continue to grieve over his absence because they do not know what the bird has done with him. Yet if they only knew they would wish as he wished. This, the teller of the story observes, should be the belief of the Sincere Brethren about those whose death precedes theirs. For the lower world resembles that island, and its inhabitants resemble the apes. Death is like that bird, and the friends of God are like the shipwrecked people. The abode of the hereafter is like that other island where their home and their people are to be found.[11]

In the next lines the poet elaborates on the experiences of the soul in this world. At first she seems to forget her former stay in the 'protected enclosure' (*ḥimā*) which she was not satisfied to leave. Yet when the heavy burdens of physical existence bear down on her she weeps from eyes flowing without cease as she remembers her stay in that enclosure. Ibn al-Walīd comments only briefly, referring back to his previous explanations. Her weeping, he suggests, is an allusion to her repentance and distress about the loss of her true being and her containment in the confines of non-being. By this repentance her rise on the stairs of ascent comes about, as does her attachment to the rope of life that is extended to her through the guidance of the Imams and the ranks of the teaching hierarchy (*ḥudūd*).

Yet the dense shape of the body, the poem continues, holds her back like a cage from the lofty spacious summit and she remains tied to that which must stay behind, allied to the dust. Ibn al-Walīd comments that by the alliance to dust is meant the body's return to the earth from which it has come and from which it draws its nourishment, whereas the soul returns to her abode, and her parts join her whole, gaining salvation. He quotes one of the ranking teachers who said:

> Since every kind shall join its kind from a shell that remains in the abode of senses
> to a pearl that joins the Spirit of Holiness.

The poem continues: 'When the voyage to the protected enclosure with the wide open space draws near, the dove coos in excitement as the veil is lifted and she sees what cannot be perceived with drowsy eyes.' Ibn al-Walīd interprets the approach of the voyage as the arrival of the life that is trapped in matter at the human shape, which is the end of objective existence (*wujūd dhātī*) and the beginning of formal existence (*wujūd ṣūrī*), after it has traversed the inverted, crooked path and reached the straight path. If it is granted success and enters the gates of the gardens of bliss by ascent on the ladder of salvation it obtains the second perfection, flowing to the vast open space of holy spirituality. When the soul in her travel reaches this stage, which is the last gate of the world of generation and corruption, when she enters the circle of existence by obedience to the Imams of right guidance, takes cognisance of the ranks of the physical as well as the sacred spiritual hierarchy and opens up through the spiritual sciences, the veil is lifted for her from the hidden mysteries. At that time she awakens from the sleep of unawareness, seizes the opportunity to acquire the gnostic insights in the time of respite and speaks with the tongue of wisdom and reflection, while longing to join the righteous of her likes and her brethren. A witness to this is the statement of the Commander of the Faithful 'Alī b. Abī Ṭālib when he said: 'If the veil were lifted my certitude could not increase', because of his full realisation of his closeness to God and of his lofty rank. 'Alī also said, when he was struck by the sword of his murderer: 'I have won, by the Lord of the Ka'ba.' As further testimony Ibn al-Walīd quotes eight lines from a *qaṣīda* of al-Sulṭān al-Khaṭṭāb b. al-Ḥasan al-Ḥajūrī (d. 533/1138), chief of a clan of Hamdān in northwestern Yemen, *ma'dhūn* in the Ismaili teaching hierarchy, and poet. There al-Khaṭṭāb laments his long journey in this world, bidding the bodily frame that holds him back from his aims to part. Having associated with his body when a wrap covered his eye, he is, now that it has been cleared away, ready for a decisive break. Let each one of them join his kind, be it of earth or of heaven. He expects to reach his hopes as he knows, beyond all guessing, his destination when the veil is removed. The bliss that he shall find is above description by his thought and intelligence.[12]

The poet continues stating that as the dove comes to warble on the peak of a lofty height so knowledge raises the rank of the one who had not been raised. Ibn al-Walīd repeats that the soul's warbling is in response to her cognition of the divine sciences, obscure secrets, and gnostic truths and expresses her longing to join her like, who have been freed from their bodies and have left behind the rebellious opponents of the faith. The summit of the lofty height signifies her reaching the upright stature (*qāma alifīyya*) that resembles the first originational beings[13] and her rise through the ranks of the hierarchy, gaining the two perfections, the objective and the formal, and yearning to appear in the most excellent camphoric shape (*shabaḥ kāfūrī*). Ibn al-Walīd endorses, in glowing terms, Ibn Sīnā's praise of knowledge as raising the rank of the soul. How could it be otherwise, he asks, when knowledge is the greatest magnet drawing noble souls to their destination, their protector from disintegration and corruption, when it dyes them with the beautiful and splendid dye of God, joins them to the radiant lights of the highest world, removes from them evil habits and beastly traits, endows them with pleasing angelic dispositions, turns them into substances after they were counted among accidents and ordains for them permanent happiness and arrival at all goals? 'Alī b. Abī Ṭālib stated: 'When God wishes to humiliate a servant He denies him knowledge', and the Prophet said: 'God does not give a servant knowledge but that He will rescue him some day through it.'

In the next section a certain tension becomes apparent between Ibn Sīnā's poem as conventionally understood and the Ismaili interpretation of Sayyidnā Ibn al-Walīd. There are in fact some minor but significant variants between the commonly transmitted text and that quoted by Ibn al-Walīd, highlighting the different perspective of the philosopher and the religious gnostic. Ibn Sīnā first poses the question as to why the dove may have been cast from its high summit to the bottom of the lowest depth. If God caused her to descend for a wise reason it has been hidden even from the most pious of intelligent men. For Ibn al-Walīd this cannot be a real question. He states briefly that he has already explained the fall of the soul and her imprisonment in the corporeal world by her initial failure to hold on to the one above her in rank and to obey him when summoned to obedience. This offence prevented her from gaining her share of the second perfection and necessitated her dismissal to the transitory world of decay. Yet the Intellects of the world of origination turn with compassion and affection to its fallen parts and emit noble benefits to them in order to repair their deficiency and perfect their substance. That Divine Wisdom which is hidden from the minds of mankind reaches them only through the tongues of the Friends of the Truth, and becomes known only to the deserving on whom they bestow it.

The poem now presses the question further: If the fall of the dove was a due blow to make her hear when she would not hear and to make her know every obscure matter in the two worlds, then her defect has not yet been mended. The version cited by Ibn al-Walīd turns the conditional 'if the fall was' (*in kāna*) into a categorical affirmation 'no doubt the fall was' (*lā shakka*), and the apodosis of the conditional sentence introduced by 'then' (*fa-*) is changed into a clause introduced by 'while' (*wāw ḥāliyya*). Ibn al-Walīd comments that the poet seems to refer by this to the concealed sciences and protected wisdom through which the soul obtains the perfection of her substance and nobility of her constitution and to her cognition of the mysteries of the two worlds, that of density and that of purity, before her deficiency has yet been mended by her arrival at these sciences and before she has been freed from her slavery by taking cognisance of them.

In its conventional form the poem continues: Time has cut short the path of the dove such that she 'set outside the place of rising' (*gharaba bi ghayr al-maṭlaʿ*). The cutting short of her path is naturally to be understood as referring to death, while her setting far from the place of rising suggests its finality. The anonymous commentator quoted by B. Carra de Vaux sees in it, not unreasonably, a repudiation of metempsychosis (*tanāsukh*) by Ibn Sīnā.[14] In Ibn al-Walīd's reading of the text, *bi ghayr al-maṭlaʿ* is replaced by *bi-ʿayn'l-maṭlaʿ*, implying that she declined in the very place of rising.[15] Ibn al-Walīd then interprets time's cutting short of the soul's path in the context of her cosmological voyage in exile. He suggests that the poet meant that the soul, when entering under the rule of time, among the movements of the spheres and the mixture of the elements, becomes united with the forces of the elements and in the mixture joins the first of the realms of nature, that of the minerals. That is the final stage of her descent, from where her ascent and return to the original spiritual beings begin. The poet alluded by the places of setting and rising to this stage. In confirmation of this interpretation Ibn al-Walīd cites Ḥamīd al-Dīn al-Kirmānī, who in his *Kitāb maʿālim al-dīn*[16] mentioned the first stage of the minerals, which is gypsum, stating: 'That is where Nature appears in reverse, returning to parallel the First (Intellect).' On this, Ibn al-Walīd adds, the eminent shaykh ʿAlī b. al-Ḥusayn b. al-Walīd based his treatise known as *Risālat al-ḍilʿ*,[17]

where he describes the right side (*ḍilʿ*) of a cosmological triangle drawn by him as the path of descent in objects (*dhawāt*), the left side as the path of ascent in forms, and the base of the triangle as the place of the realms of nature, which are the end of the fall and the beginning of the rise.[18] The mineral realm, which constitutes the first stage, is thus the place of both setting and rising. Similarly Sayyidnā Ḥamīd al-Dīn Abū ʿAlī Bāb al-Abwāb stated in his *Kitāb al-dhāt waʾl-ṣūra* that the world of compulsion (*ʿālam majbūr*) consists of physical objects (*dhawāt*) without form, while the world of free choice (*ʿālam mukhtār*) consists of abstract forms without objects. Whatever is between them is both objects and forms.[19] Our descent from that world to this world thus was in objects, and our ascent from this world to that world will be in forms.

The final line of the poem likens the dove, or her exile on earth, to a bolt of lightning that flashes in the enclosure and then vanishes as if it had never shone. Following its vain search for the wisdom that lies behind her exile, the poem thus seems to end on a note of pessimism or agnosticism.[20] The Ismaili gnostic, certain of possessing the key for understanding the cause of the soul's exile, reads the line rather as an admonition to the faithful. The poet, he suggests, meant by this the state of the soul when she appeared in the human mould and was embodied in the Adamic shape, her short life span, the closeness of its end and the readiness of her composite body to disintegrate. He represented all that by the flashing of the lightning and the speed of its disappearance. The poet then admonished the righteous out in front to gather provisions for the day of return, to hasten to perform good deeds and to exertion, to restrain the irascible soul from reprehensible morals and evil acts, which is the reality of jihad, to resolve upon acts of worship and the acquisition of enduring pious works, to adorn themselves with the mark of the fear of God, which consists in combining the two kinds of worship: that of knowledge and that of work, to be friends of the Friends of God and the members of the hierarchy, who are the best of mankind, so that their souls may gain eternal blessings in the hereafter, emanations of the luminous Intellects and everlasting joys. Let therefore every prudent, knowledgeable, and sensible person, every vigilant, consummate, and refined character take advantage of this short life and avail himself of the period of brief respite, which may be likened to a flash of lightning because of the speed of its passing and disappearance, before the Lender demands back His loan, lest repentance befall them when there is no time for repentance and before the One to whom destiny leads seizes the souls, when man will meet the acts he has performed and there will be no helper to be called upon. Ibn al-Walīd concludes his commentary with a prayer for himself and all believers that God might seal their lives as He seals those of His close Friends.

## Notes

1. Aḥmad Amīn held that the poem by its poetical inspiration stood in clear contrast with the generally clumsy Arabic style of Ibn Sīnā in both his prose and poetry. He suggested that the real author of the poem was the poet, philosopher and ascetic Muḥammad b. al-Ḥusayn b. al-Shibl al-Baghdādī (d. 473/1080–1081). Aḥmad Fu'ād al-Ahwānī, on the other hand, expressed doubts on Ibn Sīnā's authorship because the contents of the poem do not agree with some of his views about the human soul. Especially, he argued, the depiction of the soul at the beginning of the poem as pre-existing the body was in conflict with Ibn Sīnā's commonly upheld view that the soul originates with the body. See F. Kholeif (Khulayf), *Ibn Sīnā wa-madhhabuh fi'l-nafs* (Beirut, 1974), pp. 131–136. Kholeif rejects these doubts. He notes in particular the similarity of some of the terms and metaphors used by Ibn Sīnā in both the *ʿAyniyya* and his *Risālat al-ṭayr* (pp. 155–158).

2. Notes from an anonymous commentary are provided by B. Carra de Vaux in his edition and translation of the poem, 'La Ḳaçîdah d'Avicenne sur l'âme', *JA*, 9th ser. vol. 14. It is to be noted that the reference to this article in *GAL*, SI, p. 818 is erroneously to *JA*, 9th ser. vol. 4. The mistaken reference has been copied by both G. Anawati, *Mu'allafāt Ibn Sīnā* (Cairo, 1950), p. 155 and Y. Mahdavī, *Fihrist-i nuskhahā-yi muṣannafāt-i Ibn-i Sīnā* (Tehran, 1954), p. 197. F. Kholeif gives a few quotations from four commentaries on the poem.

3. W. Ivanow, *A Guide to Ismaili Literature* (London, 1933), p. 59; I. K. Poonawala, *Biobibliography of Ismāʿīlī Literature* (Malibu, CA, 1977), p. 159. The sixth *Risāla ramaḍāniyya* of Sayyidnā Ṭāhir Sayf al-Dīn, entitled *Durār al-hudā al-muḍī'a*, was published in Bombay 1341/1923. The excerpts from the *R. al-mufīda* are on pp. 44–61. The present study is based on four manuscripts belonging to The Institute of Ismaili Studies in London.

4. See W. E. Gohlman, *The Life of Ibn Sīnā* (Albany, NY, 1974), pp. 18–19.

5. Al-Subkī, *Ṭabaqāt al-shāfiʿiyya al-kubrā* (Cairo, 1905–1906), vol. 4, p. 79.

6. See H. Corbin, *Trilogie Ismaélienne* (Tehran and Paris, 1961), pp. 135–136.

7. The same division of the rebellious spiritual forms is described by al-Ḥusayn b. ʿAlī b. al-Walīd, the son of ʿAlī b. Muḥammad and eighth *dāʿī muṭlaq*, in his *Risālat al-mabda' wa'l-maʿād* (ed. H. Corbin in *Trilogie Ismaélienne*, Arabic text, p. 106). The repentant forms constitute the ether, the perplexed ones make up the other three elements – air, water, earth – and the recalcitrant become the rock (*ṣakhra*) at the centre of the earth.

8. *Al-Risāla al-jāmiʿa*, ed. J. Ṣalībā (Damascus, 1949), vol. 2, pp. 38–39; ed. M. Ghālib (Beirut, 1974), pp. 354–355.

9. The *Jāmiʿat al-jāmiʿa* quoted here is a work belonging to the literature of the Ṭayyibīs and is not yet published. It differs from the *Jāmiʿat al-jāmiʿa* edited by ʿĀrif Tāmir (Beirut, n.d.).

10. Al-Kirmānī, *Rāḥat al-ʿaql*, ed. M. Ghālib (Beirut, 1967), pp. 269–270. Al-Kirmānī's identification of nature with life, form, motion and soul is thoroughly analysed by D. De Smet, *La Quiétude de l'Intellect* (Leuven, 1995), pp. 324–331.

11. *Risālat bayān iʿtiqād Ikhwān al-Ṣafā'* in *Rasā'il Ikhwān al-Ṣafā'*, ed. Kh. al-Ziriklī (Cairo, 1928), vol. 4, pp. 102–104.

12. Al-Khaṭṭāb's lengthy poem is edited by I. Poonawala in his *al-Sulṭān al-Khaṭṭāb: Ḥayātuh wa-shiʿruh* (Cairo, n.d.), pp. 121–129. The lines quoted by Ibn al-Walīd are on p. 124, nos. 35–42, as noted there by the editor.

13. The spiritual beings of the *ibdāʿ* world possess upright *alif* stature like the human stature. They are, however, distinguished by exceeding purity, luminosity and splendour so that they cannot be perceived by physical senses or described by corporeal attributes. See the question and answer no. 1 in R. Strothmann, *Gnosis-Texte der Ismailiten* (Göttingen, 1943), Arabic text, p. 111.

14. *JA*, 9th ser., vol. 14, pp. 164–165, 172.

15. Kholeif, *Ibn Sīnā*, p. 131 n. 4, notes the variant *bi-ʿayn* from the *Dīwān Ibn Sīnā*, ed. Ḥ. ʿA. Maḥfūẓ (Tehran, 1957).

16. The *Kitāb maʿālim al-dīn* is commonly known as *al-Risāla al-waḍīʾa fī maʿālim al-dīn*. The quoted passage is in the edition by Muḥammad ʿĪsā al-Ḥarīrī (Kuwait, 1987), on p. 127.

17. See Poonawala, *Biobibliography*, pp. 140, 146. It is alternatively known as *Risālat tuḥfat al-ṭālib wa-umniyyat al-bāḥith al-rāghib*. The author, ʿAlī b. al-Ḥusayn b. Jaʿfar b. Ibrāhīm b. al-Walīd (d. 554/1159), was an uncle and the first teacher of ʿAlī b. Muḥammad b. al-Walīd.

18. In the manuscripts of the *Risālat al-ḍilʿ* the descent appears to the onlooker in fact on the left side of the triangle and the ascent on the right side.

19. The *Kitāb al-dhāt waʾl-ṣūra* has so far been known only through a reference to it, without the name of the author, in al-Bhārūjī's *Kitāb al-azhār*, ed. ʿĀdil al-ʿAwwā, *Muntakhabāt Ismāʿīliyya* (Damascus, 1958), vol. 1, p. 198. See Poonawala, *Biobibliography*, p. 321. There is a brief quotation from it in ʿAlī b. al-Ḥusayn's *Risālat al-ḍilʿ*: 'The worshipper's raising of his hands at the *takbīr* is an indication that the world of acts (*ʿālam al-afʿāl*) will return to the world of statements (*ʿālam al-aqwāl*).' ʿAlī b. al-Ḥusayn takes the world of acts as referring to the descent and the world of statements as referring to the ascent in his cosmological triangle. The author of the *Risālat al-dhāt waʾl-ṣūra* is called by ʿAlī b. al-Ḥusayn merely Bāb al-Abwāb. The author to whom it is ascribed here by Ibn al-Walīd seems to be identical with the early Fatimid *dāʿī* Abū ʿAlī al-Ḥasan b. Aḥmad Bāb al-Abwāb (d. 321/933), who, according to Ibn Ḥawqal, had earlier been known as Ḥamdān Qarmaṭ (see Madelung, 'Ḥamdān Qarmaṭ and the Dāʿī Abū ʿAlī', in *Proceedings of the 17th Congress of the UEAI*, St. Petersburg, 1997, pp. 115–124) The name Ḥamīd al-Dīn may be an erroneous addition by an early scribe, induced by the occurrence of it a few lines before referring to al-Kirmānī, or it may have been intentionally added as an honorific title (suggestion by I. Poonawala in a letter dated 27/9/1999). It is not known if the book is extant. The terminology employed in it, contrasting *dhāt*, in the sense of a physical, corporeal object, with *ṣūra*, abstract form, is unusual in Ismaili literature. Ibn al-Walīd, however, uses it in several passages of his commentary.

20. See the comments of Carra de Vaux, *JA*, 9th ser., vol. 14, p. 173.

# 14

# *Āyat al-Nūr*: A Metaphor for Where We Come From, What We Are, and Where We Are Going

*Soraya Mahdi Hajjaji-Jarrah*

*Āyat al-nūr* (Qur'an 24:35) whose metaphors are a fascinating fusion of spirituality and aesthetics gives, as Goldziher once wrote, 'the most profound concise mystic conception of God in any language'.[1] The *āya* speaks of this conception by bringing together two polarities: the transcendental *nūr* and the temporal '*nūr*', the eternal and the transient. And in this meeting lie both its enigma and concision. It is thus no accident that this linking occurs in the poetic expressions of *āyat al-nūr*, so powerfully that both Ibn Sīnā (d. 428/1037) and al-Rāzī (d. 606/1209) ambitiously sought, through its metaphors, to deal with some of the most profound metaphysical theories which speculate on the fundamental nature of reality. In their endeavour both thinkers draw upon the discipline of *ta'wīl* in the field of Qur'anic exegesis as well as upon rational philosophical discourse.[2] However, even though the two thinkers appear to display a vast difference in terms of premise and approach, their conclusions, as we shall see, intertwine into an indissoluble union. This paper proposes to shed some light on how Ibn Sīnā and al-Rāzī construct arguments intended to define something perhaps indefinable hidden behind the metaphors of the *āya*. The focal point of comparison in this study must be the possibility of amalgamating the fundamental dichotomy between rational thought and religio-poetic expression.

By way of introduction, it must be noted that while Ibn Sīnā's *ta'wīl* of the *āya* is discussed in its entirety, al-Rāzī's reading of its first phrase, '*Allāhu nūru al-samawāti wa'l-arḍ*', constitutes the other portion of the study. Given the limited scope of this study, and more importantly our contention that his *ta'wīl* of the selected phrase yields a justifiable comparison with Ibn Sīnā's, as we shall demonstrate, drawing such a boundary is particularly essential. This, it must be pointed out, is a preliminary investigation of al-Rāzī's thought. For although his vastly inclusive thought been the subject of dynamic transformation and evolution, our knowledge of his thought is still rudimentary. This is evident from the fact that al-Rāzī has not received due attention from either Muslim or non-Muslim modern scholarship.[3]

Ibn Sīnā's attention has evidently been captured by the sublime imagery of the *āyat al-nūr*. Its interpretation is central in his treatise *Fī ithbāt al-nubuwwāt* and integrated in his major work *al-Ishārāt*.[4] His *ta'wīl* of the *āya* in *Fī ithbāt* is well defined though it does not cover the whole passage; it breaks off at the verse's most dramatic moment: *nūrun 'alā nūrin*.[5] The resulting suspense is somewhat relieved as Ibn Sīnā resumes his discussion of some aspects of his ontological theory with which he begins his interpretation, in the process, tying together the conclusion and the introduction. In *al-Ishārāt* Ibn Sīnā shifts from an *ishāra* to the interpretation of the *āya* with a recapitulation of his 'earlier' *ta'wīl* in *Fī ithbāt*. Here the organisation of the passage is torn out of its original order and only a few of its symbols receive attention. Ibn Sīnā departs from the *āya* to another *ishāra* as abruptly as he has approached it. His *ta'wīl* of the *āya* in both works is devoted to reinforcing his theory on prophethood which he perceives as the epitome of intellectual and spiritual perfection, as a point of contact between the temporal and the eternal realm, if not essentially belonging to a realm beyond all temporality. More on Ibn Sīnā's *ta'wīl* later on.

Dissimilar to Ibn Sīnā's supra non-canonical approach to *tafsīr*, al-Rāzī's *ta'wīl* of *āyat al-nūr* is a fusion of his unique contribution to the tradition and its established rules. He, in a typical Razian fashion, transmutes the passage into a sixteen-page 'web' of a complex intellectual discussion vis-à-vis Ibn Sīnā's four-page condensed commentary. Al-Rāzī divides his commentary into three sections (*fuṣūl*), with numerous subsections. The first two *fuṣūl* are what concern us here. The first *faṣl*, which is dedicated to discussing the attribution of the term *nūr* to God, is a paraphrasing of, and a verbatim citation of, a large portion of al-Ghazālī's commentary on the *āya* in his *Mishkāt* as well as al-Rāzī's own idiosyncratic reading of the Qur'anic term. In the second *faṣl* and without any introduction, al-Rāzī shifts his *ta'wīl* to interpreting a non-canonical, albeit famous, *ḥadīth*, or what H. Landolt calls the 'Veils-Tradition': '*inna lillāhi sab'īna ḥijāban min nūrin wa-ẓulmatin law kashafahā lā'aḥraqa subuḥāti wajhihi kulla mā adraka baṣaruhu*.'[6]

The overall discussion of al-Rāzī's *ta'wīl* evolves around the overwhelming interaction and tension between temporal light and eternal light; both are, as intimated earlier, central in the *āya*. At the initial phase a partial release is achieved through an *argumentum ex contrario*. In this argument he reduces the literal meaning of *nūr* into its transient component elements. He invalidates them one by one, negating the possibility of attributing such literal meaning to the One who is not an accident, is never extinct, eternal, unchangeable, non-corporeal, essentially existent in Himself.[7] However, the situation is more complex. Since there are Qur'anic verses which clearly refer to God as being unlike anything else (42:11), and others where the term *nūr* is attached to God (*āyat al-nūr*), *ta'wīl* is rendered 'mandatory' '*lā budda mina al-ta'wīl*'. At this point, al-Rāzī abandons the ontology of being and draws upon other Qur'anic verses, previous authorities, poetry and Arabic language usages in order to infer a meaning for the term in the Qur'anic passage. His conclusion here has the sense of probability rather than certainty: 'for most probably what is intended by *al-nūr* is guidance in intellectual and practical endeavours'.[8] Al-Rāzī, however, does not seem satisfied with probabilities. He is after certitude. He thus shifts to where he appears to believe, as we shall see, certitude may lie. In so doing al-Rāzī's final discussion of the Qur'anic expression '*Allāhu nūru al-samawāti wa'l-arḍ*', constitutes what he calls a *muḥaṣṣil* of al-Ghazālī's interpretation of the phrase in his *Mishkāt al-anwār* where al-Ghazālī alleged (*za'ama*) that God in reality is *nūr*, 'or better still the *nūr* is nothing else but Him (*laīsa al-nūr illā Huwa*)'. Al-Rāzī justifies the inclusion of this extraordinarily long citation as being 'by way' ('*alā sabīl*) of an examination in order to reach an impartial judgement (*inṣāf*) of al-Ghazālī's statements.[9]

Al-Rāzī's 'leap' to *al-Mishkāt* transmutes his reading of the verse to the Ghazalian *ta'wīl*. The initial stage of this *ta'wīl* constitutes a grand ascending scale of an epistemological hierarchy where the term *nūr* assumes a different connotation at each stage until it reaches the Summit or the Ultimate source of all the *anwār*: *Nūr al-anwār*. The intensity of illumination (understood as knowledge) at each stage depends on its proximity to the Ultimate *Nūr*. The ascent begins from the debased *nūr* of the physical eye (*al-baṣar*), progressing to the *nūr* of the human rational faculty (*al-baṣīra*). At the subsequent stage *al-nūr* is identified with the divine Word and the souls of the prophets. At this point *al-nūr* passes over the terrestrial boundaries and rises through the celestial spirits (*arwāḥ*). Its definition as the divine Word of revelation and the souls of the prophets represents the link between the terrestrial rational lights (*al-anwār al-'aqliyya al-sufliyya*), and the celestial lights (*al-anwār al-'ulwiyya*).

Once the scale moves into the world of the Spirits ('*ālam al-arwāḥ*), the hierarchy ceases to have an overriding epistemological theme; it does not acquire a definite ontological motif either. The motion of ascent, however, continues in the Higher World which is charged with the lights of the Angelic Substances (*jawāhir al-malā'ika*). Its structure is made up of countless degrees of proximity to the source of all lights. At the summit, the epistemological approach to defining *al-nūr* takes a profoundly ontological stance. Here *al-nūr* is no longer identified with knowledge; rather it turns to denoting existence in its absolute and essential 'form', namely God or the Necessary Existence who is *al-Nūr al-Muṭlaq*. At this point, all the previous identifications of *al-nūr* are negated and reduced to metaphors of the only Real

Light. Consequently, the lights of all creation are transmuted into contingent existence which is synonymous, in reality, with pure darkness and pure nonexistence (*ẓulma maḥḍa, 'adam maḥiḍ*).[10]

Subsequently this 'unconventional' ontological stance is carried further to its 'ultimate frontiers' where the flowing of the lights of existence from the primordial wellspring of lights, *Nūr al-Anwār*, takes the form of total identification between being and non-being, between the real and the metaphor. It is a type of identification which is similar to the intensity of union (*shiddat al-ittiḥād*) between light and colour as a result of which light 'cannot be independently discerned'. The relationship between God and creation is established in the same way. Everything in existence can only be apparent through the eternally present Divine light (*al-Nūr al-Ilāhi*) with which it is united. The illuminating agent and the illuminated subject are so intensely united and inseparable that the Divine light is rendered hidden and indiscernible. Paradoxically, however, 'His hiddenness is [precisely] due to the intensity of His manifestation'.[11]

The above-cited Ghazalian commentary in al-Rāzī's *Mafātīḥ*, provides a remarkable glimpse of what Landolt calls 'al-Ghazālī's "monism"' or what 'Afīfī calls 'a curious proximity to the doctrine of *waḥdat al-wujūd*, even though al-Ghazālī does not clearly say that God and creation are one, like Ibn 'Arabī did'.[12] What appears quite puzzling at this stage, however, is al-Rāzī's decision to cease citing al-Ghazālī. For even though al-Ghazālī concludes the first *faṣl* of *al-Mishkāt* by nullifying his preceding statements through asserting that 'God is before, above and the Revealer (*muẓhir*) of everything from one aspect (*wajh*), He is also with everything from another *wajh*',[13] al-Rāzī chooses not to cite al-Ghazālī's 'abrogation'. Instead he accepts the Ghazalian commentary as a series of satisfactory statements (*kalām mustaṭāb*) and concludes, in very few lines, that after verification (*ba'da'l-taḥqīq*) it amounts to 'identifying God as light with God as creator (*khāliq*) of the universe and creator of the perceptive powers', as well as being the 'guide (*ḥādī*) of the inhabitants of the heavens and the earth'. The latter identification is his own, as he properly states.[14]

Another seemingly bewildering stance is taken by al-Rāzī in his second *faṣl*. He interrupts his commentary on the *āya* by inserting an interpretation of the Veils-Tradition which occupies the third section of the known recension of the *Mishkāt*.[15] However, al-Rāzī at this point no longer refers either to al-Ghazālī or to the *Mishkāt*. Nevertheless he follows in its footsteps, adopting a philosophical argument to negate the attribution of 'veiledness' to God due to His Necessary Existence. Just like the standard version of the *Mishkāt*, the veils are divided into three classes: veils of total darkness, veils of a mixture of light and darkness, and veils of sheer light. To the first class belong those who are veiled from inferring the existence of God by the darkness of their preoccupation with their own passions. In the second category are the philosophical rationalists whose veils of light are due to their realisation that the existence of creation is dependent on an affecting agent. However, their attribution of this agent to someone or thing other than God constitutes their veil of darkness.[16] The last class consists of those who are veiled by the infinite veils of the light of the Divine attributes or what Landolt calls 'the theological attributes'.[17] His unique reality, al-Rāzī concludes, is infinitely veiled (*muḥtajaba*) from all.[18]

The striking, albeit covert, affinity between the *Mafātīḥ* and the standard *Mishkāt* is perhaps more conclusive in al-Rāzī's short treatise *Asās al-taqdīs*. In its seventh *faṣl*, entitled *al-hijāb*, lies the crux of the matter.[19] Its highly condensed statements are demonstrative of al-Rāzī's ontological views. Here the Veils-Tradition is given in two variants; one variant is identical to that in *al-Mafātīḥ* and the other differs from both *al-Mafātīḥ* and the *Mishkāt* versions. What all these variants have in common is the certainty of the action of burning by the splendours of the Divine face, should His 'veil/s' be removed. Moreover, the theoretical and linguistic basis for applying the term veil to God and to His creation is in disagreement with that of the *Mafātīḥ* and consequently with the *Mishkāt*'s. In the latter two, veiledness is held to be inapplicable to God who is 'manifest in Himself and for Himself' (*mutajallī fī dhātihi li-dhātihi*);[20] in *Asās al-taqdīs*, al-Rāzī insists that God is *self-veiled* rather than being veiled. Furthermore, while in his discussion of the Veils-Tradition in the *Mafātīḥ*, he elaborates on the observable contingency of creation and its subsequent realisation of its need (*iḥtiyāj*) for an affecting agent (*mu'athir*), this view in *Asās* is given as an axiom. The infinity of the veils of light, interpreted in *Mafātīḥ* as being the negative and relational Divine attributes, is cast here in stages of perfection (understood as existence). Existence, he explains briefly, can only be ascertained in the affecting agent in its strongest and most perfect form. Any kind of existence which occurs to an affected entity (*athar*) is obtained from the affecting agent. And since the giver of all existence in its entirety is undoubtedly the Transcendent Truth, the existence of all the ontologically possible (*al-mumkināt*), that is to say the entirety of the physical and spiritual world (*'ālam al-ajsām wa-'ālam al-arwāḥ*), when compared with the existence of God 'is more deserving to be called nonexistence' (*'adam*).[21]

Moreover, while we find no reference to 'attainment' (*wuṣūl*) in the *Mafātīḥ* version, this notion and the human spirit's annihilation of the *Mishkāt*'s third section bring al-Rāzī's interpretation of the Divine veils of light in the *Asās* to a precise conclusion. The attainers, here, are the human spirits who reach 'the lowest spheres of real existence' (*adnā martaba min marātib tilka al-kamālāt*). They burn and perish (*taḍmaḥil*) by 'the Splendours of His Face which burn everything reaching Him by his sight (or reached him by His Sight)'.[22] The Razian ontological drama concludes with the dropping of His Veils, and the 'Ultimate Reality of [His] "Light" turns out to be the "Fire" [of His Existence which] ... burns everything other than Itself of whatever "existence" it may wish to claim of its own'.[23] This is indeed the infinite dominion of essential existence over contingent existence through which al-Rāzī perceives the 'existence' of the entirety of creation: since creation is only possible in itself, it is null and void, and only the One exists, in reality, by virtue of His essential existence.[24]

While the preceding mystical notion of ascent and *wuṣūl* is essentially ontological, the drama of another sort of ascent is associated with the metaphors of *āyat al-nūr*. The proponent is Ibn Sīnā whose *ta'wīl* is profoundly epistemological. Both his interpretation of the term *nūr* and his *ta'wīl* rest on philosophical premises 'pertaining to the nature of essential and accidental inherence, actual and potential existence'.[25] In his *Ithbāt* he defines *nūr* as 'an equivocal term partaking of two meanings, one essential, the other metaphorical'[26] both of which can only be applied to God. The basis of his propositions is laid down in condensed statements. Since light is essentially the perfection of the transparent, inasmuch as it is transparent, and in the metaphorical sense since God is essentially that which is good, He is actual Good and the cause behind bringing Good from potentiality to actuality.

In most of his *ta'wīl* Ibn Sīnā uses the Qur'anic simile of *al-nūr*, and the apparatus and material that produce it to elucidate the stages of potentiality and actuality of the rational human soul's knowledge. Ibn Sīnā holds that the 'niche' (*al-mishkāt*) represents the unadulterated potentiality of the rational human soul which exists in all men with varying degrees of intellectual capabilities (*al-ʿaql al-hiyūlānī*). The 'glass' (*al-zujāja*) stands for the intellect by positive disposition (*al-ʿaql bi'l-malaka*). Here the potential of the human rational faculty has been partly actualised through acquiring the first intelligibles. It is, however, still in a stage of potentiality in relation to the succeeding stage, because it has not as yet received the secondary intelligibles. The 'lamp' (*al-miṣbāḥ*) of the *āya* is a symbol of the acquired intellect (*al-ʿaql al-mustafād*) which receives the second intelligible. The human soul travels from potentiality to actuality via two routes. On the first route it receives the secondary intelligibles from the Active Intellect (*al-ʿaql al-faʿʿāl)* through its cogitative power which is represented in the *āya* by the 'blessed olive tree' (*shajaratin mubārakatin*). The second route is through its intuition (*zayytūnatin*) whose metaphor, in Ibn Sīnā's view, is the almost-luminous 'oil' (*yakādu zaytuha yuḍī'*) of the verse. This human soul endowed with intuition (*ḥads*) possesses the holy power (*al-quwwa al-qudsiyya*) of the prophets.[27] To Ibn Sīnā, this unique soul is the Qur'anic honourable 'glass' which represents the perfection of the actualisation of the human soul's intellect. Its receipt of the secondary intelligibles is actualised through their visible apparition in its intellect (*mushāhada mutamāthila fī'l-dhihin*).[28] This is the meaning of the Qur'anic metaphor of 'the glass [whose] oil almost shines even if no fire touched it, light upon light'. The 'fire' (*al-nār*) of the verse represents the Active/ Universal Intellect[29] which draws Its own *nūr* from the essential source of *al-nūr*, viz. God. Henceforth Ibn Sīnā's *ta'wīl* is implying that the holy intellect is possessed by an autonomous or 'an almost autonomous' human soul who is the exemplary model of the ascent of the degrees of intellectual and spiritual perfection.

The direction of the rational human soul's celestial ascent to perfection is the 'East', the region of pure light. Ibn Sīnā's use of the antithesis of East and West, light and dark transmutes existence into a 'sacred geography'.[30] Its horizontal directions 'rest' on an axis of ascent and descent. In his *ta'wīl* of the Qur'anic statement 'neither from the east nor from the west' (*lā sharqiyyatin wa-lā gharbiyyatin*), Ibn Sīnā interprets the West as a region of utter darkness where matter, represented by 'animal power' (*al-quwwa al-hayawaniyya*), reigns supreme. The East is the point of uninterrupted *nūr*; it is the world of pure rational power (*al-quwwa al-maḥḍiyya al-nuṭqiyya*).[31] To reach the sacred East and attain intellectual perfection, the human rational soul rises above its physical conditions, leaves the terrestrial frontiers and joins the heavenly spheres. The middle ground where light and dark, East and West, intersect, is interpreted by Ibn Sīnā as the cogitative power of the human soul (*al-quwwa al-fikriyya*). This power is the 'blessed olive tree' of the Qur'an, standing at the threshold of East and West, between potentiality and actuality, and uniting the psychic energies and the sensible elements of the human soul.[32] The instantaneous embarkation on the journey to the East, however, occurs through the energies of the human soul which possesses the gift of *ḥads*. It is the Ibn Sinian superior human soul, the Qur'anic *brilliant star* (*al-kawkab al-durrī*) of *āyat al-nūr*, and the honourable *lamp* of Ibn Sīnā's *ta'wīl*. This soul almost gives off light even if no *fire* (the Active/Universal Intellect) has touched its oil (its rational powers). It is a perfect and almost autonomous human soul, because it is already burning with intuition (*tashtaʿilu ḥadsan*).[33] It is the prophetic soul on whose *nūr* is God's *nūr*, and what the Qur'an describes as being *nūrun ʿalā nūrin*. This stage represents the climax of the human soul's degrees of *nūr*, where it reaches the transcendent highest heights, where it enters the brilliant and splendid realm of the Divine *nūr* and where the distinction between *al-anwār* becomes blurred.[34] It is also the stage of arrival of the soul of the *ʿārif*. The *ʿārif* is the theosopher who has perfected discursive knowledge as well as attaining spiritual illumination through travelling the road to Truth. The climax of the *ʿārif*'s journey is when he 'plunges into the depths of the "sea" of arrival' (*lujjat al-wuṣūl*)[35] and attains union with the Divine.

The implications of the human soul's climb up the steps of knowledge and its ascent of the degrees of spirituality are compelling. Upon its arrival, the rational human soul perfects in itself the appearance of all existence and accomplishes the most exalted form of knowledge: the knowledge of God and the meaning of His existence.[36] The soul's arrival is the summit of its spiritual and intellectual experience. Through this dual experience the soul ascends the hierarchy of being. In each zone, a different faculty of the human soul comes into play. The end of the 'ladder' is when the human soul is 'transformed into an intelligible world analogous to the entire existence, which becomes a witness to utter Splendour, utter Goodness and real Beauty, and becomes *united with It*' (*wa-muttaḥidān bihi*).

The dazzling drama of the coming together of the two *anwār* or more precisely the *nūrun ʿalā nūrin* of the *āya* achieves a remarkable manifestation. It is the blinding brilliance of the fusion of the two *anwār* when the perfected rational human soul is almost luminous. Its near luminosity suggests the notion that its capacity to emit *nūr* transcends that of the *al-ʿaql al-faʿʿāl* or the Qur'anic *fire* of *āyat al-nūr*. Moreover in *al-Ishārāt*, Ibn Sīnā says that the apex of perfection of the intelligible substance (*al-jawhar al-ʿāqil*) lies in its becoming identical to quiddity (*al-dhāt*) understood as divine quiddity.[37] Al-Ṭusī comments on the station of arrival of the *ʿārif* saying it is where the *ʿārif* and God become identical, and it is the station of attaining knowledge through which all distinctions are abolished, and where what is known is inexpressible.[38] It is the total union at the instant of the human soul's separation from its terrestrial bonds. Better still it is the combining of union and separation in the same instant. Consequently the arrival (*al-wuṣūl*) of the perfected rational human soul as a result of its intellectual and spiritual ascent represents the zenith of the human soul's role in the Ibn Sinian universe.

Ibn Sīnā's *ta'wīl* of *āyat al-nūr*, though disguised by seemingly impenetrable rational expressions, rattles the iron cage of previous discourse and echoes with a subtle poetic thought that appears to have been motivated by the powerful metaphors of the *āya*.[39] Perhaps Ibn Sīnā has interpreted the profoundest Qurʿanic statement of God through his perception of the human soul's ability to reach spiritual and intellectual perfection for a deep-seated reason. Both the human soul's ascent into the East, and the symbols of the Qurʿanic *āya* terminate with an *ittiḥād*, a coming together, an identification where all distinctions are abolished: this is indeed the sublime Qurʿanic panorama of *nūrun ʿalā nūr*. Ibn Sīnā must have perceived *āyat al-nūr* as being intended to announce 'something' that cannot be expressed otherwise. He saw the *āya* as a unique expression of the thing symbolised. This 'thing' is a reality which in itself transcends all expressions.[40]

These commentaries on *āyat al-nūr* give a panoramic view of the overarching philosophical, ontological and epistemological systems in which it is discussed. These systems describe the cosmogonic unfolding of the universe from a single source of creation, and the ascent of the fulfilled and perfected individual human soul to the ontological point of origin of the whole of creation.[41] The ontological drama takes place in successive stages of illumination from God through the spiritual substances of *ʿĀlam al-Malakūt* until it reaches the terrestrial world (*al-ʿālam al-asfal*). In the celestial process each spiritual substance (*jawhar rūḥānī*) shines down on another celestial substance. The intensity of their illumination depends on their proximity to the First Principle, the *Nūr al-anwār*. This movement is similar to the reflection and refraction of sunlight on the moon which is in turn reflected onto a mirror, then onto another mirror, from there onto a bucket of water from where it is reflected onto the ceiling.[42] The movement of descent in the lower world begins from the *anwār* of the prophets who are at the threshold of *al-ʿālam al-ʿulwī* and *al-ʿālam al-suflī*. However, since all these *anwār* are only possible in themselves, they are darkness and nothingness without their reflective relation to the Principle Source of 'their' *anwār*.

In the theory of human knowledge the cosmic drama is reversed. It redeems itself through the progression of the intellect of the human soul. It is from stage to stage from *the niche*, (*al-ʿaql bi'l-quwwa*), to *the glass* (*al-ʿaql bi'l-malaka*), to *the lamp*, (*al-ʿaql al-mustafād*), to the honourable *glass*, (*al-ʿaql al-qudsi*) respectively, represented by one of the degrees of the intellectual refinement, that the human soul accomplishes its ascent towards perfection and closes the cycle of the cosmic drama. In its journey of ascent the rational human soul restores the cosmos back to its origins. And in this act of restoration, the perfected rational human soul is, in effect, practising a *ta'wīl* of the entire universe.[43]

## Notes

1. I. Goldziher, *A Short History of Classical Arabic Literature*, tr. J. Desomogyi (Berlin, 1966), p. 29. For an excellent English rendering of *āyat al-nūr*, see M. Marmura, 'Avicenna: On the Proof of Prophecies and the Interpretation of the Prophets Symbols and Metaphors', in R. Lerner and M. Mahdi, ed., *Medieval Political Philosophy* (Ithaca, NY, 1986), p. 116. Throughout the discussion, some of Prof. Marmura's translations of the expressions of the *āya* are occasionally referred to.

2. H. Corbin takes a great interest in *al-ta'wīl* in tr. W. Trask, *Avicenna and the Visionary Recital* (London, 1960), pp. 29 ff. (hereafter cited as *The Visionary Recital*) and offers a searching analysis of the linguistic connotations of the term. The doctrine of the duality (*ẓāhir* and *bāṭin*) of the Qur'anic meanings is in line with Ibn Sīnā's own views in his *Risāla aḍhawiyya fī amri'l-maʿād*, ed. S. Dunya (Cairo, 1949), pp. 44 ff; *al-Najāt* (Cairo, 1939), pp. 304 ff; *Fī ithbāt al-nubuwwāt wa-ta'wīl rumūzihim wa-amthālihim*, ed. with an Introduction by M. Marmura (Beirut, 1968), pp. 48 ff. on an elitist epistemic status assigned to prophets and philosophers (*al-ḥukāma'*) as an exclusive instrument in deciphering divine revelation which in its entirety is couched in a symbolic language. This elitism is seen by Ibn Sīnā to be a divine design intended for the common good of human society. For had the commoners (*al-ʿawām)* been able to unravel the knowledge of God hidden in the *bāṭin* meanings of the revelation, they would be confused, might deny the truth and engage in civil dissent. See also M. Marmura, 'Avicenna: Healing and Metaphysics,' in R. Lerner and M. Mahdi, ed., *Medieval Political Philosophy* (Ithaca, NY, 1986), pp. 103 ff.

Though al-Rāzī and Ibn Sīnā share a common denominator viz., epistemic elitism, differences in their approach to *al-ta'wīl* are readily discernible. Al-Rāzī insists that hermeneutically *ta'wīl* is only permissible when the apparent (*ẓāhir*) meanings are impossible and inaccessible beyond any shadow of doubt. For al-Rāzī, *al-ta'wīl* is a '*mawḍuwʿ ʿaẓīm*' that is to say a very serious issue. His discussions of *al-ta'wīl*, and his reservations, can be found in his *Asās al-taqdīs*, ed. A. al-Saqqā (Cairo, 1986), pp. 234 ff.

3. Compare, for instance, al-Rāzī's intellectual formulations on the question of human knowledge in his voluminous Qur'anic commentary *Mafātīḥ al-ghayb* (known as *al-Tafsīr al-kabīr*) (Cairo, 1976), vol. 2, pp. 412 ff., with his views on the issue in his *Lubab al-ishārāt*, ed. A. al-Saqqā (Cairo, 1986), p. 173. On the compulsory necessity of the existence of a prophet, for example, see al-Rāzī, *al-Mabāḥith al-mashriqiyya*, ed. with a commentary by al-Baghdādī (Beirut, 1966) vol. 2, pp. 555 ff. Interestingly his 'un-Ash'arī' views here are almost a verbatim quotation from Ibn Sīnā's *al-Najāt*, pp. 304 f. Al-Rāzī elsewhere, however, upholds the Ash'arī doctrine of the absolute divine freedom of will *'lā yajibu 'alā Allāhi shayy'*. See F. al-Rāzī, *Muḥaṣṣil afkār al-mutaqadimīn wa'l-muta'khirīn mina al-'ulamā' wa'l-ḥukamā' wa'l-mutaklimīn*, ed. with an Introduction by T. Sā'īd (Beirut, 1984), p. 295.

4. See Ibn Sīnā, *Fī ithbāt*, pp. 48 ff and *al-Ishārāt wa'l-tanbihāt*, with a Commentary by Nasīr al-Dīn al-Ṭūsī, ed. S. Dunya (Cairo, 1958), pp. 365 ff. Ḥ. 'Āṣī holds that we neither have indications that Ibn Sīnā intended to interpret the whole Qur'an, nor any evidence that he produced more, now lost, Qur'anic commentaries. At any rate, 'Āṣī continues, Ibn Sīnā selected for his meagre interpretations passages that could be subordinated to his philosophical system. Ḥ. 'Āṣī, *al-Tafsīr al-Qur'ānī wa'l-lugha al-ṣūfiyya fī falsafa Ibn Sīnā* (Beirut, 1983), pp. 24 f. Curiously, however, 'Āṣī includes a two-page manuscript found at the University Library in Istanbul (no. 1458, n.d.) attributing it to Ibn Sīnā and claiming it is a variation of Ibn Sīnā's *ta'wīl* of *āyat al-nūr*, see 'Āṣī, *al-Tafsīr al-qur'ānī*, pp. 84 ff. Though discussing its authenticity is beyond the scope of this essay, a few observations must be made. Not only does the interpretation in the manuscript exhibit no subordination to any philosophical system, but the most salient characteristics of Ibn Sīnā's thought are also absent. Furthermore, the lack of any methodological or structural relationship between the manuscript and Ibn Sīnā's well-authenticated works makes attributing it to him highly problematic. The same source from this manuscript appears in the bibliography of P. Heath's monograph *Allegory and Philosophy in Avicenna (Ibn Sina)* (Philadelphia, PA, 1992), p. 219 without any comment.

5. The exceptional sense of drama in this phrase will be demonstrated below.

6. Al-Rāzī, *Mafātīḥ al-ghayb*, 23: 222 ff. In his article 'Ghazālī and "Religionswissenschaft"', *EA*, 14 (1991), p. 25 Landolt gives the English rendering of this *ḥadīth*. Given the ambiguity of the pronoun '*hu*' in *baṣaruhu* in terms of whether it refers to the human vision or that of God, I have opted to quoting it in Arabic following al-Rāzī's version, al-Rāzī, *Mafātīḥ al-ghayb*, 23: 230 f.

7. Al-Rāzī, *Mafātīḥ al-ghayb*, 23: 223.

8. These two distinctly different approaches appear to be related to the religious orientations of the addressees. He refers to this relationship quite clearly when he concludes his negation of attributing the literal meanings of light to God by stating that it is intended to refute the Manicheans' belief that God is the Greatest Light, and when he introduces the second part of his discussion by saying: 'As for the corporealists who acknowledge the authenticity of the Qur'an …', al-Rāzī, *Mafātīḥ al-ghayb*, 23: 223.

9. Al-Rāzī, *Mafātīḥ al-ghayb*, 23: 224. In his well-known mystical treatise *Mishkāt al-anwār*, ed. with an Introduction by A. 'Affīfī (Cairo, 1964), pp. 39 ff., al-Ghazālī dedicates a major section to the interpretation of *āyat al-nūr*.

10. Al-Rāzī, *Mafātīḥ al-ghayb*, 23: 224 ff. Al-Rāzī's citation of al-Ghazālī is not without his own additions and occasional interferences. Upon reaching the stage of identifying the term

*nūr* with the Divine word, al-Rāzī's argument takes a different route to that of al-Ghazālī's in his *Mishkāt*. Al-Rāzī alerts the reader of this different course by stating 'We say' (*fa-naqūl*). Here he holds that since the rational faculty is susceptible to error, it needs the guidance of the divine Word. Consequently, al-Rāzī concludes, the Qur'an is more deserving to be called *nūr* than the human intellect. Al-Rāzī, *Mafātīḥ al-ghayb*, 23: 228. Al-Ghazālī, on the other hand, does not acknowledge the possibility of such an error '*al-ʿaql munazzah ʿanhā*', al-Ghazālī, *Mishkāt*, p. 47. When the term *nūr* is finally identified with Essential Existence, Who 'overflows' the light of existence on His creation, al-Rāzī adds also the overflowing of knowledge: 'He has caused (*afāḍa*) the lights of knowledge before which [His creation] was in the darkness of ignorance to overflow,' al-Rāzī, *Mafātīḥ al-ghayb*, 23: 229. This addition is absent in the *Mishkāt*, and it is amalgamated with al-Ghazālī's statements without alerting the reader to such an addition. See al-Ghazālī, *Mishkāt*, pp. 54–56. On the reasons behind the rational powers being more deserving to be called *nūr* than sense-perception al-Rāzī's additional thirteen proofs, to al-Ghazālī's seven, are announced at the outset. However some of these additional proofs are either partial repetitions of al-Ghazālī's seven or a paraphrasing of some of them. Consider the following examples, al-Rāzī's proof no. 17 is derived from al-Ghazālī's proof no. 7; al-Rāzī's proof no. 19 is a paraphrase of al-Ghazālī's proof no. 6; al-Rāzī's proof no. 20 is a summary of al-Ghazālī proof no. 7. See al-Rāzī, *Mafātīḥ al-ghayb*, 23: 227–228; al-Ghazālī, *Mishkāt*, pp. 46–47.

11. Al-Rāzī, *Mafātīḥ al-ghayb*, 23: 230: *wa-yakūnu khafa'ūh li-shiddati ẓuhūra*.

12. Landolt, 'Ghazālī', p. 59; al-Ghazālī, *Mishkāt*, p. 14. Despite these supra-rational doctrines of being, al-Rāzī does not include any reference to al-Ghazālī's interpretation of Q. 28: 88. This interpretation constitutes what Landolt calls al-Ghazālī's 'theologically shocking doctrine of the divine "face"'. Landolt, 'Ghazālī', pp. 60 ff. In the first section of the *Mishkāt* al-Ghazālī reads the verse as meaning that nothing exists except God and His face, for everything has always been perishing and shall always be eternally perishing (*azalān wa-abadān*), al-Ghazālī, *Mishkāt*, p. 56.

13. Al-Ghazālī is aware of his inconsistency. Thus he seems to find it imperative to give an explanation. He insists that his statements are only seemingly contradictory and cannot be understood by the intellectually incompetent or the immature (*al-qāṣirin*) whose intellectual deficiencies called for this seeming contradiction. Al-Ghazālī, *Mishkāt*, p. 64.

14. Al-Rāzī follows his phrase '*kalām mustaṭāb*' by '*wa-lakin*' before giving his verdict on al-Ghazālī's statements. This *wa-lakin* raises the question of al-Rāzī's real judgement, as Landolt rightly observes. Landolt, 'Ghazālī', p. 66 n. 159. The phrase *wa-lakin* which is followed by *baʿda al-taḥqīq* may have been intended to convey the following: 'Even though al-Ghazālī's statements appear heretical, after a close reading, however, we can conclude that they actually amount to no more than saying … .' Al-Rāzī, *Mafātīḥ al-ghayb*, 23: 230.

15. In his argument for the authenticity of the third section of the *Mishkāt*, Landolt attributes al-Rāzī's inclusion of the Veils Tradition in the 'middle' of his *tafsīr* of *āyat al-nūr* to the possibility that al-Rāzī was using a different recension of the *Mishkāt* to the standard version we have today. Landolt, 'Ghazālī', p. 65.

16. The notion of the observable contingency of creation and the consequent inference (*istidlāl*) of its need of an affecting agent who is essentially existent occupies a central place in al-Rāzī's thought. See, for example, his *Kitāb al-arbaʿīn*, pp. 86 ff. However, he does not refer here to any sort of veils.

17. Landolt, 'Ghazālī', p. 67.

18. Al-Rāzī, *Mafātīḥ al-ghayb*, 23, pp. 230 f.

19. Al-Rāzī, *Asās al-taqdīs*, pp. 129 ff.

20. Al-Rāzī, *Mafātīḥ al-ghayb*, 23, p. 231; al-Ghazālī, *Mishkāt*, p. 84.

21. Al-Rāzī, *Asās al-taqdīs*, pp. 132 f.

22. Ibid., p. 133; al-Ghazālī, *Mishkāt*, pp. 9 f.

23. Landolt, 'Ghazālī', p. 62.

24. This ontological view obviously extends beyond al-Rāzī's and al-Ghazālī's *Ash'arism*. Note how al-Ghazālī begins stating this view in the *Mishkāt* by saying '*aqūl walā ubālī* ...', al-Ghazālī, *Mishkāt*, p. 54.

25. M. Marmura, 'Avicenna's Psychological Proof of Prophecy', *JNES*, 21 (1962), p. 52.

26. Marmura, 'Avicenna: On the Proof of Prophecies', p. 116. This entire article (pp. 112–121) is an English rendering of Ibn Sīnā's treatise *Fī ithbāt al-nubuwwāt* by Prof. Marmura.

27. For Marmura's discussion of Ibn Sīnā's views on the essential autonomy of certain rational human souls, which possess the prophetic faculty (*al-quwwa al-nabawiyya*), see Ibn Sīnā, *Fī ithbāt*, pp. 32 f.

28. Ibn Sīnā, *al-Ishārāt*, p. 366.

29. Ibn Sīnā interprets *al-nār* in *Fī ithbāt*, p. 52 as the Universal Intellect, and as being the Active Intellect in *al-Ishārāt*, p. 376.

30. S. H. Nasr, *Three Muslim Sages: Avicenna - Suhrawardī - Ibn 'Arabi* (Delmar, NY, 1964) p. 65.

31. Ibn Sīnā, *Fī ithbāt*, p. 51. See also Ibn Sīnā, *al-Najāt*, p. 168.

32. 'By *kindled from a blessed tree, an olive,* is meant the cogitative power, which stands as subject and material for the intellectual acts in the same way that oil stands as subject and material for the lamp.' M. Marmura's translation of Ibn Sīnā's commentary on *āyat al-nūr*. See Marmura, 'On the Proof of Prophecies', p. 117.

33. This autonomy is strongly implied by Ibn Sīnā in his *Shifā'*: 'This potentiality [to acquire knowledge] may be so intense in some people that they do not require much contact with the Active Intellect, it is as though their capability to acquire the second intelligibles is innate ... this condition of the material intellect must be called the holy intellect, it is some kind of an angelic intellect.' F. Rahman, ed., *Avicenna's De Anima: Being the Psychological Part of Kitāb al-Shifā'* (London, 1959), p. 240.

34. Ibn Sīnā explains in his *al-Ishārāt* that the Qur'anic similitude of *al-kawkab al-durrī* refers to the human soul which possesses the gift of intuition (*ḥads*). It is the prophetic soul that possesses the holy intellect (*al-'aql al-qudsī*). Such a soul receives the middle terms and second intelligibles instantaneously without any cogitative (*fikriyya*) or estimative efforts, and with or without wish and longing (*bi-shawq aw bi-ghayri shawq*). To Ibn Sīnā, the human who has the highest level of intuition has the highest level of the human rational faculties, and represents the highest level of prophecy. See Ibn Sīnā, *al-Ishārāt*, pp. 365 ff.; Ibn Sīnā, *al-Najāt*, pp. 167 f. The expression the 'highest heights' is derived from Ibn Sīnā's Ode on the Soul in which he describes the summit of the soul's intellectual ascent. F. Khulayf, *Falāsifat al-Islām Ibn Sīnā, al-Ghazālī, Fakhr al-Dīn al-Rāzī* (Alexandria, 1976), p. 151.

35. Ibn Sīnā, *al-Ishārāt*, p. 841. See also al-Ṭūsī's commentary on the arrival of *al-'ārif.* It is also imperative to see the *namaṭ al-tāsi'* of Ibn Sīnā's *al-Ishārāt*, pp. 789–852. This section

describes the characteristics of *al-ʿārif*, who can also be a prophet and the journey of his soul to spiritual perfection.

36. Ibn Sīnā, *al-Najāt*, p. 293; Ibn Sīnā, *al-Ishārāt*, p. 764.

37. Ibid., pp. 64 f.

38. Ibid., p. 841. Al-Ṭūsī is commenting on Ibn Sīnā's extremely condensed statement on the station of arrival of *al-ʿārif*.

39. Ironically a host of commentators do not seem to reach beyond the 'surface' of Ibn Sīnā's *taʾwīl*. Consider, for instance, A. Muhammad who states, in his commentary on al-Shahristānī's work *al-Milal wa'l-niḥal*, that in Ibn Sīnā's attempt to reconcile philosophy with religion, he has 'forced' a philosophical interpretation on *āyat al-nūr* where his strenuous efforts 'reduced' the *āya* to mere symbols of Platonic and Aristotelian terms which deleted its clarity. See Abu'l-Fatḥ al-Shahrastānī, *al-Milal wa'l-niḥal*, ed. with commentary by A. Muhammad (Beirut, 1990), p. 643. 'Āṣī joins in by observing that Ibn Sīnā's *taʾwīl* of the Qur'anic passages represents his 'loyalty' to philosophy and manifests his belief that revelation is, in reality, symbols to truths unattainable to the common believers. Consequently Ibn Sīnā forcibly 'pressures' the Qur'anic verse into accommodating his philosophical views. 'Āṣī, *al-Tafsīr al-qurʾānī*, pp. 25 f. Khulayf's comments are no different. He holds that Ibn Sīnā has adopted a curious (*gharīb*) approach in his *taʾwīl* of *āyat al-nūr* forcing an Aristotelian philosophical 'garb' on the *āya* that the Qur'anic parables are transformed into symbols and corroborating evidence to this philosophy. Khulayf, *Falāsifat al-Islām*, pp. 175 f.

40. In his discussion of the differences between symbol and allegory, Corbin states 'The symbol is not an artificially constructed *sign*; it flowers in the soul spontaneously to announce something that cannot be expressed otherwise; it is the *unique* of the thing symbolised as of a reality that thus becomes transparent to the soul, but which in itself transcends all expression', Corbin, *The Visionary Recital*, p. 30.

41. Heath, *Allegory and Philosophy*, p. 36.

42. Al-Rāzī, *Mafātīḥ al-ghayb*, 23, p. 229.

43. Note Ibn Sīnā's and al-Ṭūsī's observations on this restoration of the universe (*al-wujūd*) to its perfect 'Origin', through the ascent of the rational human soul in Ibn Sīnā's *al-Ishārāt*, pp. 671 f.

# Part Two

# Medieval Islam

# 15

# Reading al-Ghazālī: The Case of Psychology

*Peter Heath*

Al-Ghazālī's use of ambiguous language and shifting terminology in his various writings has long been noticed by his readers. Professor Richard Frank in his two recent studies on al-Ghazālī – *Creation and the Cosmic System: al-Ghazālī and Avicenna*, and *al-Ghazālī and the Ash'arite School* – raises this issue several times.[1] In his first study, for instance, Frank notes 'that the diversity of his work and the ambivalence with which he [al-Ghazālī] frequently expresses himself make it difficult to come to a clear judgement' regarding certain of al-Ghazālī's theological positions. (p. 9) In his second book, Frank remarks that

> Al-Ghazālī is an extremely complex figure. His writings differ greatly from one another in form and rhetoric as well as in topic and focus and in trying to trace the course of his thought and discern his commitments, one has sometimes the impression of attempting to follow the movements of a chameleon, so varied are the hues and postures he assumes from one place to another. (p. 3)

Frank is in good company when he expresses these sentiments; they are shared by most serious readers of al-Ghazālī, including some early, very prominent ones. Ibn Ṭufayl, for example, states in *Ḥayy ibn Yaqẓān* that 'al-Ghazālī's works, because he preached to the masses, bind in one place and loose in another. First he says a thing is rank faithlessness, then he says it's permissible.' (p. 15, Goodman tr. p. 101) A few lines later, Ibn Ṭufayl continues: 'Most of what he said was in the form of hints and intimations, of value to those who hear them only after they have found the truth by their own insight or to someone innately gifted and primed to understand.' (p. 16, tr. p. 101)[2]

Ibn Rushd was more irritated with al-Ghazālī's equivocations. At one point in his *Faṣl al-maqāl*, he complains that the latter 'adhered to no one doctrine in his books but was an Ash'arī with the Ash'arīs, a Sufi with the Sufis and a philosopher with the philosophers'. (p. 52, Hourani tr. p. 61)[3]

The ambiguities of al-Ghazālī's style and use of terminology have influenced how some scholars have interpreted him. For example, in his *Encyclopedia of Islam* article on the thinker, Montgomery Watt stated:

> But there is no reason for thinking that, even if al-Ghazālī had different levels of teaching for different audiences, he ever in the 'higher' levels directly contradicted what he maintained in the lower levels. (*EI2*, 2:1039)

This judgement affected Watt's acceptance of the authenticity of certain texts or parts of texts, causing him to reject sections of *Mīzān al-'amal* and *Mishkāt al-anwār*.[4] In similar vein, Lazarus-Yafeh contends in her *Studies on al-Ghazzālī* that:

> It seems to me therefore that those books attributed to al-Ghazzālī in which the philosophical terminology appears should be considered as not having been written by him. It may well be that this linguistic approach leaves less room for any other approach to the matter. While al-Ghazzālī could always have been expressing new ideas, contradicting those he had outlined before (and even his authentic books abound in contradictions and changes of opinion), it seems hardly conceivable that al-Ghazzālī would change his linguistic habits entirely while dealing with the same religious issues as before, even if he did express new and contradictory ideas. (p. 254)

On this basis, she concludes that: 'There is no ground for the assumption that al-Ghazzālī had a secret doctrine, which totally contradicted his widely known traditional ones.' (p. 362)[5]

Beyond the significant issues of verbal ambiguity and hermeneutic framework, other serious obstacles confront the student of al-Ghazālī. One crucial problem is the state of our knowledge of his texts. We lack critical editions of most of his works, major and minor, and there has been little focused philological study of the textual and manuscript history of individual works. As a result, the authenticity of several treatises attributed to him, and even of portions of texts otherwise accepted as authentic, is still a matter of uncertainty. This situation makes it difficult to determine whether ideas or doctrines in such texts should be attributed to him.[6]

A second problem is the breadth of al-Ghazālī's learning and the large extent to which he synthesises the intellectual traditions on which he relied. That he had an intimate knowledge and mastery of the major intellectual currents of this time poses a two-fold problem for anyone who wishes to interpret his thought. First, one must be well acquainted with the major currents of Muslim law, theology, philosophy, mysticism and Ismailism with which al-Ghazālī was working. This is a challenging prerequisite. Secondly, in relying on the studies of previous scholars, one must evaluate their (and one's own) statements on the basis of their own intellectual background and hermeneutical assumptions. Because al-Ghazālī is multifaceted, theologians tend to see the theologian in him, students of mysticism seize upon the mystical strain of his thought, while, alternatively, experts in Islamic philosophy tend to focus only on the book that al-Ghazālī wrote against philosophy, the *Tahāfut al-falāsifa* ('Incoherence of the Philosophers') and to ignore his – so-called – non-philosophical writings. In short, scholars emphasise those dimensions of al-Ghazālī's thought that accord with their own training and interests. One might suppose that one solution to this problem would be to limit oneself to studying only al-Ghazālī's texts. However, because he appropriates so much from the diverse intellectual currents of his day, this is perhaps the worst way to proceed. All this makes using the writings of previous students of al-Ghazālī almost as complicated as understanding the thinker's own works.

Despite al-Ghazālī's ambiguous and shifting terminology, scholars have been able to penetrate the veils of his rhetorical style in order to discern the underlying doctrines. Ibn Rushd certainly knew his al-Ghazālī extremely well. And recently, a number of scholars, such as Richard Frank, Hermann Landolt, Marie Bernhard and Herbert Davidson have succeeded in clarifying our general picture of the sources for, and the nature of, the overall outlines and the particular details of al-Ghazālī's thought.[7] This process of pinning down al-Ghazālī is not yet complete. Nevertheless, it already promises to transform the standard image of the thinker.

Traditionally, al-Ghazālī has been viewed as the theologian who struck the death-knell of Islamic philosophy in the East with his work *Tahāfut al-falāsifa*, while he simultaneously discounted the value of speculative theology in favour of the mystical intuition and the meditative practices of Sufism. It is now becoming clear that al-Ghazālī was a major agent in reducing the disciplinary distance between philosophy and theology by introducing philosophical doctrines (mainly based on Ibn Sīnā's system) into Islamic theology (and from there into Sufism as well – but that is another story). If there has long been a consensus that this was the case in regard to logic, it is becoming increasingly clear that it was also the case in regard to many metaphysical and cosmological doctrines as well. There is no doubt that al-Ghazālī used peripatetic philosophy for his own purposes, and in ways of which the philosophers did not approve. Nevertheless, careful examination of his overall relationship with philosophy reveals how influential it was on the general structure of his theological thought. Rather than a figure who discarded philosophy and speculative theology to focus on Sufism, one now confronts a major theological thinker who was willing to bend philosophical thought, the traditional legal and theological doctrines of the schools and the rapidly developing apparatus of mystical terminology, all to serve his own specific theological vision. It is a stunningly ambitious enterprise!

It can be claimed, of course, that al-Ghazālī's immediate influence was limited.

Within a century of his death, Ibn Rushd had discounted the validity al-Ghazālī's arguments against philosophy, Fakhr al-Dīn al-Rāzī (d. 606/1209) had bypassed him in theology to confront Ibn Sīnā directly, and mainstream representatives of *taṣawwuf* proceeded along their own paths, apparently being little influenced directly by al-Ghazālī's writings, his individual example or his intellectual achievement. Yet despite these individual achievements, al-Ghazālī's writings, particularly his *Iḥyā' 'ulūm al-dīn* ('Revivification of the Religious Sciences') have exerted immense influence over the centuries.[8] To this day, he remains the most widely read pre-modern Muslim theologian and religious thinker. Nonetheless, the precise history of al-Ghazālī's 'reception' over the centuries remains to be charted so that we can attain a more calibrated picture of when and how the thinker influenced later generations.

In the course of this ongoing re-evaluation of al-Ghazālī's thought and historical influence, it is useful to confront head-on the issue of his rhetoric, rather than viewing it as a side issue that one complains of in the course of attempting to delineate specific doctrines or theological positions. Instead of making al-Ghazālī's shifting use of language and terminology an ancillary if annoying problem, we must make it a specific subject of investigation. If al-Ghazālī is a chameleon in his use of language, we should first inquire into why this is the case and then attempt to delineate his theory and practice of language – in other words, we must elucidate his rhetorical method. To do this in a complete and systematic way is not possible here. Such a task would require extensive, detailed examination of many of al-Ghazālī's numerous works. Nevertheless, it is possible to set forth some general principles that can be used to facilitate the process of understanding why al-Ghazālī writes as he does, why he is an 'Ash'arī with the Ash'arīs, a Sufi with the Sufis, and a philosopher with the philosophers'. Then, we offer as a case study of how to read him a discussion of his varied presentations of his psychological theory.

In reading al-Ghazālī, the first principle to be aware of is that of overlap and economy of texts. We cannot read only one of al-Ghazālī's texts and believe that we therefore understand his ideas. Rather, his method of writing demands that we consult as many texts as seem relevant. For instance, we must be aware – as far as it is possible – of al-Ghazālī's sources. One may read his work on ethics, *Mīzān al-'amal* ('The Criterion of Action') by itself, but this provides no guarantee of truly understanding what he intends to accomplish in it. To attain a better degree of comprehension, one must first consult his summary of the doctrines of the philosophers, *Maqāṣid al-falāsifa* ('Intentions of the Philosophers') to see how he understands their ethical theory there, and then, preferably go back to compare his version of it with those of Ibn Sīnā and al-Fārābī directly. Thereafter one must also compare the *Mīzān* with al-Rāghib al-Iṣfahānī's (d. between 501–503/1108 or 1109) *al-Dharī'a ilā makārim al-sharī'a* ('The Expedient Path to the Noble Characteristics of the *sharī'a*'), since al-Ghazālī appropriates significant sections of this work more or less word-for-word.[9] In both cases, we must notice what exactly al-Ghazālī takes from his predecessors and what he ignores. At this point, we have caught up with al-Ghazālī on a textual basis and can thus concentrate on how he uses his sources and why he alters them or keeps them the same.

Such a procedure is not part of examining the thinker's rhetoric *per se*, but it is a necessary preliminary to it. Nor does this process end here. Al-Ghazālī often incorporates versions of his earlier works into his later ones. Hence, we must look forward in the sequence of his compositions as well as back. For example, it is easier to appreciate what he is doing and not doing in the *Mīzān* when one compares it to the first book of the *Iḥyā' ʿulūm al-dīn*, the 'Book of Knowledge' (*Kitab al-ʿilm*), since he incorporates sections of *Mīzān al-ʿamal* into this treatise. Likewise, it will be difficult to appreciate what he is doing in the 'Book of Knowledge' unless one has completed a survey of earlier (and later) works whose subject matter overlaps with its subject matter.

We must use this principle of overlap not only in regard to al-Ghazālī's text but also with his use of terminology. For example, when we examine his presentation of levels of psychological apprehension (external senses, internal senses, the stages of the intellect) in various works: *Maqāṣid al-falāsifa, Mīzān al-ʿamal, Kitāb al-ʿilm* from the *Iḥyā', al-Munqidh min al-ḍalāl* ('Deliverance from Error'), and *Mishkāt al-anwār* ('Niche of Lights') – to restrict ourselves only to writings whose authenticity is not doubted – we discover that in each of these texts al-Ghazālī changes his presentation either in regard to technical terminology or in matters of emphasis. Yet he is not being inconsistent here. Rather what we face are diverse presentations whose point of focus varies because they are directed at different audiences, or because of their particular relation to the specific topic under discussion. As we shall see, the doctrines themselves tend to remain the same even if their presentations differ.

What then are these doctrines? Or more precisely, how can we discern a unified doctrine beneath varying presentations. Here we come to a second principle or method of analysing al-Ghazālī's use of language and terminology. The underlying structure tends to be philosophical that is derived from *falsāfa*. Nevertheless, he simultaneously strives to conceal this fact by changing the way he presents his discussion, although less in terms of general conceptual structures or distinctions than in regard to technical terminology, points of emphasis and strategies of presentation. For example, the best way – or, rather, the only way – to understand al-Ghazālī's theory of knowledge is to read it against Ibn Sīnā's. If one does not know Ibn Sīnā, one will not understand al-Ghazālī. Conversely, however, we must not mistake this appropriation of conceptual structures with a complete congruence of doctrine. Al-Ghazālī, no matter how much influenced by the philosophers, is not a crypto-philosopher. He is a theologian whose doctrinal differences with the philosophers are in certain areas very real. Nonetheless, since he finds their conceptual categories and intellectual structures more sophisticated than those of his fellow *mutakallimūn*, he tends to adopt them. For instance, in the *Kitāb al-ʿilm*, he introduces the two categories of *ʿilm al-muʿāmala* and *ʿilm al-mukāshafa* (the knowledge of practical religion and of revelation, respectively). What he intends by these terms must be worked out in context, yet such a process is hastened when one realises that the distinction is based on that of the *al-ʿilm al-ʿamalī* and *al-ʿilm al-naẓarī* (practical and theoretical knowledge) dichotomy developed by philosophers since Aristotle.

The third principle to be aware of is that al-Ghazālī is acutely aware of the philosophical theory of logic-based poetics. In fact, Ibn Rushd is angry with al-Ghazālī in his *Faṣl al-maqāl* precisely because he knows that al-Ghazālī is well versed in this theory but violates its principles (in Ibn Rushd's opinion) to use it for his own purposes.

This theory is based on the elitist concept that different levels of discourse are appropriate to use to convince different classes of people, according to their dominant levels of psychological apperception. For those in whom sense-based imagination dominates, i.e. the common folk, one uses concrete images and stories (poetic mimesis) or the emotive evocations of rhetoric. For those convinced by logical arguments based on pre-accepted precepts, suppositions, teachings or accepted opinions (*ẓann*), one uses dialectic arguments. Such is the appropriate discourse for theologians, who rather than exploring the nature of God freed of preconceptions, for example, already assume His existence and aspects of His agency and then proceed from there. Finally, there are individuals who accept only rational arguments based on logical demonstration. This group, the philosophers, only use this level of discourse with one another, since they realise that only they can comprehend it and work on its level. Ibn Rushd's annoyance with al-Ghazālī stems from the fact that the latter is willing openly to submit the rationalist positions of philosophy to the dialectic standards of theological discourse in order to discredit them. To Ibn Rushd's horror, even though al-Ghazālī is intelligent enough to know the rules of proper discourse, he violates and twists them to suit his own purposes.[10]

Ibn Rushd is correct in this evaluation. Al-Ghazālī does understand this philosophical theory of levels of rhetorical discourse and he uses it constantly in his writings as he directs different levels of argumentation at different groups. This can be seen again in 'The Book of Knowledge' section of the *Iḥyāʾ*. When analysed, the conceptual structure of this work's notion of knowledge is philosophical, yet al-Ghazālī only gets to this point at the book's end. Most of its earlier sections consist of pronouncements regarding the purpose of knowledge cited from the Qur'an, *ḥadīth* and the traditions of the Companions or early theological leaders of the community. In other words, al-Ghazālī first relies on the sensual images of the imagination or the pre-accepted authority of religious belief to make his point; only thereafter does he briefly intimate his real, philosophically-structured views on the matter.

Understanding al-Ghazālī's use of this method of discourse does much to clarify and explain his seeming ambiguities, inconsistencies or shifts in position. A final example can illustrate this point. Ibn Rushd notes in *Faṣl al-maqāl* that al-Ghazālī mentions five levels of existence in his *Fayṣal al-tafriqa bayn al-Islām wa'l-zandaqa* ('The Decisive Criterion Separating Islam and Atheism'): essential existence (*dhātī*), sensual (*ḥissī*), imaginative (*khayālī*), intellectual (*'aqlī*) and figurative (*shabahī*). This is a full listing in a work directed at intelligent and sophisticated theologians. In a much later work, however, *Iljām al-'awwam 'an 'ilm al-kalām* ('Restraining Commoners from the Science of Theology', pp. 5–9), al-Ghazālī mentions only four levels of possible existence: as objects existing externally (*fi'l-khārij*), in minds (*al-adhhān*), in linguistic expression (*lisān*) or in written expression (*kitāba*). (*Iljām*, 280 in *Majmū'a; Faṣl al-maqāl*, pp. 46–47, n. 3.)

Is al-Ghazālī being inconsistent in these two presentations of the levels of existence? Has he changed his mind with the passage of years? I do not believe this to be the case. In the first work, al-Ghazālī addresses himself to intellectuals, hence his categories are based on a conceptual structure taken from *falsāfa*; in the second work, however, he addresses non-specialists, i.e. a general audience of *'ulamā'* and others on whose intellectual sophistication he cannot rely. Hence, he changes his first category from the abstract term 'essential' to the concrete term 'object existing externally', he collapses the intellectual levels of intellect and imagination into the less sophisticated and more general term 'mental', and he replaces the term 'figurative' (*shabahī*) with the more concrete 'linguistic' and 'written'. Despite these changes in terminology and presentation, al-Ghazālī has not altered his intellectual position, he has simply modified it to fit his audience's level of understanding.

Once the three principles outlined above are understood – that is, the principle of textual overlap and the necessity of intertextual comparison, the fact that philosophical conceptual structures underlie much of the theologian's thought and the fact that al-Ghazālī employs different levels and forms of address for different groups – then most of the theologian's supposed ambiguities and inconsistencies are clarified. This perhaps, does not make him easier to read, since one cannot rely on what he says in any one text without reference to other texts. Nevertheless, in the long run, appreciating these principles does lessen the frustration with which one confronts his writings. As with any thinker, one must understand why al-Ghazālī writes as he does. Only then can we understand what he is trying to say.

## II

For an example of how to use these principles in interpreting al-Ghazālī's thought, let us turn to the case of psychological epistemology. In al-Ghazālī's view, this is an area of concern which includes significant aspects of epistemology. Al-Ghazālī had various sources to draw on for his psychological theory, stemming from theology, philosophy, and mysticism. Understanding his use of these sources in this area should help to begin the process of solving some of the larger problems I have mentioned above. Let us begin examining al-Ghazālī's psychological theory by comparing two late works whose authenticity scholars have not doubted.

In *al-Munqidh min al-ḍalāl* (written ca. 499–502/1106–1109), al-Ghazālī states that 'humans, in their original condition (*aṣl al-fiṭra*), are created in blank simplicity (*khāliyy*an *sādhij*an). (p. 51, tr., p. 96) They then derive knowledge of the worlds around them according to four stages (*aṭwār*) of perception (*idrāk*):

1. The five external senses *(al-ḥawass)*, touch, sight, smell, hearing, taste.
2. Discernment (*al-tamyīz*), a faculty beyond (*zā'ida*) the senses that appears around the age of seven.
3. The intellect (*al-'aql*), through which humans 'perceive the necessary, the possible, the impossible, and things not found in the previous stage'. (p. 53, tr., p. 97)
4. A stage beyond the intellect in which 'another eye is opened, by which humans see the hidden and what will take place in the future, and other things from which the intellect is as far removed as the power of discernment is from the perception of intelligibles and the power of sensation is from the things perceived'. (p. 53, tr., p. 97)

Among the potential capabilities of this last faculty are 'prophetic perceptions' (*mudrikāt al-nubuwwa*). Al-Ghazālī proceeds to assert that 'men endowed with intellect have no way of attaining such knowledge by intellectual resources alone. The properties of prophecy ... can be perceived only by fruitional experience (*al-dhawq*) as a result of following the way of Sufism'. (p. 54, tr., p. 99)

Let us compare al-Ghazālī's statements in *Mishkāt al-anwār* (written ca. 499/1106; pp. 76–77, tr., 143–49). Here he delineates five faculties, or 'spirits' (*arwāḥ*), of perception.

1. The sensory spirit (*al-rūḥ al-ḥassās*), the domain of the five senses.
2. The imaginative spirit (*al-rūḥ al-khayālī*), the 'recorder of the information conveyed by the senses. It keeps that information filed and ready at hand, so as to present it to the intellectual spirit above it, when the information is called for'. (p. 76, tr., p. 144)
3. The intellectual spirit (*al-rūḥ al-'aqlī*), whose domain is 'ideas beyond the spheres of sense and imagination ... such as axioms of necessary and universal application'. (p. 77, tr., p. 145)
4. The discursive spirit (*al-rūḥ al-fikrī*), which 'takes the data of pure reason and combines them, arranges them as premises, and deduces from them informing knowledge'. (p. 77, tr., pp. 145–146)
5. The sanctified, prophetic spirit (*al-rūḥ al-qudsī al-nabawī*), which is 'the special

characteristic of prophets and some saints. By it the tablets of the unseen world (*lawaʿiḥ al-ghayb*) and the statutes of the Hereafter (*aḥkām al-ākhira*) become manifest, together with the totality (*jumla*) of the sciences of the celestial (*malakūt al-samāwāt*) and terrestrial realms, no rather, of the divine sciences (*al-maʿārif al-rabbāniyya*) that the intellectual and discursive souls are unable to comprehend'. (p. 77, my tr.)

Again al-Ghazālī chastises those who rely on rational perception alone, saying 'O you who cling to the world of the intellect, it is not far-fetched that there is another stage beyond the intellect in which appears that which does not appear in the intellect; just as it is not far-fetched that the intellect represents a stage beyond discernment and the senses in which are wonders and marvels that the senses and discernment cannot grasp'. (pp. 77–78, my tr.) [11]

There is some variance of terminology between these two descriptions, but it is fair to say that al-Ghazālī is describing three basic levels of perception: one based on the senses and sensual images (the five senses, imagination and some aspects of discernment); one stemming from the intellect working with intelligibles (some aspects of discernment, intellectual first principles and discursive reasoning), and a level that one can argue appears to be supra-rational (the sanctified prophetic soul), a level of perception whose entry proceeds from Sufi practices from which fruitional experience (*dhawq*) and divine unveiling (*kashf*) appear. And it also appears clear that al-Ghazālī awards pride of place to the experiential perception of mysticism over the discursive reasoning of philosophy. One might conclude, therefore, that mysticism is the main source for his apparent category of supra-rational perception.

This impression, however, is erroneous. It is incorrect to conclude that al-Ghazālī considered *kashf* to be a supra-rational stage of perception or that he was anti-rationalist in his psychology or in his epistemology. On the contrary, he adopted his psychology, including this apparently supra-rational element, almost totally from the rationalist psychologies of the Muslim peripatetic philosophers, al-Fārābī and Ibn Sīnā.

Al-Ghazālī's whole relationship with philosophy must be evaluated carefully. The purpose of the *Tahāfut* is not to promote anti-rationalism; it is rather to demonstrate that there is no contradiction between the tenets of Islam and 'true philosophy'. The book, he states, sets 'forth the doctrines of the philosophers as those doctrines really are. This will serve the purpose of making it clear to the hide-bound atheists of our day that every piece of knowledge, whether ancient or modern, is really a corroboration of the faith in God and in the Last Day. The conflict between faith and knowledge is related only to the details superadded to these fundamental principles.' (p. 39, tr., p. 3)

The *Tahāfut*, in fact, is not a diatribe against philosophy in itself, but rather against philosophers, who are 'a class of men who believe in their superiority to others because of their greater intelligence and insight. They have abandoned all the religious duties Islam imposes on its followers. They laugh at the positive commandments of religion which enjoin the performance of acts of devotion, and the abstinence from forbidden things. Not only do they overstep the limits prescribed by it, but they renounce the Faith altogether, by having indulged in diverse speculations.' (p. 37, tr., p. 1)

The heresy of the philosophers has two causes: first, 'an uncritical acceptance ... of whatever one hears from others or sees all around', and second, 'theoretical inquiries which are the outcome of stumbling – skeptically, misguidedly, and stupidly – upon fanciful notions'. (pp. 37–38, tr., pp. 1–2; compare his discussion of the philosophers in the *Munqidh*).

Al-Ghazālī is therefore not so much opposing philosophy as the unfounded – that is, the irrational – speculations of certain philosophers. He presents a critique of philosophy in the *Tahāfut* not on the basis of its rational approach but rather because philosophers have used their supposed rationalism to make claims that cannot be rationally demonstrated. To this end, he does not need to prove that these beliefs are incorrect to make his case, he only has to confirm that their ideas cannot be logically proven to be true. This is what he sets out to do.

In the *Tahāfut*, he says nothing about the psychological theories of the philosophers, an understandable situation given that he does not oppose their ideas in this area. In fact, the best place to attain a comprehensive picture of al-Ghazālī's understanding of psychology is to consult his own summary of the tenets of contemporary philosophy: his book on 'The Aims of the Philosophers' (*Maqāṣid al-falāsifa*; written between 484/1091–1092 and 487/1094; see pp. 346–349, 356–363). The faculties of human perception, he states there, are as follows:

1. The five external senses (*al-ḥawāss al-ẓāhira*, as above)
2. The five internal senses (*al-ḥawāss al-bāṭina*)
   a. common sense (*al-ḥiss al-mushtarak*)
   b. the representative faculty (*al-quwwa al-mutaṣawwira*)
   c. the imaginative faculty (*al-quwwa al-mutakhayyila*)
   d. estimation (*al-quwwa al-wahmiyya*)
   e. recollection (*al-quwwa al-dhākira*)
3. The intellect (*al-ʿaql*), whose levels include:
   a. the practical intellect (*al-quwwa al-ʿamaliyya*), which uses intellectual knowledge (such as the knowledge that oppression is evil) to guide actions
   b. the theoretical intellect (*al-quwwa al-naẓariyya*), which itself has various stages (*maratib*)
   i. the material intellect (*al-ʿaql al-hayūlānī*), completely potential in nature
   ii. the habitual intellect (*al-ʿaql bi'l-malaka*)
   iii. the intellect in actuality (*al-ʿaql bi'l-fiʿl*)

iv. the acquired intellect (*al-ʿaql al-mustafād*)

The divine agency that moves the intellect from complete potentiality to complete actualisation is the Active Intelligence *(al-ʿaql al-faʿʿāl)*. This agent emits constant emanations of intelligibles onto human souls. First, it actualises the soul to receive universal concepts and thus initiates the process of its attaining 'the knowledge of the realities of things as they truly are' (*al-ʿilm bi-ḥaqāʾiq al-ashyāʾ ʿalā mā hiya ʿalayhā*). Among the kinds of knowledge (*maʿārif*) that pertain to the nature of the intellectual faculty are 'the knowledge of God and His angels, and His books, and His messengers, and how existence issues from Him, and similar kinds of knowledge'. (p. 374) Furthermore, the more developed the abilities of individuals are to receive divine emanation, the more their intellects can perceive, beginning with dreams requiring interpretation, then veridical dreams, then saintly inspiration from the invisible world (*ʿālam al-ghayb*) and ending with prophetic revelation. Each of the latter two levels of knowledge can give recipients control over natural phenomena, so that they become able to enact saintly or prophetic miracles.

All humans are naturally attracted to the happiness that ensues from intellectual perception. Nevertheless, many people become preoccupied with sensual pleasures and the concerns of the body and thus turn away from it. As al-Ghazālī states, 'their longing and desire (*al-shawq waʾl-raghba*) are not strengthened in this, now, because of the lack of experiencing it (*li-ʿadam dhawqihi*)'. (p. 374)

The conceptual structure of this psychological model is pure Ibn Sīnā; yet the challenge that al-Ghazālī faces as a theologian and spiritual leader differs from that of the philosopher. Ibn Sīnā was content to accept his psychology with its explicit assumption of intellectual elitism intact. Only a few individuals were endowed with and could develop intellectual superiority; such was the nature of things. Al-Ghazālī could not accept a situation in which most people are condemned to remain unable to participate in spiritual realities. Starting from a presumption that most individuals are potentially able to experience religious 'realities', his problem is how to strengthen their longing and desire in order to increase their attention to and happiness derived from participation in the divine intellectual world. This, in turn, becomes an issue of knowledge and action (*al-ʿilm waʾl-ʿamal*), a duality of concerns that becomes the major theme of al-Ghazālī's subsequent writings, most significantly in his masterpiece, *Iḥyāʾ ʿulūm al-dīn*. This predicament therefore explains the configuration of his discussion of the intellect (*al-ʿaql*) at the end of the 'Book of Knowledge', the first book of the *Iḥyāʾ*. There he explains the division of the theoretical intellect in exactly the same terms that he used in *Maqāṣid al-falāsifa* (material, habitual, actual, acquired). Although he admits that it is a given that human beings differ in regard to the power of their intellects, he still praises the utility of the intellect and criticises those who discount its importance. Simultaneously, he also asserts that disparity among humans may 'also be the result of differences in the mastery of knowledge which reveals the evils of the other appetites' (p. 87, tr., p. 232), continuing that if such disparity is 'due to knowledge, then we shall call this knowledge intellect'. (p. 88, tr., p. 233) Providing knowledge that assists its possessors to resist the temptations of the lower appetites then becomes the subject of the rest of the *Iḥyā'*.

Accordingly, the acquisition of true knowledge rather than the fruitless display of intellectual cleverness becomes the true purpose of intellectual and spiritual pursuit. As a result, philosophers must be weaned away from the false elements of their doctrines (this is the task of the *Tahāfut al-falāsifa*); religion must be understood correctly (this is the purpose of such works as *Jawāhir al-Qur'ān* ('Jewels of the Qur'an'), *al-Munqidh min al-ḍalāl* and *Mishkāt al-anwār*); and new, more effective methods of activity must be advocated to direct individuals towards more fruitful paths of action. Developing these methods of activity becomes the goal of first the *Mīzān al-ʿamal* and subsequently, and more elaborately, the *Iḥyā' ʿulūm al-dīn*.

Al-Ghazālī soon decided, it appears, that Sufi religious exercises were the most efficient way of promoting individual participation in the divine realm. Nonetheless, close examination of his psychological theories reveals that it would be incorrect to assume that he would claim that participation in this realm was supra-rational or that it differed in any significant way from that understood by the philosophers. The advantage of Sufism was its efficacy: it moved individuals directly into this realm without subjecting them to the complex, and potentially heretical, tangles of false doctrine in which philosophical speculation might involve them. The knowledge attained from the correct pursuit of either path, however, has, for al-Ghazālī, the same source. The knowledge that the philosophers claimed came through the medium of the acquired intellect was that which al-Ghazālī decided to call inspiration (*ilhām*) and unveiling (*kashf*), it was the 'light', (according to his famous statement in the *Munqidh*) that God had 'cast into his heart'.

This point can be illustrated by a story from *Mīzān al-ʿamal*. (pp. 225–226) Al-Ghazālī tells how artists from Greece (Rūm) and China were equally famous for their skills in sculpting and painting. One day a king ordered a group of artists from each country to decorate one side of a porch (*ṣuffa*) to see whose artistic skills were the greatest. From the middle of this porch the king lowered a curtain, so that members of each group could not see what the other was doing. The Greeks gathered innumerable unusual colours of paint and set to work. The Chinese, however, used their time to shine and polish their side of the porch. At last, the Greeks announced that they had finished, and the Chinese said the same. In surprise, the audience asked the Chinese how that could be so, since they had not used any paint. When the curtain was raised, however, the Chinese artists' side was so polished that all the hues and patterns of the Greek side were reflected in its brilliant mirror-like surface.

This story, states al-Ghazālī, shows how the methods of the philosophers and the mystics relate. One group creates a replica of divine knowledge through the use of discursive reasoning; the other polishes their souls, until the replica shines directly into them by means of divine emanation. Al-Ghazālī ends the story by saying that as long as each method is properly followed, each representation will be correct. Furthermore, he argues that to value one medium of knowledge over the other would be a mistake. However, for most people, it is easier to achieve success following the path of practical spiritual exercise that Sufism advocates, and hence this method is preferable.

Al-Ghazālī's psychology is a mixture of the ideas of al-Fārābī and Ibn Sīnā. He does not mention the latter's concept of *ḥads* (intuition) in the *Maqāṣid*, for example, although he appears to rely on a version of it for his own theory of inspiration. Nevertheless, examination of his psychology reveals the large debt that al-Ghazālī owes to the philosophical tradition in this area. His modifications involve changes of terminology rather than any drastic restructuring of conceptual framework. Moreover, since al-Ghazālī's terminology shifts in his many writings, one can only understand his psychology, and how to interpret his various presentations of it, by first having recourse to its source, which in this case is philosophy, and then tracing his elaboration of the subject through his successive works.

## III

May we conclude from this survey of al-Ghazālī's psychological terminology that he was a crypto-philosopher? Such an interpretation would be erroneous. First and foremost, I would argue, we should consider al-Ghazālī to be a theologian, although a theologian of a very special kind. Al-Ghazālī considered himself to be master of all the disciplines of the religious sciences of his day, which meant that he could employ them as he saw fit. He worked within the delimitations of Shāfiʿī *fiqh* in works of *uṣūl*, such as the *al-Mustaṣfā*.[12] Similarly, Richard Frank has demonstrated how he stayed within the boundaries of Ashʿarī *kalām* in his works devoted specifically to *kalām*, while he ignored them when elucidating his own systems of thought. In other words, reforming or revising the tenets of *fiqh* or *kalām* were not part of his programme of religious revival. He did not want to reform what his fellow Muslims believed, but rather how they did so. He opposed specifically both the *fuqahā*ʾ and the *mutakallimūn* less than he did the whole ethos of *taqlīd* (thoughtless imitation) among the *ʿulamāʾ* in general. As countermeasure, he argued – in various ways in different works –– for a personal relationship toward religious belief based on Sufi noetics as interpreted through the conceptual prism of philosophical psychology and epistemology.

Although this summary of al-Ghazālī's method can serve as a working hypothesis, we must finally recognise that we are still in the initial stages of the process of piecing together the full range of ways that al-Ghazālī attempted to carry out his programme. Beyond the crucial tasks of establishing critical editions of his texts, we must also investigate in greater detail how exactly he used the sources that he so greatly borrowed from, al-Rāghib al-Iṣfahānī's *al-Dharīʿa* in the case of *Mīzān al-ʿamal*, for example, or Abū Ṭālib al-Makkī's *Qūt al-qulūb* in the case of the *Iḥyāʾ*.[13] Before the mysteries of al-Ghazālī's thought can be solved, we must further and more specifically delineate his use of terminology, elucidate the nature of his appropriation of texts, and analyse his use of style and rhetoric. We still have a long way to go.

## Appendix: Chronology of al-Ghazālī's Cited Works

1. *Maqāsid al-falāsifa* (ca. 486/1094)
2. *Tahāfut al-falāsifa (488/1095)*
3. *Mīzān al-ʿamal* (ca. 488–1095)
4. *Iḥyāʾ ʿulūm al-dīn* (ca. 489–490/1096–1097)
5. *Jawāhir al-Qurʾān* (ca. 499/1106)
6. *Mishkāt al-anwār* (ca. 499/1106)
7. *Al-Munqidh min al-ḍalāl* (499–502/1106–1109)

## Notes

1. Richard Frank, *Creation and the Cosmic System: al-Ghazālī and Avicenna* (Heidelberg, 1992), and R. Frank, *al-Ghazālī and the Ashʿarite School* (Durham and London, 1994).

2. Aḥmad Amīn, ed., *Ḥayy ibn Yaqẓān li-Ibn Sīnā, Ibn Ṭufayl, waʾl-Suhrawardī* (Cairo, 1952), tr. Lenn E. Goodman, *Ibn Tufayl's Hayy ibn Yaqzān: A Philosophical Tale* (New York, 1972).

3. Ibn Rushd, *Faṣl al-maqāl fī mā bayn al-ḥikma waʾl-sharīʿa min al-ittiṣāl*, ed. Muḥammad ʿAmmāra (Cairo, 1972), tr. George F. Hourani, *Averroes on the Harmony of Religion and Philosophy* (London, 1976).

4. For example, W. Montgomery Watt, 'A Forgery in al-Ghazālī's *Mishkāt*?', *JRAS* (1949), pp. 5–22; and 'The Authenticity of Works Attributed to al-Ghazālī', *JRAS* (1952), pp. 25–45, where he discusses the *Mīzān al-ʿamal*. See also the responses to these articles in Hermann Landolt, 'Ghazālī and "Religionswissenschaft": Some Notes on the *Mishkāt al-anwār*', *AS/EA*, 45 (1991), pp. 19–78, and Mohammed Ahmed Sherif, *Ghazali's Theory of Virtue* (Albany, NY, 1975), respectively.

5. Hava Lazarus-Yafeh, *Studies in al-Ghazzali* (Jerusalem, 1975); see also, Lazarus-Yafeh, 'Philosophical Terms as a Criterion of Authenticity in the Writings of al-Ghazālī', *SI*, 25 (1966), pp. 111–121.

6. Current bibliographies of al-Ghazālī's works are Maurice Bouyges, *Essai de chronologie des œuvres d'al-Ghazālī (Algazel)*, ed. M. Allard (Beirut, 1959); ʿAbd al-Raḥmān Badawī, *Muʾallifāt al-Ghazālī* (Cairo, 1961), 2 vols., and George F. Hourani, 'A Revised Chronology of al-Ghazali's Writings', *JAOS*, 104 (1984), pp. 289–302. We have yet to move beyond these useful general works to examine the manuscript traditions of individual texts.

7. For the studies by Frank and Landolt, see notes 1 and 4, respectively. Marie Bernand, 'al-Ghazālī: Artisan de la fusion des systèmes de pensée', *JA*, 278 (1991), pp. 223–254; and Herbert Davidson, *Al-Fārābī, Avicenna, and Averroes on Intellect: Their Cosmologies, Theories of the Active Intellect, and Theories of Human Intellect* (New York and Oxford, 1992), which also discusses al-Ghazālī.

8. The editions of works by al-Ghazālī referred in this study are as follows: *Iḥyā' 'ulūm al-dīn* (Beirut, n.d.), 5 vols.; *Jawāhir al-Qur'ān*, ed. Muḥammad Rashīd Riḍā al-Qayyānī (Beirut, 1985), Muḥammad Abul Qasem, tr., *The Jewels of the Qur'an: al-Ghazālī's Theory* (London and New York, 1983); *Maqāṣid al-falāsifa*, ed. Sulaymān Dunyā (Cairo, 1961); *Mishkāt al-anwār*, ed. Abu'l-'Alā' 'Afīfī (Cairo, 1963), W. H. T. Gairdner, tr., *al-Ghazzali's Mishkāt al-anwār ('The Niche of Lights')*, Royal Asiatic Society Monographs, 19 (London, 1924; repr. Lahore, 1952); *Mīzān al-'amal*, ed. Sulaymān Dunyā (Cairo, 1964); *al-Munqidh min al-ḍalāl*, ed. Muḥammad Muḥammad Jābir (Cairo, n.d.), Richard J. McCarthy, tr., *Freedom and Fulfillment: An Annotated Translation of al-Ghazālī's al-Munqidh min al-Dalal and Other Relevant Works of al-Ghazālī* (Boston, MA, 1980); *Tahāfut al-falāsifa*, ed. Maurice Bouyges; rev. Majid Fakhri (4th ed., Beirut, 1990), S. A. Kamali, tr., *al-Ghazālī's Tahāfut al-Falāsifah (Incoherence of the Philosophers)* (Lahore, 1958). See now the superior *al-Ghazālī: The Incoherence of the Philosophers: A Parallel English-Arabic Text*, translated, introduced and annotated by Michael E. Marmura (Provo, UT, 1997).

9. Al-Rāghib al-Iṣfahānī, *al-Dharī'a ilā makārim al-sharī'a*, ed. Abu'l-Yazīd al-'Ajamī (Cairo, 1985); for an initial discussion of the influence of this work on al-Ghazālī's *Mīzān*, see Wilferd Madelung, 'Ar-Ragib al-Iṣfahānī und die Ethik al-Gazālīs', in his collection of articles, *Religious Schools and Sects in Medieval Islam* (London, 1985).

10. For overviews of the theory of philosophical rhetoric, see Peter Heath, *Allegory and Philosophy in Avicenna (Ibn Sīnā), including a Translation of the* Mi'rāj-nāma (*The Book of Muhammad's Ascent to Heaven*) (Philadelphia, PA, 1992) and Deborah L. Black, *Logic and Aristotle's Rhetoric and Poetics in Medieval Arabic Philosophy* (Leiden, New York, Cologne, 1990).

11. Notice the similarity of this argument to his famous sceptical 'proof' in the first section of *al-Munqidh min al-ḍalāl*.

12. Al-Ghazālī, *al-Mustaṣfā min al-uṣūl* (Beirut, 1995), 2 vols.

13. Abū Ṭālib al-Makkī, *Qūt al-qulūb* (Cairo, 1980), 2 vols.

# 16

# Stories of Aḥmad al-Ghazālī 'Playing the Witness' in Tabrīz (Shams-i Tabrīzī's Interest in *shāhid-bāzī*)

*Nasrollah Pourjavady*

## Introduction

In the history of Sufism, the personality of Aḥmad al-Ghazālī has three special qualities that are worthy of investigation and distinguish him from other Sufi masters of his age. First, he was an expert and eloquent preacher. Second, he was one of the exponents of the practice of 'playing the *shāhid*' by choosing a beautiful young person to contemplate (*naẓar-bāzī*). Here the term *shāhid* will be used to mean a young person (almost inevitably a young man) singled out by his beauty and grace to be the object of a Sufi's affection, intimacy and contemplation.[1] Thirdly, Aḥmad al-Ghazālī was constantly travelling, mainly between the cities of Western Iran where he apparently had followers who called him periodically to guide them. Upon his arrival in a city he would call a public assembly and preach in sessions that were famous in his own lifetime. In fact, our knowledge about the travels of Aḥmad al-Ghazālī and his residence in these cities comes from the extant accounts of his public meetings and his practice of 'playing the witness' (*shāhid-bāzī*).

Tabrīz was one of the cities in which Aḥmad al-Ghazālī had a *shāhid*. According to several narratives, Aḥmad al-Ghazālī went there especially to visit his *shāhid* and there is evidence that he stayed there at least once for a considerable period of time. For example, the introduction of one manuscript of al-Ghazālī's *Sawāniḥ* provides a clue that it was written in Tabrīz in 508/1114–1115.[2] There are narratives of his journeys to Tabrīz in Shams-i Tabrīzī's 'Discourses' (*Maqālāt-i Shams-i Tabrīzī*). In this article, I will analyse the narratives given by this Sufi master.[3]

## Part I
## The Narratives of Shams-i Tabrīzī

### *Shams' acquaintance with Aḥmad al-Ghazālī*

Shams al-Dīn Muḥammad Tabrīzī is a famous figure in the history of Iranian Sufism. However, the details of his life and his relationships with other Sufi masters remain obscure. Some sources claim that at the beginning of his spiritual training his master was Shaykh Abū Bakr Sallah Bāf-i Tabrīzī.[4] Others say that his master was Bābā Kamāl Khujandī, or that he was a disciple of Rukn al-Dīn Sajāsī.[5] If it is correct that Shams-i Tabrīzī was a disciple of Rukn al-Dīn, then his initiation was in the line derived from Aḥmad al-Ghazālī. It would be separated from al-Ghazālī by only two mediating masters, since Rukn al-Dīn was a disciple of Quṭb al-Dīn Abharī who was a disciple of Abū al-Najīb Suhrawardī who took an oath of initiation from the hands of Aḥmad al-Ghazālī. Whether or not this claim is accurate, we can safely say that Shams-i Tabrīzī recognised Aḥmad al-Ghazālī as one of the great Sufi masters.

Several times in the *Maqālāt*, Shams-i Tabrīzī recalls incidents related to Aḥmad al-Ghazālī directly or indirectly. Five stories and two quatrains are directly related.[6] In general, they reveal that Shams-i Tabrīzī regarded Aḥmad al-Ghazālī as a Sufi master, one who performed miracles, who was aware of the thoughts of others (in a way similar to Abū Saʿīd b. Abī al-Khayr), a man of enlightened conscience and a lover of human beauty (*shāhid-bāz*). In one of these incidents, Shams-i Tabrīzī recalls Aḥmad al-Ghazālī's relationship with his famous brother, Abū Ḥāmid al-Ghazālī.[7]

### *Aḥmad al-Ghazālī and his brother, Abū Ḥāmid Muḥammad al-Ghazālī*

But what Shams is mainly concerned with are the intellectual and spiritual achievements (*kamālāt*) of Aḥmad and Muḥammad (more commonly known as Abū Ḥāmid). Shams calls the former 'the Sulṭān of all in the intuitive knowledge (*maʿrifa*) of God' while the latter was without peer in the scholarly traditions (*ʿulūm-i ẓāhirī*) of Islam and wrote many famous books. However, we know that Aḥmad, in his youth, also studied the scholarly traditions; when his brother, Abū Ḥāmid, experienced a spiritual crisis (*inqilāb-i rūḥī*) in Baghdad and abandoned his teaching position at the Niẓāmiyya Madrasa, Aḥmad took over his teaching commitments for a time. Aḥmad also wrote books in Arabic on *kalām* and Qur'anic commentary (*tafsīr*). He produced an abridgement of his brother's famous *Iḥyā' ʿulūm al-dīn* ('Revival of the Religious Sciences'), which he entitled *Lubāb al-iḥyā'* ('Essence of the Revival').[8] However, Shams-i Tabrīzī apparently was unaware of these scholarly achievements and believed that Aḥmad al-Ghazālī had 'never studied these exoteric disciplines of knowledge'[9] and that he was 'unlettered' (*ummī*).

However, Shams-i Tabrīzī mentions the titles of two books that he imagined were written by Abū Ḥāmid al-Ghazālī: *al-Dhakhīra* ('The Treasury') and *al-Lubāb* ('The Heart'). In the catalogue of the works of Abū Ḥāmid al-Ghazālī, there is no reference to *al-Dhakhīra*, and so the editor of *Maqālāt-i Shams*, Muḥammad 'Alī Muwaḥḥid, conjectures that Shams might have been referring to a work by Aḥmad called *al-Dhakhīra fī 'ilm al-baṣīra* ('The Treasury on the Science of Perspicacity'). Similarly, he suggests that the citation of *al-Lubāb* was meant to refer either to Abū Ḥāmid al-Ghazālī's *Lubāb al-naẓar* ('The Heart of Analysis') or Aḥmad al-Ghazālī's text *Lubāb al-iḥyā'* ('The Heart of the Revival').[10] Ascribing Aḥmad al-Ghazālī's Arabic work to his brother is not uncommon in older sources. As regards Shams-i Tabrīzī's accounts, it is important to note that he had no knowledge of Aḥmad al-Ghazālī's Persian works, such as his famous *Sawāniḥ*. Nevertheless, he was aware of the fact that Aḥmad al-Ghazālī composed poetry, since he quotes one of Aḥmad al-Ghazālī's quatrains.

The story about the two al-Ghazālī brothers relates how some scholars who were jealous of Aḥmad told Muḥammad that Aḥmad was teaching various religious sciences although they claimed 'he actually knows nothing of any of them'.[11] So, Abū Ḥāmid al-Ghazālī decided to test his brother. He gave a *faqīh* copies of 'The Treasury' and 'The Heart', and sent him to Aḥmad. The *faqīh* was asked to carefully observe all of Aḥmad's reactions. The jurist went to the *khānqāh* of Aḥmad al-Ghazālī where he found Aḥmad al-Ghazālī seated happily. When from afar Aḥmad al-Ghazālī saw his brother's emissary, he said something that made the jurist tremble: 'You have brought books for me!' He explained that he was unlettered (*ummī*) and asked the jurist to read out some passages from the books. At this point, Shams-i Tabrīzī interrupts the account to explain that to be 'unlettered' means one does not know how to read or write: '*Ummī* means that one does not know the use of letters.' However, it may well be that such 'unlettered' people have intuitive knowledge and the eyes of their hearts can see. In contrast to the *ummī* 'unlettered' person is the *'āmī* or 'common' person. Such a person, says Shams-i Tabrīzī, has a heart whose vision is blocked even if they are proficient in many disciplines of outward learning. In this case they are lacking in religious knowledge. Thus Abū Ḥāmid al-Ghazālī's emissary, even though he was a jurist and scholar of religious science, lacked true knowledge of religious matters.

The jurist read some passages for Aḥmad al-Ghazālī. The latter then asked the jurist to inscribe this startling quatrain as an epigram in the introduction to the book:

In search of love's treasure my body is ruined
Over the flames of passion my heart is roasted
What have I to do with reading a 'Treasury' or 'Heart'
Since I have the healing liquor of my lover's lip[12]

Following this account, Shams-i Tabrīzī presents four more short stories.[13] Each of them is meant to demonstrate the spiritual status of Aḥmad al-Ghazālī and his miraculous powers. Three of them are specifically about Aḥmad al-Ghazālī's practice of 'playing the witness' with young men whom he loved. All apparently take place in Tabrīz.

### *An Obstacle Confronts Aḥmad al-Ghazālī*

The first story is about a spiritual problem or obstacle that confronted Aḥmad al-Ghazālī and which he struggled unsuccessfully to overcome. He endured his burden until 'a voice called out to him or an inspiration inhabited his heart that said, "This obstacle can be solved only by being present before Khwāja Sangān (or Sinjān)". He set off immediately. On the day he arrived, an assembly of passionate devotional music (*samā'*) was being held. During the musical sitting, his inner obstacle was lifted.'[14]

The point of the story is that Aḥmad al-Ghazālī, like Shams himself, did not believe in the efficacy of extended periods of (*chilla-nashīnī*) solitary worship and meditation. This, especially for a period of forty days (*arba'īn*), had become customary in some Sufi communities. But Shams-i Tabrīzī explicitly declared this practice to be in error: 'The Prophet Muḥammad never sat in isolated retreat.' In his opinion it was a form of illegitimate religious innovation (*bid'a*). According to Shams-i Tabrīzī, Aḥmad al-Ghazālī confirmed his opinion, because he 'never sat in isolated retreat'. However, Shams-i Tabrīzī emphasised that Aḥmad al-Ghazālī practised many ascetic and contemplative disciplines (*riyāḍa*) in secret. He claimed that 'anything that others relate of his ascetic practices is mere fancy or outright lie'.[15]

Where was Aḥmad al-Ghazālī living when this spiritual crisis confronted him? Shams-i Tabrīzī does not tell us until the end of the narrative, when he simply adds that 'he headed back to Tabrīz'.[16]

### *Aḥmad al-Ghazālī's return to Tabrīz to meet his 'Witness'* (shāhid)

According to Shams, Aḥmad al-Ghazālī was an exponent of 'meditation through gazing at an exemplary beauty' (*naẓar-bāz*) and loved a young man (*shāhid-dust*) and this practice was public knowledge in Tabrīz. Shams-i Tabrīzī was intimately familiar with *naẓar-bāzī* and rather than finding fault further justifies it. However, although Shams-i Tabrīzī accepts Aḥmad al-Ghazālī's 'playing the witness', he does not feel quite comfortable when he talks about it saying, 'It is not good to speak of that'.

There was good reason for Shams-i Tabrīzī to feel uneasy speaking of Aḥmad al-Ghazālī's erotic love-mysticism. Despite the fact that this passionate love for his male lover was 'Platonic' and chaste (*'afīf*), ordinary people saw it as a kind of bodily lust (*shahwānī*). Some Sufis did not consider this form of 'playing the witness' a virtuous practice permitted by religious law and even Abū Ḥāmid al-Ghazālī, who was a staunch defender of Sufi practices, did not consider 'sitting with young men, listening to devotional music with them, becoming intimate with them and speaking at length with them' proper Sufi behaviour. He held that anyone who engaged in such practices 'did not deserve the appellation of Sufi'.[17] More vituperative opposition also came from those who were against Sufis altogether. For this reason, Shams-i Tabrīzī and people like him, who believed the witness game to be a justified Sufi practice, are nonetheless unable to discuss it openly without awkwardness.

Even so, Shams tells us quite plainly that Aḥmad al-Ghazālī 'inclined to loving beautiful faces'. But he was careful to say, 'If you opened up his heart you could not find any trace of lust inside him.' This special kind of gazing the early Sufis called *naẓar-i 'ibrat*, 'a gaze of transcendental contemplation' as did Aḥmad al-Ghazālī himself.[18] Shams alluded to this when he said, 'Those things that he [Aḥmad al-Ghazālī] saw others didn't see'.

Shams said, 'On the swiftness of Aḥmad al-Ghazālī's return, the people of Tabrīz believed that he came solely for the sake of seeing a young man he had chosen as his beloved (*shāhid*).' At the end of the account, he indicates that they were right; Tabrīz was famous for having very handsome young men. Five centuries later Amīn Aḥmad Rāzī described the city in this way: 'Its men are of exceptional physical beauty and possess graceful manners. There are many fine young men of surpassing beauty and charm there with whom to keep company.' And he quoted a verse to illustrate how the young men of Tabrīz were so beautiful that all the young women fell madly in love with them:

Tabrīz is full of beautiful boys
All arrayed in clothes of finest silk.
The boys all have the beauty of Joseph
Forcing girls to learn from Zulaykhā's ilk.[19]

The rest of Shams-i Tabrīzī's story shows that ordinary Tabrīzīs did not like Aḥmad al-Ghazālī's love-play with his *shāhid* going on in their city and tried to keep him away. When they heard he was returning, they sent an old woman to wait for him by the roadside to tell him that his *shāhid* had died. On hearing this false report, Aḥmad al-Ghazālī made the caravan he was travelling with stop and bowed his head to meditate for a long time. At dawn the next day, he pronounced, 'This woman is not telling the truth! I have scanned all the souls that have left their bodies and passed from this world, from the time of Adam until the present day. I have looked over each of them individually, and the soul of that dear young man is not among them.'[20] He let the caravan continue until it reached Tabrīz: 'When he arrived in Tavriz [Tabrīz], the whole population of the city was disturbed.'

*Aḥmad al-Ghazālī's 'playing the witness' in the bathhouse and his foot not being burned by the coals*

Shams-i Tabrīzī then explains the feelings of the people of Tabrīz towards Aḥmad al-Ghazālī and his 'playing the witness'. People's opinions differed on this matter, thinking sometimes that his action was free of lust, but at other times denouncing him. One man vacillated so much that he championed Aḥmad al-Ghazālī a hundred times and denounced him a hundred times. In the end people went to the local ruler, the *Atābeg*. At this point, Shams-i Tabrīzī begins a new story which describes a miracle that happened at the hand of Aḥmad al-Ghazālī:

> One day, the people of Tabrīz sent a message to Atābeg, saying 'If you don't believe what we are reporting, come see for yourself with your own eyes! Come, look into the bathhouse through a peephole and see him [Aḥmad al-Ghazālī] lying down with one foot extended alongside that young man as we have told you, while a censer full of hot coals burns with fragrant aloe and ambergris'. Atābeg came and peered through the peephole into the bathhouse. What he saw made him recoil in total rejection. At that moment, the shaykh [Aḥmad al-Ghazālī] said in a loud voice, 'You puny Turk, look closely!' Atābeg took another look, and saw that his other leg was laid across the censer burning with coals so that his foot was in the midst of the hot embers. Atābeg was stunned and begged forgiveness. In wonder, he left the scene.[21]

The scene that Shams-i Tabrīzī depicts for us is a strange one, quite different from another story recounted by Ibn Jawzī about Aḥmad al-Ghazālī's erotic mysticism. According to Ibn Jawzī, one day Aḥmad al-Ghazālī was sitting with a beautiful young man, with a rose in one hand. One moment he would gaze at the youth and the next at the rose.[22] But here he stretches out his leg alongside the youth, while the heady fragrance of aloe and ambergris fills the air. His foot, lowered into the hot coals, does not burn, demonstrating that he is not a captive to the flames of lust but has already conquered this internal fire.

*Aḥmad al-Ghazālī's disciple who professed faith in him and then rejected him*

The Atābeg's vacillation is one example of the reaction of the people of Tabrīz. Another example is that of a scholar, a renowned teacher learned in many arts. He had become a devoted disciple of Aḥmad al-Ghazālī. However, the behaviour of Aḥmad al-Ghazālī with his beloved 'witness' (or perhaps his behaviour with yet a different young man) troubled and bewildered him. The scholar's confusion and his succumbing to the temptation of doubt comprises a narrative about the proper behaviour of a disciple in recognising and honouring a spiritual teacher, even when in the throes of a spiritual test. Aḥmad al-Ghazālī tested the sincerity of this learned scholar through 'playing the witness'.

The *Maqālāt-i Shams* has several different references to this incident. Reading them in sequence allows us to reconstruct the whole story. At the end of the story of the Atābeg, Shams-i Tabrīzī makes a decontextualised reference to the scholar: 'That scholar, who was learned in several disciplines and a respected teacher and who had become a disciple of his [Aḥmad al-Ghazālī's], began to believe in him after the miracle of the pulpit (*minbar*) rising into the air.'[23] Here, Shams-i Tabrīzī refers to another miracle when, at the end of a sermon (*wa'iẓ*) in the congregational mosque, the pulpit rose up at Aḥmad al-Ghazālī's command and remained suspended in the air. In another passage of his *Maqālāt*, Shams-i Tabrīzī refers to this as one of his miracles. They also include placing his foot in the fire and discovering that the old woman was lying about the death of his young 'witness'.

In this passage Shams says, 'From among his miracles is that, when he commanded planks of wood [the pulpit] to move, the planks would be set in motion. At that moment the wooden pulpit was set in motion. It went down one cubit into the ground, until he said, "I'm not talking to you, O Pulpit, get back in your place!"'[24] Elsewhere in the *Maqālāt* this miracle is attributed to a different preacher by the name of Shaykh Manṣūr Hafẓa.[25] Editors of the *Maqālāt* have conjectured that this might refer to a preacher in Tabrīz named Abū Manṣūr Hafḍa (d. 571/1175–1176).[26] But this is a weak conjecture, because in this very narrative Shams-i Tabrīzī talks about the same learned scholar becoming a disciple of Aḥmad al-Ghazālī. For this reason, it is more sound to attribute the miracle of the floating pulpit to Aḥmad al-Ghazālī alone.

Let us return to the scholar. He was a teacher of the exterior (*ẓāhir*) religious disciplines and had many students, yet a strong desire to become Aḥmad al-Ghazālī's disciple was sparked in him. So strong was this that he would always accompany and serve the master, following his horse around the city with the master's saddlecloth on his shoulder. His extreme humility and abasement before his master provoked some of the scholar's students and fellow dignitaries to censure him. But he paid no attention.

> Despite his great social status, he always trailed behind his master. He had a hundred students, all of them learned in many scholarly disciplines. A group of these noble people began to blame the scholar for his attachment to the master. He replied to them, 'By God, the Creator of us all, if you knew the power of even a single hair of his head the way that God has made me aware of this, you would grab the saddlecloth from my hand the way you grab worldly positions from each other and feel jealous of each other for these positions!' Thus in complete faith, he would follow the retinue of the master.[27]

Despite the apparent firmness of his belief in Aḥmad al-Ghazālī, the learned scholar had to be put to the test. In this context, the subject matter of 'playing the witness' occurs again. Once Aḥmad al-Ghazālī was riding on a horse, while the scholar ran behind carrying the saddlecloth on his shoulder. Suddenly the scholar noticed that the master was paying no attention to him or to any of the others in his retinue. Another Sufi master passed by, greeting Aḥmad al-Ghazālī with '*al-Salāmu 'alaykum*' but the master paid him no attention. However, when a good-looking young man passed down the road, Aḥmad al-Ghazālī greeted him warmly and began following the young man and gazing at him.

At this point, the scholar became ensnared by the temptation of doubt and was in turmoil. At times, he would try to justify the behaviour of the master in order to keep his faith in him as firm as it had been before. But at other times he was so overwhelmed by doubt that he found that he could no longer believe in his master. The text of the *Maqālāt* describes this scene and the scholar's struggle with this temptation in three separate places. In one passage it relates:

> With that young man holding onto the master's stirrups (*fitrāk*), the master would whisper secrets to him and make intimate gestures to him. All the while the scholar was following along behind, lugging the saddlecloth. Ten times, he began to deny his master, saying he should drop the saddlecloth and go. After each time, he returned to his faith and thought that he would bare his head in shame and beg forgiveness for harbouring such doubts, that he would fall at the hooves of his master's horse, beseeching him for deliverance from such doubts.[28]

In another passage, the text relates:

> Though he was a distinguished scholar, he would pick up the saddlecloth and run before the master's horse. Along the way, at each moment, he would lose faith and denounce his master. He would say to himself, 'That other Sufi master came along and greeted him, but he didn't even turn to look at him. But right after that, along comes some pretty boy and the master greets him warmly! How should I not mistrust his sincerity?' Then he would repent. Again he would clutch the saddlecloth, fearing that his master might turn away from him. One moment he was a believer (*muslim*), the next an infidel (*kāfir*), and so on until he arrived at the master's house with the saddlecloth weighing on his shoulder.[29]

In a different passage, it says:

> Thus the situation developed that, on the way to his master's house, he would approve confidently of him, and then disown him several times. He would ask himself, 'Why would the master show such humble cordiality to a boy who could be the cause of lust? But then he would say, 'What harm would it be for him, since he is the very mine of anti-lust medicine, the mine of *Allāh has been forgiving your sins in what preceded and in what follow.* And he is the ocean of *Allāh exchanges their former sins for current good deeds*.'[30]

This internal struggle between sincere faith and vituperative denunciation was not concealed from the master. Indeed, it was the master himself who had deliberately created it: 'The master observed both states in his disciple, who was in his firm embrace, like a child who is made to cry one moment and to laugh the next'.[31]

In another passage, Shams expresses his opinion by putting words into the mouth of Aḥmad al-Ghazālī, saying that it is the master himself who was deliberately testing his disciple. This comes when Shams discusses how masters interact with the souls of their disciples and gives examples:

> When the master looked upon him with a caring gaze, he projected these good and wholesome thoughts onto his mind. Then, when the master turned his gaze away, the disciple fell under the shadows again and dark doubts whispered, 'Supposing that he's achieved such a lofty spiritual station, what manliness is there then in misleading people with such public behaviour and throwing them into such misgivings and into having second thoughts?' The master witnessed all of this in his disciple, saying, 'Hello! How are you feeling about me? Have you forgotten me again? Do you think that I allow you the freedom to accept me or reject me? *Day and night revolve in endless change* (Qur'an 24:44). Several times He casts down into the ocean of darkness, and several times burns down the darkness with the flame of the light of day. *Do the people think they will be left alone to say 'We believe' without ever being tried and tested?* (Qur'an 29:2). In this world, is there anything that is accepted without being tested first? Is there anything that is rejected without first being tried? As for you, if God wills, you will end up taking the right path and choosing the best option. Then you will know who and what you really are'.[32]

The scholarly disciple went home burdened by all these intellectual and existential doubts, anxieties and turmoil. All night he swung between trust and repudiation. The next day, he went to the master to ask his forgiveness:

> That next day, he went out to see his master as usual, while making the Tempter, *Iblīs*, ineffective with a thousand strategies, like saying via his conscience, 'There is no power or ability except with God'. When he reached the master's house, he saw that his master was sitting with the son of the ruler, playing chess. In a flash, he rejected his master and turned away.[33]

In this passage, Shams provides some crucial evidence about Aḥmad al-Ghazālī and his *shāhid*. This was no ordinary youth but the son of a prominent noble (*ra'īs*), probably the son of that very ruler of Tabrīz, the Atābeg, who had spied on Aḥmad al-Ghazālī in the bathhouse. Later, in another narrative, the young man is the son of the local chief of police. A further important detail is that Aḥmad Ghazālī is playing chess with his beloved 'witness'. This is a new scenario to add to other forms of 'playing the witness'. In the view of Islamic jurists (*fuqahā'*), the types of behaviour described earlier were not actually forbidden (*ḥarām*) although they were blameworthy.[34] But there is some ambiguity over playing chess. In the view of this scholarly disciple, undoubtedly learned in Islamic law, chess was not permitted especially when played with an attractive young man. He held this opinion despite the fact that in Shāfiʿī jurisprudence it is not absolutely forbidden but is seen as allowable in ordinary people, though not meritorious in the pious.[35]

After this incident, the scholar went home to bed. Whilst asleep he had a vision of the Prophet turning his face away from him which convinced him to renew his relationship with the master. The Prophet averted his face because the scholar had repudiated one rightfully empowered as his follower:

> In his dream, he saw the chosen Prophet [Muḥammad]. He meant to rush forward and greet the Prophet. But the Prophet turned his face away from him. He cried out, 'Oh Prophet of God, don't turn away from me!' The Prophet replied, 'How many times will you deny me? How many times will you denounce me?' The scholar answered, 'Oh Prophet of God, when did I ever denounce you?' He said, 'You have denounced my beloved friend [*dust*]. He comes under the saying, *each person is counted among those he loves.* He is of the believers about whom it is said, *the believers are like one person.*[36]

This exchange between the scholar and the Prophet in a dream is described differently in another passage:

> He said, 'Oh Muḥammad, why are you turning away from me?' He replied, 'You have turned away from my brother'. He pleaded, 'If I turn back to him, will you turn back towards me?' The Prophet said, 'Of course!'[37]

In his dream the scholar repented and fell in the dust before the Prophet, crying. He resolved to visit his master. The Prophet gave him a handful of nuts and raisins before he left. When the scholar awoke, he discovered he actually had the nuts and raisins with him. Picking them up, he rushed to his master's home. He imagined that they would meet face to face and that he would take the master's hand to renew his vow. The moment he arrived at the master's house, Aḥmad al-Ghazālī was in the middle of a game of chess with his beloved 'witness'. On seeing this, the scholar vowed to leave immediately and never return. Suddenly the master called out, 'Yet again? Have you no shame before the Prophet (*Sayyid*)?'

Upon hearing the master's exclamation, the scholar fell at his feet, realising that the Sufi knew all about his vision. Aḥmad al-Ghazālī then gave another demonstration of how he knew all the thoughts that passed through his disciple's mind. He ordered that a tray be brought before him. When it was brought, the scholar saw that it was the exact tray on which the Prophet had carried the nuts and raisins in his dream. He looked closer and saw it had an empty space where a handful of nuts and raisins might fit. Aḥmad al-Ghazālī said to him, 'Go on, drop the raisins onto the tray from which the Chosen Prophet took them'.[38]

*Creating a 'witness'*

This narrative of the scholarly disciple and his crisis over his faith in Aḥmad al-Ghazālī has another conclusion in one of the discourses of the *Maqālāt*. In it the name of the scholar is given as Muḥammad and it comes out that, after his experience with the tray, 'he became a real Muslim – the spiritual work of that Shaykh Muḥammad came to fruition in the company of his master'. Then Aḥmad al-Ghazālī sent him after his 'witness' on three occasions to call him to come. But each time the young man made his excuses. The reason for this is that Aḥmad al-Ghazālī, although apparently sending someone to get him, secretly did not want him to come: 'Inwardly, he [Aḥmad al-Ghazālī] was preventing him from coming although outwardly he was calling on him to come.' In the end, al-Ghazālī actually created a 'witness'. 'He said, "Now, why am I dependent on him? Let me create a witness so that you can adore him". He threw a rose into the air and it turned into a beautiful form.'[39]

*Requesting his 'witness' from the pulpit*

The last story of the *Maqālāt-i Shams*, about the witness play of Aḥmad al-Ghazālī in Tabrīz also, apparently, involves the Atābeg's son. One day, Aḥmad al-Ghazālī went to the congregational mosque. After the prayer, he climbed up the pulpit (*minbar*) to deliver a sermon (*wa'ẓ*). He was expected to recite the Qur'an, give praise to God and deliver a discourse on believing in divine unity (*tawḥīd*). But instead he recited this quatrain:

> That idol whose presence our gathering does beautify
> Is not present here, I don't know where he's dissembling
> How tall he is, how fine, like a cypress his body resembling
> Without him I'm in turmoil, as if the day of resurrection's nigh[40]

This 'idol' of beauty was the son of the Atābeg. With all the people there waiting for an inspiring sermon, he refused to go on: 'Until that young man arrives, I'm not going to speak!' The Atābeg was present and commanded people to go and bring the young man. Messengers were sent all over in search of him and found him in the bathhouse. 'He was shampooing his head in the bath. He quickly poured water over his head, cleaned himself up and left the bathhouse. They rushed him to the assembly. He was seated directly in front of the pulpit. Only then did the Master begin his sermon.'

## Part Two
## Shams-i Tabrīzī as a Player of the 'Witness Game'

This concludes Shams-i Tabrīzī's stories of how Aḥmad al-Ghazālī played the contemplative and erotic 'witness game'. We can now consider why Shams-i Tabrīzī related these stories in such detail, praised Aḥmad al-Ghazālī and criticised those who did not understand and denounced him. The conclusion is not difficult (though it might be surprising to some). Through these stories Shams expounded his own Sufi beliefs and defended the practice of contemplating God by 'playing the witness', which was integral to them. He did this by demonstrating that his authoritative guide in these practices was the famous Aḥmad al-Ghazālī. These accounts serve as a mirror apparently reflecting an image of Aḥmad al-Ghazālī behind which is a second face, that of Shams-i Tabrīzī himself.

Most contemporary scholars are strangely silent about Shams's practice of 'playing the witness'. Some, like Helmut Ritter, have even written that Shams was an opponent of such practices.[41] This notion is fundamentally flawed, since it relies on a report that was first put in circulation by the Sufi chronicler, Shams al-Dīn Aflākī, who popularised two stories about Shams-i Tabrīzī which continue to enjoy currency. But we do not know Aflākī's sources since he merely says 'It is related that' or 'Someone has said that etc'.

### *The story of Shams-i Tabrīzī and a witness-playing Sufi master*

According to one of Aflākī's stories, on a journey Shams met a Sufi shaykh 'who was sick as a result of the practice of playing the witness and gazing upon a beautiful face'. Shams asked him, 'What are you doing?' The Sufi answered, 'Beautiful faces are like mirrors. I can witness the True One reflected in them, as it is said in poetry:

> When I contemplate you with vision pure,
> Look not with lust's murk and desire's lure.
> Your beautiful face is a mirror reflecting God's beauty,
> Contemplating you I observe God's beauty, be sure!'[42]

Aflākī considered the practice of witnessing the True One reflected in the surface of sensory and sensual forms and bodies or, as Aflākī calls it, 'gazing upon a beautiful face (*tafarruj-i ṣūrat*)', a kind of personal flaw or spiritual illness. He did not like this habit among Sufis and spoke out against it. We can see this in the robust answer that Shams-i Tabrīzī is presented as giving to his fellow-traveller: 'You idiot! Why search for the image of the True One in water and clay [i.e. in the human body, which is made of clay] rather than in the heart and spirit? Why don't you search for the True One in the truth rather than in some image?' This is also, more generally, the dogma held by Sufi masters of the Mevlevī order. To establish this, they have to project it retrospectively so as to demonstrate that it was held not just by Rūmī but also by his spiritual master, Shams-i Tabrīzī. Shams-i Tabrīzī's swift response, tinged with insult, is most effective. Aflākī writes, 'The Sufi immediately bowed his head, begging forgiveness of God. With a single caring glance [from Shams-i Tabrīzī] he was guided and reached spiritual perfection. He realised his own state, and the truth (or reality) of God was revealed to him.'[43]

### *The story of Shams-i Tabrīzī and Awḥad al-Dīn al-Kirmānī*

The second of Aflākī's accounts about Shams-i Tabrīzī's opposition to playing the witness has a similar structure and moral intent. The major difference is that Shams-i Tabrīzī's opponent is not an anonymous Sufi in an unspecified place but one of the renowned Sufi masters of the age, Awḥad al-Dīn al-Kirmānī. And the setting is apparently Awḥad al-Dīn's own *khānqāh*. Just like the previous story the narrative begins with a question from Shams: 'What are you up to?' Awḥad al-Dīn gives an answer similar to that of the anonymous Sufi: 'I'm contemplating the moon reflected in a basin of water'. Again Shams's reproof is somewhat insulting: 'Unless you've got a boil on the back of your neck, why not gaze at the moon in the sky?' In the earlier narrative, Aflākī himself called 'playing the witness' a weakness or illness; here, he gives these words to Shams-i Tabrīzī. Throughout the dialogue with Awḥad al-Dīn, Shams gives him unsolicited spiritual guidance, saying 'Now go and see a doctor so that you can be cured, so that whatever you gaze upon you may see the true object of contemplation'. Awḥad al-Dīn reacts like the anonymous Sufi and he is immediately transformed, saying, 'After today, I want to become your disciple.'[44]

These two simple narratives represent a very common type of baseless story that adherents of a Sufi order usually invent about the past great masters of their order so as to establish and clarify the formal teachings of the order. Even today, such stories are created and told. Accordingly, the stories that Aflākī relates (especially the one that insults and demeans a powerful and well-respected Sufi master like Awḥad al-Dīn, who is a historical figure) make us wonder if they reflect Shams' true opinion. Instead, they may well reveal to us the mind-set of their creator and narrator. What is more, no matter how reliable they seem, they are being narrated by a third person, namely Aflākī. He claims to have heard them from yet others, without specifying whom. As evidence for the real opinions of Shams-i Tabrīzī, they pale into insignificance when compared with the many accounts that come directly from the mouth of Shams-i Tabrīzī and which so vividly reflect his opinion of Aḥmad al-Ghazālī 'playing the *shāhid*'. If Shams-i Tabrīzī were indeed an opponent of 'playing the *shāhid*' and, as depicted in Aflākī's stories, despised it and called it a 'sickness' then why is there no criticism of Aḥmad al-Ghazālī in the *Maqālāt-i Shams*? On the contrary, here Shams-i Tabrīzī praises him and justifies fully his practice of 'playing the *shāhid*'.

*Shams-i Tabrīzī's desiring a witness*

In the *Maqālāt*, Shams-i Tabrīzī refers to the practice of 'playing the *shāhid*' in contexts that go beyond the immediate discussion of Aḥmad al-Ghazālī. In one place, Shams-i Tabrīzī clearly shows his own opinion of this practice: 'Search for a *shāhid* for yourself that you may become his lover! And if you can't become completely engrossed in loving him, then find another who can turn you into a lover!'[45] This is exactly what defenders of metaphorical love (*'ishq-i majāzī*) in Sufism maintain, that to become a true lover of God one must begin by being the passionate lover of a human being.

By the term *shāhid*, did Shams mean that the man who wants to progress along the path of love for God must become the lover of a woman (conditioned, of course, by her being a woman to whom he could, within the bounds of the *sharī'a*, become intimate)? This proposition is simply naive. Throughout Persian Sufi literature, the term *shāhid* refers to a young man or an adolescent (*amrad)* whose beard is not fully grown. There is a story about Shams-i Tabrīzī desiring a beardless young man as his witness related by Shams al-Dīn Aflākī himself on the authority of 'Ārif Chalabī. The source for this is far more reliable than those for the stories about Shams-i Tabrīzī criticising Awḥad al-Dīn and the unknown Sufi. 'Ārif Chalabī derives the story from Sulṭān Valad, the son of Mawlānā Rūmī (the closest follower of Shams-i Tabrīzī).

> One day, Mawlānā Shams al-Dīn (Shams-i Tabrīzī) by way of testing and being greatly provocative, asked my father [Rūmī] for a good-looking person (*shāhid*). My father took his wife, Kirā Khātūn, by the hand and presented her to him. With her good looks and perfection, she was the beauty of her day and age, a second Sarah. As for her chastity and sinlessness, she was the Mary of her era. Shams al-Dīn said, 'She is the sister of my soul. She is not suitable. Rather, I want the graces of a delicate beautiful boy (*shāhid pisarī*) who will serve me'.[46]

Rūmī then produced his own son, Sulṭān Valad, who was as beautiful as Joseph. Mawlānā Rūmī said, 'I hope he will be suitable to satisfy your needs and serve you'. Then Shams-i Tabrīzī asked Rūmī for wine. Aflākī maintains Shams-i Tabrīzī desired neither a young man nor wine but he requested them 'only as a test' of Rūmī's forbearance and patience.[47]

*Shams-i Tabrīzī plays with a European lad*

There is another story that is linked to Shams-i Tabrīzī's 'playing the *shāhid*' similar to the one about Aḥmad al-Ghazālī. This time, the object of his affection is a young European man (*farangī*). One day after Shams-i Tabrīzī left Qunya for Damascus, Rūmī called his son, Sulṭān Valad, and ordered him, 'Go to Damascus with some companions and search for Mawlānā Shams al-Dīn. Take with you a good amount of silver and gold and pour it into the shoes of that sultan of Tabrīz and turn his blessed shoes in the direction of Rūm (Turkey). And convey my greetings to him and present him with my lover-like prostrations.'[48] Sulṭān Valad made ready as his father had ordered. Rūmī gave him detailed instructions:

> Now when, happily, you come to Damascus, there is a well-known caravansarai on the *Ṣāliḥiyya* mountain. Go straight there. You will see Mawlānā Shams al-Dīn gambling at backgammon with a beautiful Frankish boy. When at last he wins, he will take the money from the Frankish boy but when he loses the boy will slap him.[49]

The scene that Mawlānā Rūmī depicts of Shams-i Tabrīzī's 'playing the witness' is more dynamic than Shams-i Tabrīzī's description of Aḥmad al-Ghazālī and his chess game. This scene was later retold in the famous *Majālis al-'ushshāq* ('The Assemblies of Lovers'), with a slight variation. In that version Shams-i Tabrīzī's 'witness' is called 'a young Christian boy' and the game they play together is chess.[50]

What Mawlānā Rūmī foretold, of course, came true. When Sulṭān Valad and his travelling companions arrived in Damascus and came to the house on the hill, they saw exactly what Rūmī had described. They fell to the ground and performed 'the prostration of true lovers (*sajda-yi 'āshiqān*)' at his feet. At this, the lad grew frightened, thinking, 'Who is this noble person who I've been gambling with in so familiar a manner?'

Of course, Mawlānā Rūmī and his followers must explain away this famous scene of Shams-i Tabrīzī's 'playing the witness'. So, Aflākī says that according to Mawlānā Rūmī this European lad was actually one of the axial saints of the age (*quṭb*), who had not as yet recognised his own true nature. Later it would become apparent and he would grow up to be a great man, adopt the Islamic faith and become a spiritual guide. He would vow to return to the Frankish lands, to take the hand of European disciples and oversee their spiritual progress. In Europe he would achieve his true status as an axial saint. In this way, it is suggested, Shams was playing games with the young man and let himself to be slapped by him for the sake of the lad's spiritual instruction and the guidance of his soul.

### *Shams-i Tabrīzī's view of women*

In another story related by Aflākī, Rūmī tells of the famous Sufi Bāyazīd Basṭāmī, whom he depicts as playing with beardless young men (*amrad-bāz*): 'God appeared to him [Bāyazīd] in the image of a beardless young man'.[51] However, he adds, that God loved Shams-i Tabrīzī so much that he would appear to him in whatever form Shams desired, and the form he loved best was that of his wife, Kīmiyā Khātūn. Aflākī adds another naive story as illustration. Once Shams-i Tabrīzī had a quarrel with his wife and she was upset and resentful. When Rūmī went to their tent, he saw that 'Shams al-Dīn was talking gently with Kīmiyā Khātūn and touching her with his hand (*dast-bāzī*)'.[52]

In this story, Aflākī does not oppose the practice of adoring a *shāhid*. He even acknowledges that the famous early Sufi, Bāyazīd Basṭāmī, adored young men and was intimate with them. Further, Aflākī notes that Shams-i Tabrīzī himself believed that the beauty of God can be witnessed in the form of human beauty, despite his earlier claims. Only in this story, Shams-i Tabrīzī differs from Bāyazīd Basṭāmī in that Bāyazīd loved intimacy with young men while Shams-i Tabrīzī loved intimacy with a woman; to make this morally acceptable, Aflākī adds that the woman of Shams' choice was none other than his legal spouse, Kīmiyā Khātūn. This naive story lacks the polemic of Aflākī's two earlier accounts, but the claims in this story about Shams-i Tabrīzī's passionate love for and intimacy with a woman (in particular with his wife) are baseless. Aflākī himself told many other stories about Shams-i Tabrīzī which establish the contrary and show him denigrating women; in these, Shams-i Tabrīzī is presented as saying that the majority of women are incapable of experiencing a spiritual love of God and that their experience of love cannot rise above the level of sexual desire. In such instances, Aflākī depicts an obscene portrait of the lustfulness of female love. He tells another obscene story that he attributes to Shams-i Tabrīzī about the behaviour of a shaykh, named 'Alī Ḥā'irī, with the wife of the caliph.[53] Shams-i Tabrīzī in the end grows resentful of his wife and this leads to the poor woman's death.[54]

We see this same disgust for women in the discourses in the *Maqālāt*. In one place he says, 'Women are incapable of becoming Sufi masters'. To be sure, he admits that certain women achieve a degree of spiritual receptivity (*futūḥāt*) and achieve a certain spiritual status, for instance Fāṭima and 'Ā'isha (the daughter and the wife of the Prophet respectively). However, his view is that women cannot become saints and are incapable of guiding the spiritual progress of others. He is so rigid and bigoted that he says, 'If it were possible for Fāṭima and 'Ā'isha to achieve the status of spiritual master, I would stop believing in the Prophet Muḥammad!' In his opinion, women should stay at home, engaged in domestic labour: 'If God would open up the spirit of a woman, she would remain silent behind her veil, never leaving her housework and her spinning'.[55] After such statements, one cannot imagine that Shams-i Tabrīzī would chose a woman to 'play the *shāhid*' as described above.

On the one hand, we have the discourses of Shams-i Tabrīzī and the stories he tells about Aḥmad al-Ghazālī 'playing the witness' in Tabrīz. On the other hand, we have Aflākī's obscurantist, inconsistent and mutually contradictory narratives. It is evident that, for Aflākī and for members of the Mevlevī order in general, 'playing the *shāhid*' is a despicable practice, despite the fact that according to their own traditions Shams-i Tabrīzī openly and wholeheartedly engaged in it. There is contextual evidence to show that 'playing the witness' was a common and regular practice among the Sufis of Tabrīz. Like Shams-i Tabrīzī himself, poets and writers contemporaneous with him in the seventh/thirteeth century did not hesitate to speak openly and confidently on the subject even giving it an ethical justification.

## Conclusion

These seventh-century interpretations of Aḥmad al-Ghazālī's 'playing the witness' in Tabrīz, as offered by Shams-i Tabrīzī, clarify two historical points for us. The first point is about Aḥmad al-Ghazālī's biography; they show that Aḥmad al-Ghazālī travelled to Tabrīz, resided there and engaged in passionate love for a *shāhid* (or several of them) there. The second point is more specifically about the practice of 'playing the *shāhid*'; they demonstrate how the interpreter himself, Shams-i Tabrīzī (rather than the protagonist of his narratives, Aḥmad al-Ghazālī) 'played the *shāhid*'. The issue of Aḥmad al-Ghazālī 'playing the witness' comes as no surprise, for it was previously well known. Authors of *Tadhkira* literature and Sufi biographies (*tarājim*) agree on this and there are many stories about it set in other cities, including a particular story of Aḥmad al-Ghazālī practising the loving gaze with a son of Sulṭān Malikshāh, namely Sanjar, and kissing his cheek.[56] Because there are so many accounts we know that al-Ghazālī made no effort to conceal this practices. Even in the middle of a sermon, he acknowledged it openly.[57]

The narratives of Shams-i Tabrīzī place tales of Aḥmad al-Ghazālī's 'playing the witness' alongside accounts of miracles manifested at his hand. Of course, other Sufi authors attribute miracles to Aḥmad al-Ghazālī. However, linking his miracles with 'playing the witness' is particularly important to Shams-i Tabrīzī. By establishing this connection, Shams as a Sufi master wanted to emphasise that contemplative gazing at young men and passionate love for a male 'witness' was in complete accord with Islamic religious custom and Sufi spiritual practice.

But why would Shams-i Tabrīzī want to make this passionate and possibly erotic mysticism as a religiously and spiritually acceptable practice integral to Islam? This question can be answered from two different perspectives. From a rational analytical perspective, Shams and many other Iranian Sufis knew passionate love for a *shāhid* as 'metaphorical love' (*'ishq-i majāzī*) which was the first step towards arriving at the true love (*'ishq-i ḥaqīqī*). In respect of Shams-i Tabrīzī, we can say that he (like Aḥmad al-Ghazālī before him) acknowledged that love for a 'witness' was one of the many stages in the phenomenal and sensual world through which one can pass on the ascent towards true divine love. True love is a single all-pervading reality, but one that possesses many levels and stages. In all of these various stages, love is love. In other words, love spans the range of ambiguous dimensions between the absolute and the relative. In just the same way, philosophically oriented Sufis who advocated the 'unity of being' (*waḥdat al-wujūd*) discursively placed 'being' as the constant within the fluctuating ambiguity of different levels of existence. Shams-i Tabrīzī appears to confirm Aḥmad al-Ghazālī's position on the primacy of love.

The question can also be answered from an historical and sociological perspective. It is no accident that Shams-i Tabrīzī emphasises 'playing the *shāhid*' and physical love of young men. He was from Tabrīz. Because of this, he highlighted the stories of Aḥmad al-Ghazālī practising 'playing the *shāhid*' in his city. This demonstrates several things. First, we can assume that 'playing the *shāhid*' was a well-established practice in Tabrīz. Secondly, in the seventh/thirteenth century the practice increased among the ordinary people of Tabrīz and became fused with accepted religious customs and Sufi practice. There were also other poets and authors, mainly from Fārs, Jibāl and Āzarbaijān who were well known for such practices including Awḥad al-Dīn al-Kirmānī, Fakhr al-Dīn 'Irāqī and Sa'dī Shīrāzī. The proof is found in their poetry where they speak about 'gazing in contemplation' and passionate love for a 'witness'. Tabrīz was one of these cities that nurtured practitioners of 'playing the witness' among Sufis, poets and chroniclers. Shams-i Tabrīzī is a clear example of this.

The collected works of the Sufi poet, Humām Tabrīzī, also contains many couplets describing the 'witness' and erotic-mystical love. Humām Tabrīzī's *Ṣuḥbat-nāma* describes passionate love of a limited, phenomenal form as a 'diversion so as to lure oneself into contentment' (*ta'allul*). This is a technical term that Aḥmad al-Ghazālī had earlier brought into use in the introduction to his famous poetic treatise on erotic mysticism, *Sawāniḥ* ('Intuitions on Love'). According to him, a human being is created in primordial time as a lover. Human love was originally directed to the creator as the primordial beloved:

When the Divine beloved mixed Adam's clay
Deep inside the seed of his own love he did lay

Because this seed of love is implanted in human nature, all lovers essentially long for union with the Divine creator. But not everyone has the strength, and conviction to reach the Divine beloved, so some pursue a 'lesser' form of love, a diversion (*ta'allul*), a passionate intimacy with some beautiful earthly form:

Lovers are ecstatic from the beloved's fragrance
To offer love to others they never give a chance
To be bonded to others' love they do not aspire
To achieve union with the one beloved they desire
But if one should incline toward the sensuous
Be it love for a beautiful face or a song melodious
It is not absolute dependence but an intermediate means
Whether the metaphor is a beautiful person or garden scenes.[58]

Another scholar and Sufi master of Tabrīz who lived at the time of Humām was

Amīn al-Dīn Ḥājjī Bulah. He also accepted Aḥmad al-Ghazālī's position on passionate love and its spiritual function. Ḥājjī Bulah's son, 'Uthmān, wrote an epistle under the influence of Aḥmad al-Ghazālī, entitled 'Delight of Lovers' (*Nuzhat al-'āshiqīn*), because he had fallen in love with a young man. All of this shows that in the seventh/thirteenth century, 'playing the witness' was an important practice among the Sufis of Tabrīz. They traced it back to the paradigmatic personality of Aḥmad al-Ghazālī, who, in their opinion, was a famous saint (*walī*) who performed miracles and whose practice of 'playing the *shāhid*' was an act of pious rectitude and spiritual profundity.

## Notes

I would like to thank Scott Kugle who translated this paper from the Persian.

1. The issue of the *shāhid*'s gender will be discussed in detail in this article, but he is inevitably a male in the loving regard of a male Sufi. His age is more ambiguous. He is always younger than the admiring Sufi, so this article translates the term as 'beautiful young man'. Some translators use 'boy' to translate the Persian word *pisar* which often describes the *shāhid*, as in John O'Kane, tr., *The Feats of the Knowers of God:* Manaqeb al-'Arefin *by Shams al-Dīn Aḥmad-e Aflākī* (Leiden, 2002). However, this could lead to misinterpretation by a contemporary Anglophone audience, for it raises questions about the age of maturity, consent and ethical responsibility which are not raised by the term *shāhid* in its medieval Persian context. In one solution to these ambiguities, Helmut Ritter defined *shāhid* as 'a beautiful person' (*insān ṣāḥib-i jamāl*) without addressing the issue of age or gender; see Aḥmad al-Ghazālī, *Sawāniḥ*, ed. Helmut Ritter (Tehran, 1943), p. iv, n. 7.

2. See Pourjavady, *Sulṭān-i ṭarīqa* (Tehran, 1358 Sh./1979), p. 15.

3. Comparable stories were also recorded by the poet who composed 'The Song of Lovers' (*'Ushshāq-nāma*)(which is sometimes known by the alternate title 'Song of Love' (*'Ishq-nāma*) that is falsely ascribed to Fakhr al-Dīn 'Irāqī.

4. Shams al-Dīn Aflākī, *Manāqib al-'arifīn*, ed. Tahsin Yaziqi (Ankara, 1961), vol. 1, p. 85; 'Abd al-Rahmān Jāmī, *Nafḥāt al-uns*, ed. Maḥmūd 'Ābidi (Tehran, 1370 Sh./1991), p. 466.

5. Ibid.

6. Shams-i Tabrīzī's 'Discourses' (*Maqālāt*) seem to consist of notes taken down by several people. The text has been edited and published twice: first by Aḥmad Khoshnevis (Tehran, 1349 Sh./1970) and then M. A. Muwaḥḥid (Tehran, 1369 Sh./ 1980) in two volumes and with extra material and notes. I have generally referred here to both editions, first to Muwaḥḥid and then to Khoshnevis.

7. Muwaḥḥid's edition, vol. 1, p. 320; in Khoshnevis this incident does not exist.

8. For Aḥmad al-Ghazālī's works, see Pourjavady, *Sulṭān-i ṭarīqa*, pp. 265–277; and also 'Gazālī, Aḥmad', *EIr*.

9. *Maqālāt*, ed. Muwaḥḥid, vol. 1, p. 321.

10. Ibid., p. 462.

11. Ibid., p. 321.

12. Ibid., p. 321. This quatrain (*rubā'*) is transmitted with slight variations in the same

text, p. 137, without being attributed explicitly to Aḥmad al-Ghazālī. The idea is that the poet needs no wine since the liquor of kissing the beloved's mouth intoxicates him. Similarly, why need to read these texts called 'The Heart' or 'The Treasure' when the Sufi has tasted real spiritual experience, having become a ruin by searching for the treasure buried in ruined places and letting the heart become scorched with love. This couplet alludes to an Arabic verse quoted in the introduction (*muqaddima*) to Aḥmad al-Ghazālī, *Sawāniḥ* (Tehran, 1348 Sh./ 1969), p. 3:

> If I've not tasted the water of her mouth / Let me drink in replacement potent wine.
> How can wine compare to her lip?/ It's just a way to occupy my sickened heart.

13. In the Muwaḥḥid edition, after this quatrain comes a discourse on a topic unrelated to Aḥmad al-Ghazālī, which continues for two pages, pp. 321–323. Muwaḥḥid has arranged the speech of Shams in one discourse, in such a way that Shams' continuous speech about Aḥmad al-Ghazālī, apparently spoken in one sitting, appears cut into two parts.

14. *Maqālāt*, ed. Muwaḥḥid, vol. 1, p. 324; this story is not found in Khoshnevis' edition.

15. Ibid., p. 323.

16. Ibid., p. 324.

17. Pourjavady, ed., 'Two Writings of Imām Muḥammad Ghazālī', *Ma'ārif*, 8 (1370/ 1991), p. 29.

18. In transcendental contemplation, one transcended the physical beauty of the object gazed at. For more on this idea in Aḥmad al-Ghazālī's Sufism see Pourjavady, *Sulṭān-i ṭarīqa*, pp. 59–60 and Pourjavady, 'Bādah-i 'Ishq' in *Nashr-i dānesh*, 12/1 (1950–1951), pp. 10–13.

19. Amīn Aḥmad Rāzī, *Haft iqlīm*, ed. Javād Fāḍil (Tehran, n.d.), vol. 3, p. 209. The term for 'beautiful boy' here is literally a 'Chinese idol' so beautiful as to inspire worship, derived from the name of Buddha (*but*). Zulaykhā is the wife of Potiphar (or 'Azīz) who fell in love with Joseph but was spurned.

20. *Maqālāt*, ed. Muwaḥḥid, vol. 1, p. 324; ed. Khoshnevis, p. 197.

21. *Maqālāt*, ed. Muwaḥḥid, vol. 1, p. 325; this story is narrated somewhat differently in ed. Khoshnevis, pp. 197 and 374.

22. Ibn Jawzī, *Talbīs Iblīs* (Cairo, n.d.), p. 259 and *Sulṭān-i ṭarīqat*, p. 56.

23. *Maqālāt*, ed. Muwaḥḥid, vol. 1, p. 325.

24. *Maqālāt*, ed. Khoshnevis, pp. 197–198. This account is not found in Muwaḥḥid's edition. Compare with *Maqālāt*, ed. Muwaḥḥid, vol. 2, p. 44.

25. *Maqālāt*, ed. Muwaḥḥid, vol. 1, pp. 284–285; ed. Khoshnevis, p. 339.

26. This article will discuss later the issue of the attribution of this miracle to two different shaykhs, Aḥmad al-Ghazālī and also Manṣūr Hafẓa (or Abū Manṣūr Hafḍa).

27. *Maqālāt*, ed. Muwaḥḥid, vol. 1, p. 285; ed. Khoshnevis, p. 197.

28. *Maqālāt*, ed. Muwaḥḥid, vol. 1, p. 325.

29. *Maqālāt*, ed. Muwaḥḥid, vol. 2, p. 19. ed. Khoshnevis, p. 156 records the words of Shams in a slightly varied way.

30. Here the scholar quotes Qur'an 25:70. *Maqālāt*, ed. Muwaḥḥid, vol. 1, p. 285; ed. Khoshnevis, p. 340.

31. *Maqālāt*, ed. Muwaḥḥid, vol. 1, p. 325.

32. *Maqālāt*, ed. Muwaḥḥid, vol. 1, pp. 285–286; ed. Khoshnevis, pp. 340–341.

33. *Maqālāt*, ed. Muwaḥḥid, vol. 2, p. 19; ed. Khoshnevis, p. 156.

34. For critics who absolutely reject 'playing the *shāhid*', see Ibn Jawzī, *Talbīs Iblīs* (Cairo, n.d.), pp. 256–268.

35. Fakhr al-Dīn Rāzī, *Jāmiʿ al-ʿulūm* (Bombay, 1322/1904–1905), p. 220. The dominant legal method in Aḥmad al-Ghazālī's circle was the Shāfiʿī one.

36. *Maqālāt*, ed. Muwaḥḥid, vol. 2, p. 19; ed. Khoshnevis, p. 373.

37. *Maqālāt*, ed. Khoshnevis, p. 198.

38. *Maqālāt*, ed. Muwaḥḥid, vol. 2, p. 19.

39. Ibid., p. 218; ed. Khoshnevis, p. 198.

40. *Maqālāt*, ed. Muwaḥḥid, vol. 2, p. 20.

41. Helmut Ritter, *Das Meer der Seele* (Leiden, 1978 [1955]), p. 476.

42. Aflākī, *Manāqib al-ʿārifīn*, vol. 2, p. 230.

43. Ibid., p. 631.

44. Ibid., pp. 616–617.

45. *Maqālāt*, ed. Muwaḥḥid, vol. 2, p. 43.

46. Aflākī, *Manāqib al-ʿārifīn*, vol. 2, p. 621. English translation from O'Kane, *Feats*, p. 427. This same story is related in Farīdūn Sipah-Sālār, *Zindagī-nāma-yi Mawlānā Jalāl al-Dīn Mevlevī* (Tehran, 1325 Sh./1946), pp. 182–183; and Jāmī, *Nafaḥāt al-uns*, pp. 471–472.

47. Aflākī, *Manāqib al-ʿarifīn*, vol. 2, p. 622.

48. Ibid., p. 695. English from O'Kane, *Feats*, p. 482. (In O'Kane's translation the last sentence is altered to correspond with the meaning intended by the author.)

49. Aflākī, *Manāqib al-ʿarifīn*, vol. 2, p. 695. English from O'Kane, *Feats*, p. 482.

50. Ḥusayn Gāzurgāhī, *Majālis-i ʿushshāq*, ed. Ghulām-Riḍā Ṭabāṭabāʾī Majd (Tehran, 1375 Sh./1996), pp. 153–154.

51. Aflākī, *Manāqib al-ʿarifīn*, vol. 2, p. 638.

52. Ibid.

53. See Aflākī, *Manāqib al-ʿarifīn*, vol. 2, pp. 640–641 for reference to Ḥāʾirī. This person is apparently the same as Shaykh ʿAlī Kurdī, who was one of the 'wise fools' (*ʿuqalāʾ-i majānīn*) who lived in Damascus. Jāmī, *Nafaḥāt al-uns*, pp. 577–579 comments on him, saying that he did not perform formal prayers, went around most of the time naked, and in Damascus he met Shihāb al-Dīn al-Suhrawardī, the author of *ʿAwārif al-maʿārif*.

54. *Manāqib al-ʿarifīn*, vol. 2, p. 642.

55. *Maqālāt*, ed. Muwaḥḥid, vol. 2, pp. 157–158.

56. See Pourjavady, *Sulṭān-i ṭarīqat*, pp. 23–26.

57. See ʿAbd al-Karīm Rāfiʿī Qazwīnī, *al-Tadwīn fī akhbār Qazwīn*, ed. ʿAzīz Allāh ʿAṭārudī (Beirut, 1987), vol. 4, pp. 98–99.

58. 'Kitāb-i ṣuḥbat-nāma', in *Dīwān-i Humām Tabrīzī*, ed. Rashīd ʿAywaḍī (Tabrīz, 1351 Sh./1972), pp. 268–269.

# 17

# Reason (*ʿaql*) and Direct Intuition (*mushāhada*) in the Works of Shihāb al-Dīn al-Suhrawardī (d. 587/1191)

*Roxanne D. Marcotte*

Reason and intuition are amongst the concepts with which Islamic philosophy was to wrestle throughout its history.[1] In this paper I would like to propose an overview of how reason and, more generally, the philosophical venture are related to intuition and the mystical or gnostic experience, particularly in the philosophical works of Shihāb al-Dīn (Yaḥyā b. Ḥabash b. Amīrak) al-Suhrawardī (549–587/1153–1191), the *Shaykh al-Ishrāq*, or the *Shaykh al-Maqtūl*.[2] The task at hand will be to investigate the role reason plays in his own works, and how reason is conceived, defined and interpreted in light of his newly-formulated terminology and division of knowledge with its emphasis on mystical experience. Reason is central in the works of the philosophers or, as al-Suhrawardī calls them, the Peripatetics, a reference to the Peripatetic philosophy of Avicenna. Such an investigation into the thought of al-Suhrawardī would not have been possible had it not been for the *pīr*, Professor Landolt, who introduces his students to the Persian language with the poetry of Ḥāfiẓ and the allegorical tales of al-Suhrawardī, such as *ʿAql-i surkh* and *Safīr-i sīmurgh*.

## Reason (*ʿaql*) and Direct Intuition (*mushāhada*)

It has been proposed that the shift made by al-Suhrawardī from reason to mystical or direct intuition is not one of substance, but rather one of emphasis; and that what is really called for in his works is the predominance of a 'philosophical intuition' (*ḥads-i falsafa*).[3] The main difficulty which arises from such a claim is that al-Suhrawardī's notion of intuition appears to be slightly different in its nature and in its function from a purely philosophical intuition.[4] In Aristotle's works, philosophical intuition is usually understood as a type of immediate knowledge or the faculty responsible for this type of knowledge. The role of this type of philosophical intuition is, first, to perceive (*intuit*) particulars of sense directly from the experienced world; and, second, to perceive (*intuit*) universals, or generalisations, and abstractions from the particulars (of sense). In Arabic, intuition is often rendered by '*ḥads*', in the sense of 'hitting correctly upon the mark', which is closely related to the notion of 'acumen'.[5] This Aristotelian notion found its way into the Arabic tradition through translations of Aristotle's works; it was later taken up by Avicenna in whose works it plays a similar role in the acquisition of knowledge through demonstration.[6] In the works of Avicenna, intuition is integrated into a greater philosophical system considerably influenced by religious considerations.[7] And finally, intuition becomes an essential method for grasping metaphysical truths.[8]

The Aristotelian or, more accurately, the Peripatetic (Avicennan) notion of intuition does, indeed, remain part of al-Suhrawardī's Peripatetic outlook. For instance, he often appeals to the judgements of intuition (*aḥkām al-ḥads* or *ḥukm al-ḥads* or *yaḥkum al-ḥads*).[9] Again, in the *Physics* of his *al-Lamaḥāt*, a handbook of Peripatetic philosophy, he mentions that 'the second [disposition of the soul] is its state when it acquires the first intelligibles (*ma'qūlāt*) and when it acquires the secondary (*thawānī*) [intelligibles], either by means of thought [or the cogitative process] (*bi'l-fikr*) or by intuition (*bi'l-ḥads*); and it [i.e. this disposition] is called the habitual intellect (*'aql bi'l-malaka*)'.[10] This particular passage is part of a psychological discussion which is essentially Avicennan in nature.[11] Furthermore, in a less Peripatetic work, his *Ḥikmat al-ishrāq* (*The Philosophy of Illumination*), a whole discussion, in the section on Logic, is dedicated to 'intuitive premises' (*ḥadsiyyāt*).[12]

In spite of the existence of similar Peripatetic discussions pertaining to the notion of intuition in al-Suhrawardī's works, an important characteristic of his philosophy of illumination (*ishrāq*) seems to be the existence of an understanding of intuition that can be better characterised, or better defined as 'mystical'. A central feature of al-Suhrawardī's thought is the contemplative thrust that he imparts to Peripatetic philosophy which will be conducive to the development of a conception of a distinct 'direct intuition'. Consequently, mystical contemplation (*mushāhada*) will become essential as the basis for judgements. Direct intuition or mystical contemplation now acquires a new status, superior to that of demonstration. In his introduction to the *Ḥikmat al-ishrāq*, al-Suhrawardī alludes to this fact when he states that traditional logical demonstration becomes, at the stage of mystical contemplation, superfluous.[13] The conceptual knowledge with which philosophical intuition is usually associated would, therefore, seem to be relegated to a secondary position. In this scheme, preeminence is attributed to the function of receptivity which is, as an epistemological function, seen as going beyond the traditional rational functions with which it is usually associated. The process of 'direct intuition' has now been given a novel inferential character; it is essentially articulated to account for knowledge acquired through illumination (*ishrāq*) and, moreover, it can ultimately account for revelation.[14] For al-Suhrawardī, 'direct intuition' is intrinsically linked to the mystical experience; accordingly, such terms as '*dhawq*', or mystical perception or vision, '*kashf*', and '*mukāshafāt*', or mystical revelations, all correspond to different aspects or stages of a more general notion of mystical intuition.

In al-Suhrawardī's works, the more general notion of mystical intuition is, perhaps, best defined by appealing to his own idea of 'mystical contemplation' (*mushāhada*), the 'witnessing' of metaphysical truths. One can also resort to the expression of 'direct intuition' as an English equivalent for al-Suhrawardī's 'mystical contemplation' (*mushāhada*). It is perhaps less with the term 'mystical', that is, in such expressions as 'mystical contemplation', that the problem resides than with the expression 'contemplation' which can, at times, mean a sort of spiritual meditation, especially in Christian religious practice, for instance, the focusing of one's mind and of one's soul upon the nature of God. The term contemplation can also mean a process by which one becomes deeply engrossed in one's thoughts, consisting of long considerations or observations of a particular thing. The latter could define the more spiritual elements at the heart of al-Suhrawardī's philosophy. Nonetheless, 'direct intuition' – perhaps philosophically more neutral – is here taken as an equivalent of al-Suhrawardī's 'mystical contemplation' (*mushāhada*), the notion at the heart of his conception of direct knowledge.[15]

## The Discursive (*baḥthiyya*) and the Experiential (*dhawqiyya*)

In the preface he wrote to the *Ḥikmat al-ishrāq*, Shams al-Dīn Muḥammad al-Shahrazūrī (d. after 687/1288) summarises the types of knowledge he found in al-Suhrawardī's works. He distinguishes between two types of knowledge – both essential: on the one hand, there is a discursive or demonstrative (*baḥthiyya*) knowledge, a knowledge that is similarly intellectual and theoretical (*naẓariyya*) and, on the other hand, there exists an 'experiential' (*dhawqiyya*) knowledge, primarily dependent on and the result of mystical perception (*dhawq*) – sometimes identified as a mystico-theosophical perception (*ḥikma dhawqiyya*)[16] – and it is closely related to mystical vision (*kashfiyya*).[17] These two essential, although different, types of knowledge will naturally call upon different methods: for the former, a philosophical method will be necessitated while, for the latter, a mystical or gnostic method will be required. Both methods are, nonetheless, quite distinct. The discursive method of the philosophers is essentially conceptual and Aristotelian in its origins; in addition, it resorts to 'observations of the sensibles' in order to produce knowledge and is, therefore, responsible for the origination of the different sciences.[18] It relies basically on the faculty of reason (*ʿaql*) and, in a broad sense, on the use of demonstrative (syllogistic) methods. Essentially discursive in nature, the process of thought (*fikr*) relies on concepts and their representations which, in turn, necessitate both forms and mental images.[19] In the *ishrāqī* terminology, this latter type of knowledge is known as acquired knowledge (*ʿilm ḥuṣūlī*). According to al-Suhrawardī, it is a valid method, albeit of a limited scope, useful for explaining what can be known by means of another superior process, that is, direct intuition.[20] Presumably, reason – or intellect – ranks quite high in the realm of discursive knowledge. For al-Suhrawardī, however, the criterion for truth in the realm of intuitive knowledge – which gives access to the realm of the divine through the experiential – cannot rest on reason, or intellect, alone if at all.

Al-Suhrawardī, in addition to his endorsement of the method of the Peripatetics, therefore, puts forward a spiritual means that becomes more adapted at grasping what lies beyond the sublunar realm. These spiritual means are such *ishrāqī* notions as those of vision (*ibṣār*), mystical contemplation (*mushāhada*) and mystical vision (*kashf*) which ultimately become the sole guarantors of the acquisition of any true knowledge. The spiritual method he proposes, and which shares much with the method of the mystics and the gnostics, rests on the 'observation of some of the spiritual realities' from which true knowledge can be derived.[21] A glimpse of what al-Suhrawardī alludes to can be observed in passages where he notes that what he has written in his book was not the result of 'discursive thought' (*fikr*), but rather it was achieved by 'another means' (*bi-amr ākhar*): it actually corresponds to the fruits of his own personal experience.[22] In fact, he mentions that he is addressing those who, like him, are already 'accomplished spiritual seekers (s. *mujtahid*) experienced in mysticism … or who aspire to it'.[23] He is now speaking of a different method as the source of most of his own knowledge of the ineffable realities.

Mystical perception would, therefore, seem to correspond to a more 'direct method' specifically adapted for the perception of the divine realm. It would be better organised and better ruled than the discursive methods used by the philosophers; in addition, it would require less effort in order to yield any results. Immediate knowledge, however, could only be achieved through a process of mystical and direct intuition by which the unveiling presence of the one susceptible of being known would occur to the knower and not when the imprinting of a form would occur – as was the case with the Peripatetics' adoption of the principles of Aristotelian psychology. This type of mystical knowledge has come to be known as a presential knowledge (*ʿilm ḥuḍūrī*). Moreover, the principle at the heart of this experiential method is essentially illumination and, in al-Suhrawardī's terminology, it also becomes the principle of an *ishrāqī* relation (*al-iḍāfa al-ishrāqiyya*).[24] Illumination and the principle of an *ishrāqī* relation are both capable of offering an explanation for the immediate and atemporal character of this particular type of knowledge.[25] As a means of grasping the essence of the object, this type of knowledge, essentially of a direct, unmediated nature (as the term itself – *ḥuḍūrī* – implies), precludes the use of any logical or demonstrative method.[26] Furthermore, there is no place for the mediation of such entities as concepts or logical categories. It is the whole being that must be the locus of experience.

Although al-Suhrawardī situates direct intuition alongside reason as a means of acquiring knowledge, he argues, nonetheless, that certainty only lies within the reach of the 'experiential' (*dhawqī*) method, that is, of mystical perception.[27] The personal experience of the true seeker (*mujtahid*), conceived as direct intuition, is at the heart of his mystical contemplation. Accordingly, this personal experience possesses a distinctive and unique character that precludes it from being conceived of as a kind of mediating agent on a par with such entities as concepts or logical categories. It would, therefore, seem unjustified to simply equate direct intuition with any type of 'philosophical intuition', or with the Aristotelian notion of 'acumen', involved at the conceptual level of the thinking process, even at its most abstract level.[28] In al-Suhrawardī's works, it would seem to correspond to a higher experiential level.

It is significant that al-Suhrawardī introduces mystical knowledge, alongside the more traditional discursive type of knowledge. One reason for such a position is most certainly a consequence of his own ontology of Light, in which Light is the essence of everything. Mystical contemplation and illumination become two epistemological principles, at the heart of the only 'true' knowing process, and this as a corollary of his ontology. There is no doubt that, for al-Suhrawardī, it is the spiritual level which is the realm of pure existence. On this metaphysical horizon, the relations that are established between the different levels of Light are conceived either in terms of contemplation or of illumination. In other words, a contemplation of the superior Lights is complementary to an illumination of the lower Lights by the higher ones. Knowledge at this level combines the Light's self-consciousness of its divine essence, that is, the nature of its Light, and the realisation of being itself an illumination of the first principle, the Light of Lights. The same type of relationship that prevails between the Lights at the metaphysical level also prevails at the physical level.[29] Lights, which manifest themselves to others are also manifest *by* themselves and *to* themselves. It is interesting to note that these Lights conceived as self-conscious are able to be cognisant in a manner quite similar to the cognisance attributed to Neoplatonic Intelligences. Having defined the essence of existence as Light, al-Suhrawardī can then proceed to make this type of mystical knowledge an immediate knowledge rooted in the spiritual experience of the Lights (that is, those that become apparent, or manifested).[30] On the whole, the ontological underpinning of the spiritual experience is the *ishrāqī* ontology of Light.

The spiritual experience is only one of the elements of al-Suhrawardī's psychology which, on the whole, shares some similarities with the psychology proposed by Avicenna. In al-Suhrawardī's works such as *al-Lamaḥāt* (the section on Physics or the *Naturalia*), the division of the internal senses of the soul is a quite familiar scheme: the *sensus communis*, the faculty of representation, the imaginative faculty, the estimative faculty, and the recollective faculty.[31] In spite of these similarities with Avicennan psychology, the essential Peripatetic distinctions established between each of the different faculties of the soul are rejected by al-Suhrawardī, in order that the essentially Peripatetic configuration of his psychology may make way for his ontology of Lights. For instance in his *Ḥikmat al-ishrāq*, al-Suhrawardī lumps together all the preceding faculties (by drawing an analogy with the classical *sensus communis*), an original reworking of the Avicennan psychology whose precedent can be found in Abu al-Barakāt al-Baghdādī's (d. ca. 559/1164) original psychology.[32] As for al-Suhrawardī's classification of the different functions that characterise the rational soul, it does not greatly depart from the classical distinctions made between the different intellects: the hylic intellect, the intellect *in habitu*, the intellect *in actu*, and the acquired intellect.[33] But, once again, the traditional distinctions are reinterpreted by al-Suhrawardī. The distinctiveness of each of these functions with the rational soul gives way to the more general ability of the soul to receive Light. Peripatetic psychology thus serves as one of the building blocks at the heart of al-Suhrawardī's own epistemology to which he can then introduce and substitute his own Light terminology. With his ontology of Lights, he introduces such notions as those of the commanding Light (*nūr isfahbad*) to correspond to the managing rational soul, or the notion of the triumphal Light (*al-nūr al-qāhir*) to correspond to the Intelligence, and so on.[34] It is, it seems, this new emphasis on the process of a direct intuition, as a means of acquiring 'true' knowledge, that serves to fill the gap that exists between two types of perception – both physical and spiritual.

Direct intuition is, in the works of al-Suhrawardī, not really a faculty but, rather, a function operating not so differently than the function of vision on which al-Suhrawardī dwells at length and from which he derives many of his analogies. Direct intuition, as vision or as mystical contemplation (*mushāhada*) of the abstract Lights, acquires a novel and significant epistemological function. Vision of the abstract Lights through contemplation becomes the mediator between the knowledge of the physical world (that is, the perception of the manifestations of the physical Lights) and the knowledge of the spiritual world (that is, the perception of the pure and abstract Lights). However, for al-Suhrawardī, it is only the second type of knowledge which corresponds to the real and essential goal sought by all genuine seekers of truth.

Al-Suhrawardī now adds an experiential and essentially mystical foundation where there previously had been mostly a rational foundation to certainty (as in the Aristotelian and Peripatetic philosophical traditions), save in the case of prophetic knowledge: certainty consists of divine knowledge obtained by divine inspiration that befalls human beings. Mystical perceptions such as direct intuition

– a combination of inspiration and revelation – acquires a new necessity. Light reveals itself at the individual level and, consequently, direct intuition, or immediate perception of this Light, now becomes the ultimate source of truth.

It is interesting to learn that one of al-Suhrawardī's commentators, Muḥammad Sharīf b. al-Harawī (fl. 11th/17th century), notes that what is acquired by prophets – as well as by those who might be labelled Theosophists (*ḥukamā'-yi ilāhī*) – is one of the following states: (i) mystical revelation (*mukāshafa*), (ii) presential experience or mystical contemplation (*mushāhada*), (iii) revelation (*waḥy*) as well as (iv) inspiration (*ilhām*).[35] These four states would seem to constitute varying degrees of divine manifestation as well as varying degrees of experiential perceptions. The religious implication of al-Suhrawardī's position for the traditional Islamic theory of revelation cannot be, therefore, minimised. As a matter of fact, it should not be forgotten that al-Suhrawardī was put to death on charges of allegedly claiming the possibility of the advent of another prophet.[36] Furthermore, this divine knowledge, in a way ineffable, can only find its expression through symbols which, al-Suhrawardī mentions, are such that they are non-refutable by means of logical demonstrations, and they thus, quite obviously, possess their own intrinsic truth criteria. This type of apprehension of divine matters is, therefore, beyond both the logical and rational realms.

Al-Suhrawardī, nonetheless, does appeal to both reason and direct intuition. He seems to want to integrate both the demonstrable and the 'experiential' aspects that belong to two different experiences – the intellectual and the mystical – within a more general framework. However, the fact that he posits the pre-eminence of the experience of direct intuition (that is, mystical contemplation) with his philosophico-mystical explanation should not be underestimated. It becomes evident that knowledge acquired through philosophy and knowledge acquired through mystical experience are not identical or equivalent. Moreover, the shift from reason to direct intuition is indicative of the new mystical orientation of *ishrāqī* philosophy and of the importance of its ascetic elements. This is highlighted by Quṭb al-Dīn al-Shīrāzī (d. 710/1311) who writes that the *ishrāqī* method rests primarily on 'mystical perception, internal revelations, due to continuous practice of spiritual exercises'.[37] In any case, al-Suhrawardī himself states that knowledge corresponds, first and foremost, to the actual mystical perception or personal experiencing of these truths. It is only after such experience that philosophical proofs can find a place within his epistemology, and even then they serve only an explanatory function.[38]

## Epistemology and Religious Authority

In the introduction of his *Ḥikmat al-ishrāq* al-Suhrawardī dwells on the relation reason and direct intuition must enjoy. Although direct intuition is of capital importance, reason, the principle at the heart of the philosophical tradition, is not to be discarded: some Peripatetic principles, attainable only by means of the discursive process, remain valid and essential. Consequently, reason must be incorporated and, indeed, it will find its place within al-Suhrawardī's *Ishrāqī* philosophy. For instance, he elaborates a hierarchy of the different stages attainable by sages and which can serve as an illustration of the relation reason and direct intuition should enjoy within his philosophical system. The most perfect sage (*ḥakīm*) is the one who has achieved the utmost level of perfection in philosophical knowledge, along with the utmost level of perfection in mystical experience. It is to such a sage that the responsibility of the supreme authority (*ri'āsa*) over the community and of the vice-regency of God (*khilāfat Allāh*) falls.[39] In this particular instance, both reason and direct intuition (that is, mystical contemplation) would appear to have the same heuristic value. Al-Suhrawardī, however, goes on to say that in the absence of such a perfect individual able to simultaneously develop these two faculties to their utmost perfection, the individual who possesses the greatest amount of mystical experience, whether that person lacks great philosophical knowledge or possesses none whatsoever, will deserve the responsibility of the supreme authority and the vice-regency of God over the community.[40] Discursive knowledge alone is, in fact, quite insufficient for the true seeker. Moreover, it is insufficient for anyone who would aspire to become the religious leader of the community, a matter much more crucial for the Islamic community as a whole.

The appointment to the office of God's vice-regency requires more than the above mentioned abilities; it also requires the existence of a 'direct appointment' in order to confirm the mission of a true prophet.[41] For al-Suhrawardī, the same holds true at the level of the mystical knowledge that results from illumination and mystical contemplation. The seekers of the truth are in need of a living proof (*quṭb*) who is one of those capable of witnessing or who have already witnessed these divine truths.[42] Consequently, the followers of al-Suhrawardī's own philosophical tradition of 'illumination' must, in order to be able to penetrate the secrets of the philosophy of Light, have already received some sort of divine inspiration (*barq ilāhī*); while others, he notes, will not be able to benefit at all from what his book *Ḥikmat al-ishrāq* has to offer; in which case, the latter group will have to depend on someone already inspired for its interpretation.[43] It is, therefore, apparent that for al-Suhrawardī direct intuitive knowledge is of the utmost importance, because only those who have received it, or perceived it, are able to guide either individuals or the community.[44]

## Al-Suhrawardī's Approach

Al-Suhrawardī posits that knowledge is acquired through two distinctive, although interrelated operations: rational demonstration and mystical contemplation (*mushāhada*). On the whole, the latter has logical and epistemological priority over the former. However, this pre-eminence of direct intuition over philosophical reasoning is, to a great extent, ontological in nature. Al-Suhrawardī's ontology, with its hierarchy of Lights, makes Light the essence of everything and the principle at the heart of the epistemological process. As such, Light is the fundamental principle responsible, on the one hand, for the dissemination and distribution of divine illumination and, on the other hand, of its correlate, that is, mystical contemplation. Reason, although excellent and invaluable in the realm of the sensible and the abstract (in an Aristotelian perspective), is limited in its capacity to grasp these divine truths; while direct intuition, responsible for a more immediate and instantaneous access to these Lights, embraces the whole spectrum of the divine effusion. Reason is deficient since it is hampered in its efforts at grasping truths; whereas, direct intuition – as a door open to the divine – is most capable of direct apprehension guaranteeing it immediate and unhampered access to certainty and divine truths.

In this respect, al-Suhrawardī's classification of learned individuals according to their respective merits in philosophy and mystical experience is revealing, since it is direct intuition or mystical contemplation that is ascribed the predominant role, as opposed to reason. A case in point is al-Suhrawardī's statement that only mystics, such as Sahl al-Tustarī (d. 283/896), Abū Yazīd al-Bistāmī (d. 261/874 or 264/877) and al-Ḥallāj, the famous disciple of al-Tustarī and Junayd (d. 298/910), executed for blasphemy in 309/922, [45] have 'achieved union (*ittiṣāl*) with the Active Intellect ... they have surpassed discursive philosophy through their personal experience'.[46] Another reason for the pre-eminence of this direct intuitive function appears to be essentially religious in nature and linked to al-Suhrawardī's prophetology; for him, only the most perfect sage who can witness these truths is said to deserve to hold God's vice-regency, whether he is embodied in a living proof (*quṭb*) or is in occultation.

Whereas previous philosophers such as al-Fārābī and Avicenna had extolled primarily intellectual faculties, al-Suhrawardī brought direct intuition, in the sense of mystical contemplation (*mushāhada*), to the forefront as an alternative – albeit more reliable – foundation for certainty. Moreover, he attempted to formulate the basis of what has been characterised as an 'esoteric philosophy'.[47] His attitude towards the methods of both the philosophical and the mystical traditions paved the way for his own personal expression of mystical speculations embedded in philosophical terminology and *a posteriori* demonstrations. Inescapably, his mystical outlook is unable to avoid emphasising intuitive knowledge as the ultimate source and criterion of true knowledge.[48]

## Notes

1. This paper has greatly benefited from the judicious remarks made by Professors Hermann Landolt, Todd Lawson and Parviz Morewedge. It was presented at the SSIPS (Society for the Study of Islamic Philosophy and Science) / SAGP (Society for Ancient Greek Philosophy) 15th Annual Conference 1996, at Binghamton University, SUNY (25–27 October 1996), and a modified version of this article appeared in *Anaquel de estudios árabes*, 7 (1996), pp. 109–126.

2. He had befriended al-Malik al-Ẓāhir, son of Ṣalāḥ al-Dīn Ayyūbī and governor of Aleppo. Opposition by the *'ulamā'* and their accusation that he was claiming the role of prophet, led to his death in Aleppo (587/1191) ordered by Ṣalāḥ al-Dīn himself, cf. Seyyed Hossein Nasr, *Three Muslim Sages* (Cambridge, 1964), pp. 52–82; cf. Henry Corbin, *En Islam iranien; aspects spirituels et philosophiques*, vol. 2, *Sohrawardî et les platoniciens de Perse* (Paris, 1971), pp. 9–19. Some have argued (i.e. Mehdi Ha'iri Yazdī, Seyyed Hossein Nasr, Henry Corbin, Sayyid Jalāl al-Dīn Āshtiyānī) that al-Suhrawardī's texts are essentially mystical in nature, ranking philosophy and its method a good second while, for others (i.e., Hossein Ziai, John Walbridge, Mehdi Amin Razavi), his works combine both the mystical and the philosophical, as two complementary methods or 'options' able to attain, or to 'ultimately "see" the same reality'. More specifically, concerning these two methods, some have argued (e.g. Yazdī) that he has proposed a process which starts with philosophy as a stepping stone that leads to a higher level, that of mystical experience, while others have argued (e.g. Nasr) that through asceticism and philosophy one arrives at the mystical stage, while still others have proposed (e.g. Amin Razavi), that besides the use of philosophy, as a valid method to attain truths, 'it was practising asceticism that resulted in illumination', cf. Mehdi Amin Razavi, 'Suhrawardī's Theory of Knowledge' (Ph.D., Temple University, 1989), pp. 142–144. It is quite obvious that interpretations regarding the Suhrawardian method do not inspire unanimity.

3. On '*ḥads-i falsafa*', cf. Hossein Ziai, 'Mushāhada, rawish-i Ishrāq, wa-zabān-i shi'r. Baḥthī pīrāmūn-i niẓām-i falsafa-yi Ishrāq-i Shihāb al-Dīn Suhrawardī (Mystical Contemplation, *Ishrāqī* Method and Poetic Language. A Study on the System of Suhrawardī's Philosophy of Illumination)', *Iran-nāma*, 8 (1990), pp. 83–84.

4. Intuition, derived from the Latin, means 'as contemplation' (*intuitio*), or 'to gaze upon' (*intueri*), or 'to look at' (*tueri).*

5. In the *Posterior Analytics* and the *Nichomachean Ethics*, cf. Dimitri Gutas, *Avicenna and the Aristotelian Tradition. Introduction to Reading Avicenna's Philosophical Works* (Leiden, 1988), pp. 166–168, esp. p. 166; cf. Gutas, 'Avicenna v. Mysticism', *EIr.*

6. Gutas states that 'Avicenna … is not interested in the ethical but the epistemological function of the concept *ḥads* (*eustochia*, not *anchinoia*)', cf. Gutas, *Avicenna and the Aristotelian Tradition*, p. 169 and 'Avicenna v. Mysticism', p. 80a.

7. For example, Avicenna also uses the term *fiṭra* ('anthropological level') as a means of acquiring knowledge within a broader Islamic theological context, i.e. 'the concept of natural intelligence providing innate, *a priori* knowledge, as expressed in the Qur'anic *fiṭra* … and *fiṭra* is precisely the term Avicenna uses to describe Intuition in theological terminology' to which corresponds such terms as '*waḥy* (revelation), *ilhām* (inspiration), and particularly *badīha* (self-evident, spontaneous, or *a priori* knowledge)', cf. Gutas, *Avicenna*

*and the Aristotelian Tradition*, p. 170; cf. John Walbridge, *The Science of Mystic Lights. Quṭb al-Dīn Shīrāzī and the Illuminationist Tradition in Islamic Philosophy* (Cambridge, 1992), pp. 34–35.

8. Gutas says, regarding the notion of intuition, that, 'It [*ḥads*] is a mental act whereby the human intellect comes into contact (*ittiṣāl*) with the active intellect (*'aql fa''āl*) and receives what Avicenna frequently describes as 'divine effluences' (*fayẓ ilāhī*), i.e. knowledge of the intelligibles through the acquisition of the middle terms. *Ḥads* constitutes the *only* point of epistemological contact, in Avicenna's thought, between the sublunar and the supralunar realms, or between the mundane and the transcendental, and it refers to a strict and precise syllogistic process. Avicenna admits no other way to a knowledge of the intelligible world and ultimately of the Necessary Existent (*wājib al-wujūd*)', cf. Gutas, 'Avicenna. v. Mysticism', pp. 79b–80a.

9. Al-Suhrawardī, *al-Talwīḥāt* [*Intimations*], in al-Suhrawardī, *Opera metaphysica et mystica*, ed. Henry Corbin (Istanbul, 1945; 2nd ed., Tehran, 1993), vol. 1, p. 57; cf. his *al-Mashāri' wa'l-muṭāraḥāt* [*The Paths and Havens*], in *Opera*, vol. 1, p. 440; cf. his *Ḥikmat al-ishrāq* [*The Philosophy of Illumination*], in *Opera*, vol. 2, p. 109. The *Ḥikma* has been translated into French, save for the section on Logic, cf. al-Suhrawardī, *Le livre de la sagesse orientale*, tr. Henry Corbin, ed. Christian Jambet (Paris, 1986). Al-Suhrawardī goes on to mention in the *Physics* of his *al-Lamaḥāt* that, 'thought (*fikr*) is a movement (*ḥaraka*) belonging to the soul, by which it can acquire principles (*mabādī'*) ... intuition (*ḥads*) is the excellence (*jūda*) of this movement which does not require any effort (*ṭalab*)', cf. al-Suhrawardī, *al-Lamaḥāt* [*The Flashes of Light],* ed. Emile Maalouf (1969; 2nd ed., Beirut, 1991), p. 120.

10. Al-Suhrawardī, *al-Lamaḥāt*, p. 119, ll. 13–15.

11. Ibn Sīna, *Kitāb al-najāt fi'l-ḥikmat al-manṭiqiyya wa'l-ṭabī'iyya wa'l-ilāhiyya* [*The Book of Deliverance Regarding Logical, Natural and Metaphysical Wisdom*], ed. Majid Fakhri (Beirut, 1405/1985), pp. 204, 206. For an English translation of the *Naturalia*, cf. Fazlur Rahman, *Avicenna's Psychology. An English Translation of Kitāb al-Najāt, Book II, Chapter VI with Historico-Philosophical Improvements on the Cairo Edition* (London, 1952), pp. 34–36.

12. Al-Suhrawardī, *Ḥikmat al-ishrāq*, pp. 40–42. The whole discussion is about demonstration (*burhān*) (it is also found in the *al-Talwiḥāt*) in which intuitive premises play a role in acquiring real knowledge. These are either empirical or traditional and are not obtained by induction; and proofs 'based on intuition are shared by those with the same intuitive capabilities only', cf. Hossein Ziai, *Knowledge and Illumination. A Study of Suhrawardī's Ḥikmat al-ishrāq* (Atlanta, GA, 1990), pp. 71–72.

13. Al-Suhrawardī mentions that a 'valid intuition (*al-ḥads al-ṣaḥīḥ*) judges without any appeal to a proof (*ḥujja*) [required in] a logical demonstration (*burhān*)', cf. al-Suhrawardī, *al-Talwīḥāt*, p. 57.

14. In one of his notes to the French translation of the *Ḥikmat al-ishrāq*, Christian Jambet writes that 'Q.D. [Quṭb al-Dīn Shīrāzī] explique le rapport entre la *mokāshafa* et la *moshāhada*: celle-ci serait ici une "visualisation" plus qu'une "vision mentale". En effet, la *moshāhada* est plus particulière, plus spéciale que la *mokāshafa*. La différence entre les deux est celle du *général* et du *propre*. Cependant dans *Le Livre du Verbe du Soufisme* (chap. III: 'De l'âme pensante comme Verbe'), Sohravardî disait: "La *mokāshafa*, c'est l'actualisation d'une connaissance par l'âme, soit par une déduction, soit par inférence, soit par une intuition secrète se rattachant à une chose particulière échéant dans le passé ou dans l'avenir." ... En

bref, la *mokāshafa*, au sens le plus général, est révélation-intérieure, intuition, vision-mentale, inspiration imaginative. La *moshāhada* est visualisation, perception-visionnaire, organe des apparitions', cf. al-Suhrawardī, *Le livre de la sagesse orientale*, p. 86 n. d.

15. Direct intuition is one of the possible ways of translating *mushāhada* proposed by Corbin, cf. Suhrawardī, *Le livre de la sagesse orientale*, p. 198, ll. 3–4.

16. Cf. the *Introduction* by Shahrazūrī, cf. al-Suhrawardī, *Ḥikmat al-ishrāq*, pp. 5, 79n. a.

17. Al-Suhrawardī, *Ḥikmat al-ishrāq*, pp. 5–6.

18. Al-Suhrawardī's major criticism of Peripatetic principles is of their notion of definition in which it is impossible to truly know anything because knowledge is acquired by concepts. He substitutes for it, as a consequence of his own ontology, a theory of definition based on a direct knowledge of things divine. This, in turn, becomes the model for his epistemology and, in fact, for his whole cosmology. Cf. Walbridge, *The Science of Mystic Lights*, p. 101.

19. It is conceptual *(taṣawwur)* and assertorial (*taṣdīq*), cf. Suhrawardī, *Ḥikmat al-ishrāq*, p. 15.

20. Al-Suhrawardī, *Ḥikmat al-ishrāq*, p. 12. Some principles of *ishrāqī* philosophy are sound Peripatetic principles, i.e. their methods and conclusions which he has not rejected and which he considers a major part to be generally valid, cf. Walbridge, *The Science of Mystic Lights*, p. 33.

21. Al-Suhrawardī notes that, 'we contemplate (*nushāhidu*) things from the spiritual realities (*rūḥāniyyāt*); thereafter, we build upon these observations', cf. al-Suhrawardī, *Ḥikmat al-ishrāq*, p. 13.

22. Al-Suhrawardī, *Ḥikmat al-ishrāq*, p. 10.

23. Ibid., p. 12.

24. It is the result of a 'knowledge based on illumination and presence' *('ilm al-īshrāqī al-ḥuḍūrī*) established by the existence of an 'illuminationist relation' (*al-iḍāfa al-ishrāqiyya*)', cf. al-Suhrawardī, *Ḥikmat al-ishrāq*, pp. 97–103; cf. Ziai, *Knowledge and Illumination*, pp. 140–143.

25. Both of these types of knowledge enjoy an ontological relation such that acquired knowledge (*'ilm ḥuṣūlī*) can be reduced to presential knowledge (*'ilm ḥuḍūrī*), cf. Sayyid Muḥammad Reza Hijazi, 'Knowledge by Presence. A Comparative Study Based on the Epistemology of Suhrawardī (d. 587/1191) and Mullā Ṣadrā Shīrāzī (d. 1050/1640)' (M.A., McGill University, 1994), pp. 43–44; cf. Mehdi Ha'iri Yazdi, *The Principles of Epistemology in Islamic Philosophy. Knowledge by Presence* (New York, 1992).

26. Knowledge by presence is restricted to immaterial existents and excludes any possibility of ascribing true-false judgements, hence it is free from falsity, cf. al-Suhrawardī, *Ḥikmat al-ishrāq*, p. 10.

27. Ibid., pp. 232 and 121; cf. Hijazi, 'Knowledge by Presence', pp. 43–44.

28. As was briefly mentioned earlier, the mystical aspect seems to be less prevalent in Avicenna's use of the notion of intuition; he used it in the sense of intellectual astuteness – even acumen. However, Ziai mentions that Avicenna's concept of intuition (*ḥads*), linked to the intellect *in habitu* (*'aql bi'l-malaka*) and which ultimately occurs as a result of the divine intellect (*'aql qudsī*), exerted an influence on al-Suhrawardī; intuition in the latter's work is responsible for grasping the intelligibles without temporal extension and does not require the help of instruction at the hand of a teacher, cf. Ziai, 'Mushāhada', p. 83 and *Knowledge*

*and Illumination*, p. 155.

29. Walbridge, *The Science of Mystic Lights*, p. 109; cf. al-Suhrawardī, *Ḥikmat al-ishrāq*, pp. 110–113.

30. Al-Suhrawardī, *al-Mashāriʿ wa'l-muṭāraḥāt*, in al-Suhrawardī, *Opera*, vol. 1, pp. 194–195.

31. Al-Suhrawardī, *Ḥikmat al-ishrāq*, pp. 209 f. and pp. 220–224.

32. Wheeler M. Thackston, *The Mystical and Visionary Treatises of Shihabuddin Yahya Suhrawardī* (London, 1982), p. 18 n. 19; cf. with the important review of Hermann Landolt, 'Suhrawardī's 'Tales of Initiation', Review Article', *JAOS*, 107 (1987), pp. 475–486, esp. 480; cf. al-Suhrawardī, *Ḥikmat al-ishrāq*, pp. 207 ff.; cf. Abu al-Barakāt al-Baghdādī, *Kitāb al-mu'tabar fī'l-ḥikma*, ed. A. al-ʿAlawī, M. al-Qudūsī and Z. al-Mawsawī (Hyderabad, 1939), 3 vols., vol. 2, pp. 318–319.

33. Al-Suhrawardī, *Kitāb al-lamaḥāt*, pp. 113–121 and, in the same work, cf. 'Preface', pp. xii–xiv; another edition of the text exists, but it only comprises the metaphysics, cf. al-Suhrawardī, *Sih risāla az Shaykh-i Ishrāq: al-Alwāḥ al-ʿimādiyya, Kalimāt al-taṣawwuf, al-Lamaḥāt*, ed. Najaf-Gholi Habibi (Tehran, 1397/1977); cf. with the Introduction by Thackston, *The Mystical and Visionary Treatises*, pp. 11–13.

34. Al-Suhrawardī, *Ḥikmat al-ishrāq*, pp. 147 and 154 respectively; cf. Walbridge, *The Science of Mystic Lights*, pp. 194–195. Walbridge identifies the immaterial light with the intellect and the accidental light with intellection, cf. *The Science of Mystic Lights*, p. 60.

35. Quoted by Ziai, 'Mushāhada', p. 94, n. 15; cf. Muḥammad Sharīf Niẓām al-Dīn Aḥmad b. al-Harawī, *Anwāriyya. 11th c. A.H. Persian Translation and Commentary on Suhrawardī's Ḥikmat al-Ishrāq [Philosophy of Illumination]*, ed. Hossein Ziai (n.p. 1357 Sh./1978; 2nd ed. Tehran, 1363 Sh./1984).

36. Beside his claims for the absolute omnipotence of God, al-Suhrawardī, nevertheless, opened the door to the possibility of prophetic claims on this very 'experiential' basis. It is interesting to note that Ibn al-ʿArabī's concept of '*waḥdat al-wujūd*', with all its religious and theological implications, was also vehemently opposed and attacked by the '*ulamā*'.

37. For Quṭb al-Dīn al-Shīrāzī's commentary on the *Ḥikmat al-ishrāq* tr. Corbin, cf. al-Suhrawardī, *Le livre de la sagesse orientale*, p. 241 n. 23; cf. *Le livre*, p. 241 n. 24, on certainty.

38. Walbridge mentions that 'Suhrawardī states that the truths of the Science of Lights are derived in the first instance from mystical intuition', cf. Walbridge, *The Science of Mystic Lights*, p. 42; cf. al-Suhrawardī, *Ḥikmat al-ishrāq*, pp. 162–165. Walbridge also adds that '*The Philosophy of Illumination* is philosophy, not mysticism; Suhrawardī constructs rational proofs of his intuitions both for the sake of his own continued certainty and correct interpretation of those intuitions and for the guidance of those without the experience', cf. Walbridge, *The Science of Mystic Lights*, p. 42.

39. Hossein Ziai, 'The Source and Nature of Authority: A Study of al-Suhrawardī's Illuminationist Political Doctrine', in Charles E. Butterworth, ed., *The Political Aspects of Islamic Philosophy. Essays in Honor of Muhsin S. Mahdi* (Cambridge, 1992), pp. 324–334.

40. Al-Suhrawardī, *Ḥikmat al-ishrāq*, p. 12.

41. Ibid.

42. Al-Suhrawardī mentions that these proofs (s. *quṭb*) are essential, whether they are living, or in occultation; and what is alluded to here is the whole doctrine of prophets and

prophetology, cf. *Ḥikma*, pp. 11, 12; cf. Corbin, *En Islam iranien*, vol. 2, pp. 69–72.

43. Al-Suhrawardī, *Ḥikmat al-ishrāq*, pp. 12–13. Al-Suhrawardī also alludes to the existence of a '*qā'im al-Kitāb*', or a 'maintainer of the Book' who will guide the seeker that is unable to 'truly' understand the esoteric meaning of his work, especially the *Ḥikmat al-ishrāq*.

44. The theme of the importance of the master-disciple relationship is prevalent in al-Suhrawardī's works.

45. Al-Suhrawardī, *al-Talwīḥāt*, pp. 70–74. For a general introduction to the historical background of the early Sufi tradition, cf. Annemarie Schimmel, *Mystical Dimensions of Islam* (Chapel Hill, NC, 1975), pp. 42–77.

46. Al-Suhrawardī, *al-Talwīḥāt*, pp. 73–4; quoted in Ziai, *Knowledge and Illumination*, p. 21 n. 3; cf. *Knowledge and Illumination*, pp. 21–22, p. 21 n. 2; cf. Henry Corbin, *Les motifs zoroastriens dans la philosophie de Sohrawardî, shaykh-ol-Ishrāq (ob. 587/1191)*, preface by M. Pouré-Davoud (Tehran, 1325 Sh./1946), pp. 28–29.

47. Toshihiko Izutsu, 'Ishrāqiyya', *ER*.

48. Hermann Landolt, 'Mystique iranienne: Suhravardī Shaykh al-Ishrāq (549/1155–587/1191) et 'Ayn al-Quẓāt-i Hamadānī (492–525/1098–1131)', in Charles J. Adams, ed., *Iranian Civilization and Culture* (Montreal, 1972), p. 25.

# 18

# Al-Suhrawardī on Body as Extension: An Alternative to Hylomorphism from Plato to Leibniz

*John Walbridge*

Among the *sophismata* of al-Suhrawardī's *Philosophy of Illumination* are several chapters on the nature of bodies, the central conclusion of which is that bodies are simply self-subsistent extensions – magnitudes or dimensions with accidents. This is a curious claim and not one that has been much discussed by modern students of al-Suhrawardī. It is, it turns out, one of the clearer examples of al-Suhrawardī's adoption of a distinctively Platonic doctrine, in this case following a particular tradition of late Neoplatonic interpretation.

## Al-Suhrawardī and his Doctrine of Space

Shihāb al-Dīn Yaḥyā al-Suhrawardī, who was executed in 587/1191 at the order of the great Saladin, is the central figure in the revival of Neoplatonism in post-classical Islamic philosophy. Trained in the philosophy of Avicenna, he was converted to Platonism, he says, through a dream in which Aristotle appeared to him, testified to the superiority of Plato and the mystics over the Peripatetics, and taught him the doctrine of knowledge by presence. Al-Suhrawardī's most important work – used here as the main source for his view – is the *Ḥikmat al-ishrāq* ('The Philosophy of Illumination'), in which he lays out his metaphysics of light. The third chapter of the Logic of this work, nominally devoted to sophistics, contains a series of attacks on characteristic doctrines of the Islamic Neo-Aristotelianism of Avicenna: essential definition, the Peripatetic proof of the immortality of the soul, the Peripatetic rejection of the Platonic Forms, and so on.[1]

Later Islamic philosophers identified two central principles of al-Suhrawardī's system: knowledge by presence and the primacy of quiddity. Knowledge by presence is the doctrine that all knowledge involves the unmediated presence of what is known to the knower. Vision, to cite his paradigmatic case, results when a sound eye is in the unobstructed presence of an illuminated object; there is no transfer or imprinting of intermediate forms. Not unlike the slightly later William of Ockham, al-Suhrawardī was deeply suspicious of theories of perception involving intermediate entities. Being a Sufi he carried this theory into the metaphysical realm, holding that an intellectual or spiritual intuition of immaterial entities was possible and indeed necessary for reliable philosophical discovery. Conversely, what could not be seen in some sense was not likely to be real.[2] Primacy of quiddity – not al-Suhrawardī's own term – was the view that it was the individual entities that were ultimately real, not substrates like existence or matter. Al-Suhrawardī held that the individuals that are all that exist are neither compounds of existence and quiddity, as Avicenna might be understood as saying, nor differentiations of a common underlying existence, as Mullā Ṣadrā and his supporters were later to insist.[3]

Aristotelian hylomorphism is one of al-Suhrawardī's chief targets in the *sophismata* of *The Philosophy of Illumination.* He writes:

> The Peripatetics argue that body admits of connection and division, but connection does not admit of division. Therefore, something must exist in the body that admits of both; this is prime matter. They further argue that magnitude does not enter into the reality of bodies, since all bodies share in corporeality yet differ in magnitudes – and because a single body may become smaller or larger with compression and rarefaction.[4]

The argument is probably taken directly from Avicenna, who wrote at the beginning of his discussion of body in the Physics in the *Hints and Admonitions:*

> You know that body is connected solid magnitude and that it accepts division and separation. You also know that that which is connected by essence does not accept both connection and division in such a way that it can be identically described by both. Therefore, the potential to accept [both] is not the existence of that which is actually accepted, nor is it its state and form.[5]

That which does allow both connection and division is Aristotle's prime matter. Al-Suhrawardī replies that the problem can equally well be solved by saying that body is simply magnitude extended in three dimensions. This curious doctrine goes back to Plato through a very interesting history of interpretation of the *Timaeus* and the hylomorphism of the *Physics.*

### The Problem of the Receptacle in the *Timaeus*

When Plato turns to describing the 'works of necessity' in the *Timaeus*, he mentions an entity that he calls the 'Receptacle' (*ὑποδοχή*).

> For our earlier discourse the two were sufficient: one postulated as model, intelligible and always unchangingly real; second, a copy of this model, which becomes and is visible. A third we did not then distinguish, thinking that the two would suffice; but now, it seems, the argument compels us to attempt to bring to light and describe a form difficult and obscure. What nature must we, then, conceive it to possess and what part does it play? This, more than anything else: that it is the Receptacle – as it were, the nurse – of all becoming … . For the present we must conceive three things: that which it becomes; that in which it becomes; and the model in whose likeness that which becomes is born. Indeed we may fittingly compare the Recipient to a mother, the model to a father, and the nature that arises between them to their offspring. Further, we must observe that, if there is to be an impress presenting all diversities of aspect, the thing in which the impress comes to be situated, cannot have been duly prepared unless it is free from all those characters which it is to receive from elsewhere.[6]

The 'one' is the world of being, which is to say the Forms, and the 'second' is the world of becoming, the familiar world of physical objects where we live. The Receptacle would then be the substrate in which material things come to be. Plato compares the Receptacle to gold being continually moulded but denies that it has any properties of its own, lest it mix its own qualities with the qualities of that which is impressed in it. It is thus not any one of the elements. Plato also refers to this entity as *χώρα*, 'space', *τόπς*, 'place' and *ἕδρα*, 'seat'. Aristotle helpfully adds two more terms: *μεταληπτκόν* and *μεθεκτικόν*, both meaning 'capable of receiving or participating'.[7] Like so much of the *Timaeus* this passage has puzzled commentators.[8]

Galen's epitome, the channel through which Muslims knew the *Timaeus*, would not have been much help to Muslim philosophers trying to find out about the Receptacle. In the Arabic version Galen writes:

> He discusses the transmutation of earth, fire, water and air into each other and names the thing that includes all of them and which remains during transmutation 'the Mother' and the 'Nurse of Becoming'. He says that she is existent *(mawḍūʿa)* since the beginning, prepared to acquire her resemblance to the Father, for the universe comes to be and is generated from matter and form (*ḥadatha wa-tawallada ʿan al-mādda wa'l-ṣūra*).[9]

For the reader of the Arabic Galen the problem is solved by omission; the mysterious 'Receptacle' is nowhere to be found. The 'Mother' and 'Nurse' remain, but they are obviously just metaphorical expressions for matter.

The reader of Aristotle's *Physics* 4.2 will find another interpretation of the Receptacle. The following is translated from the Arabic of Isḥāq b. Ḥunayn. The translation has a clarity and fidelity close to modern academic translations, but certain specific renderings will be significant for us:

> If the place (*makān*) is the first container of each body, then it is the limit (*nihāya*). If so, the place would be considered to be the existent form or shape (*ṣūra aw khilqa*) of each thing, that by which its magnitude and the matter of its magnitude (*hayūlā miqdārihi*) were bounded. Thus, it would be the limit of each of them.
>
> If we follow this approach, the place of each thing would be its form, but if it is considered with respect to the place being the dimension (*buʿd*) of the magnitude, [the place] would be the matter, for the dimension is different from the size (*al-ʿaẓm*). The dimension is that which the form encompasses (*yashtamil*) and bounds, as you would say that the surface and limit encompass it. This is an attribute of matter and of what is not bounded, for if you abstract from matter the sphericity, limit and qualities, nothing remains except matter.
>
> For that reason Plato said in his book attributed to Timaeus that matter and space (*al-mawḍiʿ*) were the same thing. That is because the Receptacle (*al-qābil ʿalāʾl-istidlāl*) and space are the very same thing. However, he describes the Receptacle differently here than he does in those of his opinions known as the 'Untitled', but he did state clearly that place and space are the very same thing. All agree that place is something, but he alone tried to find out what it was.[10]

The questions we would want to sort out are: What exactly did Plato mean by 'Receptacle'? How can it be translated into the standard terminology of Aristotle and the Peripatetics? Are Plato and Aristotle in general agreement or general disagreement on this issue? How did the intervening philosophical tradition understand the problem? We can then return to al-Suhrawardī and see what sense his views make in the light of the general tradition of interpretation of the Receptacle in the *Timaeus* and the places in Aristotle's writings where it is discussed, particularly *Physics* 4.2.

There are two major approaches to understanding the Receptacle: (1) it is matter, and thus Plato and Aristotle are in general agreement on the question of a material substrate; or (2) it is space, and Plato and Aristotle disagree. The first view, roughly speaking, reduces space to body; the second, body to space. The second is, approximately, al-Suhrawardī's view. Since I do not wish or need to bury myself in the complexities of the traditions of interpretation of the *Timaeus* and the *Physics*, my accounts will be schematic.

## The Receptacle as Matter

In their attempt to bring scientific coherence to the understanding of the *Timaeus*, Brisson and Meyerstein reduce the doctrine of the Receptacle to an axiom:

> *Axion T7: The demiurge orders a primordial stuff, the* khora.
>
> *Khora* is at the same time that in which sensible particulars are found, i.e. space or place, and that of which they are made, i.e. something approximating matter.

> We translate *khora* as 'spatial medium'. . . .
>
> The spatial medium is at the same time 'that in which' and 'that from which' the sensible world is made.[11]

Thus, for Brisson and Meyerstein the Receptacle is both space and matter. In this view, they have support from Plato's text, for he refers to the Receptacle as 'space' but later likens it to gold constantly being moulded into new shapes. By identifying the Receptacle as a 'spatial medium', they show themselves moving towards the Aristotelian position in which space and place are subordinate to matter.

The doxographer Aetius identifies the difference between Plato and Aristotle as the following:

**On place**

> Plato thinks that place is the Receptacle of forms, which he metaphorically calls 'the element'. For him it is like something that receives the element.
>
> Aristotle thinks that place is the limit of the surrounding thing that touches what it surrounds.[12]

Place for Aristotle is the surrounding body, and makes sense only in the context of other bodies. There can be no vacuum and nothing outside the universe because without body there is no place.

After Aristotle there was a consistent tradition identifying the Receptacle with matter, part of the larger tradition that minimised disagreements between Plato and Aristotle. Examples are Galen in his epitome – at least the Arabic version, which is what counts for us – and Calcidius, whose Latin commentary on the *Timaeus* was a critical text for early medieval European science.[13]

The identity of the Receptacle with Aristotelian matter is still defended in our time:

> On seven major counts, Aristotle's 'prime matter' may rightfully be said to resemble Plato's 'Receptacle'. The differences cannot be denied; but they are not insuperable, and can be accounted for. The two entities must surely be the same. Our conclusion is, therefore, that Aristotle did understand his master's view of the Receptacle, and that he adopted it and developed it in his own view of prime matter.[14]

Such a view of the Receptacle as prime matter or something close to it is the dominant one in the later Greek philosophical tradition. Even al-Suhrawardī's own Illuminationist school did not follow him in his outright rejection of hylomorphism, although his objections to it were noted.[15]

The difficulty with the Aristotelian solution is that it does not quite give a satisfactory account of space. While a self-subsistent absolute space made of nothing is a difficult notion, so too is the idea that space is nothing but the relations of bodies. An unexplained absolute space remains in the background of the Aristotelian system. Moreover, a vacuum is nowhere near as unthinkable as the Peripatetics would like us to think, and many rather ordinary physical problems can most naturally be explained by recourse to vacuum. Once the Medievals began performing thought experiments involving such notions as moving the entire universe laterally, the whole Aristotelian theory of space was doomed.

## The Receptacle as Space

The strength of the Receptacle-as-matter theory is that it seems obvious – or at least it used to seem obvious – that there must be *something* that everything is made of. Its weakness is that the Peripatetics' account of this stuff, which is never known in its pure form, does not inspire a lot of confidence. Hylomorphism may be the child of entirely respectable parents – Pythagorean mathematics and Heracleitan scepticism about appearances – but its grandparents include the naive materialistic physics of the Ionians. No matter how abstractly one might talk about 'prime matter', *ὕλη*, is still wood and at best a social-climbing granddaughter of Thales' water. In philosophy, as in families, blood will tell.

As a result, some took the radical step of identifying the Receptacle, and therefore the basic material of bodies, as space, pure and simple. This interpretation has the textual virtue that Plato did say that the Receptacle was *χώρα* 'space'. More important, it eliminates an entity: prime matter. It has gained plausiblity for us, now that general relativity and quantum mechanics have warped our conceptions of space and matter. Richard Sorabji has pointed out that such a rejection of prime matter in favour of self-subsistent magnitude or extension was a characteristic theme of certain late Neoplatonic commentators on Aristotle, notably Simplicius.[16] For them body was simply extension possessing physical properties: 'For it seems that extension has four meanings: … (3) a material extension endowed with physical qualities and resistances, such as a body.'[17]

## Body as Extension: al-Suhrawardī, Descartes, Leibniz

Al-Suhrawardī's critique of hylomorphism is complex and densely argued, the product of more than fifteen centuries of continuous philosophical debate about the nature of body and substance. In *The Philosophy of Illumination* he criticises several aspects of the Peripatetic theory of matter and form in a multipart argument spanning several short chapters. Al-Suhrawardī's theory of body raises too many questions to be analysed in detail here, particularly since there have been no serious studies, or even editions, of the physical sections of his three mature Peripatetic works. What can be said on the basis of the *sophismata* of *The Philosophy of*

*Illumination* is that he holds that body is a compound of extension and properties, just as Simplicius had done.[18]

Al-Suhrawardī seems to reject hylomorphism out of a dislike of non-sensible entities. Aristotle's theory requires several layers of such entities: matter and form, specific and generic forms, and the forms of the elements. Al-Suhrawardī wonders how these various forms and entities can be distinguished from the sensible properties of the body. He fundamentally disagrees with the Peripatetics about the role of accidents in causation. The Peripatetics, he claims, had wished to avoid making accidents part of the causes of substances, but for al-Suhrawardī it is important that accidents be able to constitute causes, for it is the causality of accidents that makes it possible to explain the existence of the Platonic Forms and ultimately to explain the diversity of the celestial and sublunar realms. The Peripatetics have it backwards, he says. Even they admit that the individuals of a species are distinguished by accidents. If this is so, then are not these accidents – which make possible the concrete existence of the individuals of the species – more worthy of being considered substances? When we look closely at the Peripatetic arguments, we find that when it is convenient they do allow accidents to figure in the causes of substance. Accidents like heat play a role in the transmutation of the four elements. On the loftiest level, the emanation of the body of the sphere, according to the Islamic Peripatetics, is caused by the intellect's intellection of its own contingency.

Al-Suhrawardī's rejection of hylomorphism is an instance of his general rejection of the reality of nonsensible entities; he constructed his theory of knowledge on the model of perception. Therefore, entities that cannot be perceived either by physical senses or by nonsensible intuition cannot be known, and if they exist, it is only as mental constructs.

He also takes this opportunity to criticise the Peripatetic treatment (or, lack thereof) of the intensity of substances and accidents. Al-Suhrawardī rejects Aristotle's list of ten categories, arguing that the ten can be reduced to five – substance, motion, relation, quantity, quality – and that intensity should be added to the list. The remaining Aristotelian categories – place, time, possession, position, action and passion – can be reduced to relation. He cites the ancient Pythagorean Archytas as his authority for changing the number of categories.[19] The Peripatetics, he complains, tried to explain change in intensity of qualities by means of differentiae. It is absurd to think that heat, for example, varies by a differentia of some sort. It is obvious that one instance of heat is simply more or less hot – more or less intensely heat. Likewise, their rejection of the application of the category of intensity to substances is found to be based on nothing more than ordinary linguistic usage. When they say that one animal is not more or less animal than another, this is just a function of language, not of reality.[20]

When al-Suhrawardī goes on to construct his metaphysics, these concepts become important. It is by intensity that the immaterial lights differ in the first instance. Bodies are barriers, simply things that acquire properties from the lights. They have no activity in themselves. In a system in which things must either be immaterial lights, dark inert bodies, or light or dark accidents, it is difficult to know what sort of things the forms of species or elements could be. They are not lights or luminous accidents, since they are not directly manifest, yet they cannot be dark barriers or dark accidents, since they are active. Al-Suhrawardī is happy to rid his universe of vague entities like secondary substances and the forms of elements.

This issue arises once again, much later in the history of metaphysics, in the form of a disagreement between Descartes and Leibniz over the nature of material bodies. Descartes, in his search for philosophical clarity, had reduced the conception of body to extension alone:

> That the nature of body consists not in weight, nor in hardness, nor colour and so on, but in extension alone.
>
> In this way we shall ascertain that the nature of matter or of body in its universal aspect, does not consist in its being hard, or heavy, or coloured, or one that affects our senses in some other way, but solely in the fact that it is a substance extended in length, breadth and depth.[21]

Descartes comes to this conclusion from a different direction than that taken by al-Suhrawardī five centuries earlier, but the objections that each feels called upon to answer are very similar, and by the time they are done, each has covered much the same philosophical territory. Both philosophers see the problem of compression and rarefaction as the obvious objection to their theory, and each answers it by explaining rarefaction as the presence of gaps filled with subtle bodies. Each argues that his theory demonstrates the non-existence of vacuum. Each rejects the indivisible atom on the grounds that, however small it might be, it would nonetheless be potentially divisible in thought.

It is possible that these similarities reflect some common source, perhaps Neoplatonic authors like Simplicius. Certainly, there are structural similarities between the two systems, for Descartes' search for clear conceptions parallels al-Suhrawardī's quest to rid philosophy of non-sensible forms. It is tempting to link these theories with contemporary physics in which the distinctions of matter, space and energy blur. While there are certainly commonalities of metaphysical style, such an analysis would take us too far afield.

Half a century later Descartes' radical reduction of body to extension was challenged by Leibniz, who proved to his own satisfaction that extension and body were different things. In his *Discourse on Metaphysics* he argues that:

> **XVIII** *The distinction between force and the quantity of motion is, among other reasons, important as showing that we must have recourse to metaphysical considerations in addition to discussions of extension if we wish to explain the phenomena of matter....*

> It appears more and more clear that although all the particular phenomena of nature can be explained mathematically or mechanically by those who understand them, yet nevertheless, the general principles of corporeal nature and even of mechanics are metaphysical rather than geometric, and belong rather to certain indivisible forms or natures as the causes of the appearances, than to the corporeal mass or to extension. In this way we are able to reconcile the mechanical philosophy of the moderns with the circumspection of those intelligent and well-meaning persons who, with a certain justice, fear that we are becoming too far removed from immaterial beings and that we are thus prejudicing piety.[22]

Leibniz is arguing that there needs to be more to material bodies than simple extension if the varying properties of bodies of the same size and shape are to be explained. Leibniz' opinion, that Descartes' attempt to reduce knowledge to analytic geometry and a handful of its first cousins had gone much too far, may perhaps be summed up in the title of a chapter a few pages earlier in the same book: 'That the opinions of the theologians and of the so-called scholastic philosophers are not to be wholly despised.'[23]

How then are we to make sense of the project of al-Suhrawardī, who was certainly not indifferent to the 'fear that we are becoming too far removed from immaterial beings and that we are thus prejudicing piety'? Al-Suhrawardī had no interest in Descartes' project of the mathematisation of nature and knowledge, and so we would expect to find him on the side of Leibniz in such issues. Yet 'the theologians and the so-called scholastic philosophers' whose authority Leibniz invoked are the Peripatetics, whom al-Suhrawardī detested and believed to be threats to the true, spiritual, Platonic philosophy. The explanation is that the roads followed by al-Suhrawardī and Descartes simply happened to run together for a time, long enough to produce similar theories of body on the basis of similar arguments, criticising the same philosophers in the process, but their fundamental philosophical projects were quite different. Descartes sought to re-establish knowledge on the basis of clear and distinct, innate ideas. The hierarchy of forms required by the Aristotelian theory of body, as al-Suhrawardī pointed out, contained much that was obscure – as witness the fact that people could disagree on something so simple as the nature of air and water. Extension, however, is a clear and distinct idea. Al-Suhrawardī, on the other hand, sought to reduce knowledge to perception – the theory of 'knowledge by presence'. For him the problem with such entities as prime matter and the forms of elements, species and genera was that they could not be seen, either literally or by mystical or intellectual intuition. In this case, the two approaches produce similar results, but the motivations for reducing body to extension are as different as they can be.

In a more fundamental way, al-Suhrawardī would have found Descartes' philosophical project utterly wrongheaded. Descartes knew that perception could be deceptive, so he dismissed it as a fundamental source of knowledge. In the end, this radical doubt drove him to solipsism, from which he could escape only with the aid of self-evident innate ideas – that is, if one believes that he actually was able to escape. Al-Suhrawardī believed exactly the opposite. 'Clear and distinct innate ideas' were *iʿtibārāt ʿaqliyya*, beings of reason or intellectual fictions, and did not necessarily correspond to real distinctions. On the other hand, the soul has a window through which it can be in the unmediated presence of that which it knows, whether by sensation or by intuition. Moreover, al-Suhrawardī's universe is full of lights, full of life and living beings. It is not the cold material universe of Descartes and Newton. We are only 'removed from immaterial beings' when we fail to open our spiritual eyes and apprehend the immaterial lights. A philosophical project which purports to show that we are in principle unable to be in direct contact with other immaterial lights – for, of course, each of us is such a monad – is likewise utterly wrongheaded.

So in fundamental ways al-Suhrawardī is in the same camp as Leibniz; indeed, the similarity of his immaterial lights to Leibnizian monads is striking. How then would he answer Leibniz' objection to the extension theory of body, that it fails to explain the diverse properties of bodies of the same extension? The answer is the immaterial beings whose banishment from the universe Leibniz had feared. Al-Suhrawardī is perfectly well aware that bodies have properties not reducible to extension. These are caused by the immaterial lights. As has been mentioned before, al-Suhrawardī had rejected the Avicennan theory that limited the immaterial intellects to ten, with perhaps ten souls driving the planets. Al-Suhrawardī did not think that this small number of intellects – immaterial lights, as he would call them – was sufficient explanation for the complexity that we observe in the world. Instead, there are vast numbers of immaterial lights existing on the same ontological levels – having the same intensity but differing from each other in accidents of light and darkness. Certain of these lights are the Platonic Forms, whose solicitude is the cause of the consistency of species. Others are souls of planets, men and animals. Still others are manifested in such features of the material universe as the four elements. Because these lights are able to interact directly with matter, al-Suhrawardī has no need to posit non-sensible forms in material objects. There need be no form of water or earth in a human body since the immaterial light that is the metaphysical cause of water and earth is sufficient to explain the existence of the attributes of water and earth in a given body. Leibniz needed to posit 'metaphysical considerations' in order to explain the properties of bodies, by which he seems to have meant something like the various forms posited by Aristotle. Al-Suhrawardī, having his 'metaphysical considerations' safely placed above the moon, can dispense with metaphysical natures implanted in bodies. It is a piece of metaphysical economy that the continental rationalists of the seventeenth century might have understood and appreciated.

## Notes

1. There is no comprehensive and satisfactory account of al-Suhrawardī's philosophy. There are two quite different approaches to interpreting al-Suhrawardī: a 'theosophical' interpretation associated with the late Henry Corbin and a 'logical' or 'philosophical' interpretation, of which Hossein Ziai and I are at present the most active defenders. The latter is assumed in the present article. The theosophical interpreters tend to privilege the allegorical elements of al-Suhrawardī's works; the philosophical interpretation the metaphysical and logical ones.

The 'philosophical interpretation': On al-Suhrawardī and his own view of his place in the history of philosophy, see my *The Leaven of the Ancients: Suhrawardī and the Heritage of the Greeks* (Albany, NY, 2000), which also contains an account of his life and works, as well as a full bibliography, and *The Wisdom of the Mystic East: Suhrawardī and Platonic Orientalism* (Albany, NY, 2001). On his metaphysics see my *The Science of Mystic Lights: Quṭb al-Dīn Shīrāzī and the Illuminationist Tradition in Islamic Philosophy* (Cambridge, MA, 1992), especially chapters two and three, which analyse the relationship between Illuminationist metaphysics and the Islamic Peripatetic tradition of Avicenna. On logic see Hossein Ziai, *Knowledge and Illumination: A Study of Suhrawardī's Ḥikmat al-Ishrāq* (Atlanta, GA, 1990); and for a more general account, Hossein Ziai, 'Shihāb al-Dīn Suhrawardī: Founder of the Illuminationist School' and 'The Illuminationist Tradition', in Seyyed Hossein Nasr and Oliver Leaman, ed., *History of Islamic Philosophy* (London, 1996), vol. 1, pp. 434–496.

The 'theosophical interpretation' is assumed in Henry Corbin's many works, notably the introductions to his editions and translations of al-Suhrawardī's works and in his *En Islam iranien* (Paris, 1971), vol. 2, *Sohravardī et les Platoniciens de Perse*. Corbin's interpretation is given in a more accessible form in the works of Seyyed Hossein Nasr, *Three Muslim Sages* (Cambridge, MA, 1964), Chapter 2 and 'Suhrawardī', in M. M. Sharif, ed., *A History of Muslim Philosophy* (Wiesbaden, 1963), vol. 1, pp. 372–398. See also Mehdi Amin Razavi, *Suhrawardi and the School of Illumination* (Richmond, Surrey, 1997) which I reviewed in *IJMES*, 30 (1998), pp. 615–617. The difference between the two interpretations may be seen in the two translations of *Ḥikmat al-ishrāq* (hereafter cited as *HI*), Corbin's *Le Livre de la Sagesse Orientale, Kitāb Ḥikmat al-Ishrāq*, ed. Christian Jambet (Paris, 1986), and Ziai and Walbridge, *The Philosophy of Illumination* (Provo, UT, 1999).

2. On knowledge by presence see Walbridge, *Leaven*, chap. 10, and *Science*, pp. 89–109; Ziai, *Knowledge*, pp. 129–161; and Mehdi Ha'iri Yazdi, *The Principles of Epistemology in Islamic Philosophy: Knowledge by Presence* (Albany, NY, 1992).

3. I develop this view in *Science*, chap. 2. See also Toshihiko Izutsu, *The Concept and Reality of Existence* (Tokyo, 1971), a brilliant study of ontology in post-classical Islamic philosophy.

4. *HI*, para. 72.

5. *Kitāb al-ishārāt wa'l-tanbīhāt ma'a sharḥ Naṣīr al-Dīn al-Ṭūsī*, ed. Sulaymān Dunyā (Cairo, 1957–1960), 4 vols. in 3, vol. 2, pp. 168–171 (vol. 2, chap. 6, pp. 1–4).

6. *Timaeus*, 48E–49A, 50C–E, tr. Cornford.

7. *Timaeus*, 52A–B; *Physics*, 4.2, 209b12,14, 35, 210a2.

8. On Plato and Aristotle's doctrines of space, matter and the Receptacle, I have used A. E. Taylor, *A Commentary on Plato's Timaeus* (Oxford, 1928), and Francis Cornford, *Plato's*

*Cosmology: The Timaeus of Plato Translated with a Running Commentary* (London, 1937), especially the latter; Luc Brisson and F. Walter Meyerstein, *Inventer l'universe* (Paris, 1991); rev. tr. *Inventing the Universe: Plato's Timaeus, the Big Bang, and the Problem of Scientific Knowledge* (Albany, NY, 1995); Keimpe Algra, *Concepts of Space in Greek Thought* (Leiden, 1995); George S. Claghorn, *Aristotle's Criticism of Plato's 'Timaeus'* (The Hague, 1954); W. K. C. Guthrie, *A History of Greek Philosophy* (Cambridge, 1975), vol. 5; Harold Cherniss, *Aristotle's Criticism of Plato and the Academy* (Baltimore, MD, 1944). I have consulted the following editions and translations of Aristotle's *Physics*, IV: P. H. Wickstead and F. Cornford (Cambridge, 1929), R. P. Hardie and R. K. Gaye, in *The Complete Works of Aristotle: The Revised Oxford Translation* (Princeton, NJ, 1984), vol. 1, pp. 315–446; Hippocrates G. Apostle, *Aristotle's Physics* (Bloomington, IN, 1969); and in Arabic, Isḥāq b. Ḥunayn, *al-Ṭabīʿa*, ed. ʿAbd al-Raḥmān Badawī (Cairo, 1385/1965).

9. Galen, 'Jawāmiʿ Kitāb *Ṭīmāwus*', in Plato, *Aflāṭūn fī'l-Islām*, ed. ʿAbd al-Raḥmān Badawī (Tehran, 1974), p. 98. The phrase 'prepared to acquire her resemblance to the Father' is obscure and my translation is a guess. Both Kraus and Badawī proposed emendations; Galen, 'Jawāmiʿ Kitāb *Ṭīmāwus*', p. 98, n. 3.

10. Aristotle, *Physics*, 209b1–16; my translation of Aristotle, *al-Ṭabīʿa*, tr. Isḥāq b. Ḥunayn, pp. 284–286.

11. Brisson and Meyerstein, *Inventing*, pp. 22–23.

12. Aetius 1.19, my translation from the Arabic.

13. I owe this particular fact to my friend Paul Spade, who also points out that Calcidius' influence can be easily traced through his literal translation of *ὕλη* 'matter' as *silva* 'wood', which was its original meaning in Greek.

14. Claghorn, *Aristotle's Criticism*, p. 19.

15. Al-Suhrawardī's commentator, Quṭb al-Dīn Shīrāzī, retains matter and form; Walbridge, *Science*, pp. 98–99. Likewise, Mullā Ṣadrā does not reject the matter/form distinction.

16. Richard Sorabji, *Matter, Space, and Motion: Theories in Antiquity and their Sequel* (Ithaca, NY, 1988), pp. 3–43, who speculates that al-Suhrawardī might be relevant to the issue. A collection of related texts with a useful introduction is Shmuel Sambursky, *The Concept of Place in Late Neoplatonism: Texts with Translation, Introduction, and Notes* (Jerusalem, 1982).

17. Sambursky, *Place*, p. 137, translating Simplicius, *In Phys.*, 623.15–20.

18. Al-Suhrawardī's discussion of matter and form, summarised here, is in *HI*, paras. 72–88.

19. *Al-Talwīḥāt*, para. 3, in *Opera Metaphysica et Mystica I* (Tehran, 1976), p. 12. Archytas was a friend of Plato. There are two works on the categories attributed to him. One, Καφολικοὶ λογοὶ δέκα (The Ten Universal Terms), was transmitted separately and the other, *Περὶ τῶν καφόλου λόγων* (On The Universal Terms), is mainly known through quotes in the Greek commentaries on the *Categories*, mainly that of Simplicius, although a full text has recently been discovered. Both are pseudepigraphic adaptations of Aristotle's *Categories*. Later Neoplatonists cited these books as evidence that Aristotle's philosophy was based on that of Pythagoras. There is no evidence of an independent translation of Archytas, so it is likely that al-Suhrawardī knew of Archytas through a commentary on the *Categories*.

Al-Fārābī knew that the works on categories attributed to Archytas were pseudepigraphic and attributed them to Themistius; cf. al-Farābī, *Kitāb al-alfāẓ al-mustaʿmala fi'l-manṭiq*, ed. Muhsin Mahdi (Beirut, 1968), pp. 108–109.

20. *Talwīḥāt*, paras. 2–5, in *Opera*, vol. 1, pp. 5–14.

21. Descartes, *The Principles of Philosophy*, 2.4, in Elizabeth S. Haldane and G. R. T. Ross, tr., *The Philosophical Works of Descartes* (Cambridge, 1969), vol. 1, pp. 255–256; cf. 2.5–20, 1:256–264, for the continuation of the discussion.

22. In Philip P. Wiener, ed., *Leibniz: Selections* (New York, 1951), pp. 316–318.

23. *Discourse on Metaphysics*, 11, in Wiener, ed., p. 303.

19

# *Miʿrāj al-kalima*: de la *Risāla Qushayriyya aux Futūḥāt Makkiyya*

*Michel Chodkiewicz*

Dans la notice du *Rūḥ al-quds* qu'il consacre à l'un de ses premiers maîtres, Abū Yaʿqūb Yūsuf b. Yakhlaf al-Qummī,[1] Ibn ʿArabī déclare: 'Je n'avais alors jamais vu la *Risāla* d'al-Qushayrī ni aucun ouvrage semblable et j'ignorais ce que signifiait le mot *taṣawwuf*.'[2] Il raconte ensuite qu'un jour Yūsuf al-Qummī, partant à cheval vers une montagne située à une courte distance de Séville, lui ordonna de l'y rejoindre avec un de ses compagnons. Ce dernier portait un exemplaire de cette *Risāla* dont Ibn ʿArabī répète qu'il ignorait tout de son contenu comme de son auteur. Les deux jeunes gens, ayant retrouvé leur shaykh au sommet de la montagne, accomplirent la prière de midi derrière lui, dans une mosquée bâtie à cet endroit. Puis, 'tournant le dos à la *qibla*, [le shaykh] me tendit la *Risāla* et me dit: "Lis!" Or la crainte révérentielle que j'éprouvais me rendit incapable de prononcer deux mots de suite et le livre tomba de ma main. Il dit alors à mon compagnon: "Lis!" Ce dernier commença à lire et le shaykh se mit à faire un commentaire sans interruption jusqu'au moment où nous accomplîmes la prière du *ʿaṣr*.'

Une date mentionnée à deux reprises dans les *Futūḥāt* à propos de Yūsuf al-Qummī suggère qu'Ibn ʿArabī connut ce shaykh en 586/1190. Il était donc âgé alors de vingt-six années lunaires. Moins de dix ans plus tard, les premiers ouvrages qu'il rédige témoignent qu'il a acquis une parfaite maîtrise du vocabulaire technique du *taṣawwuf* et que les grands textes classiques lui sont devenus familiers. Dans un livre composé, il est vrai, beaucoup plus tard, la *Muḥāḍarat al-abrār*,[3] Ibn ʿArabī donne une liste des auteurs dont il a tiré une partie des matériaux de ce recueil de miscellanées: la *Risāla* y figure en bonne place à côté d'œuvres d'al-Sulamī, d'Abū Nuʿaym, d'Ibn al-Jawzī par exemple. Elle n'est néanmoins citée qu'assez rarement dans les écrits du Shaykh al-Akbar,[4] en général lorsque celui-ci rapporte un propos attribué à l'un des *rijāl* de la *Risāla*. En dépit de cette relative rareté des renvois explicites, il n'en demeure pas moins qu'Ibn ʿArabī reconnaît à l'ouvrage d'al-Qushayrī le statut d'une référence majeure comme le vérifie un examen attentif des *Futūḥāt Makkiyyāt*.

La structure des *Futūḥāt* peut être considérée de plusieurs points de vue, ce qui entraîne parfois des confusions quant à l'emplacement exact d'une citation mentionnée par tel ou tel des commentateurs anciens qui n'avaient à leur disposition que des manuscrits. Il y a, tout d'abord, une subdivision matérielle de l'ouvrage en trente-sept volumes (*asfār*) dans le manuscrit autographe sur lequel est basée l'édition entreprise par O. Yahia. Chacun de ces volumes comporte à son tour sept parties, soit un total de deux cent cinquante-neuf *ajzāʾ*. Plus significative quant à l'architecture de cet *opus magnum* est la répartition en six section (*fuṣūl*) dotées chacune d'un titre qui en annonce le contenu. Intervient enfin la division en 560 chapitres (*abwāb*),[5] le nombre des chapitres de chaque *faṣl* ayant manifestement un caractère symbolique.[6]

C'est sur la deuxième section – le *faṣl al-muʿāmalāt* – que notre attention va se porter ici. Elle compte 115 chapitres. Ce nombre trouve son explication dans un *ḥadīth*, cité par Ḥakīm al-Tirmidhī dans son fameux questionnaire, selon lequel 'Allāh a 117 caractères'.[7] Ibn ʿArabī, dans ses réponses aux trois questions qui se rapportent à ce dit prophétique, déclare d'abord que seuls les prophètes peuvent éprouver en plénitude la 'saveur' (*dhawq*) de ces 'caractères divins' mais que les *awliyaʾ* bénéficient cependant d'une participation à ces jouissances spirituelles. Puis il précise qu'à la différence des autres *rusūl* qui, en proportions variables selon leur rang dans la hiérarchie des Envoyés, n'ont accès dans le meilleur des cas qu'à 115 des *akhlāq* divins, Muḥammad en possède la totalité. Dans le contexte de la prophétologie akbarienne, l'explication la plus probable de ces deux parts exclusivement réservées au Prophète de l'Islam est qu'elles constituent un privilège lié aux deux aspects par lesquels sa fonction se distingue de celle des autres *rusūl* – à savoir son antécédence ('J'étais prophète alors qu'Adam était entre l'eau et la boue')[8] et son caractère final puisque la Révélation est définitivement 'scellée' par la descente du Qur'an ('Pas de prophète après moi').[9] La signification du nombre des chapitres[10] devient ainsi évidente. Les *awliyaʾ* Muhammadiens sont, en leur qualité d''héritiers des prophètes antérieurs',[11] en droit d'espérer goûter la saveur de 115 des *akhlāq* divins en passant par les trois étapes que sont le *taʿalluq* ('l'adhérence' aux caractères divins), le *takhalluq* (l'appropriation de ces caractères) et le *taḥaqquq* (leur pleine réalisation).[12]

La section initiale des *Futūḥāt* est le *faṣl al-maʿārif* et la finalité de cet exposé des connaissances doctrinales fondamentales est indiqué par le très long chapitre 73 qui en est le terme: on y trouve en effet une analyse extrêmement détaillée de la nature, de la fonction, des modalités et des degrés de la sainteté.[13] L'enseignement dispensé dans les chapitres précédents a donc clairement pour objet de préparer le disciple à entreprendre le cheminement qui le conduira à la *walāya*. Encore lui faut-il mettre en œuvre les connaissances qu'il a reçues. C'est à ce passage à un stade opératif que va être consacré le *faṣl al-muʿāmalāt*, ce dernier mot ayant ici un sens très différent de celui qu'il a dans les traités de *fiqh*.

À titre de première approximation on peut, à partir d'un examen de la table des matières, conclure que la section des *muʿāmalāt* (du chapitre 74 au chapitre 188 inclus) traite de l'exercice des vertus: si la pratique 'héroïque' de celles-ci n'est pas dans l'enseignement akbarien, comme elle l'est dans la procédure de canonisation de l'Église romaine,[14] un critère décisif de sainteté, il va de soit qu'elle en est une condition nécessaire. On va voir que, sans être fausse, cette évaluation du contenu de ces chapitres demeure très insuffisante. Mais une constatation s'impose en outre dès que l'on s'interroge sur l'*ordre* des matières, c'est-à-dire sur la structure du *faṣl*: il apparaît très vite que cette structure est rigoureusement calquée sur celle de la *Risāla Qushayriyya*.[15] Cette *Risāla*, on le sait, après une introduction qui est une sorte de bref mémorial des *mashāyikh al-ṭarīq*, et une série d'exposés sur la signification d'une quarantaine de termes techniques en usage dans le soufisme,[16] est constituée, pour l'essentiel, de chapitres qui seront, annonce l'auteur, consacrés à l'explication (*sharḥ*) des 'stations' puis des 'états' de la Voie.

Relevons la liste des thèmes successivement abordés dans les treize premiers chapitres de cette partie centrale de la *Risāla*, tels que les énoncent les titres de ces chapitres: 1) *tawba*, 2) *mujāhada*, 3) *khalwa*, 4) *ʿuzla*, 5) *taqwā*, 6) *warāʿ*, 7) *zuhd*, 8) *ṣamt*, 9) *khawf*, 10) *rajāʾ*, 11) *ḥuzn*, 12) *jūʿ*, 13) *mukhālafat al-nafs*. On constate sans peine, au simple vu des titres choisis par Ibn ʿArabī, que l'ordre des thèmes, au début de la deuxième section des *Futūḥāt*, est exactement identique. Mais, alors qu'al-Qushayrī traite cette matière en treize chapitres, il n'y en a pas moins de trente-neuf dans la partie correspondante du *faṣl al-muʿāmalāt* en raison d'une démultiplication du traitement de chacun des sujets abordés. C'est ainsi que le thème de la *khalwa*, objet chez al-Qushayrī d'un seul chapitre qui associe la notion de *khalwa* et celle, connexe, de *ʿuzla*, se déploie chez Ibn ʿArabī en six chapitres: deux sur la *khalwa*, deux sur la *ʿuzla* et deux sur le *firār*, la 'fuite' vers Dieu, corollaire du 'retrait' du monde. On constate un enrichissement analogue à propos de la notion de *taqwā*, envisagée sous différents aspects dans quatre chapitres que complète un ensemble de trois autres chapitres consacrés aux principes (*uṣūl*) dont dérivent les statuts légaux puis aux *farāʾiḍ*, les actes obligatoires, et aux *nawāfil*, les actes surérogatoires. Ibn ʿArabī précise[17] qu'il eût été plus logique de parler des *uṣūl al-sharʿ* avant la série de chapitres du premier *faṣl* relatifs aux *ʿibādāt* mais que l'ordre des matières ne résulte pas, dans son ouvrage, d'un choix personnel et compare cette incohérence apparente à l'enchaînement déconcertant dans le Qurʾan de versets qui semblent n'avoir aucun rapport entre eux.[18] Cette affirmation n'est pas isolée: à maintes reprises, Ibn ʿArabī déclare que ses écrits sont rédigés sous l'emprise d'une inspiration qui lui en dicte non seulement le contenu mais aussi l'agencement.[19] On peut toutefois observer que le passage de la notion de *taqwā* à celle de Loi sacrée s'explique assez bien puisque la *sharīʿa* définit les règles de cette 'piété révérentielle' qui est l'une des significations du mot *taqwā*. Il s'agit, comme le dit al-Qushayrī, 'de se préserver par l'obéissance à Dieu [c'est-à-dire à sa Loi] de son châtiment'.[20]

Le parallélisme entre la structure de la *Risāla* et celle de la section des *muʿāmalāt* se poursuit sans le moindre écart d'un bout à l'autre. Illustrons-le par un second exemple concernant, cette fois, les derniers thèmes traités dans cette partie de la *Risāla*. Les huit chapitres finaux ont pour sujets 1) *al-khurūj min al-dunyā,* 2) *al-maʿrifa,* 3) *al-maḥabba,* 4) *al-shawq,* 5) *ḥifẓ qulūb al-mashāykh,* 6) *al-samāʿ,* 7) *al-karāmāt,* 8) *al-ruʾyā*. On retrouve ces thèmes, dans le même ordre, dans les *Futūḥāt*, répartis cette fois en treize chapitres. Au total, le nombre des chapitres est plus que doublé chez Ibn ʿArabī puisqu'aux cinquante et un chapitres de la *Risāla* correspondent cent quinze chapitres des *Futūḥāt.*

Il ne s'agit pas, toutefois, d'un simple développement quantitatif, d'une glose extensive d'un texte concis qui ne se distinguerait guère en cela de la pratique commune des commentateurs. Bien que la *Risāla* ne soit citée qu'une fois, brièvement et de manière critique dans le *faṣl al-muʿāmalāt,*[21] il est fort probable que c'est à al-Qushayrī qu'Ibn ʿArabī emprunte un certain nombre des *verba seniorum* qu'il rapporte.[22] Aucun doute n'est cependant possible dans plusieurs cas – lorsque, par exemple, dans le chapitre sur la 'certitude' (*al-yaqīn*) il mentionne – en la déclarant erronée – l'interprétation d'un *ḥadīth* par Abū ʿAlī al-Daqqāq, maître et beau-père d'al-Qushayrī: or cette interprétation figure précisément dans le *bāb al-yaqīn* de la *Risāla.*[23] La *Risāla* ou, plus exactement, les sentences des maîtres qu'elle rassemble sur chaque thème, sont pour Ibn ʿArabī un point de départ. Mais le *faṣl al-muʿāmalāt* est tout autre chose qu'un commentaire de l'ouvrage d'al-Qushayrī.

C'est à ma collègue et amie Su'ād al-Hakīm, dont la thèse est une remarquable analyse du vocabulaire d'Ibn ʿArabī, que l'on doit l'expression de *miʿrāj al-kalima* que j'ai donnée pour titre à cet article.[24] Cette forte image me paraît la plus propre à rendre compte de la démarche du Shaykh al-Akbar dans la deuxième section des *Futūḥāt* et, plus généralement, à éclairer dans toutes ses œuvres la nature du rapport qu'il entretient avec le lexique technique du *taṣawwuf.* Héritier d'une tradition déjà longue, Ibn ʿArabī ne méconnaît pas sa dette envers elle. C'est avec révérence et gratitude qu'il parle de ses propres maîtres (dans le *Rūḥ al-quds* et la *Durra fārikha* en particulier) mais aussi d'illustres soufis défunts dont il se fait à l'occasion l'hagiographe comme c'est le cas pour Dhū'l-Nūn al-Miṣrī.[25] Il paie en bien des occasions un juste tribut à des hommes comme al-Tustarī, al-Tirmidhī, al-Niffarī, Ibn Barrajān. Qu'il émette ici ou là des réserves sur tel ou tel des comportements ou des paroles de l'un ou l'autre ne doit pas surprendre: les grands *shuyūkh* de Baghdad ou du Khurasān, au 3ème siècle de l'hégire, tenaient parfois eux aussi les uns sur les autres des propos assez rudes qui traduisaient de légitimes différences de points de vue et ne sont pas à prendre au pied de la lettre; on sait qu'Ibn ʿArabī, à diverses reprises (dans les *Futūḥāt*, dans les *Tajalliyāt*, dans la *Risālat al-intiṣār*) formule des critiques à l'égard d'al-Ḥallāj – ce que Massignon ne lui a jamais pardonné .... Mais la sévérité de ces jugements ne l'empêche pas de citer souvent ses vers[26] ni de souligner qu'on lui doit deux *iṣṭilāḥāt* (*ṭūl* et *'arḍ*) qui appartiennent à la 'science des lettres', c'est-à-dire à la 'science christique' (*al-'ilm al-'isawī*) dont le rôle est fondamental à ses yeux.[27]

Ce riche langage de l'expérience spirituelle que lui ont légué les générations antérieures, Ibn 'Arabī en valide les acceptions usuelles, qui relèvent de l'ethos soufi, tout en s'appliquant, sur bien des points, à les préciser. Mais il ne s'en tient pas là. Son souci constant – on le vérifie tout particulièrement dans le *faṣl al-mu'āmalāt* – est en quelque sorte d'exhausser les 'mots de la tribu' et, par ce *mi'rāj al-kalima*, d'en faire surgir des significations plus hautes. Du domaines des pratiques vertueuses et des disciplines ascético-mystiques auquel il s'applique à un premier niveau, le vocabulaire traditionnel est ainsi conduit par degrés à expliciter les vérités métaphysiques dont il est implicitement porteur et qui fondent son emploi dans la pratique du soufisme. Cette 'ascension sémantique' revêt souvent une forme très paradoxale et l'on s'explique sans peine les multiples mises en garde de la littérature confrérique contre une diffusion imprudente des œuvres d'Ibn 'Arabī – pour ne rien dire des condamnations sans appel émanant de certains *fuqahā'*.[28] Une rapide analyse de quelques chapitres du deuxième *faṣl* des *Futūḥāt*, dont nous avons montré l'étroite relation structurelle avec la *Risāla Qushayriyya*, permet d'observer concrètement la méthode akbarienne et d'en évaluer les effets sur la compréhension de la *koinè* des hommes de la Voie.

La table des matières du *faṣl* met en évidence un aspect significatif de cette méthode: dans trente-quatre cas, le chapitre traitant d'une des 'stations' (*maqāmāt*) qui se succèdent chez al-Qushayrī est suivi d'un chapitre traitant de l''abandon' (*tark*) de cette station.[29] Loin de représenter une attitude blâmable cet abandon, on va le voir, doit être interprété chaque fois comme un dépassement du *maqām* précédent, une purification visant à libérer le *sālik* de ce qui subsistait de dualité dans la station qu'il avait atteinte. C'est donc, on le devine, envisagée en elle-même ou dans ses conséquences doctrinales, la *waḥdat al-wujūd* qui constitue la clef de voûte de cette architecture complexe.

Si, à propos de la *khalwa*,[30] Ibn 'Arabī évoque brièvement la signification commune de ce terme, celle de 'retraite cellulaire', c'est de son fondement *in divinis* qu'il veut instruire son disciple. Citant le *ḥadīth* 'Allāh était et rien n'était avec Lui', il voit dans ce vide primordial (*al-khalā'*) le principe de la *khalwa*: est véritablement en retraite, qu'il soit ou non reclus dans une cellule, celui dont le cœur est vide de tout ce qui n'est pas Dieu. Mais ce *maqām* reste imparfait puisqu'il suppose encore l'illusion séparative (Dieu/autre que Dieu). Il doit donc être 'abandonné': 'Quand l'homme ne voit que Dieu en toute chose, la *khalwa* est impossible.' Les deux chapitres sur la 'fuite' (*al-firār*)[31] qui, nous l'avons dit, n'ont pas d'équivalents dans la *Risāla*, sont en rigoureuse cohérence avec ce qui précède. Ibn ʿArabī opère en premier lieu une distinction, scripturairement justifiée, entre *al-firār min* – la fuite qui se définit par ce que l'on fuit, celle de Moïse (Qur'an 26:21) – et *al-firār ilā* – celle qui se définit par ce vers quoi l'on fuit, celle de Muḥammad (Qur'an 51:50). Si la première a pour but de se préserver, la seconde a pour but de se perdre en Dieu. Mais, 'où fuir, alors qu'il n'y a que Dieu ? . . . . Toute chose que tu vois, cela est Dieu!' Et le Shaykh al-Akbar de conclure que si, néanmoins, Dieu ordonne aux croyants de fuir vers Lui (dans le verset 51:50: *fa firrū ilā Llāh*) c'est seulement parce qu'ils ne parviennent pas à cette contemplation de Son universelle présence. Pour celui qui l'obtient la fuite – 'de' ou 'vers' – est au contraire une station dépassée.

La plupart des propos sur l''humilité' (*al-khushūʿ*) que cite al-Qushayrī[32] ont, comme c'est généralement le cas chez lui, un caractère descriptif ou prescriptif en accord avec la finalité pratique de la *Risāla*: 'L'homme est humble, dit Abū Yazīd, quand il ne s'attribue ni station, ni état et ne voit dans l'univers personne qui soit pire que lui.' Pour Junayd, que cite aussi al-Qushayrī, l'humilité c'est 'l'abaissement du cœur devant le Connaisseur des mystères'. Ibn ʿArabī, quant à lui, montre que l'humilité véritable est toujours produite par une théophanie (*tajallī*). Cependant, 'quand le serviteur est voilé à lui-même par son Seigneur' (*maḥjūb ʿan dhātihi bi-rabbihi*), il 'abandonne' nécessairement le *maqām al-khushūʿ* car il est absent de lui-même et le *tajallī* ne rencontre qu'un miroir qui le réfléchit vers sa source. Or 'Celui qui s'épiphanise à Lui-même, comment éprouverait-il l'humilité?' L'auteur des *Futūḥāt* ajoute toutefois aussitôt, car il n'ignore pas que ce qu'il vient d'énoncer ne concerne que des êtres d'exception: 'Abandonner l'humilité est blâmable chez quiconque ne possède pas cet état spirituel; et s'il l'abandonne, il sera rejeté (*maṭrūd*).'

Si le *tawakkul*, la 'remise confiante à Dieu', est unanimement reconnu comme une des règles fondamentales de la Voie, les débats à son sujet se focalisent le plus souvent sur un problème concret: le soufi doit-il gagner sa vie en pratiquant un métier, demeurant ainsi prisonnier des causes secondes (*al-wuqūf maʿa al-asbāb*)? Doit-il plutôt s'en abstenir, attendant de Dieu seul sa subsistance?[33] Les exemples sont nombreux dans l'hagiographie de saints personnages qui entreprennent la traversée des déserts sans se munir d'aucun provision. Mais le *tawakkul* peut servir aussi de pieux prétexte à une mendicité abusive. La position la plus communément acceptée est celle qu'exprime Sahl al-Tustarī, cité par al-Qushayrī: 'le *tawakkul* était l'état (*ḥāl*) du Prophète mais le *kasb* (l'acquisition par le recours aux causes secondes) était sa *sunna*.' Ibn ʿArabī n'ignore pas ces débats et son point de vue, exprimé à diverses reprises dans ses écrits, correspond à celui d'al-Tustarī.[34] Le *tawakkul* que prescrit la Révélation consiste à ne chercher appui qu'en Dieu en toute circonstance sans ressentir aucun trouble si l'on constate l'absence des *asbāb* sur lesquels les âmes ont l'habitude de s'appuyer. Il s'agit d'une disposition intérieure et non d'une impossible 'sortie des causes secondes' car Dieu opère *en* elles (et non *par* elles: *fī'l-asbāb lā bi'l-asbāb*): elles sont les voiles derrière lesquels Il se cache.[35] Mais le *tawakkul* légal (*mashrū'*) n'est pas le *tawakkul ḥaqīqī*, lequel n'appartient proprement qu'à ce qui est dépourvu d'être (*al-ma'dūm fī ḥāl 'adamihi*). La 'remise confiante à Dieu' par le *'abd* signifie qu'il charge Dieu du soin de ses intérêts. Elle est donc encore l'expression d'une volonté propre. Or Dieu ayant disposé toutes choses selon Sa Sagesse, il ne reste rien au sujet de quoi la créature devrait chercher un appui en Dieu puisqu'elle a reçu de Lui tout ce qui lui revient.[36]

Sur la 'gratitude' (*al-shukr*) al-Qushayrī rapporte un propos d'al-Shīblī selon lequel elle consiste à 'voir le Bienfaiteur plutôt que le bienfait'.[37] Cette définition coïncide avec celle que donne Ibn 'Arabī du *shukr 'ilmī*, la 'gratitude connaissante', qu'il distingue de celle qui se manifeste en paroles ou en actes (le mot de 'reconnaissance' serait d'ailleurs sans doute le plus adéquat pour traduire l'expression arabe). Il ne s'agit pas, bien entendu, d'un savoir théorique mais d'une connaissance fondée sur l'évidence: quel que soit l'agent apparent, le bienfait doit être *vu* comme venant de Dieu. Ici encore, une dualité subsiste pourtant qui trahit l'imperfection de ce *maqām*, si éminent qu'il soit. Il faut donc le quitter pour accéder au *tark al-shukr*, lequel consiste à voir Dieu comme étant à la fois *al-shākir* et *al-mashkūr*, le 'reconnaissant' et celui à qui s'adresse la reconnaissance.

'Aucune chose ne se répète dans l'existence en raison de l'infinité divine', déclare Ibn 'Arabī au début du chapitre sur 'l'abandon de la certitude' (*tark al-yaqīn*).[38] C'est pourquoi ce que les théologiens disent des accidents – à savoir qu'ils ne durent pas deux instants de suite – est vrai aussi des substances. Dès lors, en l'absence d'objets stables auxquels l'appliquer, sur quoi la certitude pourrait-elle se fonder? Les hommes de Dieu renoncent par conséquent à tout effort pour l'acquérir et ne l'acceptent que lorsqu'elle leur est octroyée. La soumission totale à la volonté divine exclut le repos et la stabilité. Rechercher la certitude est une présomptueuse tentative d'enfermer l'inépuisable nouveauté de Dieu. Le mot de *ḥayra* – la 'stupéfaction', le vertige que produit l'éblouissante procession de théophanies dont chacune est sans pareille – n'est pas prononcé ici. Mais c'est lui qui résume le mieux ce par quoi la certitude doit être dépassée. 'Le parfait (*al-kāmil*)', écrira l'auteur quelques pages plus loin, 'c'est celui dont la *ḥayra* est la plus grande.'[39]

De multiples versets qur'aniques exhortent les croyants à la patience (*al-ṣabr*) et leur proposent comme modèles l'exemple d'Abraham et de son fils, de Jacob, de Job ou du Prophète de l'Islam. Al-Qushayrī, entre autres définitions, retient celle de Ruwaym: 'la patience, c'est de renoncer à se plaindre.'[40] Ibn 'Arabī ne cite pas ce propos mais, sans le dire, c'est manifestement lui qu'il complète et rectifie en déclarant: 'la patience ne consiste pas à s'abstenir de se plaindre à Dieu pour obtenir qu'il soulage l'affliction ou l'écarte, elle consiste à s'abstenir de se plaindre *à autre que Dieu*.' Se plaindre à Dieu n'est pas une infraction au devoir de patience car si Dieu afflige ses serviteurs c'est précisément pour qu'ils Lui adressent leurs plaintes. L'exemple qur'anique invoqué à l'appui de ce point de vue est celui de Job qui, dans son malheur, fait appel à Dieu (Qur'an 21:83) et dont Dieu dit pourtant *Inna wajadnāhu ṣābiran* (Qur'an 38:44). Ce thème sera d'ailleurs amplement développé dans le chapitre 19 des *Fuṣūṣ al-ḥikam*. À contre courant de la tonalité de la plupart des textes classiques sur le *ṣabr*, le Shaykh al-Akbar, aussitôt après cette mise au point, célèbre avec jubilation la *raḥma* divine:

> Réjouissez-vous, ô serviteurs de Dieu de l'universalité et de l'immensité de la Miséricorde qui se répand sur toute créature, fût-ce après un délai! Car, lorsque disparaîtra le monde d'ici-bas, disparaîtra avec lui l'affliction de quiconque est affligé et par là même disparaîtra la patience.

Cette Miséricorde, il l'affirme ici comme il l'affirme, inlassablement, dans toute son œuvre, s'étendra même à ceux qui sont condamnés à demeurer dans la géhenne: si coupables que soient les hommes la patience divine est, elle, sans limite car Dieu est *al-ṣabūr*, le Patient par excellence.[41] L''abandon' de la patience – qui doit être compris comme le degré le plus parfait de celle-ci – s'oppose donc à la conception commune du *ṣabr*. Etre stoïque devant l'épreuve, c'est prétendre tenir tête à la force de Dieu (*al-qahr al-ilāhī*). La perfection c'est au contraire, pour le *ʿabd*, d'avouer son impuissance et sa pauvreté (*ʿajzhu wa-faqruhu)*.

Deux des chapitres les plus significatifs de la section des *muʿāmalāt* sont ceux qui correspondent à celui qu'al-Qushayrī consacre à la *ʿubūdiyya*.[42] Les titres qui leur sont donnés par Ibn ʿArabī doivent retenir l'attention: tandis que le premier est 'sur le *maqām* de la *ʿubūda*', le second est 'sur le *maqām* de l'abandon de la *ʿubūdiyya*'. Bien qu'il arrive au Shaykh al-Akbar d'employer ces mots l'un pour l'autre,[43] ils ont dans sa doctrine – et notamment ici – des significations bien distinctes, et c'est ce qui permet de comprendre l'inhabituelle modification du vocabulaire dans ces intitulés successifs. Trois termes de même racine sont en fait à considérer pour éclairer ce problème: *ʿibāda*, *ʿubūdiyya*, *ʿubūda*. Al-Qushayrī, citant al-Daqqāq, les mentionne dès le début de son exposé mais se borne à les mettre respectivement en rapport, d'une part avec le ternaire 'commun des fidèles' (*ʿāmma*), 'élite', 'élite de l'élite', d'autre part avec les degrés de la certitude (*ʿilm*, *ʿayn*, *ḥaqq*). J'ai proposé, pour rendre ces trois vocables par des mots français également de même famille, de les traduire par 'service', 'servage' et 'servitude'.[44] La servitude (*ʿubūda*) est, chez Ibn ʿArabī, le statut ontologique de la créature. Le *ʿabd*, l'esclave, ne possède rien, ne se possède pas lui-même. Il n'a pas d'être qui lui soit propre. Le nom même de *ʿabd* ne lui appartient pas.[45] Ce statut est donc irrévocable et c'est pourquoi il ne peut être 'abandonné'. Le servage, la *ʿubūdiyya* est, dit Ibn ʿArabī, 'relation à la *ʿubūda*', elle en dérive: elle est concrètement la condition à laquelle le *ʿabd* est voué en raison de son statut; et le service – la *ʿibāda* – représente l'ensemble des devoirs qu'implique cette condition servile. 'La station de la *ʿubūdiyya*, c'est la station de l'avilissement et de l'indigence'; définition commentée par la relation d'un dialogue fameux au cours duquel Abū Yazīd al-Bistāmī demande à Dieu: 'Par quoi m'approcherai-je de toi ?'

'Par ce qui ne m'appartient pas.' 'Mais, Seigneur, qu'est-ce qui ne t'appartient pas?' 'L'avilissement et l'indigence.'[46] Cette condition de servage, à laquelle la créature doit se soumettre en ce monde pour se conformer à son statut originel, nul ne l'a plus parfaitement réalisée que le Prophète et c'est pourquoi, dans le verset (Qur'an 17:1) relatif au glorieux épisode du 'voyage nocturne', il n'est pas désigné par un autre mot que celui de *ʿabd*.[47]

La fin du chapitre 130 annonce l'idée directrice du chapitre suivant: le *maqām* de la *ʿubūda*, de la servitude, exclut – à la différence du *maqām* de la *ʿubūdiyya* – toute relation avec Dieu ou avec quoi que ce soit: il est pauvreté absolue, nudité radicale; or la créature, en raison de sa contingence, ne peut subsister en l'absence de toute relation; elle disparaît donc, et il n'y a plus que Dieu se manifestant dans le *ʿabd*. '*Fa huwa ʿabd$^{un}$ lā ʿabd$^{un}$*.' Celui dont l'individualité est totalement éteinte dans la *ʿubūda* 'abandonne' la *ʿubūdiyya* car il réalise que les possibles (*al-mumkināt*) ne sont jamais sortis de leur néant, qu'ils n'ont 'jamais respiré le parfum de l'existence',[48] qu'ils ne sont que les lieux d'apparition de l'unique Apparent car 'Dieu seul possède l'être'. Autrement dit, la *ʿubūdiyya* s'évanouit pour celui qui 'revient' (car il ne l'a qu'illusoirement quitté) à l'état qui était le sien dans le *thubūt*: présent à Dieu mais s'ignorant lui-même.[49] La *ʿubūda* est résorption dans l'unicité principielle: la *ʿubūdiyya* perd toute raison d'être quand cette résorption est accomplie ou, pour mieux dire, quand le *ʿabd* découvre qu'il n'était jamais sorti de l'unicité. Le thème de la *waḥdat al-wujūd* est largement développé dans la suite de ce chapitre où Ibn ʿArabī a recours à un symbolisme qui lui est cher, celui de la procession des nombres à partir du un[50] et s'appuie sur des références scripturaires (Qur'an 15:85; 8:17) dont il use souvent quand il aborde ce sujet. Ces pages, comme toutes celles que nous avons signalées au cours de cette brève étude, mériteraient une analyse détaillée. Mais notre propos n'était pas ici de saisir dans toute sa profondeur et toute son étendue l'enseignement doctrinal que le Shaykh al-Akbar a consigné dans cette section des *Futūḥāt*: il se bornait à déceler de quelle manière s'opère le changement de registre qui confère à des termes classiques des significations qui peuvent apparaître comme un retournement paradoxal des acceptions traditionnelles.

De ce point de vue, le couplage systématique *maqām/abandon du maqām* est spécialement digne d'attention. Citons un dernier exemple, celui de la 'rectitude' (*istiqāma*). Selon les propos des maîtres transmis par al-Qushayrī,[51] elle consiste à éduquer l'âme passionnelle, à émonder le cœur, à sortir de l'enchaînement des habitudes, à agir comme si chaque instant était celui de la Résurrection. Il s'agit, en somme, de s'appliquer à redresser ce qui est tordu. Or, pour Ibn ʿArabī, toute chose possède la rectitude qui convient à sa nature: 'la rectitude d'un arc consiste dans sa courbure.' En conséquence de quoi, il ne craint pas de dire que la désobéissance d'Adam à l'ordre divin fait partie de sa rectitude, c'est-à-dire de sa conformité à la finalité de sa création: *felix culpa* puisque, sans la chute qu'elle entraîne, il n'aurait pu exercer sur terre la *khilāfa* en vue de laquelle il est venu à l'existence. Abandonner tout effort qui tendrait à instaurer la rectitude est chez le *ʿārif* le signe même de la rectitude et témoigne qu'il est 'avec Dieu en tout état'.[52] Pour lui, il n'y a pas de courbure (*iʿwijāj*) dans l'univers: tout est droit.

Rien ne serait pourtant plus contraire à l'enseignement d'Ibn ʿArabī que d'imaginer, sur la base de ces assertions provocantes, qu'il juge superflue la *via purgativa* sur laquelle mettent l'accent les soufis cités dans la *Risāla*. Les disciplines rigoureuses, que dans les *Futūḥāt* ou dans d'autres écrits il exige du *murīd*, sont exactement identiques à celles que prescrivent les saints dont al-Qushayrī invoque l'autorité. Mais le Shaykh al-Akbar décèle aussi le pélagianisme implicite que menace d'engendrer la conscience des efforts accomplis: l'ascèse, qui vise à effacer l'ego, peut aboutir à le consolider. Toute station est un piège et risque de devenir une prison.

Un *maqām* n'est pas autre chose que l'*habitus* d'une vertu. Mais c'est, comme l'énoncent toutes les définitions traditionnelles y compris celles d'Ibn ʿArabī, un *habitus* acquis (*muktasab*).[53] Abandonner un *maqām* n'est pas abandonner l'exercice de la vertu à laquelle il est associé. L''abandon' désigne ce qui se produit lorsqu'à l'*habitus* acquis la grâce divine substitue un *habitus* infus qui reconduit l'être à sa *ʿubūda* primordiale. Alors, Dieu est 'l'ouïe par laquelle il entend, la vue par laquelle il voit, la main par laquelle il saisit, le pied avec lequel il marche'.[54] *Wa-qad jā'a'l-ḥaqqu wa-zahaqa'l-bāṭil* (Qur'an 17:81): le *tark al-maqām* n'est donc rien d'autre, en définitive, que l'abandon d'une illusion.[55]

## Notes

1. *Rūḥ al-quds fī muḥāsabat al-nafs* (Damas, 1964), pp. 49–50. Sur ce shaykh, mentionné à plusieurs reprises dans d'autres notices du *Rūḥ al-quds* (pp. 55, 61, 75, 78, 84), voir aussi *Futūḥāt* (Būlāq, 1329/1911), vol. 1, p. 616 et vol. 2, p. 683.

2. Sur les premières étapes de la vie spirituelle d'Ibn ʿArabī, voir l'article de G. Elmore, 'New Evidence on the Conversion of Ibn ʿArabī to Sufism', *Arabica*, 45 (1988), pp. 50–72, et la mise au point de C. Addas, 'La conversion d'Ibn ʿArabī: certitudes et conjectures', *ʿAyn al-ḥayat*, 4 (1998), pp. 33–64.

3. *Muḥāḍarāt al-abrār wa-musāmarāt al-akhyār* (Beyrouth, 1968), p. 11. Selon une information que nous avons recueillie en 1987, un manuscrit autographe de cet ouvrage, daté de Malatiya en AH 612, serait actuellement en la possession d'un universitaire tunisien. Précisons qu'en dépit de l'interpolation dans le texte de scolies tardives l'attribution de ce livre à Ibn ʿArabī, contrairement à une hypothèse de Brockelmann, ne fait absolument aucun doute.

4. Voir, par exemple, *Fut.*, vol. 1, pp. 221, 527, 605; vol. 2, pp. 117, 245; *Kitāb nasab al-khirqa*, ms. Esad Ef. 1507, f. 98a.

5. À ces 560 chapitres il convient d'ajouter la longue *khuṭba* initiale, le *fihris* (dans lequel les titres des chapitres ne coïncident pas toujours avec ceux qui figurent en tête des *abwāb*) et la *muqaddima*, l'ensemble représentant 47 pages de l'édition de AH 1329, (correspondant aux pp. 41–214 de l'édition d'O. Yahia).

6. Ce caractère symbolique est évident dans le cas du 4ème *faṣl*, celui des *manāzil*, dont le

nombre (114) est celui des sourates du Qur'an, le premier *manzil* correspondant à la sourate 114, le deuxième à la sourate 113 et ainsi de suite jusqu'au *manzil* de la *Fātiḥa* (voir là-dessus notre *Un Océan sans ravage*, Paris, 1992, chap. 3). Il est évident aussi dans le 5ème *faṣl* (*al-munāzalāt*), où le nombre des chapitres (78) est celui des occurrences des *ḥurūf nūrāniyya* dans le Qur'an, compte tenu des répétitions, ainsi que dans le 6ème (*al-maqāmāt*) qui compte 99 chapitres, soit le nombre des noms divins des listes traditionnelles. Les chapitres 2 à 73 du premier *faṣl* (*al-maʿārif*) correspondent aux 72 *darajāt al-basmala* selon le *jazm ṣaghīr*, le chapitre 1, celui où est décrite la rencontre visionnaire qui va générer l'ouvrage tout entier, devant être considéré comme un prologue non inclus dans le *faṣl*. Nous allons revenir sur la signification des 115 chapitres du 2ème *faṣl* (*al-muʿāmalāt*). Quant au 3ème (*al-aḥwāl*), qui comporte 81 chapitres, il semble en relation avec les 78 *shuʿāb al-īmān* sans que nous puissions expliquer de façon certaine l'addition de trois chapitres supplémentaires. Au sujet du nombre des *fuṣūl*, rappelons d'autre part que le six (comme la lettre *wāw* dont il représente la valeur numérique) est un symbole de l'*insān kāmil* (voir par exemple *Fut.*, vol. 3, p. 142). Une correspondance semble en outre probable entre ces six sections et six des *asmāʾ al-dhāt*, le septième de ces Noms correspondant au premier chapitre qui constitue en quelque sorte la matrice des *Futūḥāt*. La mention dans ce premier chapitre (vol. 1, p. 50) de la Kaʿba, des sept tournées rituelles et des sept *ṣifāt* mériterait de ce point de vue un long commentaire qui permettrait de mieux comprendre pourquoi les *Futūḥāt* sont *Makkiyya*. Voir *Un Océan sans rivage*, pp. 49–50 et 126–128. Signalons enfin que 560 – date de naissance d'Ibn ʿArabī – est aussi le nombre des mots de la sourate *al-fatḥ* dont la relation avec la notion de *Futūḥāt* nous semble évidente.

7. *Khatm al-awliyāʾ*, ed. O. Yahia (Beyrouth, 1960), p. 210; B. Radtke, *Drei Schriften des Theosophen von Tirmīd* (Beyrouth, 1992), pp. 22–23. Ce *ḥadīth* est de nouveau cité par al-Tirmidhī p. 411 dans l'édition O. Yahia, p. 99 dans l'édition Radtke. Pour les réponses d'Ibn ʿArabī voir *Fut.*, vol. 2, pp. 72–74 (questions 48-49-50).

8. Ce *ḥadīth* d'authenticité très contestée, notamment par Ibn Taymiyya, est fréquemment cité par Ibn ʿArabī: voir, *inter alia*, *Fut.*, vol. 1, pp. 134, 143, 243; vol. 3, pp. 22, 141, 456.

9. Bukhārī, *Faḍāʾil aṣḥāb al-nabī*, p. 9; Ibn Māja, *Muqaddima*, p. 11, etc. Pour une analyse exhaustive des données scripturaires relatives à ce caractère final, voir Y. Friedmann, *Prophecy Continuous* (Berkeley, CA, 1989), chap. 2.

10. Le manuscrit autographe de la seconde rédaction des *Futūḥāt* permet de vérifier que cette deuxième section ne comporte que 115 chapitres et non 116 comme l'indique la table des matières figurant au début de l'ouvrage (vol. 1, p. 17) et comme l'affirme O. Yahia dans son édition (vol. 1, p. 30; vol. 13, p. 53).

11. Sur la notion de *wirātha* et son importance dans l'hagiologie d'Ibn ʿArabī voir notre *Le Sceau des saints* (Paris, 1986), chap. 5.

12. Sur ces trois notions, auxquelles Ibn ʿArabī a souvent recours, voir notamment *Fut.*, vol. 1, pp. 363, 373; vol. 2, p. 39; vol. 3, p. 126.

13. Sur le chapitre 73 des *Futūḥāt* voir nos remarques dans *Un Océan sans rivage* (p. 67 s.) et notre article 'Les Malāmiyya dans la doctrine d'Ibn ʿArabī', dans N. Clayer, A. Popovic et Th. Zarcone, ed., *Melāmis-Bayrāmis* (Istanbul, 1998).

14. Depuis Urbain VIII (1642), c'est en effet cette 'héroïcité des vertus' théologales et cardinales (et non les grâces mystiques) que l'on prend en compte dans les procès de canonisation,

le code de droit canonique de 1983 se bornant à introduire, dans les positiones *super vita et virtutibus*, certaines nouveautés méthodologiques (recours aux sciences humaines).

15. Nous utiliserons ici l'édition de la *Risāla* publiée au Caire en 1957. Il n'existe, à ce jour, aucune traduction française de cet ouvrage fondamental. La traduction allemande de R. Gramlich, *Das Sendschreiben al-Qusayrīs über das Sufitum* a été publié à Wiesbaden en 1989. Il existe une traduction anglaise partielle par B. R. von Schlegell, *Principles of Sufism* (Berkeley, CA, 1992).

16. La *Risāla* se conclut par un chapitre de 'conseils' destinés aux *murīd*. Or le schéma de ce chapitre inspire manifestement celui sur lequel est construit un court traité d'Ibn 'Arabī, le *Kitāb al-amr al-muḥkam al-marbūṭ*, écrit à Qunya en 602/1205–1206.

17. *Fut.*, vol. 2, p. 163.

18. L'exemple cité dans ce passage est celui des versets 2:235–241 où l'injonction d'observer la prière intervient entre des prescriptions relatives au mariage, au divorce et aux dispositions testamentaires.

19. Voir *Fut.*, vol. 1, pp. 59, 152; vol. 3, pp. 101, 334, 456; vol. 4, pp. 62, 74.

20. *Risāla*, p. 52.

21. Dans le chapitre 150 sur la *ghayra* (vol. 2, p. 245).

22. Probable seulement car ces propos des maîtres se trouvent aussi dans d'autres ouvrages qu'Ibn 'Arabī déclare avoir lus, comme la *Ḥilya* d'Abū Nu'aym, dont il a composé un abrégé ainsi qu'il le signale dans le *Fihris* et l'*Ijāza*.

23. *Risāla*, p. 84; *Fut.*, vol. 2, p. 204.

24. *S. al-Ḥakīm, al-mu'jam al-ṣūfī* (Beyrouth, 1981), Introduction, p. 19. Dans un bref mais suggestif essai publié à Beyrouth en 1991 sous le titre *Ibn 'Arabī wa-mawlid lugha jadīda*, S. al-Hakīm évoque brièvement le parallélisme entre la structure du *Faṣl al-mu'āmalāt* et celle de la *Risāla* (voir p. 53) mais sans procéder à une comparaison entre ces deux textes. Son propos, il est vrai, est surtout, comme l'annonce le titre de son livre, d'examiner les développements considérables que donne Ibn 'Arabī au vocabulaire traditionnel du soufisme par la création de termes ou d'expressions dont une liste (qui occupe une centaine de pages) est donnée *in fine*. L'ouvrage du Dr 'Abd al-Wahhāb Amīn Aḥmad, *al-Mughāmarat al-lughawiyya fī'l-futūḥāt al-Makkiyyāt* (Le Caire, 1995) – qui ignore les travaux les plus récents et notamment ceux de S. al-Hakīm – est assez décevant.

25. On doit à Roger Deladrière une élégante et érudite traduction de cet ouvrage (*al-Kawākib al-durriyya*) dont il n'existe pas encore d'édition critique: *La Vie merveilleuse de Dhū' l-Nūn l'Egyptien* (Paris, 1988). Mais Ibn 'Arabī est également l'auteur d'un ouvrage sur Abū Yazīd et d'un autre sur Ḥallāj (respectivement nos. 461 et 651 du répertoire général d'O. Yahia) dont les manuscrits n'ont pas été retrouvés jusqu'à présent.

26. Voir par exemple *Fut.*, vol. 1, p. 364; vol. 2, pp. 337, 361; vol. 3, pp. 104, 117; vol. 4, p. 194.

27. *Fut.*, vol. 1, pp. 169, 176; vol. 4, p. 332, etc. Voir aussi *Dīwān* (Beyrouth, 1996), p. 299 où Ibn 'Arabī parle de Ḥallāj comme de son 'frère' dans la connaissance des secrets des lettres.

28. Sur la portée réelle de ces condamnations, voir notre communication au symposium *Sufism and its opponents* (Utrecht, 1995), 'Le procès posthume d'al-'Arabī' dans *Islamic Mysticism Contested* (Leyde, 1999).

29. Nous ne considérons ici que les cas où le terme d''abandon' est employé dans le titre.

Mais la même démarche est évidente dans des cas où ce mot n'apparaît pas: la station du 'silence' *(al-ṣamt)* est ainsi suivie de celle de la 'parole', celle de la pauvreté (*faqr*) est suivie de celle de la 'richesse', celle de la veille (*sahar*) de celle du 'sommeil', etc.

30. *Fut.*, chap. 78–79; al-Qushayrī, *Risāla*, pp. 50–52.

31. *Fut.*, chap. 82–83. Sur le thème du *firār* voir aussi *Fut.*, vol. 4, pp. 156 et 183.

32. *Fut.*, chap. 110–111; *Risāla*, pp. 68–71.

33. Voir par exemple les *'Awārif al-ma'ārif d'al-Suhrawardī*, chapitres 19 et 20.

34. Tustarī est cité à plusieurs reprises dans le long chapitre de la *Risāla* consacré au *tawakkul* (pp. 75–80). Sur la position d'Ibn 'Arabī, outre les chapitres 118–119 du *Faṣl al-mu'āmalāt*, voir *Fut.*, vol. 4, pp. 153–154 et 280.

35. Sur l'impossibilité de *khurūj 'an al-asbāb*, *Fut.*, vol. 3, pp. 72 et 249.

36. Sans doute est-ce de cette manière qu'il faut interpréter une phrase de Ḥallāj citée par Kalābādhī – mais attribuée en termes vagues à 'l'un des grands maîtres' – selon laquelle *ḥaqīqat al-tawakkul tark al-tawakkul* (*Kitāb al-ta'arruf*, Le Caire, 1960, p. 101).

37. *Risāla*, pp. 80–82; *Fut.*, chap. 120–121.

38. *Risāla*, pp. 82–84; *Fut.*, chap. 122–123. L'affirmation du caractère irrépétable des choses, liée à la notion de 'création perpétuelle' et donc toujours nouvelle (*khalq jadīd*) est fréquente dans l'œuvre d'Ibn 'Arabī. Voir, par exemple, *Fut.*, vol. 1, p. 735; vol. 3, pp. 127, 159; *Fuṣūṣ al-ḥikam* (Beyrouth, 1946), vol. 1, p. 202.

39. *Fut.*, vol. 2, p. 212. Sur la *ḥayra*, thème récurrent lui aussi, voir par exemple le chapitre 50 (vol. 1, pp. 270 s.); *Fuṣ.*, vol. 1, pp. 72–73. La notion d''épectase' correspond assez bien, en théologie mystique chrétienne, où elle est d'ailleurs très controversée, à celle de *ḥayra*. Voir l'article s.v. dans *Dictionnaire de Spiritualité*, vol. 4, col. 785–788.

40. *Risāla*, pp. 84–88; *Fut.*, chap. 124–125. Dans le chapitre 124, Ibn 'Arabī cite à propos de Shiblī une anecdote rapportée par al-Qushayrī p. 85.

41. Sur le nom *al-ṣabūr*, voir *Fut.*, vol. 4, p. 317. Des précisions que nous ne pouvons donner ici seraient nécessaires sur l'inclusion finale des *ahl al-nār* dans la *raḥma*. Voir à ce sujet *Fut.*, vol. 3, pp. 164, 207, 550; *Fuṣ.*, vol. 1, pp. 93–94, entre autres passages où Ibn 'Arabī traite de l'universalité de la Miséricorde.

42. *Risāla*, pp. 90–92; *Fut.*, chap. 130–131.

43. La distinction entre *'ubūda* et *'ubūdiyya*, bien que perçue, est rarement prise en compte de façon rigoureuse chez les auteurs arabes (voir *Lisān al-'arab*, vol. 3, p. 271). Signalons que, dans le manuscrit de la première rédaction des *Futūḥāt* (postérieur à Ibn 'Arabī, l'original étant perdu) on lit *'ubūdiyya* dans le titre du chapitre 130.

44. *Un Océan sans rivage*, pp. 152 s.

45. *Fut.*, vol. 2, p. 350.

46. Ibn 'Arabī précise qu'il y a au sujet de ce dialogue un secret qu'il ne peut dévoiler. On peut, croyons-nous, deviner là une allusion au fait que, métaphysiquement parlant, il n'est *rien* qui n'appartienne à Dieu, y compris ce que la perfection divine paraît exclure, idée exprimée notamment dans le poème liminaire du chap. 127 et qui s'appuie sur des données scripturaires (par exemple Qur'an 73:23) ou sur le *ḥadīth qudsī*, parallèle à Matt. 25, 41–45, où Dieu dit: 'J'ai été malade et tu ne M'as pas visité', (sur ce *ḥadīth*, voir *Fut.*, vol. 1, p. 407; vol. 3, p. 304; vol. 4, p. 451).

47. Cette référence au verset de la sourate *al-isrā* est faite également par Abū 'Alī al-Daqqāq dans un propos que cite al-Qushayrī.

48. Cette image n'est pas employée ici mais on la rencontre fréquemment sous la plume du Shaykh al-Akbar et de ses disciples. Voir par exemple, *Fuṣ*, vol. 1, p. 76 (où il faut lire *wujūd* et non *mawjūd* comme l'a fait Afīfī).

49. Sur ce 'retour', voir *Fut.*, vol. 2, p. 672 ('La noblesse de l'homme, c'est de revenir dans son existence à son état d'inexistence') et vol. 3, p. 539.

50. *Fut.*, vol. 3, p. 494; *Kitāb al-alif* (Hyderabad, 1948); *Fuṣ.*, vol. 1, pp. 77–78.

51. *Risāla*, pp. 94–95; *Fut.*, vol. 2, chap. 132–133. Voir aussi *Risāla fī mā lā yu'awwal 'alayhi* (Hyderabad, 1948), p. 9.

52. Des idées analogues sont développées dans le chapitre 10 des *Fuṣūṣ*, avec les mêmes références qur'aniques (Qur'an 11:56 en particulier).

53. *Fut.*, vol. 2, p. 385.

54. Ces formules sont empruntées à un *ḥadīth qudsī* qu'Ibn 'Arabī a inclus dans son *Mishkāt al-anwār* et qu'il a commenté en de multiples occasions dans la plupart de ses œuvres. Nous sommes bien conscient de donner ici à l'*habitus* infus, en cohérence avec la doctrine akbarienne, une signification plus forte que celle qu'il a habituellement dans le langage de la théologie mystique chrétienne.

55. L'interprétation par Ibn 'Arabī du *ḥadīth* précité souligne que, lorsque Dieu est 'l'ouïe, la vue, la main, le pied' du serviteur, rien n'advient en fait qu'un 'dévoilement' (*kashf*) à ce dernier de ce qui toujours fut et toujours sera (*Fut.*, vol. 1, p. 406).

# 20

# Al-Shahrastānī's Contribution to Medieval Islamic Thought

*Diana Steigerwald*

He who has dived into the sea's depths does not long for a shore and he who has ascended to the summit of perfection is not scared of a descent.[1]

The richness and originality of al-Shahrastānī's philosophical and theological thought is manifested in his major works. He was certainly not an Ash'arī theologian, as has often been argued, even if he borrowed certain basic concepts shared commonly by various Muslim thinkers. Al-Shahrastānī is a difficult person to evaluate because he juggled many different sorts of philosophical and theological vocabulary. Recognised as an influential Muslim theologian and as an historian of religions, he was one of the pioneers in the development of a scientific approach to the study of religions. He was both a theologian and a philosopher, and his works combine an objective description of various religious beliefs with critical analyses of those aspects he considered inordinately irrational. In highlighting the complexity of his thought, one comes to appreciate the subtleties of his argumentation as well as its importance in Islamic thought as a whole. Three systems of thought influenced his own: Ash'arism, Avicennism and Ismailism; to reduce their influence to one tradition would limit the depth and richness of his contribution. The first of these systems is the traditional Sunni theological view which rests on the authority of scripture; the second is the Hellenic philosophy of Ibn Sīnā; the third is the Ismaili form of Shi'ism with its emphasis on the sacred authority of the divinely guided Imam. Normally these three medieval Islamic schools are regarded as more or less mutually exclusive, but al-Shahrastānī adopts specific Ash'arī and Avicennian concepts which are reconcilable with Ismailism.

Al-Shahrastānī was an astute thinker, since the intricacies of the three traditions (Ash'arism, Avicennism and Ismailism), their points of conjunction and disjunction, and finally the Shiʿi notion of the Guide are found in his thought. This article shows the importance and the originality of his contribution, which presents a theology with a philosophical background coloured by Ismailism. Al-Shahrastānī had many reasons to speak in somewhat allegorical terms. He was an extremely subtle author who often spoke indirectly by means of symbols. He preferred his personal vocabulary to the traditionally accepted one. For this reason, his position is hard to determine. It may well be that ideological considerations led him to speak indirectly; perhaps he assumed that those familiar with the symbols, notably other Ismailis, would be able to unravel his elusive ideas. For all these reasons, many scholars who studied al-Shahrastānī were misled as far as his religious identity was concerned.

During the Abbasid caliphate (132–656/750–1258), the golden age of Islamic literature, many schools elaborated their major works of medieval Islamic thought. *Kalām* (Islamic theology) developed gradually and slowly gained the respect of the *ʿulamāʾ*. The most creative work was undertaken by the Ashʿarī school, which tried to reconcile different schools of thought. But in the seventh/twelfth century, Ismailism and Avicennism were regarded with more suspicion than in earlier centuries, and the Ashʿarī position became the dominant school of theology.

Shiʿism has particularly influenced the destiny of Islam in the political and, even more so, in the philosophical domain. Ismailism belongs to the Shiʿi mainstream in Islam. From its inception, the Islamic community was divided into two main groups: the Sunni and the Shiʿa. The Shiʿa affirm that the Prophet Muḥammad designated ʿAlī as the first Imam (divine Guide) and his direct descendants as his successors, since according to the tenets of Islam, Muḥammad was the last prophet, the one who closed the prophetic cycle. The Shiʿa believe that humanity still needs a spiritual Guide: the cycle of prophecy is succeeded by the cycle of *imāma*. The prerogative of the Imam is to provide the true interpretation of the Qur'an and to gradually reveal its esoteric meaning. Since the Ismailis were Muslims, the Qur'an lay at the centre of their thinking. But in common with other Shiʿa, the Ismailis were not content to dwell on the external meaning of the text, making use as well of the subtle method of textual exegesis known as *ta'wīl*. Every verse of the sacred book, indeed every word and even every letter, is found to have an esoteric significance, the *bāṭin*, which is additional and complementary to the exoteric meaning, the *ẓāhir*.

The Ismailis advocated and practised a prudent public masking of their true beliefs. The concealment of one's true beliefs in times of adversity was a practice which continued up until recent times. For the Ismailis, it is important not to disclose secrets to those who have no belief.[2] They gained prominence in scholarly circles, keeping carefully within the bounds of accepted teaching. From Ismaili works of the time, a picture emerges of Ismailism that is very different from the one found in Sunni sources. The Ismailis attempted to raise human consciousness to a higher plane and were not at all irreligious libertines as their adversaries so often depicted them. On the contrary, they were dedicated to a life of service and self-improvement. Their goal was wholly spiritual. Ismailism is neither a philosophy nor a theology, but has features of both of these; it is best referred to by the term theosophy in its original sense of 'Divine wisdom'. The Ismailis built one of the most remarkable speculative systems from i) the Qur'an, which contains hidden meanings, ii) the science of the cosmos, which has an esoteric significance and iii) Neoplatonism, which provided the philosophical framework. These three elements were interwoven to give a rich and coherent world view and by these means the Ismailis sought to understand the cosmos and our place within it.

As for Ashʿarism, it belongs to the Sunni mainstream of Islam, emerging at the end of the third/ninth century. Abu'l-Ḥasan al-Ashʿarī (d. 424/935) was originally a Muʿtazilī, rejected their ideas and founded the Ashʿarī school of theology. The expansion of Ashʿarism did not give it complete control within Sunnism, as is commonly thought, but nonetheless it became the dominant school. This was achieved largely through the influence of the famous Persian vizier Niẓām al-Mulk (d. 1092). Ashʿarīs believed in the necessity of using moderate reason to apprehend revelation.

## Literary Review

In the early twentieth century, al-Shahrastānī (479–548/1086–1153) was seen as an 'Ashʿarī' theologian, and as an historian of religions. But recently some scholars such as Muḥammad Riḍā Jalālī Nā'īnī, Muḥammad Taqī Dānishpazhūh, Wilferd Madelung and Guy Monnot have put forward arguments in favour of an Ismaili identity for al-Shahrastānī.[3]

William Cureton (d. 1864), the editor of the *Kitāb al-milal wa'l-niḥal* (The Book of Sects and Creeds), like most scholars of his time, took for granted the biography available in the *Wafayāt* of Ibn Khallikān. It was he who described al-Shahrastānī as an Ashʿarī theologian. Western scholars started to become familiar with al-Shahrastānī through Theodor Haarbrücker's translation of the *Milal*, published in 1846. In 1964 Jalālī Nā'īnī[4] first brought a new text by al-Shahrastānī, the *Majlis*, to the attention of other scholars. This short treatise is in the form of talk in Persian delivered in a mosque, most probably in front of a Twelver Shiʿi audience and it was written during the mature period of his life. The *Majlis* is clearly one of al-Shahrastānī's works because it is possible to establish so many parallels with his other writings (*Milal*, *Nihāya*, etc.), thus showing clearly the continuity of his thought.[5] In his introduction, Jalālī Nā'īnī put forward the hypothesis that al-Shahrastānī was probably an Ismaili. His arguments were based al-Shahrastānī's description in the *Mafāṭīḥ al-asrār wa-maṣābīḥ al-abrār* (The Keys of the Mysteries and the Lamps of the Righteous), of his initiation in the Qur'an by an anonymous teacher.[6]

In 1968, Muḥammad Tāqī Dānishpazhūh[7] believed that al-Shahrastānī was an Ismaili when he was at the court of Sanjar and in Khwārazm. He noticed that in the *Milal* al-Shahrastānī was sympathetic to both Ash'arīs and Ismailis. According to him, the *Mafāṭīḥ al-asrār* contains many Ismaili concepts such as: i) the constant physical transformation (*musta'naf*) of the world in contrast with the possibility of attaining a perfect spiritual state (*mafrūgh*), ii) opposition (*taḍāḍḍ*) and ranks (*tarattub*), iii) universality (*'umūm*) and particularisation (*khuṣūṣ*), iv) creation (*khalq*) and Divine Command (*amr*).

In 1976, Wilferd Madelung[8] noted in a short article that al-Shahrastānī in his *Muṣāra'at al-falāsifa* (The Struggle with Philosophers) criticised Ibn Sīnā's doctrines by emphasising some uniquely Ismaili arguments on the division of beings. He argued that the certain contemporary accusations of al-Shahrastānī's affinities with Ismailism[9] were true, since it could clearly be seen that he had Ismaili convictions (*gesinnung*). Then in 1977, Madelung[10] further pointed out that Naṣīr al-Dīn Ṭūsī, in the *Sayr wa-sulūk*, regarded al-Shahrastānī as part of the Ismaili *da'wa*.

Finally, the annotated translation of the *Milal* by Daniel Gimaret, Guy Monnot and Jean Jolivet analyses the various influences on al-Shahrastānī's thought and points to the apparent contradictions which account for his problematic religious identity. Guy Monnot has continued to work on the *Mafātīḥ al-asrār*. During the course of his long and fruitful research, he has found a great deal of evidence in support of an Ismaili identity for al-Shahrastānī. Between 1983 and 1988, he discovered many Ismaili elements in al-Shahrastānī's *tafsīr* that supported the thesis of Jalālī Nā'īnī, Dānishpazhūh and Wilferd Madelung.

In 1983, Guy Monnot embarked on a detailed analysis of the *Mafātīḥ al-asrār*[11] and year after year he discovered more and more Ismaili elements in it. In 1986–1987, Monnot[12] was surprised to discover that al-Shahrastānī believed in an Imam present in the world in the Shi'i sense of the term. The only group which believed in a living Imam at that time were the Nizārī Ismailis. Later on in 1987–1988, he became convinced that al-Shahrastānī was in fact an Ismaili because, in the *Mafātīḥ al-asrār*, he attributes the expression 'Our God is the God of Muḥammad'[13] to the true believers. This same expression is used in the Nizārī section of the *Milal*.[14] At this point, Monnot concluded: 'Al-Shahrastānī, author of both the *Milal* and the *Mafātīḥ al-asrār*, undoubtedly belongs to the Nizārī [Ismaili] tradition.'[15] This decisive conclusion will modify all future research on the works of al-Shahrastānī. And it is probable this discovery would have been impossible without the first initiative of Jalālī Nā'īnī.

There are many discrepancies in al-Shahrastānī's so-called 'Ash'arī' thought and the relevant aspects of his real convictions will be pointed out. It is important to bear in mind his numerous affinities with Ismailism. For example, al-Shahrastānī places the Shi'i concept of the Guide at the centre of religion. In the *Milal*,[16] he puts the double negation of the Fatimid thinker Abū Ya'qūb al-Sijistānī[17] in the mouth of al-Ash'arī. Al-Sijistānī uses this method of two-fold negation as the only way to attain understanding of the perfect unity (*tawḥīd*) of God. For example, in the following example 'God is *not* not limited', the second negation is repeated to deny the first negation and at the same time to negate the negation.[18]

Unlike the Ash'arīs, al-Shahrastānī presented a gradation in creation (*khalq*). He gives a definition of prophetic impeccability (*'iṣma*) that was opposed to the Ash'arī tradition, maintaining that it subsists in the Prophet as part of his real nature. In the *Nihāyat al-aqdām fī 'ilm al-kalām* (The End of Steps in the Science of Theology), in the chapter concerning *Imāma*, al-Shahrastānī does not reveal his own point of view, since he does not talk about the *Ahl al-ḥaqq* (the People of the Truth) and the *ḥunafā'* (pl. of *ḥānif*: a follower of the original religion founded by Abraham) whom he normally favours. He exposes on the one hand the view of the Ash'arīs and on the other hand the general Shi'i point of view. But al-Shahrastānī does not systematically attack all the Shi'i arguments instead he presents certain essential Shi'i ideas without attacking their foundation. In order to understand this Nizārī Ismaili author, this paper will describe briefly his ideas on four basic themes: the Concept of God, Theories of Creation, Prophecy (*nubuwwa*) and *Imāma*.

## God

Some aspects of the Ash'arī doctrine on God are commonly shared by Ismailism; al-Shahrastānī insists on these specific issues. The meaning (*ma'na*) and the expression (*'ibāra*) used by al-Ash'arī are part of the Shi'i vocabulary in use well before al-Ash'arī was born.[19] These technical terms refer respectively to the inner (*bāṭin*) and the outer (*ẓāhir*) meaning of the revelation. The God of the Ash'arīs is not the Pure Being in opposition to the Necessary Being (*Wājib al-wujūd*) of Ibn Sīnā. He is the One who gives existence (*mūjid*) to the beings. On this point, the Ash'arī description of God has some similarities to the Ismaili notion of the Originator (*mubdi'*) beyond Being and non-Being. The Ismaili concept of God is similar to the Jewish idea that the true Name of God cannot be uttered. In fact, as far as the Ismailis are concerned, God should not be named at all since every name is composed of letters, and letters, being created things, cannot designate God, who is beyond all conception.

Al-Shahrastānī accuses Ibn Sīnā of having an anthropomorphic conception of God as part of his ontology. He argues that using the tripart term 'Necessary Being in his essence' contradicts the Divine unicity.[20] Like al-Ghazālī, al-Shahrastānī sternly criticises Avicenna's Necessary Being, who knows the universal but not the particular. Al-Shahrastānī, particularly in the *Muṣāra'at al-falāsifa*, displays an Ismaili conception of the Originator beyond Being and non-Being. He argues convincingly for the existence of Divine attributes, but he does not ascribe them directly to God. True worship means *tawḥīd* – declaring the unicity of God. This includes the negation of all attributes with which humans would endow God, the Ultimate One, who is totally different and transcendent. He is unknowable, indefinable, unattainable and above all human comprehension.

Al-Shahrastānī is frequently inspired by Shiʿi Islam, maintaining that God is knowing because he is the One who gives knowledge. Like Abū Yaʿqūb al-Sijistānī, he places the Originator above attributes. And like the Nizārī Ismaili Ḥasan-i Ṣabbāḥ, al-Shahrastānī asserts in the *Mafātīḥ al-asrār* that: 'Our God is the God of Muḥammad.' In the *Nihāya*, the most 'Sunni' of his works al-Shahrastānī does not define the Divine command (*amr*) as an essential attribute of God.[21] He rejects the Ashʿarī concept of the Divine command[22] as an attribute inherent to the Divine essence. Like Ismailis, he conceives of the Divine command as a principle beyond attributes.[23]

## Creation

As for the theory of creation, Ashʿarism and Ismailism distinguish the Divine command (*amr*) beyond time from physical creation (*khalq*). In the *Nihāya*, al-Shahrastānī insists on the fact that God is the sole Creator and Agent, and he takes over the Ashʿarī theory of acquisition (*kasb*). But in the *Majlis* and in the *Mafātīḥ al-asrār*, the angels play a dominant role in physical creation.[24] And in these last two works al-Shahrastānī leaves out the theory of acquisition (*kasb*). In Ismailism God is the source of all creation while at the same time being uninvolved with creation. We are unable to affirm anything about how the creation happens since it is prior to human logic. Creation occurs simply by virtue of the Divine command executed by the angels and the Intellects.

Al-Shahrastānī criticised Avicenna's theory of creation according to which all things come from the knowledge of the Necessary Being (*Wājib al-wujūd*); this theory does not agree with the principle 'from One only One derives'. Like al-Ghazālī, he pointed out the contradiction in Avicenna's argument which maintains that emanation is universal whereas in fact it can only be applied to a limited number of Intellects. Al-Shahrastānī rejected the physical world of the Falāsifa and their definition of *ḥudūth* (temporal origination) and he was also sceptical about the possibility of an eternal physical creation.[25]

His theory of the Divine word (*kalima*) has similar patterns to those in Ismailism;[26] for example his hierarchy of angels and Divine words (*kalimāt*) are conceived as the causes of spiritual beings. Al-Shahrastānī in the *Nihāya*[27] writes: 'His [Divine] command (*amr*) is pre-existent and his multiple *kalimāt* are eternal. Through his command, *kalimāt* become the manifestation of it. Spiritual beings are the manifestation of *kalimāt* and bodies are the manifestation of spiritual beings. *Ibdāʿ* (origination beyond time and space) and *khalq* (physical creation) become manifest [respectively in] spiritual beings and bodies. As for *kalimāt* and letters (*ḥurūf*), they are eternal and pre-existent. Since his command is not similar to our command, his *kalimāt* and his letters are not similar to our *kalimāt*. Since letters are elements of *kalimāt* which are the causes of the spiritual beings who govern corporeal beings; all existence subsists in the *kalimat Allāh* preserved in his command.' Al-Shahrastānī also developed a different interpretation of *ex-nihilo* creation, so that it does not mean creation out of nothing, but creation made only by God.[28]

In the *Majlis*, al-Shahrastānī divides creation into two worlds: the spiritual world (i.e. the world of the origination of spirits, *ibdāʿ-i arwāḥ*) in an achieved (*mafrūgh*) state and the world of physical creation (*khalq*) in a state of becoming (*musta'naf*). He partakes of an Ismaili cosmology in which God has built his religion in the image of creation.

## Prophecy

The concept of prophecy developed in the *Nihāya* is closer to that of the Ismailis and the Falāsifa than to that of the Ashʿarīs, since al-Shahrastānī establishes a logical link between miracles and prophetic impeccability (*ʿiṣma*). As far as he is concerned, the proof of the veracity (*ṣidq*) of the prophet is intrinsic to his nature and is related to his impeccability.[29] He adopts the exclusively intellectual approach of the philosophers; like Ibn Sīnā, the prophet represents the highest human perfection, because he becomes one with the angel of revelation. The concept of cyclical time is developed explicitly in the *Milal*, the *Majlis* and the *Mafātīḥ* whereas it is only implicit in the *Nihāya*.

In the *Majlis*, his understanding of the dynamic evolution of humanity is similar to that found in Ismailism, in which each Prophet opens a new cycle. He recovers the mythical Qur'anic story of Moses and the Servant of God inspired by the *Risālat al-mudhhiba* of al-Qāḍī al-Nuʿmān. Along with Ḥasan-i Ṣabbāh, he presents a new understanding of the Nizārī tradition. During the Alamūt period, Moses corresponds to the speaking-prophet (*nāṭiq*) at the rank of the universal soul (*nafs-i kullī*). He is part of the ephemeral world, whereas Khiḍr, the *ḥujja* (the Proof), at the rank of the universal intellect (*ʿaql-i kullī*), belongs to the eternal world. Al-Shahrastānī relates the spiritual evolution of Abraham in the same way as Abū Ḥātim al-Rāzī does in his *Kitāb al-iṣlāḥ* and al-Qāḍī al-Nuʿmān in his *Asās al-ta'wīl*. These Ismaili authors relate the initiation of Abraham by the *dāʿī* (summoner symbolised by the star), then by the *ḥujja* (proof symbolised by the Moon) and finally by the Imam (symbolised by the Sun) before reaching the prophetic level.[30]

## Imāma

Al-Shahrastānī, in the *Milal*,[31] takes the position of the *ḥunafā'* against the Qur'anic Sabians on the necessity of a human Guide being gifted with impeccability (*ʿiṣma*).

In the *Nihāya*, he insists on the fact that the Prophet confirms the validity of his predecessors while proclaiming his successor. Like al-Ash'arī, he takes over the idea of an implicit designation (*naṣṣ khafī*) of a successor to Muḥammad. Even if he seems to give importance to *ijmā'* (consensus), he cautions the Muslims that God did not send prophets so that the people might exercise their own individual competence.[32] He omits to speak about the theory of *tafḍīl* concerning the order of preference of the four caliphs, but he praises 'Alī showing his preference for the *Ahl al-bayt (the Family of the Prophet).*

In the *Majlis*, al-Shahrastānī clearly distinguishes different spiritual ranks: Moses as the judge of *sharī'a*, Khiḍr as the Deputy (*nā'ib*) of the Judge of the Resurrection (*qiyāma)* and 'Alī as the Riser (*qā'im*). Two forms of light were inherited from Abraham: a visible light (*nūr-ī ẓāhir*) and a hidden one (*nūr-ī mastūr*). These two lights recall the Shi'i concepts of the *nūr al-nubuwwa* (the light of prophecy) and the *nūr al-Imāma* (the light of the *Imāma*).

In the *Mafātīḥ al-asrār*, he asserts that 'the people and the awaiting Shi'a (*al-Shī'at al-muntaẓira*) do not profess anything except an absent and awaited Imam, while God has on earth (21:26 f.): "Honoured Servants (*'ibād mukramūn*) [who] speak not before He speaks, and act [in all things] by His Command"; (35:32): "He chose the Servants as heirs of His Book". Whoever fights them, fights God; whoever loves them, loves God; whoever obeys them, obeys God; whoever prostrates himself before them[33] prostrates himself before God.'[34] In the *Nihāya*, he cites a *ḥadīth* generally quoted by the Shi'a according to which 'the earth will never be deprived of an Imam [acting according to] the Divine command (*amr*)'.[35]

In most of his writings, al-Shahrastānī demonstrates his fidelity to 'Alī and the *Ahl al-bayt*. In his *Milal*, he adopts Shi'i criticism (*maṭā'in*) of the actions of the first three caliphs while the Prophet was on his deathbed.[36] He regards 'Alī as the *Amīr al-mu'minīn* (Prince of believers).[37] He cites a *ḥadīth* saying that: "Alī was with the truth and the truth was with him'.[38] Al-Shahrastānī was certainly not a Twelver Shi'a since in the *Milal*, he criticises Twelver Shi'i notions of *ghayba*[39] and of Divine versatility (*badā'*).[40] But he seems to profess Ismailism since he believes in the existence of a living Guide physically present in this world.

In the *Milal* al-Shahrastānī criticised certain peculiar aspects of Twelver Shi'i doctrine. Since the *Majlis* is a discourse delivered to a Twelver audience, he does not reinforce the fundamental aspects which differentiate the Ismailis from the Twelver Shi'a (i.e. the concepts of *badā'*, *ghayba*, *mahdī* and the fourteen Impeccable beings, *chahārda ma'ṣūm*). He propounds certain Ismailis ideas such as *amr* (command) versus *khalq* (creation), 'Alī at the level of the first command (*amr-i awwal*) and Ḥasan as the heir of the revelation (*tanzīl*). The *Majlis* lays emphasis on the necessity of a Guide who belongs to both the spiritual and physical world. For each spiritual level there is a teacher (*mudabbir*).[41] The *dā'ī* (summoner symbolised by the star), the *ḥujja* (proof symbolised by Moon) and the Imam (symbolised by the Sun) are manifested in the world. Al-Shahrastānī explains clearly that on the day of the Resurrection, ʿAlī will have the function of the Riser (*qāʾim*) who separates those deserving Paradise from those deserving hell. The description of ʿAlī as the *qāʾim* has an Ismaili (more particularly Nizārī) imprint,[42] since the Twelver Shiʿi traditions consider the twelfth Imam (Muḥammad al-Mahdī) as the *qāʾim al-qiyāmat* (the Lord of the Resurrection).[43] Abū Isḥāq-i Quhistānī (d. 904/1448), a Nizārī writer, refers to a Prophetic tradition describing ʿAlī as *qāʾim*. He quotes: 'And Muṣṭafā (Muḥammad) said that ʿAlī b. Abī Ṭālib, may God beautify his countenance!, on the day of Resurrection, will raise the banner of the *qiyāma* single-handed.'[44]

## Conclusion

Al-Shahrastānī was an able and learned man of great personal charm. He made a profound study of earlier Ismaili literature but was also attracted by philosophy and theology. He fused these three traditions in a bold new synthesis. The real nature of his thought is neither completely philosophical nor theological but has features of both and is best referred to by the term theosophy. However al-Shahrastānī was certainly not totally against theology nor philosophy[45] even if his criticisms of the philosophers and the theologians were very severe. As he explained in the *Majlis*, in order to remain on the right path, one must preserve a perfect equilibrium between intellect (*ʿaql*) and audition (*samʿ*).[46] A philosopher or a theologian must use his intellect until he reaches the limits of the rational. Beyond this limit, he must listen to the teaching of Prophets and Imams. So al-Shahrastānī's thought is not philosophical in the modern sense, but a theosophy or a Divine wisdom.

The true philosophers of the past, as far as al-Shahrastānī was concerned, were the disciples of the seven pillars of wisdom (Thales, Anaxagoras, Anaximenes, Empedocles, Pythagoras, Socrates and Plato). The Ismailis like to stress that their thinking agrees with that of some of the ancient Sages, as al-Shahrastānī does at the beginning of his *Nihāya*. For al-Shahrastānī, the true philosophers were those who used their intellect within the parameters of faith defined by the Imam of the time (*imām al-zamān*). His works reflect a complex interweaving of three intellectual strands: Ashʿarism, Avicennism and Ismailism. His thought is a unique synthesis of the fruitful historical period. Al-Shahrastānī includes many of the elements of Fatimid thought in his *Majlis*, because he is one of the first representatives along with Ḥasan-i Ṣabbāḥ, of the Nizārī Ismaili tradition. He introduces some new specifically Nizārī elements that later Ismaili thinkers were to develop in their philosophy and theology. It is evident that al-Shahrastānī belongs to the Nizārī Ismaili tradition. This decisive conclusion modifies all future research on his writings.

In his concepts of God, creation, prophecy and *imāma*, al-Shahrastānī adopted many Ashʿarī as well as Avicennian elements. But all these specific elements could be reconciled with Nizārī Ismailism. The necessity of a Guide belonging both to the spiritual and the physical world is primordial to his scheme, since the different Guides are manifested in the world as *dāʿī*, *ḥujja* and Imam. Even though he does not directly mention the different dignitaries in the *Majlis*, he describes them through symbols (star, Moon and Sun) shared by Fatimid and Nizārī Ismailis. The enigmatic role of Khiḍr gives the *Majlis* a Sufi colouring. Khiḍr may be associated with the *ḥujjat al-imām* (Proof of the Divine guide) in Nizārī Ismaili doctrine, since he is the Deputy (*nāʾib*) of the Judge of the Resurrection, (*qiyāma*). ʿAlī has the prestigious role of the Riser (*qāʾim*) in the salvation of each soul.

## Notes

1. Al-Shahrastānī, '*Muṣaraʿat al-falāsifa*', ed. and tr. Wilferd Madelung and Toby Mayer in *Struggling with the Philosopher: A Refutation of Avicenna's Metaphysics* (London, 2001), text, p. 4, tr., p. 21.

2. D. Steigerwald, 'La dissimulation (*taqiyya*) de la foi dans le shīʿisme ismaélien', *Studies in Religion/Sciences religieuses*, 27 (1998), pp. 39–59.

3. For an extensive discussion of al-Shahrastānī's identity (Ashʿarī or Ismaili?), cf. D. Steigerwald, *La pensée philosophique et théologique de Shahrastani (m. 548/1153)* (Sainte-Foy, Québec, 1997), pp. 298–307.

4. J. Nāʾīnī, *Sharḥ-i ḥāl wa-āthār-i Ḥujjat al-Ḥaqq Abu'l-Fatḥ Muḥammad b. ʿAbd al-Karīm b. Aḥmad Shahrastānī* (Tehran, 1343 Sh./1964), pp. 47, 51.

5. Cf. the comments of Diana Steigerwald concerning the authenticity of the Majlis in Al-Shahrastānī, *Majlis-i maktūb-i Shahrastānī munʿaqid dar Khwārazm*, ed. Muḥammad Riḍa R. Jalālī Nāʾīnī and trans. into French by Diana Steigerwald in *Majlis: Discours sur l'ordre et la création* (Sainte-Foy, Québec, 1998), pp. 27–28.

6. Al-Shahrastānī, *Mafātīḥ al-asrār* (Tehran, 1369 Sh./1990), vol. 1, f. 2r., l. 13 to 2v., l. 11; Nāʾīnī, *Sharḥ-i ḥāl wa-āthār-i Ḥujjat al-Ḥaqq*, p. 49, l. 13 to p. 50 l. 9; G. Monnot, 'Islam: exégèse coranique', *Annuaire de l'École Pratique des Hautes Études*, 92 (1983–1984), p. 306.

7. M. T. Dānishpazhūh, 'Dāʿī al-duʿāt Tāj al-Dīn-i Shahrastāna', *Nāma-yi Āstān-i Quds*, 7 (1346 Sh./1968), pp. 73–74; 8 (1347 Sh./1969), p. 62.

8. 'Ash-Shahrastānīs Streitschrift gegen Avicenna und ihre Widerlegung durch Naṣir ad-dīn at-Tūsī', *Akten des VII. Kongresses für Arabistik und Islamwissenschaft, Abhandlungen der Akademie des Wissenschaften in Göttingen*, 98 (1976), pp. 251, 258.

9. Ismaili history can be divided into six important phases: i) the first period extends from Imām ʿAlī to Imām Jaʿfar al-Ṣādiq (d. 148/765) and is shared also by the Twelvers; ii) the second period from Ismāʿīl to Raḍī al-Dīn ʿAbd Allāh is the pre-Fatimid period. The Imāms were hidden (*masātīr*); iii) the Fatimids start with ʿAbd Allāh al-Mahdī and end with al-ʿĀḍid (d. 567/1171). At the death of al-Mustanṣir bi-Allāh, a split occurred between the western Ismailis and the eastern Ismailis; iv) the Alamūt period extends from Nizār to Rukn al-Dīn Khurshāh (d. 655/1257). Ḥasan-i Ṣabbāḥ and al-Shahrastānī lived during this period; v) the ginānic period begins with Shams al-Dīn Muḥammad and ends with Khalīl Allāh III (d. 1233/1817) in the Indo-Pakistan subcontinent; vi) lastly the modern period which starts

with the first Aga Khan. Ismailism has multiple facets: i) synthesis with Neoplatonism in the Fatimid period; ii) synthesis with Sufism in the Alamūt and post-Alamūt period and iii) synthesis with Vaishnavism in the ginānic period.

10. W. Madelung, 'Aspects of Ismāʿīlī Theology: the Prophetic Chain and the God beyond Beings', in Seyyed Hosein Nasr, ed., *Ismāʿīlī Contributions to Islamic Culture* (Tehran, 1977), pp. 62–63.

11. Al-Shahrastānī, *Mafātīḥ al-asrār*, vol. 1, f. 121v., l. 25 to 122r., ll. 1–6 and 9–11.

12. Monnot, 'Islam: exégèse coranique', *Annuaire de l'École Pratique des Hautes Études*, 95 (1986–1987), pp. 255–256.

13. Al-Shahrastānī, *Mafātīḥ al-asrār*, vol. 2, f. 266r., ll. 5–13.

14. Al-Shahrastānī, *Kitāb al-milal wa'l niḥal*, ed. Muḥammad Fatḥ Allāh Badrān (Cairo, 1366–1375/1947–1955), 2 vols., vol. 1, pp. 444–445.

15. Monnot, 'Islam: exégèse coranique', *Annuaire de l'École Pratique des Hautes Études*, 96 (1987–1988), p. 240; 'Al-Shahrastānī', *EI2*, vol. 9, pp. 220–222.

16. Al-Shahrastānī, *Kitāb al-milal wa'l niḥal*, vol. 1, p. 152.

17. Abū Yaʿqūb al-Sijistānī, *Kitāb al-iftikhār*, ed. Muṣṭafā Ghālib (Beirut, n.d.), p. 24.

18. P. E. Walker, *Early Philosophical Shiism: The Ismaili Neoplatonism of Abū Yaʿqūb al-Sijistānī* (Cambridge, 1993), p. 78.

19. Ibid., pp. 121, 127–128.

20. Al-Shahrastānī, *Muṣāraʿat al-falāsifa*, ed. Suhayr M. Mukhtār (Cairo, 1396/1976), p. 40.

21. Al-Shahrastānī, '*Nihāyat al-aqdām fi ʿilm al-kalām*', ed. and partial trans., Alfred Guillaume in *The Summa Philosophiae of al-Shahrastānī* (Oxford, 1934), p. 385.

22. For more details on divine Attributes, cf. W. M. Watt, *The Formative Period of Islamic Thought* (Oxford, 1998), pp. 245–246.

23. D. Steigerwald, 'L'Ordre (*amr*) et la creation (*khalq*) chez Shahrastānī', *Folia Orientalia*, 31 (1995), pp. 163–175.

24. Al-Shahrastānī, *Majlis*, p. 82; al-Shahrastānī, *Mafātīḥ al-asrār*, vol. 1, f. 109v., l. 24 to f. 110r., l. 1.

25. Al-Shahrastānī, '*Nihāyat al-aqdām fi ʿilm al-kalām*', pp. 21, 44–45.

26. D. Steigerwald, 'The Divine Word' (*Kalima* in Shahrastānī's *Majlis)', Studies in Religion, Sciences religieuses*, 25 (1996). pp. 335–352.

27. Al-Shahrastānī, '*Nihāyat al-aqdām fi ʿilm al-kalām*', p. 316.

28. Ibid., pp. 18–19.

29. Ibid., pp. 444–445.

30. Steigerwald, *La pensée philosophique*, pp. 294–295.

31. Al-Shahrastānī, *Kitāb al-milal wa'l-niḥal*, vol. 1, pp. 560–562.

32. Al-Shahrastānī, '*Nihāyat al-aqdām fi ʿilm al-kalām*', p. 486.

33. Those who oppose the Friends of God and consider themselves superior to them, repudiate the Qur'anic verses concerning prostration, cf. Abū Ḥanifā al-Nuʿmān, '*Al-Risālat al-Mudhhiba*', in *Khams Rasāʾil Ismāʿīliyya*, ed. ʿĀrif Tāmir (Beirut, 1956), p. 38.

34. Al-Shahrastānī, *Mafātīh al-asrār*, vol. 1, f. 121v., ll. 25 to f. 122r., ll. 1–6 and 9–11; Monnot, 'Islam: exégèse coranique', pp. 255–256.

35. Al-Shahrastānī, '*Nihāyat al-aqdām fi ʿilm al-kalām*', pp. 478–479.

36. Al-Shahrastānī, *Kitāb al-milal wa'l-niḥal*, vol. 1, pp. 18 f.

37. Ibid., pp. 21, 24, 192, 196.

38. Ibid., p. 24; al-Shahrastānī, '*Nihāyat al-aqdām fi 'ilm al-kalām*', p. 494.

39. Al-Shahrastānī, *Kitāb al-milal wa'l-niḥal*, vol. 1, pp. 360–361.

40. Ibid., pp. 335 f.; D. Gimaret and G. Monnot, *Livre des religions et des sects* (Belgium, 1986), vol. 1, p. 485 n. 55.

41. Al-Shahrastānī, *Majlis*, p. 95.

42. Al-Sijistānī, *Kitāb al-iftikhār*, p. 50: 'Alī as the *asās* is potentially the Riser (*qā'im*); al-Shahrastānī could not possibly be acquainted with the *Haft bāb-i Bābā Sayyidnā* but I notice that this same idea is shared by later Nizārī works. This doctrine was probably introduced by Ḥasan-i Ṣabbāḥ. Cf. *Haft bāb-i Sayyidnā*, ed. Wladimir Ivanow in *Two Early Ismaili Treatises* (Bombay, 1933), p. 16, extract translated by Marshall G. S. Hodgson in *The Order of Assassins* (New York, 1980), p. 295: "Alī (bless him) b. Abī Ṭālib will come and lift the standard of the Qiyāma. And there are many proofs of this sort that Mawlānā will be *qā'im* of the *qiyāma*.'

43. See the beginning of the 11th chapter of the *Kitāb al-irshād* of Shaykh al-Mufīd. According to the early traditions, every Imam is Qā'im, cf. A. A. Sachedina, *Islamic Messianism* (Albany, NY, 1981), pp. 61–62.

44. Abū Isḥāq-i Quhistānī, *Haft bāb*, ed. and tr., Wladimir Ivanow (Bombay, 1959), p. 40.

45. See G. Monnot's review of Diane Steigerwald, *La pensée philosophique et théologique de Shahrastani (m. 548/1153)* in *BCAI*, 15 (1999), pp. 79–81.

46. Al-Shahrastānī, *Majlis*, p. 99.

# 21

# The Pertinence of Islamic Cosmology: Reflections on the Philosophy of Afḍal al-Dīn Kāshānī

*William C. Chittick*

My recollections of Professor Landolt go back to the 1970s when he used to come to Tehran to do research at the Tehran Branch of the McGill Institute of Islamic Studies. At the time I was busy with my Ph.D. dissertation at Tehran University and later teaching at Aryamehr Technical University. Although I remember that Professor Landolt was often present during academic events, I recall specifically only one of his lectures. That was an impressive Persian talk in the Faculty of Letters at Tehran University on the theories of the Sufi 'Alā' al-Dawla al-Simnānī. To my regret, I never had the chance to profit personally from his great erudition, which he reserved mainly for his direct students.

More recently, it was the good fortune of me and my wife to be staying with our old friends Mehdi Mohaghegh and Nushin Ansari in Tehran in May of 1999, right after an international congress on Mullā Ṣadrā. Professor Landolt was also staying with them, though we hardly had time to talk because he was so busy meeting friends. Then, however, a bureaucratic snafu kept him in Tehran three days longer than he had planned, and we had plenty of opportunity to discuss various matters of mutual interest. Among other things, we spoke about my recent work on the philosopher Afḍal al-Dīn Kāshānī, and I was delighted to hear that he had read Kāshānī carefully and that his estimate of Kāshānī's place in the philosophical tradition coincided more or less with my own. Given the interest Professor Landolt expressed in my work, I thought it would be appropriate to offer an article on Afḍal al-Dīn to him in his *Festschrift*.

Afḍal al-Dīn Kāshānī, usually known in Iran as Bābā Afḍal (d. ca. 610/1213–1214), was one of the two or three Muslim philosophers who wrote mainly in Persian rather than Arabic. His collected Persian works include six longish treatises, four translations from Arabic of works by Greek philosophers, many short essays, seven letters to disciples, and a good number of quatrains and other poems. He was a contemporary of Averroes, al-Suhrawardī and Ibn ʿArabī, but his philosophical position is perhaps closest to the Neoplatonism of the Ikhwān al-Ṣafāʾ. He considered himself someone who stood squarely in the Greek tradition and the only philosophers he mentions by name are Aristotle and Hermes.

In contrast to most philosophers, Bābā Afḍal does not beat about the bush. He goes directly to the heart of philosophy as received by the Islamic tradition. This heart can be expressed most succinctly in the Delphic maxim, 'Know thyself'. Bābā Afḍal writes with the goal of clarifying the nature of the quest for self-knowledge that must animate all philosophy worthy of the name, and he holds that true philosophy remains inaccessible to those who do not know themselves. Those who investigate and study things that do not illuminate their understanding of themselves are wasting their time.

In the later tradition Bābā Afḍal was perhaps better known as a poet than a philosopher. His philosophical works were partly forgotten not because of any lack of originality or profundity, but because Arabic remained the language of serious philosophy in Iran down to the nineteenth century, and any work in Persian appeared peripheral to students of the discipline. No doubt he influenced the later tradition, but his influence has not been studied, so it is difficult to provide concrete evidence for it. However, Mullā Ṣadrā was familiar with his writings and I suspect that a careful comparison of their works will show that he appropriated Bābā Afḍal's ideas in many places. One proof of this assertion is that Mullā Ṣadrā translated Bābā Afḍal's *Jāwidān-nāma* into Arabic, making a good number of modifications and additions, but without mentioning the fact that Bābā Afḍal was the original author. He called the new version of the treatise *Iksīr al-ʿārifīn*.[1]

Bābā Afḍal's orientation towards the achievement of self-knowledge and the practice of philosophy as a spiritual discipline throws light on a contemporary issue concerning which most scholars have concluded that pre-modern philosophy has nothing to say. This is the domain of cosmology, or the understanding of the nature of the universe. It appears that modern scholars have paid little attention to this philosophical cosmology because they consider it to have been superseded by science. Nonetheless, many historians and philosophers have recently begun to question the epistemological authority of science, and this should allow us to reconsider the whole question of how philosophical cosmology might speak to us in modern times.

Before I address the issue of Bābā Afḍal's cosmology, however, I need to say something about his general philosophical perspective, since his cosmology cannot be isolated from his other concerns. Two discussions need to be summarised – ontology and psychology. It is in the relationship between these two domains that the practical orientation of Bābā Afḍal's philosophy becomes completely clear.

The essence of Bābā Afḍal's position can perhaps be summed up in one sentence: 'The fullness of being is identical with the fullness of self-awareness.' I want to explain very quickly what this sentence means, leaving aside, of course, all the arguments that Bābā Afḍal presents to prove the truth of the assertion.[2]

Bābā Afḍal does not follow the usual tripartite analysis of *wujūd* (existence or being) into necessary, possible and impossible. His basic position on Ultimate Reality is that it lies outside philosophical investigation. Everything that we can investigate has *wujūd*, but the Ipseity (*huwiyya*) or Essence (*dhāt*) – the Neoplatonic 'God-above-thinking-and-being'[3] – cannot enter into philosophical discussion. This leaves us with things that exist in modalities accessible to our experience. When we investigate these things, we find that they can be divided into four primary categories or levels.

In describing the four levels of experienced reality, Bābā Afḍal takes advantage of the Persian language to bring out two basic meanings of the word *wujūd*. Although the term is normally translated into English as 'existence' or 'being', outside philosophical discourse it is just as likely to mean 'finding' or 'being found'. Bābā Afḍal tells us that *wujūd* can be divided into two sorts. One sort is 'being' (*būdan*, *būd*, *hastī*), and the other sort is 'finding' (*yāftan*, *yāft*). It is immediately obvious that finding is a higher level than being, because everything that finds also has being, but everything that has being does not necessarily find. The finder finds existent things, but existent things qua existent things do not find the finder or other existent things. To find is always to be, but to be is not always to find.

Having divided *wujūd* into two levels, Bābā Afḍal subdivides each level into two sorts. The lowest level of *wujūd* is 'potential being' (*būdan-i bi-quwwa*). An example would be the existence of a tree in a seed. The second level is actual being (*būdan-i bi-fiʿl*) and is represented by all objects in the external world, like the tree itself. The third level is potential finding. This is the level of the 'soul' (*nafs*), which is identical with the 'self' (*khwud*). The fourth and highest level is actual finding, which is the level of the intellect or intelligence (*ʿaql*, *khirad*). In Avicennan terms, this fourth level is identical with the 'active' or 'fully actualised' intellect (*ʿaql-i faʿʿāl*).

It becomes clear in Bābā Afḍal's very description of *wujūd* that philosophers have a practical goal. In his view, the lover of wisdom sets out to know existence per se and, as a function of knowing existence, to know all things that exist. But, to grasp *wujūd* in its totality is the same as to grasp the knowing self in its totality. 'To be' in the full sense of the word is to have total awareness (*āgahī*). Absolute being is absolute knowledge. The philosopher strives to know *wujūd* qua *wujūd*, but he can only do so by knowing self qua self. In other words, the philosopher is striving to know intellect as the intellecter, or to know his own pure and disengaged (*mujarrad*) intelligence as the only true object of knowledge. This is the stage of the unification of the intellecter, the intellect and the intellected (*ittiḥād-i ʿāqil u ʿaql u maʿqūl*), a position supported most vocally among Muslim philosophers by Mullā Ṣadrā.

In short, the practical goal of the philosopher is to know all things. But in order to know all things, the philosopher must know the principle of all things, a principle that is at one and the same time the knower of all things and the fullness of being. This knower is the 'intellect', which is the fully actualised soul, or the self that is totally aware of self, or, as Bābā Afḍal sometimes calls it, the 'radiance of the Ipseity' (*furūgh-i huwiyya*).

In short, Bābā Afḍal discusses psychology and ontology in terms of a progression of both being and awareness that culminates in the perfection of self and existence. In the fullness of their actualisation, self and existence are identical. In both, there is a clear unfolding from the lowest inanimate level to the highest level of self-awareness, which is the fully actualised intellect, where existence and awareness are one. It follows that the disciplines of psychology and ontology both focus on the ascent from potentiality to actuality. Hence, we also need an explanation of how things come to exist in a state of potentiality in the first place, and this is the basic role of cosmology.

The philosophers commonly discuss coming into existence and the subsequent ascent to the final goal as *mabda' wa-maʿād*, 'the origin and the return'. In discussing the return, they elaborate upon a basic human intuition. People know innately that they have 'come up' and can go up further. An adult has come up from childhood, a child from the womb and a knowing person from ignorance. People can assist their upward climb by their own efforts. They can climb up through their aptitudes and talents, and they can set their goals as high as they wish. All concepts of education, learning, improvement, progress, evolution and directed development are based on this fundamental understanding that things can be changed in an 'upward' direction. The idea is so basic to human life that people rarely bother to reflect upon it, but simply take it for granted. In the mythic terms of the Western monotheisms, amongst others, the goal towards which the upward movement is oriented correlates with the celestial, starry realms as well as with paradise, or the happy domain after death. Refusal to undertake the upward movement is correlated with the lower reaches of existence and with hell.

The philosophers discuss the upward, returning movement in terms of both ontology and psychology, but they discuss the downward, originating movement mainly in terms of cosmology. The question is this: Where did this world come from and how do we happen to be here? In answering the question, the philosophers elaborate upon an intuition that is as basic to pre-modern humanity as the perception of upward movement. This is that nothing can go up that has not come down in the first place. As Bābā Afḍal puts it in passing, 'Whatever does not fall down from heaven does not rise up from earth'.[4]

We are now down. The proof is that we aspire to higher things, and we often achieve them. But if we are down, our aspiration must correspond to something within us that knows what it means to be up. True knowledge of 'upness' presupposes some mode of previous awareness of what 'upness' is, and that in turn means that something of the 'up' must have come down to us.

Mythic formulations of the precedent 'upness' are practically universal. The scientific myths of evolution and progress may be the only examples of myths that speak of the upward movement while denying the primal descent. In modern myths, we situate ourselves at the top and look back at the bottom. The alpha is one thing, far behind and below us, and we are the omega, or at least the current omega. In the pre-modern myths, people saw themselves as if situated on a trajectory that began on high, with God or the gods. Then human beings came to be low, and now they are in the process of going back in the direction from which they came. The alpha and the omega are ultimately one.

Some versions of the modern myth suggest that the process has its own necessity – we have been forced up because of the impersonal laws of evolution, and we will keep on going up as we evolve further. The pre-modern myths offer no guarantee of ascent, not at least in any meaningful future. If there is to be an ascent, people must strive to achieve it. We can as easily move further away from the Ultimate Reality as we can move closer to it. We can be left in dispersion and multiplicity indefinitely. Even versions of the pre-modern myths that speak of an inevitable return to the personal and loving God, as does the Islamic, insist that human beings must exert their own efforts if they are to return by a route that will leave them happy with the journey. If they are not ready for the climb, they will go back under constraint, and they will suffer because of the lack of congeneity and harmony with what they meet on the way and at the destination. Bābā Afḍal and others explain suffering in the afterlife along these lines.

The underlying rationale for the pre-modern myths is the perception of invisible qualities in the world and the self, that is, the understanding that there is more to existence than meets the eye, not in terms of physical inaccessibility, but in terms of spiritual distance. The myths all acknowledge a realm of superior, intelligible and intelligent things that we can glimpse through the beauty and goodness that we find in ourselves and in the world. We must reach up for this realm if we are to make contact with it, and those who reach with sincerity, love and devotion achieve it more fully than those who go through the motions perfunctorily, or those who make no attempt to undertake the journey. In short, the world is perceived as bathed in the supernal qualities, and a whole and healthy human self is understood to be one that is drawn in the direction of those qualities, which are the source of all awareness and everything that is good, beautiful, desirable and lovable.

The rationale for the modern myths seems to be the inability to see quality beyond quantity. All so-called 'qualities', if real in any way, are explained away in reductionist, quantitative terms. By indefinite division and analysis – by taking things back to genes or social conditioning or atomic particles – we can explain away all the echoes of the divine that were seen by 'primitive' and 'backward' peoples. We ourselves then stand in a privileged position at the peak of the evolutionary upsurge. We alone are finally able to understand the truth behind the cosmos – or, what is more likely nowadays, that there is no truth behind the cosmos. Holy mother science has allowed us to see clearly that pre-modern peoples were labouring under primitive illusions and living in self-serving dreams, inventing all sorts of myths to act as psychological crutches. We do not reflect on the psychological crutches that we put to use with our own myths of science and superiority.

In short, perception of quality allows people to see things as diaphanous screens within which the signs of God are displayed, but inability to see anything but quantity breeds a sort of thinking that understands only in terms of reduction to the least common denominator.

For Islamic thinking in general, knowing the qualitative domain towards which we are aspiring demands knowing the qualitative domain from which our aspirations have descended. Those who want beauty aspire to it because they have a sense of what it means, and that sense drinks from the same well as beauty itself. But, in order to find the goal, one has to know the route by which aspiration came to us in the first place. Bābā Afḍal explains this in a letter to a student:

> You must know that searching out and exploring things and investigating the origin and return of the self does not rise up from bodily individuals. If searching and yearning for the meanings and for the road of reality rose up from human individuals inasmuch as they are individuals, this wanting would be found in every particular individual, but that is not the case. This is because the wish to encompass both worlds is fitting for someone for whom it is possible to encompass them. But it is impossible for any particular individual in respect of individuality to encompass another individual – not to speak of both worlds. Hence this wish does not rise up from the individual. Rather, it rises up from the soul that is radiant with the divine light.[5]

The philosophers investigated the Origin in order to understand the Return. Origin and Return represent the two basic movements demanded by *tawḥīd*, the assertion of God's unity. Asserting that the Ultimate Reality is one demands recognition that it is both First (*awwal*) and Last (*ākhir*). Everything comes from the Real and everything returns to it. In order to understand how we will return to the First, we need to discover how we came to be separated from the First. To do so, we must grasp the true nature of our faculties and powers, including the senses and intelligence. We also need to ask if the compulsory return to the First that is now driving us towards death is sufficient for the achievement of true humanity, or if – what seems to be much more likely if not self-evident – we need to employ our cognitive and practical powers to achieve that humanity, just as we employ these powers to achieve everything else that we achieve.

The Muslim philosophers thought that the study of the human soul was fundamental to the 'quest for wisdom', which is the very definition of philosophy. And they looked for the roots of the soul in the First. They considered ethics an important science, because ethics is nothing if not a discussion of how the soul achieves harmony with the First in keeping with the manner in which it came out from the First at the beginning. The soul appeared in the world because of a compulsory descent (*nuzūl-i iḍtirārī*), in the sense that none of us were asked if we wanted to come. Or, in the light of a certain Neoplatonic approach, human freedom (*ikhtiyār*) was already manifest in the choice of the human self to come into this world. Whether or not we chose to come, we have come, and now we must go back where we came from. We have sufficient freedom to make some choices, and what freedom we have must be put to good use if there is to be any possibility of achieving ultimate happiness.

According to the philosophers, human beings in their present situation are in the process of going up, which is to say that they are moving from the potency of the fertilised egg towards the pure actuality of the disengaged intellect (*'aql-i mujarrad*). Because of the compulsory return, they have gathered together the stages of inanimate nature, the plant soul and the animal soul, and they possess the powers and faculties of all these stages. Now they stand at the level of the human soul, so they are free to direct their own ascent. No one is forcing them to continue the upward movement. If they prefer to do so, people can stay where they are and go about actualising the animal traits to a degree undreamed of by any non-human animal.

Unquestionably, human beings possess the power of intelligence. To deny this in any sort of meaningful way would be to contradict oneself. Given that people have this power, they can use it as they see fit. But this is not to say that how they use it is indifferent and that all will necessarily be for the good. Just as they need discipline and guidance to become pianists or soccer players, so also they need discipline and guidance to become fully intelligent, which is to say, fully human, since intelligence alone is their uniquely *human* characteristic.

I do not wish to suggest that intelligence is their only human characteristic. Rather, it is the highest human trait and the pinnacle of human possibility, because the fullness of intelligence is identical with the fullness of being. It perhaps needs to be stressed, however, that the soul has two perfections, the theoretical and the practical, and both need to be actualised. Practical perfection demands the fullness of ethical and moral being, or the actualisation of all the virtues (*faḍā'il*). Neither theoretical nor practical perfection can be achieved in isolation. Perfection of intelligence cannot be achieved without perfecting all the soul's aptitudes, and most of these are named by the names of the virtues – love, compassion, justice, forgiveness. Ethical activity and beautiful character traits are inseparable from striving for human status.

In order to move from potential intellect to actual intellect, people need to know what they are striving for. In general, the religious tradition looks for knowledge of the final goal in the Qur'an and the *ḥadīth*, and it looks for knowledge of the praxis that allows the goal to be reached in the Sunna and the *sharīʿa*. But the philosophers maintain that knowledge of the final goal and of the praxis needed to achieve it require thought (*andīsha*) and reflection (*tafakkur*). To the extent that people put the power of their own intelligence to work by coming to understand the nature of things, they will actualise intelligence, and gradually they will move from potential intellect to fully actualised intellect.

Philosophical discussions of the Return focus on the two basic ways of going back to the First – the road that people will be compelled to follow and the road that they are free to follow if they choose to do so. Discussions of the Origin focus on how they arrived at their starting place. If they can go up to intelligence, they must have come down from intelligence. If they can go up to intelligence by ascending through the stages of soul, they must have come down into this world by descending through the stages of soul. The Return is the mirror image of the Origin. In later texts, Origin and Return are often discussed as the two arcs of a circle, the 'descending arc' (*qaws-i nuzūlī*) and the 'ascending arc' (*qaws-i ṣuʿūdī*).

The descending route of the Origin is well known. The basic outline is the same as that already present in the *Theology* of Plotinus – intellect, soul, heavenly spheres, four elements. Bābā Afḍal sticks to this simplest of schemes, though some philosophers had developed it into several degrees, as for instance al-Fārābī and Avicenna.

One should not be thrown off track by the language of these discussions and think that, for example, the philosophers are reifying the concepts of intellect and soul, much as people today reify the concept of God; or that they are describing the planets and celestial spheres with anything like the concerns of modern astronomy. Discussion of intellect and soul has to do with what we can retrace in our own selves, and discussion of the spheres has to do with what we can discern with the naked eye. By studying the heavens, the philosophers want to know what we can learn about what is 'up' by looking in that direction. The 'upness' of the physical domain is an analogue of the 'upness' of the spiritual domain, which is to say that what is 'up' in terms of our sense perception is a marker of realities that are 'up' in respect of our intelligence and understanding. If we look up in the outside world, we see the planets and stars, and if we look up in the inside world, we see soul and intelligence. The key is looking, gazing, thinking, reflecting, pondering, meditating and contemplating.

In short, discussion of the heavens pertains to the investigation of the qualities and characteristics that are 'higher' than we are in our corporeal – though not our intellective – nature. Inasmuch as the heavens pertain to the Origin, they represent descending stages through which the self, in coming down from intellect and entering the womb, becomes more and more differentiated from other selves and immersed in multiplicity. Inasmuch as the heavens pertain to the Return, they represent stages that the self must pass through in order to actualise its potentiality, harmonise its diverse powers, unify its multiple aptitudes and finally rejoin the intellect from which it arose. The mythic model for this Return is provided by the accounts of the Prophet's *miʿrāj*.

The philosophers were able to read spiritual significance into what they saw of the celestial spheres because they were reflecting upon themselves. They saw that they themselves, beginning in the womb, had risen up from mineral, to plant, to animal, to human, and that they were now striving to rise to the fullness of self-knowledge, the intellect that knows itself and all things. In their view, the way to achieve a truly useful knowledge of the spheres – that is, useful in the quest to become human – is to investigate how the celestial realms display the qualities and characteristics of our own intellective nature. To study the heavens is to study realities that bring together many other realities and embrace and encompass the evanescent world below. The heavens reflect much more directly than the sublunar realm the nature of the intelligent self, which is incorruptible and everlasting.

When reading historical discussions of Islamic cosmology, we are sometimes left with the impression that the (First) Intellect and the (Universal) Soul – that is, the initial stages of descent from the Origin – were concepts lifted from Neoplatonic sources without much reflection on the part of those who did the lifting. The two can appear as rather odd suppositions that have nothing to do with the real world – though it is understandable, we may be led to believe, that the 'unimaginative Muslims', relying as usual on the Greeks, should borrow this notion as an easy and ostensibly 'rational' explanation for the origin of the universe. But there is no reason to think that these ideas were taken over without critical assimilation on the part of those who took them over. Philosophy is nothing if not the sober consideration of what we can know, the sifting of supposition from real knowledge. It is a certain breed of historian that has seen the history of ideas as an unreflective collecting of ideas from the past as if they were precious artifacts.

If we are to make any sense of the Intellect and the Soul as the dual progenitors of the cosmos, we have to stop and reflect on what the philosophers were trying to say. As human beings, we know innately that all things have been born from the Soul, because our own souls embrace nature along with the plant, animal and human faculties. We know innately that the Intellect is the all-embracing origin, because it is precisely our own intelligence that knows all this, arranges all this, becomes all this and embraces all this. If our microcosmic intelligence is able to conceive of the whole world, it can do so only because it is already, at some level, of itself an intelligence that conceives of the whole universe. What goes up must have come down in the first place.

Once we re-evaluate Islamic cosmological teachings in such terms, it will be obvious that it is premature to abandon its perspective because it does not coincide with modern theoretical constructs. Rather, we should ask ourselves: What is the goal of studying the universe? What are the self-imposed limits of those who study? The modern study of the universe and the accompanying theories all stop short at the surface of reality. Islamic cosmology was always focused on the depths of reality, and the depths of reality are inseparable from the human self.

In effect, modern science and the modern disciplines have abandoned the study of the human self. Instead, people study subjects that allow them to go out and get things done, or at least to make money. For Islamic philosophy, to abandon study of the self is to abandon humanity, to give up any claim to human status. Knowledge that does not help us understand who we are is not, in fact, knowledge. Theories that purport to give knowledge divorced from the knowing subject are simply systematic ignorance. Such theories can be enormously useful for manipulating the world and establishing power relationships, but they do not and cannot aid in the quest for wisdom.

In short, in the view of Islamic philosophy in general and Bābā Afḍal in particular, to be human is to seek after knowledge that will increase one's humanity. Humanity's defining characteristic is the self-aware intelligence and knowing that intelligence intelligently demands focusing one's energies on self-knowledge. Any knowledge that does not aid in the quest for self-knowledge is in fact ignorance, and its fruit can only be the dissolution and destruction of human nature.

## Notes

1. William C. Chittick, *Mulla Sadra, the Elixir of the Gnostics: A Parallel English-Arabic text* (Provo, UT, 2003).

2. Details can be found in my study of Bābā Afḍal's writings: *The Heart of Islamic Philosophy: The Quest for Self-knowledge in the Teachings of Afdal al-Din Kashani* (Oxford, 2001).

3. I take the expression from Philip Merlan, *Monopsychism, Mysticism, Metaconsciousness: Problems of the Soul in the Neoaristotelian and Neoplatonic Tradition* (The Hague, 1963), pp. 20–21.

4. Afḍal al-Dīn Kāshānī, *Muṣannafāt*, ed. M. Mīnuwī and Y. Mahdawī (Tehran, 1331–1337 Sh./1952–1958), p. 325.

5. Ibid., p. 688.

# 22

# The Sciences of Intuition and the Riches of Inspiration: Najm al-Dīn Kubrā in Jāmī's *Nafaḥāt al-uns*

*Elizabeth Ross Alexandrin*

This paper is an examination of textual composition in 'Abd al-Raḥman al-Jāmī's (d. 897/1492) medieval Persian Sufi hagiography, *Nafaḥāt al-uns min ḥaḍarat al-quds*. Drawn from historical, doctrinal and oral sources, Sufi hagiography reveals much about the codification and creation of texts in medieval Islamic societies. Hagiography often shares the stylistic features and format of religious history, oral traditions and biographical accounts.

In a similar manner, the Sufi *silsila* also reflects the verbal and non-verbal elements of religious instruction within the context of the traditional religious sciences as well as the master-disciple relationship. As an encapsulation of multiple transmissions of exoteric and esoteric religious knowledge from various shaykhs, the Sufi *silsila* details the composite and the sphere of the individual's knowledge and authority to instruct and train others. In order to discern the composite of the Central Asian Sufi, Najm al-Dīn Kubrā's (539–c.617/1145–1221) religious education, this paper will first examine the standard forms of textual transmission in medieval Islamic societies, as established primarily during the second to third/eighth to ninth centuries as well as the life and training of Najm al-Dīn Kubrā. The second part of the paper will concern itself with Najm al-Dīn Kubrā's initial mystical experiences as a student of the religious sciences and his later abilities as a perfected Sufi master.

## The Modes of Transmission

The Qur'an has four aspects: *tafsīr*, which the scholars know, and *'arabiyya*, which the Arabs know, and *halāl wa-ḥarām*, the knowledge of which is indispensable to the people, and *ta'wīl*, which only God knows.[1]

As both the sciences of Arabic grammar and Qur'anic exegesis developed in their second/eighth-century social and political contexts, treatises on asceticism (*zuhd*) and scholastic theology (*kalām*) began to be transmitted and recorded.[2] The early mystical commentaries (*tafsīr*), attributed to the likes of Ḥasan al-Baṣrī (d. 109/728), Ḥasan b. Muḥammad b. al-Ḥanafiyya (d. ca.99/718), and Ja'far al-Ṣādiq (d. 148/765), quoted and interpreted verses from the Qur'an.[3] The method that the early scholars undertook in order to craft a specific doctrinal focus for their commentaries did not differ greatly from their more 'popular' counterparts – the preacher (*wā'iẓ*) and the Qur'anic storyteller (*qaṣṣ*).[4] The substance of the oral sermon and the written treatise relied on the Qur'an and propounded the implications of its often unclear and ambiguous verses. From this vantage point, the learned scholar and the local preacher alike, in their respective social and religious roles, instructed the *umma* in matters of the applicability of the Qur'an and of the religious laws and meanings it embodied.[5]

There was, in fact, a great deal of fluidity between the oral and written transmission of texts in the context of religious instruction. In reference to the early uses of the Qur'an and its levels of interpretation, there was another category of specialists amongst the emerging, yet overlapping, groups of religious scholars, ascetics and local preachers. The Qur'an reciters (*qurrā'* or *mudhakkirūn*), however, occupied a much more ambiguous role in relation to the authority to transmit legitimate interpretations (*ta'wīl*) of the Qur'an. Though the *mudhakkirūn* were active in sustaining and spreading the word of the Qur'an as one of the daily practices of the Muslim community, other individuals concerned with textual interpretation and its modes of transmission came to consider the Qur'an reciter's role in the following way: 'whosoever recites the Qur'an without knowing its *ta'wīl*, is illiterate in it.'[6]

The example of the *mudhakkirūn* in the early development of the Islamic religious sciences also relates back to the above-mentioned nature of oral and written texts and the adaptation of these texts in the process of religious instruction and attaining a higher degree of knowledge.[7] In more specific terms, in order to lay the foundations for this discussion of Najm al-Dīn Kubrā's religious biography from Jāmī's *Nafaḥāt al-uns* (compiled 882/1478), the differing forms of instruction constantly refer back to written documents (i.e. the Qur'an or the *ḥadīths*).[8] Through first reflecting upon a perceived hierarchy in the methods of transmitting religious knowledge during the early years of Islam, we may then examine and elucidate similar processes in Najm al-Dīn Kubrā's scholastic and Sufi training. This approach will allow us to discuss how Kubrā's mystical experiences under the guidance of his Sufi shaykhs serve to clarify, comment upon and encapsulate the knowledge he acquired through his scholastic education. As well, it will provide us with the opportunity to examine one particular example of the transition, as Ernst has recently discussed, 'from oral teaching to written text in Sufism'.[9]

## The Religious Sciences

Sezgin's theory of the development of *ḥadīth* points out that there were three standardised methods for transmitting texts from written sources in the first two centuries of the hijra (7th–9th centuries CE).[10] The transmission of the text through the teacher's and student's personal contact (*al-riwaya ʿalā'l-wajh*) could be separated into two categories – *samāʿ*, hearing the teacher recite the *ḥadīth* and then reciting it back, and *qirāʾa*, the teacher reading the *ḥadīth* and the student then reading the text back to the teacher.[11] A third mode of transmission was termed *kitāba* (a transference of previously codified notes or reports), in which the student was granted permission (*ijāza*) from his teacher to transmit the texts incorporated in the *kitāba* to other individuals even though the student's knowledge was not actually tested.[12]

Sezgin also points out that the latter mode was more often criticised than the former two, particularly in reaction to the codification of *ḥadīth*s as a written corpus. This cautious attitude towards writing down *ḥadīth*s might be related to early reactions to the notion that a collection of *ḥadīth* was equal to the authority of the Qurʾan in deciding religious and legal matters.[13] In more fundamental ways, deriding the *mudhakkirūn*'s 'mere recitation' remained comparable to the methods of *kitāba*, where the student's critical abilities and actual knowledge of the text was not tested. Of course, the idea of the examination is to see if the student is able to reapply and re-identify the principles behind the generalisations learnt from the teacher's examples and placed in a specific order and set context. The solid and sound knowledge of texts also entails an ability to draw readily upon the memorised material in settings not necessarily related.[14] Mere memorisation, with this understanding, does not necessarily entail anything more than a schematic framework of knowledge in terms of what was memorised.[15]

At the same time, the modes of transmission may be extended to other genres of religious texts besides *ḥadīth* literature. Schoeler suggests that there was no prioritisation of the written texts over the oral transmission as Islamic literature developed during the early years of the Muslim community.[16] In ways that are useful for the purposes of this paper, Schoeler also makes a distinction between two types of sources of textual knowledge used by later works and compilations.[17] As we will point out in the discussion of Najm al-Dīn Kubrā's biography, in the case of a set transmission of teachings from one specific authority, additions or glosses by later transmitters were often regarded as instances of 'co-authorship'. The second type of source consisted of a chain of authorities transmitting both teachings and sayings from one teacher to another.[18] Again, in the first case, the author's comments and glosses on a text added to the knowledge it encapsulated and were not viewed as a 'corruption' or distortion of an original work, but rather as part of the transmission.

Before discussing the applicability of Schoeler's and Versteegh's ideas on the modes of transmission and textuality to Jāmī's account of Najm al-Dīn Kubrā, it is necessary to give a brief synopsis of the life of the Kubrawī Sufi order's eponymous founder. The most often used source for Kubrā's life is Jāmī's *Nafaḥāt al-uns*. The information which Jāmī himself collected came from the works of two different, later branches of the Kubrawī order.[19] These works were written by Iqbāl al-Sistānī (d. 8th/14th century) and by Kamāl al-Dīn Ḥusayn al-Khwārazmī (d. 836/1433).[20] According to the sources, Kubrā was born in the southern part of Khwārazm in the city of Khīwa (located in present-day Uzbekistan). When he was a young student (then known by his proper name of Abu'l-Jannāb Aḥmad b. 'Umar b. Muḥammad b. 'Abd Allāh al-Ṣūfī al-Khīwaqī al-Khwārazmī), people began to call him by the *laqab* of 'The Great Calamity' (*al-Ṭāmma al-Kubrā*) 'because in the years of his youth he occupied himself with acquiring knowledge and he could overpower whomsoever held debates and discussions with him'.[21]

There are also references in Kubrā's own works to his zeal for the scholastic life.[22] Jāmī's account details his travels to Egypt and Khūzistān to collect *ijāza*s in *ḥadīth*s and *kalām* from individuals with 'lofty credentials'.[23] In terms of the structure of Kubrā's biography, we may also note at this time that two of his most important mystical experiences are recounted directly after incidents that took place during journeys to Tabrīz, Alexandria and Dizfūl (in Khūzistān) to collect *ijāza*s in order to be able to transmit *ḥadīth*s on his own authority.[24]

Later Kubrawī accounts note and discuss Kubrā's links of spiritual authority (*silsila*s) to three shaykhs he met in his years travel. For the purpose of discussing the textuality of Sufi hagiography, however, it is not of vital importance to trace Kubrā's *silsila* all the way back to the Sufi shaykhs of earlier times (e.g. Aḥmad al-Ghazālī, d. 519/1126). What is more telling is that only two of the four shaykhs linked to Kubrā through spiritual transmissions may themselves be traced back through their *silsila*s to the Prophet Muḥammad or to other early Sufi figures.[25] One shaykh is not incorporated into the Kubrawī lineage or *silsila* in any clear way. The authority of the four shaykhs to transmit a complete rendition of esoteric knowledge and the manner in which they may do so may also be separated from one another in four distinct ways.[26] The method of the 'initiatory' shaykh, Bābā Faraj al-Tabrīzī, will be referred to again and discussed in connection with excerpts from Kubrā's religious biography. Keeping in mind Schoeler's and Versteegh's views, this method will be compared to the modes of transmission, after two more aspects of the earliest part of the Kubrawī tradition have been summarised.

It is possible to understand the environment of Kubrā's life and the degree of social acceptance that Sufi teachings found in Central Asia through the hagiographies of Sufi shaykhs of other orders based in seventh/thirteenth-century Khurāsān and Khwārazm, as well as through other types of sources.[27] As stated, however, in Jāmī's account as well as in accounts collected from other sources, Kubrā returned to Khwārazm, to the city of Gurganj, around 583–584/1188–1189, after he had finished his travels for his training in both the exoteric and esoteric sciences.[28] For the remainder of his life, which coincided with the reigns of the Khwārazmshāhs 'Alā' al-Dīn Tekesh (r. 567–598/1172–1200) and his son, 'Alā' al-Dīn Muḥammad (r. 598–616/1200–1220), Kubrā established a Sufi lodge (*khānqāh*) and taught. In the words of Jāmī, however, 'He came to Khwārazm and the path became widespread and many disciples gathered around him and he occupied himself with showing the correct path.'[29]

Jāmī's account of Kubrā's death at the hands of the 'Tatar' invaders of Khwārazm stands as one of the more dramatic of the historical events in the hagiography. It also serves as a concrete example of Schoeler's theory of collective authorship.[30] Though this discussion will utilise Schoeler's ideas in a more paradigmatic form, in reference to the transmission of differing levels of religious knowledge from Sufi shaykhs to disciples, this example serves as a point of entry into the structure of Jāmī's work.

Jāmī draws upon excerpts from the Arabic biographical dictionary compiled by 'Afīf al-Dīn al-Yāfi'ī and a later Kubrawī commentary on Rūmī's *Masnawī*, Ḥusayn al-Khwārazmī's *Jawāhir al-asrār*, to illustrate Kubrā's refusal to leave the city of Gurganj when Chingiz Khan's invasion of Khwārazm began, and his subsequent death.[31] Whilst one earlier passage from Yāfi'ī's work appears in its original Arabic form and is cited, the final passage dealing with Kubrā's death records the statements he made to his disciples at the time of the invasion as well as the date of his 'martyrdom' in Arabic, but without any sort of acknowledgment. And where there are excerpts translated from the Arabic original there are no references to the original.[32] In a somewhat different manner, one of Rūmī's *ghazal*s is associated with Kubrā through the intermediary source of the *Jawāhir al-asrār* and is then incorporated into the text. While Jāmī cites Rūmī's *ghazal* and suggests its implications for the connections between the history of the Kubrawī order and Persian mystical poetry, the fact that it was selected from Ḥusayn al-Khwārazmī's commentary passes without comment.[33]

As a switch in emphasis that will lead directly into a discussion of Kubrā's religious education, it is quite useful to take note of the works attributed to Kubrā. Kubrā's principal Arabic literary project was his Qur'anic *tafsīr* entitled *'Ayn al-ḥayāt* – a project which two of his disciples continued and completed.[34] Kubrā also composed a variety of treatises in Arabic on the Sufi path and mystical practices as well as on the rules and regulations of the mystic's life.[35] Taken as a whole, Kubrā's literary works embody a strict rule for religious practice as well as methods for interpreting – a hermeneutic for – the Qur'an and perceptions of religious experience.[36]

> Send me however much copper you have so that I may change it into pure gold and send it back to you. – Rūzbihān[37]

The opening passages of the account of Kubrā in Jāmī's *Nafaḥāt al-uns* suggest an individual, whose training and mystical experiences have perfected him, shaping him into a shaykh with powers over the seen and unseen forces of the world. The passage dealing with Kubrā's discussion with his disciples concerns the well-known sura of the Cave (Qur'an 18:1–23). Therefore, the miraculous events that follow the discussion also are grounded in and inspired by Qur'anic interpretations and remain part of Kubrā's method of instructing his disciples as well. The passage is as follows:

> One day a critical discussion was taking place concerning the Companions of the Cave. Shaykh Sa'd al-Dīn Ḥamūya,[38] may God's peace be upon him, who was among the students of the shaykh, had a passing thought, 'Which person among this group could have an effect on dogs because of his companionship?'
>
> The shaykh knowing things through the light of clairvoyance, got up went to the door of the *khānqāh*, and waited. Suddenly a dog turned up there and waited, and it was wagging its tail. The shaykh's gaze fell upon it in his state of blessing and the dog was dumbfounded and it lost consciousness. It turned from the town and went to the graveyard, and it rubbed its head in the dirt, until it was related that wherever the dog went, fifty or sixty dogs would gather around it, forming a circle, and they would keep their paws placed together, and would not bark loudly, and would not eat anything and would stand out of reverence. Finally, when the dog died, the shaykh ordered them to bury it and construct a tomb over it.[39]

This passage depicts Kubrā as the refined and completed product of his esoteric and exoteric training. His status in this passage as a shaykh with a circle of disciples clearly indicates that he has already completed the tasks his teachers set before him. In this situation, he now has the authority to transmit his own rendition of their collective teachings, similar to Schoeler's conceptualisation of the first type of source. In actuality, this passage serves as one point in the circular path of Kubrā's biography, where his zeal for the exoteric sciences and learning was finally balanced by his cumulative mystical understandings and perceptions through his Sufi training.[40] At the end of his scholastic and Sufi training, however, Kubrā is a 'codified' version of both of Schoeler's modes of textual redaction. He may cite and transmit *ḥadīths* and interpret the Qur'an on the authority of his learned teachers as well as recreate and elaborate upon the instructive mystical experiences he has had under the guidance of his Sufi shaykhs. The question that still remains is what is the exact relation between these two bodies of religious knowledge?

To refer back to Schoeler and Versteegh, the next passage in Jāmī's account of Kubrā's life tells of the turning-point in his religious education. Kubrā's meeting with Bābā Faraj al-Tabrīzī, an ecstatic Sufi, indicates a shift away from codified texts and the standard forms of transmitting religious knowledge in Kubrā's biography:

> In Tabrīz, the shaykh was among the students of Muḥyī al-Sunna, who had superior credentials. He was reading the book *Sharḥ al-sunna*. He was reading

> the latter parts of it seated in the presence of the teacher and he was among the group of imams who were reading *Sharḥ al-sunna*, when a dervish whom he did not recognise came in. But the shaykh underwent a complete change as a result of watching him and lost his ability to read. He asked, 'Who is this?' He [the teacher] said, 'This is Bābā Faraj al-Tabrīzī,[41] who is one of the people attracted to God and one of the Beloved Ones of God, may he be praised.'[42]

Having lost the ability to read, and also to indicate to the teacher his knowledge of the text, Kubrā decides to find Bābā Faraj so that he can ask him for an *ijāza* instead.[43] He gathers together the teacher and the Imams to go along with him and then he experiences the following:

> Then we came before Bābā Faraj and we sat. After that, a momentary state changed Bābā Faraj and he appeared glorious in his bodily form. When the sun grew harsh, he tore off the cloak he was wearing. After an hour, he returned to his senses. He got up and put the cloak on me and said, 'Don't read books. It is time you became the title page of the world!' This state changed me and my interior became cut off [detached] from anything other than the Real.
>
> When we came out of that place, the teacher said, 'Some parts of *Sharḥ al-sunna* are still left. We will read it for three more days and the rest is up to you.' When I went to the lesson, I saw Bābā Faraj, who came in and said, 'Yesterday you passed through a thousand stations of the wisdom of certainty. Today you are going back to the beginning of wisdom.' I abandoned the lesson and occupied myself with the hardships of solitude. The sciences of intuition and the riches of inspiration revealed themselves to me. I said, 'It would be such a shame if they slipped away.' I was writing that and I saw Bābā Faraj, because he came in through the door, and he said, 'Satan is troubling you. Do not write these words.' I threw the inkstand [away] and was completely done with these thoughts.[44]

How do these two passages correspond to Schoeler's and Versteegh's ideas of the overlap between oral and written forms of texts as well as the hierarchy of modes of transmitting religious knowledge? First of all, it is important to note and focus upon the construction of the second passage and its relation to the first passage from the *Nafaḥāt al-uns*. In the second passage, Kubrā is engaged in typical scholarly pursuits and the mere sight of Bābā Faraj draws him out of his usual understandings and expectations of the religious teacher as well as out of everyday reality. He is drawn out of Muḥyī al-Sunna's scholarly circle. The dialogue and process of instruction, however, does not commence until the second passage, when Kubrā sits in the circle that Bābā Faraj heads rather than that of the esteemed religious scholar. Kubrā, as well as his fellow scholars and his teacher, witness Bābā Faraj's mystical experience. That experience, in many senses, symbolises the lesson and the 'text' studied for the day. The cloak bestowed upon Kubrā also takes the symbolic place of the usual *ijāza* conferred when a student finished the substance of the lesson and was permitted to teach the work.

The third passage is unique because it reinforces the conceptual understanding that the esoteric 'text' which Bābā Faraj transmits to Kubrā consists of a knowledge which is not to be recorded in words. It is not meant to form the substance of a written text.[45] The instructional element of the passage co-exists with the refutation of codified texts yet it still takes on the form of a spiritual discourse. Kubrā, the scholar who is noted for his great skills in debate and in the exoteric sciences, is refuted and corrected three times in the second passage.[46] Once Kubrā is aware of the situation (or understands the lesson), he throws his inkstand away and forgets about recording such visions in writing, which would also constitute a translation of the experience.[47]

Perhaps because the third passage dwells on Kubrā's initiation into the Sufi path through the guidance of Bābā Faraj, it is not yet possible to reconcile the exoteric and esoteric sciences. In fact, Kubrā is rebuked for returning to Muḥyī al-Sunna's class to finish *Sharḥ al-sunna*. Once the Sufi method of instruction has begun, the focus is no longer on the written text. In ways that are connected, returning to the scholastic mode of acquiring knowledge nullifies all the progress that might have been made on the Sufi path before the training is properly completed. Instead, the student's focus is on Sufi practices and he comes to rely on the Sufi shaykh for guidance and instruction rather than on written texts – a process that perhaps allows for a more critical evaluation of the knowledge the student has acquired and his mystical experiences. It also seems that the relationship between the two modes of transmitting religious knowledge (exoteric and esoteric) must be momentarily suspended until the student becomes less dependent on the accepted forms (i.e. books) through which knowledge is supposed to be revealed.

Then again, there is another detail in the second passage which allows this paper to relate these reflections back to the example of the early Qur'anic commentators and the highly valued abilities of deduction and discernment. It again may be related to the nature of religious education and the shaykh's method of instructing disciples. In Jāmī's account, Bābā Faraj is the first of four shaykhs who will instruct and train Kubrā. Yet Bābā Faraj's 'esoteric' instruction through the example of a mystical experience parallels his standing as a shaykh in the Kubrawī *silsila*. That is to say, his role as an 'initiatory' shaykh is not recorded in the *silsila*, and thus, neither incorporated into the Kubrawī lineage nor legitimised. It is important to reflect upon this while examining the third passage, particularly when Kubrā is seized with the desire to record and fix in language the unripe fruits of his first mystical experiences. In a manner comparable to the study of the more 'exoteric' branches of Islamic learning, Kubrā is not allowed to comment on or interpret these experiences (experiences which are thus analogous to the Qur'an and *ḥadīths*) until he has been thoroughly trained on the path. Once he has been trained, he is granted these critical abilities and the authority to use them. The fact that he was eventually able to integrate the two branches of Islamic knowledge as a Sufi shaykh was first shown in the passage concerning the discussion on the Companions of the Cave.

It is important to note one more matter concerning the nature of orality and the transmission of esoteric knowledge before concluding. In ways that were presumably clear throughout the preceding discussion, the relation of the oral religious text to its written and codified counterpart changes according to the individual's level of understanding and their authority to instruct and teach others. From this perspective, this paper intended to show how Najm al-Dīn Kubrā, a sixth–seventh/thirteenth-century religious scholar and Sufi shaykh acquired a certain degree of esoteric knowledge through his initial encounter with the personage of Bābā Faraj al-Tabrīzī. At the same time, he was unable to draw upon his previous training in the exoteric sciences until he had completed his Sufi training. It was originally assumed, as stated above, that examining Jāmī's account of Kubrā's life would enable us to discern the ontology of religious knowledge through its particular ordering and arrangement of exoteric to esoteric, of the traditional religious sciences to the mystical experience. Though the actual hierarchy of religious knowledge was not ascertained, it can be seen that elements of a scholastic training could be displaced in favour of the Sufi path. It was also possible, after the completion of one type of instruction, to reconcile the two methods and bring them together in an arrangement that was not necessarily hierarchical.

## Notes

1. Al-Muqātil, *Tafsīr*, vol. 1, p. 27, cited in C. H. M. Versteegh, *Arabic Grammar and Qur'ānic Exegesis in Early Islam* (Leiden, 1993), p. 64.

2. See G. Böwering, *The Mystical Vision of Existence in Classical Islam* (Berlin, 1980), Introduction, and Versteegh, *Arabic Grammar and Qur'ānic Exegesis*, p. 42.

3. Versteegh, *Arabic Grammar and Qur'ānic Exegesis*, pp. 41–62. For additional information on Ḥasan al-Baṣrī, see A. Schimmel, *Mystical Dimensions of Islam* (Chapel Hill, NC, 1975), pp. 30–31 and M. Sells, *Early Islamic Mysticism* (New York, 1996), pp. 17–20. For further information on Ibn al-Ḥanafiyya, see W. al-Qadi, 'The Development of the Term *Ghulāt* in Muslim Literature with Special Reference to the *Kaysaniyya*', *Akten. VII. Kong. Arabistic Gottigen*, ed. A. Dietrich (Gottingen, 1976), pp. 295–319. See also M. A. Amir-Moezzi, *The Divine Guide in Early Shi'ism*, tr. D. Streight (Albany, NY, 1994), pp. 17–49, who discusses in great detail the sixth Shi'i Imam Ja'far al-Ṣādiq's commentary on the Qur'an (*ad* 7:143). This commentary is widely acknowledged to be one of the first mystical *tafsīrs*, though its textual authenticity is highly debatable. Sells has recently translated this *tafsīr*, see *Early Islamic Mysticism*, pp. 78–79.

4. See J. Pedersen, 'The Islamic Preacher: *Wā'iẓ, Mudhakkir, Qaṣṣ*', in S. Löwinger and J. Somogyi, ed., *Goldziher Memorial Volume*, 1 (Budapest, 1948), pp. 227–232, and Versteegh, *Arabic Grammar and Qur'ānic Exegesis*, p. 42.

5. G. Makdisi, *The Rise of Humanism in Classical Islam and the Christian West*

(Edinburgh, 1990), pp. 173–177; see also Pedersen, 'The Islamic Preacher', p. 239 and Versteegh, *Arabic Grammar and Qur'ānic Exegesis*, pp. 64–65.

6. Al-Muqātil, *Tafsīr*, vol. 1, p. 27, ll. 8f cited in Versteegh, *Arabic Grammar and Qur'ānic Exegesis*, p. 64.

7. Makdisi, *The Rise of Humanism*, p. 202, states the following with respect to the perceived hierarchy in the process of acquiring knowledge through memorising:

> Memory played a crucial role in the process of learning. It was a tool in the service of humanism, as well as in that of scholasticism. Memorising involved great quantities of materials, their understanding and their retention through frequent repetition at close intervals of time. When limited to mere transmission, memorising was simply the attribute of the common man among the men of learning, e.g. the scholars of *ḥadīth*, the lexicographers. Above this rudimentary level, the humanist, like the scholastic, aimed at the higher level of emulation. The road to creativity called for progression from authoritative reception and transmission, *riwāya*, to understand the materials transmitted, *dirāya* and finally, with personal effort, pushed to its limit, *ijtihād*, to creating one's personal ideas, in one's own words and, in an elegant style, expressed with eloquence.

8. For further information on the compilation of the *Nafaḥāt*, see D. DeWeese, 'The *Kashf al-hudā* of Kamāl al-Dīn Ḥusayn al-Khwārazmī: A Fifteenth-Century Sufi Commentary on the *Qasidat al-Burda* in Khwarazmian Turkic' (Ph.D. dissertation, Indiana University, 1985), p. 11. As an additional point, Versteegh, p. 49, states that the process of instruction remained firmly grounded in written documents. In order to use his idea with a greater degree of flexibility in our examination of Kubrā's biography, it is of great benefit to view this process either as a means of reinforcing the text or as a polemic against the written text. In this way, an actual reference to a written text may be based upon absolute consensus (agreement) or complete refutation. In yet another way, as we shall see in the case of Kubrā's education, the very concept of the written text may be refuted as well, while it still refers back to the idea of instruction and a corpus of knowledge.

9. C. Ernst, *The Eternal Garden* (Albany, NY, 1992), p. 63. The role of texts and that of the Sufi shaykh in the process of religious instruction was first discussed by Meier in his classic study, 'Khurāsān un das ende der klassichen ṣūfik', now in Glassen and Schubert ed., *Bausteine. Ausgewählte Aufsätze zur Islamwissenschaft* (Istanbul and Stuttgart, 1992), vol. 1, pp. 131–156. This article, amongst many others, has now been translated into English in J. O'Kane and B. Radtke, ed. *Essays on Islamic Piety and Mysticism* (Leiden, 1999), pp. 189–219. Meier addresses in particular the issue of 'textbooks and transition' in Sufism in his article entitled 'The Mystic Path', in B. Lewis, ed., *The World of Islam* (London, 1976), pp. 118–128. See also Muhsin Mahdi with regard to texts and Sufism, 'The Book and the Master as Poles of Cultural Change in Islam', in S. Vyronis, ed., *Islam and Cultural Change in the Middle Ages* (Wiesbaden, 1975), pp. 3–16.

10. Versteegh, *Arabic Grammar and Qur'ānic Exegesis*, p. 49. This detail is pointed out in Sezgin's introduction to his *Geschichte des arabischen Schriftums* (Leiden, 1967), vol. 1, p. 58, n. 67. G. Schoeler's articles, 'Die Frage der schriftlichen oder mündlichen Überlieferung der Wissenschaften im frühen Islam', *Der Islam*, 62 (1985), pp. 201–230, 'Mündliche Thora und Ḥadīth: Überlieferung, Schriebverbot, Redaktion', *Der Islam*, 66 (1986), pp. 213–251,

'Schreiben und Veröffentlichchen: zu Verwendung und Funktion der Schrift in den ersten islamischen Jahrhunderten,' *Der Islam*, 69 (1992), pp. 1–43, are also relevant for ascertaining both the oral and written character of *ḥadīth*s in the early Islamic period.

11. Böwering, *The Mystical Vision of Existence*, pp. 1–18; Makdisi, *The Rise of Humanism*, pp. 98 and 202.

12. Versteegh, *Arabic Grammar and Qur'ānic Exegesis*, p. 49.

13. Goldziher, *Muslim Studies*, ed. S. M. Stern, tr. C. Barber and S. M. Stern (London, 1967–1971), 2 vols., vol. 2, pp. 131–152; Pedersen, 'The Islamic Preacher', pp. 231–239; Sezgin, *Geschichte*, pp.62–63.

14. Makdisi, *The Rise of Humanism*, pp. 202–207.

15. Ibid.

16. Schoeler, 'Die Frage der schriftlichen', p. 224.

17. Ibid., pp. 220f.

18. Ibid., pp. 220–224; Versteegh, *Arabic Grammar*, p. 53. Concerning the modes of transmission, see also A. Buehler, *Sufi Heirs of the Prophet* (Columbia, 1998), pp. 83–84 for the following relevant point:

> In many respects these Sufi genealogical chains resemble *isnāds* (s. *sanad*, literally support, backing), which have been used to certify that the transmission of a given *ḥadīth* actually originated with the Prophet or a Companion … . In Islam this *isnād* principle also applies to the transmission of knowledge in general, Qur'an recitation, the religious sciences (*tafsīr*, *ḥadīth*, *fiqh*) and history (*ta'rīkh*, *sīra*, *maghāzī*). As a general principle, the *isnād* mechanism is an Islamic knowledge-validation principle designed to guarantee connection to the Prophet and His Companions.

19. DeWeese, '*Kashf*', p. 11; R. Gramlich, *Die Shiitischen Derwischorden Persiens* (Wiesbaden, 1976), vol. 2, p. 174. DeWeese and Paul have directed their attention to the development of the genre of Sufi hagiographies in the middle and late medieval periods. In ways that are important to the present discussion of Jāmī's *Nafaḥāt al-uns*, DeWeese, in 'An "Uvaysī" Ṣūfī in Timurid Mawarannahr', *Inner Asian Studies* (Bloomington, IN, 1993), p. 11, describes the *Nafaḥāt* as one of the 'collective hagiographical works,' organised along the lines of the Sufi *silsila*, but without promoting the merits of one specific order or lineage. Paul remarks, with a specific reference to DeWeese's statements, that the *Nafaḥāt* is 'un livre de *silsila* ou même de "silsilisation"'. See J. Paul, 'Au début du genre hagiographique dans le Khorassan', in D. Aigle, ed., *Saints orientaux* (Paris, 1995), p. 35.

20. The most thorough summaries of Kubrawī sources are included in the works of DeWeese, in addition to the work cited above, these are: 'The Eclipse of the Kubravīyah in Central Asia', *Iranian Studies*, 21 (1988), pp. 45–83; 'Sayyid 'Alī Hamadānī and Kubrawī Hagiographical Traditions', in L. Lewisohn, ed., *The Legacy of Medieval Persian Sufism* (New York and London, 1992), pp. 121–58. See also the following three works focusing in turn on 'Alā' al-Dawla al-Simnānī, his teacher Nūr al-Dīn al-Isfarāyinī and finally Kubrā himself: J. Elias, *The Throne Carrier of God* (Albany, NY, 1995); H. Landolt, *Le Revélateur des mystères* (Paris, 1986); F. Meier, *Die Fawā'iḥ al-gamāl wa-fawātiḥ al-galāl des Najm al-Dīn Kubrā* (Wiesbaden, 1957). See this last, pp. 23–24, for details of the two Kubrawī transmissions of Kubrā's biography and the implications for the differences between accounts.

It is important to note here that Jāmī specifically cites Amīr Iqbāl al-Sistānī's work, *Chihil majlis*, starting from the passage where al-Sistānī mentions how al-Simnānī himself collected Kubrā's sayings (*sukhanān*) that had been transmitted to him, see *Chihil majlis*, ed. ʿAbd al-Rafīʿ Ḥaqīqat (Tehran 1358/1979), pp. 80–83. The narrative diverges from the *Nafaḥāt*, on p. 83, ll. 10ff. *Chihil majlis* also mentions, in the middle of the narrative discussing Kubrā's training in the exoteric sciences, that Shaykh ʿAlī Lālā was at Aḥmad Yasawī's *khānqāh* in Turkistan at the same time as Kubrā.

21. *Nafaḥāt al-uns*, ed. M. Tawḥīdīpūr (Tehran, 1336 Sh./1957), p. 419, ll. 3–4. All citations are based on this edition, unless otherwise indicated. Kubrā is also mentioned in this account as the 'carver of God's friends' (*walī-tarash*). See also DeWeese, '*Kashf*, p. 99, n. 13 and Meier, *Die Fawā'iḥ*, p. 23.

22. See F. Meier, 'Sharaf al-Dīn Balkhī and Majd al-Dīn Baghdādī', p. 248, n. 5 in *Essays on Islamic Piety* (cited above); M. Molé, 'Traités mineurs de Nağm al-din Kubrā', *Annales Islamologiques*, 4 (1963), p. 4. Both scholars take note of the story Kubrā relates in his work, *Risāla ilā al-hā'im* – that he was inspired by the devil to pursue *ḥadīth* studies.

23. DeWeese, '*Kashf*, p. 11; *Nafaḥāt*, p. 421, ll. 3–8.

24. *Nafaḥāt*, p. 420, ll. 4–9 and p. 421, ll. 5–8.

25. See in particular, DeWeese, '*Kashf*, p. 12, who notes that Ḥusayn al-Khwārazmī indicates that Kubrā's *silsila* may be traced back through Aḥmad al-Ghazālī to the 'Junayd' school of Sufism, and may also be traced back to Ḥasan al-Baṣrī, as is the case with most post-Mongol period constructions of the Kubrawī *silsila*. Whether or not the Kubrawī tradition has a tendency towards Shiʿism, or if its *silsila* includes ʿAlī, as discussed and debated in the scholarly literature, must be considered within the context of the order's historical development while allowing for the possibility of regional variations. For an appraisal of this ongoing discussion, see DeWeese, 'Eclipse' and 'Sayyid ʿAlī' (cited above). In addition, see J. Elias, 'The Sufi Lords of Bahrabad: Saʿd al-Din and Sadr al-Din Hamuwayi', *Iranian Studies*, 27 (1994), pp. 53–75; Landolt, *Revélateur*, pp. 19–26; M. Molé, 'La version persane du traite de dix principles de Najm al-Dīn Kubrā par ʿAlī ibn Shihāb al-Dīn Hamdānī', *Farhang-i Īrān Zamīn*, 6 (1958), pp. 38–66 and his 'Professions de foi de deux Kubrawis: ʿAlī Ḥamdānī et Muḥammad Nurbakhsh', *Bulletin de l'Institut Français de Damas*, 17 (1961–1962), pp. 133–204. See Schimmel, pp. 57–59 and Sells, pp. 251–257 for a general introduction to Junayd's (d. 298/910) life and doctrines.

26. DeWeese, '*Kashf*, pp. 12–13 notes that Kubrā is linked to the Prophet Muḥammad through the two Khūzistānī shaykhs mentioned in Jāmī's account, ʿAmmār b. Yāsir al-Bidlīsī and Ismāʿīl al-Qarṣī. According to other sources, Kubrā received the *shajarat-i irādat* (initiatory genealogy of doctrinal inclination) from al-Bidlīsī, and the *shajarat-i khirqat* (the lineage of the physical transmission of the Sufi cloak/*khirqa*) from al-Qarṣī. The fact that the third, more 'ecstatic' Sufi, mentioned in Kubrā's biography – Bābā Faraj al-Tabrīzī – is not incorporated into the Kubrawī lineage is telling, especially in relation to the previously mentioned theories about codification and the transmission of religious knowledge from two forms of sources, according to Schoeler. The issue will be discussed together with the passage concerning the esoteric transmission of knowledge between Bābā Faraj and Kubrā. For more information on Kubrā's lineage, see Gramlich, *Die Shiitischen*, vol. 2, p. 174 and Meier, *Die Fawā'iḥ*, pp. 16–17 and 19. In addition to the above, the role of Shaykh Rūzbihān, who serves as an 'intermediary' instructor, is worthy of further speculation, but is beyond the reaches

of the present paper. See, however, *Nafaḥāt*, p. 422, ll. 5–7, where 'Ammār orders Kubrā to become a disciple of Rūzbihān, for 'he can drive this existence (*hastī*) out of your head with one blow'. See also *Nafaḥāt*, pp. 417–419, for Jāmī's biographies of 'Ammār, Rūzbihān and al-Bidlīsī, as individuals linked to Kubrā as well as to Abū Najīb al-Suhrawardī. Also see L. Lewisohn's recent monograph on the poet and mystic al-Shabistārī, *Beyond Faith and Infidelity* (Richmond, Surrey, 1995). Due to his use of diverse sources he is able to present a more thorough synopsis of Bābā Faraj's life and background.

27. DeWeese, '*Kashf*', pp. 92–93, n. 25, n. 26; Paul, 'Hagiographische Texte als historische Quelle', *Saeculum*, 41 (1990), pp.17–43.

28. DeWeese, '*Kashf*, p. 13; Meier, *Die Fawā'iḥ*, pp. 40–47.

29. *Nafaḥāt*, p. 423, ll. 4–5.

30. See Schoeler, 'Die Frage', pp. 220–224.

31. DeWeese, '*Kashf*, pp. 13–15; Meier, *Die Fawā'iḥ*, pp. 53–56. DeWeese also indicates that al-Yā'fi'ī's work, *Mir'at al-jinān*, differs from other accounts that narrate the events leading to Kubrā's death.

32. *Nafaḥāt*, p. 419, ll. 5–9, p. 423, ll. 16–17 and p. 424, l. 4. See for example the introduction and the reference to Kubrā as 'The Great Calamity' (*Nafaḥāt*, p. 419, ll. 6–10), where a form of direct citation is used, as compared to the end of the account (*Nafaḥāt*, pp. 423–424, ll. 20–24 to 1. 4):

> He is Abū Jinnāb and his name is Aḥmad b. 'Umar al-Khīwaqī, and his *laqab* is Kubrā .... And they called him by the surname 'The Great Calamity'. Then they took away 'Calamity' and called him by 'Kubrā', and they found it correct to call him this as he relied on a group of his companions. Some of them said that it was correct as the *fātḥa* elided with the long vowel and as Najm al-Dīn Kubrā completely broke the great. It is so in the history of Imām al-Yāfi'ī, may the mercy of God the Most High be upon him.

33. *Nafaḥāt*, p. 423, ll. 23–24 to p. 424, l. 3.

34. See in particular, M. T. Dānishpazhūh, '*Sharḥ-i ḥadīs "kuntu khanzan makhfiyyan"*', *Sophia Perennis*, 3.2 (1977), pp. 28–31; DeWeese '*Kashf*, p. 15; Elias, *Throne Carrier*, pp. 3, 203–212.

35. DeWeese '*Kashf*, p. 17; M. I. Waley, 'A Kubrawī Manual of Sufism: The *Fuṣūṣ al-adab* of Yaḥyā Bākharzī', in Lewisohn, ed., *Legacy*, p. 290.

36. Landolt's and Meier's ground-breaking works are fundamental for the study of Kubrawī dream/vision interpretation and have not been surpassed in any regard. For a concise introduction to the topic of Kubrawī dream interpretation, and its subsequent influence on post 15th-century Naqshbandī Sufism, see Buehler, pp. 107–109.

37. *Nafaḥāt*, ed. M. 'Ābidī (Tehran, 1373 Sh./1994–1995), p. 426, ll. 8–9.

38. For more detailed information on Ḥamūya's life and doctrinal thought, see in particular see H. Landolt, 'Sa'ad al-Dīn al-Ḥammū'ī', *EI2*; DeWeese, '*Kashf*, pp. 24–25; Elias, 'Sufi Lords', pp. 53–75; Lewisohn, *Beyond Faith*, pp. 126–128; Meier, *Die Fawā'iḥ*, p. 42. As for the importance of this family at the Mongol court and in the conversion of Ghāzān Khān, see Landolt, *Revélateur*, p. 31 and C. Melville, 'Pādishāh-i Islām: The Conversion of Sultan Maḥmūd Ghāzān Khān', in C. Melville, ed., *Pembroke Papers* (Persian and Islamic Studies

in Honour of P. W. Avery) (Cambridge, 1990), pp. 159–177, esp. pp. 159–161, 165.

39. *Nafaḥāt*, p. 419, ll. 19–25 and p. 420, ll. 1–3; *Nafaḥāt*, ed. ʿĀbidī, p. 423, ll. 6–14.

40. *Nafaḥāt*, p. 419, ll. 1–3; R. Gramlich, *Die Wunde des Freunde Gottes* (Wiesbaden, 1987), p. 178, indicates the importance of this very same passage and translates it in full in the context of his discussion of the power of the gaze of God's friends (*awliyāʾ*). Gramlich also provides two other references to other hagiographies besides the *Nafaḥāt*, namely Dārāshikūh's *Safīnat al-awliyāʾ* and Ghulām Sarwar-i al-Lāhawrī's *Khazīnat al-aṣfiyāʾ*, which contains the same passage.

41. See DeWeese, *'Kashf*, p. 12; Lewisohn, *Beyond Faith*, pp. 121–126; Meier, *Die Fawāʾiḥ*, p. 16, for more information on the personage of Bābā Faraj.

42. *Nafaḥāt*, p. 420, ll. 4–9; *Nafaḥāt*, ed. ʿĀbidī, p. 423, ll. 15–19.

43. *Nafaḥāt*, p. 420, ll. 9–12; *Nafaḥāt*, ed. ʿĀbidī, p. 423, ll. 19–22.

44. *Nafaḥāt*, p. 420, ll. 14–24; *Nafaḥāt*, ed. ʿĀbidī, p. 424, ll. 2–12. Also see Lewisohn, *Beyond Faith*, pp. 122–124, who bases his own translation of this passage on Ibn al-Karbalāʾī's hagiography, *Rawḍāt al-jinān*.

45. *Nafaḥāt*, p. 420, ll. 22–24.

46. Ibid., p. 420, ll. 14–24.

47. Ibid., p. 421, ll. 1–2.

# 23

# Two Narratives on Najm al-Dīn Kubrā and Raḍī al-Dīn ʿAlī Lālā from a Thirteenth-Century Source: Notes on a Manuscript in the Raza Library, Rampur

*Devin DeWeese*

The study of the Kubravī Sufi tradition – unlike that of many other Sufi traditions that began to take shape in Eastern Iran and Central Asia between the twelfth and fourteenth centuries CE (for example the Khwājagānī/Naqshbandī, Yasawī and Khalwatī communities) – has been well supplied, not only with an abundance of written sources produced by some of the earliest figures associated with that tradition, but with a select group of outstanding scholars engaged in the study, publication and analysis of these sources. The present contribution, offered in honour of one of those scholars, Hermann Landolt, is intended to introduce a small source, hitherto unknown, that contains interesting narratives involving two figures associated with the earliest phase of the Kubravī tradition: Najm al-Dīn Kubrā (d. 618/1221) himself and his disciple Raḍī al-Dīn ʿAlī Lālā (d. 642/1244).

### A Note on Kubravī Hagiographical Material

While the doctrinal writings of the shaykhs linked to the Kubravī tradition have been relatively well studied, the legacy of hagiographical narratives evoked by these shaykhs remains largely unexplored. The neglect of such narratives, indeed, may stem precisely from the relative abundance of seemingly more reliable biographical data, preserved in early works of known provenance, on many members of the Sufi circle of Najm al-Dīn Kubrā and the highly personal writings of Kubrā, Majd al-Dīn Baghdādī, or ʿAlāʾ al-Dawla Simnānī, for instance – which not only provide self-conscious descriptions of experiences during their individual mystical endeavours, but also illuminate their relationships with masters and disciples and associates

– can lend the strength of autobiographical accounts to any reconstruction of the lives of these shaykhs. The availability of such direct and authentic testimony has perhaps made the body of hagiographical narratives circulated about these shaykhs seem less interesting and less valuable as biographical sources than might be the case for shaykhs who left few writings of their own, or none at all.

The study of these narratives, however, can often provide important insights into various aspects of the Kubravī tradition's history. In some cases, the narratives and biographical information preserved in sources deemed 'legendary', or considered 'too hagiographical' to be reliable, can be corroborated from other early sources. The narratives themselves may offer a glimpse of a shaykh's 'public' profile, which in many cases took shape at the same time that his literary, initiatory and 'managerial' legacies were being cultivated by other claimants to his memory. Competing narratives can often be traced, offering evidence of communal tensions and rivalries that were negotiated in part through the medium of hagiography. And, at the very least, exploring the development and distribution of particular narratives can help us draw significant conclusions about historical developments within the Sufi communities that linked their mystical practice, their doctrinal orientation and their very 'corporate' identities, to a given shaykh.[1]

The body of hagiographical material associated with the Kubravī tradition, as circulated in various venues, spans the eight centuries between Najm al-Dīn Kubrā's Sufi career and the present, and we cannot fully review the material or its sources here. In the case of Najm al-Dīn Kubrā himself, we still lack even a full inventory of the hagiographical narratives about him as they appear in sources produced within the later Kubravī tradition. While Fritz Meier painstakingly analysed the early biographical material dealing with Kubrā,[2] he paid less attention to the development of hagiographical traditions about the shaykh, in part because particularly important sources were then unavailable to him.[3] In compiling such an inventory, however, and in analysing the development of particular hagiographical motifs surrounding Kubrā and his circle, it will be important to include not only the 'internal' sources, produced within Sufi communities claiming initiatory ties to Kubrā, but narratives preserved in sources originating in other Sufi circles as well. These 'external' accounts not only offer a different perspective on the early development of the Kubravī tradition,[4] but often preserve much earlier recordings of stories about Najm al-Dīn Kubrā and his disciples than we find in sources produced within the lineages linked directly to Kubrā.

Examples of such accounts include: 1) the long narrative focused on Kubrā (as well as others dealing with his disciples) found in the anonymous life of the famous shaykh Awḥad al-Dīn Kirmānī (d. 635/1238), produced probably in the second half of the thirteenth century;[5] 2) the story of how Raḍī al-Dīn ʿAlī Lālā met Najm al-Dīn Kubrā, recounted in somewhat different versions in two hagiographies devoted to the famous Rūzbihān Baqlī (d. 606/1209) of Shīrāz, likewise compiled in the later thirteenth century;[6] 3) an account of how Sayf al-Dīn Bākharzī became Kubrā's disciple, in the *Fawā'id al-fu'ād*, a collection of discourses of the Chishtī saint Niẓām al-Dīn Awliyā', compiled in the later fourteenth century,[7] and 4) a distinctive account of Kubrā's martyrdom preserved in another Chishtī source from the early fourteenth century.[8] None of these works, incidentally, is noted in Meier's list of sources on Kubrā's life.[9]

To these accounts, which appear in published sources, may be added other narratives that remain less accessible owing to their preservation only in still-unpublished and often little-known works; my aim here is to present two such narratives, preserved in an interesting Persian source produced, evidently, early in the second half of the thirteenth century. These narratives offer glimpses of the relations between Najm al-Dīn Kubrā and Raḍī al-Din 'Alī Lālā respectively, and an obscure Sufi shaykh of Khurāsān. Their depiction of Kubrā and Lālā naturally differs from the image offered in sources generated and transmitted within the Sufi circles from which the later Kubravī order emerged, insofar as Kubrā and Lālā appear in these stories as secondary figures and their role is to underscore the greatness of another master who was, we may presume, the central figure for the author or community responsible for recording or transmitting the narratives. Nevertheless, these accounts may offer valuable insights not only into the lives and images of two saints who were pivotal figures in the development of the Kubravī tradition, but also into the broader environment in which the Sufi communities linked to the legacy of Najm al-Dīn Kubrā took shape.

The narratives, preserved in a single manuscript, are presented in translation below, with a brief discussion of their contents and significance. In order to assess these narratives, and the unique source in which they appear, we must first consider the textual environment in which the accounts survive, and then look more closely at what has come down to us of the work in which they were included.

## The Rampur Manuscript

The manuscript of interest here, a *majmū'a* containing a large number of Sufi works, is preserved in the Raza Library in Rampur, as No. 764 under the classification '*sulūk fārsī*' (i.e. Persian manuscripts on mysticism). I was able to examine it in July of 1988, during a series of research visits to Islamic manuscript collections in India.[10] There was no full description of the manuscript as a whole, but the separate works preserved in it were recorded in a two-volume handlist (unpublished) of the library's Persian manuscripts.[11] I had too little time in Rampur to permit me to verify the handlist's identification of most works, and indeed the work containing the narratives of interest here was not accurately identified (it was listed as a collection of letters). However, I was able to photograph portions of the manuscript (including the chief work under consideration), and the following discussion is thus based on information derived from the handlist, on notes from my own examination of the manuscript in 1988 and on the photographs of selected works.

The manuscript contains in all 352 folios, but there is a substantial gap in their numbering, suggesting that a portion of the original manuscript has been lost (or is, perhaps, preserved elsewhere as a separate fragment). Following f. 186b, at the end of one work, the next folio (where another work begins) is marked 243, and the foliation thus runs 1–186 and then 243–407. Each folio bears seventeen lines; the script is a relatively neat small *nastaʿlīq*. The colophon of one work preserved in the manuscript (f. 62b) indicates that the work was copied in Ramaḍān, with the year given in figures as 919 (i.e. November 1513), but given in words as 929 (July–August 1523). Presumably the latter is to be preferred. Nearly the entire manuscript appears to have been copied by the same hand, and it is likely that the other works were copied within the same year.

The extant portions of the manuscript contain over thirty Sufi treatises; to judge from the contents, it was most likely copied in Khurāsān by a Sufi linked with Kubravī circles, but with ties also to other Sufi communities of the region active in the late fifteenth and early sixteenth centuries. There are several treatises either unascribed or ascribed to assorted Sufi authors, without further identification. The authors named range from Aḥmad al-Ghazālī and ʿAbd Allāh Anṣārī to Sayyid Sharīf Jurjānī.[12] There is also a single brief treatise, untitled and unascribed, that appears to stem from Naqshbandī circles,[13] framing three types of mystical discipline – the *ṭarīq-i dhikr*, the *ṭarīq-i tawajjuh wa-murāqaba* and the *ṭarīq-i rābiṭa bi-pīr* – with the latter emphasised as the best.[14] One of the most valuable sections of the manuscript is an excerpt (17 folios in all, incomplete at the end) from an otherwise unknown work presented as the *Malfūẓāt* of Zayn al-Dīn Khwāfī, an important shaykh of Harāt during the late fourteenth and early fifteenth centuries and eponym of the Zaynī order.[15]

By far most of the works in the manuscript, however (twenty in all), are ascribed to (or appear to be linked with) figures associated with the Kubravī tradition. Most of these are known works of the important fourteenth-century shaykh Sayyid ʿAlī Hamadānī.[16] At least eleven treatises ascribed to him are represented in the Rampur manuscript,[17] and it seems likely that the compilation of the manuscript as a whole was the work of someone at least loosely connected with a Kubravī *silsila* line stemming from Hamadānī through the lineage Hamadānī>Khwāja Isḥāq Khuttalānī>Sayyid ʿAbd Allāh Barzishābādī>Rashīd al-Dīn Bīdwāzī,[18]>Shaykh Shāh ʿAlī Bīdwāzī>Ḥājjī Muḥammad Khabūshānī. The latter figure was the master of the pivotal sixteenth-century Kubravī shaykh of Central Asia, Ḥusayn Khwārazmī, as well as of the martyred ʿImād al-Dīn Faḍl Allāh.[19] The Rampur manuscript includes not only a treatise ascribed to Khabūshānī himself,[20] but also the text of the 'certificate of licensure' (*khaṭṭ-i irshād*) given by Khabūshānī to ʿImād al-Dīn Faḍl Allāh in 897/1492.[21]

The manuscript also includes potentially valuable material from earlier figures in the central Kubravī lineage. The final text in the manuscript is a work by 'Alā' al-Dawla Simnānī;[22] another very short work, on the 'stations of the mystical voyagers', is ascribed to Simnānī (it is not immediately recognisable among Simnānī's works, but the ascription may be correct).[23] Three works in the manuscript are ascribed to Simnānī's master, Nūr al-Dīn 'Abd al-Raḥmān Isfarāyinī (who is typically ascribed, in these texts, the *nisba* 'Khurāsānī' as well): two of these[24] do not correspond to any of the works of Isfarāyinī published by Landolt (but perhaps are to be found among the still-unpublished treatises preserved in the manuscripts Landolt discussed[25]), but the third, assigned the title '*al-Risāla al-nūriyya*' in the Rampur handlist, corresponds closely to the text of a letter published by Landolt.[26] The Rampur manuscript, however, not only prefaces the text with an interesting introduction evidently not found in the copy consulted by Landolt,[27] but also includes a substantial passage (amounting to a little over one side of a folio in the manuscript) that is omitted from the published version.[28]

The Rampur manuscript's material linked to the Kubravī tradition includes, lastly, a brief Sufi treatise ([11] ff. 102b–105a) ascribed in the text to 'Raḍī al-Milla wa'l-Dīn, Junayd al-Zamān, Burhān al-Ḥaqīqat Abu'l-'Alā' 'Alī b. Sa'īd b. 'Abd al-Jalāl al-Juwaynī al-Ṣūfī known as Lālā' – i.e. the disciple of Najm al-Dīn Kubrā[29] through whom the most important 'Kubravī' *silsila* line is customarily traced (i.e. Kubrā>Raḍī al-Dīn 'Alī Lālā>Aḥmad Gūrpānī>Isfarāyinī>Simnānī>Maḥmūd Mazdaqānī>Sayyid 'Alī Hamadānī). While there are no personal references or particulars to support or undermine the treatise's attribution to Lālā, its focus is in keeping with the content and style of works by his predecessors.[30] In view of the other contents of the Rampur manuscript – which appears to preserve old and possibly unique material and suggests a collection of writings handed down within a lineage stemming from Lālā – there seems good reason to accept this brief treatise as the only literary work of Shaykh Raḍī al-Dīn identified to date.[31]

### The Fragment from the Life of Ḍiyā' al-Dīn al-Ḥātimī

The text of primary interest here is a brief excerpt, evidently, from a work on an unknown Sufi shaykh of Khurāsān who must have lived in the late twelfth and early thirteenth centuries; the excerpt gives no indication of the work's author and I have not been able to trace any other copy or any citation of or allusion to the work or its subject. The excerpt appears on ff. 348b–361b (No. 30 in the sequence of surviving sections) and begins with the heading, 'These letters and sayings are related from the *Maqāmāt* of his holiness, the Perfect and Perfecting master, the *quṭb al-mashā'ikh*, Shaykh Ḍiyā' al-Dīn Abū Bakr b. Abu'l-'Alā' al-Ḥātimī'. This Ḍiyā' al-Dīn's father, also a Sufi, is identified in the text as Shaykh Sa'd al-Dīn Abu'l-'Alā' al-Ḥātimī. The surviving portion of the text gives no hint regarding the meaning of the *nisba* borne by father and son, which unfortunately leaves their place of origin unknown.[32]

Despite Shaykh Ḍiyāʾ al-Dīn's obscurity,[33] the excerpts from his *Maqāmāt* preserved in the Rampur manuscript provide considerable evidence on his sphere of activity and on the period in which he lived. The most prominent Sufis mentioned in the excerpts are Najm al-Dīn Kubrā (d. 618/1221) and his disciple Raḍī al-Dīn ʿAlī Lālā (d. 642/1244), each of whom is the subject of a narrative outlining his relationship with Ḍiyāʾ al-Dīn. These two narratives, explored below, naturally highlight Ḍiyāʾ al-Dīn's spiritual eminence, as affirmed by the two better-known shaykhs (whose relationship with one another, incidentally, is never mentioned in either narrative), but offer interesting glimpses of these figures careers as framed in stories that must have been already in circulation in the thirteenth century. The narrative involving Kubrā also provides some further chronological and geographical information: in it, the anonymous author mentions a daughter and grandson of Shaykh Ḍiyāʾ al-Dīn and implies that his work was written already when the grandson was a grown man (suggesting, in turn, that the author may have been a disciple of one of Ḍiyāʾ al-Dīn's successors and not of Ḍiyāʾ al-Dīn himself). The author also affirms that Shaykh Ḍiyāʾ al-Dīn maintained a *khānqāh* in 'Khudāshāh' or 'Khurāshāh',[34] a village in western Khurāsān usually assigned to the province of Juwayn. These indications, together with the *nisbas* of Ḍiyāʾ al-Dīn's associates as recorded in the text, the likely identifications of the political figures mentioned therein, and the towns and cities in which particular stories about Ḍiyāʾ al-Dīn are set, all make it clear that Ḍiyāʾ al-Dīn's activity as a Sufi shaykh was centred in Khurāsān during the early part of the thirteenth century (in all likelihood, both before and after the Mongol invasion). Taken together, the excerpts provide a glimpse of an apparently small Sufi community in Khurāsān during the period and near the place in which Najm al-Dīn Kubrā's Sufi circle was also taking shape.

The excerpts from the *Maqāmāt* of Shaykh Ḍiyāʾ al-Dīn al-Ḥātimī, begin with the texts of seven letters written by Ḍiyāʾ al-Dīn (ff. 348b–354a).[35]

1. The first is a personal letter addressed to the author's father, Shaykh Saʿd al-Dīn Abu'l-ʿAlāʾ al-Ḥātimī, and was sent from Baghdad. It alludes to the son's recovery from a serious illness, notes his plans to complete his journey to Mecca and Medina after his return to full health, and asks for his father's continued prayers.
2. The heading to the second letter (ff. 348b–349a) affirms that Shaykh Ḍiyāʾ al-Dīn wrote it in Nīshāpūr, at the time when he had been sent to arrange peace between the '*Amīr-i kabīr*, Ṣalāḥ al-Dīn Ṭughril', ruler of Quhistān and a certain 'Kamāl al-Dīn Masʿūd'. The latter is identified only as a 'lord' (*ṣāḥib*) and it is not clear whether he should be understood as an equal of Ṣalāḥ al-Dīn Ṭughril, or as his subordinate. I have so far been unable to identify either of these figures; the

letter's actual addressee is not named in the text, but he was evidently a ruler and was undoubtedly the sovereign or vizier to whom the two quarrelling men were subordinate.[36] In any case, the mediation was unsuccessful, as both the heading and the text itself make clear.[37]

3. The third, and longest, letter (ff. 349a–350b), according to its heading, was written to 'Sulṭān Jalāl al-Dīn', at an unspecified time characterised only as 'the height of his glory' (*dar waqt-i 'ulūw-i shān*). The letter sets out to explain, however, the reason for an unidentified ruler's fall from power and subsequent ruin, and cautions the addressee against involving himself in injustices that would lead to his destruction as well.[38] While it is not inconceivable that the addressee was merely a local ruler, otherwise unknown, it is likely, considering the time and place of Shaykh Ḍiyā' al-Dīn's Sufi career, that 'Sulṭān Jalāl al-Dīn' could mean only the son of the Khwārazmshāh 'Alā' al-Dīn Muḥammad (r. 596–617/1200–1220), the famous Jalāl al-Dīn Mengburnī. The era in question provides abundant candidates for identification with the fallen ruler, of course, but the letter implies that he was 'replaced' by a non-Muslim,[39] and its cautionary tale may well allude to the fate of 'Alā' al-Dīn Muḥammad himself. If this interpretation is correct, the letter presumably would have been written some time between the father's death (617/1220) and the son's (628/1231), most likely relatively early in this period (after Jalāl al-Dīn's return from India, but before his ventures further west in Iraq, Syria, Georgia, Azerbaijan and eastern Anatolia). The letter, as is mentioned both in the heading and in the text itself, was sent to the sultan with a certain 'Shams al-Dīn Tashtī',[40] who is identified only as an 'ascetic shaykh' but was presumably also a follower of Ḍiyā' al-Dīn. Otherwise the only name mentioned in the text is that of a certain 'Shams al-Dīn *'amīd*', to whose sayings and adages the addressee is urged to pay heed. It is possible that the figure intended here is Shams al-Dīn Juwaynī (i.e. a native of the region in which Shaykh Ḍiyā' al-Dīn's activity was centred), who served both the Khwārazmshāh Muḥammad and his son Jalāl al-Dīn as '*ṣāḥib-dīwān*' (finance minister) and who was the grandfather of the historian Juwaynī.[41]

4. The fourth letter (ff. 350b–352a) is addressed to 'Sulṭān Ghiyāth al-Dīn', who is identified as a hereditary ruler (he is called in the text 'our noble son, the eminent *sulṭān-zāda*'), and who was evidently active in Khurāsān.[42] It is possible that the addressee was the Ghūrid ruler Ghiyāth al-Dīn Maḥmūd, who ruled briefly (602–609/1206–1212) in the western Ghūrid domains with claims on Khurāsān, following the death of his uncle, Shihāb al-Dīn Muḥammad; or the letter might refer to this Ghiyāth al-Dīn's father, Ghiyāth al-Dīn Muḥammad (d. 599/1202–1203).[43] It appears more likely, however, that the Ghiyāth al-Dīn referred to here is Ghiyāth al-Dīn Pīr-shāh, a younger son of the Khwārazmshāh Muḥammad and a half-brother of the preceding letter's addressee.[44] The chief drawback to this identification is perhaps the author's characterisation of the addressee's

'late father', who is praised for his devotion to the counsel of dervishes.[45] This contrasts sharply not only with the preceding letter's apparent criticism of 'Alā' al-Dīn Khwārazmshāh for having countenanced oppression, but also with the broader hostility towards the Khwārazmshāh that seems to have prevailed in Sufi circles of the early thirteenth century (above all, that of Najm al-Dīn Kubrā, as seen most dramatically in accounts of the Khwārazmshāh's responsibility for the death of Kubrā's disciple Majd al-Dīn Baghdādī). There are unfortunately no other details in the letter that help resolve this question; the '*malik* Ẓahīr al-Dīn' whose habit of showing forgiveness and mildness towards the oppressed population is lauded in the text remains unidentified.[46] The letter was carried to Ghiyāth al-Dīn, the heading tells us, by 'Shaykh ʿAbd al-Raḥmān Hamadānī' and 'Shaykh Imām Ṣafī al-Dīn T.f.l.šī'.[47] However, the text itself refers to 'the bearers of this appeal' as 'the pious shaykh Kamāl al-Dīn ʿAbd al-Wāḥid and Imām Ṣafī al-Dīn'.

5. The fifth letter (ff. 352a–b), according to its heading, was addressed to 'Atābak Muẓaffar al-Dīn Atsïz b. Saʿd b. Zangī'; in the text itself he is called 'the epitome of the kings of Persia' (*khulāṣa-i mulūk-i ʿajam*), and his relative youth is implied when the author addresses him as 'son' (*farzand*, and once as *jawān-farzand*). This figure's father is clearly the well-known Salghūrid ruler of Fārs (r. 594–623/1198–1226), who was for a time subject to the Khwārazmshāh 'Alā' al-Dīn Muḥammad and later to his son Jalāl al-Dīn, but it is not certain whether 'Muẓaffar al-Dīn Atsïz' refers to Abū Bakr Muẓaffar al-Dīn b. Saʿd (r. 623–658/1226–1260), who was eventually accorded the title 'Qutlugh Khān' by the Mongols, or should be understood as the name of yet another, unknown, son of Saʿd b. Zangī.[48] The letter, as is clear from the heading and the text itself, was sent in response to an earlier message from the addressee and praises the latter's inclination toward justice and good works (with a reminder that rejecting what God prohibits is better than a thousand *rakʿa*s of supererogatory prayer), as well as his inclination towards dervishes. It refers also to the benedictions of 'a party of servants', of whom three are mentioned by name: '*ṣāḥib* Ẓahīr al-Dīn ʿAbd al-Raḥīm' (perhaps the '*malik* Ẓahīr al-Dīn' of the preceding letter?), 'Fakhr al-Dīn Ḥaydar' and 'the *ṣadr* Shams al-Dīn Masʿūd'.[49]
6. The sixth letter (ff. 352b–353a) is quite short (a little over five lines) and is addressed to Shaykh Jamāl al-Dīn Āmulī – presumably a disciple or associate of Shaykh Ḍiyā' al-Dīn – in Nasā.
7. The seventh and final letter (ff. 353a–354a) is addressed to 'Jalāl al-Dīn'; this may refer again to the son of the last Khwārazmshāh, but he is called here only '*ṣāḥib*', not '*sulṭān*', and this Jalāl al-Dīn may have been a vizier or high-ranking official rather than a ruler himself. The letter alludes to a complaint brought before the shaykh by a man identified in the text only as 'Badr al-Dīn', who is assigned the ambiguous appellation '*mihtar*'. It is not clear whether we should understand this

to mean that Badr al-Dīn was merely an 'elder' or that he was himself an official subordinate to Jalāl al-Dīn, though presumably he was a man of some standing. The complaint was that the addressee sought to destroy Badr al-Dīn's house in order to construct a garden (*bāgh*) on the site for his (the addressee's) son. Ḍiyā' al-Dīn's letter begins by chiding Jalāl al-Dīn for not heeding the counsel of dervishes. Rather, 'I have heard that he is destroying the homes of several people in order to make a *bāgh* for [his] son; before God, this affair is far removed from religion and honour (*dīn wa-murūwwa*) and in this construction (*'imāra*) the paths of Satan are well ordered (*ma'mūr*).' The shaykh further reminds Jalāl al-Dīn of past kings and viziers who bestowed blessings on their children, but acted oppressively in acquiring those blessings, and cautions him that those oppressions remain with them in their graves, while nothing enduring remains for the children (the 'blessings' instead becoming a burden and the cause of their impoverishment and destruction). 'And if he does not believe, let him take note of the situation of the late *ṣāḥib*, 'Amīd al-Dīn, and his son Mas'ūd, who is alive.' Once again, these figures remain difficult to identify, but it is possible that their names reflect those of prominent officials under the Khwārazmshāhs or, more likely, under the Salghūrids.[50] The letter counsels Jalāl al-Dīn, finally, to give up his designs on the home of Badr al-Dīn and to put the latter's mind at ease.

The seventh letter is followed (at f. 354a) by a heading that signals 'some of the sayings that came from his tongue'. A series of brief utterances and longer anecdotes, some recounted by specific disciples of Shaykh Ḍiyā' al-Dīn, follows.[51] In the first, for example, the shaykh is said to have declared, 'Whoever performs *namāz* so that he can eat bread because of it makes his performance of *namāz* the equivalent of eating bread; and whoever eats bread in order to perform *namāz* through its power makes his bread-eating the equivalent of performing *namāz*'. The shaykh's response to a question – submitted in a letter, we are told – by a certain 'Shaykh Nūr al-Dīn Guwāshirī'[52] is then related, followed by several brief narratives set during Ḍiyā' al-Dīn's visits to Ṭūs, Iṣfahān and Baghdad. Another saying was prompted by a question from 'Shaykh Jamāl al-Dīn' (who may be the addressee of the sixth letter noted above, a native of Āmul in Māzāndarān, and who is mentioned also in the anecdote about Raḍī al-Dīn Lālā recounted below), who told the shaykh, 'The common people come constantly to us, and love for them is keeping us from religious matters (*kār-i dīn*)'. The shaykh replied, 'Lend something to those who are poor, and ask for something from those who are rich, so that both groups will neither come back to you, nor remain in your company, except seeking religion.'[53]

A series of other brief sayings follows, including one of particular interest because of the questioner who prompted it. This was one of Shaykh Ḍiyā' al-Dīn's *murīds*, we are told, called 'Khwāja Imām 'Umar Isbanjī Arghiyānī',[54] who is in all likelihood to be identified with the 'Imām 'Alā' al-Dīn 'Umar b. Muḥammad

b. Ḥākim Arghiyānī' mentioned, in a fourteenth-century source, as an associate of Saʿd al-Dīn Ḥammūyī. According to the source in question,[55] this 'Alā' al-Dīn 'Umar Arghiyānī studied with Saʿd al-Dīn a juridical work (the famous *Maṣābīḥ al-sunna*) by Rukn al-Dīn Ḥusayn al-Baghawī, known as 'Muḥyī's Sunna' (d. 510/1117),[56] in Jumādā I–II 629/March–April 1232.[57] The mention of this figure in the excerpts from the *Maqāmāt* of Shaykh Ḍiyā' al-Dīn not only supports its authenticity and antiquity, but confirms again the connections between the obscure, and apparently small, Sufi community of Khudāshāh and other groups in nearby regions – whether other parts of Khurāsān or farther away, in Khwārazm – and the pattern of overlapping Sufi circles (to speak of 'orders' is certainly premature) that characterised the geography of Sufism in the later twelfth and early thirteenth centuries. Saʿd al-Dīn Ḥammūyī, of course, was yet another pupil of Najm al-Dīn Kubrā and maintained close ties with many shaykhs of Khurāsān (and more distant regions), forged through extensive travels, before he established himself at his ancestral home in Baḥrābād, just a short distance from Shaykh Ḍiyā' al-Dīn's base in Khudāshāh.[58]

This series of brief sayings is followed by four somewhat longer narratives, each marked simply by the heading '*ḥikāyat*'. The first is the story about Najm al-Dīn Kubrā given below in translation. The second is a story ascribed to a certain 'Shaykh Abū Naṣr Yūzdār',[59] followed by the author's note that this Ḥājjī Abū Naṣr later performed the *ḥajj* four times in Shaykh Ḍiyā' al-Dīn's company. Next comes a story, related about himself, by 'Ḥāmid Majnūn-i Ṭūsī', another disciple of Ḍiyā' al-Dīn, involving his shaykh's intervention to save him from sin at a nearby *khānqāh*.[60] The fourth is the story recounted by, and about, Shaykh Raḍī al-Dīn ʿAlī Lālā likewise given in translation below.

The end of the last narrative may, in fact, mark the end of the excerpts from the *Maqāmāt* of Shaykh Ḍiyā' al-Dīn. What follows it, without any heading or introduction, on f. 360b, is a story about the Prophet related on the authority of Anas b. Mālik.[61] This story comes to an end on f. 361b, with another anonymous narrative (about Jaʿfar al-Ṣādiq) beginning, with no heading, on f. 362a.

The excerpts from the *Maqāmāt* thus provide considerable evidence on Shaykh Ḍiyā' al-Dīn's sphere of activity, not only through the localities mentioned in specific narratives – his *khānqāh* in Khudāshāh, his disciple's stay in Āzādvār, his apparent connections with Māzāndarān, Ṭūs, Nīshāpūr and Nasā, his travels elsewhere in Iran – but through the *nisba*s of his disciples as well. The latter, indicating natives of Āmul, Hamadān, Qāyin (in Quhistān) and Guwāshir (Kirmān), as well as of regions closer to his base such as Arghiyān and Ṭūs, suggest the range of his reputation, as do, in a different way, the references in the letters to the political figures of the era who seemingly put some stock in Shaykh Ḍiyā' al-Dīn's counsel. One notable issue absent from the excerpts preserved in the Rampur manuscript, however, is that of the basis of the shaykh's authority as a Sufi teacher. We are told nothing about Shaykh Ḍiyā' al-Dīn's own master or his *silsila*. It is possible that we should avoid construing this silence as evidence that Ḍiyā' al-Dīn's Sufi community paid less attention than some others known from the thirteenth century to matters of formal spiritual transmission and succession. On the other hand, the mention of Ḍiyā' al-Dīn's father might suggest that this small Sufi circle reflected the continued predominance in this era of local hereditary shaykhs (for example, the familial successors of Shaykh Aḥmad-i Jām based to the south and east of Shaykh Ḍiyā' al-Dīn), whose communities remained relatively unaffected by the developments that were leading other Sufi communities in the direction of actual 'orders' organised around the principle of succession defined in terms of *silsila* relationships.

We will return briefly to these issues; now we may turn to translations of the two narratives from the text that are arguably of greatest interest, the first dealing with Najm al-Dīn Kubrā and the second with Raḍī al-Dīn 'Alī Lālā.

## The Narrative about Najm al-Dīn Kubrā (ff. 356Aa–357b)

I have [received] a narrative (*riwāya*) from the shaykh of illustrious virtue, the pious *muftī*, Sa'd al-Dīn al-Qāyinī (may God bless him), who was among our Shaykh's *murīds* and one of the esteemed ones of the community (*ṭā'ifa*), and was for years a friend of the Shaykh, attending to him and serving him on journeys and in his presence, and whose blessed head the Shaykh shaved with his own hands, and who received the *khirqa* from the blessed hands of the Shaykh at the sanctuary of the Ka'ba. He said that at the beginning of the career of our Shaykh (may God bless him), the shaykh of shaykhs, Najm al-Dīn Kubrā, the Sufi (may God bless him), had gone to the Ḥijāz and performed the pilgrimage, and was returning to Khwārazm. And at the time when he had left his home, he had made a vow (*nadhr*), saying, 'Wherever I go, I will observe the custom of presenting a prayer rug and staff to a worthy saint among the saints of God.'

When at last he came to Khudāshāh[62] and stopped at the *khānqāh* of our Shaykh, with seven Sufis accompanying him, [our Shaykh's] servants (*khādimān*)[63] brought him from the *khānqāh* to the dervishes' place of devotions (*muta'abbad*). After awhile the Shaykh entered and they embraced. Our Shaykh wished to seat Shaykh Najm al-Dīn Kubrā (may God bless them both) at his right side, and said so several times. But Shaykh Najm al-Dīn Kubrā did not respond. Then they sat down and spoke in signs and allusions and exchanged pleasantries until the first course (*sufra-i awwal*). When they brought in the first course and presented it, Shaykh Najm al-Dīn Kubrā's servant (*khādim*) rose and with his own hands presented the bowls of food, bypassing the servants of our Shaykh.

And Shaykh Najm al-Dīn, after [spending] three days, with our Shaykh's permission, in that room where he had [first] taken lodging, spent [another] three days in a devotions room (*mutaʿabbad-khāna*) adjacent to a cell (*ḥujra*) in which running water had been brought, next to the Shaykh's private quarters (*ḥaram*), and next to the [first] devotions-hall (*mutaʿabbad*), which was connected to that place through a doorway. Then he sought to take leave and prepared to depart. He came out to our Shaykh, and they sat together; then our Shaykh said, 'Today I have a criticism regarding Sufi etiquette to bring up with you.[64] With your permission, I will tell you.' Shaykh Najm al-Dīn was gracious and inquired about what he had in mind. The Shaykh said, 'There are three points. The first is that on the first day, when the Shaykh came to us, I wished, in accord with the injunction, "Honour your guest and you will be honoured", that you would sit by my side on my cushion, and so I requested; but you did not agree, and did not observe the custom [described by the saying,] "I sit where you sit".' Shaykh Najm al-Dīn confirmed this and said, 'I accept this point.'

Then [our Shaykh] said, 'The second is that for many years the inhabitants of this building (*buqʿa*) have been performing service, be it good or bad, for dervishes. It is a snare they have set, and they have fed a hundred sparrows, thinking that one day a falcon would come to the snare, and food would reach its gullet by means of their hands. Yet when they wished to present food before you in the proper manner, you directed your own servant (*khādim*) [to do so], and that company was left disappointed and desolate.' Shaykh Najm al-Dīn confirmed this and said, 'This point is also accepted.'

[Then our Shaykh said,] 'As for the third, when you reach Khwārazm, you will remember; there is no need for me to say it.' And however much Shaykh [Najm al-Dīn] pressed him, our Shaykh would not divulge that third thing. And Shaykh Najm al-Dīn himself, however much he pondered, could not reach the secret of that third matter. He apologised and became humble and resigned himself, insisting upon his fairness in giving what is due (*inṣāf*) and showing repentance; and both were content. Afterwards, Shaykh Najm al-Dīn revealed his wish to leave, and they began the musical performance (*samāʿ*). States of mystical joy (*dhawq*) were opened up, and there was much ecstatic fervour (*khirqa-bāzī*) and daring mystical intensity that evening. After the music, our Shaykh and Shaykh Najm al-Dīn (may God bless both of them) spent that night in communion and conversation (*mudhākira wa-mufāwaḍa*) until dawn.

Then the next day Shaykh Najm al-Dīn set out for Khwārazm; and by the time he reached Khwārazm, he remembered what our Shaykh had said he would remember in Khwārazm. He said to himself, 'I had made a vow (*ʿahd*) that wherever I came to a worthy saint, I would present to him a prayer rug and staff; but I came to his holiness Shaykh Ḍiyā' al-Dīn and forgot completely!' At once he assigned Shaykh 'Alā' al-Dīn Khujandī and Akhī Yūsuf Shahristānī to go from Khwārazm with a prayer rug and staff to take to the holy Shaykh. And he wrote a long letter and begged his pardon:

'That which the Shaykh said – namely, "When you reach Khwārazm, the settling of the unpaid debt and the fulfilment of the unmet obligation that were the subject of the third point will become known to you" – has indeed become known, and the attainments and stations of the Shaykh have also become known. Be assured that Abu'l-Jannāb[65] says, "If I had known that there was such a great man and such a servant of God in a small corner of a country town (*dar gūsha-i rūstāqī*), I would never have travelled throughout the world." And be assured that Abu'l-Jannāb has directed all his resolve so that after he has gone to Khwārazm and seen his kinsmen (*aqārib wa-ʿashāʾir*), at the earliest possible time he will return to you and spend several days in your service.'

And so, the great Imām Khwāja Saʿd al-Dīn al-Qāyinī said, 'One day after the midday prayer, our Shaykh was sitting, with his companions seated in his presence, and the Shaykh was in an extremely expansive and cheerful frame of mind (*munbasiṭ wa-kushāda*). Suddenly in the midst of his words, he began to recite verses of Shaykh Najm al-Dīn Kubrā (may God bless him) and said, "This very hour word will come of our faithful brother (*birādar-i ḥaqqānī*), and he will send his words and message to us."' He [al-Qāyinī] says, 'One hour had passed after he said this when those two dervishes came in, and after embraces and handshakes they presented the Shaykh's letter and message, and brought forth the bequests (*amānāt*) of Shaykh Najm al-Dīn. Our Shaykh honoured [the two dervishes] and after three days sent them on.'[66]

And our Shaykh had a piece of woollen cloth (*saqirlāṭ*), brightly coloured and equal in length and breadth, upon which he performed his prayers (the Shaykh always used it as his prayer rug in summertime and, with a patched mat, in wintertime). He sent it as a gift to Shaykh Najm al-Dīn Kubrā. And he treated those two messengers of his graciously and put the *khirqa* on them; and when they said that Shaykh Najm al-Dīn had asked for [our Shaykh's] assistance in his spiritual aspiration (*istimdād-i himmat karde-ast*), it brought tears to his eyes. Then the dervishes left and went back to Khwārazm.

That prayer rug and staff were in our Shaykh's private quarters (*ḥaram*), among the *khirqa*s of all [his] shaykhs, until it was left as a legacy to our Shaykh's child, 'Azīza Khwātūn [*sic*], and from her to her son, Shaykh Muʿīn al-Dīn Muḥammad Ḥafada.[67]

This story about Kubrā is of interest not only for confirming elements of Shaykh Ḍiyāʾ al-Dīn's life – one of his pilgrimages to Mecca, his *khānqāh* in Khudāshāh, the hereditary transmission of his Sufi 'gift' from Najm al-Dīn to his daughter and grandson (a transmission implicitly separate from the disposition of the *khirqa*s he had received from numerous shaykhs) – but also for its references to initiatory practice within Ḍiyāʾ al-Dīn's Sufi circle (i.e. the author's mention, in connection with Saʿd al-Dīn al-Qāyinī, of the shaving of the head and the transmission of the *khirqa*) and the glimpses it offers of life and Sufi custom in the setting of the *khānqāh*. As for Kubrā himself, the narrative supports the assumption that he performed the *ḥajj* at least once after he returned to Khwārazm following the extensive travels on which he undertook his Sufi training.[68] Unfortunately the account does not identify the 'seven Sufis' who accompanied Kubrā during his visit to Ḍiyā' al-Dīn's *khānqāh* (and presumably on his pilgrimage as well), but it does mention two additional disciples, 'Alā' al-Dīn Khujandī and Akhī Yūsuf Shahristānī.

The first of these figures might be identified with 'Alā' al-Dīn Abū Muḥammad Thābit b. Muḥammad b. Aḥmad b. Thābit al-Khujandī, mentioned in the biographical compendium of Ibn al-Fuwaṭī (d. 723/1323) as a leading figure of Balkh, with his date of death given as 637/1239–1240. This 'Alā' al-Dīn belonged to an illustrious family that hailed originally from Khujand, but had gained prominence in Iṣfahān,[69] and clearly the same figure (despite the different details of his lineage) is mentioned by al-Dhahabī and in Junayd Shīrāzī's *Shadd al-izār*, where he is referred to once simply as 'Shaykh 'Alā' al-Dīn al-Khujandī'.[70] Unfortunately none of our other sources mentions any connection between this figure and Najm al-Dīn Kubrā (or between Kubrā and any other figure plausibly represented by this designation[71]), and despite its chronological suitability we cannot be sure of the identification. The other disciple mentioned in the narrative, meanwhile, Akhī Yūsuf Shahristānī, would appear to have been a native, or resident, of the town of Shahristāna, near Nasā, where, according to another of Kubrā's lesser-known disciples, a *khānqāh* linked to Kubrā's Sufi circle was located.[72]

The reference in the narrative to Kubrā's 'vow' to offer a prayer rug and staff to 'worthy' shaykhs he met – the issue, in fact, on which the entire story hinges – is of considerable interest as well, insofar as Kubrā's gift of a prayer rug and a staff figures in a story told about a thirteenth-century saint of Tashkent known as Zangī Ata. It is first recorded in a seventeenth-century Yasawī hagiography, the *Lamaḥāt min nafaḥāt al-quds*. In this story, Kubrā sends a prayer rug and a staff to Zangī Ata and the latter – a figure consistently portrayed as a rustic cowherd – at once breaks the staff in two for use as a yoke for his cattle, and rips up the prayer rug to prevent the yoke from chafing.[73] The echo of this motif in the *Maqāmāt* of Shaykh Ḍiyā' al-Dīn supports the supposition that this narrative element was already attached to Kubrā's memory in the thirteenth century. The element of Kubrā's vow to deliver these tokens in person is not mentioned in connection with Zangī Ata, but the parallel with the narrative involving Shaykh Ḍiyā' al-Dīn is nevertheless quite close (since the latter story likewise ends with Kubrā merely dispatching the gifts). Zangī Ata's rough treatment of Kubrā's offerings in the *Lamaḥāt*'s account may reflect a polemical, or perhaps merely didactic, adaptation of an earlier narrative, but even here we may find a similarity in the use of the theme, albeit more mildly, to underscore the spiritual virtues of Shaykh Ḍiyā' al-Dīn (rather than those of Kubrā).

The mildness of the narrative may in fact also be significant, since this account of Kubrā, though clearly designed to underscore the preeminence of Shaykh Ḍiyā' al-Dīn, is free of the pejorative and downright derogatory tone that often appears in the hagiographical narratives, circulated in later times, that pit one shaykh against another. Such narratives often provided an important means of asserting a particular Sufi community's claims of spiritual superiority, and typically result in the deflation or confounding (or worse) of a shaykh linked with a rival community, but in this case Kubrā is treated quite respectfully (and the second narrative also maintains a quite positive tone towards Lālā, as we will see). Whether this suggests some closer connection, in the thirteenth century, between the Sufi community linked to Najm al-Dīn Kubrā and the group centred upon Shaykh Ḍiyā' al-Dīn remains difficult to judge. (We will return to this problem below.)

More broadly, the narrative itself offers an illustration of the connections maintained by Kubrā and his Sufi community based in Khwārazm, with various Sufi centres of Khurāsān. It is, to be sure, quite difficult to suggest the precise nature of the affiliations between Kubrā's Sufi circle and other Sufi groups active at the time in nearby regions. As noted, we have evidence that a *khānqāh*, linked to Kubrā's circle, was maintained in Shahristāna, near Nasā, while the letters of Majd al-Dīn Baghdādī allude to *khānqāhs* linked with Kubrā not only in Nasā, but in Nīshāpūr and Marw as well; Baghdādī's mention of the appointment of a *khādim* at yet another *khānqāh* in Khurāsān[74] may suggest that Kubrā exercised some degree of administrative authority over these *khānqāhs*, but there was undoubtedly a larger network of *khānqāhs* in the region run by Sufi shaykhs – such as Ḍiyā' al-Dīn al-Ḥātimī – who maintained connections and good relations with Kubrā's community and with still other Sufi lodges, but without any structures of hierarchical authority being clearly recognised among them. It is undoubtedly anachronistic to understand any of these *khānqāhs*, or the shaykhs who administered them, in the context of distinct Sufi 'orders' (just as it makes no sense to regard Kubrā himself as having consciously sought to establish a 'Kubravī' Sufi organisation). Yet even in the case of *khānqāhs* that seem to have been more closely linked with Kubrā's circle, we have very little information for this period about the actual management of the communities, or about the impact of notions about the extent of a shaykh's authority and that authority's transmission, upon the practice of administering a Sufi *khānqāh* and the affairs of its residents.

In the absence of such evidence, the available narrative material may hold our only clues to the patterns of communal boundaries and communal interconnections that prevailed in thirteenth-century Khurāsān – boundaries and connections that were inevitably obscured in the later reconstructions of communal history in terms of *silsila*-based Sufi 'orders'. In this regard the second narrative, focused on Raḍī al-Dīn 'Alī Lālā, may be revealing as well.

## The Narrative about Raḍī al-Dīn ʿAlī Lālā (ff. 359a–360b)

Shaykh Raḍī al-Dīn ʿAlī Lālā (God's mercy be upon him) related, 'When I entered the Shaykh's service and conceived of travelling the mystical path, the Shaykh (God's mercy be upon him) prescribed a seclusion (*khalwa*) for me; and with him I performed two forty-day retreats (*arbaʿīns*). God opened the gates of proximity and grace to me and through the blessing of the Shaykh's company, numerous secrets of the angelic realm became clear within me. After that I proposed to go to India; the Shaykh gave me his permission (*ijāza*) and gave me also a tunic made of fine cloth from Nīshāpūr,[75] which he had worn, putting it on me with his own hands. I asked for his initiatory license, and the Shaykh consented and wrote it out.[76] And he said to his servant (*khādim*), Jamāl al-Dīn,[77] "Go to the shop of the master Aḥmad, the cutler (*sakkāk*), and buy a good file blade and bring it here." Presently he brought it, and the Shaykh gave it to me; and he said, "God in God, and paradise in worship and pious deeds, 'As a reward for what they have done.'"[78] Then he said, "Raḍī al-Dīn, do not forget these words of mine; and sew up this file in your *khirqa*. Do not be negligent in the service of God or in acquiring attainments and virtues, for life is passing by."

'Then he saw me off as far as the vestibule (*dihlīz*),[79] and he embraced me and sent me on. I was completely unable to understand the secret behind these words, and I did not comprehend the significance of that file. But I knew that the words and allusions and intimations of that great one would not be devoid of secrets, and so I obeyed and followed the Shaykh's commands: I sewed the file blade into my *khirqa*, and I repeated those words so much that I memorised them.

'Then I set off for India, passed Maʿbar and Q.lībār, and came to K.w.k.r.[n].[80] The air was extremely warm, such that I was unable to endure staying in that place. I spent the day in discomfort until the evening, and went out during the evening – for I could not bear to stay still – because of the intensity of the heat, nor could I move about by day, because it was so hot. When I reached the [city's] gate and made several cries for help, they allowed me to go out, and I went out. I had travelled for awhile when a band of men came by searching for a bandit. They supposed that I was the bandit, and seized me, and however much I tried to deflect their suspicions, they would not listen. They dragged me down and beat my arms and legs unsparingly with sticks and whips. Then they put a rope around my neck, and whenever I begged for mercy, they beat me harder still – since they regarded me as a foreigner and did not understand my speech – until they had injured all my limbs and I was unable to move. At last I resigned myself to God's decree and kept silent. Then they took me and shut me up in a room, and the next morning they brought me before their ruler (*shāh*). But however much I spoke and declared my innocence, no use came of it. They sentenced me to be placed in an underground dungeon (*bi-zindān dar maṭmūra*), and they put both my feet in strong chains. With me, nearby, there were several other persons, in chains, in the dungeon. Every day they would bring each one [of us] a small amount of rice, with butter and a piece of bread, and then go away until the next day.

'I was left in that misery for nearly five or six months; and not once did I think of that file, until one night I was scratching myself, and suddenly the tip of the file pushed a hole through my *khirqa*, and part of it came out and nicked my hand. I remembered it and became elated and overjoyed; and I performed a prostration in thanks, and said a prayer for my Shaykh. Then when part of the evening had passed, I took out the file; it was a new file, fine and sharp, and in the blink of an eye I broke both bonds. At once I made my escape and set out towards several islands, and God delivered me from the midst of those infidels (*bī-dīnān*). For three days I waited in those islands and then set out for another country.

'And in truth it became clear that God had set me free through the blessing of the Shaykh's noble resolve (*himma*), and I knew that the Shaykh had given me the file for those bonds. But still the understanding of those two sayings did not become clear to me until I came to Kirmān. One day I was sitting in the mosque speaking with a group of Bukhārans (*bā jamʿī-i bukhārāʾī*). In the course of our discussion someone voiced an objection to me, saying, "In what can the Imam find God, and in what can he find paradise?" I searched in myself for something both comprehensive and refined to say in response to him. All at once the words of my Shaykh (may that which he has earned of God's favour come upon him) came to my mind, and I said, "[One finds] God in God – that is, in an inclination and attraction (*irāda wa-jadhba*) towards Him; and [one finds] paradise in pious deeds, 'As a reward for what they have done.'"[81] The man came and placed his head at my feet.

'When these two impediments that had fallen upon my path during this journey were thus removed through the Shaykh's blessing, I set out to return to the Shaykh; and for some time further I served at his threshold and was favoured with the honour of his companionship and solicitude (and it is God who favours and guides).'

This second narrative portrays Raḍī al-Dīn ʿAlī Lālā beginning his mystical pursuits under Shaykh Ḍiyāʾ al-Dīn's guidance, then journeying to India, and returning to Ḍiyāʾ al-Dīn following yet another demonstration of his foreknowledge, this one in Kirmān.[82] The account of Lālā is both more direct and personal than the narrative involving Kubrā, and less explicitly evocative of the atmosphere of *khānqāh* life and Sufi *adab*. It is nevertheless of some interest in connection with one aspect of Sufi custom – that of service to multiple masters, often in the course of extensive travels – which was quite the norm in the thirteenth century, but eventually, in the era of actual Sufi orders, came into conflict with the ethos of discipleship under a single shaykh (even though it was never effectively suppressed in practice). In the case of this narrative, to be sure, Shaykh Ḍiyāʾ al-Dīn has become Lālā's only significant master, and this too may hint at the context in which the story was circulated. But the story deals with their relationship in the context of Lālā's travels in general, and his journey to India in particular, and it is worth noting the other evidence that has survived on these issues.

The notion that Raḍī al-Dīn ʿAlī Lālā travelled widely and served numerous shaykhs is implicit in the account of his time in Shīrāz, found in the thirteenth-century biographies of Rūzbihān Baqlī noted earlier. Among sources produced within the Sufi lineage traced through Lālā, the earliest biographical details about him appear in the works by and about ʿAlāʾ al-Dawla Simnānī from the early fourteenth century. In the *Chihil majlis*, a collection of Simnānī's discourses compiled by a disciple, Simnānī is cited for an extended account of the way in which Lālā came to be Kubrā's disciple; the account refers to Lālā's travels 'throughout the world', for several years in search of Kubrā (whom he had seen in a dream).[83] A somewhat fuller account of Lālā's travels (without reference to the dream about Kubrā) appears in a brief treatise by Simnānī, entitled *Hidāyat al-mustarshidīn wa-waṣīyat al-murshidīn*, completed in 705/1306. There, in a discussion of the frequent need for multiple masters (which he illustrates also with the example of Kubrā being sent successively to numerous shaykhs in order to remove additional obstacles on the path), Simnānī affirms that Lālā had travelled through the inhabited part of the world, and had visited 113 eminent shaykhs of his time, undertaking seclusions[84] and practising austerities, before receiving licensure (*ijāzat al-irshād*) from Kubrā. Even then, Simnānī added, Lālā was in need of further 'refinement' under the direction of Majd al-Dīn Baghdādī, who then also wrote an *ijāza* for him and dispatched him to Isfarāyin.[85]

The specific mention of India as one of Lālā's destinations, however, is found only in somewhat later sources and appears in connection with a link claimed between Lālā and 'Bābā Ratan', a famous *muʿammar*, a long-lived saint (i.e. suitable for conveying *ḥadīth*s, or some other legacy, directly from the Prophet to much later generations).[86] The link with Bābā Ratan is first mentioned in the *Khulāṣat al-manāqib*, a biography of Sayyid ʿAlī Hamadānī dating from the late fourteenth century,[87] which affirms that Bābā Ratan handed over to Lālā three unidentified 'legacies' intended for Lālā by the Prophet himself. In this account, however, Lālā's meeting with Bābā Ratan is not explicitly set in India, and only from the later fifteenth century do we find explicit discussion of Lālā's journey to India, in Dawlatshāh's *Tadhkirat al-shuʿarā*,[88] and in Jāmī's *Nafaḥāt al-uns*.[89] Both of these sources affirm that Lālā travelled to India, met Bābā Ratan there, and recieved from him a comb that had belonged to the Prophet. Dawlatshāh mentions the story of the comb after affirming that Lālā travelled throughout the world and received licensure (*ijāzat al-irshād*) from 400 shaykhs, before his discipleship under Kubrā, while Jāmī affirms that Lālā received *khirqa*s from 124 shaykhs (of which 113 remained after his death, echoing the figure given in Simnānī's *Hidayat al-mustarshidīn*), and gives a somewhat more elaborate version of the story of the Prophet's comb (he ascribes the story to a work – evidently in Arabic – by 'Alā' al-Dawla Simnānī,[90] and says that the latter received the comb together with a *khirqa* that had also been transmitted by Bābā Ratan).

After all, a narrative claiming that a certain shaykh – especially one held up as a spiritual ancestor in an initiatic chain through which a particular Sufi community claimed its distinct identity – had received spiritual sanction from the Prophet himself through the medium of a *mu'ammar* such a Bābā Ratan was clearly of use, potentially, in such competitive environments.

The Sufi circles that might have responded to communal rivalries in part through the circulation of a story linking Lālā to Bābā Ratan, we may suppose, were those that were defining themselves, by the late fourteenth century, in terms of spiritual descent from Najm al-Dīn Kubrā through Lālā. In this connection the total silence, in the thirteenth-century *Maqāmāt* of Shaykh Ḍiyā' al-Dīn, about Lālā's relationship to Kubrā may be of interest as well. We might argue that it was simply unnecessary to mention a relationship that was quite well known; but it is also possible that the 'separation' of Kubrā and Lālā in the anecdotes linking them to Shaykh Ḍiyā' al-Dīn may hold clues both about the fate of the narratives themselves – to which we find no echo or allusion in any other extant source – and about the environment in which the stories were circulated.

In the first regard, a narrative recounting Lālā's journey to India and his deliverance through the foresight of Ḍiyā' al-Dīn, without mention of Kubrā, was undoubtedly of little interest, and of little use, for self-consciously 'Kubravī' communities. The survival of such communities, and the eventual disappearance of any Sufi circle that had cultivated the memory of Shaykh Ḍiyā' al-Dīn, may explain why the story of Lālā and Ḍiyā' al-Dīn survives only in a single known manuscript fragment, and finds no echo in the body of narrative material preserved in sources produced within the Kubravī Sufi tradition.

As for the environment in which the narratives were circulated, it may be of further significance that Shaykh Ḍiyā' al-Dīn's *khānqāh* was located in the region of Khurāsān that became the chief centre of activity of the shaykhs who came to be incorporated into the central Kubravī lineage: Lālā himself, as noted, was sent to nearby Isfarāyin, and was later buried in that region, in the village of Gūrpān, which was the native village of his principal successor, Shaykh Aḥmad Gūrpānī; Gūrpānī's career appears to have been centred there as well, and his chief successor, Nūr al-Dīn 'Abd al-Raḥmān Isfarāyinī, was likewise active there for a good part of his life, before moving to Baghdad; and the only other disciple of Lālā mentioned in available sources was a certain Shaykh 'Abd Allāh of Nasā, whose small agricultural community of dervishes there is depicted in Isfarāyinī's writings.[91] The Sufi circles that traced their origins through Lālā may thus have been direct competitors, by the later thirteenth and early fourteenth centuries, with whatever communal legacy we may envisage for the Sufi group, centred on Juwayn, that had been led by Shaykh Ḍiyāʾ al-Dīn. The competition between these groups might plausibly have fostered a claim, on the part of Ḍiyāʾ al-Dīn's group, that Lālā – the spiritual ancestor of their rivals – had in fact been trained and protected by Ḍiyāʾ al-Dīn; this is the implication of the second narrative, which portrays Lālā as subordinate to Shaykh Ḍiyāʾ al-Dīn, but ignores Lālā's ties with any another shaykh (even one – Kubrā – who is depicted as honouring Ḍiyāʾ al-Dīn). The same competitive atmosphere might likewise have fostered the circulation of counterclaims among Lālā's spiritual descendants, with stories stressing Lālā's independent sanction by the Prophet, through the medium of Bābā Ratan, with no more than an echo of one element of the account told by their rivals (i.e. the journey to India). As the competitive environment that had fostered the development and circulation of these narratives eventually changed (through the dissolution or absorption of Ḍiyāʾ al-Dīn's Sufi circle), we may suppose that the original purpose of the narratives was no longer relevant, and no longer remembered. And by the early sixteenth century, the inclusion of part of the *Maqāmāt* of Ḍiyāʾ al-Dīn, including narratives about Kubrā and Lālā, in a volume devoted primarily to 'Kubravī' treatises could hardly have posed any further threat to the Kubravī community; it had very different competitors by then.

On the other hand, the quite positive tone with which Lālā is treated in the *Maqāmāt* of Ḍiyāʾ al-Dīn suggests that the narrative about him was not the product of a simple effort to discredit the spiritual ancestor of a rival community, or even to subordinate that spiritual ancestor to Ḍiyāʾ al-Dīn (thereby asserting preeminence for the latter's community over the group centred on Lālā). If the target of those who produced and circulated the *Maqāmāt* of Ḍiyāʾ al-Dīn was simply the community of Lālā's spiritual descendants, we might expect to find Lālā himself disparaged or portrayed as clearly inferior to Ḍiyāʾ al-Dīn, but this is not the case in the *Maqāmāt* (despite his inordinate delay in recalling the key to his freedom). Lālā, instead, is spoken of respectfully, as is Najm al-Dīn Kubrā. What seems significant is not the attitude towards these figures, but their separation, and the narrative from the *Maqāmāt* of Ḍiyāʾ al-Dīn may intend not to slight Lālā, but to claim him for Ḍiyāʾ al-Dīn's circle of disciples – thereby undermining even the spiritual ancestry presumably claimed by their rivals. To be sure, Lālā is not explicitly identified in the text as Ḍiyāʾ al-Dīn's disciple, unlike other figures who appear in anecdotes from the *Maqāmāt*; but the story is told in the first person, and Lālā himself is portrayed speaking of a quite formal relationship of training and supervision by Ḍiyāʾ al-Dīn, and of a longer period in his service following the shaykh's protective intervention in India.

We must also consider the possibility, however, that the omission of Kubrā from the account of Lālā might reflect not simply (and again, in all likelihood, anachronistically) a polemical tactic used by the partisans of Shaykh Ḍiyāʾ al-Dīn, but the actual sequence of Lālā's training, in which Kubrā's role was effectively erased. Perhaps, that is, the *Maqāmāt*'s silence regarding a connection between Lālā and Kubrā reflects the actual sequence of Lālā's Sufi training, in which his time with Shaykh Ḍiyā' al-Dīn (and his journey to India) indeed followed his earlier, incomplete training under Kubrā. In this case, we would have to assume that, despite later 'Kubravī' efforts to depict Kubrā and Baghdādī as Lālā's final and decisive masters, Lālā's relationship with Shaykh Ḍiyā' al-Dīn in fact came after Lālā's association with Kubrā and Majd al-Dīn. It would thus be those later 'Kubravī' accounts that were manipulating Lālā's biography in order to obscure his training with another master *after* Kubrā's death.

In this connection we may note that although some later accounts of Kubrā's death name Lālā among the disciples whom Kubrā sent out from Khwārazm just before the Mongol invasion – a story that may sound suspicious on several counts – our evidence on Lālā's association with both Kubrā and Majd al-Dīn Baghdādī suggests that it might have occurred well before that time. We know, for instance, that Kubrā had already given Lālā an *ijāzat-nāma*, authorising him to train disciples in his own right, in 598/1202.[92] The extant versions of the *ijāzat-nāma* given to Lālā by Majd al-Dīn Baghdādī bear no date,[93] but what is most likely our best source on the date of Majd al-Dīn's death would suggest that his licensure of Lālā must have come in or before 606/1209.[94] Lālā himself lived on, presumably near Isfarāyin, until 642/1244. And while it is possible that Lālā's time with Shaykh Ḍiyā' al-Dīn occurred before he began his association with Kubrā and Baghdādī (as we would suppose if we credit the later 'Kubravī' accounts saying that Lālā's time with these two shaykhs marked the culmination of his spiritual training), the narrative linking Kubrā with Ḍiyā' al-Dīn implies that the latter had just begun his Sufi career when the already renowned Kubrā came to visit, while most of the other personal associations reflected in Ḍiyā' al-Dīn's *Maqāmāt* suggest his activity in the 1220s, after Kubrā's death.

It is thus quite plausible that the subsequent narrative tradition within the lineages traced through Lālā to Kubrā may have restructured Lālā's biography so as to make Kubrā (or Baghdādī[95]) his final master; and it is only the greater success and longevity of the Kubravī tradition (and the higher survival rate of its representatives' writings), that might incline us to doubt the possible implications of the first-person account of Lālā as recorded in Shaykh Ḍiyā' al-Dīn's biography. Moreover, we may suggest, there may well have been Sufi circles that traced their origins through Lālā, but did not yet, in the thirteenth century, emphasise Lālā's connection to Najm al-Dīn Kubrā as the central initiatic or organisational focus of his Sufi career. Perhaps what is at work here, after all, is not a conflict between the 'Kubravī' successors of Lālā and the successors of Shaykh Ḍiyā' al-Dīn, but a conflict between a Sufi community that sought to align itself, and Lālā, with the legacy of Najm al-Dīn Kubrā, and another Sufi community that claimed Lālā as a successor to Shaykh Ḍiyā' al-Dīn (both groups could have regarded themselves, in turn, as successors to Lālā, whatever his further affiliation).

These scenarios remain, of course, speculative. It may well be that we should understand Lālā's time in Khudāshāh as part of the time of travels spoken of in 'Kubravī' sources, and Shaykh Ḍiyā' al-Dīn as one of the 113 (or 124, or 400) shaykhs whom he served, according to those same sources. We need not assume, however, that the narrative from the *Maqāmāt* of Ḍiyā' al-Dīn was crafted explicitly for polemical purposes in order to draw some lessons from it regarding the early phases of the Kubravī tradition. The story, indeed, has a distinctly non-polemical tone, and the lack of evident polemical aims makes it all the more likely that the narrative should be regarded as an authentic record of Lālā's first-hand report. As such, furthermore, the *Maqāmāt*'s account of Lālā would appear to reflect a time before the coalescence of particular Sufi communities around the principle of *silsila*-based succession – a process that *did* occasion the polemical adaptation of hagiographical narratives – and this in itself may serve to set in relief both the narrative style and content that we can begin to recognise as characteristic of that later, competitive environment, and the organisational patterns of communal life, and of relationships between 'master' and 'disciple', that predominate in each period.

It is important, indeed, to point out that our understanding of the relationships among the loosely affiliated Sufi communities of thirteenth-century Khurāsān may in fact be hampered by assumptions about the organisational implications of initiatic relationships and *silsila* ties – assumptions that may suit a later era of fully developed Sufi 'orders', but may be quite misleading for the period reflected in the *Maqāmāt* of Shaykh Ḍiyā' al-Dīn. That is, it is quite possible that Sufi communities linked to figures typically depicted, in later times, as 'disciples' of Kubrā, for instance, were associated with him in quite different ways. Later accounts of Sufi organisational history are marked by a tendency to reduce a specific type of Sufi relationship (i.e. based on transmission of a particular practice, book, or item of Sufi insignia) into a more general and seemingly all-encompassing 'master-disciple' relationship, and by a parallel tendency to distil a complex pattern of associations into a simple *silsila.*

In the light of this, it is quite problematical, after all, to speak of sources 'internal' and 'external' to a tradition that we should understand to have been just then developing. The narratives translated above, preserved in a source reflecting a Sufi community that was clearly in close contact with the Sufi circle linked to Najm al-Dīn Kubrā, are a case in point. Thus it is perhaps anachronistic to assume that they were produced in a Sufi community that should be regarded as 'external' to the community from which the later Kubravī tradition emerged. Our understanding of the emergence of the 'Kubravī' order as a distinct and self-conscious Sufi community, I would argue, will be enhanced by entertaining the possibility that contacts and associations as loose as those between Shaykh Ḍiyā' al-Dīn al-Ḥātimī and both Najm al-Dīn Kubrā and Raḍī al-Dīn ʿAlī Lālā, as depicted in these narratives, might in later times be construed as initiatory relationships. It is equally possible that an authentic intiatory bond between Kubrā and a particular figure was not itself a guarantee of that figure's inclusion among the recognised disciples of Kubrā, much less of the classification of that figure's own spiritual descendants as 'Kubravī' Sufis.

That is, we know of disciples of Kubrā who are never named among his prominent successors in the standard accounts of his Sufi circle (e.g. Majd al-Dīn al-Muwaffaq al-Khāṣī, or here the two figures mentioned in the first narrative as Kubrā's envoys to Shaykh Ḍiyāʾ al-Dīn). We know of Sufis who had genuine initiatory links to Kubrā, and who are typically named among his prominent disciples, but who undoubtedly should not be regarded as founders of 'Kubravī' initiatory lineages. Among such figures are Saʿd al-Dīn Ḥammūyī (who seems to have stood somewhat apart from the rest of Kubrā's disciples, and to have been shaped as much by a hereditary association with Sufism, through his familial tradition centred on the community at Baḥrābād, as by his ties to Kubrā) and Najm al-Dīn Rāzī (whose ties to Kubrā are clear, but who also trained with many other shaykhs, and who cannot be regarded as continuator of a specifically Kubravī communal legacy), as well as, to some extent, Sayf al-Dīn Bākharzī (whose legacy, as transmitted primarily through his natural descendants, included initiatic bonds not only with Kubrā, but with other less prominent shaykhs as well, and whose only substantial communal legacy linked with his *silsila* transmission through Kubrā – the Indian Firdawsiyya – did not define itself as part of a 'Kubravī' tradition). At the same time, we know of Sufis customarily listed among Kubrā's disciples whose links to him, whether authentic or not, have left few traces even of an association with him, much less of any substantial legacy transmitted through him in terms of doctrine, practice, or communal organisation (e.g. Jamāl al-Dīn Gīlī – whose memory was retained in later summary accounts of the Kubravī tradition, such as Jāmī's – or the shaykhs of Shīrāz, mentioned in fourteenth-century sources, noted already by Meier – who were entirely ignored in later presentations of Kubrā's circle of disciples). And finally, we know of later Sufi lineages that were projected back onto Kubrā through assertions, found only in relatively late sources, that their founding figures (whether prominent or obscure) were Kubrā's disciples (e.g. the father of Jalāl al-Dīn Rūmī, and the spiritual ancestor of the Khalwatī Sufi communities active in Māwarāʾ al-Nahr, Khurāsān, and other regions during the fourteenth and fifteenth centuries).

Only in two cases can we link a Sufi community active in, say, the fifteenth century with a figure whose initiatory ties to Kubrā can be clearly established on the basis of thirteenth-century sources: one is the Central Asian community stemming from Bābā Kamāl Jandī (which seems to have disappeared by the end of the fifteenth century), and the other is the Kubravī order of Khurāsān and Central

Asia that emerged out of the *silsila* traced through Raḍī al-Dīn ʿAlī Lālā (which led to Simnānī, Sayyid ʿAlī Hamadānī, and the lineages stemming from ʿAbd Allāh Barzishābādī). And even in these cases, we should assume that the actual organisational continuity of the tradition, and even the actual pattern of initiatic ties of each link in the *silsila*, were considerably more complex than is suggested by the simple, lineal development implied in the sources that were engaged, in effect, in a retrospective definition and formulation of an authoritative (and organisationally significant) *silsila*. Those later depictions, we must remember, may have more to do with subsequent developments among the Sufi communities linked with each figure than with a simple effort to sort out the nature of each figure's connections with the others. Had there been an ongoing, independent Sufi community to cultivate the legacy of Shaykh Ḍiyā' al-Dīn al-Ḥātimī, the narratives involving his association with Kubrā might well have been adjusted in order to highlight claims of initiatory ties (in either direction!), or, alternatively, in order to emphasise the unambiguous superiority of one or the other master.

In the end, the narratives drawn from works such as the *Maqāmāt* of Shaykh Ḍiyā' al-Dīn may remind us that the construction of Sufi communities, and the development of some of them into 'orders' such as the Kubraviyya, were shaped not only by Sufi teaching and practice, and by innovations or refinements in the organisation and management of Sufi institutions, but also by the formulation, adaptation, transmission, and manipulation of hagiographical anecdotes, for didactic and celebratory, but also competitive and polemical, purposes.

## Notes

1. I have explored some of these potential uses of hagiographical narratives, in connection with one shaykh linked to the Kubravī tradition, in 'Sayyid ʿAlī Hamadānī and Kubravī Hagiographical Traditions', in *The Legacy of Mediaeval Persian Sufism*, ed. Leonard Lewisohn (London, 1992; repr. as *The Heritage of Sufism*, Oxford, 1999, vol. 2), pp. 121–158.

2. See his discussion of Kubrā's life and Sufi career in the introduction to his edition of one of Kubrā's works, *Die Fawā'iḥ al-Ǧamāl wa-Fawātiḥ al-Ǧalāl des Naǧm al-Dīn al-Kubrā: eine Darstellung mystischer Erfahrungen im Islam aus der Zeit um 1200 n Chr* (Wiesbaden 1957), pp. 8–64.

3. Meier was sceptical, for instance, of material he attributed to the 15th-century shaykh Ḥusayn al-Khwārazmī, whose *Jawāhir al-asrār* he knew only through excerpts preserved in a very late source, but certain elements of this work's presentation find confirmation in early sources unavailable to Meier; similarly, Meier did not have access to the 16th-century work of 'Ibn Karbalā'ī', the *Rawḍāt al-jinān wa-jannāt al-janān*, ed. Jaʿfar Sulṭān al-Qurrā'ī (Tehran, 1344–1349 Sh./1965–1970), which cites considerable material from a *Maqāmāt* of Najm al-Dīn Kubrā, confirming the existence of a now-lost hagiographical work that may well have been in circulation already by the early 15th century. Meier was likewise unfamiliar with the later body of hagiographical literature produced within Central Asian Kubravī circles.

4. For a discussion of one narrative motif focused on Kubrā, reflected in both 'internal'

and 'external' sources, see my 'Dog Saints and Dog Shrines in Kubravī Tradition: Notes on a Hagiographical Motif from Khwārazm', in Denise Aigle, ed., *Miracle et karāma: Hagiographies médiévales comparées* (Turnhout, 2000), vol. 2, pp. 459–497.

5. Badīʿ al-Zamān Furūzānfar, ed., *Manāqib-i Awḥad al-Dīn Ḥāmid b. Abi'l-Fakhr Kirmānī* (Tehran, 1347 Sh./1968); the narrative dealing with Kubrā is No. 52, pp. 202–207. The story recounts how Kirmānī, visiting Kubrā's *khānqāh* in Khwārazm incognito, learned that a famine in the region was responsible for the paltry food offered to him by the shaykh, and surreptitiously arranged for Sulṭān Muḥammad, the Khwārazmshāh, to send a huge amount of gold to the *khānqāh*; the ruler did so, sending along his infant son Jalāl al-Dīn as well (whose future greatness Kirmānī duly predicted), but just as Kubrā began to realise who his remarkable guest was, al-Kirmānī departed and could not be found, leaving the Khwārazmshāh, who came to Kubrā's *khānqāh* in search of the guest, likewise disappointed.

6. Both works were edited by Muḥammad Taqī Dānishpazhūh, in *Rūzbihān-nāma* (Tehran, 1347 Sh./1968), with the narratives in question appearing at pp. 24–25 and 199–200 (the two versions differ markedly from the story of the relationship between Lālā and Kubrā as told in traditions found in the writings of later members of the Sufi lineage traced through the two shaykhs; the earliest such account appears in works focused on 'Alā' al-Dawla Simnānī). They recount how Lālā's suspicion of Rūzbihān's maintenance of ritual purity led Rūzbihān to send Lālā on to Kubrā, and how yet another initial suspicion led Kubrā to consign Lālā to his disciple Majd al-Dīn Baghdādī for further refinement; his suspicion of Kubrā was evoked by seeing the latter playing chess with the 'handsome youth' Baghdādī, a narrative element reflected also in the *'Ushshāq-nāma* of the famous Sufi poet Fakhr al-Dīn 'Irāqī (d. 688/1289); see *The Song of Lovers ('Ushshāq-nāma) by 'Irāqī*, ed. and tr. A. J. Arberry (Oxford, 1939), text pp. 77–78, tr., pp. 46–47, and Saʿīd Nafīsī, ed., *Kulliyāt-i Shaykh Fakhr al-Dīn Ibrāhīm Hamadānī mutakhallaṣ bi-'Irāqī* (Tehran, 1335 Sh./1956), pp. 308–309; 'Irāqī's version of the story about Kubrā and Majd al-Dīn Baghdādī was also outlined in V. A. Drozdov, 'Chetyre legendy iz poèmy Fakhr al-Dina Iraki "Ushshak-name"', *Izvestiia Akademiia nauk Tadzhikskoi SSR, ser. Vostokovedenie, istoriia, filologiia*, 1, 1987, pp. 52–59). Julian Baldick, in 'The Authenticity of 'Irāqī's "'Ushshāq-Nāma"', *SIr*, 2 (1973), pp. 67–78, rejects this work's attribution to 'Irāqī, but his arguments are not altogether convincing, and in any case affect only the authorship of the work, not its antiquity.

7. See the translation of Bruce B. Lawrence, *Nizam al-Din Awliya, Morals for the Heart: Conversations of Shaykh Nizam al-Din Awliya recorded by Amir Hasan Sijzi* (New York, 1992), pp. 366–367. Additional hagiographical material on both Kubrā and Bākharzī is found in the 15th-century *Manāqib al-aṣfiyā*, produced in the Firdawsī Sufi community that traced its lineage to Bākharzī.

8. Amīr Khūrd, *Siyar al-awliyā'* (repr. of the Delhi lithograph of 1302/1885; Islāmābād, n.d.), pp. 528–529.

9. Meier, *Fawā'iḥ*, pp. 1–5.

10. I am grateful to Akbar 'Ali Khan Arshizada, the then officiating director of the Raza Library, for his exceptional kindness and hospitality in facilitating my work in Rampur.

11. Imtiyāz 'Alī 'Arshī, ed., *Fihrist-i makhṭūṭāt-i fārsī*; the section on '*Sulūk Fārsī*' is in vol. 1, pp. 85–223. The Rampur collection also includes several other manuscripts of interest for the Kubravī tradition, noted in the same section of the handlist, including:

- No. 752 (ff. 18a–27a, dated 845/1441–1442), described as a '*Risāla dar bayān-i ʿaql wa-ʿishq*' and ascribed to Najm al-Dīn Kubrā;
- No. 842, a copy of the *Chihil majlis* of Amīr Iqbāl Sīstānī, on the discourses of ʿAlāʾ al-Dawla Simnānī, and No. 844, *Rasāʾil al-nūr fī shamāʾil ahl al-surūr*, ascribed in the handlist to Simnānī, but in fact a compilation, by Simnānī, of the writings of his master Nūr al-Dīn Isfarayinī (Nos. 842 and 844 both belong to the same volume, which was copied in 989/1581, and which bears the designation '*Sulūk Fārsī* No. 637', according to an older numbering system; the newer handlist somewhat confusingly refers to the copy of the *Chihil majlis* as occupying ff. 149b–202a of MS *Sulūk* 842, and to the copy of the *Rasāʾil al-nūr* as occupying ff. 1–149a of MS *Sulūk* 844); versions of the *Chihil majlis* are now available in three published editions; on which see Jamal J. Elias, *The Throne Carrier of God: The Life and Thought of ʿAlāʾ al-Dawla as-Simnānī* (Albany, NY, 1995), pp. 176–178, the most complete listing of manuscript copies, and Hartwig Cordt, *Die Sitzungen des ʿAlāʾ al-dawla as-Simnānī* (Zürich, 1977), pp. 39–45, the best account of the work's development; neither author mentions the Rampur copy), while most of the works included in the *Rasāʾil al-nūr* have not yet been published; see the discussion of this collection, known from two other manuscripts, in Hermann Landolt, ed., *Correspondance spirituelle échangée entre Nuroddin Esfarayeni (ob. 717/1317) et son disciple ʿAlaoddawleh Semnani (ob. 736/1336)* (Tehran and Paris, 1972), pp. 22–28, and in Nûruddîn Abdurrahmân-i Isfarâyinî, *Le Révélateur des mystères (Kâshif al-Asrâr)*, ed. Hermann Landolt (Paris, 1986), pp. 9–16; in the latter work, pp. 11–12, Landolt discusses two redactions of the *Rasāʾil al-nūr*; unfortunately I was not in a position to confirm which redaction the Rampur copy represents;
- No. 886, an apparently unique copy (dated 1020/1611–1612), in 52 ff., of a treatise of Khwāja Abu'l-Wafā Khwārazmī, on whom see Hermann Landolt's article in *EIr*, 1, p. 394, and the comments in my 'Bābā Kamāl Jandī and the Kubravī Tradition among the Turks of Central Asia', *Der Islam*, 71 (1994), pp. 58–94, pp. 92–93;
- and numerous copies (Nos. 761, 773, copied in 951/1544–1545, 787, 855) of the works of Sayyid ʿAlī Hamadānī (see below).

12. These miscellaneous treatises include (with the number of their sequence in the manuscript indicated), (1) ff. 1b–31a, *Tabṣirat al-mubtadī wa-tadhkirat-i muntahī*, evidently the work by that title ascribed to Ṣadr al-Dīn Qūnawī; see *GAL*, vol. 1, p. 450; *GALS*, vol. 1, p. 808; (2) ff. 32b–42a, a *Risāla* ascribed to Aḥmad al-Ghazālī; (3) ff. 42b–52a and (4) ff. 52a–56b, two treatises ascribed to ʿAbd Allāh Anṣārī; (5) ff. 56b–62b, an unascribed '*Risālat al-anwār*' (this work bears the copy-date noted above); (12) ff. 105a–118a, an unascribed *Risāla* beginning with a citation of 'one of the pupils of ... Imām Muḥammad al-Ghazālī'; and (13) ff. 118a–121b, a *Risāla* ascribed to Sayyid Sharīf Jurjānī. Here too may be noted (24) ff. 243a–291a, a '*Risālat-i shuhūdiyya*' ascribed to Sharaf al-Dīn ʿAlī al-Yazdī; this work immediately follows the gap in folio numbering noted above.

13. (8) ff. 83b–86a, with explicit reference to the *silsila-yi khwājagān* and discussions of such notions as *wuqūf qalbī* and *khalwat dar anjuman*.

14. On the question of *rābiṭa*, see the recent discussion of Jürgen Paul in 'Doctrine and Organisation: The Khwājagān-Naqshbandīya in the First Generation after Bahāʾuddīn', *Anor*, 1 (1998), pp. 34–44, with further references.

15. This section of the manuscript ([6] ff. 63a–79b) is discussed in a forthcoming study; it's inclusion in the Rampur manuscript may owe as much to Khwāfī's connections with

shaykhs in Harāt, and elsewhere in Khurāsān, who were linked also to Kubravī lineages, as to any substantial cultivation of a hagiographical tradition within the Zaynī circles themselves.

16. On this figure and his works, see Muḥammad Riyāẓ, *Aḥwāl wa-āthār wa-ash'ār-i Mīr Sayyid 'Alī Hamadānī (bā shish risāla az vay)* (Islamabad, 1364 Sh./1985); J. K. Teufel, *Eine Lebensbeschreibung des Scheichs Alī-i Hamadānī (gestorben 1385): Die Xulāṣat ul-Manāqib des Maulānā Nūr ud-Dīn Ca'far-i Badaxšī* (Leiden, 1962); G. Böwering, "'Alī b. Šehāb al-Dīn b. Moḥammad Hamadānī', *EIr*, vol. 1, pp. 862–864; and my own 'Sayyid 'Alī Hamadānī and Kubravī Hagiographical Traditions'.

17. Works ascribed to Sayyid 'Alī Hamadānī:

(15) ff. 128a–138a, *Risāla-yi dhikriyya*; Teufel, pp. 54–55, No. 44; Riyāẓ, pp. 117–120, No. 6, and the text edition at pp. 527–545;

(16) ff. 138a–142a, *Makātīb-i Amīriyya*; Teufel, p. 51, No. 23; Riyāẓ, pp. 120–125, No. 7; cf. Muḥammad Riyāẓ Khān, ed., 'Matn-i maktūbāt-i Mīr Sayyid 'Alī Hamadānī', *Majalla-i dānishkada-i adabiyāt wa-'ulūm-i insānī*, 21 (1353 Sh./1974–75), pp. 33–66;

(17) ff. 142b–154a, *Risāla-yi futūwwatiyya*; Teufel, p. 55, No. 47; Riyāẓ, pp. 171–172, No. 40, and the longer discussion at pp. 243–377, including a text edition, pp. 341–366; cf. M. Molé, 'Kubrawiyat II: 'Alī b. Şihābaddīn-i Hamadānī'nin Risāla-i futuwwatīya'si', *Şarkiyat Mecmuası*, 4 (1961), pp. 33–72, and Muḥammad Riyāẓ Khān, ed., 'Futuwwat-nāma az Mīr Sayyid 'Alī Hamadānī', *Ma'ārif-i islāmī*, 10 (1348 Sh./1969), pp. 64–69; 11 (1349 Sh./1970), pp. 32–39;

(18) ff. 154a–160b, *Risāla-yi Bahrāmshāhiyya*; Teufel, p. 54, No. 42; Riyāẓ, pp. 128–129, No. 10; the Rampur handlist suggests that this work may instead be Hamadānī's *Risāla-yi wāridāt*, on which see Teufel, p. 58, No. 67, and Riyāẓ, pp. 131–132, No. 12;

(19) ff. 161a–165b, an untitled treatise ascribed to Hamadānī;

(20) ff. 166a–174b, *Risāla-yi awrādiyya*; Teufel, p. 54, No. 40, apparently different from Hamadānī's famous *Awrād-i fatḥiyya*; however, Riyāẓ does not list a separate work by this title, though he does mention among Hamadānī's Arabic works a *Risālat al-awrād*, pp. 190–191;

(21) ff. 175a–178b, *Dah qā'ida*; a translation of Najm al-Dīn Kubrā's *al-Uṣūl al-'ashara*; Teufel, p. 47, No. 5; Riyāẓ, pp. 132–136, No. 13; cf. M. Molé, ed., 'La version persane du Traité de dix principes de Najm al-Din Kobrā par 'Alī b. Shihâb al-Din Hamadânī', *Farhang-i Īrān Zamīn*, 6 (1958), pp. 38–66;

(22) ff. 179a–184b, *Risāla-yi 'aqabāt*; Teufel, p. 53, No. 37; Riyāẓ, pp. 143–146, No. 19; a note added at the end of this treatise, however, identifies it as a '*risāla-yi qudsiyya*' from among the compositions of 'Alā' al-Dawla Simnānī;

(28) ff. 332a–341b, *Risāla-yi 'aqliyya*; Teufel, p. 53, No. 38; Riyāẓ, pp. 125–127, No. 8;

(29) ff. 342a–347b, *Risāla-yi manāmiyya*; Teufel, p. 48, No. 7; Riyāẓ, pp. 137–138, No. 15;

(33) ff. 385a–391b, *Kitāb-i i'tiqādiyya*; Teufel, p. 56, No. 53; Riyāẓ, p. 141, No. 17; cf. M. Molé, ed., 'Professions de foi de deux Kubrawīs: 'Alī-i Hamadānī et Muḥammad Nūrbakhsh', *Bulletin d'études orientales de l'Institut français de Damas*, 17 (1961–1962), pp. 133–204.

18. The Rampur manuscript includes one work that may tentatively be ascribed to Rashīd al-Dīn Bīdwāzī ([14] ff. 122a–127b); it is identified in the library's handlist as a '*Risāla-yi Rashīd*', and in the text itself, 'Rashīd' is named only in a poem by the author (f. 125a). The work was inspired, the author writes, by an unnamed dervish's recitation of two *rubā'īs* of Sa'd al-Dīn Ḥammūyī in Mecca on 14 Rajab 867/4 April 1463; this date fits the lifetime

of Rashīd al-Dīn Bīdwāzī, but, pending a closer study of this figure's life and works, it is primarily the predominance of the works of other Kubravī shaykhs in the manuscript that suggests this treatise's attribution to Bīdwāzī.

19. On these figures, and the lineage from Hamadānī down to Ḥusayn Khwārazmī, see my 'The Eclipse of the Kubravīyah in Central Asia', *Iranian Studies*, 21 (1988), pp. 45–83.

20. (25) ff. 301b–309b (the author identifies himself as 'Ḥājjī Muḥammad').

21. (26) ff. 309b–311b; the handwriting here is different from that found in all other sections of the manuscript. Essentially the same text is preserved (somewhat more completely) in a manuscript (copied in the later 17th century) from Islamabad, described in Aḥmad Munzawī, ed., *Fihrist-i nuskhahā-yi khaṭṭī-yi Kitābkhāna-i Ganjbakhsh* (Islamabad, 1982), vol. 4, pp. 2082–2083, Title No. 2473, MS No. 5765, *majmūʿa* No. 5250, part 2, pp. 102–106.

22. (34) ff. 392a–407a, Simnānī's *Sirr bāl al-bāl li-dhawī'l-ḥāl* (published in Najīb Māyil Harawī, *Muṣannafāt-i fārsī-i ʿAlā' al-Dawla Simnānī* (Tehran, 1369 Sh./1990), pp. 127–151, and in W. M. Thackston, Jr., ed., *ʿAlā'uddawla Simnānī: Opera Minora* (Cambridge, MA, 1988), pp. 151–167; cf. Elias, *Throne Carrier*, p. 186.

23. (23) ff. 185a–186b: the text appears without mention of an author or title either in the beginning or in a colophon; the heading identifies it as a '*Risāla-yi Maqāmāt-i sālikān*' by Simnānī (the 'title' is given in the handlist as '*Risāla dar maqāmāt-i sālikān*'). No such title is registered in the fullest list of Simnānī's works compiled so far (that of Elias, *Throne Carrier*, pp. 165–212); Teufel lists a work entitled *Maqāmāt al-sālikīn* among the writings of Sayyid ʿAlī Hamadānī (*Lebensbeschreibung*, p. 51, No. 26), but Riyāẓ does not mention it (referring only to a '*Maʿāsh al-sālikīn*', pp. 175–176 and an Arabic '*Manāzil al-sālikīn*', pp. 188–189). The work in the Rampur manuscript begins by affirming that 'travellers on the *ṭarīqa* are of two divisions', namely the '*aṣḥāb-i bidāya*' and the '*arbāb-i nihāya*'; the 'beginners' are further subdivided into three classes (defined in terms of particular types of luminous appearance: first, the *aṣḥāb-i liwā'iḥ*, who perform austerities; second, the *aṣḥāb-i lawāmiʿ*; and third, the *aṣḥāb-i ṭawāliʿ*, who have slain the carnal soul (*nafs*) through austerities, but are still not wholly free of the filth of the carnal soul), while the '*arbāb-i nihāya*' too are said to belong to three types: first, the *aṣḥāb-i muḥāẓara* – who have purified the mirror of their being of the 'dirt' of the carnal soul; second, the *aṣḥāb-i mukāshafa* – who have purified the mirror of the heart; and third, the *aṣḥāb-i mushāhada* – who are said to be able to move about the unseen world at will, with the text citing Bisṭāmī, Junayd, and al-Ḥallāj on this condition.

24. The longer of these ([9] ff. 86a–94b) is ascribed to "Abd al-Raḥmān al-Khurāsānī al-Isfarāyinī' in the heading (and the beginning of the text itself refers to 'Nūr al-Millat wa'l-Dīn ʿAbd ar-Raḥmān'). The shorter treatise ([7] ff. 80a–83b) is ascribed to Isfarāyinī in the handlist, but contains no details confirming the identification internally; it discusses, among other matters, the need for the Sufi master to hide his status from the common people, a point underscored by a passage attributed by the author to his own shaykh (i.e. presumably Aḥmad Gūrpānī, assuming the work is Isfarāyinī's): 'People spend their common coin (*fulūs*) in the bazaar. You too should spend the same kind of common coin, for if someone brings out pure gold, people will say, "Where did he get that?" or "He stole it from the sultan's treasury" or "He has come upon a treasure", and they will harass him, or perhaps even kill him. Or they may not be like the moneylenders, and may not know real gold, and so they will say, "This is not real gold", or "This fellow is a counterfeiter"' ('this', the author adds, 'was a lesson to me about hiding my own status as a *pīr*, and a metaphor for

the Path'). The only name mentioned in this shorter text is that of a certain 'brother', Ḥājjī Quṭb al-Dīn, whose need to persevere in discipline, in order to obtain spiritual 'unveilings', is briefly discussed (f. 83a). This figure is not immediately recognisable among the disciples of Isfarāyinī and/or Simnānī. The name might refer to Quṭb al-Dīn Yaḥyā Jāmī Nīshāpūrī, who according to Jāmī associated with Simnānī (among other shaykhs of the early 14th century) and was known for having performed the *ḥajj* seven times; he died in 740/1339 and was buried in Harāt; see Nūr al-Dīn 'Abd al-Raḥmān Jāmī, *Nafaḥāt al-uns*, ed. Mahdī Tawḥīdīpūr (Tehran, 1336 Sh./1957), pp. 577–578; Maḥmūd 'Ābidī, ed. (Tehran, 1370 Sh./1991), pp. 575–576. Another possibility is the Quṭb al-Dīn 'Abd Allāh b. Muḥammad b. Ayman al-Iṣfahīdī who wrote a Sufi treatise entitled *al-Risāla-yi al-makkiyya fī khalwat al-ṣūfiyya*; see the description of the only known manuscript, in Maulavi Abdul Muqtadir, ed., *Catalogue of the Arabic and Persian Manuscripts in the Oriental Public Library at Bankipore*, vol. 13 (Calcutta, 1928), pp. 175–185, No. 959, and the notice in Ḥājjī Khalīfa's *Kashf aẓ ẓunūn*, ed. G. Flügel, *Lexicon Bibliographicum et encyclopaedicum* (London, 1835–1858), vol. 3, p. 445, No. 6368; this figure too was a disciple not of Isfarāyinī directly, but of the latter's disciple 'Burhān al-Dīn al-Samarqandī' – who is to be identified, undoubtedly, with Burhān al-Dīn Sāgharjī of Samarqand, a figure identified in later sources as a disciple of al-Isfarāyinī.

25. On the manuscripts containing Isfarāyinī's works, see Landolt, ed., *Correspondance spirituelle*, pp. 22–28, and *Révélateur*, pp. 9–16.

26. (10) ff. 95a–102a, found in Landolt, ed., *Correspondance spirituel*, pp. 15–28 (text), No. V.

27. The introduction (MS, f. 95a) recounts the circumstances that led to Isfarāyinī's response to a letter by Simnānī: 'Shaykh Rukn al-Dīn 'Alā' al-Dawla had not yet entered the service of Shaykh Nūr al-Dīn 'Abd al-Raḥmān, who was his shaykh, externally, but had received both instruction in the *dhikr* and the *jāma* from Shaykh Sharaf al-Dīn Ḥasan Simnānī, whom the aforementioned Shaykh [Isfarāyinī] had sent to Simnān through an inspiration (*ilhām*), writing on the cover of a book that "When you find someone among the *aṣḥāb-i wuzarā* to whom a divine attraction (*jadhba*) has come and who is avoiding the company of people, serve him, instruct him in the *dhikr*, and invest him with the *jāma*." And when [Simnānī] had received instruction in the *dhikr* from him, he engaged in *khalwa* and *'uzla* with a group of sincere dervishes who were of like mind, by the order of Shaykh Nūr al-Dīn 'Abd al-Raḥmān. And after Arghūn had made [Simnānī] turn back from the road to Baghdād, the Shaykh [Isfarāyinī] had written him a letter [instructing Simnānī] to "Engage in the *awrād* that I have written, and consider that I am in your presence". Then Shaykh Rukn al-Dīn 'Alā' al-Dawla wrote an appeal to express his apologies, and explained the experience that is described in this treatise; and this is the response [he received]. The first question he had posed was about the meaning of this *ḥadīth*...' (at this point the text as published by Landolt begins). The account here reflects the period soon after Simnānī's renunciation of service to the Ilkhānid ruler Arghūn, and appears to be drawn from the Persian translation of Simnānī's *al-'Urwa li-ahl al-khalwa wa'l-jalwa*, ed. Najīb Māyil Harawī (Tehran, 1362 Sh./1983), p. 318, which alone among accounts of Simnānī's early Sufi training names his 'messenger' from Isfarāyinī 'Akhī Sharaf al-Dīn Ḥasan Simnānī'; in the Arabic version of the work, and in other writings by Simnānī (see *Opera minora*, ed. Thackston, pp. 1, 118, 161), he is called Akhī Sharaf al-Dīn Sa'd Allāh b. Ḥanawayh Simnānī (cf. Elias, *Throne Carrier*, pp. 22–29).

28. The texts coincide very closely down to Landolt, *Correspondance*, p. 15, line 8 = Rampur 764, f. 95b, line 1, and then resume at Landolt, p. 15, line 12 = Rampur, f. 96a, line 6 (thus p. 15, lines 8–12 in the edited text replace nearly all of f. 95b and the first six lines of f. 96a in the Rampur manuscript; Landolt made note of the apparently defective text at this point). The passage missing from Landolt's edition includes a reference (at the bottom of f. 95b) to yet another apparent member of Isfarāyinī's circle of disciples, called 'Ḥājjī Shams al-Dīn Muḥammad b. Abī Bakr b. Jaʿfar al-Nāyinī', and identified as a '*farzand-i ṭarīqa*'. On Nāyin, in central Iran northwest of Yazd, southwest of Naṭanz, and east of Iṣfahān, see Dorothea Krawulsky, *Īrān - Das Reich der Īlḫāne: Eine topographisch-historische Studie* (Wiesbaden, 1978), p. 288; he is surely to be identified with the 'Muḥammad Nāyinī' mentioned (with some irritation) in a treatise by Simnānī, the brief *Hadiyyat al-mustarshidīn wa-waṣiyyat al-murshidīn*, which he completed in 705/1306 (Thackston, ed., *Opera minora*, pp. 170–171: the context is a passage in which Simnānī discourages *murīd*s who are having trouble with their own shaykh, who is also Simnānī's disciple, from seeking better treatment from Simnānī himself; Simnānī acknowledges that he would effectively dismiss Muḥammad Nāyinī from his mind so long as Nāyinī was not on good terms with Simnānī's 'son in the *ṭarīqa*', a certain 'Akhī Muḥammad Pahlavān').

29. As discussed below, Lālā is sometimes shown as a disciple of Majd al-Dīn Baghdādī, another of Kubrā's disciples, and is sometimes assigned directly to Kubrā, in later presentations of the Kubravī *silsila*, but clearly received licensure from both Kubrā and Baghdādī.

30. After an introduction stressing the need for the spiritual master – the *murīd* without a *pīr* is compared to a motherless child – this treatise affirms two foundations of the Sufi path, the first being austerities (*riyāẓat-i nafs*) and the second being retirement and seclusion (*khalwa wa-ʿuzla*); the latter foundation, further, depends on eight conditions: the first six are phrased in terms of persistence (*dawām*) in seclusion (*khalwa*), ablution (*wuẓu'*), fasting (*rūza*), silence (*sukūt*), *dhikr*, and repelling idle thoughts (*nafī-i khawāṭir*); the seventh is 'the fixation of the heart on the master' (*rabṭ-i qalb bi-shaykh*); and the eighth is 'abandoning resistance to God' (*tark al-iʿtirāẓ ʿalā'llāh taʿālā*). These conditions are essentially the same as those affirmed in Kubrā's *Fawā'iḥ*, ed. Meier, text, pp. 2–3 (though in a slightly different order: as the conditions of 'the Path of Junayd' are mentioned there persistence in ablution, fasting, silence, seclusion, the *dhikr* (with the formula '*lā ilāha illā'llāh*'), and then *rabṭ al-qalb bi'l-shaykh*, *dawām nafī'l-khawāṭir*, and *dawām tark al-iʿtirāẓ ʿalā'llāh*).

31. A poem ascribed to Lālā is cited in one of Simnānī's works (*Opera minora*, ed. Thackston, p. 111; *Muṣannafāt-i fārsī*, ed. Māyil Harawī, p. 1). In one of his works published by Landolt, Isfarāyinī cites a saying of Lālā found 'in his *kalimāt*' (*Révélateur*, text, pp. 125–126) – a phrase not clearly indicating a written source – in which the centrality of *dhikr* is stressed, but there is no close textual correspondence with the brief treatise found in the Rampur manuscript.

32. If the *nisba* implies a claim of descent from the famous paragon of proverbial generosity, Ḥātim al-Ṭā'ī, nothing is made of such descent in the text itself; see C. van Arendonk, 'Ḥātim al-Ṭā'ī', *EI2*, vol. 3, pp. 274–275. Ḥātim was the subject of popular romances in several languages, and of Persian literary treatment in Ḥusayn Wāʿiẓ Kāshifī's *Risāla-yi Ḥātimiyya*, from 891/1485, which was published in Ch. Schefer, *Chrestomathie persane* (Paris, 1883), vol. 1, pp. 174–203, text, pp. 190–204, see notes; Kāshifī, a native of Sabzawār, not far from the centre of activity of Shaykh Ḍiyā' al-Dīn, gives no hint of awareness of a local family of

'Ḥātimī' shaykhs. In his *Kitāb al-ansāb* from the 12th century, Sam'ānī identifies 'al-Ḥātimī' simply as an ancestral *nisba*, and mentions several scholars known by it from the 10th to early 12th centuries; one, who died in 393/1003, was a native of Ṭūs, while another (d. 513/1119) was a native of Nasaf in Māwarā' al-Nahr; 'Abd al-Karīm b. Muḥammad al-Sam'ānī, *Kitāb al-ansāb*, ed. 'Abd al-Raḥmān b. Yaḥyā (Hyderabad, 1384/1964), vol. 4, pp. 1–3.

33. Given Ḍiyā' al-Dīn's apparent connection with the Salghūrid rulers based in Fārs (see below), it might be appealing to identify him with the poet 'Ḍiyā' al-Dīn Fārsī', part of whose *qaṣīda* written on the occasion of 'Alā' al-Dīn Muḥammad Khwārazmshāh's victory over the Qarākhiṭāy in 607/1210 is recorded in Juwaynī's *Tārīkh-i Jahān-gushā*; Juwaynī, *The History of the World-Conqueror*, tr. J. A. Boyle (Cambridge, MA, 1958; repr. Seattle, 1997), p. 346; see also 'Alī Akbar Dihkhudā, ed., *Lughāt-nāma* (Tehran, 1337–1352 Sh./1959–1974), vols. 18–19, s.v. 'Ḍiyā' ad-Dīn Khujandī Fārsī'. A manuscript of this poet's *Dīwān*, copied in 981/1573, was noted by D. S. Robertson, 'A Forgotten Persian Poet of the Thirteenth Century', *JRAS* (1951), p. 103, and is preserved at the library of the School of Oriental and African Studies in London; Robertson deferred to the comments of Vladimir Minorsky and Reuben Levy, to whom he had shown the manuscript, regarding the poet's identity and period (judged primarily, it would seem, on the basis of references in the poetry itself), and writes that the poet was a native of Fārs who later established himself in Khujand, that dates mentioned in the text range from 600/1204 to 638/1240, and that one poem includes an allusion to the Mongol invasion of Māwarā' al-Nahr; on this manuscript, see also Robertson's note accompanying the article of Mas'ūd Ḥasan, 'Diyā-yi Fārsī', *JRAS* (1952), pp. 105–107, and the fuller discussion in K. A. Shidfar, 'O divane Ziia-i-Farsi', *Narody Azii i Afriki* (1965), pp. 113–117, with further details on the poet's dates and sphere of activity. Unfortunately, despite Shaykh Ḍiyā' al-Dīn al-Ḥātimī's apparent connections with the Khwārazmshāhs, as well as with the Salghūrids, and aside from his chronological suitability for identification with Ḍiyā' al-Dīn Fārsī, we have no evidence with which to link Shaykh Ḍiyā' al-Dīn personally with Fārs, or with Khujand, or indeed with any region beyond the region of western Khurāsān where the brief text in the Rampur manuscript situates him; he emerges from this text, rather, as a local shaykh of a small Sufi community based in a minor town of Khurāsān, and his possible identification with Ḍiyā' al-Dīn Fārsī remains purely speculative.

34. The reading of this name, and the location of the town to which it refers, remain problematical; its single occurrence in the Rampur manuscript could be read either 'Khudāshāh' or 'Khurāshāh'. The place most likely intended in the *Maqāmāt* of Shaykh Ḍiyā' al-Dīn is the town known as Khudāshāh in the province of Juwayn (the site is shown on Map 7 in Dorothea Krawulsky, *Ḫorāsān zur Timuridenzeit nach dem Tārīḫ-e Ḥāfeẓ-e Abrū (verf. 817–823 h.)*, Übersetzung und Ortsnamenkommentar (Wiesbaden, 1984), about 55 km southwest of Isfarāyin, and approximately 23 km west-northwest of Baḥrābād); its name often appears as 'Khurāshāh' or even 'Khūrāshāh' in sources ranging from the 13th to 16th centuries, and the latter forms of the name seem to be reflected in the name of another town, near 'Khudāshāh', both of which evidently still exist. In her earlier study of the historical geography of Iran, published in 1978, Krawulsky opted for the reading 'Khudāshāh' and discussed only one town referred to by the various forms of this name (see Krawulsky, *Īrān*, pp. 88, 93, and Map 4); she noted that the geographical work of Ḥāfiẓ-i Abrū, from the early 15th century, gives 'Khudāshāh', as does a manuscript variant noted in the edition of Ḥamd Allāh Mustawfī's *Nuzhat al-qulūb* from the early 14th century (for which the text edition adopts the reading

'Khūrāshāh'), and cited also a *nisba* form, 'Khudāshāhī', from the early 15th-century history of Muʿīn al-Dīn Naṭanzī. Krawulsky also referred there to the important study of Jean Aubin, 'Réseau pastoral et réseau caravanier: Les grand'routes du Khurassan a l'époque mongole', *Le Monde iranien et l'Islam: Sociétés et cultures*, 1 (1971), pp. 124 and 129, n. 105); Aubin had adopted the spelling 'Khurāshāh', noting this spelling in the 15th-century *Mujmal-i Faṣīḥī* as well; Faṣīḥ Khwāfī, *Mujmal-i Faṣīḥī*, ed. Maḥmūd Farrukh (Mashhad, 1341 Sh./1962), vol. 3, pp. 240, 250, in both cases clearly referring to the town in Juwayn, and in the second instance noting a manuscript variant 'Khudāshād'. In her later study (1984), based on Ḥāfiẓ-i Abrū, however, Krawulsky adopted the reading 'Khurāshāh', without comment, not only for the town in Juwayn (pp. 65, 244–245), but for another town, in the province of Jūrbad, some 55 km northwest of the 'Khurāshāh' in Juwayn (pp. 58, 214), implying that the former is Ḥāfiẓ-i Abrū's reading for the modern village of Khudāshāh, and that the latter is today 'Khurāshāh'; Krawulsky does not mention it in either work, but the same distinction was asserted already in G. Le Strange, *The Lands of the Eastern Caliphate: Mesopotamia, Persia, and Central Asia from the Moslem conquest to the time of Timur* (London, 1905; repr. New York, 1966), p. 392 (Le Strange insisted, see n. 1, that 'Khudāshāh' and 'Khurāshāh' are the names of separate towns, at roughly equal distances from the town of Āzādvār, see below, n. 60, the former east of it and the latter north of it). Whatever their contemporary status (to judge from Krawulsky's figures, the modern Khurāshāh is slightly larger than Khudāshāh), it seems clear from 15th-century sources, at least, that the historically significant town was Khudāshāh in Juwayn; the variant spellings, however, make it difficult to be certain which town was intended in the *Maqāmāt* of Shaykh Ḍiyāʾ al-Dīn – if, indeed, the town today called Khurāshāh was known at all in the 13th or 15th centuries, since it is clear that all the variant spellings were used for the town in Juwayn. In addition to the *Mujmal-i Faṣīḥī* and Ḥāfiẓ-i Abrū's geographical work, for instance, the recent edition of Ḥāfiẓ-i Abrū's *Zubdat al-tawārīkh* gives the forms 'Khūrāshāh' and 'Khudāshāh', clearly referring to the same town; Ḥāfiẓ-i Abrū, *Zubdat al-tawārīkh*, ed. Sayyid Kamāl Ḥājj Sayyid Jawādī (Tehran, 1372 Sh./1993), vol. 2, p. 718, an itinerary passing from Baḥrābād to 'Khūrāshāh' and then to Jājarm, p. 797, specified as 'Khudāshāh in Gūyān', i.e. in Juwayn; Sharaf al-Dīn 'Alī Yazdī mentioned the death of Timur's uncle, Ḥājjī Barlās, at 'Khūrāshah' (*sic*), which he identified as 'a village in the district of Juwayn in the province of Sabzavār', Shäräfuddin Äli Yäzdiy, *Zäfärnamä*, facs. ed. A. Urunbaev (Tashkent, 1972), f. 99b; Le Strange noted Yazdī's reference to the town. Evidently the town in Juwayn is also meant in Khwānd Amīr's discussion of the events of 920/1514 in Khurāsān; 'Khūrāshār' in the printed edition, *Ḥabīb al-siyar*, ed. Jalāl al-Dīn Humāʾī (3rd ed., Tehran, 1362 Sh./1983), vol. 4, p. 395.

35. In view of the nature of these letters it seems unlikely that any of them would have been included in the epistolary collections of the late 12th and early 13th centuries; on these, see Heribert Horst, *Die Staatsverwaltung der Grosselǧūqen und Ḫōrazmšāhs (1038–1231)* (Wiesbaden, 1964), pp. 10–12, and Jürgen Paul, '*Inshāʾ* Collections as a Source on Iranian History', *Proceedings of the Second European Conference of Iranian Studies, Bamberg, 1991*, ed. Bert G. Fragner, Christa Fragner, *et al.* (Rome, 1995), pp. 535–550); most of these collections, moreover, are too early to reflect the activity of Shaykh Ḍiyāʾ al-Dīn, but I have been unable to consult the collection prepared, evidently, for Ghiyāth al-Dīn Pīr-shāh (see below) described by Horst (*Die Staatsverwaltung*, p. 12). I have also been unable to check whether some of these letters might have made their way into the large 15th-century epistolary

collection compiled by a descendant of Shaykh Aḥmad-i Jām, the *Farā'id-i Ghiyāthī*; none appear in the sections published to date (in two volumes), and Shaykh Ḍiyā' al-Dīn is not mentioned among the authors of letters included near the beginning of the work; see Jalāl al-Dīn Yūsuf-i Ahl, *Farā'id-i Ghiyāthī* (ed. Ḥishmat Mu'ayyad, Tehran, 1336 Sh./1957), vol. 1, pp. 10–19).

36. When the text of the letter alludes to the directive, conveyed by Shaykh Ḍiyā' al-Dīn, that had been disobeyed by the two hostile parties, it refers to it as the 'obligatory command' of 'my lord' (*mawlawī*), with the latter term followed by the blessing, 'May God multiply his glory' (*ḍā'afa'llāh jalālahu*). Given the time and place in which Shaykh Ḍiyā' al-Dīn lived, and the region (Quhistān) named as the domain of Ṣalāḥ al-Dīn Ṭughrīl, both the latter and '*ṣāḥib* Kamāl al-Dīn Mas'ūd' would most likely have recognised the suzerainty of the Khwārazmshāhs. The text of the letter itself, incidentally, does not mention Ṣalāḥ al-Dīn by name, though it does once refer to '*ṣāḥib* Kamāl al-Dīn'; the title '*Amīr-i kabīr*' assigned to Ṣalāḥ al-Dīn in the heading, however, suggests that he was a relatively high-ranking military official whose role in Quhistān might well have been only temporary. Unfortunately, neither of our chief 'local' sources on this era offers a suitable candidate for identification with either of the two rivals. Juwaynī mentions a Ṣalāḥ al-Dīn al-Nasā'ī among the officials of Jalāl al-Dīn, the son of the Khwārazmshāh Muḥammad, and identifies him as governor of Ghazna in 618/1221 (Juwaynī, *History*, p. 461); Nasawī calls the same figure 'Ṣalāḥ al-Dīn Muḥammad Nasā'ī' see Shihāb al-Dīn Muḥammad al-Nasawī, *Sīrat al-sulṭān Jalāl al-Dīn Minkbrati (Zhizneopisanie Sultana Dzhalal ad-Dina Mankburny)*, ed. and tr. Z. M. Buniiatov (Moscow, 1996), p. 118, an appellation that does not preclude his having borne the name 'Ṭughrīl' as well, but there is no further basis for identifying him with the Ṣalāḥ al-Dīn who figures in this letter.

37. The letter begins by noting that a command – evidently, to make peace – had been duly conveyed to both men, and that they had each received it humbly and had accepted it; 'but they persist in the same old errors', and remain enemies with one another, Shaykh Ḍiyā' al-Dīn complains, affirming that both are equally guilty for the continuation of hostility (he compares their mutual recriminations to the Qur'anic portrayal, see 2:113, of the Jews and Christians declaring the positions of their rivals baseless, with each party using the same language). He singles out '*ṣāḥib* Kamāl al-Dīn', however, as particularly deceitful and ignoble (among his offences was to send a certain 'Akhī Ibrāhīm' to Ḍiyā' al-Dīn, to learn, ahead of his rival, whether the peacemaker would stay or depart). The heading simply affirms that the shaykh's effort to make peace 'did not succeed'.

38. The reason for the unnamed ruler's ruin, according to the letter, is that 'he witnessed the injustice of the oppressor upon the oppressed, and despite his power and ability to stop that oppression, he consented to it'; consequently, 'his situation was altered, and at once his rule came to an end'. The letter further enjoins the addressee to refrain from oppression, not to consent to oppression, and not to be left unaware of any act of oppression by his lieutenants (*gumāshtagān*), 'for if he is aware of it and consents to it, he is a partner to the oppressor in that affair'.

39. The letter affirms that the unnamed fallen ruler had governed the country so long as he followed the path of justice and rectitude, but that when he 'turned from the path of justice' (*rāstī*), the name 'oppressor' had adhered to him as well, and the kingdom had been taken from him and 'transferred' to another, in accordance with the saying that dominion

remains with unbelief, but not with injustice. The latter detail, of course, implies that the unnamed ruler who assumed power after the oppressor's fall was not a Muslim, and this in turn suggests that the letter alludes to the collapse of the Khwārazmshāh's power and the establishment of Mongol rule.

40. This figure's *nisba* is twice clearly written in the form 't.š.tī', but I have been unable to identify its referent (it may mask the name of 'Sast', a village near Isfarāyin, see Krawulsky, *Īrān*, p. 79, or an adaptation of '*dasht*', a common toponymic element, or perhaps even the *nisba* 'Tustarī' or 'Shustarī'/ 'Shushtarī').

41. Juwaynī, *History*, tr. Boyle, p. 170 (and see Boyle's introduction, p. xxviii, on Shams al-Dīn's death, apparently in 626/1229); Nasawī, *Sīrat*, tr. Buniiatov, pp. 220, 236–237; and see also the early 14th-century work of Nāṣir al-Dīn Munshī Kirmānī on the lives of noted viziers: *Nasāʾim al-asḥār min laṭāʾim al-akhbār dar tārīkh-i wuzarā*, ed. Mīr Jalāl al-Dīn Ḥusaynī Urmawī 'Muḥaddith' (Tehran, 1338 Sh./1959), p. 101. The epithet ascribed to this Shams al-Dīn by both Nasawī and Kirmānī – *mūy-i dirāz* ('long-haired') – might suggest a reputation for wisdom and aphoristic counsel.

42. The letter counsels Ghiyāth al-Dīn to preserve his realm from oppression, for 'every king and sulṭān who became ruler over Khurāsān and established the foundations for the practices of disobedience and corruption and oppression and wickedness' soon collapsed.

43. On these figures, see C. E. Bosworth, 'Ghūrids', *EI2*, vol. 2, pp. 1099–1104, and *The New Islamic Dynasties* (New York, 1996), pp. 298–299.

44. As we know from the histories of Nasawī and Juwaynī, Ghiyāth al-Dīn Pīr-shāh established himself in the region of Kirmān in the aftermath of the first Mongol attack, and was then briefly active in Fārs and Khūzistān before moving north to Rayy; he subsequently spent considerable time at the Ismaili stronghold of Alamūt (not far west of Shaykh Ḍiyāʾ al-Dīn's centre of activity), and then returned to Kirmān, where he was killed (around 625/1227–1228) by his former *atabek*, the Qarākhiṭāy officer in the Khwārazmshāh's service, Barāq Ḥājib, who was then consolidating his rule in Kirmān (see Nasawī, *Sīrat*, tr. Buniiatov, pp. 65, 112–117, 127, 134–139, 145–147, 180–185; the date of Ghiyāth al-Dīn's death is uncertain; see the editor's discussion, p. 347, notes 8–9; cf. Juwaynī, *History*, tr. Boyle, pp. 417–420, 436–437, 468–474, 476–479). The use of '*farzand*' in the letter to address 'Sulṭān Ghiyāth al-Dīn' befits the relative youth of Ghiyāth al-Dīn Pīr-shāh, who was five years younger than Jalāl al-Dīn.

45. The letter says that Sulṭān Ghiyāth al-Dīn's father 'constantly listened to the words of the dervishes with the ear of submission and obedience, and regarded their sayings as his guide'; it urges the son as well to pay heed to the counsel of dervishes and to put an end to oppression, so that, just as rulership came to him from his late father, so he too will pass it on to his son.

46. He is perhaps identifiable with the 'Ẓahīr al-Dīn Masʿūd b. al-Munawar al-Shāshī' who served as provincial vizier of Nasā under 'Alāʾ al-Dīn Muḥammad (Nasawī, *Sīrat*, tr. Buniiatov, p. 62); the title '*malik*' ('viceroy', in this context) was indeed often borne by provincial governors (see Horst, *Die Staatsverwaltung*, pp. 24, 44, 110–113; the title may have indicated hereditary status in a local ruling dynasty, beyond a specific function in the Khwārazmshāh's service), but despite the rough correlation of place and time, the identification remains purely speculative. Two figures called 'Malik Ẓahīr al-Dīn' are mentioned in Jūzjānī's *Ṭabaqāt-i Nāṣirī* among the viceroys of the Ghūrid ruler Muʿizz al-Dīn (Shihāb al-Dīn) Muḥammad

(d. 602/1206), but without a clear indication of where they served; *Ṭabaḳāt-i Nāṣirī*, tr. H. G. Raverty (Calcutta, 1881; repr. New Delhi, 1970), vol. 1, p. 490. Either one might be the figure mentioned in Ḍiyā' al-Dīn's letter, which we would then have to assume was addressed to one of the Ghūrid rulers known as Ghiyāth al-Dīn, but here too the evidence is too thin for a clear identification.

47. The latter figure's *nisba* is presumably an error for 'Tiflīsī', but may also reflect a conflation with a *nisba* of another town such as 'Tafrish' (Krawulsky, *Īrān*, p. 317, southwest of Tehran) or 'Turshīsh' (the latter a variant of 'Turshīz' in Quhistān, south of Nīshāpūr; see Krawulsky, *Īrān*, pp. 132–133). A native of Tiflīs is mentioned in the life of Awḥad al-Dīn Kirmānī (*Manāqib*, ed. Furūzānfar, pp. 132–136) as a disciple of Kirmānī who once met Sa'd al-Dīn Ḥammūyī in Āmul, in Māzāndarān; this 'Tiflīsī' is assigned the *laqab* 'Shams al-Dīn', however.

48. On these figures, see C. E. Bosworth, 'Salghūrids', *EI2*, vol. 8, pp. 978–979, and Bosworth's *New Islamic Dynasties*, p. 207; cf. T. W. Haig and C. E. Bosworth, 'Sa'd (I) b. Zangī', *EI2*, vol. 8, p. 701. The *laqab* 'Muẓaffar al-Dīn' was assigned to several Salghūrid rulers, including Sa'd b. Zangī himself, and it is possible that the addressee's name has been transmitted incorrectly; on the other hand, it is quite possible that Muẓaffar al-Dīn Abū Bakr b. Sa'd bore also the Turkic name 'Atsïz', even if we assume that 'Abū Bakr' is used in this case as an *ism* rather than as a *kunya*. Nasawī refers to Abū Bakr b. Sa'd, who received the title Qutlugh Khān, as 'Nuṣrat al-Dīn' (Nasawī, *Sīrat*, tr. Buniiatov, pp. 58–59), but Juwaynī calls him 'Muẓaffar al-Dīn Abū Bakr' (*History*, tr. Boyle, p. 419); Juwaynī mentions also three other sons of Sa'd b. Zangī – Zangī, Salghūr-shāh, and Tahamtan (pp. 234, 365–366, 418) – but not an 'Atsïz'. A daughter of Sa'd b. Zangī was given in marriage to the Khwārazmshāh's son Jalāl al-Dīn; see J. A. Boyle, 'Djalāl al-Dīn Khwārazm-shāh', *EI2*, vol. 2, pp. 392–393, as well as the biographies of Sa'd b. Zangī and of his son Abū Bakr in Jūzjānī, *Tabaḳāt-i Nāṣirī*, tr. Raverty, I, pp. 176–180, in Aḥmad b. Zarkūb Shīrāzī's *Shīrāz-nāma*, from the first half of the 14th century, ed. Bahman Karīmī (Tehran, 1350 Sh./1971), pp. 52–53, 55–56, and in Junayd Shīrāzī's *Shadd al-izār fī ḥaṭṭ al-awzār 'an zuwwār al-mazār*, from the later 14th century, ed. Muḥammad Qazwīnī and 'Abbās Iqbāl (Tehran, 1328 Sh./1949), pp. 215–219.

49. These figures too remain unidentified. The third name mentioned here recalls that of Shams al-Dīn Mas'ūd Harawī, a vizier of the Khwārazmshāh Tikish mentioned by Juwaynī (*History*, tr. Boyle, p. 162), but this figure died considerably earlier than most of those mentioned in Shaykh Ḍiyā' al-Dīn's letters; cf. Z. M. Buniiatov, *Gosudarstvo Khorezmshakhov-Anushteginidov, 1097–1231* (Moscow, 1986), pp. 94–95; according to Ibn al-Athīr, he died in 596/1200, and his lifetime would thus have briefly overlapped the reign of Sa'd b. Zangī. The same figure is called 'Ṣadr al-Dīn Mas'ūd b. 'Alī al-Harawī' in Nāṣir al-Dīn Munshī Kirmānī's work from the early 14th century (*Nasā'im al-asḥār*, pp. 94–95). Shams al-Dīn Mas'ūd is mentioned also, as an antagonist of Bahā' al-Dīn Muḥammad b. al-Mu'ayyad al-Baghdādī, the author of an epistolary collection, *al-Tawassul ilā'l-tarassul*, and brother of the Sufi Majd al-Dīn Baghdādī, in 'Awfī's *Lubāb al-albāb*, ed. E. G. Browne (London, 1903–1906), vol. 1, p. 139.

50. The names might reflect those of Shihāb al-Dīn Mas'ūd and his father Niẓām al-Mulk Muḥammad b. Ṣāliḥ: the father had been vizier under 'Alā' al-Dīn Muḥammad, and the son Mas'ūd was appointed *ustādh al-dār* under Jalāl al-Dīn, in 624/1227; see Nasawī, *Sīrat*, tr. Buniiatov, p. 221; cf. Buniiatov, *Gosudarstvo*, p. 99, and on the father, Kirmānī, *Nasā'im*,

pp. 96–97, but we have no indication that the father also bore the *laqab* "Amīd al-Dīn' (in addition to the 'official' *laqab* 'Niẓām al-Mulk'), and it is not clear how their lives and careers might have served the admonitory purpose intended in the letter. Alternatively, in view of Shaykh Ḍiyā' al-Dīn's ties with the Salghūrids, the 'late ʿAmīd al-Dīn' mentioned here might more likely be identified with the vizier of the Atābak Saʿd b. Zangī, ʿAmīd al-Dīn Abū Naṣr Asʿad b. Naṣr Abzarī, who was imprisoned, together with his son, by Abū Bakr b. Saʿd soon after the latter's accession, upon his father's death, late in 623/1226; a few months later, in the spring of 624/1227, ʿAmīd al-Dīn was executed, and his son, though released, was ruined (see the accounts of this ʿAmīd al-Dīn in the 14th-century *Shīrāz-nāma*, ed. Karīmī, pp. 54–57, including the detail that ʿAmīd al-Dīn was sent by Saʿd b. Zangī as an envoy to the Khwārazmshāh, and met Fakhr al-Dīn Rāzī during his mission, and in Junayd Shīrāzī's *Shadd al-izār*, ed. Qazwīnī and Iqbāl, pp. 215–216, in the account of Saʿd b. Zangī, especially the editors' discussion at pp. 215–216, n. 2, and Qazwīnī's discussion of ʿAmīd al-Dīn's life, pp. 517–527, citing additional sources; cf. A. E. Khairallah, 'Abzarī', *EIr*, vol. 1, pp. 411–412). While we are not told precisely the reasons for his execution, the case of this ʿAmīd al-Dīn seems to fit the situation reflected in Shaykh Ḍiyā' al-Dīn's letter, which alludes to the father's death (though not explicitly his execution), affirms that the son was still alive, and implies that the fate of both father and son were the result of injustices the father had committed in an effort to secure the son's welfare (in both the *Shīrāz-nāma* and the *Shadd al-izār*, moreover, the father is typically referred to as '*ṣāḥib* ʿAmīd al-Dīn'); unfortunately, however, 'Amīd al-Dīn's son is called in the sources 'Tāj al-Dīn Muḥammad', evidently precluding his identification with the son 'Masʿūd' ascribed to 'the *ṣāḥib* ʿAmīd al-Dīn' by Shaykh Ḍiyā' al-Dīn. ʿAmīd al-Dīn may have had another son, of course; and according to the editors' notes in the *Shadd al-izār*, a *qaṣīda* composed by ʿAmīd al-Dīn while imprisoned was written down by his son and given to a cousin of ʿAmīd al-Dīn, Imām Ṣafī al-Dīn Masʿūd Sīrāfī, d. 678/1279–1280; see the accounts of this Masʿūd and his son, with the editors' notes, in *Shadd*, pp. 430–433, whose name was perhaps confused with that of ʿAmīd al-Dīn's son. If the letter does indeed refer to this ʿAmīd al-Dīn and his son, it must have been written in or after 624/1227.

51. MS, ff. 354a–356Aa (there are two folios marked '356'; I have called the second '356A' and otherwise maintained the numbering found in the manuscript).

52. His *nisba* links him with Guwāshīr, an old name for the chief town of the province of Kirmān (see Krawulsky, *Īrān*, p. 140; cf. A. K. S. Lambton, 'Kirmān', *EI2*, vol. 5, p. 150); Juwaynī gives the Arabised spelling, 'Juwāshīr' (*History*, tr. Boyle, pp. 417–418, 469, 477), but uses also the form 'Kuvāshīr' (p. 475), while Nasawī gives the form 'Kuwāshīr' (*Sīrat*, tr. Buniiatov, p. 134, text, p. 117).

53. This counsel is echoed, albeit with a more ironic twist, in the *Gulistān* of Saʿdī (d. 691/1292), where it is presented simply as a *pīr*'s response to a *murīd*'s complaint about the pressure of people visiting him: 'Lend something to those who are poor, and ask for something from those who are wealthy, so that they will not come to you again' (ed. Nūr Allāh Irānparast, Tehran, 1348 Sh./1969, p. 71). It is possible that Saʿdī adapted this passage from the *Maqāmāt* of Shaykh Ḍiyā' al-Dīn, or from oral tradition surrounding him (Saʿdī's well-known connections with the Salghūrid court perhaps offer a point of contact with the Shaykh's reputation), but the aphoristic character of the master's advice suggests that it may have been a floating motif adapted independently by Saʿdī and by the author of our text.

54. MS, f. 356b. His first *nisba* must refer to the village known as Isfanj, in the province

of Arghiyān, in western Khurāsān, between Isfarāyin and Nīshāpūr (see Krawulsky, *Īrān*, p. 66, citing the form 'Isfanj' from Sam'ānī in the 12th century, Yāqūt, who gives also the form 'Sabanj' in the 13th, and Ḥāfiẓ-i Abrū in the 15th century; cf. Krawulsky, *Ḫorāsān*, pp. 66, 256–258). The location of Arghiyān has occasioned some confusion. Le Strange (*Lands of the Eastern Caliphate*, p. 392) identified it with Jājarm, a view also adopted in Brian Spooner, 'Arghiyān: The Area of Jājarm in western Khurāsān', *Iran*, 3 (1965), pp. 97–107; Krawulsky follows the conclusions of Aubin, who discusses the sources at length ('Réseau pastoral', pp. 109–116) and locates the region well east of Jājarm, just south and west of Khabūshān (Arghiyān was thus a region bordering Juwayn, where Khudāshāh was located, on the east).

55. The work is the *Murād al-murīdīn*, written by Khwāja Ghiyāth al-Dīn, a great-grandson of Sa'd al-Dīn Ḥammuyī, in the middle of the 14th century; the material it includes pertaining to Sa'd al-Dīn's life was outlined by Muḥammad-Taqī Dānishpazhūh in his review of Aḥmad Mahdawī Dāmghānī's edition of the *Kashf al-ḥaqā'iq*, a work by Sa'd al-Dīn's pupil 'Azīz-i Nasafī (the review appears in *Farhang-i Īrān Zamīn*, 13, 1344 Sh./1965, pp. 298–310).

56. On the work, see *GAL*, vol. 1, p. 363; *GALS*, vol. 1, p. 620.

57. Dānishpazhūh, review of *Kashf al-ḥaqā'iq*, ed. Dāmghānī, p. 302; *Murād al-murīdīn*, MS Tehran University 2451, f. 30b.

58. On Sa'd al-Dīn, and the illustrious family to which he belonged, see Jamal J. Elias, 'The Sufi Lords of Bahrabad: Sa'd al-Din and Sadr al-Din Hamuwayi', *Iranian Studies*, 27 (1994), pp. 53–75, with a discussion of possible readings of the familial *nisba* (this study does not take account, however, of several important sources, including the *Murād al-murīdīn* as discussed by Dānishpazhūh).

59. The latter term is vowelled with *ḥarakāt*, and might be read '*yūzvār*' or '*yūzavār*'; '*yūzdār*', denoting a keeper of panthers used in hunting (see Dihkhudā, *Lughāt-nāma*, vol. 33, p. 292), is apparently the form intended, but the story recounted by him (MS, ff. 357b–358b) involves his occupation as a melon-grower (the account centres on a vision in which Khiḍr correctly told him that his melons were ripe well before he believed they could be). Alternatively, the form might be emended to read 'Nūzwār', the name of a village of Khwārazm; see W. Barthold, *Turkestan Down to the Mongol Invasion*, tr. V. and T. Minorsky, ed. C. E. Bosworth (4th ed., London, 1977), pp. 148–149, 155; the site is mentioned in Juwaynī, *History*, tr. Boyle, p. 322, but the form given is clearly not a *nisba*, and the construction 'Abū Naṣr-i Nūzwār', while plausible, is not typical for this text.

60. MS, ff. 358b–359a. According to the tale, Shaykh Ḍiyā' al-Dīn sent Ḥāmid, early in his discipleship, on a journey to Māzandarān; when he reached Āzādwār – a town of Juwayn barely 15 km west of Khudāshāh, in the direction of Māzandarān (Krawulsky, *Īrān*, pp. 67–68, and *Ḫorāsān*, pp. 65, 247; cf. Aubin, 'Réseau pastoral', pp. 123–125, 128–129, and Le Strange, *Lands*, pp. 391–392, noting that Khudāshāh is 'a stage east' of Āzādvār, which he terms the major town of Juwayn), thus making the point that the disciple had not gone far at all – he stopped at the *khānqāh* of a certain 'Shaykh Abu'l-Qāsim', where he tarried, becoming enamoured of a merchant's servant-girl. He planned to seduce her, but was stopped by a vision of his shaykh, and repented; he then continued on to Māzandarān to take care of the shaykh's business, and returned to Shaykh Ḍiyā' al-Dīn, avoiding his master's eyes for shame, but then repenting again once he realised that the shaykh was aware of what he had intended. 'Abu'l-Qāsim' is hardly an uncommon *kunya*, but a letter evidently written by Majd

al-Dīn Baghdādī early in the 13th century refers to an 'Abu'l-Qāsim' in connection with the affairs of *khānqāh* management in a village (called 'Arḥad' [?]) near Nīshāpūr, not far east of the region discussed here (see the text of the letter in Muḥammad-Taqī Dānishpazhūh, 'Khirqah-i hazār-mīkhī', *Collected Papers on Islamic Philosophy and Mysticism*, ed. M. Mohaghegh and H. Landolt (Tehran, 1350 Sh./1971), Persian section, pp. 149–178/pp. 168–169); this Abu'l-Qāsim would seem to have had some ties with the Sufi community centred upon Najm al-Dīn Kubrā and Majd al-Dīn Baghdādī, and it is quite possible that the same figure is intended here.

61. The account presents a series of 'wishes' posed to the Prophet, and his succinct responses (e.g. 'I want to be the wisest of men', to which the Prophet replies, 'Then fear God', f. 360b; 'I want to know by what deed servants come closest to God', to which the Prophet replies, 'By *jawānmardī*', f. 361a).

62. Or 'Khurāshāh'; see above, n. 34.

63. The term '*khādim*' typically refers not to a 'servant' in general, but to the 'steward' entrusted by a shaykh with attending to the needs of residents of, and visitors to, the *khānqāh*, above all arrangements for food and lodging; in the present narrative, however, Najm al-Dīn Kubrā is shown with his own *khādim*, who was evidently travelling with him.

64. *Amrūz mā-rā bar khidmat-i shaykh giriftī-i ṣūfiyāna ast.*

65. This is the *kunya* by which Kubrā is typically known; its acquisition (or more precisely its change to this form from the form 'Abu'l-Janāb') is the subject of a brief account by Kubrā himself (see Meier, *Fawā'iḥ*, pp. 9–10, and the text, pp. 79–80).

66. This seems to mark the end of the passage quoted from al-Qāyinī, since the departure of the two dervishes is recounted again.

67. The term '*ḥafada*' ('grandsons', 'descendants') is evidently to be understood as an honorific here, i.e. 'Shaykh Muʿin al-Dīn Muḥammad the [shaykh's] grandson'.

68. On the question of Kubrā's possible pilgrimage and/or other journeys westwards following his initial travels, see Meier, *Fawā'iḥ*, p. 38.

69. Ibn al-Fuwaṭī, *Talkhīṣ Majmaʿ al-ādāb fī muʿjam al-alqāb*, ed. Muṣṭafā Jawād (Damascus, 1962–1965), vol. 4, part 2, p. 1011.

70. *Shadd al-izār*, ed. Qazwīnī and Iqbāl, pp. 419–420, with reference to al-Dhahabī (who calls him ''Alā' al-Dīn Abū Saʿd Thābit b. Aḥmad b. Muḥammad b. Abū Bakr al-Khujandī al-Iṣfahānī'); in the text of the *Shadd* itself, he is accorded a brief biography (in which his *laqab* is omitted and he is called 'Abū Muḥammad'), but elsewhere, in an account of a figure who studied under him, the same figure is mentioned as 'Shaykh ʿAlā' al-Dīn al-Khujandī' (p. 325). Both sources affirm that he died in 637/1239–1240.

71. Another famous shaykh of Khujand, Maṣlaḥa al-Dīn, is shown as Kubrā's contemporary, and is visited by an unnamed disciple of Kubrā, in a story first recorded in the late 15th century, in two of the biographies of Khwāja Aḥrār (Mīr ʿAbd al-Awwal Nīshāpūrī, *Malfūẓāt*, MS Lucknow, Taṣawwuf Fārsī 172/2457, ff. 73b–74a; Mawlānā Muḥammad Qāḍī, *Silsilat al-ʿārifīn*, MS Aligarh, Subhanullah no. 297.7/72, ff. 66b–67a).

72. On this disciple, Majd al-Dīn al-Muwaffaq al-Khāṣī, see Fritz Meier, 'Der unbekannte schriftsteller al-Muwaffaq al-Ḫāṣī', *Der Islam*, 66 (1989), p. 313, noting al-Khāṣī's mention of a stop, on his journey away from Khwārazm, at Kubrā's *khānqāh* in Shahristāna; Meier assumed that this referred to a 'Shahristān' in Jurjān, but it seems more likely that the site intended was Shahristāna near Nasā (see Juwaynī, *History*, vol. 1, p. 157; Nasawī, *Sīrat*, p. 99;

cf. Barthold, *Turkestan*, p. 153, n. 16, citing Yāqūt). Another 'Shahristānī', evidently a disciple of Majd al-Dīn Baghdādī, added a note to a manuscript (of al-Qushayrī's famous Sufi treatise) that was copied in 582/1186–1187, 'in Jurjāniyya of Khwārazm', by Majd al-Dīn Baghdādī, and checked by Najm al-Dīn Kubrā. The manuscript is noted in the late 19th-century work of Muḥammad Bāqir al-Khwānsārī, *Rawḍāt al-jannāt fī aḥwāl al-'ulamā' wa'l-sādāt* (Tehran, 1390/1970), vol. 1, pp. 298–299; the account is discussed also in Qazwīnī's notes to the edition of the *Shadd al-izār*, p. 44, n. 1 and in Badī' al-Zamān Furūzānfar, *Sharḥ-i aḥwāl wa-naqd wa-taḥlīl-i āthār-i Shaykh Farīd al-Dīn Muḥammad 'Aṭṭār Nīshābūrī* (Tehran, 1339–1340 Sh./1960–1961), pp. 22–24; see also Dānishpazhūh, 'Khirqah-i hazār-mīkhī', p. 151, suggesting this figure's identity with the 'Shams al-Dīn' to whom two letters of Majd al-Dīn Baghdādī are addressed.

73. I have noted this story briefly in 'The Yasavī Order and Persian Hagiography in Seventeenth-Century Central Asia: 'Ālim Shaykh of 'Alīyābād and his *Lamaḥāt min nafaḥāt al-quds*', in Leonard Lewisohn and David Morgan, ed., *The Heritage of Sufism*, vol. III: *Late Classical Persianate Sufism (1501–1750), The Safavid and Mughal Period* (Oxford, 1999), p. 408; the passage appears in the facsimile publication of a late manuscript of the *Lamaḥāt*, prepared by Muḥammad Nadhīr Rānjhā; Muḥammad 'Ālim Ṣiddīqī, *Lamaḥāt min nafaḥāt al-quds* (Islamabad, 1406/1986), pp. 134–135. As noted already by Cordt (*Sitzungen*, pp. 223–224, n. 3), a story from the *Chihil majlis* may refer to the dervish who inspired the figure of Zangī Ata as an associate of Kubrā and of Majd al-Dīn Baghdādī; a fuller study of the Yasawī tradition, including these issues, is in preparation.

74. See the texts in Dānishpazhūh, 'Khirqah-i hazār-mīkhī', pp. 162, 168, 173–174, regarding these matters of *khānqāh* administration.

75. The phrase used here *('jubba-i 'adanī')* refers to a shirt or tunic made of a fine cloth woven, despite its name, in Nīshāpūr (see Dihkhudā, *Lughāt-nāma*, vol. 22, p. 127).

76. *Istijāza kardam, shaykh marā ijāza dād wa-bi-niwisht.*

77. This is probably the same 'Shaykh Jamāl al-Dīn Āmulī', then in Nasā, to whom the sixth, and shortest, letter was addressed (ff. 352b–353a); elsewhere in the text (f. 356a), 'Shaykh Jamāl al-Dīn' asks a question that prompts a doctrinal discussion by Shaykh Ḍiyā' al-Dīn.

78. '*Khudā-rā bi-khudā wa-bihisht-rā bi-ṭā'a wa-'amal-i ṣāliḥ 'jazā'an bi-mā kānū ya'malūna*' (the Arabic passage is from the Qur'an, 56: 24; 32: 17); the significance of the phrase becomes clear near the end of the narrative.

79. This is the only allusion, in this second narrative, to the likely setting for Lālā's association with Shaykh Ḍiyā' al-Dīn (i.e. a *khānqāh* maintained by the latter).

80. This brief 'itinerary' would appear to make it clear that Raḍī al-Dīn travelled by sea, but may simply reflect an offhand mention of places associated with India, perhaps to emphasise the exotic setting of the story, rather than an actual sequence of places on the way to Raḍī al-Dīn's destination. Of the the three places named, only '*m.'.b.r*' is easily recognisable, and refers to a region that hardly seems appropriate as the first landmark in an actual itinerary of a traveller from Khurāsān: 'Ma'bar' was the usual Muslim name for the coastal region ('Coromandel') of southeastern India, across from Sri Lanka (see A. D. W. Forbes, 'Ma'bar', *EI2*, vol. 5, pp. 937–938). The second name, written '*q.l.y.bār*', looks somewhat like an error for 'Mulaybār' (or 'Malībār'), referring to the Malabar coast of southwestern India (see Forbes, 'Malabar', *EI2*, vol. 6, pp. 206–207) – in which case the sequence would have

Raḍī al-Dīn travelling from east to west – but the initial *qāf* is quite clearly written in the text, and seems an unlikely error for 'Mulaybār'; perhaps it indicates a copyist's omission of a name from a longer list and a conflation of '*m.l.y.bār*' with another name (for example, that of Qāliqūt, Calicut, then one of the chief ports of Malabar). As for the third name, we might expect it to be transmitted more faithfully, as the site of Raḍī al-Dīn's torment and eventual deliverance, but the form given in the text – which could be read as '*k.w.k.r*' or '*k.d.k.r*' – is difficult to identify, and any plausible suggestion requires us to assume, again, a copyist's error. The form may mask the name of the region well north of the Malabar coast (south of present-day Mumbai) called Konkan, a name written by Ibn Baṭṭūṭa as '*k.w.k.n*'; see *Voyages d'Ibn Battûta*, ed. and tr. C. Defrémery and B. R. Sanguinetti (Paris, 1854; repr. Paris, 1969), vol. 3, pp. 335–336; cf. Peter Jackson, *The Delhi Sultanate: A Political and Military History* (Cambridge, 1999), p. 204; and Irfan Habib, *An Atlas of the Mughal Empire* (Delhi, 1982, repr. 1986), Map 14A and p. 55; this identification may also be attractive in view of the proximity of the site called 'Jazīra', not far south of Mumbai, to which we might find a garbled reference in the seemingly vague mention, later in the narrative, of Lālā's escape to 'some islands' (*baʿẓī jazīrahā*); on the other hand, there were Muslim communities in many of the islands off the southwest coast of India, including some as distant as the Maldives, that would presumably have served as a suitable refuge for Raḍī al-Dīn. Alternatively, the form '*k.w.k.r*' may be even more likely to represent, with a simple omission of a final *nūn*, the name of the coastal town of Gokarn (Habib, *Atlas*, Map 16A and p. 63), not far south of Goa, and approximately midway between Calicut and the region of Konkan (I am indebted to Carl Ernst and Richard Eaton, respectively, for these suggestions). Further afield, the form in the text might conceivably mask the name of Kunakār, a major town of Sri Lanka visited by Ibn Baṭṭūṭa; see M. N. M. Kamil Asad, 'Ibn Battūtah's Account of Malabar and Saylān (Sri Lanka)', *Journal of the Pakistan Historical Society*, 42 (1994), pp. 329–339, p. 334; and, were we willing to assume that Lālā's journey was not by sea, but by land into the Punjab, we might see in '*k.w.k.r*' a representation of the name of the Hindu Khokars (which Juwaynī writes as '*k.w.kār*', *History*, 2, p. 414; cf. Abdus Subhan, 'Khokars', *EI2*, vol. 5, p. 31). On balance, however, either Konkan or Gokarn, on the western coast, seems a more likely candidate. If 'Q.lībār' may indeed be taken as a garbled reference to a site on the Malabar coast, and 'K.w.k.r' refers to either the region of Konkan or the town of Gokarn, then the text does give a reasonable itinerary, but one that would appear to reflect Raḍī al-Dīn's return journey, from east to west, and not the sequence of sites he passed after first setting off for India; it may be that the author of the *Maqāmāt* of Shaykh Ḍiyā' al-Dīn omitted a portion of Lālā's narrative in order to focus on the story of his deliverance.

81. *Khudā-rā bī-khudā, yaʿnī bī-irāda wa-jadhba-i ū, wa-bihisht-rā bī-ʿamal-i ṣāliḥ, 'jazā'an bi-mā kānū yaʿmalūna'* (here '*ṭāʿat wa*' is omitted before '*ʿamal-i ṣāliḥ*').

82. The brief mention of Lālā's stay in Kirmān, and the presence of 'Bukhārans' there, following his return from India, is of interest in connection with the ties between another of Kubrā's disciples, Sayf al-Dīn Bākharzī, and Kirmān; one of Bākharzī's sons moved there, and Shaykh Ḥasan Bulghārī, who spent time in Bukhārā with Bākharzī, made Kirmān his destination after his stay in Central Asia, both enjoyed the patronage of the Qarākhiṭāy dynasty based in Kirmān; see Nāṣir al-Dīn Munshī Kirmānī, *Simṭ al-ʿulā li'l-ḥaẓrat al-ʿulyā*, ed. ʿAbbās Iqbāl (Tehran, 1328 Sh./1949), pp. 43–44. Lālā's stop in Kirmān following his return from India may also reflect ties between the Salghūrid dynasts ruling Fārs and Kirmān and

Muslim communities of the Indian coast; according to the 14th-century *Shīrāz-nāma* (ed. Karīmī, pp. 55–56), the name of Muẓaffar al-Dīn Abū Bakr b. Saʿd b. Zangī (see above, n. 48) was mentioned in the *khuṭba* 'in some of the towns of Hind' (cf. Jackson, *Delhi Sultanate*, p. 193).

83. Simnānī, *Opera minora*, ed. Thackston, p. 216; Cordt, *Sitzungen*, pp. 191–192.

84. The reference here to the *khalwat*s undertaken by Lālā echoes the specific mention, in the *Maqāmāt* of Shaykh Ḍiyā' al-Dīn, that the latter had prescribed seclusions for Lālā, as well as the passage in the *Chihil majlis*, near the end of Simnānī's account of Lālā's search for Kubrā (*Opera minora*, ed. Thackston, p. 218; Cordt, *Sitzungen*, p. 195), in which Lālā is portrayed undertaking a *khalwat* in Turkistān on the instructions of Shaykh Aḥmad Yasawī (who is, aside from Rūzbihān Baqlī, the enigmatic Bābā Ratan [noted below], and now Shaykh Ḍiyā' al-Dīn al-Ḥātimī, the only shaykh named explicitly among the many with whom Lālā is said to have spent time).

85. Simnānī, *Opera minora*, ed. Thackston, p. 172.

86. On this figure, see J. Horovitz, 'Bābā Ratan, the Saint of Bhatinda', *Journal of the Panjab Historical Society*, 2 (1913–1914), pp. 97–117, and Muḥammad Shafīʿ, 'Ratan', *EI2*, vol. 8, pp. 457–459.

87. Teufel, *Lebensbeschreibung*, p. 93.

88. Dawlatshāh Samarqandī, *Tadhkirat al-shuʿarā*, ed. M. Ramaḍānī (Tehran, 1338 Sh./1959), p. 166.

89. *Nafaḥāt*, ed. ʿĀbidī, pp. 438–439.

90. I have not identified any such account in the published works of Simnānī, and it is possible that Jāmī adopted it from some other source (it appears, for instance, in the *Laṭā'if-i Ashrafī*, a work evidently compiled in the middle of the 15th century based on the sayings of Sayyid Ashraf Jahāngīr Simnānī); it may indeed appear among the unpublished works of ʿAlā' al-Dawla Simnānī, however. The *Gulzār-i abrār*, a hagiographical compendium completed in India around 1022/1613 by Muḥammad Ghawthī b. Ḥasan b. Mūsā Shaṭṭārī, also ascribes the story of the Prophet's comb to Simnānī, but goes further, affirming that Lālā himself had dated his meeting with Bābā Ratan to 620/1223 (MS Calcutta, Asiatic Society of Bengal, D262, described in W. Ivanow, *Concise Descriptive Catalogue of the Persian Manuscripts in the Collection of the Asiatic Society of Bengal*, Calcutta, 1924, pp. 96–108, No. 259, f. 8a); the accounts noted earlier all imply that Lālā's travels, and his association with Bābā Ratan, occurred prior to his discipleship under Kubrā.

91. Landolt, *Révélateur*, text, pp. 21–24; tr. pp. 149–152; cf. intro., pp. 24–26.

92. The text, with the date, appears in Ibn Karbalā'ī, *Rawḍāt al-jinān*, vol. 2, pp. 306–308; an incomplete version of the text, drawn from manuscripts of the 15th-century *Farā'id-i Ghiyāthī*, was published in Dānishpazhūh, 'Khirqah-i hazār-mīkhī', pp. 162–164.

93. The *ijāzat-nāma* given by Baghdādī to Lālā was edited by Dānishpazhūh, 'Khirqah-i hazār-mīkhī', pp. 165–168, from versions found in the 15th-century *Farā'id-i Ghiyāthī* and in a 15th-century manuscript preserved in Paris; essentially the same text appears in Ibn Karbalā'ī, *Rawḍat al-jinān*, vol. 2, pp. 308–310.

94. Baghdādī's disciple Najm al-Dīn Rāzī, who says he was with his master until the time of his martyrdom, dates that event to 606/1209 (it is also dated to 607/1210, 613/1216, and 616/1219 in relatively early sources); see William Shpall, 'A Note on Najm al-Dīn al-Rāzī and the *Baḥr al-ḥaqā'iq*', *Folia Orientalia*, 22 (1981–1984), pp. 69–80.

95. The same questions may arise, of course, in connection with the complex relationship among Kubrā, Majd al-Dīn Baghdādī, and Lālā; their relationship – too complex to be depicted adequately through a simple recitation of a chain of transmission – was dealt with, in subsequent depictions of 'Kubravī' history, in several ways, both through the narratives noted above, recounting how Lālā came to Kubrā and was then handed over to Baghdādī, and through the more straightforward explanation, by Simnānī, of Lālā's need for additional 'refinement' even after his licensure by Kubrā (Simnānī's writings, in fact, reveal a subtle shift over time, from highlighting Kubrā alone as Lālā's shaykh, to stressing the role of Baghdādī). Yet Baghdādī may have died as much as ten years before Kubrā's death; what kind of ties pertained between Lālā and Kubrā after Baghdādī's death? Did Lālā's licensure by Baghdādī indeed follow his licensure by Kubrā, as Simnānī's accounts claim? Or did Lālā in fact come to Kubrā after his time with Baghdādī (and perhaps even after his death)? Majd al-Dīn's letters (as published in Dānishpazhūh, 'Khirqah-i hazār-mīkhī') suggest that he was an independent shaykh and *khānqāh* manager who maintained good ties with Kubrā; and while there is no good reason to doubt the initiatory relationship between Kubrā and Baghdādī, there is also no good reason to assume that this initiatory relationship lent Kubrā any significant authority over the *khānqāh*s and communities directed by Baghdādī or by others who had been his formal disciples (as would often be the case for a senior shaykh in later times, through the structures proper to actual Sufi orders as known from the later 15th and 16th century). It may be that Baghdādī's connections with other Sufi communities were more significant than the interest he still took in the affairs of Kubrā's circle in Khwārazm. Moreover, if Majd al-Dīn indeed sent Lālā off, with his *ijāza*, to serve as a shaykh (and, presumably, to manage a *khānqāh*) in Isfarāyin, then Lālā too was clearly functioning as an independent shaykh even during Kubrā's lifetime, with, quite possibly, the same pattern of connections with both Kubrā and other Sufi communities. These questions, again, highlight how little we yet know about the relationship – if any – between the initiatic structures of Sufi transmission and the organisational structures of Sufi communities for the period – the 12th and 13th centuries – in which it is customary to assume that Sufi 'orders' were taking shape.

# 24

# Ibn Sīnā and Meister Eckhart on Being

*Etin Anwar*

This essay will compare the similarities and differences of the notion of Being in the thought of two of the greatest medieval philosophers of Being: Ibn Sīnā[1] (370–428/980–1037) and Meister Eckhart[2] (1260–1328). They are comparable for several reasons. First, they were the primary metaphysicians of their time; their metaphysical ideas have been highly influential in their respective philosophical systems.[3] Second, although both philosophers were in many respects influenced by Aristotle, they were not merely commentators on his work.[4] Indeed, both share with Aristotle the subject matter of metaphysics, i.e. Being qua Being; nonetheless, Ibn Sīnā's notion of Being, in all its variety, is his original contribution to Islamic philosophy, whereas Eckhart's reflection on Being brought with it a deeper understanding of Christian theology. Last but not least, Eckhart himself acknowledges his debt to Ibn Sīnā. This link has not been explored in any detail; nevertheless, scholars such as Davies,[5] Kelly,[6] and Tobin[7] have shown how Eckhart's philosophical background points to Ibn Sīnā's influence.

Having indicated the commonalities between Ibn Sīnā and Eckhart, I will compare the notion of Being as it is found in Ibn Sīnā's 'Flying man'[8] and Eckhart's *Commentary on Exodus*: 'I am who I am.'[9] In particular, I will examine the implication of the theory of Being for the proof of the existence of God. I will argue that both Ibn Sīnā's and Eckhart's notions of Being provide the ground for the ontological proof of the existence of the ultimate Being relevant to their respective traditions. In an attempt to demonstrate both arguments for the existence of the Ultimate Being, the first section will compare Ibn Sīnā's 'Flying man' with Eckhart's 'I am who I am'. The second section will examine the similarities and differences in Ibn Sīnā's and Eckhart's theories of Being. The last section will present the proofs for the existence of God deriving from Ibn Sīnā's and Eckhart's definitions of Being.

## Ibn Sīnā's 'Flying man' versus Eckhart's '*Ego sum qui sum*'

Ibn Sīnā employs the account of the 'Flying Man' in a number of his works, such as *al-Najāt* and *al-Ishārāt wa'l-tanbīhāt*, in order to illustrate his theory of Being.[10] However, in this paper, reference to the original idea for the 'Flying Man' will chiefly be made from his *al-Aḍḥawiyya fi amr al-ma'ād*. Under the heading 'On Man's Stable Individual Existence', he proposes the concept of individual human being (*anniyyatihā*) as grounded in the self (soul). Ibn Sīnā writes:

> If a man were to contemplate the thing (entity) by virtue of which he is called 'he' (*huwa*) and to which he himself refers as 'I' (*anā*), he would at first think that this ['he' (*huwa*) or 'I' (*anā*)] consists of his corporeal body. Then, once he thinks deeply, he will see that if his hands and legs, his ribs and other manifest parts of his body did not exist, it would not negate the meaning referred to; and through this he will understand that these parts of the body are not included in the concept [of 'he or I'].[11]

This passage demonstrates the existence of the self as a substance different from the body. Ibn Sīnā describes the self using the personal pronoun 'I' or the word 'he' because this concept signifies individual human existence. Even though the self is an inherent constituent of individuality, it is not merely composed of the members of the body, such as the heart and the limbs; for if we were to imagine that such bodily members were spread out, the person would still be cognisant of his individual being (*anniyyatihā*) as an immaterial entity.[12] Here, Ibn Sīnā insists that the self is a substance which is able to exist independ of body.[13]

The second hypothetical example of the 'Flying Man' appears in his work *al-Ishārāt wa'l-tanbīhāt*. In this treatise, Ibn Sīnā presents his idea in brief as follows:

> Return to your self and reflect whether, being whole, or even in another state, where, however, you discern a thing correctly, you would be oblivious to the existence of your self (*dhātaka*) and would not confirm your self (*nafsaka*)? To my mind, this does not happen to the perspicacious – so much so that the sleeper in his sleep and the drunk in the state of his drunkenness will not miss knowledge of his self, even if his presentation of his self to himself does not remain in his memory.
>
> And if you imagine your self (*dhātaka*) to have been at its first creation mature and whole in mind and body, and it is supposed to be in a generality of position and physical circumstance where it does not perceive its parts, where its limbs do not touch each other but are rather spread apart, and that this self is momentarily suspended in temperate air, you will find that it will be unaware of everything except of the 'fixedness' (*thubūt*) of its individual existence (*anniyyatihā*).[14]

The above passages highlight the existence of the human self that has self-knowledge regardless of his/her physical condition.

With the example of the 'Flying Man' in mind, one may question the relevance of the idea of the self to the Necessary Existent (the Ultimate Being). In response, it should be kept in mind that Ibn Sīnā uses the simplest means of showing the birth of human consciousness.[15] He shows that this consciousness is reached without any medium other than the self.[16] This self or non-physical aspect of a person exists as 'the receiver of *a priori* truths'.[17] Human self-knowledge, by implication, reaches as far as the Ultimate Being, or what Ibn Sīnā refers to as the Necessary Existent or the Necessary Being.

Meister Eckhart discusses the theory of Being in a number of his sermons. In the *Commentary on Exodus*, he deals with the ontological significance of God's self-identification to Moses: 'I am who I am.' (Exodus 13:14) Eckhart offers five interpretations of the phrase. Firstly, he notes that the three words 'I', 'am' and 'who' refer only to God.[18] 'I' is the first pronoun that indicates 'the pure substance, without any accident, without anything foreign, the substance without quality, without this or that form, without this or that'.[19] The word 'who' is an unlimited expression that fits with God.[20] The term 'am' is 'a substantive word' in the sense of 'the Word was God' (John 1:1), and of 'upholding all things by the Word of His power'. (Hebrews 1:3)[21]

Secondly, the word 'am' is the predicate, which refers back to God's statement, 'I am', which indicates 'the pure naked existence of the subject which is the subject itself or the essence of the subject'.[22] It also demonstrates that in the case of God essence and existence are the same thing. Furthermore, in an apparent reference to Ibn Sīnā's concept of essence and existence, Eckhart explains that the 'what-it-is' that belongs to God is his 'that-it-is'. This is because for God, there is no 'what-it-is' beyond 'that-it-is', which in turn indicates his being.[23]

Thirdly, the saying 'I am who I am' is principally an indication of 'the purity of affirmation excluding all negation from God'.[24] Another implication that derives from this passage is that of the process of emanation, which he describes as follows:[25]

> It should be noted that the repetition of 'am' in 'I am who I am' indicates the purity of affirmation, along with the exclusion of everything negative from God; as well as a turning back and reversion of his existence (*esse*) into and upon itself, and its dwelling and inherence in itself; all this, as well as a certain *bullitio*[26] and self-birth (*parturitionem sui*) – see the thing in/into itself (*in se*), and in and into itself melting and bubbling. Light in light and into light, utterly interpenetrating itself, turned completely upon itself and reflected upon itself from all sides. As the wise man said: 'Monad begets – or begat – monad, and reflected its love or ardour into itself.'
>
> For this reason it is said in the first chapter of John: 'In Him was Life.' 'Life'

> indicates a certain pushing out by which something swells up in itself, pouring out and boiling over. Thus, it is said that the emanation of the persons in the divine realm (*in divinis*) is a reason (*ratio*) and a precursor (*praevia*) of creation. Thus, in John 1 it is said: 'in the beginning was the Word', and a little later on: 'all things were made through it'.[27]

A detailed explanation of emanation is beyond the scope of this paper, but it should at least be noted that Eckhart's emanation has something to do with the passage, 'I am who I am'.

Eckhart's fourth point is that in Latin the expression 'who' is properly used after a name, in a similar manner to Priscian here: 'Who, father, is that man who thus accompanies him on his way?' Accordingly, the terms the terms 'who' and 'what' may be used to inquire into the essence of a thing, which can be indicated by its name and/or definition.[28] In making this point, Eckhart establishes the distinction between the essence and the existence of created beings.

The last point is that the first 'I am' in the passage signifies 'the thing's essence'; and it is 'the subject or what is dominated'. The second 'I am' on the other hand indicates 'the thing's existence' and it is 'the predicate or denominator and denomination'.[29] This interpretation actually refers to Maimonides'[30] understanding of the passage, 'I am who I am'. According to Eckhart, Maimonides apparently understood this to mean 'the name of Tetragrammaton',[31] which is 'sacred, separated, written and not pronounced, and alone signifies the naked and pure substance of the creator'.[32] As a result of this interpretation, God's essence is self-sufficient and 'such sufficiency is proper to God alone'.[33] Thus, according to Eckhart's understanding of 'I am who I am', God is a being that is what it is, and would therefore be the Necessary Existent. Accordingly, God exists as who he is, as in the verse: 'I am who I am; he who sent me'; therefore, God is the Necessary Existent.[34]

While Ibn Sīnā's and Eckhart's concepts of Being point to a certain degree to Necessary Existence, it would be interesting to discover in what way their notions of Being are compatible and, given their different intellectual backgrounds, how their notions of Being depart from one another. The following section will attempt to answer these questions.

## The Theory of Being

It has already been pointed out that Ibn Sīnā's 'Flying Man', demonstrating the immateriality and individuality of the self,[35] paves the way for the discussion of the concept of Being.[36] Ibn Sīnā's concept of Being is fundamental to a direct understanding of the Ultimate Being.[37] This allows Ibn Sīnā to establish that Being *qua* Being is the subject matter of metaphysics, which is the highest form of knowledge.[38] In Ibn Sīnā's understanding, the cause of all existents, without reducing them all to a common category, is Being. This Being is beyond distinction and polarisation, and is also the cause of the world of multiplicity in which its existence is manifested in a variety of quiddities (*māhiyyāt*).[39]

Similarly, Eckhart perceives Being as falling within the domain of metaphysics.[40] Even in his German works he employs Latin terms, such as *ens*, *esse* and *essentia*,[41] when presenting his theory of Being. However, it should be noted that Eckhart usually uses the terms *esse* or *ens* in reference not only to created Being, but also sometimes to God.[42] And yet although both God and his creatures are in fact beings, nevertheless God's *esse* is infinite and necessary, whereas the creature's *esse* is finite and dependent on God.[43]

From the same perspective, Ibn Sīnā's and Eckhart's theories of Being rely on two basic distinctions identifying their ontology.[44] The first distinction relates to essence (*māhiyyāt*) and existence (*wujūd*). The second concentrates on the concept of the necessary and contingent beings. These distinctions appear to be similar. Of course, this is not surprising since both Ibn Sīnā and Eckhart share a common Aristotelian background. However, in spite of this, there are some differences.

The difference between essence and existence is applicable to all actual and potential beings, but not to God.[45] Thus essence or quiddity, for human beings, is independent of existence.[46] Another central implication that of Ibn Sīnā's distinction between essence and existence is the use of the three modalities: 'necessity (*wājibī*), contingency (*mumkinī*) and impossibility (*mumtaniʿī*).'[47]

But there is no distinction between essence and existence in the case of the Necessary Existent. From this starting point, Ibn Sīnā contends that God is definitely simple in His Being.[48] This is to say that God is 'a single atomic element in a single being'.[49] Thus, God's existence is identical with His essence.

Eckhart believes that the distinction between essence and existence applies to the creation, but not to God.[50] Essence gives a certain identity to all beings. For example, human beings, horses and trees are in existence and they are different beings in reality, but what differentiates their beings is their essence.[51] Essence can also refer to a thing that is not in existence, since the existence of that thing may be conceived. Here again, Eckhart's theory parallels Ibn Sīnā's concept of the distinction between essence and existence.

However, when Eckhart speaks of the essence and the existence of God, he differs sharply in some respects from Ibn Sīnā, embracing a paradoxical understanding of the essence of God. In accordance with the second point made in his commentary on the phrase in Exodus, he reasons that God is a being whose essence and existence are absolutely one.[52] Elsewhere, however, he suggests that God has no essence at all since human knowledge tries to understand other essences.[53] He further reasons that it cannot be said that God is more than what He is. Similarly, saying that 'God is not' is for God neither this nor that.[54] Here, Eckhart establishes the doctrine of the negation of negation (*negatio negationis*) which determines what it is and distinguishes something that is not another thing.[55]

Eckhart's negation of the essence of God, according to Tobin, is not intended as a denial of God's existence but to demonstrate that knowledge of God should derive from an understanding of God himself as the Intellect. Furthermore, attributing a quality to God is only permissible by ascribing purity of Being (*puritas essendi*). Again, all things are perceivable in God's knowledge, even though God is not Being.[56]

Eckhart divides Being into two categories. The first, *esse*, is 'absolute Being (*esse absolutum*), simple Being (*esse simpliciter*) or Being itself (*esse ipsum*)'; the second category is 'Being that or this (*esse hoc et hoc; esse hoc aut aliud; esse huius et huius*), Being such and such (*esse tale*), or determinate Being (*esse determinatum*)'.[57] The former refers to God, 'infinite and uncontaminated by any form of admixture', the latter to creation in general or a specific being in the world.[58] The second being must depend on the first because the first generates the second. Consequently, the first being exists necessarily and voluntarily. In arguing this, Eckhart refers to Ibn Sīnā's Necessary Existent. This is why, for him, the passage 'I am who I am' may refer to the Necessary Existent.

Eckhart's division of Being coincides with Ibn Sīnā's necessary (*wājib*) and contingent (*mumkin*) beings.[59] While Ibn Sīnā's division of Being appears Aristotelian,[60] his distinction between necessary and contingent Being also relies on the *kalām* concept of a 'determinant of existence over non-existence'.[61] Indeed, Ibn Sīnā is indebted to the Aristotelian Unmoved Mover; but the *kalām* systematisation of the proof of the existence of God points Ibn Sīnā towards the transcendent Deity or the Necessary Existent.

The differentiation between necessity and contingency employed by Ibn Sīnā establishes the concept of a '*necessarily existent Being*', a being that exists voluntarily and will never cease to exist, and of a '*possibly existent Being*', that is a being for which there is the possibility to exist or not exist.[62] A sum of possibly existent beings stem from the concept of Being necessarily existent by virtue of itself and the concept of Being possibly existent by virtue of itself, necessarily existent by virtue of another. The last concept, according to Marmura, is the result of Ibn Sīnā's distinction between essence and existence.[63] From an analysis of the latter two concepts, Ibn Sīnā draws the premise that the totality of all contingent existent beings cannot resemble a being necessarily existent by virtue of itself; rather, their existence must depend on a being that is *necessarily existent by virtue of itself*, which he calls the Necessary Existent.[64]

Even though both Ibn Sīnā's and Eckhart's divisions of Being are twofold, there are differences. Ibn Sīnā's treatment of the issue reflects a profound philosophical argument, one which in fact helps him to develop an elaborate metaphysics, whereas Eckhart's twofold being depends on his theological interpretation, although presented philosophically. Furthermore, their respective understandings of God as Being are obviously dissimilar. Ibn Sīnā's concept of Necessary Existent as Being, Simple and One has much more in common with the *kalām* argument about the Oneness of God.[65] Al-Māturīdī, for instance, demonstrates the Oneness of God by using *dalīl al-tamānuʿ*, an argument of the Oneness of God by demonstrating the impossibility of having more than one god.[66] Al-Māturīdī's argument is based on Qur'anic verses such as 17:42, 21:22, 23:91 and 13:16. While he reiterates the Qur'anic vision of the concept of *tawḥīd*, he makes use of Aristotle's notion of the impossibility of unceasing motion for something that is moved and caused by a mover.[67]

Evidently, Eckhart's discussion of God has been influenced by Ibn Sīnā in a number of ways. On the one hand, the third point of his philosophical treatment of the passage 'I am who I am' concludes that God is Being, Simple and One.[68] He reasons, as Ibn Sīnā does, that 'God has no equal; for then there would be two gods, and this is not God at all'.[69] But the Eckhartian God sometimes is a reference to the central teaching of Christianity, namely the trinitarian God. In his *Tractates*, especially the one entitled 'The Kingdom of God', he states that the term God refers to a being, 'threefold in Person and onefold in his nature',[70] meaning that to speak of the Persons is to speak of the Father, Son and Holy Ghost; whereas to speak of their nature is to speak of the Godhead.[71] To understand this consider again Eckhart's emanative system in which the essence of the three Persons overflows into another essence, which is in the shape of the Godhead. This is possible because one of the Persons, i.e. the Father, has two facets. On the one hand 'He begets the Son', on the other hand, 'the Father and the Son are unbegotten, are Life as principle without principle, are self-causality',[72] which accords with Eckhart's third interpretation of the passage 'I am who I am'.

To discover which of Eckhart's opinions on the conception of God is most representative, one must put the phrase 'I am who I am' in context. Initially, this passage refers to the specific situation when God said to Moses: 'I am who I am. This is what you are to say to the Israelites: I am has sent me to you', (Exodus 3:14).[73] Therefore, it comes as no surprise that Eckhart characterises the attributes of God as being One, Simple and Self-sufficient, just as the Jewish and Muslim philosophers saw Him. Seen from Christ's point of view he states that 'He who sent me does not send me alone, he also sends every one who does the will of my Father'.[74] For this reason, in his 'Commentary on St John' Eckhart cites the passage 'But by the grace of God I am what I am' (1 Corinthians 15:10)[75] when describing Christ.

## Proofs for the Existence of God

This section discusses the implication of Ibn Sīnā's and Eckhart's theories of Being on the proof of the existence of God. It is argued that Ibn Sīnā's 'Flying Man' serves as a starting point for both cosmological and ontological proofs for His existence.[76] In a like manner, Eckhart's 'I am who I am' initiates the establishment of an ontological proof for the existence of God. This phrase has the potential to become a reference for the ontological argument because his rational intuition takes as its starting point the view that God is Being.

Returning to Ibn Sīnā's proof for the existence of God, some scholars, such as Davidson, Morewedge and Goodman,[77] argue that Ibn Sīnā never wished to establish the ontological proof. What may be inferred from the concept of *necessary* and *contingent beings* is a kind of cosmological doctrine. According to Davidson Ibn Sīnā develops his cosmological proof from philosophical principles, such as 'the principle of causality, the impossibility of an infinite linear regress of causes and the impossibility of a circular regress of causes'.[78] These principles led him to conclude that there must be an Aristotelian First Cause whose existence is *necessary by virtue of itself* and that it must cease there because an infinite linear and circular regress is impossible.[79] Morewedge also finds that Ibn Sīnā's discussion of the self can be phenomenally considered as '*a priori*' in establishing the argument for the existence of God, but this is not a direct premise of an ontological argument.[80] Goodman believes that Ibn Sīnā's cosmological argument is a mix between the possibly existent (*mumkin al-wujūd*) of *kalām* and the Aristotelian quest for the First Cause.[81]

I argue that Ibn Sīnā's ontological proof for the existence of God can be drawn from his discussion of the *necessary* and *contingent beings*. What is meant by ontological proof here is defined by Owen as the proof that departs from God's essence in the shape of *a priori* reasoning.[82] Certainly, Ibn Sīnā embraces rational intuition in establishing his 'Necessary Existent', whose being is in existence voluntarily and necessarily. For an understanding of Ibn Sīnā's cosmological and ontological proofs for the existence of God, reference may also be made to Sufism. Davidson indicates that Ibn Sīnā's cosmological proof is tinged with Sufism and traces this back to the Sufi Ibn 'Aṭā Allāh al-Iskandarī (d. 1309).[83] Landolt points out that Ibn Sīnā's 'Sufi theme' may be better traced to classical Sufism, for instance to al-Junayd's categorisation of *ma'rifa*, as Kalābādhī (d. 995) mentions in his writings.[84] Junayd (d. 910) says:

> There are two kinds of *ma'rifa*, namely the gnosis of Self-revelation (*ta'arruf*) and the gnosis of Instruction (*ta'rīf*). The first one means that God makes them know Himself, and to grasp things through Him, for as Ibrāhīm said, 'I love not the things that go down'. The meaning of the second is that He demonstrates the effect of His omnipotence in Heaven and the soul, then establishes it firmly in them; thus these things signify the Creator. This type of the gnosis belongs to the majority of the believers; whereas the first one refers to the elect (*al-khawāṣṣ*).[85]

On the one hand, it can be inferred that Ibn Sīnā's cosmological proof is in line with Junayd's *ta'rīf*, which demonstrates that the effects of God's creation lead us back to the Uncaused Cause or the Maker. On the other hand, his ontological argument also resembles Junayd's concept of *ta'arruf* in that God causes human intellection to know Him. So it is quite possible that Junayd's *ma'rifa* may have influenced Ibn Sīnā's ideas, even though the latter as a philosopher developed his own method in order to establish a proof for the existence of God that satisfied his demand for rationalism.

Ibn Sīnā also formulated a proof for the existence of God on the basis of the modalities of necessity and contingency.[86] This type of proof from Being,[87] according to Ibn Sīnā, is 'nobler' because it does not depend on contingent Being.[88] This nobler proof is attainable only by the 'saints' (*al-ṣiddīqūn*)[89] and is evidently superior to the proof of the *mutakallimūn* who relied upon the evidence of His Creation.[90] Furthermore, the word 'saints' (*al-ṣiddīqūn*) used by Ibn Sīnā, as Landolt pointed out, corresponds to the elect (*al-khawāṣṣ*) in al-Kalābādhī's work.[91] Judging from his explanation, it is possible that Ibn Sīnā regarded himself as one of the elect (*al-khawāṣṣ*).

Eckhart's passage 'I am who I am,' on the other hand, indicates an ontological proof for the existence of God. God, for Eckhart, becomes the starting point from which to establish that He exists necessarily. His fifth interpretation of the passage 'I am who I am', for example, signifies that God himself instructs human beings concerning the subject 'I am'.[92] This implies that human intellection of God comes from God, causing him to assert firmly that God exists. According to Kelly, Eckhart's method for establishing the existence of God represents true Christianity; God makes Himself known through his Self-revelation in the shape of Jesus Christ, as 'the God of the Self, unrestricted, isness and love'.[93]

Further support for Eckhart's ontological proof for the existence of God may be found in his *Tripartite Work*: The procession of *esse* from God to the human self, is direct, without any medium or cause, and therefore is one way of seeing God as the cause of all Being.[94] To reinforce his argument, Eckhart cites Romans 11:36, '*Ex ipso, et per ipsum et in ipso sunt omnia* (All that exists comes from him; all is by him and in him according to these causes.)[95] Here, Eckhart acknowledges the unity of God and of creation, but makes it clear that the creator of divine knowledge initiated such a union through the soul. As a result, God as Being and Intellect is intellectually conceivable by humans.

Eckhart's ontological proof agrees with what most Christian philosophers hold to be true. According to Gilson, the central tenet of Christian philosophy allows only for physico-metaphysical proofs that take their departure from Being as being.[96] Making God the starting point in affirming His existence perfectly accords with Christianity.[97] Letting human beings seek the existence of God in some way or another could be a mistake because they may be led to misinterpret God as 'an impersonal Absolute'.[98] However, this was not the case for Christian philosophers such as Eckhart who, like the Muslim philosopher Ibn Sīnā, held that the human self possesses an innate knowledge of God.

## Concluding Remarks

Ibn Sīnā's proof for the existence of God basically consists of a series of philosophical discussions within his metaphysical system. Although Islam (especially the discipline of *kalām*) was one of the influences on Ibn Sīnā's thought, it was not so to the extent that Christianity was on Eckhart's. Ibn Sīnā strives to synthesise the transcendent Deity of the *kalām* with the Aristotelian Unmoved Mover as the First Cause. Seen from this perspective, it is correct to say that Ibn Sīnā's theory of Being paves the way for the ontological and cosmological proofs for the existence of God, whereas Eckhart's passage 'I am who I am' is the starting point for the establishment of ontological and theological proofs.

Moreover, all of Ibn Sīnā's and Eckhart's proofs for the existence of God can be distinguished from Aristotle's proof from motion, in that a first mover and a first efficient cause are not meant to be God as such.[99] Another departure from the Aristotelian tradition is their insistence that the Ultimate Being generates matter. This distinction eventually prepares one for the idea of 'mystical union' between the deity and the human self, the latter possessing knowledge pertaining to the former.

Even though Eckhart was influenced by Ibn Sīnā, his metaphysical system, including his belief in the trinitarian God, the negation of negation and the denial of the self as well, distinguishes his concepts from those of Ibn Sīnā. It is also a matter of debate whether Eckhart's understanding of the Trinity has any correspondence with the triple reflection of Ibn Sīnā's First Intelligence,[100] for instance, or whether Eckhart's Father and Ibn Sīnā's First Intelligence are the sources for the plurality of being.

## Notes

1. For Ibn Sīnā's biography and influence, see Soheil M. Afnan, *Avicenna: His Life and Works* (London, 1958), pp. 258–288.

2. Eckhart's life and works are surveyed in Raymond Bernard Blakney's *Meister Eckhart, A Modern Translation* (New York and London, 1941).

3. For Ibn Sīnā's metaphysics see L. E. Goodman, *Avicenna* (London and New York, 1992), pp. 49–83; for Eckhart's metaphysics, C. F. Kelly, *Meister Eckhart on Divine Knowledge* (New Haven, CT and London, 1977).

4. For Ibn Sīnā, Thérèse-Anne Druart, 'The Soul and Body Problem: Avicenna and Descartes', in Thérèse-Anne Druart, ed., *Arabic Philosophy and the West: Continuity and Interaction* (Washington, 1988), p. 27; for Eckhart, see Kelly, *Meister Eckhart on Divine Knowledge, p. 27.*

5. Oliver Davies, *Meister Eckhart: Mystical Theologian* (London, 1991), p. 91.

6. Kelly, *Meister Eckhart on Divine Knowledge,* p. 29.

7. Frank Tobin, *Meister Eckhart: Thought and Language* (Philadephia, PA, 1986), p. 46.

8. See *Ibn Sīnā's work, al-Ishārāt wa'l-tanbīhāt,* with a commentary by Naṣīr al-Dīn

al-Ṭūsī (Cairo, 1958), pp. 319–320 and Ibn Sīnā, *al-Aḍḥawiyya fi'l-ma'ād*, ed. Ḥasan 'Aṣī (Beirut, 1984), pp. 127–131.

9. See *Meister Eckhart: Teacher and Preacher*, ed. Bernard McGinn (New York and Toronto, 1986), pp. 45–48.

10. Michael E. Marmura, 'Avicenna's "Flying Man" in Context', *The Monist*, 69 (1984), p. 383.

11. Ibn Sīnā, *al-Aḍḥawiyya fi amr al-ma'ād*, p. 127.

12. Fazlur Rahman, 'Ibn Sīnā', in M. M. Sharif, ed., *History of Muslim Philosophy* (Wiesbaden, 1963), vol. 1, p. 487.

13. Afnan, *Avicenna: His Life and Works*, p. 149.

14. Ibn Sīnā, *al-Ishārāt wa'l-tanbīhāt*, pp. 319–320 and its translation taken from Marmura's 'Avicenna's "Flying Man" in Context', p. 391.

15. A. M. Goichon, 'The Philosopher of Being', in *Avicenna Commemoration Volume* (Calcutta, 1956), p. 109.

16. Ibn Sīnā, *al-Ishārāt wa'l-tanbīhāt*, p. 321.

17. Parviz Morewedge, 'A Third Version of the Ontological Argument in the Sīnian Metaphysics', in Parviz Morewedge ed., *Islamic Philosophical Theology* (Albany, NY, 1979), p. 204.

18. McGinn, *Meister Eckhart: Teacher and Preacher*, p. 45.

19. Ibid.

20. Ibid.

21. Ibid.

22. Ibid.

23. Ibid., p. 46.

24. Ibid.

25. Ibid.

26. *Bullitio* literally means 'boiling' and 'boiling over'. In broader usage, this term relates to emanation. See, McGinn, 'A Glossary of Eckhartian Terms', in *Meister Eckhart: Teacher and Preacher*, pp. 391–392.

27. Michael Anthony Sells, 'The Metaphor and Dialectic of Emanation in Plotinus, John The Scot, Meister Eckhart and Ibn 'Arabi' (Ph.D., University of Chicago, 1982), p. 152.

28. McGinn, *Meister Eckhart: Teacher and Preacher*, p. 46. (Priscian was a Latin grammarian ca. 500 in Constantinople. His *Institutiones Grammaticae* became a standard text in the Middle Ages.)

29. Ibid., p. 47.

30. Maimonides, (1135–1204 CE) *'Guide for the Perplexed' (Moreh Nevukhim)* might have been read by Eckhart. See 'Maimonides' in Dan Cohn-Sherbok, *The Blackwell Dictionary of Judaica* (Oxford, 1992), p. 339.

31. Tetragrammaton is derived from Greek and means 'four letters' refering to the written word YHVH as the Hebrew name of God. See, 'Tetragrammaton' and 'Names of God' in Cohn-Sherbok, *The Blackwell Dictionary of Judaica*, pp. 538 and 182, respectively.

32. McGinn, Bernard, ed., *Meister Eckhart: Teacher and Preacher*, p. 47.

33. Ibid.

34. Ibid.

35. Michael Marmura, 'Avicenna: Metaphysics', *EIr*.

36. Julius R. Weinberg, *A Short History of Medieval Philosophy* (Princeton, NJ, 1991), p. 113.

37. Ibid., p. 74.

38. Nasr, *An Introduction to Islamic Cosmological Doctrines: The Conception of Nature and Methods used for Its Study by the Ikhwān al-Ṣāfā, al-Bīrūnī, and Ibn Sīnā* (London, 1978), p. 197.

39. Ibid., p. 198.

40. Tobin, *Meister Eckhart: Thought and Language*, p. 31.

41. The first term, *ens*, is translated as being (or beings) in reality; the second term, *esse*, is used to show the act of existing beings as they are; and the latter, *essentia* (essence), is every individual manifestation that belongs to all beings. See Tobin, *Meister Eckhart: Thought and Language*, p. 32.

42. Ibid.

43. Ibid., p. 35.

44. For Ibn Sīnā, see Seyyed Hossein Nasr's work, *Three Muslim Sages: Avicenna - Suhrawardi - Ibn ʿArabi* (New York, 1964), p. 25; for Eckhart, Davies, *Meister Eckhart: Mystical Theologian*, pp. 108–109.

45. Marmura, 'Avicenna: Metaphysics', *EIr.*

46. Nasr, *Three Muslim Sages*, p. 25.

47. Morewedge, 'Philosophical Analysis', p. 432.

48. Rahman, 'Ibn Sīnā', p. 482.

49. Ibid.

50. Tobin, *Meister Eckhart: Thought and Language*, p. 32.

51. Ibid.

52. Ibid.

53. G. R. Evans, *Philosophy and Theology in the Middle Ages* (London and New York, 1993), p. 59.

54. Ibid.

55. Sells, *The Metaphor and Dialectic of Emanation*, p. 153.

56. Tobin, *Meister Eckhart: Thought and Language*, p. 36.

57. Davies, *Meister Eckhart: Mystical Theologian*, p. 108.

58. Ibid.

59. Parviz Morewedge, *The Metaphysica of Avicenna (Ibn Sīnā): A Critical Translation-Commentary and Analysis of the Fundamental Arguments in Avicenna's 'Metaphysica' in the* Dānish-nāma-i ʿalaʾ-i *('The Book of Scientific Knowledge')* (London, 1973), p. 47.

60. Ibn Sīnā divides Being into three categories: necessary, contingent and impossible. Our discussion is limited to the first two. See also, Herbert A. Davidson, *Proofs for Eternity, Creation and the Existence of God in Medieval Islamic and Jewish Philosophy* (New York and Oxford, 1987), p. 290.

61. Goodman, *Avicenna*, p. 65.

62. Davidson, *Proofs for Eternity*, p. 290.

63. Marmura, 'Avicenna: Metaphysics', *EIr.*

64. Davidson, *Proofs for Eternity*, p. 310.

65. Ibn Sīnā argues that the nature of Necessary Existence is undivided in its meaning and quantity. See, *al-Ishārāt wa'l-tanbīhāt* (Beirut, 1970), Part III, Fourth Class, chap. 21, p. 472.

66. Abū Mansūr Muḥammad b. Muḥammad al-Māturīdī al-Samarqandī, *Kitāb al-tawḥīd*, ed. Fathalla Kholeif (Beirut, 1970), p. 35. See also Kholeif's *Analysis of the Contents*, p. xxv.

67. Aristotle, *Metaphysics*, Book 12, chap. 7, 1072a25–1072b10, in *The Complete Works of Aristotle*, ed. Jonathan Barnes (Princeton, NJ, 1984), p. 1694.

68. McGinn, *Meister Eckhart: Teacher and Preacher*, p. 162 and p. 173.

69. Ibid., p. 87.

70. Franz Pfeiffer, *Meister Eckhart*, tr. C. De B. Evans (London, 1924), p. 281.

71. Ibid., p. 283.

72. Sells, *The Metaphor and Dialectic of Emanation*, p. 175.

73. *The Holy Bible: New International Version* (New York, 1984), p. 51.

74. Halcyon Backhouse, ed., *The Best of Meister Eckhart* (New York, 1995), p. 117.

75. See 1 Corinthians 15:10.

76. For the lack of space, this paper does not consider whether Ibn Sīnā's proof for the existence of God is cosmological or ontological.

77. Goodman, *Avicenna*, p. 63.

78. Davidson, *Proofs for Eternity*, p. 299.

79. Ibid., pp. 289–302.

80. Morewedge, 'A Third Version of the Ontological Argument', p. 205.

81. Goodman, *Avicenna*, p. 63.

82. H. P. Owen, 'Arguments for the Existence of God', in Paul Edwards, ed., *The Encyclopedia of Philosophy* (New York, 1964), vol. 3, p. 348.

83. Landolt, 'Ghāzālī and Religionswissenschaft', *EA*, 45 (1991), p. 51, n. 125.

84. Ibid.

85. See Abū Bakr Muḥammad b. Isḥāq al-Kalābādhī, *al-Ta'arruf li-madhhab ahl al-taṣawwuf* (Beirut, 1993), p. 70.

86. Al-Ṭūsī, in his *Commentary on* al-Ishārāt wa'l-tanbīhāt, p. 482.

87. This proof, developed later on by 'Ain al-Quḍāt al-Hamadānī (executed in 526/1131). See, Landolt's article, 'Ghazālī and Religionswissenchaft', p. 56.

88. Ibn Sīnā, *al-Ishārāt wa'l-tanbīhāt*, Part III, Fourth Class, chapter 29, p. 482.

89. Landolt, 'Ghazālī and Religionswissenchaft', p. 51.

90. Ibn Sīnā, *al-Ishārāt wa'l-tanbīhāt*, p. 482.

91. Landolt, 'Ghazālī and Religionswissenchaft', p. 51.

92. McGinn, *Meister Eckhart: Teacher and Preacher*, p. 46.

93. Kelly, *Meister Eckhart on Divine Knowledge*, p. 54.

94. Tobin, *Meister Eckhart: Thought and Language*, p. 40.

95. Ibid., p. 41.

96. E. Gilson, *The Spirit of Mediæval Philosophy* (repr. Notre Dame and London, 1991), p. 80.

97. Kelly, *Meister Eckhart on Divine Knowledge*, p. 54.

98. Ibid.

99. Davidson, *Proofs for Eternity*, p. 238.

100. Hermann Landolt suggested this idea during a discussion on 24 May 1996.

# 25

# La Vision de Dieu dans l'Onirocritique Musulmane Médiévale

*Pierre Lory*

La question de la vision de Dieu par l'homme, on le sait, a parcouru l'histoire de la théologie musulmane. Elle est née au fil des siècles de l'exigence de cohérence doctrinale des exégètes musulmans de diverses tendances, cherchant à concilier le sens obvie de certains versets qur'aniques et *ḥadīth*s suggérant une contemplation visuelle de Dieu par les croyants, avec le dogme de l'absolue transcendance de Celui-ci (*tanzīh*). Dieu se rend-il visible dans l'au-delà seulement, ou dès ici-bas? Sa contemplation est-elle réservée à la seule élite des croyants, ou à tous les humains ressuscités? Cette vision s'entend-elle au sens physique, ou comme une sorte d'aperception intuitive du cœur? Quel serait le statut ontologique de cette forme présentée au regards? Nous ne reviendrons pas sur les implications théologiques de ces interrogations[1] mais voudrions apporter ici quelques modestes remarques sur une modalité particulière de la théophanie, celle qui se produit parfois lors d'un 'songe véridique' (*ru'yā ṣādiqa*). On se souvient que la tradition musulmane au sens large a attribué aux messages oniriques un statut à la fois considérable et ambigu, celui de complément ponctuel aux données révélées.[2] Elle a certes évacué de son domaine d'intérêt les rêves chaotiques et trompeurs (*aḍghāth aḥlām*), induits par l'action du démon, ainsi que les simples réminiscences nocturnes des préoccupations quotidiennes, mais prend en considération les songes fournissant un contenu positif, 'sain', c'est à dire utile au destin moral et religieux du rêveur. Elle s'appuie pour ce faire sur un nombre assez considérable de *ḥadīth*s. Le Prophète lui-même rêvait en effet souvent, racontait et interprétait ses propres songes à son entourage, et orienta certaines de ses décisions en fonction de messages oniriques. Les enseignements les plus fondamentaux retenus par la Tradition[3] sont les suivants:

- Après la mort du Prophète, les croyants auront à leur disposition les bonnes nouvelles (*mubashshirāt*), c'est à dire, précise le *ḥadīth*, les rêves sains. Ces nouvelles sont bonnes, non parce qu'elles seraient toujours agréables à recevoir, précisent les commentateurs – il peut s'agir de sévères avertissements – mais parce qu'elles traduisent une intention providentielle à l'endroit du rêveur destinée à le mettre sur la voie du salut.
- Ce rêve sain est la quarante-sixième partie de la prophétie.[4] Il n'est donc pas produit par la conscience du rêveur, mais correspond à un message d'origine transcendantale.
- Celui qui voit le Prophète en songe, le voit vraiment, car Satan ne peut prendre son aspect. La rencontre du Prophète en rêve est par conséquent clairement admise et confirmée. Le statut de la vision de Dieu, on le verra, se présente de façon plus équivoque.

Les recueils de *ḥadīths* et les sources historiques fournissent par ailleurs des exemples de rêves vécus par le Prophète lui-même et par certains de ses Compagnons en assez grand nombre. Or quelques unes de ces traditions évoquent la vision de Dieu Lui-même. Parmi les plus célèbres, le récit du *Miʿrāj*,[5] ou encore le fameux *ḥadīth al-ru'yā*: 'J'ai vu mon Seigneur sous la plus belle des formes… .'[6] Leur fonction est certes décisive, puisqu'ils fondent la possibilité pour un homme de percevoir le divin sous une certaine 'forme'. Mais nous limiterons notre propos ici à la question de la vision de Dieu chez le commun des croyants, non chez les personnes considérées comme saintes ou a fortiori prophètes.

Ces données traditionnelles sur le rêve ont été reprises et explicitées par plusieurs doctrinaires importants, comme al-Ghazālī[7] et Ibn Khaldūn,[8] qui ont tenté d'expliquer la nature même du processus onirique et sa fonction éventuelle dans la vie religieuse: tout rêve, y compris le plus délétère, est en définitive envoyé par Dieu. La portée spirituelle des songes fut par ailleurs largement valorisée par le courant soufi, chez qui les expériences oniriques viennent en contrepoint des états psychologiques à l'état de veille – afin de les annoncer, de les éclairer, de les amplifier voire de se substituer à elles. Mais, répétons-le, ces pages ne concernent pas des développements théologiques ou théosophiques, mais une forme de littérature à la fois plus modeste et plus proche aussi sans doute du vécu des Musulmans au Moyen-Age: les 'clés des songes', à savoir les traités de *taʿbīr al-ru'yā*.

L'interprétation des rêves connut un essor considérable durant les premiers siècles de l'ère hégirienne. Stimulée par l'aval explicite que lui conférait le *ḥadīth*, elle se développa comme une science divinatoire licite, admise par le consensus des simples croyants comme des docteurs. Des sentences en onirocritique furent attribuées de façon assez douteuse aux principaux Compagnons – Abū Bakr principalement, mais aussi 'Umar – ainsi qu'à plusieurs figures connues de la génération des Suivants: Saʿīd b. al-Musayyab, mais surtout Muḥammad b. Sīrīn (m. en 728).[9] Abū Nuʿaym, dans la notice du *Ḥilyat al-awliyā'* qu'il lui consacre, rapporte une seule parole remontant à lui et se rapportant à notre propos: 'Celui qui voit son Seigneur en songe entrera au Paradis'. Des traités plus étoffés ont été attribués à Ja'far al-Ṣādiq,[10] ainsi qu'à Abū Isḥāq al-Kirmānī, important auteur de la seconde moitié du 2/8 siècle, dont le *Dustūr fī'l-ta'bīr*, malheureusement perdu, a servi de base à la plupart des traités d'onirocritique ultérieurs. Ibn Qutayba compterait également parmi les auteurs ayant écrit dans cette discipline.[11] Quoiqu'il en soit, c'est à partir de la coupée du 4/10 siècle qu'apparaissent des compilations qui vont faire date et qui seront utilisées jusqu'à nos jours. Notre corpus, concernant la vision de Dieu dans les rêves, est constitué par les œuvres suivantes, classées dans l'ordre chronologique: le *Qādirī fī al-ta'bīr* d'Abū Sa'īd al-Dīnawarī (achevé en 397/1006) qui est l'ouvrage le plus éclectique et conséquent de l'ensemble; la *Bishāra wa'l-nidhāra fī ta'bīr al-ru'yā* d'Abū Sa'īd al-Wā'iẓ al-Kharkūshī (m. 406/1015);[12] le *Kāmil al-ta'bīr*, en persan, d'Abu'l-Faḍl al-Tiflisī (m. vers 600/1203); les *Ishārāt fī 'ilm al-'ibārāt* de Ghars al-Dīn b. Shāhīn (m. en 874/1468); le *Muntakhab fī ta'bīr al-ru'yā* d'Abū 'Alī al-Khalīlī al-Dārī (9/15 siècle), couramment connu sous le titre de *Tafsīr al-aḥlām al-kabīr* et attribué à Ibn Sīrīn; enfin le dictionnaire onirocritique *Ta'ṭīr al-anām fī tafsīr al-manām* de 'Abd al-Ghanī al-Nābulsī (m. en 1143/1731).[13] Cette littérature s'étend ainsi sur plus de sept siècles d'histoire, mais elle présente un caractère de large homogénéité. Les auteurs reprennent le matériel des ouvrages plus anciens, le recopiant souvent mot à mot. Nous n'avons absolument pas affaire à des recueils de songes individualisés, analysés en fonction du contexte particulier au rêveur, mais à des collections de songes 'types', repris et retransmis de génération en génération et de compilation à compilation. Les interprétations fournies relèvent toutes d'une 'tradition' au sens premier du mot; elles ne se renouvellent pas au fil des générations, mais se confirment plutôt l'une l'autre. A la fin de la chaîne, al-Nābulsī ne fournit plus à ses lecteurs qu'un dictionnaire, un recueil d'images stéréotypées jusque dans leur formulations accompagnées de quelques clés conventionnelles d'interprétation. Mais c'est précisément ici que ces textes nous intéressent: ils nous fournissent un relevé consensuel de ce qu'il est loisible de voir durant ce moment si étrange et privilégié qu'est le sommeil – cette petite mort qui préfigure à tant d'égards le moment de la résurrection finale. Nous n'avons pas accès ici à la subjectivité personnelle du rêveur, comme dans les récits oniriques de certains mystiques (al-Tirmidhī, Rūzbihān al-Baqlī, Najm al-Dīn Kubrā, Ibn 'Arabī pour ne citer que les plus célèbres), mais à des traits d'un imaginaire collectif qui s'aligne autant que se peut faire sur l'orthodoxie ambiante. Le témoignage de ces textes nous sont donc précieux en ce qu'ils nous renseignent sur un Islam spirituel 'moyen', commun. Car il n'est pas obligatoire d'être un grand mystique ou un profond théologien pour rêver de Dieu et d'en tirer bénéfice pour soi et pour ses proches.

Chacun des traités évoqués ci-dessus contient un chapitre consacré à la vision de Dieu proprement dite au cours de certains rêves; il est situé au début de l'ouvrage avec les autres thèmes spécifiquement religieux comme la vision des prophètes, des anges, des rituels, etc. Les descriptions de ces rêves comme les interprétations sont assez hétérogènes. Par ailleurs, des récits de rêves où une manifestation divine entre en jeu à propos de thèmes connexes se rencontrent dans d'autres passages dans le corps des ouvrages. En regroupant ces données, on constate que la vision de Dieu peut se produire selon diverses modalités:

- soit la vision d'une pure lumière, dénuée de formes ou d'attributs.[14]
- Dieu peut également apparaître sous une forme humaine. Cette forme humaine peut être inconnue, ou bien correspondre à celle d'une personne existante. Un *ḥadīth* souvent cité désigne la figure du souverain en particulier: 'L'Envoyé a dit: "la meilleure vision que vous puissiez avoir durant votre sommeil est celle de votre Seigneur, ou de son Prophète, ou de ses deux parents musulmans." On lui demanda: "Prophète de Dieu, un homme peut-il voir son Seigneur?" Il répondit: "(sous l'apparence) du souverain (*al-sulṭān*); car le souverain, c'est Dieu."'[15] Les parents ou un frère survenant en rêve peuvent également figurer la bienveillance, la compassion et la générosité que la providence divine, à l'instar des parents, porte sur le dormeur. A noter que cette bienveillance peut se traduire par des épreuves pénibles dans la vie terrestre, annonciatrices d'un surcroît de récompenses dans l'au-delà.[16] Le message divin emprunte donc les signifiants usuels des hommes concernant le pouvoir, l'amour, la fidélité, etc. Ceci dit, Dieu peut être perçu sous une grande variété de formes. Suite à une énumération de possibles théophanies, Ibn Shāhīn conclut: 'Celui qui voit Dieu en rêve sous une forme autre que celles que nous venons de mentionner, qui soit spécifique et originale tout en s'accordant à la *sharīʿa*, a dans tous les cas reçu un signe de bonne augure.'[17]
- Il peut également se manifester comme une présence physique mais dont les attributs ne sont pas spécifiés. Très souvent, nos textes parlent simplement de 'regarder Dieu' ('*wa-in raʾā-Hu*') sans autre détail.[18] C'est alors son action ou sa parole qui sont le thème du rêve. Le rêveur peut sentir que Dieu lui caresse la tête ou l'embrasse, sans que l'apparition divine ne soit décrite plus avant.[19] Ou bien, Dieu lui donne un présent – et alors, c'est la nature de ce cadeau qui est détaillée, mais non pas la manifestation de la divinité elle-même. Le don d'un vêtement par exemple indiquera que des épreuves terrestres conduisant vers une récompense *post mortem* attendent le rêveur.[20]

## Aspects de l'interprétation

Une première question qui se pose est celle, sous-jacente, de l'*anthropomorphisme* et du risque d'idolâtrie. Elle a été posée par al-Ghazālī notamment, qui a insisté sur l'idée que c'est Dieu qui, en définitive, envoie aux hommes le contenu de leurs rêves – comme celui de leurs pensées à l'état de veille. Libre à Lui donc de Se donner à voir sous la forme qu'Il juge adéquate. Mais les images oniriques ne sont pas pour autant imposées selon un pur arbitraire: le rêve est un message, ce qui implique une cohérence dans sa signification. De fait, une correspondance générale existe entre les formes des mondes célestiels et celles du monde terrestre. En ce sens, en fonction de cette homologie générale, il est possible de voir le roi sous la forme du soleil, le vizir sous celle de la lune, et Dieu comme une lumière. Ceci dit, nos auteurs onirocrites s'adressaient à un public assez vaste, qui consultait leurs livres à des fins pratiques et qui n'était pas intéressé par ce type de spéculations théologiques. Nous ne rencontrons donc pas de longs développements sur l'immatérialité de Dieu, sur sa transcendence, etc. Les remarques incidentes de nos auteurs sont toutefois fort révélatrices de leur volonté de bien marquer leur orthodoxie. La supériorité du rêve où Dieu est 'dépourvu d'attribut, de forme, de ressemblance (*mithāl*)', pour reprendre l'expression d'al-Dīnawarī, Se présentant comme une pure et splendide lumière, est soulignée: il s'agit de l'annonce d'un destin faste dans ce monde-ci ou/et dans l'autre. Le rêveur y perçoit Dieu avec son cœur – c'est à dire, en saisissant le sens de sa Présence.[21] Cette expérience se rapproche extérieurement quelque peu de celle des mystiques. De façon plus générale, il est un bon signe de percevoir Dieu comme s'Il se trouvait derrière un voile, cela par référence au verset qur'anique 42:51 'Il n'est pas donné à l'homme que Dieu lui parle autrement que par inspiration ou derrière un voile'. Par contrecoup, et un peu paradoxalement, Le percevoir sans ce voile devient un indice néfaste de déficience en matière de religion.[22] Mais le danger de l'anthropomorphisme existe bel et bien dans d'autres cas, ceux où le rêveur voit Dieu sous la forme d'une créature, et où il se met à adorer cette forme comme étant son Dieu. Un tel rêve avertit de la gravité de l'état de péché où se trouve le sujet. Or une majorité de rêves de vision de Dieu consignés dans nos traités présentent des aspects anthropomorphiques. Al-Nābulsī par exemple, dans l'article 'Allāh' de son dictionnaire d'onirocritique, précise que 'Dieu ne peut être ni défini ni désigné par analogie' et se montre sévère à l'encontre des rêves de théophanies concrètes; puis, sans relever de contradiction, il fournit plusieurs exemples flagrants de *tashbīh*. Nous nous trouvons ici devant une aporie que l'on serait tenté de résoudre par le recours à la dimension imaginale de l'être dont Henry Corbin a souligné l'importance dans la vie spirituelle des Soufis.[23] Une telle interprétation serait sans doute légitime, mais nos textes ne la suggèrent pas explicitement. On pourrait expliquer leur positions à travers certaines considérations fournies par al-Dīnawarī en particulier, dont l'œuvre est la plus construite et la plus conséquente parmi celles de notre corpus. Apparemment, ce qui est grave pour lui n'est pas tant de voir Dieu sous une forme créaturelle, mais de Le confondre avec elle:

> Si le rêveur voit une forme, un attribut, une ressemblance et qu'il lui est dit: 'ceci est ton Dieu', et qu'il se prosterne devant elle en pensant qu'il s'agit d'un dieu, qu'il l'adore, cela signifie qu'il se rapproche mensongèrement de ce que représente cette forme ou cet attribut – qu'il s'agisse d'un abstraction ou d'un être réel. Car

la vision de Dieu (*ru'ya Allāh*) ne peut se définir ni se décrire, elle ne peut exister dans le monde de la veille. Il s'agit donc d'un des songes vains (*aḍghāth*). Car Dieu Très-Haut a dit: 'Les regards ne l'atteignent pas' (Qur'an 6:103).[24]

Voir Dieu en rêve doté d'attributs qui ne Lui conviennent pas (assoupi ou endormi par exemple) ou blasphémer est aussi, tout naturellement, un indice de péché grave.[25] Quoiqu'il en soit, on le constate, le dogme fait donc partie intégrante des scénarios de rêve exposés. Dieu ne Se laisse jamais voir. La forme qu'Il envoie au rêveur pour Se représenter est un signe, une partie du message qu'Il lui destine. Elle n'est donc jamais ni complètement 'vraie', ni mensongère. Elle n'enseigne rien sur Dieu, mais uniquement sur la situation morale et religieuse du rêveur.

La *parole* accompagnant la vision est un élément essentiel du rêve. Il peut arriver que le rêve soit 'extatique' et accompagné d'un sentiment de crainte et d'exultation, et demeure alors muet; ou que Dieu, apparaissant sous forme humaine, reste silencieux, ce qui est un signe très néfaste exprimant le courroux divin. Dans de nombreux cas toutefois, il semble qu'il y ait message auditif, et le rêveur est alors tenu de recevoir ces paroles dans leur sens littéral: car si Dieu peut voiler son apparence sous des formes sensibles imaginales, son discours, lui, ne se masque pas sous des symboles. Le texte du rêve ne subit pas de *ta'wīl* comme la parole qur'anique ou éventuellement le *ḥadīth*. C'est là un des points marquant la limite du rêve – part de la prophétie certes, mais part réduite malgré tout: il s'agit d'un message ponctuel dans le temps et univoque dans son expression car adressé à une personne déterminée et pour elle seule.[26] Ces paroles sont parfois ramenées à des citations qur'aniques, comme si Dieu transmettait son message en pointant sur le verset de la Révélation adéquat à la situation du rêveur. Il arrive également que des images oniriques soient rapportées à tel passage du Texte sacré. Mais le rapport proposé entre le verset et la situation du dormeur n'est le plus souvent pas direct. Voir Dieu irrité pourra signifier que le rêveur tombera d'un endroit élevé – mur, montagne etc, en raison du verset qur'anique 20:81: 'Ma colère s'abattrait sur vous, et quiconque encourt ma colère connaîtra la chute.'[27]

Un autre point qui mérite d'être noté est la *réversibilité* du symbole de la présence de Dieu dans les rêves. On peut voir Dieu sous la forme de son père; mais à l'inverse, l'apparition de Dieu peut renvoyer à la personne du père. Par exemple, la présence de Dieu irrité désignerait la colère des parents, ou sa bienveillance leur contentement. Plus généralement, voir Dieu sous la forme d'une personne connue indique le succès et la reconnaissance promise à ladite personne.[28] Voir Dieu sous la forme d'une idole peut signifier que l'on se trouve de bonne foi dans l'erreur (cf. *supra* note 24). Ou, ainsi qu'il vient d'être signalé, percevoir en rêve la colère divine pourra tout simplement avertir de l'imminence de la chute du haut d'un mur.

Par ailleurs, un parallèle doit être tracé entre les apparitions oniriques de Dieu, et celles où des anges, des prophètes ou des saints viennent apporter des messages au rêveurs. Car nos traités d'onirocritique consacrent également de nombreuses pages à ces rêves là, détaillant la nature et l'aspect exact de chaque ange ou prophète qui se manifeste en songe. Ces rêves – et notamment ceux mettant en scène les prophètes et tout particulièrement Muḥammad – sont nombreux, beaucoup plus que les rêves d'apparitions divines. Cependant il importe de noter que le contenu même du message livré ne diffère jamais beaucoup de ceux des théophanies proprement dites. Les codes d'interprétation sont les mêmes, les diagnostics également: à l'instar de la théophanie, l'apparition d'un prophète ou de l'ange confirme le comportement vertueux, annonce le succès dans les affaires d'ici-bas et le salut dans l'au-delà. Le silence du prophète, comme celui de Dieu, ou leur éloignement, sont des signes de désapprobation grave.[29] Le parallèle est frappant, jusque dans la formulation du diagnostic. En soi, la chose n'a rien d'étrange, puisqu'en rêve comme dans le dogme, le prophète ou l'ange n'est qu'un fidèle message du Dieu souverain. Simplement, à quelques exceptions près, il ne semble pas que la manifestation de Dieu 'en personne' confère au songe un statut privilégié ou un degré de véracité supérieur à l'apparition de ses envoyés. Cela pourrait être dû à une prudence fondamentale face à une expérience directe du divin qui viendrait mettre en danger l'édifice dogmatique. Mais peut-être faut-il y voir à nouveau l'idée qu'une théophanie demeure toujours indirecte, équivoque, imparfaite, et ne doit pas être surévaluée. Par comparaison, le face à face avec le prophète paraît plus immédiat, clair, aisé à interpréter.

Quant au *contenu* des rêves – c'est à dire, aux interprétations toutes prêtes qui sont fournies dans nos recueils – ils convergent dans la plupart des cas vers la finalité morale de la vie du croyant: le respect de la morale, la promesse de la vie heureuse dans l'au-delà. Voir Dieu constitue un gage d'engagement dans la bonne voie, il s'agit fondamentalement d'un signe de bonne augure, d'une promesse de la vision béatifique du paradis – ou bien, s'Il semble irrité, une menace et un avertissement. Mais la démarche interprétative est loin d'être aussi simple qu'on pourrait le supposer au premier abord. L'intrusion de la subjectivité dans les interprétations est constante. Cette subjectivité présente un double aspect en fait.

- D'une part, la qualité morale et religieuse générale du rêveur intervient de façon décisive. La vision de Dieu en rêve doit être interprétée comme une malédiction et non une bénédiction dans le cas où le rêveur est en état de péché. Le songe est alors à recevoir comme un avertissement et une mise en garde (*indhār*, *taḥdhīr*).
- D'autre part, le ressenti subjectif du rêveur au moment ou le songe est vécu – ce qu'al-Dīnawarī appelle le *ḍamīr* du consultant – est indispensable pour que l'onirocrite accomplisse valablement son travail d'exégèse. Voir Dieu sans ressentir de crainte révérencielle par exemple est un indice de fort mauvaise augure.[30]

Nous retrouvons ici l'embarras foncier où se trouve la méthode onirocritique musulmane. Celle-ci a tenté depuis les premiers siècles de se fonder comme une science religieuse à part entière. Certains auteurs, comme Ibn Qutayba (c.à.d. le traité qui lui est attribué, cf. *supra* note 11) ou al-Dīnawarī ont tenté d'isoler des critères d'interprétation invariants des données oniriques, puisés dans le Qur'an et la Sunna et qu'ils ont désignés comme des *uṣūl*; ainsi la lumière désigne Dieu, le lait désigne la science, la chemise la piété, etc. A ces fondements, ils tâchaient d'articuler des variables, les *furūʿ*, constituées par l'apport des expériences des consultants et de leurs particularités sociales, culturelles etc. Il faut toutefois admettre que ces tentatives ont fait long feu. Les onirocrites n'ont pas réussi à maintenir des cadres d'interprétation fixes, invariantes, dans un domaine aussi labile que celui du symbolisme onirique. On ne peut mettre à jour une syntaxe et une morphologie de l'expérience qui fonctionne à l'échelle d'une société entière, fût-elle homogène dans ses repères symboliques comme l'était la *umma* musulmane au Moyen-Age. Force est de constater que l'apparition de Dieu dans les rêves demeurait elle-même profondément équivoque, et ne pouvait même pas être ramenée à quelques règles élémentaires. Elle déborde en effet du domaine de la morale et du salut, pour s'étendre à celui d'interprétations plus terre à terre: une présence divine aperçue à tel endroit assurerait la justice sociale, de bonnes récoltes, ou l'absence d'épidémie etc.[31] Et là aussi, le ressenti au moment du rêve demeure un point décisif: percevoir une lumière indescriptible sans pouvoir la rapporter (à un sentiment religieux) est une annonce de grave problèmes de santé.[32] La tradition onirocritique nous transmet des interprétations fixes de rêves typiques, mais celles-ci n'obéissent au fond à aucune logique méthodique.

Que conclure à la suite de ces quelques données? Principalement que la vision de Dieu dans un rêve ne constitue pas forcément une expérience spirituelle d'une dimension exceptionnelle. Une telle théophanie se trouve comme encapsulée dans un dispositif beaucoup plus vaste – dogmatique et juridique – qui ne le valorise pas particulièrement: aucune tentation montaniste ne semblait se manifester dans l'Islam sunnite médiéval. S'il est loisible en effet au croyant de voir son Seigneur en rêve, ainsi que le fit Muḥammad, le contenu et la portée d'un tel rêve se trouvent immédiatement limités à la sphère individuelle, et subordonnés au cadre religieux préexistant. Le rêve vient simplement expliquer au sujet où il se trouve par rapport à la ligne de la religion qu'il encadre: il le resitue dans une 'position qur'anique' de choix entre la vraie et la mauvaise foi. Un rêve dont le contenu serait déviant, comme celui d'un culte de type idolâtrique, est ipso facto disqualifié: le message dont il est porteur, c'est la mécréance du rêveur, et non une donnée du culte. Le cercle est bouclé: le croyant ne peut voir Dieu que dans le cadre de l'orthodoxie, et son rêve ne peut que le conforter dans son insertion dans cette même orthodoxie.

Une dernière remarque concernant la dimension mystique de la vision de Dieu. Nous avons précisé plus haut que nous n'avions pas à aborder la question des rêves tels qu'ils se produisent et sont interprétés par les Soufis, du fait que les traités d'onirocritique de notre corpus s'adressent à un lectorat assez large, et beaucoup plus préoccupé par les réalités terrestres sensibles que par l'union au divin ici-bas. Il n'existe toutefois pas de césure très nette entre les milieux soufis et ceux des Musulmans pieux et lettrés. Les traités d'onirocritique mentionnés ici font état de visions divines en rêve rapportées par certains Soufis connus, dont les expériences oniriques étaient visiblement incorporés à la culture commune de l'époque. C'est au cours d'un rêve en forme de *miʿrāj* qu'Abū ʿUbayd al-Bishrī intercède avec succès auprès de Dieu en faveur d'Adam.[33] Ailleurs, al-Kharrāz se fait blâmer en rêve par Dieu pour avoir eu recours aux thèmes de poésie amoureuse dans ses séances de *samāʿ*.[34] A l'inverse, les Soufis n'ont apparemment pas professé de théorie particulière concernant les visions durant le rêve. La consultation des ouvrages les plus classiques – le *Taʿarruf* d'al-Kalābādhī, la *Risāla* d'al-Qushayrī, les *ʿAwārif al-maʿārif* d'al-Suhrawardī – montre bien combien ils fondaient leurs conceptions de la *ruʾyā ṣāliḥa* sur le même socle qur'anique et traditionnel que tous les autres Musulmans. Cette position est particulièrement nette concernant la question de la vision de Dieu. Les Soufis avaient parfois été accusés de prétendre 'voir' Dieu. Or les principaux auteurs soufis qui abordent la question (jusqu'à al-Ghazālī; Ibn ʿArabī opèrera une synthèse renouvelée de ce thème) le font avec une grande prudence: la vision de Dieu est possible, mais dans l'au-delà seulement, et pour les bienheureux uniquement. Quant à la notion de *mushāhada*, si centrale dans la littérature spirituelle des mystiques, elle est définie comme l'expérience d'une totale certitude, *yaqīn*, reçue par le cœur à l'état de sobriété ou d'extase aussi forte et immédiate qu'une vision oculaire.[35] De toute évidence, l'expérience onirique n'était pas prise en compte dans la question théologique de la vision de Dieu. Mais ceci n'a pas entravé le rôle essentiel joué par les rêves dans le déroulement de la vie spirituelle des mystiques. Les novices les soumettaient à leurs shaykhs, et les grands Maîtres y trouvaient la confirmation de leur avancement spirituel.[36] Les apparitions divines durant le sommeil constituaient des compléments ou des confirmations des dévoilements reçus à l'état de veille. Leur nombre, leur poids sont tels que l'on est amené à s'interroger sur l'étanchéité séparant l'état de sommeil de celui de veille – la seule et unique source de la conscience résidant toujours, en définitive, en Dieu Lui-même – même si bien évidemment la prise de conscience proprement dite devait avoir lieu dans le second, en pleine lucidité.

## Notes

1. Au sujet desquelles on pourra consulter J. van Ess, *Theologie und Gesellschaft im 2. Und 3. Jahrhundert Hidschra* (Berlin, 1991), tome 4, D1, plus particulièrement 411 sq. et index s.v. *ruʾyat Allāh*. Voir aussi ma contribution dans le volume, *Autour du regard: Mélanges Gimaret*, éd. É. Chaumont et al. (Leuven, 2003), pp. 183–212.

2. Sur le rêve en général dans la société musulmane, on pourra consulter John C. Lamoreaux, *The Early Muslim Tradition of Dream Interpretation* (Albany, NY, 2003); Pierre Lory, *Le rêve et ces interprétations en Islam* (Paris, 2003).

3. Cf. al-Bukhārī, *Taʿbīr*; Muslim, *Ruʾyā*; Abū Dāwūd, *Ruʾyā* et *Adab, bāb mā jāʾa fīʾl-ruʾyā*; al-Tirmidhī, *Ruʾyā*; Ibn Māja, *Taʿbīr al-ruʾyā*; al-Dārimī, *Ruʾyā*.

4. *Ḥadīth* transmis avec un grand nombre de variantes dans sa formulation et dans la proportion indiquée dans les grands recueils canoniques; cf. le luxe de détails exégétiques apportés par Ibn Ḥajar dans le *Fatḥ al-bārī*.

5. Que le dogme musulman refuse d'assimiler à un simple rêve. Pour une synthèse sur cette question, v. dans éd. M. A. Amir-Moezzi, *Le voyage initiatique en terre d'Islam* (Paris, 1996), les contributions de C. Gilliot, J. van Ess, D. Gimaret, G. Monnot.

6. Les commentaires théologiques suscités par cette tradition comme par cet autre *ḥadīth* 'J'ai vu mon Seigneur sous la forme d'un jeune homme à l'abondante chevelure etc.' – qui rapportent vraisemblablement une expérience onirique – sont résumés dans D. Gimaret, *Dieu à l'image de l'homme* (Paris, 1997), pp. 143–164. Pour la question de la théophanie dans une belle forme humaine chez les Soufis, v. H. Ritter, *Das Meer der Seele* (Leiden, 1955), p. 445 s. Voir aussi maintenant la contribution du Prof. Pourjavady dans ce volume.

7. V. *Iḥyā*, IV (*Kitāb dhikr al-mawt wa-mā baʿda-hu*, 8); *Maḍnūn* (*Faṣl fī man lā yaʿrifu ḥaqīqat al-ruʾyā*); *Tahāfut al-falāsifa* (*Fī ibṭāl qawli-him inna nufūs al-samāwāt muṭṭaliʿa ʿalā jamīʿ al-juzʾiyyāt al-ḥāditha fī hādhā al-ʿālam*); *Mishkāt al-anwār*, II (*Fī sirr al-tamthīl wa-minhāji-hi*).

8. *Al-Muqaddima*, VI (*ʿIlm taʿbīr al-ruʾyā*). A noter la place très particulière de l'onirocritique dans le plan de l'ouvrage – située juste après les sciences religieuses (*fiqh*, *kalām*), et avant les sciences profanes (arithmétique, astronomie ...).

9. L'activité d'onirocrite d'Ibn Sīrīn apparaît très peu évidente dans les sources anciennes. Pour des raisons mal expliquées, sa réputation dans ce domaine s'amplifia énormément vers le 3è siècle. Plusieurs traités de taʿbīr lui sont attribués, dont le principal, le *Tafsīr al-ahlām al-kabīr*, est une compilation tardive due à Abū ʿAlī al-Dārī (cf. *infra*). Sa célébrité s'est étendue au domaine occidental, cf. Fahd, *Études d'histoire*, tome 1, pp. 112 s.

10. Il s'agit du *Taqsīm al-ruʾyā*, très certainement apocryphe, mais abondamment cité dans certaines sources postérieures comme le *Kāmil al-taʿbīr* d'al-Tiflisī. L'ouvrage représente une tentative de taxonomie complète des thèmes oniriques et des conditions de leurs interprétations.

11. Son *Taʿbīr al-ruʾyā* ne figure pas parmi les titres des œuvres connues du célèbre polygraphe, mais cette attribution figure cependant déjà dans le *Fihrist* d'Ibn al-Nadīm. T. Fahd a étudié dans le ms. Is.Saib Sincer I 4501 à Ankara le traité conservé sous ce titre et cette attribution, et n'exclut pas qu'il puisse s'agir d'un texte authentique (*La divination arabe*, Paris, 1987, pp. 316–328).

12. Bien que pratiquement contemporain d'al-Dīnawarī – et concitoyen, tous deux vivant à Nīshāpūr – Kharkūshī ne fait pas référence au *Qādirī fīʾl-taʿbīr* dans son propre traité d'onirocritique. Il est vrai qu'il représente un enseignement plus populaire, moins savant que celui de son aîné.

13. Il s'agit bien sûr ici d'un choix assez réduit d'œuvres, comparé à la liste de 158 titres établie par T. Fahd (*La divination arabe*, p. 330 s.) ou Lamoreaux, (*The Early Muslim Tradition of Dream Interpretation*, p. 175), mais nous pensons là qu'il s'agit clairement des textes les plus synthétiques et les plus consultés à l'époque médiévale.

14. V. p.ex. *Qādirī*, I, p. 117.

15. Cf. notamment *Qādirī*, I, p. 95. Ce *ḥadīth* n'apparaît pas dans les collections canoniques.

16. *Qādirī*, I, p. 119; *Ta'ṭīr*, p. 12.

17. *Ishārāt*, p. 37.

18. Ainsi par exemple *Qādirī*, I, p. 118; *Bishāra*, fol.16b.

19. *Qādirī*, I, p. 117; *Bishāra*, fol.16b; *Ishārāt*, 37; *Ta'ṭīr*, pp. 11, 12.

20. Cf. p.ex. *Qādirī*, I, p. 118; *Bishāra*, fol.16b; *Ishārāt*, p. 36. Mais le don peut indiquer un faveur bien plus concrète: le cadeau offert dans le rêve sera offert au dormeur à son réveil. Cf. *Qādirī*, I, p. 118.

21. Qādirī, I, p. 117; *Ishārāt*, pp. 35, 37, où une telle vision est précisée '*bi-lā kayfa wa-lā kayfiyya*'; *Kāmil*, fol. 23b, qui souligne le danger de l'hérésie des corporéistes; *Muntakhab*, p. 64; *Ta'ṭīr*, pp. 11, 12.

22. Qādirī, I, pp. 118, 120; *Ishārāt*, pp. 35, 38; *Muntakhab*, p. 64; *Ta'ṭīr*, p. 12.

23. Cf. tout particulièrement son *Imagination créatrice dans le soufisme d'Ibn 'Arabī* (Paris, 1958); trad. angl. *Creative Imagination in the Sufism of Ibn 'Arabī* (Princeton, NJ, 1977).

24. *Qādirī*, I, p. 122; *Muntakhab*, p. 65 où il est précisé qu'il s'agit d'un signe que le rêveur s'adonne à l'erreur en pensant qu'il est dans la vérité.

25. *Ishārāt*, p. 37, *Muntakhab*, p. 65 et *Ta'ṭīr*, p. 12 y voient l'indice de l'ingrat face aux bienfaits et au décret de Dieu.

26. *Qādirī*, I, pp. 118, 120; *Ishārāt*, p. 36; *Muntakhab*, p. 64; *Ta'ṭīr*, p. 11.

27. *Bishāra*, fol. 17a; *Ta'ṭīr*, p. 12.

28. *Qādirī*, I, p. 122; *Bishāra*, foll. 16b–17a; *Kāmil*, fol. 23a; *Ishārāt*, p. 36.

29. Comparer, à titre d'exemple, l'éloignement de Dieu ou sa colère avec celle du Prophète dans *Qādirī*, I, pp. 122 et 124. Pour une synthèse récente sur la question de la vision du prophète en rêve, v. J. Katz, *Dreams, Sufism and Sainthood* (Leiden, 1966), chap. VII.

30. *Qādirī*, I, p. 120; *Kāmil*, foll. 22b, 23a.

31. *Qādirī*, I, pp. 119, 120; *Bishāra*, fol. 17a; *Ishārāt*, pp. 36, 37; *Kāmil*, fol. 22 a et b; *Ta'ṭīr*, pp. 12, 13.

32. *Qādirī*, I, p. 119; *Bishāra*, fol. 16b.

33. *Bishāra*, fol. 16a et b; une autre version apparaît dans *Muntakhab*, p. 63, le héros en étant cette fois-ci al-Tustarī.

34. *Muntakhab*, p. 64.

35. Cf. *Sarrāj, Luma'* (*K. al-aḥwāl wa'l-maqāmāt*); al-Kalābādhī, *Ta'arruf*, XLVI; al-Hujwirī, *Kashf al-mahjūb* (*Kashf al-ḥijāb al-thāmin*); al-Qushayrī, *Risāla (Bāb tafsīr alfāẓ ...)*, où la *mushāhada* est décrite comme un état d'abolition de toute dualité. Mais cf. Marcotte dans ce volume-ci.

36. Parfois, ils en rendent compte dans leurs écrits, comme Tirmidhī dans son *Bad' sha'n*; Rūzbihān dans le *Kashf al-asrār*; Najm al-Dīn Kubrā dans les *Fawā'iḥ al-jamāl*; Ibn 'Arabī dans *al-Mubashshirāt fī'l-ru'yā* et dans bien d'autres passages de son œuvre; Dabbāgh, rapporté par Ibn al-Mubārak dans son *Ibrīz*.

# 26

# The Spiritual Journey in Kubrawī Sufism

*Leonard Lewisohn*

*Coda*: Central to Hermann Landolt's numerous studies of Islamic theosophy have been the writings of Shaykh Nūr al-Dīn al-Isfarāyinī, 'Alā' al-Dawla al-Simnānī and 'Azīz-i Nasafī, three Kubrawī Sufi masters[1] whose inspiration pervades many of his scholarly dissertations. A pivotal term of the vocabulary and doctrine of the Persian Kubrawī Sufis is the concept of *sulūk* (wayfaring, spiritual conduct). By examining the permutations of this technical term in the lexicon of early classical Persian Sufism as well as in the writings of the later Kubrawī Sufis ('Azīz-i Nasafī in particular), this essay attempts to chart the course of the 'spiritual journey' in Islamic mysticism. It is hoped that the general overview of the meaning of this term given below will shed some light on the spiritual methods of *taṣawwuf* and, at the same time, provide some insight into the philosophical approach of *ḥikma* at the heart of Professor Landolt's researches into the Kubrawī mystics.

## I. *Sulūk* in Classical Persian Sufism

> After the science of divine unity (*'ilm-i tawḥīd*) and the religious law, there is no science nobler than that of spiritual wayfaring (*'ilm-i sulūk*), and after education and pedagogy, there is no art more eminent than that of asceticism (*fann-i riyāḍāt*). In truth, just as the art of asceticism is a stimulating tonic by which lost stragglers in the Vale of Error are conveyed to the waystation of Certitude, so the science of spiritual wayfaring is a cardinal principle through which those benighted on the way of Ignorance reach their goal of Faith.
>
> Ḍiyā' al-Dīn al-Nakhshabī[2]

*Sulūk* is the Islamic term for the archetypal motif of the 'journey' that mystics of different religious traditions have used to describe the steps which must be taken to leave illusory selfhood behind and realise Union with the divine.[3] Connotations of the term in Islamic literature include: 'progression', 'method', 'behaviour', 'comportment',[4] 'demeanour', 'wayfaring', 'conduct' and 'manners'.[5] Derived from the Arabic triliteral root S-L-K, *sulūk* means 'to travel' or 'to follow a road', depending on the context. However, in the particular lexicon of Muslim mysticism, *sulūk* denotes 'methodical progress on the "*via mystica*" or *ṭarīqa*, the process of ascension and advancement – psychical, ethical and spiritual – which the Sufi 'wayfarer' (*sālik*) experiences in his pursuit (*ṭalab*) of God. It is, as Victor Danner defined it, the method of 'progression on the Path towards divine Reality' being 'the opposite of *tanazzul* and the same as *taraqqī*'.[6]

Constituting the principal 'course of practice' on the Sufi Path, *sulūk* involves an integral method of spiritual progress based on spiritual struggle (*mujāhada*) and inner intuitive 'unveiling' (*kashf*), combining what in Christian mystical theology are known as the via purgativa and the via illuminativa into a broad-based mystical highway. Thus, the term *sulūk* designates – as J. S. Trimingham aptly put it – 'the scala perfectionis of the orders'.[7] *Sulūk* is the not merely proper 'wayfaring', but 'spiritual correctness' (as is conveyed by the modern Persian expression *ḥusn-i sulūk*, 'good behaviour' or 'becoming conduct') as well, the 'travelling manners' appropriate spiritual attitude and proper ethical comportment which should be possessed by any road-wise Sufi 'wayfarer' (*sālik*) who wishes to traverse the stations of the Way. Such a 'wayfarer', comments the great Akbarian master 'Abd al-Razzāq Kāshānī, is 'one who is travelling towards God, being midway between the novice (*al-murīd*) and one who has attained the end of the Path (*al-muntahī*)'.[8]

The later Sufi conception of *sulūk* especially as the term featured amongst the Kubrawiyya from the late thirteenth century onwards is more or less identical in connotation to the term *al-ṭarīq* (Way), which is referred to throughout the Qur'an,[9] as Su'ād Ḥakīm points out. The eminent Kubrawī Shaykh Najm al-Dīn Rāzī (d. 654/1256), for instance, introduced the term in precisely this sense in the exordium of his *Mirṣād al-'ibād* where he emphasises that his work is devoted to 'expounding the modes of proper conduct on the Sufi Path (*bayān-i sulūk-i rāh-i ṭarīqat*)'.[10] In Aristotelian terms, one might say that while the Sufi Path (*ṭarīq*) is the *substance* of the archetypal Journey of the Muslim mystic, *sulūk* incarnates the *form*, the very process of travelling, of wayfaring upon it.[11]

In many Sufi works *sulūk* is contrasted, on the one hand, to 'attraction' (*jadhba*) and to 'spiritual travel' (*sayr*) on the other. Sometimes paired as two different polar opposites to *sulūk*, and sometimes coupled to the term for the sake of rhetorical effect, the term takes on some interesting nuances.[12] Also contrasted with *sulūk* in Sufi terminology are terms such as *sayr* (visionary voyage) and *ṭayr* (spiritual flight), denoting higher degrees or levels of the same spiritual journey. The pair '*sayr* and *sulūk*', 'flight of spiritual vision' vs. 'methodical progression' on the Path, are the most popular of such terms, belonging to those famous linguistic pairs of opposites – I refer to such pairs as *waṣl* vs. *faṣl, talwīn* vs. *tamkīn*, etc. – whose alliterative rhyming is manipulated to great rhetorical effect by the Sufi writers.[13] The *sayr* and *sulūk* relationship, however, is complementary rather than hierarchically distinct; instead of considering the former as a higher stage of the latter, each should be seen as depending on the other: *sayr* being the fruit of the tree of *sulūk*.[14]

It was only with the rise of institutional Sufism in the early fifth/twelfth century that the term *sulūk*, denoting the progression of the mystic pilgrim on his path, comes to the fore in its formal technical usage. Hence arose the conspicuous omission of *sulūk* from Louis Massignon's *Essai sur les origines du lexique technique de la mystique musulmane.*[15] This omission is also symptomatic of the term's absence from nearly all the early – third/tenth- to fourth/eleventh-century classical Sufi texts written in Arabic.[16] However, as an integral concept in the Sufi lexicon of technical terms, *sulūk* becomes, a century later, regularly featured throughout mystical literature in Arabic and Persian to denote the traditional course of Sufi discipline.

Abū Ḥāmid al-Ghazālī (d. 505/1111), for instance, gave a detailed description of the practical requirements of *sulūk* in Sufism taught to neophytes in his *Iḥyā ʿulūm al-dīn*,[17] a mystical usage further underlined in the *Tamhīdāt* composed by his brother's (Aḥmad al-Ghazālī's) disciple ʿAyn al-Quḍāt al-Hamadhānī (d. 525/1131) who drew a distinction between 'the people of religion on the religious way' (*ahl-i dīn dar rāh-i dīn*) and 'the people of spiritual conduct who follow the mystical method' (*ahl-i sulūk dar rāh-i sulūk*). *Sulūk* principally related to the 'conduct' of the elect who tread the Sufi *ṭarīqa,* and is only secondarily treated as an affair of the *sharīʿa* (that is shared in common among all Muslims), according to ʿAyn al-Quḍāt.[18] A few decades later, Ibn Munawwar in his *Asrār al-tawḥīd* (composed between 553–588/1158–1192) used the term in exactly the same sense to describe the saintly manner of 'conduct on the course of the Sufi Path' (*sulūk-i ṭarīq-i ṭarīqat*) as was observed by the holy companions of Abū Saʿīd b. Abi'l-Khayr (d. 440/1049).[19]

During the medieval (twelfth–fourteenth-century) revival of Sufism in Anatolia and Persia,[20] numerous works devoted to elucidation of the intricacies of the Sufi 'Pilgrim's Progress' were composed that adopted the notion of *sulūk* as their central theme. The most famous of such works are the great poem *Naẓm al-sulūk* or 'The Gnostic's Progress' by Ibn al-Fāriḍ (d. 633/ 1235) of Egypt[21] and the *Silk al-sulūk* or 'The Method of Spiritual Progress' by the Chishtī Sufi master Ḍiyā' al-Dīn al-Nakhshabī (d. 751/1350).[22]

## II. The Spiritual Journey (*Sulūk*) in Kubrawī Sufism

A century after ʿAyn al-Quḍāt's martyrdom in 1131, in the introduction to a major tract on *sulūk*, the eminent Kubrawī theosopher Shaykh ʿAzīz-i Nasafī (d. between 1281–1300), one of the first exponents and interpreters of Ibn ʿArabī's theosophy in the Persian language,[23] discerned, like him, two broad religious types (*sulūk bar dū nawʿ-ast*) among the adherents of *sulūk*:

i. those who attempt to know God through their powers of memory and efforts at intellectual study, that is, adherents of the exoteric path of the Law (*sharīʿa*);
ii. those who tread the path (*ṭarīqa*) of *unlearning*, striving daily to forget where others strive to learn, burnishing their heart bright and white with *dhikr* where others with pens make paper black with ink.[24]

While not rejecting the former, more pedestrian and intellectual, method of legalistic study – recognising in it, indeed, some deeper truth – Nasafī, like all true Sufis, did not regard such knowledge either as being on a par with the visionary path of *sulūk* or as equal in its aims to those of the Sufi *ṭarīqa*.[25] Yet despite Nasafī's (and ʿAyn al-Quḍāt's) important distinction between the mystical and exoteric kinds of *sulūk*, the *sharīʿa* basis of the Sufi 'course' was always recognised and preserved by Muslim mystics in general and Sufis of the Kubrawī school in particular.

This is apparent from Hermann Landolt's definitive critical edition and translation of a treatise partially consecrated to the issue of Sufi *sulūk* (*Risāla dar rawish-i sulūk wa-khalwat-nishīnī*, 'The Method of Conduct and Spiritual Retreat'). Here, the renowned Kubrawī Shaykh Nūr al-Dīn Isfarāyīnī (d. 717/1317) wrote of the Sufis:

> Their journey and practice (*sayr u sulūk*) is based on the way of the Muḥammadan *ṭarīqa*. Now, the *ṭarīqa* is the inner mystery of the *sharīʿa*. Therefore, the Sufis endeavour to keep their external selves upright and virtuous through obedience to the *sharīʿa* while rectifying their inner selves through compliance with the *ṭarīqa*. This is because wayfaring (*sayr u sulūk*) the *ṭarīqa* is an esoteric and hidden affair. When the disciple (*murīd*) is sluggish in following the *ṭarīqa*, he will be unsuccessful in mystical progression (*sulūk*) and his inner being will remain devoid of virtue.[26]

This connotation of *sulūk* as constituting the special 'course' or 'method' of Sufi spiritual discipline is consistently brought out in most of the Sufi works composed by the later Kubrawī masters. For example, the great Akbarian Sufi poet al-Shabistarī (d. after 740–741/1340) whose affiliation to the Kubrawiyya can be described as uncertain but probable,[27] notes: 'The wayfarer (*musāfir*) is one who moves in haste: to forsake and raze the "self" utterly away, like fire from smoke./ Know his course (*sulūk*) to be a voyage of inner revelation (*sayr-i kashfī*) from Possibility to Necessity by casting off deficiencies and flaws.'[28] The celebrated Sufi

Kubrawī master and poet Muḥammad Lāhījī (d. 912/1507)[29] in his commentary on the poem states that *sulūk* in these verses connotes 'traversing the waystations and stages [of the Sufi Path] by the travelling wayfarer (*sālik-i musāfir*) – from possible being and its individual determinations unto the very threshold of the Necessary Being'.[30] As Shabistarī's and Lāhījī's descriptions illustrate, the process of *sulūk* is connected with the appearance of mystical revelation or *kashf*, 'the unveiling' of the mysteries of faith through the heart's vision. Rather than merely *intellectual* advancement, *sulūk* denotes the progression through, by realisation of the realities of, the waystations *of the heart*.

Incidentally, it should be pointed out that *sulūk*'s meta-rational – by no means *irrational* – mode of understanding was also emphasised in many early Persian Sufi texts. In his commentary on the sayings of great Sufi poet Bābā Ṭāhir (fl. fifth/eleventh century) Muḥammad Ibrāhīm Khaṭīb Wazīrī had pointed out:

> Progression on the Path to God (*sulūk-i rāh-i ḥaqq*) by means of reason (*'aql*) only creates confusion, since reason has no authority outside the realm of possible being and thus no access to the Necessary Being. However, only when *sulūk* is undertaken by means of the Light of God and divine grace, and no recourse to reason or the passions (*nafs*) is had, will one attain salvation.[31]

Another later Kubrawī master, Najm al-Dīn Rāzī (Shabistarī's contemporary) also affirms this visionary perspective of *sulūk* when he relates how the process of asceticism and purification of the heart allows the wayfarer (*sālik*) 'to traverse and fare (*'ubūr wa-sulūk*) through both the sensible and suprasensible worlds so that in every spiritual station he experiences, relative to his condition, a fresh "unveiling" (*kashf*)'.[32] The teleology of *sulūk* is similarly linked to a certain non-discursive and intuitive kind of 'contemplation' or 'meditation' (*tafakkur*). Thus, Lāhījī points out:

> The meditation, travelling, voyaging and wayfaring (*tafakkur u raftan u sayr u sulūk*) about which the unitarian mystic travellers discourse, refers to a journey of direct 'unveiling' (*sayr-i kashfī-yi 'ayānī*); it is *not by way of ratiocinative knowledge* … for in relation to the gnosis of divine 'unveiling', ratiocinative knowledge is sheer ignorance.[33]

The eminent Central Asian Kubrawī master and Akbarian exegete Tāj al-Dīn Ḥusayn b. Ḥasan Khwārazmī (d. 840/1436–1437) also stressed this contemplative bias of the Sufi spiritual journey. *Sulūk*, he states, involves maintaining an awareness of the ascending degrees of divine Omnipresence, 'from God's effects [in creation] (*āthār*) to his Acts (*af'āl*) and from his Acts to the all-Majestic and Beauteous Names (*asmā'*) and Qualities; from his Names and Qualities towards the Oneness of the divine Essence'.[34]

Among some of the non-Kubrawī mystics of the Mongol period, *sulūk* had rather abstruse technical connotations. In his *Fuṣūs al-ḥikam*, for example, Ibn 'Arabī identifies the 'science of *sulūk*' as pertaining to a special 'lore of the feet' (*'ilm al-arjul*) which directs the mystic upon 'the Straight Path (*al-ṣirāṭ*)' of the Prophets.[35] Khwārazmī, commenting on this conception of spiritual travel, notes that spiritual progression (*sulūk-i ma'nawī* or *sulūk-i bāṭinī*) is to be distinguished from simple progression in the realm of material form (*sulūk-i ṣūrī* or *sulūk-i ẓāhirī*); whereas the latter is but physical 'travelling on foot', the former is realised by 'walking with steps of sincerity and feet of creative aspiration (*himmat*)'.[36]

From the standpoint of comparative religion, the most interesting aspect of the various taxonomies of the science of *sulūk* among the Kubrawiyya was their attempt to integrate it into an entire programme of mystical discipline and spiritual pedagogy through underlining the importance of the varieties of human psychological types. The recognition by Kubrawī masters that there is a plurality of ways to approach God, a multiplicity of social contexts in which salvation may be realised, is of great significance for modern man who inhabits, by necessity if not always by choice, a pluralistic religious universe. In the context of the contemporary study of religious pluralism, the Presbyterian philosopher-theologian John Hick has pointed out that the comparative study of religion has increasingly led to 'the realisation that religious language expresses our apprehension of the divine in mythic pictures, and that these pictures are human and culturally conditioned', opening up for some 'the possibility that the different mythologies of the great religious traditions may constitute alternative, or rather complementary, rather than rival ways of picturing the divine reality'.[37] While grounded in the specificity of the forms of the Islamic faith based on the Qur'anic doctrine of Unity (*tawḥīd*), the Kubrawī vision partook of the traditional Islamic perspective which, in the words of the contemporary Muslim philosopher S. H. Nasr, 'is already blessed with the perfume of the sacred', envisaging

> ... in the multiplicity of sacred forms, not contradictions which relativise, but a confirmation of the universality of the Truth and the infinite creative power of the Real that unfolds Its inexhaustible possibilities in worlds of meaning which, although different, all reflect the unique Truth.[38]

As one sifts through and explores the various Kubrawī doctrines of *sulūk*, it becomes obvious that there exists no one, single, exclusively 'correct' form of conduct on the Path, insofar as divergences in 'mystical procedure' are tolerated, if not sympathetically embraced by most masters of this school. Despite the rather strict requirements for *sulūk* in Sufi spiritual discipline according to the masters of this Order there still exists wide scope for individual variation in 'conduct' – due to contrasting types of esoteric orientation and character differences – that is theoretically unlimited.

Abu'l-Mafākhir Yaḥyā Bākharzī (d. 776/1261), a major figure in the Central Asian Kubrawiyya, for instance, devotes an entire chapter of his Sufi manual, the

*Fuṣūs al-ādāb*,[39] to the subject of the 'divergent ways', or 'different strokes for different folks' (*ikhtilāf al-masālik*) among the Sufis. In this work, he cites some nine different approved methods of *sulūk* or ways of spiritual conduct.[40] First, states al-Bākharzī, comes the Way of Devotee:

1. One group base their conduct on the Path of Devotion (*sulūk-ṭarīq-i 'ibādat*), focusing their practice on water [for ritual ablutions] and the prayer niche, occupying themselves intensively with *dhikr*, supererogatory devotions and litanies.

The categorisation continues as follows:

2. 'the Ascetic' (*sulūk-ṭarīq-i riyāḍat*)
3. 'the Solitary', (*sulūk … khalwat*)
4. the 'Itinerant Traveller and Voluntary Exile' (*sulūk … siyāḥat wa-safar wa-ghurbat*)
5. the way of Service and Charitable preference of one's Sufi brethren over oneself (*sulūk … khidmat wa-badhl-i jāh dar khidmat-i īn ṭā'ifa*)
6. the Way of Spiritual Struggle (*sulūk … mujāhadāt*)
7. the Way of Self-humiliation and Self-abasement before people (*sulūk bi īn ṭarīq mīkunand ki jāh-i khwud rā bi nazdīk-i khalq sāqiṭ mīkunand va āb-i rū-yi khwud rā mībirīzand*)
8. the way of [conscious] helplessness and weakness (*sulūk …'ajz u shikastigī*)
9. the way of teaching [religious] knowledge and keeping the company of scholars, listening to the 'traditions' [of the Prophet and his companions] and preservation of knowledge (*sulūk-i ṭarīq-i ta'līm-i 'ilm u mujālisat bā 'ulamā' u samā'-i akhbār u ḥifẓ-i 'ulūm*).

Bākharzī is careful to emphasise that each of these *sulūk*-types has its own proper conditions and etiquette (*ādāb*) to be observed 'exactly as the masters have taught or else the wayfarer will be halted and never reach the goal'.[41]

Bākharzī's contemporary, 'Azīz-i Nasafī (mentioned above) also reflected on a similar plurality of mystical approaches to God which the methodology of *sulūk* offers the spiritual seeker. 'Wayfaring denotes seeking (*sulūk ṭalab-ast*)', states Nasafī – and as if propounding a Sufi parallel to Matthew Arnold's Stoic maxim that 'the aids to nobler life are all within' – declares:

> The seeker (*sālik*) may be either in a [Sufi] *khānqāh*, a [Christian] church, or even be king upon his throne. Thus, whoever is a seeker is a wayfarer, but the wayfaring of some people is subject to certain conditions whilst the wayfaring of others lacks them. The gist of all my discourse is that there are four degrees in Sufism:
>
> One, devotional commitment (*irāda*) with conditions. Two, service (*khidma*) with conditions. Three, methodical progression on the path (*sulūk*) with its

conditions. Four, holding spiritual company during a religious retreat (*ṣuḥbat bā 'uzlat*) subject to the conditions of the retreat.[42]

Bākharzī's and Nasafī's cosmopolitan perspective and broad tolerance of religious differences typifies the sympathetic humanity of the Persian Sufis' traditional religious outlook, which, as Marshall Hodgson insightfully observes,

> … was as naturally tolerant of local differences as the *Sharʿī ʿulamā'* tended to be intolerant. The *ʿulamā'* had to concentrate on matters of external conformity, as dictated by the *sharīʿa*, in order to maintain the legal and institutional framework for social unity. … For the Sufis, on the contrary, externals were secondary. For many of them, especially by the Earlier Middle Period, *even the difference between Islam and other cultural traditions such as Christianity was of secondary importance in principle*; of still less moment were the various differences in social custom within the community of Muḥammad. What mattered was the inner disposition of the heart to God.[43]

Nasafī's ecumenical approach to religious diversity and his ideal conception of *sulūk* as a kind of universal esoteric path – that may be traversed within a Christian church, whilst among common Muslims or humble *fuqarā'* or 'even in a palace' – lies at the heart of the Kubrawī religious outlook in general. It also reflects the 'moral universalism', as Wilfred Cantwell Smith termed it, of the Persian Sufi outlook on Christian-Muslim relations in particular.[44] The endless tales which reappear in Sufi literature respecting inter-religious tolerance can in fact all be read in this context. Abū Saʿīd b. Abi'l-Khayr's (d. 440/1049) friendly acceptance of Christians and Abu'l-Ḥasan al-Kharaqānī's (d. 426/1034) toleration of Christians posing as Sufis, are good examples of this.[45]

The major work on *sulūk* among the Kubrawiyya is Nasafī's 'Exposition of Wayfaring' (*Risāla dar bayān-i sulūk*), being the fifth treatise of his collection of treatises published in the 'Book of the Perfect Man' (*Kitāb al-insān al-kāmil*). Here, Nasafī recorded in abundant detail the entire human/divine continuum and spectrum of meanings of *sulūk*, the central principles of which may be summarised as follows:

I. *Sulūk* occurs as a natural process within the psycho-spiritual development of man whereby the hierarchical degrees (*marātib*) of his inner microcosm (*ʿālam-i ṣaghīr*) are gradually revealed. 'All the stations of the Way are within man: the wayfarer is you, the Way is you and the waystation also you', he declares.[46]

II. Proper intention (*niyyat*) is paramount. The *sālik* should not consciously 'seek God'; rather, he or she should become truly 'human' (*ādam*) so that the hierarchical degrees of humanity (*marātib-i insānī*) naturally mature within the psyche. At this point, all other desiderata of the mystical Path: manifestation of the virtues, purity, gnosis, the unveiling of lights and revelation of mysteries, are attained. True and permanent knowledge is solely that which is drawn from the well of the heart; transient knowledge (obtained through the ear) is like pouring water from another man's well into your own; it quickly stagnates.[47]

III. *Sulūk* has six ethico-spiritual conditions: (i) renunciation of property, social status and position, behaviour discordant with religious injunctions, and bad character traits; (ii) peace with all mankind, doing harm to no one with either hand or tongue, acting with total compassion towards everyone, recognising that all people are as helpless, infirm and needy as oneself;[48] (iii) seclusion; (iv) silence; (v) hunger; (vi) wakefulness.

IV. For success in *sulūk*, four types of knowledge are requisite:

1. Knowledge of the Supreme Object (*ma'rifat-i maqṣad*) = the perfection of the Self (*kamāl-i khwud*).

2. Knowledge of the wayfarer-to-this-Object, which al-Nasafī defines as the wayfarer's own inner being (*bāṭin*). This inner being is 'known by different names: soul (*nafs*), spirit (*rūḥ*), heart (*qalb*), reason (*'aql*), and the Light of God (*nūr Allāh*), but it is actually only one substance: the essential Human Reality (*jawhar-i ḥaqīqat-i ādamī*)'.[49]

3. Knowledge of the way to this Object, which is conditioned by several stages, according to al-Nasafī, 'beginning with learning and memorisation (*taḥṣīl u tikrār*) and terminating in spiritual struggle and invocation of divine Names (*mujāhida u adhkār*). These stages he explains as follows:

> First, he goes to the madrasa and acquires of Islamic legal knowledge (*'ilm-i sharī'a*) what is necessary. Then, he should study beneficial knowledge so that he becomes quick-witted and fathoms subtle expressions, since the understanding of learned discourse which is acquired in the madrasa is an extremely important pillar of this subject. Then, he goes to the *khānqāh* and affiliates himself as a disciple to a shaykh, devoting himself to his threshold, contenting himself with one shaykh alone, learning what is necessary of the 'science of the mystical path' (*'ilm-i ṭarīqa*). Then, he devotes himself to reading the tales of the [Sufi] shaykhs, that is, he should study their ascetic practices, their spiritual struggle, piety and abstinence, as well as their stations and states. Then, he renounces all books, and occupies himself with whatever the shaykh deems appropriate.[50]

Although al-Nasafī (and here 'Ayn al-Quḍāt may also be recalled) notes that there are two ways to attain to the Supreme Object, the first being the 'Path of learning' pursued by the 'wayfarers on the lane of the *sharī'a*', and the second being 'the Path of spiritual struggle and invocation' that is pursued by 'adherents of the Sufi *tarīqa*', the second path ('far more secure and close at hand'[51]) is al-Nasafī's sole concern in his treatise.[52]

4. Knowledge of the Guide (the shaykh) to this Object. Total obedience to the Guide is the fundamental principle which embraces all six pillars of spiritual progression (*arkān-i sulūk*), these being:

   i. 'The spiritual Guide' himself, 'without whom no progression is possible' (*bī hādī sulūk muyassar nashavad*);
   ii. discipular commitment to and love of the Guide (*irādat u maḥabbat*);
   iii. total obedience to the Guide, both in faith and practice;
   iv. abandonment of personal volition/willfulness and individual thinking;
   v. abandonment of objection to and denial of the Guide;
   vi. 'long years of constant and stable adherence to the conditions and principles of "wayfaring" (*thabāt u davām bar sharā'iṭ u arkān-i sulūk sālhā-yi bisyār*).'[53]

Only strict observance of these 'pillars' combined with adherence to the 'six ethico-spiritual conditions' mentioned above will secure success in *sulūk*, states Nasafī.

## III. The Finale of *Sulūk*

Descriptions in classical Sufi writings of the terminus of the degrees (*maqāmāt*) of *sulūk* are unanimous on one point: that the goal of the Sufis' progress is in the attainment of *fanā' fī'llāh,* annihilation of the self in God, and the realisation of the perfection of existential Oneness (*tawḥīd*), which pertains to the level of the 'transconscious' (*khafī*).[54] Among the Kubrawiyya, however, perhaps in line with the elaborate theories and conceptions of visionary experience presented by masters of this school, descriptions of the consummation of the spiritual journey and the finale of *sulūk* are often quite distinctive. Nasafī's comments on the sublime degrees attained by the highest adepts in spiritual conduct are summarised below, forming a fitting conclusion to this study of the spiritual journey in the Kubrawī tradition.

Those who have realised the heights of the transcendental Unity of Being, al-Nasafī dubs the 'people of unity', (*ahl-i waḥda*). These unitarian mystics are in turn divided into two categories of 'terrestrial' and 'celestial wayfarers', novices and adepts.

Illuminating the role of inspired contemplative reflection (*fikr*) in Sufi spiritual practice, Nasafī gives precise information about the spiritual method, principles and path pursued by the second category (celestial wayfarers). These adepts mount the mythical 'winged steed' of inspired contemplative reflection (*burāq-i fikr*), and ride upon the Pegasus of vision (*mushāhada*), which possesses four 'wings' (symbolic of the four archetypal faculties) by which it soars aloft in the hierocosmos of contemplation.

The first wing of the steed is *correct audition,* which Nasafī describes as 'hearing things perfectly, as the words are in their essence, as a wise man would hear them spoken'. By this, he implies the perfection of the ear of the heart, the refining of the faculty of intuition.

The second wing is *correct vision,* described as 'seeing things as they actually are'. Correct audition and vision are described as the wings which provide the mystic with a 'manifest inspiration' (*waḥy-i jahr*).

'Reflection' (*fikr*) is itself the third wing, and this is given profuse treatment by Nasafī:

> Everyone calls reflection (*fikr*) by a different name. Some say it is a 'mystical state' (*ḥāl*), some say it is the condition [which the Prophet described when he remarked]: 'I have a time with God,'[55] some call it 'absence' (*ghayba*). Now all these expressions imply that a person experiences within himself a certain mystical time (*waqt*) in which he is so immersed and absorbed in something that the activity of his external senses ceases such that his inner being becomes completely concentrated upon that thing. For some people this mystical state lasts an hour, for others a day or several days, and in others it may even last up to ten days.[56] … The experience of reflection causes others in the midst of ritual prayer to become abstracted from themselves. Others, in the midst of eating, may find themselves caught up in contemplative thought, remaining absorbed therein for up to one or two days, while holding a morsel of food in their hand or mouth![57]

Nasafī's definition of reflection is a definition of contemplation itself, a description of the experience of rapture and ecstasy (*ḥāl*) – indeed, a purely 'celestial reflection' – rather than related to the process of reasoning or even 'meditation' on divine Qualities. The fourth and final degree or 'wing' of contemplation is termed 'inspiration' (*ilhām*) and, like reflection, is understood by different people to mean different things, being called by various names:

> Some call it an inspiration (*ilhām*), others call it a heralding (*adhan*), others a passing thought (*khāṭir*), but the meaning of all these diverse expressions is that it is a moment in which a certain knowledge appears in a person's heart, so that he becomes aware of the circumstances of the past and future, without prior reflection or having been informed by anyone.[58]

Nasafī maintains the last two 'wings' – reflection and inspiration – constitute 'a non-manifest inspiration', that is to say, they are types of consciousness belonging to the innermost depth of contemplative thought or reflection.

From the above précis, we can conclude that the path of reflection contains four hierarchical degrees: *audition, vision, reflection* and *inspiration*, all subsumed under the rubric 'reflection' as being the highest mode of contemplation and the spiritual discipline utilised by the most advanced Sufi adepts. According to Nasafī's description, it is characterised by the sharpening of all the inner senses, the perfecting and spiritualising of the faculties of audition and vision. By such immersion in 'reflection', consciousness of temporality and the spatial delimitation of the human condition is swept aside. (His view of reflection here would seem similar to that of Suhrawardī Maqtūl).[59] Reaching the final degrees of reflection, the celestial wayfarer is lent the 'wing of inspiration', transporting him beyond time into the future, tearing aside the veil which is suspended before the *nunc aeternum*:

> When the wayfarer puts recollection behind him and when reflection presents itself and overwhelms him, he soars beyond the realm of the body and reaches the world of the spirits (*'ālam-i arwāḥ*). When he transcends reflection, inspiration presents itself, enabling him to transcend the world of reason (*'aql*) and reach the world of love (*'ishq*). When he transcends the level of inspiration, contemplative vision (*'iyān*) presents itself, whereupon he transcends the world of love and attains to the spiritual station of stability (*tamkīn*).[60]

Once the Sufi reaches stability in all these disciplines, his spiritual journey is completed. The wayfarer transcends all fluctuation and mutation (*talwīn*) until he realises total self-control in all his spiritual practices, such that

> ... if he wishes, he engages in recollection (*dhikr*); if he wishes, he occupies himself with contemplative thought, or else, he negates both of these practices in order to be receptive to inspiration (*ilhām*), and thus becomes informed of events bygone or yet to come. That is, he burnishes the mirror of his heart clean from the images of both worlds, so that the image of whatever is happening in the world, either in the present or future, will be cast into his heart.[61]

## Notes

1. For an overview of Kubrawī Sufism, see Muḥammad Isa Waley, 'Najm al-Dīn Kubrā and the Central Asian School of Sufism', in S. H. Nasr, ed., *Islamic Spirituality II: Manifestations* (New York, 1991), pp. 80–104. Nasafī's affiliation with the Kubrawī Order should be described as probable but ultimately uncertain. Hermann Landolt argues in his article 'Le paradoxe de la "face de Dieu": 'Azîz-e Nasafî (VII$^{e}$/XIII$^{e}$ siècle) et le "monisme ésotérique" de l'Islam', *SIr*, 25 (1996), p. 175, that Nasafī's esoteric doctrines often do not accord with typical Kubrawī Sufi teachings.

2. *Silk al-sulūk*, ed. Ghulām-'Alī Āryā (Tehran, 1369 Sh./1990), pp. 2–3.

3. R. A. Nicholson pointed out: 'Mystics of every race and creed have described the progress of the spiritual life [*sulūk*] as a journey or a pilgrimage. Other symbols have been used for the same purpose, but this one appears to be almost universal in its range.' *The Mystics of Islam* (London and Boston, MA, 1963), p. 28.

4. In political theory, the term usually carries the implication of 'conduct' or 'comportment'. A medieval Persian treatise by Faḍl Allāh b. Rūzbihān al-Khunjī, composed 920/1514, concerning the proper 'comportment' which various types of leaders in the religious and

political sphere should observe is appropriately entitled 'The Conduct of Kings', *Sulūk al-mulūk*, ed. M. 'A. Muwaḥḥid (Tehran 1362 Sh./1983). In the same fashion, even such a Sufi author as Najm al-Dīn al-Rāzī (d. 654/1256) devoted all eight divisions (*faḍl*) of the final chapter of his monumental conspectus of Sufi doctrine, the *Mirṣād al-'ibād*, ed. M. A. Riyāḥī (Tehran, 1374 Sh./1995) to the 'proper conduct (*sulūk*) to be observed by kings, ministers, deputies, the learned classes, the rich, landowners, merchants, businessmen and artisans'.

5. For other relevant meanings, see 'Alī Akbar Dihkhudā, *Lughāt-nāma* (Tehran, 1947–1973), s.v. '*sulūk*'.

6. Ibn 'Aṭā' Allāh, *Ṣūfī Aphorisms* [*Kitāb al-ḥikam*], tr. Victor Danner (Leiden, 1973), p. 78.

7. *The Sufi Orders in Islam* (London, 1973), p. 140.

8. 'Abd al-Razzāq Kāshānī, *Isṭilaḥāt al-ṣūfiyya*, ed. Muḥammad Ibrahīm Ja'far (Cairo, 1981), no. 259.

9. Su'ād Ḥakīm, *al-Mu'jam al-Sūfī* (Beirut, 1981), p. 720; e.g. 46:30 – although the exact construction *sulūk* does not occur in the Qur'an, there is one reference to *salaka*: 20:53.

10. *Mirṣād al-'ibād*, ed. M. A. Riyāḥī (Tehran, 1372 Sh./ 1993), p. 11.

11. The 'adepts in spiritual conduct' (*ahl-i sulūk*) – according to 'Izz al-Dīn Maḥmūd Kāshānī's (d. 735/1335) taxonomy in his mystical textbook *Miṣbāḥ al-hidāya wa-miftāḥ al-kifāya*, ed. Jalāl al-Dīn Humā'ī (Tehran 1325 Sh./1946) – are divided into three categories: Mutaṣawwifa, Malāmatiyya and Sūfiyya. The first two groups are veiled (for various reasons) from attainment of the supreme goal of 'total selflessness', while only the last group, the Sufis, enjoy, 'by grace of the attraction of the Eternal Being, complete serverance from selfhood'. (*Miṣbāḥ al-hidāyat*, pp. 115–116). Most Sufis, however, were far less exacting in their terminology. Rāzī thus considers the 'company of spiritual progression' or *ahl-i sulūk* to be the true Sufis (*Mirṣād*, p. 311) and refers to the *arbāb-i sulūk u ma'rifat* ('the adepts in spiritual progress and gnosis') as denoting those advanced on the Path (*Mirṣād*, p. 29).

12. Concerning the dichotomy of *Jadhba/Sulūk*, Khwārazmī, for instance, states that 'Attraction' (*jadhba*) by God before undergoing *sulūk*, 'is the quality of beginners', whereas 'the experience of "attraction after *sulūk*" belongs to the most advanced and perfect adepts', Khwārazmī, *Sharḥ-i fuṣūs al-ḥikam Muḥyī al-Dīn Ibn 'Arabī*, ed. N. M. Harawī (Tehran, 1989), p. 235. 'Izz al-Dīn Maḥmūd Kāshānī (d. 735/1335) also describes *sulūk* as an initial stage leading to *jadhba*. Only two sorts of mystics are worthy to become guides (*shaykh*) on the Sufi Path, affirms al-Kāshānī, 1: 'The 'wayfarer who later becomes an ecstatic' (*sālik-i majdhūb*), must first traverse all the deserts and perils of the qualities of the lower passions with the feet of *sulūk*, until by grace of divine attraction (*jadhabāt*) he surpasses all the degrees of the heart and hierarchical levels of the Spirit, attaining to the realm of mystical unveiling and certitude (*kashf wa-yaqīn*).' 2: 'The "ecstatic who later becomes a wayfarer" (*majdhūb-i sālik*), who by grace of divine attraction crosses the wide expanse of the stations (*maqāmāt*), attains to the world of unveiling and direct vision (*'iyān*), only later re-experiencing the stages and levels of the Path (*ṭarīq*) through pedestrian *sulūk*, finding the reality of his spiritual disposition (*ḥaqīqat-i ḥāl*) in the form of knowledge (*ṣūrat-i 'ilm*).' *Miṣbāḥ al-hidāya wa-miftāḥ al-kifāya*, p. 110; based on the *'Awārif al-ma'ārif* of Shihāb al-Dīn Abū Ḥafṣ 'Umar al-Suhrawardī, (d. 632/1234). In a similar vein, Tahānawī contrasts *sulūk* with the personal 'effort' (*kūshish*) of the *sālik* and *jadhba* with the fore-ordained 'pull' (*kishish*) of God. *Kashshāf iṣṭilāḥāt al-funūn, A Dictionary of the Technical Terms Used in the Sciences*

*of the Musalmans*, ed. M. Wajih, 'Abd al-Haqq, G. Kadir and Nassau Lees (Calcutta, 1862), 2 vols., p. 686; cf. also p. 661. As an example of typical usage of the *jadhba/sulūk* polarity in medieval Persian Sufism, see Sa'īd al-Dīn al-Farghānī, *Mashāriq al-darārī: Sharḥ-i Tā'iyya Ibn Farīḍ*, ed. Jalāl al-Dīn al-Āshtiyānī (Tehran, 1979), *jadhba/sulūk*, pp. 307–310; and for *sayr/sulūk* see pp. 60, 72, 77, 108, 144, 147, 150, 175, 203, 337, 261, 271, 292, 380, 511, 544, 573, 590.

13. What is interesting here is not only the typological difference of *sayr* and *sulūk* but also their analogical relationship, aimed at creating an equilibrium between such apparently polar opposites. Thus, Maḥmūd al-Kāshānī observes that 'The visionary voyage (*sayr*) of lovers through the hierarchical levels of the spiritual stations (*maqāmāt*) cannot be undertaken except by correct methodical order and gradation. As long as the lover has not fulfilled the requirements of a lower station he or she cannot attain to a higher one. ... Hence, no progress (*taraqqī*) will be made unless each station is traversed step by step in proper methodological order by following [the process of] the "journey within" (*sayr*) and "conduct without" (*sulūk*). Then and only then shall his conduct (*sulūk*) be transformed into divine attraction (*jadhba*) and his inner voyage (*sayr*) culminate in spiritual flight (*ṭayr*)'. *Miṣbāḥ*, p. 110.

14. Some Sufis, on the other hand, did not discriminate between *sayr* and *sulūk* and considered them as synonyms. Thus, Nasafī states: 'Know that *sulūk* designates *sayr*, and there are [the two types of] the journey to God (*sayr ilā Llāh*) and the journey within God (*sayr fī Llāh*). The journey to God has a limit, whereas the journey within God is unlimited. By the journey to God is meant that the wayfarer (*sālik*) journey to such an extent that his being is annihilated and he becomes alive through God's own existence – living, knowing, seeing, hearing and speaking through God. By the journey within God is meant that the wayfarer comes to realise the reality and the wisdom of everything en vérité, both through extensive, broad-based knowledge and through intimate, personal verification'. *Kitāb al-insān al-kāmil*, ed. Marijan Molé (Tehran and Paris, 1962), pp. 12–13.

15. Louis Massignon, *Essai sur les origines du lexique technique de la mystique musulmane* (Paris, 1928).

16. Perhaps the earliest known usage of the term to describe the progression of the mystic on the Path under the supervision of a teacher is to be found in al-Qushayrī's *Tartīb al-sulūk* analysed by Fritz Meier, 'Qushayrī's *Tartīb as-sulūk*', *Oriens*, 16 (1963), pp. 1–39. *Sulūk* is notably not featured in either Nicholson's index of technical terms to his critical edition of Abū Naṣr al-Sarrāj's (d. 378/988) *Kitāb al-luma' fi'l-taṣawwuf*, nor in the *Kitāb al-ta'arruf li-madhhab ahl al-taṣawwuf* by Abū Bakr Muḥammad al-Kalābādhī (d. 380/990), nor in the *Qūt al-qulūb* of Abū Ṭālib al-Makkī (d. 386/996), nor in the *Ṭabaqāt al-ṣūfiyya* of Abū 'Abd al-Raḥmān al-Sulāmī (d. 412/1021), nor in the *Ḥilyāt al-awliyā'* of Abū Nu'aym al-Iṣfahānī (d. 430/1038), nor in the *Risāla* of Abu'l-Qāsim al-Qushayrī (d. 467/1074), neither in the Persian nor in the Arabic writings of 'Abd Allāh al-Anṣārī (d. 481/1089) – those key works which played a formative role in the literary blossoming of 12th-century Sufism. Neither does any mention of *sulūk* occur in the oldest Persian treatise on Sufism, namely the *Kashf al-maḥjūb* of 'Alī b. 'Uthmān al-Hujwīrī (d. 463/1071) nor as a formal technical term in the works of Rūzbihān al-Baqlī (d. 606/1210).

17. *Iḥyā 'ulūm al-dīn* (Beirut, n.d.); *Kitāb kasr al-shahwatayn*, Bk. 23: 11, p. 75.

18. *Tamhīdāt*, ed. 'A. Osseiran (Tehran, 1341 Sh./1962), p. 71: 4.

19. *Asrār al-tawḥīd*, ed. M. Shafī'ī-Kadkanī (Tehran, 1366 Sh./1987), vol. 1, p. 4, line 2. Also

cf. ibid., pp. 7, 8 and especially p. 5, lines 12–14, where two references to the Qur'an (43:22; 6:90) contextualise the idiom *sulūk-i ṭarīq-i ḥaqīqat*.

20. On which, see Lewisohn, ed., *The Heritage of Sufism, vol. 2: The Legacy of Mediæval Persian Sufism* (Oxford, 1999), pp. 33–36.

21. On which, see Stefan Sperl, '*Qaṣīda* Form and Mystic Path in 13th-Century Egypt', in S. Sperl. C. Shackle, *Qasida Poetry in Islamic Asia and Africa* (Leiden, 1996), vol. 1, pp. 65–81.

22. See note 1 above.

23. See I. de Gastines' (tr.) introduction to Nasafī's *Le Livre de l'Homme Parfait* (Kitāb al-insān al-kāmil) (Paris, 1984), p. 10. *Kashf al-ḥaqā'iq*, ed. Aḥmad Mahdavī-Dāmghānī (Tehran, 1359 Sh./1980), introduction, p. 8.

24. *Kashf al-ḥaqā'iq*, p. 120.

25. See L. Ridgeon, *'Azīz Nasafī* (London, 1997), pp. 118–119.

26. *Nuruddin Isfarayini: Le Révélateur des mystères: Traité de soufisme*, ed. Hermann Landolt (Paris, 1986), pp. 120–121. The same distinction between the *sulūk* of the Law and the Path was also maintained by Isfarayīnī, *Le Révélateur*, p. 146.

27. See L. Lewisohn, *Beyond Faith and Infidelity: The Sufi Poetry and Teachings of Maḥmūd Shabistarī* (London, 1995), chap. 1.

28. *Gulshan-i rāz*, ed. Ṣamad Muwaḥḥid, *Majmū'a-yi āthār-i Shaykh Maḥmūd Shabistarī* (Tehran, 1365 Sh./1986), p. 79, vv. 313–314.

29. On Lāhījī, see M. Glünz, 'Sufism, Shi'ism and Poetry in Fifteenth-Century Iran: The Ghazals of Asiri-Lahiji', in Lisa Golombek and Maria Subtelny, ed., *Timurid Art and Culture: Iran and Central Asia in the Fifteenth Century* (Leiden, 1992), pp. 195–200; B. Zanjānī, ed., *Dīwān-i ash'ār wa-rasā'il-i Asīrī Lāhījī* (Tehran, 1978), N. Anṣārī's introduction.

30. *Mafātīḥ al-i'jāz fī sharḥ-i Gulshan-i rāz*, ed. Barzgār and Karbāsī (Tehran, 1371 Sh./1992), p. 205.

31. *Al-Futūḥāt al-rabbāniyya fī mazj al-ishārāt al-Hamadāniyya*, in Muḥammad Javād Mashkūr, ed. *Sharḥ-i aḥwāl u āthār u dūbaytīhā-yi Bābā Ṭāhir* (Tehran, 1354 Sh./1975), p. 852.

32. *Mirṣād*, ed. Riyāḥī, p. 289.

33. *Mafātīḥ*, ed. Barzgār and Karbāsī, p. 10.

34. Khwārazmī, *Sharḥ-i fuṣūs al-ḥikam Muḥyī al-Dīn Ibn 'Arabī*, p. 375. A similar type of metaphysically oriented *sulūk* is also found in some of the earliest Persian Sufi poetry, such as the didactic *mathnawī*s of Sanā'ī (d. 525/1131): cf. his *Ḥadiqat al-ḥaqīqat*, ed. M. Raḍawī (Tehran, 1359 Sh./1980), p. 113: 6–8.

35. *Fuṣūs al-ḥikam*, ed. Abu al-'Alā 'Afīfī (Beirut, n.d.), vol. 1, p. 107: 7.

36. *Sharḥ-i fuṣūs*, ed. Harawī, p. 368: 11–13.

37. John Hick, *Problems of Religious Pluralism* (London, 1985), pp. 13–14.

38. S. H. Nasr, *Knowledge and the Sacred* (Albany, NY, 1989), p. 281. For a comparison between Nasr's and Hick's philosophies of religious pluralism, see Adnan Aslan, *Religious Pluralism in Christian and Islamic Philosophy* (London, 1998).

39. On which, see M. I. Waley, 'A Kubrawī Manual of Sufism: the *Fuṣūs al-ādāb* of Yaḥyā Bākharzī', in Lewisohn, ed., *The Heritage of Sufism*, vol. 2, pp. 289–310.

40. It may be noted that his taxonomy of *sulūk* below is nearly a verbatim translation of the relevant section in Abu'l-Najīb al-Suhrawardī's (d. 563/1168) *Ādāb al-murīdīn*, ed. N. M. Harawī, Arabic text with a Persian translation (Tehran, 1363 Sh./1984), pp. 231 ff.

41. *Fuṣūs al-ādāb*, (Tehran, 1358 Sh./1979), pp. 55–56.

42. *Kashf al-ḥaqā'iq*, p. 126.

43. *The Venture of Islam*, vol. 2, p. 220. Italics mine.

44. Wilfred Cantwell Smith, *The End and Meaning of Religion* (London, 1963), p. 329, n. 9. On the metaphor of the spiritual path in Christian-Muslim ecumenism, see William Phipps, *Muhammad and Jesus: a Comparison of the Prophets and their Teachings* (London, 1996), pp. 232–233. See also my 'The Esoteric Christianity of Islam: Interiorisation of Christian Imagery in Mediæval Persian Sufi Poetry', in L. Ridgeon, ed., *Muslim Interpretations of Christianity* (London, 2001), pp. 127–156.

45. See M. R. Shafī'ī-Kadkanī, ed., *Asrār al-tawḥīd fī maqamāt-i Shaykh Abī Sa'īd* (Tehran, 1371 Sh./1992), p. 210. Also M. A. Jamnia and M. Bayat, *Under the Sufi's Cloak: Stories of Abu Sa'id and His Mystical Teachings* (Maryland, 1995), pp. 53–55. See J. Nurbakhsh, 'The Key Features of Early Persian Sufism', in Leonard Lewisohn, ed., *The Heritage of Sufism, I, Classical Persian Sufism: from its Origins to Rūmī*, p. xxxiii.

46. *Risāla dar bayān-i sulūk*, ed. Marijan Molé (Tehran/Paris, 1962), p. 85.

47. Ibid., pp. 86–87.

48. Ibid., p. 95. Cf. 'Aṭṭār's (d. 618/1221) *Ilahī-nāma*, ed., H. Ritter (Tehran, 1359 Sh./1980) p. 54: 2, 10) where this explicitly ethical dimension of *sulūk* figures prominently. 'Aṭṭār thus recounts how 'Alī encountered an ant on the road which aroused in him a state of terror, only to be later informed by the Prophet in a dream of the ant's exalted spiritual rank. 'Aṭṭār employs this *ḥadīth* as an *exempla* to moralise: 'If ever you hurt an ant on the road, you are unconscious of your conduct (*sulūk*). If you are absolutely ignorant in your conduct (*sulūk*), you are a total pauper even though you be a prince.'

49. *Risāla dar bayān-i sulūk*, pp. 91–92.

50. Ibid., p. 92.

51. Ibid., p. 93.

52. Ibid., p. 95.

53. Ibid., p. 97.

54. Nonetheless, the mystics varied considerably in their comportment whilst bidding 'farewell to wayfaring'. Cf. 'Ayn al-Quḍāt al-Hamadhānī, *Tamhīdāt*, p. 317; Tāj al-Dīn al-Ushnawī (d. ca. 610/ 1213), *Majmū'a-yi āthār-i fārsī ... Shaykh Tāj al-Dīn Ushnawī*, ed., N. M. Harawī (Tehran, 1368 Sh./1989), p. 93.

55. Alluding to a famous saying of the Prophet: 'I have a time with God which no other prophet finds, nor angel knows, not even the purest spirit – who is Gabriel.' See Badī' al-Zamān Furūzānfar, *Aḥadīth-i Mathnawī* (Tehran, 1956), no. 100.

56. *Kashf al-ḥaqā'iq*, p. 139.

57. Ibid.

58. Ibid.

59. Cf. Y. H. Hairi, 'Suhrawardī's *An Episode and a Trance*: A Philosophical Dialogue in a Mystical Stage', in Parviz Morewedge, ed., *Islamic Philosophy and Mysticism* (New York, 1981), pp. 177–189.

60. *Kashf al-ḥaqā'iq*, p. 141.

61. Ibid., pp. 141–142.

# 27

# Notes on the Transmission of Mystical Philosophy: Ibn ʿArabī according to ʿAbd al-Wahhāb al-Shaʿrānī

*Richard J. A. McGregor*

The following will discuss the transmission of the mystical philosophy of Muḥyī al-Dīn Ibn ʿArabī (d. 638/1240) into sixteenth-century Egypt, through the efforts of the well-known compiler and author ʿAbd al-Wahhāb al-Shaʿrānī (d. 973/1565). Al-Shaʿrānī's best-known works are probably his *al-Ṭabaqāt al-kubrā* (or *Lawāqiḥ al-anwār fi ṭabaqāt al-sādāt al-akhīra*), and *al-Ṭabaqāt al-ṣughrā* (or *Lawāqiḥ al-anwār al-qudsiyya fī manāqib al-ʿulamāʾ waʾl-ṣūfiyya*), two substantial collections of hagiographies and biographies, and his theological effort *al-Yawāqīt waʾl-jawāhir fī bayān ʿaqāʾid al-akābir*. He also composed a substantial autobiography, *Laṭāʾif al-minan waʾl-akhlāq*. In his work he touched on many of the traditional sciences, but his primary concern remained mysticism.[1] Al-Shaʿrānī's accounts of saintly lives circulated widely in the late medieval period and continue to be reprinted today.[2] For this reason a close look at his editing strategies and techniques is useful, not only for students of Ibn ʿArabī, but also for anyone interested in the hundreds of other figures al-Shaʿrānī reports on. The present study will not address the important historical developments of the period in which he lived or his biography since this has been done admirably in the recent work of Michael Winter.[3] Instead we turn our attention to his writings, and more specifically, to his presentation of the thought of Ibn ʿArabī.

This study will focus on one work by al-Shaʿrānī, his *al-Kibrīt al-aḥmar*, which presents the teachings of Ibn ʿArabī almost entirely through edited and abridged excerpts presented thematically. It is essentially intended as a handbook for the Great Shaykh's *al-Futūḥāt al-Makkiyya*. As pointed out by Winter, unfortunately we do not know the details concerning the teaching and transmission of Ibn ʿArabī's works in sixteenth-century Egypt. But al-Shaʿrānī's short statement (see *al-Kibrīt al-aḥmar*, vol. 2, p. 187) that he intends to present certain of Ibn ʿArabī's teachings according to some of his own masters, suggests to us that al-Shaʿrānī was dealing with Ibn ʿArabī's work within a well-established tradition of mainstream Sufism. However, the details are scanty and this issue requires further research.[4]

Turning to al-Shaʿrānī himself, I have chosen to investigate the hitherto unexplored work entitled *al-Kibrīt al-aḥmar fī bayān ʿulūm al-Shaykh al-Akbar* (on the margin of *al-Yawāqīt wa'l-jawāhir*, Cairo, 1932 and 1959, 2 vols.). *Al-Kibrīt al-aḥmar* is in fact one of only two of his works dealing exclusively with the Shaykh al-Akbar. The second, entitled *al-Qawl al-mubīn*, apparently exists as a manuscript in Cairo's Dār al-Kutub, and at Yale University. It is described as a defence of Ibn ʿArabī against the charges of incarnationism.[5]

Surveying al-Shaʿrānī's *al-Kibrīt al-aḥmar*, I hope to show in some detail how he represents Ibn ʿArabī's position on key issues such as sanctity (*walāya*) and its relationship to prophethood, the relationship of the Law (*sharīʿa*) to mystical vision, and the 'seal' of sainthood (*khatm al-walāya*). As will be seen below, al-Shaʿrānī's presentation of Ibn ʿArabī, although limited by its summary nature, is generally true to its original. Of course al-Shaʿrānī can be accused of picking and choosing from *al-Futūḥāt al-Makkiyya*, and certainly he passed over the most provocative statements, but from my study of *al-Kibrīt al-aḥmar* it appears that his 're-presentation' of Ibn ʿArabī is largely fair to the original Akbarian doctrine. This conclusion is particularly important as a corrective to some recent scholarship which has tended to present al-Shaʿrānī as a kind of orthodox-minded reformer of Ibn ʿArabī's thought. Let us turn now to an example of such scholarship.

## One Assessment of al-Shaʿrānī

In a recent work on al-Shaʿrānī, K. V. Johnson paints a picture of medieval socio-religious crisis. The issue at hand is the tension between an upstart amoral mystical school, and the conservative mystical forms of traditional Sufism. The rise of the former led to a situation in which the antinomian actions of a few charismatic individuals, claiming divine inspiration, threaten the believing community. These inspired individuals, despite their popularity and the undeniability of their miracles (*karāmāt*), had, according to Johnson, distorted the older and more restrained tradition of sainthood or sanctity within Sufism. The image evoked is that of the rise of unscrupulous miracle-workers flouting the *sharīʿa*, and challenging the right of those saints who are their superiors in law and in sanctity. We are told that,

> In al-Shaʿrānī's time such perversions of the mystical tradition were abundantly represented by shaykhs (of the mystical orders) who used their purported link to the hierarchy of saints as a license to indulge in corruption. Those outside the orders as well could not escape the influence of a concept of sanctity in which

behaviour unacceptable to the sharīʿa was dismissed as a manifestation of divine states bestowed upon a friend of God.[6]

Historically, the severing of sanctity from the stock of the *sharīʿa*, according to Johnson, received impetus from the work of Ibn ʿArabī which provided the 'philosophical basis for the devotion to the prophets and saints which increasingly dominated the popular religious tradition'.[7] The Shaykh al-Akbar is here held up as a kind of evil genius who, through his systematisation of the theory of sanctity, undermined the positive ethical structures of 'orthodox' Sufism. We will discuss the validity of these portrayals shortly. Three centuries later, according to Johnson, it fell to al-Shaʿrānī to oppose these innovations and to come to the defence of the community. Johnson attributes two related goals to al-Shaʿrānī: the first was the restoration of *walāya* to the *sharīʿa*, and the second was to provide those around him with a means of distinguishing between the superior and inferior manifestations of sanctity.

Johnson concludes that the traditional concept of sanctity went on, with the help of Ibn ʿArabī, to be drained of its moral content: 'Unrestrained by the injunctions of the revealed Law ... the *walī* (saint) thus existed as a potent spiritual force unencumbered by moral restraints'.[8] This conclusion, however, is an over-simplification. A quick survey of early Muslim saints shows us that both law-abiding and antinomian saints have been consistently present within the mystical tradition. In addition to the figures cited by Johnson, we should include those of intoxication (*sukr*) like Abū Yazīd al-Bastāmī (d. 261/875), the so-called antinomians such as Abū Saʿīd b. Abu'l-Khayr (d. 441/1049), the tradition of *shaṭaḥāt* (ecstatic utterances), and the early Qalandariyya movement.[9] Although she does, at least on the popular level, recognise the '*walī* through obedience' and the '*walī* through grace' (p. 14), it is misleading on Johnson's part to portray classical Sufism in this one-sided way simply to set Ibn ʿArabī up as an innovator and the later al-Shaʿrānī as a great reformer. (It is worth noting that this characterisation is not drawn from the works of al-Shaʿrānī, but rather is based on Johnson's interpretation of Ibn ʿArabī.) Contrary to Johnson's claim however, our study of *al-Kibrīt al-aḥmar* will show that the superiority of 'law-abiding' saints is in fact derived from Ibn ʿArabī, and not presented by al-Shaʿrānī as a corrective.

It must be noted here that in reality Ibn ʿArabī goes to great lengths to stress the importance of the law in his mystical philosophy. A few examples will make this clear. In *al-Futūḥāt al-Makkiyya* we read:

> He who desires the path of knowledge and felicity should not let the Scale of the law drop from his hand for a single instant. ... In the same way, no one for whom the law is made incumbent (*al-mukallaf*), namely, no human being, should let the Scale established by the law drop from his hand.[10]

In the *Fuṣūṣ al-ḥikam* Ibn ʿArabī cites al-Bukhārī to the effect that mystical consciousness is necessarily linked to the *sharīʿa*: 'There are those of us in whom the Reality has become their hearing, sight, and all their faculties and limbs, according to the signs taught us by revealed Law that tells us of God.'[11] In addition to these positive statements it must be recognised that Ibn ʿArabī's view of the nature of the *sharīʿa* is rather complex.[12] Although we cannot here go into detail, the following is representative of the encompassing sense of the divine in Ibn ʿArabī's system, which forms the ground for all else:

> [O]ne may deduce that every ruling carried into effect in the world today is the decision of God, since it is only God's decisions that have any effect, in reality, even if it seems to go against the outer established ruling called the Law. That is because everything that happens in the Cosmos is according to the ruling of the divine Will and not [necessarily] in accordance with the rulings of established Law, even though its very establishment derives from the divine Will.[13]

In short, the point here is that Ibn ʿArabī cannot be seen as opposing the law – he is simply stressing that events in creation which do not follow the law are nonetheless subject to, and determined by, God's will.

### Ibn ʿArabī via al-Shaʿrānī

In the remaining pages we will pursue a few key themes in *al-Kibrīt al-aḥmar* with an eye to the claims made above by Johnson. First we will discuss briefly the presentation of the figure of Ibn ʿArabī himself, then we shall move on to survey the issues of the relationship of the *sharīʿa* to mystical vision, and finally the presentation of sanctity through the doctrine of the seal of sainthood. In the course of this survey it will become clear that al-Shaʿrānī – against the interpretation of Johnson – is much more the inheritor than the opponent or reformer of the shaykh.

Against criticism that Ibn ʿArabī does not give full due to the *sharīʿa*, al-Shaʿrānī presents the shaykh's statements on the necessity of law and its necessary connection to the attainment of *kashf* (mystical unveiling). The first example to be noted is one in which the observance of external law is a prerequisite for an intuitive or inspirational relationship with revelation. Al-Shaʿrānī quotes chapter 45 of the *al-Futūḥāt al-Makkiyya* to the effect that,

> The perfect one among men is he who has combined the call to God with the curtain of the station *(sitr al-maqām*, i.e. the specific realities of one time and place); for he calls to God by his recital of the books of *ḥadīth* and those on the subtle affinities (*raqāʾiq*), and by stories of the shaykhs; so that the people recognise them as a model. … Thus the perfect saint (*al-walī al-kāmil*) must embrace behaviour (in accord with) the law so that God opens up in his heart an eye to understanding Him, and inspiration into the meaning of the Qur'an.[14]

Here it is clear that he who is to benefit society around him with inspired understanding of the sources of revelation must first submit to the *sharīʿa*. The point being made here is not that mystical experience in its more dramatic forms should be denied, but rather that it has no place as a public spectacle. The mystic's internal progress cannot be detached from his outward observance of law. Elsewhere in *al-Futūḥāt al-Makkiyya* Ibn ʿArabī explains that the problem with ecstatic utterances is that through them the servant is attempting to climb to the level of his Lord. This movement is discouraged because it would entail the violation of one's 'essential reality' in relation to God, which is absolute servitude.[15]

## The Saint-maker

Not only is it inaccurate to say that al-Shaʿrānī is trying to restrain Ibn ʿArabī's school of mysticism, al-Shaʿrānī himself tries to impart a saintly aura to the figure of Ibn ʿArabī. In *al-Kibrīt al-aḥmar* al-Shaʿrānī makes clear in a number of statements the inspired nature of Ibn ʿArabī's writings. On page four he begins quoting various passages from the *al-Futūḥāt al-Makkiyya* in order to present its divinely inspired nature. He writes:

> In chapter 365 he said: Know that all I speak of in my teachings (*majālis*) and my writings is from the presence of the Qur'an and its treasury. I have been given the keys to understanding and the (necessary) resources; this is done so that I do not diverge from the teachings of God's truth or my intimate conversations with Him (*munājāt*) ... which are from holy inspiration (*waḥy al-quds*); however it is not like the inspiration of speech nor the inspiration of symbolic expression (*waḥy al-ishāra*) or interpretation (*ʿibāra*). So distinguish, my brother, between inspiration of words and inspiration of revelation (*waḥy al-ilhām*).[16]

The emphasis on *waḥy* is rather striking – especially in light of the traditional association of *waḥy* with the prophets and *ilhām* with saints. Al-Shaʿrānī himself has repeated this association in *al-Yawāqīt wa'l-jawāhir* (p. 89). From here he goes on in *al-Kibrīt al-aḥmar* to quote Ibn ʿArabī's implicit claim to sainthood. The passage runs:

> [A]ll that I write in this book however is from divine dictation and Lordly recitation or spiritual 'saliva' in the spirit of my being. All of this is by virtue of the heritage (*irth*) of the prophets and by (my) dependency upon them, and not by virtue of (my) independence.[17]

Although Ibn ʿArabī's claim to be inheritor of the prophets is no secret to scholarship, the significance here is that it is being stated in such a forthright manner by al-Shaʿrānī at the beginning of the book. Later on al-Shaʿrānī quotes the shaykh even more explicitly on the matter. We read from chapter fourteen: 'The number of perfect poles (*aqṭāb*) in previous generations, that is from Adam to the time of Muḥammad, is twenty-five. God showed them to me at a most holy meeting place in the Barzakh, while I was in the city of Cordoba.'[18] In light of the elevated position of visionary (and implied sainthood) al-Shaʿrānī is advertising for Ibn ʿArabī here, it is difficult to accept Johnson's claim that al-Shaʿrānī is using Ibn ʿArabī's own words with the intention of opposing him.[19]

## On Sainthood

As for the presentation of sanctity in *al-Kibrīt al-aḥmar*, the reader first encounters a number of comments on the cosmic hierarchy of the holy figures. Although we cannot cite all the instances al-Shaʿrānī quotes concerning these figures, a brief presentation should suffice to show that *al-Kibrīt al-aḥmar* reflects Ibn ʿArabī's complex teaching on the subject, even if al-Shaʿrānī does not address the details or ambiguities involved.[20] In the following we read of a four-tiered hierarchy:

> The levels of bliss reached by man are four: faith (*imān*), sanctity (*walāya*), prophethood (*nubuwwa*) and messengerhood (*risāla*); however, only to a few of each level is there tasting (*dhawq*). The *nabī* may have *dhawq* on the levels of *imān* and sanctity, but if a messenger (*rasūl*) is increased above them in *dhawq* of the level of *risāla* (it is) because he is *rasūl*, *nabī*, *walī* and *mu'min* (believer).[21]

This hierarchy is not unusual except for the introduction of the mystical term *dhawq*, which supplies an added element of discrimination between sanctified figures. Another hierarchy – this one more earthly – is set up between three classes of men. It is particularly significant because it reflects the high position of Ibn ʿArabī's version of the *malāmiyya* (i.e. those who appear unremarkable, rather than blameworthy[22]). Al-Shaʿrānī reproduces a rather lengthy passage from *al-Futūḥāt al-Makkiyya* on this:

> The men of God are of three types. The worshippers (*ʿubbād*), the Sufis and the *malāmiyya*. The perfect among men are the worshippers who are dominated by renunciation, constant devotion and outwardly praiseworthy acts. They do not see anything above themselves. They have no knowledge of the states (*aḥwāl*) and the levels (*maqāmāt*), and no inkling (lit. smell) of the divine science or the knowledge of unveilings (*kashūfāt*); and they are anxious that their actions be cautious and (always) acceptable to God. And the Sufis are above these worshippers because they see that all acts are God's, and they have in addition (to what the worshippers possess) earnestness, struggling, piety, renunciation, trust, etc., but they see that they have more than them (the worshippers) of a vision of the levels that are above them. They are of good manners (*akhlāq*) and chivalry (*futuwwa*), but they are people of frivolity and ego in the eyes of the people of the third level. … These people follow in the footsteps of Abū Bakr. They do not add anything

> to the five prayers and the supererogatory exercises. They are not distinguished from the people by any additional states by which they may be known. They walk in the markets and speak with the people in common speech, but they are alone with God in their hearts and they do not diverge from servanthood at all.[23]

In light of the primacy of the *malāmiyya* it would appear at first that these statements represent a primary source for al-Shaʿrānī's so-called 'orthodox' vision of sanctity. The inconspicuous mystic is held above the formalistic Sufi. However, if this is to be taken as evidence of an 'orthodox' Sufism, the troubling issue then arises concerning Johnson's claim that al-Shaʿrānī moved against the rise of gnostic or esoteric knowledge – as represented by Ibn ʿArabī.[24] Surely in this hierarchy just described the *malāmiyya* are gifted with a superior gnosis,[25] or at least a secret intimacy with the Divine, while the inferior Sufis only practice the Way. It would appear that in fact al-Shaʿrānī is following Ibn ʿArabī in equating higher sanctity with esoteric knowledge and an elite mystical experience.

Further on this, al-Shaʿrānī himself appends comments, extolling the *malāmatiyya* (here, those who are piously blameworthy), to his summary of Ibn ʿArabī's discussion of the modes of love. In chapter 471 of *al-Futūḥāt al-Makkiyya* (vol. 7, p. 188) Ibn ʿArabī outlines three kinds of love: the love of Providence (*ḥubb al-ʿināya*), the love of the worshipper (*ḥubb al-ʿabd*), and the love of (Divine) favour (*ḥubb al-karāma*). Al-Shaʿrānī summarises this fairly detailed discussion by saying simply, 'The love of Providence from God to the prophets is superior to (His) love of favour towards the saints' (vol. 2, p. 105). As a summary, al-Shaʿrānī's notice is certainly curt, and even misleading in as much as the prophets and saints are not clearly those to whom the discussion is referring. Nevertheless, what is more important to our discussion at hand, what is said concerning the *malāmatiyya*, is what al-Shaʿrānī adds. He writes:

> And thus the *malāmatiyya* are those who are the greatest among the people (*qawm*) (or, among the Sufis). They do not pray the obligatory (prayers), but they necessarily take upon themselves the important supererogatory prayers, since they fear that the claim will arise against them that they accomplish the obligatory prayers in a perfect way and that they excel in this. Yet (most consider) there is no supererogation except by completion of the obligatory prayer, and well they have understood! Yet further, what is superior is to multiply the supererogatory acts, securing the love of God for them. Thus they consider this (practice) a restoration for some who are lacking in their (outer) obligations; but God knows best.

From this it is clear that al-Shaʿrānī leaves open an important position to even the antinomian gnostic, as represented by the *malāmatiyya*; an unlikely stand if he were an 'orthodox-minded' reformer.

## Sanctity and its forms

The connection between the prophets and the saints is central to Ibn ʿArabī's complex position on sanctity. This connection is usually described as an inheritance (*wirātha*) passed down from a prophet to certain saints who then manifest their prophet's type of virtue and behaviour.[26] An elementary typology of the various inheritances may be attempted (e.g. a 'Moses-like' (*Mūsawī*) saint may manifest a luminous face as Moses did; a 'Jesus-like' saint may walk on water, etc.), but these outward signs of affiliation are not as important as the more subtle ethical and theological principles which characterise these prophetic inheritances. Ibn ʿArabī composed *al-Fuṣūṣ al-ḥikam* as an exposition of these inheritances. But although this practice of associating certain principles with certain prophets clearly predates Ibn ʿArabī,[27] it cannot be said that he brought this typology into clearer focus. In fact, the descriptions of prophets in *al-Fuṣūṣ al-ḥikam* often function less as typologies than they do as thematic devices for mystical speculation. Nevertheless, our main concern here is the dynamic of *wirātha* itself and al-Shaʿrānī's presentation of it. On page 40, volume 2 of *al-Kibrīt al-aḥmar* al-Shaʿrānī presents Ibn ʿArabī's account of a celestial meeting with the saints. The passage reads as follows: 'God brought me to the congregation of His prophets, and none remained unseen or unknown to me; and likewise He introduced me to their inheritors from among the saints, and I recognised (*ʿaraftuhum*) them. In each age they number at least 124,000.' Turning to *al-Futūḥāt al-Makkiyya* chapter 349 (vol. 5, p. 401) for comparison, we notice that al-Shaʿrānī's account is summary indeed. His three main points are accurate: the meeting with the prophets, with the saints and the number of these inheriting saints as 124,000. However, al-Shaʿrānī has conflated two categories of saints. Ibn ʿArabī writes, 'There must be, in every age, 100,000 saints and 24,000 saints in the line of a number of prophets … and God allots the knowledge of that prophet to those who are his inheritors.' Although the original *al-Futūḥāt al-Makkiyya* provides much more detail, for example, 'Know that God … has placed at the foot of each prophet a saint as inheritor', al-Shaʿrānī has certainly communicated the essentials of Ibn ʿArabī's doctrine of *wirātha* to his readers. Al-Shaʿrānī's account is poorer in detail than the original, but we should not read too much into his omissions. In the light of the above case, it would be hard to argue that he is trying to alter significantly the content of the material he is describing.

Another central element of the 'Akbarian' system is the so-called seal (*khatm*) of saints or sainthood. The idea – an extension of the principle of Muḥammad as the seal of prophethood – was first presented by al-Ḥakīm al-Tirmidhī in the ninth century CE, but was only developed some three centuries later by Ibn ʿArabī. Although the concept of the seal is quite complex in *al-Futūḥāt al-Makkiyya*, (with a distinction being made between the seal of universal sainthood and the seal of Muhammadan sainthood, and both being subsumed under Muḥammad's supra-mundane function as mediator between the eternal and the created), al-Shaʿrānī clearly notes one essential part. In *al-Kibrīt al-aḥmar*, volume two, p. 109, al-Shaʿrānī quotes *al-Futūḥāt al-Makkiyya*, chapter 480 (vol. 6, p. 213):

> (Jesus says) 'He made me blessed' (Qur'an 19:31) that is he honoured me by elevation *(bi-ziyāda)* not reached by any other; and that elevation (says Ibn ʿArabī) is his sealing the cycle of sainthood (*hiya khatmuhu li-dawra al-walāya*) and his descent at the end of time and his ruling by Muḥammad's law.

There is only a minor difference from the original passage in *al-Futūḥāt al-Makkiyya*, which reads simply 'his sealing of sainthood' (*khatmuhu li'l-walāya*) for 'his sealing the cycle of sainthood'.

Perhaps more interesting and more central to the question of al-Shaʿrānī's presentation of Akbarian thought is the rest of the passage, in which Jesus as seal is subordinated to Muḥammad. In *al-Kibrīt al-aḥmar* (vol. 2, p. 109) the passage continues, 'And this is so he will see his Lord on the Day of Resurrection in the Muhammadan mirror (*li-yarā rabbahu yawm al-qiyāma fī'l-mir'āti al-Muḥammadiyyati*), which is the most perfect of mirrors'. In *al-Futūḥāt al-Makkiyya* the passage is essentially the same, but ends with a different phrase. It runs, '... so that (or until) he will be, on the Day of Resurrection, among those who see their Lord as Muḥammad sees Him, (that is), in the Muhammadan form (*miʿman yarā rabbahu al-ru'yata al-Muḥammadiyyata fī'l-ṣūrati al-Muḥammadiyyati*)'. Of note here is al-Shaʿrānī's replacement of this rather elusive final phrase '*al-ru'yata al-Muḥammadiyyata fī'l-ṣūrati al-Muḥammadiyyati*' with '*al-mir'āti al-Muḥammadiyyati*'; we now turn our attention to these terms themselves.

In my research on Ibn ʿArabī I have not found any developed treatment of the two specific terms, '*al-ru'ya al-Muḥammadiyya*' or '*al-ṣūra al-Muḥammadiyya*'. Yet here al-Shaʿrānī does us a service by presenting the 'Muhammadan mirror' in their place. The mirror is a well-developed symbol for Ibn ʿArabī, and it is in drawing upon this development that al-Shaʿrānī's substitution makes sense.

In *al-Fuṣūṣ al-ḥikam* Ibn ʿArabī summarises his analogy of the mirror,

> [A] divine Self-revelation ... occurs only in a form conforming to the essential predisposition of the recipient of such revelation. Thus, the recipient sees nothing other than his own form in the mirror of the Reality.[28] ... In seeing your true self, He is your mirror and you are His mirror in which He sees His Names and their determinations, which are nothing other than Himself.[29]

Thus, one can only see oneself in the mirror that is God, although this image is in essence a contingent or partial divine Self-revelation. As for other possible mirrors, *al-Kibrīt al-aḥmar* summarises to the effect that the spiritual elite witness their Lord through the mirror of prophets, and that the lesser saints and learned ones witness at one step removed, that is, by the mirrors of the elite followers of the prophets.

> Know that the special saints and learned ones (*'ulamā'*) do not see their Lord except by the mirror of their prophet (Muḥammad), since it is the most perfect of mirrors, containing all (other) mirrors. And the non-elect among the saints and the learned ones witness by their (the elect's) mirrors while (these elect are) at the feet of the prophets; and that is because His self-revelation (*tajallī*) in the experiences (*ma'ārif*) of the hearts of the prophets is more complete and perfect than is His self-revelation in the hearts of others.[30]

Here it is made clear that there exists a hierarchy of mirrors; that is, beyond one using oneself as a mirror for the Divine, or the Divine as a mirror for oneself, one may turn to better mirrors (than oneself) for an improved view of the Divine. In *al-Futūḥāt al-Makkiyya* the apex of this hierarchy is clearly indicated. Here Muḥammad as mirror, in his function as intermediary, allows the seeker the best vision of God.

> It is known that the messengers are the most balanced *(a'dal)* of all people in constitution, since they receive the messages of their Lord. … There is no prophet who was not sent specifically to a designated people, since he possessed a specific and curtailed constitution (*mazāj khāṣṣ maqṣūr*). But God sent Muḥammad with an all-inclusive message for all people without exception. He was able to receive such a message because he possessed an all-inclusive constitution which comprises the constitution of every prophet and messenger … (But) you do not have a constitution like that possessed by Muḥammad. Whenever the Real discloses Himself to you within the mirror of your heart, your mirror will make Him manifest to you in the measure of its constitution and in the form of its shape. … Place him (Muḥammad) before you as the mirror… (and) you will come to know that God must disclose Himself to Muḥammad within his mirror. So the manifestation of the Real within the mirror of Muḥammad is the most perfect, most balanced, and most beautiful manifestation, because it is His mirror for (showing) Himself (*li-mā hiya mir'ātuhu 'alayhi*) … . And He gave to us through the Message and (the requisite) faith what the intellect without faith only curtails perception of … . And likewise our natures and the mirrors of our hearts curtail vision of what is manifested in the mirror of Muḥammad. … And inasmuch as you believe in Him concerning the Message in absence (*ghayb*, i.e. without being able to verify it rationally), so you witness Him in this prophetic manifestation directly (*'ayn*an).[31]

We see from these three notices a multi-level function for the mirror, which itself is the mediator of Divine presence. In the first instance one's own form is reflected back when the mirror is the Divine Itself, when the mediator is also the mediated. In the model of the saints using a prophet as mirror, the mediating role of the elite brings the divine Self-revelation into better focus. The final stage is that of the best mirror providing the best view – that is, providing a

Muhammadan view, which presents the Divine in the best form *(ṣūra)* possible, that of Muḥammad.

This last example of al-Shaʿrānī's editing – replacing the Muhammadan vision and form with the Muhammadan mirror – is a fitting example upon which to end our discussion. It shows a substitution into less problematic terminology, yet terminology which only makes sense in the wider context of Ibn ʿArabī's own writing and thought. The use of 'Muhammadan mirror' is not a move towards less speculative or less 'gnostic' language, rather it shows essentially al-Shaʿrānī using Ibn ʿArabī to explain Ibn ʿArabī. Nor does this example show al-Shaʿrānī explaining away some threat to the religious order of his day, instead, it shows a student struggling within a school of thought to make sense of a master's teachings.

The conclusions of this paper make clear to us that al-Shaʿrānī should be seen not only as an apologist for Ibn ʿArabī (as has been well noted by Winter and Garcin), but also as an exponent and transmitter of his thought. Although one might criticise al-Shaʿrānī for being equivocal and at times even pedestrian, it should be remembered that for many parts of the Islamic world it is his presentation of *al-Futūḥāt al-Makkiyya* that has served as the vehicle for the circulation of Ibn ʿArabī's thought. It is on the assumption that the medium is worthy of consideration, in addition to the message, that this paper has been written.

## Notes

1. See *EI* and *EI2*, s.v. 'al-Shaʿrānī'.

2. On his less well-known collection of saintly biographies, *al-Akhlāq al-maṭbūliyya* (Cairo, 1960 and 1975), 3 vols., see the recent article by C. Mayeur-Jaouen, 'Le cheikh scrupuleux et l'émir généreux à travers les Akhlāq maṭbūliyya de Shaʿrānī', in R. Chih and D. Gril, ed., *Le saint et son milieu ou comment lire les sources hagiographiques?* (Cairo, 2000).

3. M. Winter, *Society and Religion in Early Ottoman Egypt: Studies in the Writings of ʿAbd al-Wahhab al-Shaʿrani* (New Brunswick, NJ, 1982). Note also the biographies of T. Tawīl, *al-Shaʿrānī, imām al-taṣawwuf fī ʿaṣrihi* (Cairo, 1945) and Muḥammad Muḥyī al-Dīn al-Malījī, *al-Manāqib al-kubrā* composed in 1109/1697 (Cairo, 1937).

4. One might begin by looking closely at the teachers who made the greatest impact on al-Shaʿranī. See Winter, *Society and Religion*, pp. 54–58, and J.-C. Garcin's work: 'Index des Tabaqat de Shaʿrani', *Annales Islamologiques*, 6 (1963), p. 44; 'L'Insertion sociale de Shaʿrani dans le milieu Cairote', in *Colloque International sur l'Histoire du Caire* (Cairo, 1969), p. 164; 'Histoire et hagiographie de l'Egypte Musulmane à la fin de l'époque Mamelouke', in *Hommages à la mémoire de S. Sauneron, II: Egypte post-pharaonique* (Cairo, 1979), pp. 300–308.

5. It is described in A. E. Shmidt, *Abd al-Vakhkhab ash-Shaʿrani i Ego Kniga Razispannykh Zhemchuzhin* (St. Petersburg, 1914), as cited by Winter, *Society and Religion*.

6. K. V. Johnson, 'The Unerring Balance: a Study of the Theory of Sanctity (Wilaya) of ʿAbd al-Wahhab al-Shaʿrani' (Ph.D. Thesis, Harvard University, 1985), p. iii.

7. Ibid., p. 28. Unfortunately Johnson does not deal with criticisms of Sufi (and other devotional) practices from a socio-historical perspective at all. There were many more

reasons for criticism of certain practices than that identified by Johnson. For more on this see B. Shoshan, *Popular Culture in Medieval Cairo* (New York, 1993) and E. Geoffroy, *Le Soufisme en Egypte et en Syrie* (Damascus, 1995), chap. 20.

8. Johnson, *The Unerring Balance*, p. 70.

9. M. Monawwar, *The Secrets of God's Mystical Oneness (Asrār al-tawḥīd fī manāqib Abī Sa'īd)*, tr. J. O'Kane (Costa Mesa, CA, 1992) and A. T. Karamustafa, *God's Unruly Friends: Dervish Groups in the Islamic Later Period 1200-1550* (Salt Lake City, UT, 1994), chap. 3.

10. W. C. Chittick, *The Sufi Path of Knowledge* (Albany, NY, 1989), p. 179.

11. Ibn 'Arabī, *The Bezels of Wisdom*, tr. R. W. J. Austin (New York, 1980), p. 125.

12. See M. Chodkiewicz, 'Ibn 'Arabi: la lettre et la loi', in *Actes du colloque: Mystique, culture et société* (Paris, 1983). Ibn 'Arabī's understanding of the nature and function of the law, while nuanced, held it as essential for not only everyday living but also along the mystic path (for example, he does not condone ecstatic utterances) (p. 35). He also opposed the blind following of one legal school (*madhhab*) over the others (p. 30). Statements such as 'The *sharī'a* is the *ḥaqīqa*' (p. 28), and Ibn 'Arabī's assertion that any mystical unveiling contradicting the law must be rejected, certainly absolve the shaykh of any charge of simple antinomianism.

13. Ibn 'Arabī, *The Bezels of Wisdom*, p. 204.

14. *Al-Kibrīt al-aḥmar*, vol. 1, p. 22. The first sentence is quoted almost directly, while the second is a paraphrase of the following: 'The perfect inheritor (of the prophets) is a (divine) gift from among the saints who occupies himself only with God, by the law of God's prophet, to the point that God opens up in his heart the understanding of what He sent down to His prophet and messenger Muḥammad.' See *al-Futuḥāt al-Makkiyya* (Beirut, 1994), vol. 1, pp. 574, 577.

15. M. Chodkiewicz, *Seal of the Saints: Prophethood and Sainthood in the Doctrine of Ibn 'Arabī* (Cambridge, 1993), p. 111. In *al-Kibrīt al-aḥmar*, vol. 2, p. 144, al-Sha'rānī presents some of his own comments on this.

16. *Al-Kibrīt al-aḥmar*, vol. 1, p. 4. Al-Sha'rānī's quotation does not appear in chapter 365 of my edition of *al-Futūḥāt al-Makkiyya* (Cairo, 1293/1876).

17. Ibid., p. 4. From chap. 373, *al-Futūḥāt al-Makkiyya*, vol. 6, p. 287. The second sentence is not a direct quotation.

18. Ibid., p. 10. This is a paraphrase of the following: 'As for the perfect poles of preceding generations, their names were mentioned to me in the Arabic language when I witnessed them, seeing them in the Barzakh, while I was in Cordoba in a most holy place (*mashhad aqdas*).' For more on Ibn 'Arabī's visions see C. Addas, *Quest for the Red Sulphur* (Cambridge, 1993) chap. 3.

19. Johnson, *The Unerring Balance*, p. 73. This claim is made during a discussion of *al-Yawāqīt wa'l-jawāhir*, but I believe this logic, by implication, extends to *al-Kibrīt al-aḥmar*.

20. A number of discussions may be found, including, vol. 1, pp. 58, 109, 129, and vol. 2, pp. 59, 101, 190 and 198.

21. *Al-Kibrīt al-aḥmar*, vol. 1, p. 105. I am unable to locate the original version of this passage in *al-Futūḥāt al-Makkiyya*. On *dhawq* according to Ibn 'Arabī see Chittick, *The Sufi Path of Knowledge*, pp. 70, 220.

22. For more on the *malāmiyya* and *malāmatiyya* see Chodkiewicz, *Seal of the Saints*, p.

109, and al-Hujwīrī (d. 463/1071), *The Kashf al-maḥjūb*, tr. R. A. Nicholson (London, 1936), p. 63.

23. *Al-Kibrīt al-aḥmar*, vol. 2, p. 12. This passage is taken from chapter 309, *al-Futūḥāt al-Makkiyya*, vol. 5, pp. 64, 65. Al-Sha'rānī's summary leaves nothing significant out, but the phrase 'They are in the footsteps of Abu Bakr' does not appear in this section of *al-Futūḥāt al-Makkiyya*.

24. Johnson sees the threat to the traditional concept of sanctity as beginning with al-Tirmidhī in the 4th/9th century. In contrast to those before him who 'sought to accommodate the *sharī'a* and the pursuit of the Way, al-Ḥakīm al-Tirmidhī (ca. 300/910) ... offered a concept of *wilāya* based upon the attainment of gnostic wisdom (*ma'rifa*)'. (p. 64) This degeneration continued thanks to Ibn al-'Arabī's refinements which produced a 'sanctity born of gnostic contemplation' (p. 65), all of which 'led 'Abd al-Wahhāb al-Sha'rānī to propose his own theory of *wilāya* as a means by which the *sharī'a* might be restored to its rightful role'. (p. 71)

25. See Chittick, *Ibn al-'Arabī's Metaphysics*, p. 372.

26. Chodkiewicz, *Seal of the Saints*, p. 75. Note also p. 147, 'Akbarian hagiology is ultimately arranged around three fundamental notions: *wirātha, niyāba, qurba. Wirātha* – the heritage of a spiritual knowledge or, if one prefers, of a mode of knowledge of God peculiar to one of the prophetic models – explains the forms taken by sainthood.' For examples in Ibn 'Arabī's life see *al-Futūḥāt al-Makkiyya*, chap. 438, and *al-Kibrīt al-aḥmar*, vol. 2, p. 97.

27. Abū Madyan (d. 594/1198), the most frequently mentioned of Ibn al-'Arabī's teachers (although the two never met in person) mentioned in *al-Futūḥāt al-Makkiyya*, provides a beginning of a typology of prophetic heritage in his *Bidāyat al-murīd*, p. 87 of *The Way of Abū Madyan*, tr. V. Cornell (Cambridge, 1996). The 4th/9th-century al-Ḥakīm al-Tirmidhī also begins to address the characteristics of the prophets. See B. Radtke's *The Concept of Sainthood in Early Islamic Mysticism* (Surrey, UK, 1996), p. 101. Note also Qur'an (17:55) which reads, 'We have preferred some prophets over others'.

28. Ibn al-'Arabī, *The Bezels of Wisdom*, tr. R. W. J. Austin (New York, 1980), p. 65; *Fuṣūṣ al-ḥikam*, ed. A. Affifi (Beirut, 1946), p. 61.

29. Ibn al-'Arabī, *The Bezels of Wisdom*, p. 65; *Fuṣūṣ al-ḥikam*, p. 62.

30. *Al-Kibrīt al-aḥmar*, vol. 2, p. 199. (Al-Sha'rānī gives *al-Futūḥāt al-Makkiyya*, chap. 398 as his source, but I am unable to locate it there.)

31. Chittick, Ibn al-'Arabī's Metaphysics, p. 351, al-Futūḥāt al-Makkiyya, chap. 355, vol. 5, p. 479.

# Part Three

# Pre-Modern Islam

# 28

# Shāh Ṭāhir and the Nizārī Ismaili Disguises

*Farhad Daftary*

In the long reign of the Fatimid Ismaili Caliph-Imam al-Mustanṣir (427–487/1036–1094), the Fatimid state had already embarked on its course of decline. The Ismailis of Persia now became increasingly wary of the Fatimid dynasty's failing political fortunes and influence beyond the shrinking boundaries of the Fatimid state, even though the Ismaili *daʿwa* or religio-political mission had continued to be propagated in Persia and other eastern lands on behalf of the Fatimids by a network of *dāʿīs* or missionaries. By the final decade of al-Mustanṣir's rule, Ḥasan-i Ṣabbāḥ had risen to the leadership of the Persian Ismailis as their chief *dāʿī*, also initiating a revolutionary campaign against the Turkish Saljuqs, the new masters of the Abbasid caliphate, whose alien rule was detested by the Persians. Ḥasan-i Ṣabbāḥ (d. 518/1124) launched his armed revolt by seizing the mountain fortress of Alamūt in northern Persia in 483/1090. This also marked the effective foundation of what was to become the Nizārī Ismaili state of Persia and Syria.

Ḥasan-i Ṣabbāḥ was already acting somewhat independently of Cairo when al-Mustanṣir died in 487/1094 and his succession was disputed by his sons – Nizār, the original heir-designate, and his much younger half-brother Aḥmad who had been rapidly installed on the Fatimid throne with the caliphal title of al-Mustaʿlī bi'llāh. Al-Mustaʿlī was also recognised as al-Mustanṣir's successor to the Ismaili Imamate by the leaders of the *daʿwa* headquarters in Cairo as well as the Ismailis of Egypt, Yaman and some other regions. The situation was quite different in the east, where Ḥasan-i Ṣabbāḥ sided with Nizār and broke off relations with the Fatimids and the *daʿwa* headquarters in Cairo, which henceforth served the cause of al-Mustaʿlī and his successors in the Fatimid dynasty. Ḥasan had now in effect also founded the independent Nizārī Ismaili *daʿwa* centred on the stronghold of Alamūt. Nizār himself was executed in 488/1095 following the failure of his revolt to assert his claims, but the Nizārī *daʿwa* continued to be propagated in the name of Nizār and his descendants who eventually emerged as Imams in Alamūt.[1]

Despite the much superior military power of the Saljuqs and their successors, and their continued hostility towards the Shiʿi Ismailis, the Nizārī state survived for some 166 years until 654/1256, when Persia was overrun by the Mongol hordes commanded by Hūlāgū. One of the primary objectives of the invading Mongols had been the destruction of the Nizārī state in Persia, which they accomplished meticulously though with some difficulty. The Mongols systematically destroyed the bulk of the Nizārī fortresses of Persia; they also put to the sword large numbers of Nizārīs. However, despite the claims of Juwaynī (d. 681/1288), the Persian historian and functionary who accompanied Hūlāgū on his anti-Ismaili campaigns, the Nizārīs were not completely extirpated.[2] Many Nizārīs in Persia survived the destruction of their state and fortress communities. The Nizārī Ismaili Imamate too continued and was handed down among the descendants of Rukn al-Dīn Khurshāh, the last lord of Alamūt who was killed by the Mongols in 655/1257. Before Rukn al-Dīn fell into Mongol captivity, a group of Nizārī dignitaries had succeeded in taking his son and successor to the Imamate, Shams al-Dīn Muḥammad, to a safe locality in northwestern Persia. Shams al-Dīn and his immediate successors as Imams lived clandestinely under different guises without much contact with their followers.

The first few centuries after the fall of Alamūt represent an extremely obscure period in Ismaili history. The fact remains, however, that in the aftermath of the Mongol debacle, the Nizārīs who survived precariously in scattered groups and outside their traditional fortress communities, were totally disorganised and demoralised. Many migrated to adjacent lands in Afghanistan, Central Asia and Sind, where Ismaili communities already existed. The Nizārīs now also resorted widely to *taqiyya*, the precautionary dissimulation of one's true religious beliefs in the face of danger. The Ismailis had traditionally practised *taqiyya*, a basic tenet of Imāmī Shiʿism shared by Twelvers and Ismailis, since they were frequently persecuted by Sunni Muslims as 'heretics' (*malāḥida*). As a result, they had become rather skilled in adopting a variety of external guises. Nevertheless, many Nizārī groups soon either disintegrated or were assimilated into the religiously dominant communities of their milieus.

It seems that in the wake of the Mongol catastrophe, in many localities the Persian Nizārīs adopted the guise of Sunnism, then still the predominant religion of the Iranian lands. They also began to use Sufi and poetic forms of expression to camouflage their Ismaili teachings, without establishing formal affiliations with any of the Sufi *ṭarīqa*s or orders then spreading in Persia and Central Asia. The earliest evidence for these disguises is found in the writings of Ḥakīm Saʿd al-Dīn b. Shams al-Dīn, better known as Nizārī Quhistānī (d. 720/1320), a Nizārī poet and an official at the court and chancery of the Mihrabānids of eastern Persia.[3] Nizārī Quhistānī, who alludes in his still-unpublished versified *Safar-nāma* ('Travelogue') to having secretly met the Imam Shams al-Dīn Muḥammad in Azerbaijan, is the first Nizārī author to have used Sufi terminology such as *khānqāh*, *darwīsh* (dervish), *qalandar* (wandering dervish) as well as *pīr* and *murshid*, terms designating a Sufi master.[4] Nizārī Quhistānī's poetry, permeated with Ismaili idioms and concepts such as *ẓāhir*, *bāṭin*, *ta'wīl* and *qiyāma*, contain numerous Shiʿi ideas as well as the more specifically Nizārī teachings of the Alamūt period.

Shams al-Dīn Muḥammad, the first post-Alamūt Nizārī Imam, who lived secretly in Azerbaijan as an embroiderer (hence his nickname of Zardūz) died around 710/1310. An obscure dispute over his succession split the Nizārī Imamate into two rival lines, later designated as Muḥammad-Shāhī and Qāsim-Shāhī, named after the deceased Imam's progeny who claimed his heritage. This schism, which dealt another devastating blow to the Nizārī community, was first brought to the attention of the scholarly community by W. Ivanow (1886–1970), a pioneer in modern Ismaili studies.[5] Shāh Ṭāhir, the focus of our attention here, was the most famous Imam of the Muḥammad-Shāhī line, which became discontinued by the end of the twelfth/eighteenth century, while the Qāsim-Shāhī Imams, who since the earlier decades of the nineteenth century have carried the honorific title of Aga Khan (Āghā Khān), are now the sole Nizārī Ismaili Imams. It seems that initially the Muḥammad-Shāhī, also known as Mu'min-Shāhī, Imams were particularly successful in Persia and Central Asia.[6] However, by the tenth/sixteenth century, they had begun to lose their prominence to the Qāsim-Shāhī Imams.

By the middle of the ninth/fifteenth century, the Muḥammad-Shāhī Imams had acquired large followings in Central Asia, notably in Badakhshān and adjacent areas in the upper Oxus region. The Ismailis of Badakhshān, who remain particularly devoted to Nāṣir-i Khusraw (d. after 465/1072) and consider him as the founder of their communities, had acknowledged the Nizārī *daʿwa* sometime during the Alamūt period as a result of the activities of *dāʿīs* sent from Khurāsān. Subsequently, this region situated in the midst of the Pamir and Hindu Kush mountains was spared the Mongol catastrophe. Badakhshān was later annexed to the Tīmūrid empire by Abū Saʿīd (r. 855–873/1451–1469). A few decades later, Badakhshān was conquered by the Uzbeks, whose authority was intermittently resisted by a number of local rulers as well as the Ismaili *dāʿīs* who had founded dynasties of their own in Shughnān and other districts of Badakhshān.[7] It was under such circumstances that Shāh Raḍī al-Dīn II, the thirtieth Imam of the Muḥammad-Shāhī Nizārīs and Shāh Ṭāhir's father, arrived in Badakhshān and with the support of his local community established his rule over a part of the region. He had earlier lived in Sīstān and Quhistān (in southeastern Khurāsān) and led the Nizārīs of eastern Persia and some parts of Khurāsān. Shāh Raḍī al-Dīn's fortunes were reversed when his supporters began to quarrel among themselves. In the event, the Nizārī Imam was killed in 915/1509 and his head was sent to Mīrzā Khān, a local Tīmūrid ruler who was then extending his own hegemony over parts of Badakhshān.[8] Mīrzā Khān had dealt a disconcerting blow to the Nizārīs of Badakhshān who gradually switched their allegiance to the Qāsim-Shāhī line of Imams.

Indeed, by the tenth/sixteenth century, the Qāsim-Shāhī Imams were well on the way to overshadowing their Muḥammad-Shāhī rivals in the Nizārī Imamate. They had already emerged several decades earlier from their hiding places and established their headquarters in the village of Anjudān, near Qumm in central Persia, initiating the Anjudān revival in post-Alamūt Nizārī (Qāsim-Shāhī) Ismailism which lasted for some two centuries. During that period, the Qāsim-Shāhī Imams reorganised and reactivated the *daʿwa* operations under their own leadership and acquired an increasing number of followers, especially in Central Asia and India. They also won many Muḥammad-Shāhīs to their side in Persia and Badakhshān. During the Anjudān revival, Nizārī doctrinal works too once again began to be composed, reiterating the earlier teachings of the Alamūt period. The bulk of the Nizārī literature extant from the early Anjudān period, including the writings of Abū Isḥāq Quhistānī (d. after 904/1498) and Khayrkhwāh-i Harātī (d. after 960/1553), were written by authors belonging to the Qāsim-Shāhī community,[9] while the Muḥammad-Shāhīs seem to have produced very few scholars and authors – one example being Sayyid Suhrāb Walī Badakhshānī (d. after 856/1452).[10] It is to be noted that a majority of the Nizārī works written during the Alamūt and post-Alamūt periods has been preserved by the Nizārī Ismailis of Badakhshān,[11] now divided by the Oxus (Āmū Daryā) river between Tajikistan and Afghanistan, even though numerous private manuscript collections were destroyed in various ways under Soviet rule in Central Asia.

By the time the Safawids founded their state in Persia and adjacent lands, in 907/1501, relations between Nizārī Ismailism and Persian Sufism had become well established in the Iranian world. Both branches of Nizārī Ismailism had increasingly dissimulated under the mantle of Sufism, while the Sufis themselves used the *bāṭinī taʾwīl*, or esoteric exegesis, and other ideas more widely ascribed to the Ismailis. Indeed, a distinctive coalescence had developed between these two independent esoteric traditions in Islam. This coalescence, still less understood from the Sufi side, would not have been so readily possible if the Ismailis and the Sufis did not share important doctrinal affinities.[12] The Sufis too had developed their own *bāṭinī* tradition based on a distinction between the *ẓāhir* and the *bāṭin* dimensions of religion, or between the *sharīʿa* and its inner spiritual reality or *ḥaqīqa*. And in both traditions, the faithful believer (*muʾmin*) or the disciple (*murīd*) was to focus his devotion on a spiritual guide, the Imam or the Sufi master, transcending the limitations of his own separate existence. The ontological position of the Nizārī Imam, as the representative of cosmic reality, was also analogous to that of the Perfect Man (*al-insān al-kāmil*) of the Sufis, though the latter was an imperfect substitute for the Imam. The single Imam of the Nizārīs was much more than a Sufi master, one among a multitude of such guides at any moment in time.

The adoption of Persian as the religious language of the Persian-speaking Nizārīs from the time of Ḥasan-i Ṣabbāḥ had further facilitated the Ismaili-Sufi literary relations. As an instance of this unique type of coalescence, mention may be made of the famous Sufi treatise entitled *Gulshan-i rāz* ('The Rose-Garden of Mystery') composed by Maḥmūd Shabistarī (d. after 740/1339), and its later commentary by a Nizārī Ismaili author who produced esoteric interpretations of selected passages of this poem.[13] Maḥmūd Shabistarī, a Sufi master from Azerbaijan, clearly reveals his familiarity with certain Ismaili teachings, while the Ismaili commentary on the *Gulshan-i rāz* reflects its author's familiarity with Sufi doctrines. At any rate, the Nizārīs of Persia and Central Asia consider the *Gulshan-i rāz* as part of their literary heritage,[14] and this explains why it was commented upon by a Nizārī Ismaili author. The author of this commentary may have been none other than the Muḥammad-Shāhī Imam Shāh Ṭāhir who is reported to have actually written a commentary entitled *Sharḥ-i Gulshan-i rāz*.[15] Owing to the close Ismaili-Sufi ties, the Persian-speaking Nizārīs of the Iranian world have traditionally considered some of the great mystic poets of Persia, such as Mawlānā Jalāl al-Dīn Rūmī and Farīd al-Dīn ʿAṭṭār as their co-religionists, preserving selections of their works in their collections of manuscripts. The Nizārī Ismailis of Persia, Afghanistan and Central Asia have continued to use verses of Rūmī and other mystical poets of the Iranian lands in their religious ceremonies. It should be noted in passing that Twelver Shiʿism developed its own rapport with Sufism in post-Mongol Persia.

The Ismaili-Sufi interfacings are also abundantly attested to in the *Pandiyāt-i jawānmardī* ('Admonitions on Spiritual Chivalry'), a book containing the religious sermons of Mustanṣir bi'llāh II (d. 885/1480), the thirty-second Qāsim-Shāhī Imam.[16] In this work, preserved in the private libraries of Badakhshān and northern areas of Pakistan, the Nizārīs are designated by Sufi expressions such as *ahl-i ḥaqīqat* or the 'People of the Truth', while the Imam is referred to as *pīr* and *murshid*. Permeated with Sufi ideas, it is interesting to note that the admonitions in the *Pandiyāt*, in fact, start with the *sharīʿat-ṭarīqat-ḥaqīqat* categorisation of the Sufis. It is explained to the true believers seeking *jawānmardī* or high standards of ethical behaviour that *ḥaqīqat* is none other than the truths hidden in the *sharīʿat* or the positive law – truths which could be attained only by following the guidance of the Imam along the spiritual path or *ṭarīqat*. The same ideas are expressed in the writings of Khayrkhwāh-i Harātī. Still concealing their true identity, the Nizārī Imams now appeared to outsiders as Sufi masters or *pīr*s, while their followers adopted the standard Sufi guise of disciples or *murīd*s – a term first used by Nizārī Quhistānī, a contemporary of Maḥmūd Shabistarī. It is interesting to note that the Nizārī Ismailis still refer to themselves as their Imam's *murīd*s and apply the word *ṭarīqa* to their particular interpretation of Shiʿi Islam. The term *pīr*, the Persian equivalent of the Arabic *shaykh*, acquired wide usage among the Nizārī Ismailis and it came to be applied not only to the Imam himself, but also to the *dāʿī*s of higher ranks. This term was subsequently retained by the Nizārī communities of Central Asia and India. The Imams also used Sufi names such as Shāh Qalandar, adopted by the Imam Mustanṣir bi'llāh II whose mausoleum still stands in Anjudān. More generally, the Imams often added terms such as Shāh and ʿAlī to their names, similar to Sufi masters.

In the meantime, the Sufi *ṭarīqas* themselves, though overwhelmingly Sunni in their membership, played a crucial part in spreading Shiʿi sentiments and ʿAlid loyalism in Persia and Central Asia, where the bulk of the population adhered to Sunnism. In other words, most of the Sufi orders then developing in pre-Safawid Iranian world remained outwardly Sunni, while they were at the same time particularly devoted to ʿAlī b. Abī Ṭālib and the Prophet Muḥammad's family (*ahl al-bayt*), acknowledging ʿAlī's spiritual guidance (see references in note 18). As a result, a covert and popular form of Shiʿism, infused with Sufi ideas, had begun to be diffused mainly through the Sufi orders – a phenomenon designated by the late Islamicist Marshall Hodgson (1922–1968) as 'ṭarīqa Shiʿism',[17] which eventually culminated in Safawid Shiʿism. Amongst the Sufi orders which spread Shiʿi sentiments in Persia and contributed to what Professor Claude Cahen (1909–1991) once described as the 'Shiʿitisation of Sunnism',[18] particular mention should be made of the Nūrbakhshiyya, the Niʿmat Allāhiyya and the Ṣafawiyya, which eventually became fully Shiʿi *ṭarīqas*. The Ṣafawiyya order played the most active and direct political role in establishing a Shiʿi state in Persia. Although concrete evidence is lacking until the late twelfth/eighteenth century, the Nizārī Imams, notably those belonging to the Qāsim-Shāhī line, may have developed some ties with the Niʿmat Allāhiyya order even in this early period.[19] This atmosphere of religious eclecticism, together with political fragmentation of post-Mongol Persia, proved favourable for the activities of the Nizārīs and a number of other crypto-Shiʿi or Shiʿi-related movements, such as those of the Ḥurūfiyya and their offshoot the Nuqṭawiyya, which entertained millenarian aspirations and received much popular support in Persia. The Nuqṭawiyya, too, shared common doctrinal grounds with the Nizārī Ismailis and developed close relations with Persian Sufism.[20]

The advent of the Safawids and the proclamation of Twelver Shiʿism as the state religion of their realm in 907/1501 promised yet a more favourable ambience for the activities of the Nizārīs and other Shiʿi communities in Persia. Under the circumstances, the Nizārīs, who still used the *murshid-murīd* disguise and appeared to be a Sufi order, had evidently begun to reduce the intensity of their *taqiyya* practices. The Nizārī optimism was, however, short-lived. Soon the Safawids, spurred by their *sharīʿa*-minded *ʿulamāʾ*, started to persecute all popular types of Sufism as well as those Shiʿi movements that fell outside the boundaries of the Ithnāʿashariyya or Twelver Shiʿism. As a result, many Sufi orders of Persia were uprooted in the reign of Shāh Ismāʿīl (907–930/1501–1524), the founder of the Safawid dynasty, while the few remaining orders such as the Niʿmat Allāhiyya rapidly lost their earlier prominence. It was under such circumstances that the Persian Nizārīs adopted a new form of *taqiyya*, dissimulating under the mantle of Twelver Shiʿism, the 'politically correct' form of Shiʿism sponsored and actively championed by the Safawids. At the time, the Safawids were in fact relying on the efforts of a number of Twelver *ʿulamāʾ* brought from Iraq and elsewhere in the Middle East to propagate Twelver Shiʿism throughout their dominions. The Nizārīs found it relatively easy to practise this new form of *taqiyya* as they shared the same early ʿAlid heritage and Imāmī Shiʿi traditions with the Twelver Shiʿa. The available evidence indicates that Shāh Ṭāhir, who succeeded to the Imamate of the Muḥammad-Shāhī Nizārīs shortly after the foundation of the Safawid state, may indeed have been the earliest Nizārī leader to have initiated the Twelver Shiʿis disguise, which remained operative within the Persian Nizārī community until the early decades of the twentieth century. Dissimulating as Twelver Shiʿis did by and large safeguard the Nizārīs against rampant persecution by the Safawids and their successors in Persia, but its extended application also led to the acculturation of numerous Nizārī groups and their full assimilation into the dominant Twelver communities of their surroundings. In other words, the adoption of Twelver Shiʿism eventually led, after several centuries of dissimulation, to the loss of the specific religious identity of a not insignificant number of Persian Nizārī Ismailis who in fact became 'genuine' Twelver Shiʿis.

Shāh Ṭāhir al-Ḥusaynī had succeeded in 915/1509 to the Imamate of the Muḥammad-Shāhī Nizārīs on the death of his father, the thirtieth Imam Shāh Raḍī al-Dīn II. The most famous Imam of his line, Shāh Ṭāhir was a learned theologian, poet and stylist as well as an accomplished diplomat who rendered valuable services to the Niẓām-Shāhī dynasty of Aḥmadnagar in the Deccan, in southern India; hence his nickname of al-Dakkanī. The most detailed account of Shāh Ṭāhir is related by Muḥammad Qāsim Hindū Shāh Astarābādī, the celebrated historian of the Deccan, in his *Gulshan-i Ibrāhīmī*, commonly known as *Taʾrīkh-i Firishta* after the pen-name of its author.[21] Firishta, who completed his history around 1015/1606, was evidently in contact with Shāh Ṭāhir's descendants and was also aware of their Ismaili affiliation.

Shāh Ṭāhir was born and brought up in Khund, a village near Qazwīn in northern Persia, where his predecessors, known as the Khundī Sayyids (Sādāt-i Khundiyya), had lived for some time. It seems that Shāh Ṭāhir had presented himself as a Twelver Shiʿi from early on, perhaps even before he succeeded to the Muḥammad-Shāhī Imamate. At any rate, as a reflection of his *taqiyya* practices, Shāh Ṭāhir, in the course of his eventful life, composed a number of commentaries on the theological and juristic treatises of well-known Twelver Imāmī scholars such as ʿAllāma al-Ḥillī (d. 726/1325).[22] Owing to his learning and piety, Shāh Ṭāhir was invited in 920/1514 by Shāh Ismāʿīl to join other Shiʿi scholars at the Safawid court in Sulṭāniyya, in Azerbaijan. Under obscure circumstances, Shāh Ṭāhir soon aroused the anger of the Safawid monarch, perhaps because his teachings reportedly deviated from those of other *'ulamā'*. At any rate, on the intercession of Mīrzā Ḥusayn Iṣfahānī, an influential Safawid courtier who may have been a secret follower of the Imam, Shāh Ṭāhir was permitted to settle in Kāshān, like Qumm another traditional centre of Shi'i learning in Persia, and teach at a theological seminary there.

Before long, Shāh Ṭāhir's Twelver cover was seriously threatened as countless numbers from amongst his own followers (*murīds*) as well as Nuqṭawīs and others swarmed to his lectures from different localities. Firishta and other sources relate that Shāh Ṭāhir's rising popularity in Kāshān soon aroused the jealousy of the local officials and Twelver scholars, who complained to Shāh Ismā'īl about his 'heretical' teachings. Whether or not Shāh Ṭāhir propagated some form of Ismaili doctrine in his lectures cannot be ascertained. Be that as it may, Shāh Ṭāhir's Ismaili connection had now been discovered and reported to the Safawid monarch, who speedily ordered his execution. The Imam was once again saved by his friend at the court, Mīrzā Ḥusayn Iṣfahānī, who secretly informed him in time to leave the Safawid dominions. In 926/1520, Shāh Ṭāhir hurriedly left Kāshān for Fārs and then sailed to the port of Goa in India. Initially, he proceeded to Bijapur, in the Deccan, hoping to find a suitable position there at the court of Ismā'īl 'Ādil Shāh (916–941/1510–1534), whose father had been the first Muslim ruler in India to have adopted Shi'ism as the religion of his state. Disappointed with his poor reception in Bijapur, however, Shāh Ṭāhir then encountered and impressed some scholars and dignitaries from the court of Burhān Niẓām Shāh (914–961/1508–1554), who duly invited the Persian scholar to join his entourage.

In 928/1522, Shāh Ṭāhir, who now very closely guarded his Ismaili identity, arrived in Aḥmadnagar, the capital of the Niẓām-Shāhī dynasty in the Deccan, where he was to spend the rest of his life. Soon, he became the most trusted adviser and confidant of Burhān Niẓām Shāh. By this time, Shāh Ṭāhir had been extremely successful in dissimulating as a Twelver Shi'i scholar, and as such he delivered weekly lectures on different religious subjects inside the fort of Aḥmadnagar. Shāh Ṭāhir's success in disguising his true religious identity culminated in his conversion of Burhān Niẓām Shāh from Sunnism to Twelver Shi'ism, which also enabled the Deccani monarch to cultivate friendly relations with Safawid Persia. Shortly after his own conversion, in 944/1537 Burhān Niẓām Shāh adopted Twelver Shi'ism as the official religion of his realm. It is not clear whether Shāh Ṭāhir ever attempted to propagate any form of Nizārī Ismaili doctrines to the Niẓām-Shāhīs and their subjects. In all probability, after his Persian experience, the Nizārī Imam had decided to adhere fully and publicly to the Twelver form of Shi'ism in the strictest possible observance of *taqiyya*. And this explains the strange phenomenon of an 'Ismaili' Imam actively propagating 'Twelver Shi'ism'.

Henceforth, an increasing number of Shi'i scholars, including Shāh Ṭāhir's own brother Shāh Ja'far, were patronised by the Niẓām-Shāhīs to the contentment of the Safawids, who had now somehow failed to unmask Shāh Ṭāhir's true identity. At any event, Shāh Ṭahmāsp (930–984/1524–1576), the second Safawid monarch, sent an embassy and gifts to Burhān Niẓām Shāh; and the latter reciprocated by dispatching Shāh Ḥaydar, Shāh Ṭāhir's son, on a goodwill mission to the Safawid court. Subsequently, Shāh Ṭāhir rendered great services to the Niẓām-Shāhīs by participating in numerous diplomatic negotiations on their behalf. Shāh Ṭāhir died around 956/1549 and his remains were later taken to Karbalā and interred in the Imam al-Ḥusayn's shrine, in line with a well-established Twelver Shiʿi custom. According to Muḥammad-Shāhī traditions, Shāh Ṭāhir was succeeded as Imam by his eldest son Shāh Ḥaydar (d. 994/1586), who at the time of his father's death was still at Shāh Ṭahmāsp's court in Persia. Shāh Ṭāhir had three other sons, all attaining high positions at the courts of various Deccani rulers.

The Muḥammad-Shāhī Imamate was handed down in the progeny of Shāh Ḥaydar, who lived in Aḥmadnagar for several more generations before settling in Awrangabād. It seems that some eclectic form of Nizārī Ismailism, as propagated very secretly under different guises by the Muḥammad-Shāhī Imams, survived for some time with increasing difficulty in India as attested by the versified *Lamaʿāt al-ṭāhirīn*.[23] This is one of a handful of extant Muḥammad-Shāhī works composed in 1110/1698 by a certain Ghulām ʿAlī b. Muḥammad who eulogises the Imams of the Twelver Shiʿa and also alludes to the Imams of the Muḥammad-Shāhī Nizārīs. The author struggles to conceal a number of scattered Ismaili doctrines and concepts under the guises of Twelver Shiʿism and Sufism. This treatise indeed represents a curious admixture of teachings from different Shiʿi traditions so much so that its Nizārī components have become completely marginalised. It is thus safe to assume that after Shāh Ṭāhir and Shāh Ḥaydar the Muḥammad-Shāhī Imams became increasingly associated in a real sense with Twelver Shiʿism, adopted initially as a tactical disguise, and so they gradually lost their Ismaili heritage and identity. As a result, the Muḥammad-Shāhī Nizārī community too gradually disintegrated or became fully assimilated into the Twelver Shiʿi groups of India, including especially the Ithnāʿasharī Khojas. It was under such circumstances that the line of the Muḥammad-Shāhī Imams was discontinued towards the end of the twelfth/eighteenth century. The last known Imam of this line was Amīr Muḥammad Bāqir, the fortieth in the series, who died around 1210/1796. By then, the Muḥammad-Shāhī Nizārī community too had evidently disappeared completely in India – a phenomenon accentuated by the anti-Shiʿi policies of the Mughal emperor Awrangzīb (1068–1118/1658–1707). These developments also explain why Muḥammad-Shāhī texts have failed to be preserved.

In Persia and Badakhshān, by the eleventh/seventeenth century the Muḥammad-Shāhīs had completely lost their position to the Qāsim-Shāhīs who had been more successful than Shāh Ṭāhir and his successors in posing as Twelver Shiʿi while secretly retaining and practising their Nizārī Ismaili faith. However, in Persia, too, many isolated Nizārī groups were assimilated over time into the predominant Twelver community of their respective milieus. In Syria, the Muḥammad-Shāhīs did not resort to *taqiyya* practices in any guise and, therefore, they fully preserved their identity. But by the final decades of the thirteenth/nineteenth century, when they had been left without a manifest Imam for almost a century, the bulk of the Syrian Muḥammad-Shāhīs acknowledged the Qāsim-Shāhī Nizārī Imamate, then represented by Sulṭān Muḥammad Shāh Aga Khan III (1885–1957). A small minority, based in Qadmūs and Maṣyāf, refrained from switching their allegiance; and they developed the belief that their last known Imam or one of his successors was, in fact, the Mahdī who had gone into concealment. This community, numbering a few thousands, are still awaiting the reappearance of their Imām-Mahdī. These points were explained to the author by ʿĀrif Tāmir (1921–1998), the most learned member of this minority Nizārī community known locally in Syria as Jaʿfariyya or Suwaydāniyya.

In the meantime, the *daʿwa* preached on behalf of the Qāsim-Shāhī Nizārī Imams had become quite successful in South Asia, where the Hindu converts became generally known as Khojas. The *dāʿīs*, or *pīrs* as they were more commonly designated in India, did not resort to Twelver disguises as practised by their co-religionists in Safawid Persia and by the Muḥammad-Shāhī Imams after Shāh Ṭāhir in South Asia. Instead, they used distinctively acculturated conversion tactics which were designed to maximise the appeal of their message to Hindu audiences, using Hindu idioms and mythological themes to express their Ismaili teachings. The resulting indigenous Nizārī tradition developed in the Indian subcontinent, known as Satpanth or 'true path', is reflected in the religious literature of the Nizārī Khojas, devotional hymns known as *ginān*s, which are quite distinct from the Nizārī literatures produced in Syria, Persia, Afghanistan and Central Asia.

The experience of the Muḥammad-Shāhī Nizārīs in India, and to a lesser extent that of the Persian Qāsim-Shāhī Nizārīs, clearly shows that the principle of *taqiyya* may indeed prove to be a double-edged sword; while in the short-run its circumscribed and judicious use will undoubtedly assure the safety of an endangered religious minority, its extensive and long-term applications may well lead to the disintegration or total loss of the original religious identity of the dissimulating community.

## Notes

1. For overviews of the Nizārī state and the early Nizārī *daʿwa*, see Marshall G. S. Hodgson, 'The Ismāʿīlī State', in *The Cambridge History of Iran*, vol. 5, *The Saljuq and Mongol Periods*, ed. J. A. Boyle (Cambridge, 1968), pp. 422–482; F. Daftary, *The Ismāʿīlīs: Their History and Doctrines* (Cambridge, 1990), pp. 324–434, 669–699, and 'Ḥasan-i Ṣabbāḥ and the Origins of the Nizārī Ismaʿili Movement', in F. Daftary, ed., *Mediaeval Ismaʿili History and Thought* (Cambridge, 1996), pp. 181–204.

2. 'Alā' al-Dīn 'Aṭā-Malik Juwaynī, *Ta'rīkh-i jahān-gushā*, ed. M. Qazwīnī (Leiden and London, 1912–1937), vol. 3, pp. 259–278; English tr., *The History of the World-Conqueror*, tr. J. A. Boyle (Manchester, 1958), vol. 2, pp. 712–725. See also Rashīd al-Dīn Faḍl Allāh, *Jāmi' al-tawārīkh: qismat-i Ismā'īliyān va Fāṭimiyān va Nizāriyān va dā'īyān va rafīqān*, ed. M. T. Dānishpazhūh and M. Mudarrisī Zanjānī (Tehran, 1338 Sh./1959), pp. 185–195.

3. Ch. G. Baiburdi, *Zhizn i tvorchestvo Nizārī-Persidskogo poeta* (Moscow, 1968); Persian trans., *Zindigī va āthār-i Nizārī*, tr. M. Ṣadrī (Tehran, 1370 Sh./1991); Dhabīḥ Allāh Ṣafā, *Ta'rīkh-i adabiyyāt dar Īrān* (2nd ed., Tehran, 1355 Sh./1976), vol. 3, part 2, pp. 731–745; N. Eboo Jamal, *Surviving the Mongols: Nizārī Quhistānī and the Continuity of Ismaili Tradition in Persia* (London, 2002); Persian trans., *Baqā-yi ba'd az Mughūl: Nizārī Quhistānī va tadāvum-i sunnat-i Ismā'īlī dar Īrān*, tr. F. Badra'ī (Tehran, 1382 Sh./2003), and I. K. Poonawala, *Biobibliography of Ismā'īlī Literature* (Malibu, CA, 1977), pp. 263–267.

4. See, for instance, Nizārī Quhistānī's *Dīwān*, ed. M. Muṣaffā (Tehran, 1371–73 Sh./1992–94), vol. 1, pp. 583–584, 617, 632, 634, 642, 660, 674, 795, 860, 966, 1137, 1292, 1359 and elsewhere.

5. W. Ivanow, 'A Forgotten Branch of the Ismailis', *JRAS* (1938), pp. 57–79.

6. The Muḥammad-Shāhī Imams are named in a long poem by Shaykh Sulaymān b. Ḥaydar (d. 1212/1797), a Syrian *dā'ī* of that community, in his 'Qaṣīda Ḥaydariyya', ed. 'Ārif Tāmir, in his *Murāja'āt Ismā'īliyya* (Beirut, 1994), pp. 6–20. See also 'Ārif Tāmir, 'Furū' al-Shajara al-Ismā'īliyya al-Imāmiyya', *al-Mashriq*, 51 (1957), pp. 581–612.

7. See Mīrzā Sang Muḥammad Badakhshī and Faḍl 'Alī Beg Surkh Afsar, *Ta'rīkh-i Badakhshān*, ed. A. N. Boldyrev (Leningrad, 1959; repr., Moscow, 1997), pp. 227–253, and Qurbān Muḥammad-Zāda and Muḥabbat Shāh-Zāda, *Ta'rīkh-i Badakhshān*, ed. A. A. Yigānā (Moscow, 1973), pp. 87–94.

8. Mīrzā Muḥammad Ḥaydar Dughlāt, *A History of the Moghuls of Central Asia*, ed. and tr. N. Elias and E. Denison Ross (2nd ed., London, 1898), pp. 217–221; V. V. Barthold, *Guzīda-yi maqālāt-i taḥqīqī*, tr. K. Kishāvarz (Tehran, 1358 Sh./1979), pp. 326 ff.; and his 'Badakhshān', in *EI2*, vol. 1, pp. 851–854.

9. Abū Isḥāq al-Quhistānī, *Haft bāb*, ed. and tr. W. Ivanow (Bombay, 1959); Muḥammad Riḍā b. Sulṭān Ḥusayn Harātī, better known as Khayrkhwāh-i Harātī, *Faṣl dar bayān-i shinākht-i imām*, ed. W. Ivanow (3rd ed., Tehran, 1960); English trans., *On the Recognition of the Imam*, tr. W. Ivanow (2nd ed., Bombay, 1947), and his *Taṣnīfāt*, ed. W. Ivanow (Tehran, 1961). See also F. Daftary, 'Khayrkhwāh-i Harātī', *EI2*, Supplement, pp. 527–528.

10. See Badakhshānī's *Sī va shish ṣaḥīfa*, ed. H. Ujāqī (Tehran, 1339 Sh./1961); F. Daftary, 'Badakhshānī', *The Great Islamic Encyclopaedia* (Tehran, 2003), vol. 11, pp. 520–521; Poonawala, *Biobibliography*, pp. 267–268.

11. See A. Berthels and M. Baqoev, *Alphabetic Catalogue of Manuscripts found by the 1959–1963 Expedition in Gorno-Badakhshan Autonomous Region* (Moscow, 1967).

12. On Ismaili-Sufi relations in post-Mongol Persia, see Daftary, *The Ismā'īlīs*, pp. 452–471 and 'Ismā'īlī-Sufi Relations in Early Post-Alamūt and Safavid Persia', in *Heritage of Sufism*: vol. 3, *Late Classical Persianate Sufism (1501–1750)*, ed. L. Lewisohn and D. O. Morgan (Oxford, 1999), pp. 279–293.

13. This anonymous Nizārī commentary, entitled *Ba'ḍī az ta'wīlāt-i Gulshan-i rāz*, has been edited and translated into French by H. Corbin in his *Trilogie Ismaélienne* (Tehran and Paris, 1961), text pp. 131–161, tr. pp. 1–174.

14. See, for instance, Berthels and Baqoev, *Alphabetic Catalogue*, p. 83.

15. W. Ivanow, *Ismaili Literature: A Bibliographical Survey* (Tehran, 1963), p. 164, and Poonawala, *Biobibliography*, pp. 274, 351.

16. *Pandiyāt-i jawānmardī*, ed. and tr. W. Ivanow (Leiden, 1953).

17. Marshall G. S. Hodgson, *The Venture of Islam: Conscience and History in a World Civilization* (Chicago, 1974), vol. 2, p. 493 ff.

18. Claude Cahen, *'Le problème du Shīʿisme dans l'Asie Mineure Turque préottomane'*, in T. Fahd, ed., *Le Shīʿisme Imāmite* (Paris, 1970), pp. 118 ff. See also S. Amir Arjomand, *The Shadow of God and the Hidden Imam* (Chicago, 1984), pp. 66–84.

19. See N. Pourjavady and P. L. Wilson, 'Ismāʿīlīs and Niʿmatullāhīs', *SI*, 41 (1975), pp. 113–135.

20. A. Amanat, 'The Nuqṭawī Movement of Maḥmūd Pisīkhānī and his Persian Cycle of Mystical-Materialism', in Daftary, ed., *Mediaeval Ismaʿili History*, pp. 281–297. See also K. Babayan, *Mystics, Monarchs and Messiahs: Cultural Landscapes of Early Modern Iran* (Cambridge, MA, 2002) pp. 57–117.

21. Muḥammad Qāsim Hindū Shāh Astarābādī, Firishta, *Taʾrīkh-i Firishta*, ed. J. Briggs (Bombay, 1832), vol. 2, pp. 213–231; Brigg's English translation of this work under the title *History of the Rise of the Mahomedan Power in India* (London, 1829), 4 vols., does not include the section on Shāh Ṭāhir. See also ʿAlī b. ʿAzīz Ṭabāṭabā, *Burhān-i maʾāthir* (Hyderabad, 1936), pp. 251–270, 274–295, 324–325; al-Qāḍī Nūr Allāh al-Shūshtarī, *Majālis al-muʾminīn* (Tehran, 1375–1376/1955–1956), vol. 2, pp. 234–240; Maʿṣūm ʿAlī Shāh, *Ṭarāʾiq al-ḥaqāʾiq*, ed. M. J. Maḥjūb (Tehran, 1339–1345 Sh./1960–1966), vol. 3, pp. 133–150; Shihāb al-Dīn Shāh al-Ḥusaynī, *Khiṭābāt-i ʿāliya*, ed. H. Ujāqī (Bombay, 1963), pp. 40–41; Muḥammad b. Zayn al-ʿĀbidīn Fidāʾī Khurāsānī, *Kitāb hidāyat al-muʾminīn al-ṭālibīn*, ed. A. A. Semenov (Moscow, 1959), pp. 119–132; ʿĀrif Tāmir, *al-Imāma fi'l-Islām* (Beirut, 1964), pp. 202–208; Ṣafā, *Taʾrīkh-i adabiyyāt*, vol. 5, part 2, pp. 662–670, and Daftary, *The Ismāʿīlīs*, pp. 486–491, 713–714, where further references are cited.

22. See Poonawala, *Biobibliography*, pp. 271–275.

23. Ivanow, *Ismaili Literature*, pp. 166–167, and Poonawala, *Biobibliography*, p. 281. The Library of The Institute of Ismaili Studies possesses copies of the *Lamaʿāt*, divided into 110 chapters or *lamaʿāt* (lit. 'flashes of light').

# 29

# Some Notes on Shaykh Aḥmad Sirhindī and the Problem of the Mystical Significance of Paradise*

*Abdollah Vakily*

Paradise, as the ideal place for the pious, has always been at the centre of the consciousness of religious-minded people.[1] For Muslim mystics the centrality and significance of Paradise has undergone a few reinterpretations. For the first group of Muslim mystics, who were primarily ascetics, emerging gradually after the death of the Prophet as well as for the two subsequent generations, the life-formula for spiritual success was quite simple: Fear God and forsake the world, to be saved from the punishment of Hellfire; seek God's Pleasure by performing good deeds, and pray that He will grant you entry to Paradise where, purified and multiplied infinitely, all the pleasures of this world are awaiting the believers. But this view of Paradise, although in strict conformity with orthodox teachings,[2] did not remain unchallenged. It was challenged and gradually changed due to the emergence of a new generation of mystics, known as Sufis, who emphasised love for God to such a degree that eventually fear of God became utterly subordinated to it. It should be emphasised, however, that although for earlier Sufis, Paradise was a place for meeting God, they still delighted in recounting the beautiful things that awaited the faithful there. The following anecdote vividly portrays both the ascetics and early Sufis' view of Paradise:

> Hazrat Shaykh Abū Sulaymān Dārānī[3] R. A. reports, 'I set forth in the direction of Mecca with the intention of performing *ḥajj* and *ziyāra* [visiting the grave] of Rasūl Allāh Sal'am. On the way I met a young man in the prime of his youth who had the same intentions as mine. He was such a deeply religious person, that as long as our caravan went along, he kept busy reciting the Qur'an, and whenever we stopped anywhere he performed *ṣalāt*. And so he continued in *ṣalāt* throughout the night. During the day he observed fasting. This continued until we reached

> Mecca and there we separated. At the moment of separation, I asked him, "Young man, tell me, what has made you exert yourself so endlessly in *ʿibāda* [worship]?" He replied, "O Hazrat Abū Sulaymān, I have seen in a dream one of the mansions of Paradise, which like the others was built of bricks of silver and gold. So also was its top storey. On top I saw two towers and between these towers I saw a damsel who lived there. She was so beautiful that no eyes had ever seen such beauty and heavenly complexion, with such beautiful locks of hair hanging down in front. When she saw me, she smiled at me, and when she smiled the whole of Paradise lit up with the shine from her teeth, as she smiled. She said to me, 'O young man exert yourself in *ʿibāda* for the sake of God, so that I may become yours, and you become mine.' At this my eyes opened and I awoke from my dream. This is my story, and now it has become an obsession with me to exert myself in *ʿibāda*, and whatever you have seen of me is merely my means of acquiring those bounties of Paradise." I asked him to pray for me. This he did and left. After this I thought things over carefully and said to myself, "If such is his exertion and striving in order to acquire one damsel of Paradise, how much more should not be one's exertion to acquire the Lord, Master and Creator of those damsels of Paradise."'[4]

The change in the perceptions of Paradise apparent in the preceding anecdote, was intensified over time by the increased emphasis on man's love for God. The peak of Sufism thus witnessed a radicalisation of love to the point where a Sufi was required to forsake both this world and Paradise, to be concerned only with God Himself. Referring to the story of Moses in the Qur'an,[5] in which God orders Moses to remove both of his shoes and then proceed towards the burning bush, these later Sufis argued that this was a symbolic reference to leaving both worlds (this world and the hereafter), in order to be able to get closer to God. Examples of this view abound in classical Sufi sources. According to *Tadhkirat al-awliyāʾ*,[6] one day Abu'l-Qāsim Naṣr Ābādī (d. 977), a famous Sufi shaykh from Persia, was performing circumambulation around the Kaʿba. He noticed that a large group of people were talking among themselves, preoccupied with worldly affairs. Enraged over this behaviour, he collected some wood and brought it back along with some fire. When people asked what he wanted to do with the fire he said, 'I want to burn down the Kaʿba so that people become free from the Kaʿba and become concerned with God',[7] meaning that as long as people took a pragmatic, ritualistic approach to the worship of God they would not be able to pay attention to God Himself, and thus they would miss the opportunity to know God and love Him. The best-known representative of love-inspired Sufism is Rābiʿa al-ʿAdawiyya (d. 185/801), a Sufi woman of second-/eighth-century Iraq.[8] It is narrated that one day Rābiʿa fell sick. When people asked her the reason, she replied, 'This morning a desire for Paradise appeared in my heart and my Lord punished me with this illness.'[9] This negative attitude towards Paradise is further illustrated in the following anecdote, transmitted by al-Aflākī (d. 761–762/1360) in his *Manāqib al-ʿārifīn*, in which the striking similarity between Rābiʿa's view of Paradise and that of Naṣr Ābādī becomes quite obvious.

> One day a group of the people of the heart saw Rābiʿa running in haste, in one hand carrying fire, and in the other water. They asked, 'O Lady of the hereafter, to where are you running, and what are you going to do?' Rābiʿa replied, 'I am going to set Heaven afire and pour water into Hell so that both these two distracting (*do ḥijāb-i rāhzan*) veils are removed and the destination becomes clear, and the servants of God may serve God without the motive of hope and reason of fear; since if there were not the hope of Heaven and fear of Hell no one would worship God and obey [Him].'[10]

Rābiʿa's understanding of the significance of Paradise – or its insignificance for that matter – is demonstrated in a story according to which once Rābiʿa overheard someone reciting this verse of the Qur'an, 'Verily on that day, the inhabitants of Heaven will have joy in everything they do. In happiness they and their spouses will recline on couches.'[11] She remarked, 'The poor inhabitants of Heaven! To be preoccupied with their spouses.'[12] These stories – and many other anecdotes and utterances attributed to Rābiʿa – make it sufficiently clear that for Rābiʿa, the love of God is so exclusive that even Heaven is a veil that separates the mystic from the Beloved, and hence it must be discarded.

The most famous formulation of Rābiʿa's view is undoubtedly the one which appears in her supplications where she asks God:

> O My God, if I worship You out of fear of Hell, burn me in Hell, and if I worship You with the hope of Paradise, make Paradise forbidden to me, and if I worship You for Your [Own] sake, do not deprive me of Your Eternal Beauty.[13]

This prayer vividly portrays the attitude of the Sufis who were drawn to love mysticism, and therefore, it soon became the classic model for understanding the relationship between man and God; and although Rābiʿa was one of many Sufis who expressed this view of the mystical path, her image and utterances, crystallised into the concept of 'disinterested love',[14] soon became synonymous with the idea of Sufi love mysticism itself,[15] perhaps due to the fact that she was the first Sufi to change the balance of fear and hope in favour of love. Rābiʿa's impact was so profound and her influence was so great that her fame spread beyond the parameters of Sufism to gain popular notoriety so that, according to Louis Gardet, the image of Rābiʿa running with a torch and a bucket of water reached as far as France where it was incorporated into seventeenth-century literature as in the figure of *Caritée* found in the writings of Pierre Camus.[16] It was due to this understanding of disinterested love – that is love for God alone without any secondary motive – personified in the image of Rābiʿa, that giving up Paradise became a prerequisite for the mystical journey for subsequent generations of mystics.

There were, however, from time to time, exceptions to the predominant perspective of disinterested love and its concomitant notion of Paradise. Shaykh ʿAbd al-Qādir al-Jīlānī (d. 561/1166) for instance, in some poems which appear in a *diwān* ascribed to him, expressed a view that differed radically from that of Rābiʿa. For example, he boasted,

To Heaven for quite a different purpose we go,
Not for sightseeing (*tafarruj kardan)* Ṭubā and Kawthar we go.
Our purpose in travelling to Egypt, is the beauty of Joseph,
Not for receiving sugar and sugar cubes we go.
(…)
To be granted the fortune of the visit [of the Beloved] in Paradise, is what we desire,
Not for the piling up of jewellery and gold we go.[17]

Farīd al-Dīn ʿAṭṭār (d. ca.617/1220–1221) also gave a beautiful and moving description of the spiritual nature of Paradise in the form of two long poems, which appeared in his *Asrār-nāma*.[18] And Ibn al-ʿArabī (d. 638/1240), that most influential Sufi of all time, explicitly criticised Rābiʿa's view of Paradise and ascribed it to a lack of proper understanding on her part. Commenting on Rābiʿa's response upon hearing Qur'anic verses about the preoccupation of the people of Paradise, Ibn al-ʿArabī said:

> Verily she did not understand, and she herself is poor, because their preoccupation is with God … and this results from the hidden guile of God to those saints who injure other saints with undue sarcasm and criticism whereas they [the latter saints] are innocent of such accusations.[19]

Yet the influence of Rābiʿa's view was such that even this clear criticism by Ibn al-ʿArabī was unable to counter its popularity. Hence shortly afterwards, Mawlānā Jalāl al-Dīn Rūmī (d. 673/1273), who popularised love mysticism in Persian-speaking lands through his poetry, again referred to Paradise in terms similar to Rābiʿa's. According to al-Aflākī:

> One day Mawlānā's wife Karā Khātūn (may God be pleased with her) inquired [from Mawlānā] about the secret of this *ḥadīth* [and asked], 'What is the meaning of "the majority of the inhabitants of Heaven are fools"?'[20] He said that if they were not foolish they would not be satisfied with Paradise and the rivers [there]. Where there is the vision of the Beloved, [there] is not room for Heaven and the rivers [of Heaven]. He said, 'The majority of the inhabitants of Heaven are the fools, and the heights (*ʿillīyūn*) belong to the people of inner knowledge (*dhawil albāb*)',[21] and he recited this poem:
>
> In Hell, if Your hair becomes accessible to my hand, I would be embarrassed

over the state of the people of Paradise, and if I am called to Heaven without You, the Kingdom of Heaven becomes too small in my heart.

'So', [he said] 'any person of little ambition who became attached to sightseeing in the garden was deprived of the vision of the gardener.'[22]

Rūmī's overwhelming popularity further strengthened Rābi'a's view and as a result the views of al-Jīlānī and 'Aṭṭār as well as Ibn al-'Arabī's criticism, moved to the sidelines of Sufi thought and their significance gradually faded away. Apart from the popularity of Rābi'a and Rūmī, there were other factors inhibiting the spread of the alternative view presented by al-Jīlānī, 'Aṭṭār and Ibn al-'Arabī. There was a lack of coherent context within which this explanation would fit. Al-Jīlānī did not discuss the issue in his prose works and Ibn al-'Arabī's criticism had a limited scope, applied only to Rābi'a's understanding of Paradise as an isolated issue and not as part of a theoretical edifice. Consequently, the concept of 'disinterested love' and its concomitant notion of detachment from Paradise continued to dominate Sufi thought so much that Najm al-Dīn Kubrā (d. 617/1221) considered it one of the principles of the spiritual journey to refrain from asking God for Paradise.[23]

It was not until the seventeenth century that the predominant Sufi view of Paradise was vehemently challenged by the great Indian Sufi, Shaykh Aḥmad Sirhindī (d. 1624), whose view then became a permanent alternative to that of Rābi'a.[24] Sirhindī argued that although giving up Paradise and concentrating on God alone is highly desirable, it still contains elements of spiritual pride and lack of total surrender. Also, since God has prepared Paradise with all of its gifts and pleasures for His friends and lovers, it is a sign of ingratitude to want to ignore it and 'give it up'. Furthermore, Sirhindī asked, since Paradise is the only place where God's full vision is possible, how could a friend and lover of God not yearn to enter it? He also argued that the pleasures of Paradise are not to be avoided since they are devoid of 'the corruptive elements of worldliness', hence conducive to spiritual progress.

Thus Sirhindī contributed to a more profound understanding of the significance of Paradise by emphasising that it was fundamentally a spiritual state, which earlier had been underestimated both by those yearning to enter it and those striving to 'give it up'. The following is a summary discussion of Sirhindī's view of Paradise, taken from his celebrated *Maktūbāt:*

The purpose of the spiritual journey is purification of the lower ego-self and its cleansing so that salvation from the worship of false gods, which stems from the existence of the ego's desires, becomes possible, and so that in truth there is nothing left as the focal point of one's attention except one true Beloved, and one does not prefer any aim or objective over Him either amongst the religious goals or worldly affairs. [Because] although the religious goals are considered good deeds, they belong to the people who are [still] on the spiritual journey,

> and the ones who have already reached the destination and are in proximity [to God] consider it a sin and regard nothing as the goal except the One. Acquiring this fortune depends on the attainment of the state of annihilation and realisation of the essential love, in which station prize and punishment are the same, [and] there is as much pleasure from punishment as there is from endowment of blessings. In that station, if people desire Heaven, it is because it is the place of [the manifestation of] God's contentment and in its seeking lies His satisfaction. [Likewise] they seek refuge from Hell because it is the place of the anger of the Lord. Neither is the aim of seeking Paradise to indulge the ego, nor is that of escaping Hell to avoid pain and suffering there, since whatever comes from the Beloved is, for these noble ones [i.e., the people of proximity] desirable and the very object of their quest. Thus the truth of sincerity is acquired in this station and the freedom from false gods is realised here, and the proper appreciation of God's Unity (*tawḥīd*) becomes possible at this time.[25]

What Sirhindī describes in this letter is to some extent similar to Rābiʿa's view in that for lovers of God, nothing else matters except the Beloved, and their love for Him renders everything else in existence as insignificant and non-existent. However, Sirhindī drives this point to its logical conclusion by arguing that the rejection of everything other than God cannot be extended to the things related to God Himself. This is because, in Sirhindī's view, a true lover of God not only loves God, but he also loves what God loves, and dislikes what God dislikes. Thus for a true Sufi, Paradise is desirable and Hell is abhorrent not for what they symbolise in themselves but simply because God has declared them to be desirable and abhorrent respectively.

This issue is further elaborated in another letter which Sirhindī wrote to his son and successor, Muḥammad Maʿṣūm.[26] In this letter Sirhindī describes three groups of believers. The first type, the ordinary Muslim, understands the eternal pleasures of Heaven as being much the same as transitory earthly delights. Yet for the sake of gaining these permanent heavenly pleasures and in order to avoid the punishment for sin, the ordinary believer restrains himself from forbidden indulgences and devotes himself to a life of piety. The believer of the second group also sees Heaven as the projection of earthly pleasures but, in his yearning for God, he wishes for nothing except God and thus rejects the rewards of Heaven and punishments of Hell as distractions and veils. Sirhindī identifies the perspective and experience of the people of the second group as intoxication and annihilation. The believer of the third, and highest, group is he who has passed into the station of remaining in God (*baqāʾ*) which, as Sirhindī often observes, is marked not by intoxication but by sobriety. He writes

> [I]n the station of annihilation, oblivion of this world and the hereafter becomes possible, and one sees the preoccupations of the hereafter in a similar way as

> [one sees] the preoccupations of this world. But once one is honoured with the [station] of remaining in God ... [then] there is all the pain of the hereafter and seeking refuge from Hell and the desire for Heaven. The trees and rivers and angels of Heaven have no relation with the things of this world; rather these are two sides of a contradiction like the contradiction between wrath and contentment. The trees and the rivers and whatever is in Heaven are the results of right actions. The Prophet said that Heaven does not have trees, [therefore] you should plant trees there. The people asked how. He said with *taṣbīḥ* and *taḥmīd* and *tamjīd* and *tahlīl*,[27] meaning [that one should] praise God so that a tree is planted in Heaven. Thus the tree of Heaven becomes the result of praising God. As the purifying perfections of this word have been put in the garment of letters and sounds [in this world], in Heaven these perfections are hidden in the garment of a tree. Accordingly, whatever is in Heaven is the result of right action. And whatever of the Divine Perfections have been placed in the garment of goodness of words and deeds, in Heaven those perfections will be manifest in the guise of pleasures and luxuries. Thus inevitably the enjoying of pleasure and luxury is accepted and agreed [upon by God] and is a means for attaining [the vision of God].[28]

After this lengthy explanation, Sirhindī returns to the theme of his previous letter by criticising Rābiʿa as follows:

> Poor Rābiʿa, if she had known this secret she would not have thought about burning Heaven, and would not have considered its preoccupation other than preoccupation with God – contrary to enjoying the pleasure and luxury of this world whose source is impurity and wickedness and which results in disappointment in the hereafter.[29]

Thus Sirhindī indicates that Rābiʿa's view of Heaven reflects her station of annihilation, and that she has not yet reached the station of remaining in God. In other words, although her perceptions are authentic according to her mystical experiences, Rābiʿa had not yet reached the end of the spiritual path and thus mistakenly viewed the pleasures of Heaven as projections of the pleasures of the world which, according to Sirhindī, are evil at root. The implication of Sirhindī's teachings on the intoxicated, love-inspired school of Sufism personified by Rābiʿa, is that whereas the insights and experiences attained by the mystics of this group are relatively authentic, ultimately these mystics do not supersede the parameters of orthodox teachings, nor do their experiences transcend the relation between the Divine and human spheres as established and defined through revelation. Thus even though the travellers on the mystical path may find that the teachings and obligations of orthodoxy are eclipsed by the light of their mystical experiences, this eclipse is temporary and does not mean that those teachings and obligations are ultimately transcended; a fact that becomes evident once they are promoted to higher levels of mystical attainment.

In conclusion, what must be emphasised is that for Muslim mystics, particularly the Sufis, the spiritual significance of Paradise has not always been the same, rather it has developed through a historical process. This historical development, however, should not be interpreted in a reductionist fashion which results in equating different generations of ascetics and mystics themselves with phases of 'primitive', 'intermediate', and 'advanced' spirituality and mystical attainment. It should simply be taken to indicate that on the level of theoretical development, there has been a three-stage movement from a simple – perhaps at times simplistic – understanding of the significance of Paradise towards a fuller and more profound understanding and elaboration of its reality.[30] Hence the earlier ascetics and mystics tended to look at Paradise as an ideal place where they hoped to enjoy the earthly pleasures in an eternal context as a reward for their voluntary deprivations; whereas the later mystics regarded Paradise and its pleasures as distractions that veiled them from God. Consequently the early ascetics yearned for Paradise and tried their best to 'gain it', whereas the later mystics aimed at detaching themselves from any preoccupation with Paradise and tried their best to 'give it up'. It was Sirhindī's contribution to reconcile this contradiction and show the proper place of Paradise within the spiritual universe of Islam; this was the place of real and vital importance assigned to it by orthodox teachings and now confirmed – rather than negated – by mystical experience. Sirhindī's contribution here represents more than a developmental stage in Sufi doctrine, and once put in the context of his overall system has major implications for the study of Sufism and Islam as a whole, as he once again demonstrated that the dichotomy between orthodoxy and Sufism is an artificial one and that in reality there is no final contradiction between the two. The compatibility of Islam and Sufism was of course discussed and basically established much earlier, by eminent Sufi scholars such as Abu'l-Qāsim al-Qushayrī (d. 465/1072) and Muḥammad al-Ghazālī (d. 505/1111). The significance of Sirhindī's contribution in this respect, however, lies in the fact that whereas previous figures such as al-Qushayrī and al-Ghazālī had addressed their discussion mainly to the theologians and common people, Sirhindī demonstrated this compatibility for the Sufis themselves. Moreover, Sirhindī addressed the Sufis not as a theologian with theoretical discussions, but as a Sufi with unprecedented claims to authority based on his mystical experiences.

As Sirhindī's legacy continued through the successive generations of his deputies and students to the present time, the spiritual significance of Paradise has been appreciated and upheld wherever Naqshbandī-Mujaddidī Sufis have been present. Sirhindī's legacy has also continued through at least one other group of Sufis in modern times. The Deobandi Sufi *'ulamā'*,[31] whose most famous member Mawlānā Ashrāf 'Alī al-Thanawī (d. 1943)[32] was designated as the *mujaddid* of the present century,[33] along with their counterparts at Dār al-'Ulūm Saharanpur and Dār al-'Ulūm Nadwat'l-'Ulamā' also subscribe to Sirhindī's view of Paradise, even though their main Sufi affiliation is Chishtī rather than Naqshbandī. The spiritual significance of Paradise is so strongly established for these Sufis, thanks to Sirhindī, that they either take it for granted and do not see any need to emphasise it[34] or they devote a good part of their work to advertising and propagating it in terms almost identical to Sirhindī's own formulations.[35]

## Notes

*An earlier draft of this article was presented at The Annual Conference of The American Academy of Religion, Eastern International Region, held at Le Moyne College, Syracuse: New York, April 12–14, 1996.

1. Due to the particular focus of this article, a discussion of other perceptions of Paradise has been avoided. For a comparative study of the theme of Paradise and its various forms, manifestations and functions in human culture, see Richard Heinberg, *Memories and Visions of Paradise* (Los Angeles, CA, 1989).

2. The 'orthodox view' is based on a strict and literal interpretation of the Qur'an and *ḥadīth* material. In the Qur'an alone, there are 70 verses which contain references to Heaven, with sura 7, *al-A'raf* ('The Heights'), containing more references to Heaven than any other. Many of these verses describe Heaven as an ideal place for the pious and encourage man to try to be among those who will enter it. See for example: 26:90, 18:31. Similarly, the *ḥadīth* material contains many references to Heaven. Consequently all major *ḥadīth* collections have devoted an independent section to the presentation of this material. The following *ḥadīth*, narrated by 'Ubādat b. al-Ṣāmit is a particularly relevant one:

> Verily in Heaven there are a hundred degrees (levels) and the distance between the two is like the distance between the sky and the earth, and *firdaws* is the highest level of them, and the four rivers of Heaven flow from there and above it is the throne (*'arsh*); so when you ask Allah for something ask Him for *firdaws*.

See 'Āshiq Ilāhī Mirat-hi, tr. and ed., *Durar-i farā'id* (Delhi, 1931), vol. 4, pp. 727–728. This is an Urdu translation with explanatory notes of a rare manuscript of a *ḥadīth* collection, *Jam' al-fawā'id,* compiled in the 17th century in Mecca by 'Allāma Muḥammad b. Muḥammad al-Rādānī, which 'Āshiq Ilāhī published along with its Arabic original. I am grateful to Mawlānā Muḥammad Maẓhār 'Ālam for introducing this text to me, drawing my attention to this particular *ḥadīth*, and lending me his copy for consultation. Also among the personal supplications of Prophet Muḥammad which he often recited and encouraged his followers to recite too, there are several references to Paradise. The following is an example of this type of material:

> O God! I seek of You that which will make certain (for me) Your mercy, and the resolution of Your forgiveness ... and entry to Paradise, and freedom from the Fire.

Cf. Muḥammad al-Ghazālī, *Remembrance and Prayer: The Way of Prophet Muhammad*, tr. Yusuf Talal De Lorenzo (Leicester, 1986), p. 96.

3. The reference is apparently to Abū Sulaymān al-Darā'ī (d. 214–215/830). For al-Darā'ī see Farīd al-Dīn 'Aṭṭār, *Tadhkirat al-awliyā'*, ed. Muḥammad Isti'lāmī (4th ed., Tehran,

1984–1985), pp. 276–284. See also R. A. Nicholson, ed., *Tadhkirat al-awliyā'* (London, 1905), vol. 1, pp. 229–236.

4. Hazrat Shaykh Mawlānā Muḥammad Zakariyyā Ṣāḥib, *Virtues of Charity and Ḥajj*, tr., Muḥammad Masroor Khan Saroha and Yousuf Karaan (Delhi, 1982), p. 297.

5. Qur'an 20:10–12.

6. Unless otherwise stated, the translations in this article are my own.

7. 'Aṭṭār, *Tadhkirat al-awliyā'*, p. 78. This anecdote also appears in Aḥmad 'Alī Rajā'ī, ed., *Muntakhab-i rawnaq al-majālis wa-bustān al-'ārifīn wa-tuḥfat al-muridīn* (Tehran, 1975), pp. 155–156. However, the wording in this text slightly differs from that of *Tadhkirat al-awliyā'*.

8. On Rābi'a, see Barbara Lois Helms, 'Rābi'ah as Mystic, Muslim and Woman', in A. Sharma and K. Young, ed., *The Annual Review of Women in World Religions* (Albany, NY, 1994), vol. 3, pp. 1–87.

9. 'Aṭṭār, *Tadhkirat al-awliyā'*, p. 84.

10. Shams al-Dīn al-Aflākī, *Manāqib al-'ārifīn*, ed. Taḥsīn Yāzījī (Ankara, 1959–1961), vol. 1, p. 397.

11. Qur'an 36:55.

12. 'Abd al-Raḥmān al-Badawī, *Shahīdat al-'ishq al-ilāhī, Rābi'a al-'Adawiyya* (Cairo, n.d.), p. 138; cf. 'Abd al-Ra'ūf al-Munāwī, *Ṭabaqāt al-awliyā'*, Damascus, Ḥāhiriyya Library, Manuscript 4164, p. 105.

13. 'Aṭṭār, *Tadhkirat al-awliyā'*, p. 87.

14. This term was made popular by Margaret Smith in her well-known work, *Rabia the Mystic and her Fellow-Saints in Islam* (Cambridge, 1928; repr., 1984), p. 97. It paraphrases al-Ghazālī's interpretation of Rābi'a's spiritual detachment from the world through love of God. Smith, p. 105; cf. al-Ghazālī, *Iḥyā 'ulūm al-dīn.*

15. Smith has written extensively on Rābi'a and on her 'doctrine of disinterested love'. However, there are numerous problems with her use of source material, particularly concerning the position of Rābi'a, and love-inspired Sufism in general, vis-a-vis orthodox Islam. For a more reliable discussion of the relationship between Rābi'a's love mysticism and her concepts of Heaven and Hell, see Helms, especially pp. 21–30 and 37–38.

16. G. C. Anawati and Louis Gardet, *Mystique musulmane, aspects et tendances – expériences et techniques* (Paris, 1961), pp. 166–177.

17. Shaykh 'Abd al-Qādir al-Jīlānī, *Dīwān-i ghawth al-a'ẓam* (Lucknow, 1952), pp. 37–38.

18. Farīd al-Dīn 'Aṭṭār, *Asrār-nāma*, ed. Sayyid Ṣādiq Gawharīn (Tehran, 1959), pp. 46–50.

19. Al-Badawī, p. 139; cf. al-Munāwī, p. 106.

20. On this *ḥadīth*, its interpretation, evaluation and variant versions see Ismā'īl b. Muḥammad al-'Ajlūnī al-Jarāḥī, *Kashf al-khaṭa' wa-muzīl al-albās 'amma Ashtahara min al-aḥādīth 'alā alsina al-nās* (2nd ed., Beirut, 1988), Parts 1 and 2, p. 164.

21. This is a variant of the same *ḥadīth*, see below.

22. Al-Aflākī, p. 396. It is interesting that Rūmī employs the word *tafarruj* (sightseeing) to describe the approach of the people interested in Paradise. This is the same word that al-Jīlānī had used earlier, only in a negative sense, to differentiate his motive for seeking Paradise from mere sightseeing. Another important point in regard to Rūmī's view is that he made a distinction between being in Paradise and having God's vision, as if they were independent

of each other. But as we will see later, Sirhindī emphasised the interdependence of the two and explained how they are inseparable.

23. Najm al-Dīn Kubrā, *Die Fawā'iḥ al-gamāl wa-fawātiḥ al-galāl des Najm al-Dīn Kubrā*, ed. Fritz Meier (Wiesbaden, 1957), pp. 2–3. A comparison between Kubrā's statement and the *ḥadīth* mentioned in note 2 and the Prophet's own supplication for Paradise shows how the Sufi's appreciation of the significance of Paradise had grown to be different from that of earlier generations.

24. On Sirhindī see J. G. J. ter Haar, *Follower and Heir of the Prophet, Shaykh Aḥmad Sirhindī (1564–1624) as Mystic* (Leiden, 1992). Yohannan Friedmann's, *Shaykh Ahmad Sirhindī: An Outline of His Thought and A History of His Image in the Eyes of Posterity* (Montreal and London, 1971), still serves as the best introduction to Sirhindī's life and some aspects of his thought, successfully locating Sirhindī in his essential role (that of Sufi shaykh).

25. Nūr Aḥmad, ed., *Maktūbāt-i imām-i rabbānī, ḥaḍrat-i mujaddid-i alf-i thānī al-Shaykh Aḥmad-i Sirhindī* (Peshawar, n.d.), vol. 1, Book 1, Letter 35, pp. 96–97.

26. Ibid., vol. 1, Book 5, Letter 302, pp. 147–148.

27. Traditional devotional formulae for praising God, referring to, respectively, the uttering of the three formulae: *subḥān Allāh* (glory be to God), *al-ḥamdu l'illāh* (praise be to God), *lā ilāha illa Allāh* (there is no god except God), and *Allāhu Akbar* (God is the greatest), respectively, which according to *ḥadīth* material was taught personally by the Prophet to his daughter Fāṭima.

28. Nūr Aḥmad, ed., *Maktūbāt-i imām-i rabbānī*, vol. 1, Book 5, Letter 302, pp. 147–148.

29. Ibid.

30. It should be emphasised here that there are no fixed boundaries separating these three stages and preventing some elements of the former stages from reappearing in the later stages. Sirhindī's typology of three kinds of Muslims corresponds roughly with these three stages, the representatives of which could co-exist at any particular time in history, particularly from Sirhindī's time onward.

31. For Deobandī Sufis see Barbara Daly Metcalf, *Islamic Revival in British India: Deoband, 1860–1900* (Princeton, NJ, 1982). See also Syed H. Haq Nadvi, 'The Role of Resurgent 'Ulama' and Sufi Shaikhs in the Reconstruction of Islamic Education: Foundation of Deoband (1867) and Nadwa (1893)', *Muslim Education Quarterly*, 3 (1986), pp. 37–56.

32. On Mawlānā al-Thānawī, see Barbara Daly Metcalf, *Perfecting Women, Mawlana Ashraf Ali Thanawi's Bihishti Zewar* (Berkeley and Los Angeles, CA, 1990).

33. Sajida S. Alvi, 'The *Mujaddid* and *Tajdīd* traditions in the Indian Subcontinent: An Historical Overview', *Journal of Turkish Studies*, 18 (1994), p. 13.

34. For example, a prolific writer such as Shaykh Muḥammad Zakariyyā al-Kāndihlawī (d. 1982) who has numerous works on all aspects of *sharī'a* and *ṭarīqa* does not have any discussion of this subject, treating it as axiomatic.

35. See for example Mawlānā Shāh Muḥammad Ashraf 'Alī al-Thānawī, *Jazā' al-a'māl* (3rd ed., Deoband, 1965), pp. 22–24, and especially pp. 25–26.

# 30

# The Naqshbandī Mujaddidī Sufi Order's Ascendancy in Central Asia Through the Eyes of its Masters and Disciples (1010s–1200s/1600s–1800s)

*Sajida S. Alvi*

> We, rather, all Muslims of India, who are far removed (*dūr-uftāda*) and backward (*pas-mānda*), are so much indebted to the *'ulamā'* and the Sufis (*mashā'ikh*) of Transoxiana (Māwarā' al-Nahr) that it cannot be conveyed in words. It was the *'ulamā'* of the region who strove to correct the beliefs [of Muslims] to make them consistent with the sound beliefs and opinions of the followers of the Prophetic tradition and the community (*Ahl-i Sunna wa'l-Jamā'a*). It was they who reformed the religious practices [of the Muslims] according to Ḥanafī law (*madhhab*). The travels of the great Sufis (may their graves be hallowed) on the path of this sublime Sufi order (*ṭarīqa*) have been introduced to India by this blessed region.
>
> Shaykh Aḥmad Sirhindī[1]

Thus spoke the founder of the Mujaddidiyya branch of the Naqshbandī order about the transplanting of the Naqshbandī order from Central Asia to India. Sirhindī's biological and spiritual descendants in the following centuries continued to express pride in their Central Asian heritage while acknowledging their backwardness in their writings.

The Naqshbandī Sufi order, a relative latecomer to South Asia, arrived with the Mughals in the early sixteenth century. The Mujaddidī offshoot of the order that developed in India never failed to acknowledge their links with Central Asia. The other major factor contributing to the affinity of Indian Muslims to Central Asia was the role of Turco-Islamic heritage in the formation of Indo-Muslim society. The descendants of Maḥmūd of Ghazna (d. 421/1030) are credited with sowing the seeds of Turco-Islamic heritage in Indian soil. But it reached its zenith with the coming of the Mughals, the descendants of the Central Asian conqueror Amīr Tīmūr-Lang known in the West as Tamerlane (r. 771–805/1370–1405), and remained influential long after the decline of the Mughals which began in 1119/1707.[2]

Naqshbandīs and Naqshbandī Mujaddidīs have received some scholarly attention in recent times but not much has been written on the Naqshbandī Mujaddidīs in Central Asia. Two recent articles by Buehler and Foltz are relevant for this study. Buehler traces the continued presence of the Naqshbandī Central Asian legacy in Mughal India and identifies factors contributing to the popularity of the Mujaddidīs in India and Central Asia.[3] Foltz's article outlines the relations of Central Asian Naqshbandīs with the Mughal rulers.[4] This study complements these two articles although it is only preliminary and exploratory, relying of necessity on Indian Mujaddidī writings.

Shaykh Aḥmad Sirhindī, as noted earlier, took pride in the fact that the Naqshbandiyya Sufi order from Central Asia took root in the Subcontinent and returned to Central Asia in the seventeenth century with the strong reformism of its Mujaddidī offshoot. Sirhindī was a spiritual master (*pīr*), a spiritual guide (*murshid*), and a perfect living mystic consigned by God to support the cosmos (*qayyūm/quṭb al-aqṭāb*), revered by the majority of his contemporaries and criticised by some. Posterity remembers him as the custodian of the House of Islam in India in the face of a rising tide of syncretism.[5]

A contemporary scholar, ʿAbd al-Ḥakīm Sialkotī (d. 1067/1657), bestowed on Sirhindī the title of the Renewer of the Second [Islamic] Millennium (*Mujaddid alf-i thānī*). Sirhindī's grandson, ʿAbd al-Aḥad (d. 1714) viewed his grandfather's influence on Central Asian Islam as one of the manifestations (*shawāḥid*) of his being a *mujaddid*. He lauded his grandfather's conscious effort to disseminate his ideas in the 'East and the West', to make numerous converts, and to reform the religious practices and beliefs of thousands of Muslims.[6] Following generations of *ʿulamāʾ* and Sufis echoed the views. One of India's most outstanding *ʿulamāʾ* of the eighteenth and early nineteenth centuries, Shāh ʿAbd al-ʿAzīz (d. 1824), also mentioned Sirhindī's complete sway over regions of Central Asia and Afghanistan to justify his receiving the designation of *Mujaddid alf-i thānī*. In these areas, he said, the majority of the population was Sunni Muslim with no Hindus, Christians or Shiʿi, and there was no other Sufi order which actively promoted the spiritual development of the people.[7]

## The Networking

All available sources emphasise the pan-Islamic appeal of Sirhindī's message and the extensive networking of his disciples to spread the Mujaddidī *ṭarīqa:*

> In the fourteenth year of *tajdīd*, seventy disciples were sent to Turkistān and Qipchāq under the leadership of Yār Muḥammad Khān Ṭāliqānī, forty were sent to Yemen, Syria and Rūm [Turkey] under the supervision of Farrukh Ḥusayn; and Shaykh Aḥmad Barkī led a delegation of three senior *khalīfa*s to Turān, Badakhshān and Khurāsān. … After the completion of the first volume of the *Maktūbāt*, compiled by Shaykh Yār Muḥammad Jadīd Ṭāliqānī, many copies were prepared and circulated in Iran, Turān and Badakhshān which made a good impact.[8]

The specific details here from a secondary source are hard to verify, but are similar to the views of Sirhindī's biographers. Among the reliable primary sources are two biographies, *Zubdat al-maqāmāt*, and *Ḥaẓrāt al-quds*,[9] written by Sirhindī's most prominent *khalīfa*s, Muḥammad Hāshim Kishmī (probably died in 1054/1644)[10] and Badr al-Dīn Sirhindī (lived until 1048/1648) respectively.[11] Following the conventions of biographical writing in Mughal India, they give detailed accounts of Sirhindī's senior *khalīfa*s (spiritual successors) in Afghanistan and Central Asia. In the *Zubda*, Kishmī included forty-three major and minor *khalīfa*s (excluding Sirhindī's own sons) – thirteen of them non-Indians;[12] in the *Haẓrāt al-quds* nine out of nineteen,[13] and in the later and less reliable *Rawḍat al-qayyūmiyya*, fourteen out of twenty-seven *khalīfa*s were from outside India.[14] Of those who came to India only the ones who excelled spiritually were designated *khalīfa*s and received permission (*ijāza*) to initiate and train others. Some returned home and others decided to remain in India. This networking spread Sirhindī's teachings beyond Mughal India. The *khalīfa*s stayed in touch with their master through letters. The three volumes of Sirhindī's letters (*Maktūbāt*) containing 536 letters are a major source for Mujaddidī philosophy, a medium for the spread of Sirhindī's legacy, and, above all, a treasure house for the reconstruction of the mystical, intellectual and social life of the period. The compilers of the first and third volume, Yār Muḥammd Jadīd Ṭāliqānī and Muḥammad Hāshim Kishmī Badakhshānī respectively, were, as their names indicate, of Central Asian origin.

### Samples of Shaykh Aḥmad Sirhindī's Correspondence

Sirhindī wrote approximately ninety-two letters to his Central Asian and Afghan disciples. In one of two letters to Mīr Mu'min Balkhī, Sirhindī expressed his love and respect for the people of Transoxiana. This letter is quoted here at some length because it sheds light on the interaction of the Central Asian Naqshbandī Sufis and the Mujaddidiyyas in India. The first paragraph of this letter is quoted at the beginning of this paper:

> The sages of this blessed region have helped develop the understanding of such aspects of the [Naqshbandiyya order] as the stations (*maqāmāt*) of strong and

overwhelming love (*jadhba*), travelling the Sufi path (*sulūk*) … . May God, by virtue of the Prophet's blessings, protect this region from catastrophes and calamities. The friends coming from [your] great country to this lowly region convey the love and affection of the blessed individuals of the area and specially from you who are the refuge of guidance. It is encouraging to know that the Sufis of this region read and appreciate what this slave has written on branches of knowledge (*'ulūm*) and transcendental realities (*ma'ārif*). … Recently, Shaykh Abu'l-Makāram Sufi has kindly conveyed your affection [for me] anew.[15] Relying on your love, I have troubled you by writing these few sentences in order to remind you to keep me in your thoughts. Since I have despatched with the aforementioned Sufi a copy of some of my writings compiled by Brother Muḥammad Hāshim, one of my sincere friends, I have not discussed in this letter any aspect of the intricacies of this sublime order. Because of your kindness, I hope that on special occasions you might pray for my peaceful ending. Please convey my best wishes to Sayyid Mīrak Shāh Bukhārī – the embodiment of nobleness (*sharāfa*) and high-mindedness (*najāba*), and refuge of the Godly people (*Ahl-Allāh kē jā'ē panāh*), and to Mawlānā Ḥasan – a source of goodness and foremost scholar of the time, and Qāḍī Taulak – the supporter of the *sharī'a* and protector of the community, may God sustain their blessings. Please convey the greetings of my sons (*faqīrzāda*) to your sons (*makhdūmzāda*).[16]

In the *Ḥaẓrāt al-quds*, Badr al-Dīn included some Central Asian Sufis who could not visit India but beseeched Sirhindī to direct his spiritual attention to them *in absentia*. He also noted that Sayyid Mīrak Shāh, Mīr Mu'min Balkhī, Ḥasan Qubādiyānī, and Qāḍī Mawlānā Taulak sent gifts to Sirhindī with a dervish who was visiting India. The dervish delivered their letters and conveyed a message from his master, Mīr Muḥammad Balkhī, saying that but for Balkhī's old age and the long distance, he would have come in person and benefited from Sirhindī's higher stations of enlightenment. Mīr Muḥammad Balkhī implored Sirhindī to grant him spiritual attention *in absentia*. The visiting dervish also took the oath of allegiance (*bay'a*) on his master's behalf. Before he left, the dervish asked Sirhindī to write a message for the people of Balkh who were impressed with Sirhindī's understanding of gnosis. Sirhindī complied by writing a few words conveying his best wishes.[17]

### Aḥmad Sirhindī's Message

The topics covered in the letters to Central Asians and Afghans were not restricted to mystical issues. Sirhindī was a learned *'ālim*. A Sufi of profound insight, he practised and popularised the Sunna, curbed innovation in religion, provided leadership in theological and spiritual matters, and held firmly to his convictions undeterred by political pressures and intimidation. He was convinced that the teachings and practices of the Naqshbandiyya were the most efficacious for reaching God. 'What is the ultimate goal of other Sufi orders is the starting point in the Naqshbandiyya because adhering to the Sunna and shunning innovation (*bidʿa*) are the two fundamental principals of this order', he wrote to Muḥammad Ashraf Kābulī.[18] 'This order avoided the musical sessions (*samāʿ*) and dancing (*raqṣ*) and ecstasy (*tawājud*) because they were not in practice during the time of the Prophet and the Khulafāʾ-i Rāshidīn', he admonished Khwāja Muḥammad Qāsim Amkangī.[19] And to Mīr Sayyid Ḥusayn: 'In this order, self-discipline for subduing the soul which inspires evil (*nafs-i ammāra*) is achieved by observing the injunctions of the *sharīʿa* and through absolute adherence to the Sunna.'[20]

Trained as an *ʿālim*, Sirhindī was fully aware of the significance of the *ʿulamāʾ* as a class, and expected them to assume a central role in Indo-Islamic society. He categorically stated that the *sharīʿa* was not subject to abrogation (*naskh*) and change and that it was members of the *ʿulamāʾ* who should perform the function of prophet after the Prophet's death.[21] He deplored the apathy of the contemporary *ʿulamāʾ* and their lack of action against *bidʿa*.[22] In his letter to Aḥmad Barkī, he said that in his region of influence, that is Bark,[23] he should disseminate the *sharīʿa* and the intricacies of *fiqh*, and intermingle with the *ʿulamāʾ*: 'He should instruct individuals in religious sciences and popularise the ordinances of jurisprudence because these two things are the ultimate goals [of this order], and the spiritual advancement and salvation of individuals rest on these.'[24]

We can discern Sirhindī's intimate bond with and sensitivity to the welfare of his disciples in the region. In his letter of condolence on Aḥmad Barkī's death, for example, while grieving over Barkī's loss, he designated Mawlānā Ḥasan as the new *khalīfa*, outlined his new responsibilities, and asked Ḥasan's disciples in the region to respect him as their spiritual leader.[25]

More importantly, the *tajdīd* message was actively disseminated in Central Asia by the Naqshbandiyya Mujaddidiyya Sufis for at least two hundred years, from Shaykh Aḥmad Sirhindī, d. 1624, to Shāh Ghulām ʿAlī, d. 1824. This phenomenon has been documented in the *maktūbāt* and *malfūẓāt* (i.e. discourses of the Sufi master) literature produced in the Subcontinent. This literature also reflects the interest of subsequent generations in Shaykh Aḥmad Sirhindī and his writings. In order to provide some concrete examples, we now review the lives and activities of three descendants of Sirhindī, one biological, Khwāja Muḥammad Maʿṣūm (his son), and two spiritual, Mīrzā Maẓhar Jān-i Jānān (d. 1780), and his major *khalīfa*, Shāh Ghulām ʿAlī.

### Khwāja Muḥammad Maʿṣūm

Muḥammad Maʿṣūm (1599–1668), Sirhindī's third son, his successor and the second of the four *qayyūm*s inherited the charisma and spiritual grace of his father. He also received a solid education and profound mystical training from Sirhindī who spoke highly of his son's spiritual attainments.[26] Maʿṣūm, in turn took his father as a role model for every detail of his life.[27]

According to the Mujaddidī tradition, approximately fifty thousand people, including two thousand of his father's *khalīfas*, took the oath of allegiance to Khwāja Maʿṣūm. Sirhindī's deputies and the ruling elite of Transoxiana, Khurāsān and Badakhshān despatched representatives with presents to renew their allegiance.[28] His collection of letters known as the *Maktūbāt-i Maʿṣūmiyya* (published in three volumes with a total of 652 letters), was modelled after his father's collection. Maʿṣūm and his brother, Khwāja Muḥammad Saʿīd, (d. 1070/1659), and Sirhindī's other biological and spiritual descendants spread his message and charisma by circulating and interpreting his writings. Pilgrimages to Sirhindī's tomb also kept his memory alive. Abu'l-Muẓaffar Burhanpurī, Khwāja Muḥammad Maʿṣūm's *khalīfa*, for example, expressed his wish to visit Aḥmad Sirhindī's tomb about which Maʿṣūm himself also wrote with passionate enthusiasm.[29] The veneration displayed at Sirhindī's mausoleum, however, was countered by some Mujaddidī shaykhs who advised their disciples to seek guidance from the living shaykhs and discouraged them from observing the anniversaries of the deaths of their masters at their shrines.[30]

Khwāja Maʿṣūm's followers continued Sirhindī's initiative to introduce the Mujaddidī branch to Afghanistan and Transoxiana.[31] Out of the forty-one major *khalīfas* of Maʿṣūm, twenty-seven came to Sirhind from towns in Central Asia and Afghanistan. The compiler of the third volume of the *Maktūbāt-i Maʿṣūmiyya*, Ḥājī Muḥammad ʿĀshūr, was from Bukhārā and migrated to India. He was also the author of the *Sharḥ-i maʿmūlāt-i Maʿṣūmiyya* and *Adhkār-i Maʿṣūmiyya*. Like his father, Khwāja Maʿṣūm was also preoccupied with admonishing people who had become lax in religious matters. He urged Mawlānā Ḥasan ʿAlī Pishāwarī to acquire *ʿulūm-i sharīʿa* in order to curb the spread of *bidʿa* and to revive the Sunna of the Prophet during those 'dark times'.[32]

He had a close and compassionate relationship with his disciples. For example when Abū Isḥāq Turkistānī, one of his Central Asian deputies, wished to visit him in Sirhind, Maʿṣūm discouraged him from travelling because of his financial constraints and family responsibilities.[33] Another disciple, Ḥajī Ḥabīb Allāh Ḥiṣārī Bukhārī repeatedly expressed a keen desire to visit his master but Maʿṣūm discouraged him because of his duties towards his disciples.[34]

Shaykh Aḥmad Sirhindī was the first Naqshbandiyya Sufi who disseminated the Mujaddidiyya message in Central Asia, but it spread further under Khwāja Maʿṣūm. It might be argued that Shaykh Sirhindī did not have a *khalīfa* of the stature of Shaykh Muḥammad Murād who was Muḥammad Maʿṣūm's designated *khalīfa*. Shaykh Muḥammad Murād is credited with introducing and popularising the Mujaddidī branch of the Naqshbandī order in the Ottoman lands. He was born in Bukhārā and initiated by Khwāja Muḥammad Maʿṣūm. However, after his initiation, the master and the disciple apparently did not correspond since no letter in the *Maktūbāt-i Maʿṣūmiyya* is addressed to Murād.

Shaykh Murād undertook a series of journeys. In 1092/1681 he visited Istanbul where he spent five years. After travels spanning almost three decades, he returned to Istanbul in 1729 and died there the same year. A *tekke* built at his tomb became 'the fountainhead of the Mujaddidī branch of the Naqshbandī order in the Ottoman lands'.[35]

Shaykh Murād was followed by another Sufi, born in the late 1770s in Qaradāgh in the district of Shahrazūr in Kurdistan who reinvigorated the Naqshbandī Mujaddidī order in Turkey, Syria and Iraq. Known as Khalīd Rūmī, Abu'l-Bahā Ḍiyā al-Dīn Khālid Shahrazūrī was the most prominent non-Indian *khalīfa* of Shāh Ghulām ʿAlī Dihlawī, the *khalīfa* of Maẓhar Jān-i Jānān of Delhi. Khālid Rūmī, like Sirhindī, was regarded as the *mujaddid* for Sunni Muslims in general and the Naqshbandī order in particular.[36]

Mawlānā Khālid arrived in Delhi in 1810. After spending nine months there and rapidly traversing various stages on the Path, he returned to Sulaymāniyya in 1811 as Shāh Ghulām ʿAlī's *khalīfa*.[37] Shāh Ghulām ʿAlī's major *khalīfa*, and compiler of his discourses, Ghulām Muḥyī al-Dīn Quṣūrī recorded Khālid Rumī's journey to India via Peshawar, and Shāh Ghulām ʿAlī's special attentions to him. Quṣūrī ends his description with these words, 'From the visitors (to Delhi) we learn that Mawlānā is the refuge (*marjaʿ*) of all people of Rūm (Turkey)'.[38]

There are three letters from Shāh Ghulām ʿAlī to Khālid.[39] In one of them, he cautioned Mawlānā Khālid not to let an urge for vengeance overpower him. He should take no action that might give the *ṭarīqa* a bad name.[40] In another letter addressed to his *khalīfa* and successor, Shāh Abū Saʿīd (d. 1834), Shāh Ghulām ʿAlī expressed his happiness on hearing that Mawlānā Khālid had been so successful in popularising the Mujaddidiyya *ṭarīqa* in Turkey and Baghdad. He was especially pleased to learn that 500 *ʿulamā'* and a large number of his *khulafā'* had been initiated by the *mawlānā*.[41]

Another letter, addressed to the *ʿulamā'*, *fuḍalā'* (the learned), and the nobility of Turkey is of particular interest. It was written in support of Mawlānā Khālid who was caught in a conflict with the Barzinjī family and their followers in the Qādirī order. Shāh Ghulām ʿAlī was unhappy over textual fabrication in Barzinjī's Arabic translation of Sirhindī's *Maktūbāt*. He felt it was an attempt to discredit Sirhindī and his followers. Shāh Ghulām ʿAlī said that the *mawlānā* had attained higher stations of spiritual excellence under his supervision and that he had bestowed the *ijāza* and *khilāfa* on him. Note the idiom Shāh Ghulām ʿAlī used to lend his full support to Mawlānā Khālid:

> His hand is my hand, his vision is my vision, his friendship is my friendship. His rejection by the people and the animosity they show towards him adversely affect me. His acceptance by the people is like their acceptance of my Masters, namely

> Shāh Naqshband, Khwāja Aḥrār, Khwāja Muḥammad Bāqī and Ḥaẓrat Mujaddid. It is incumbent upon the Muslims of that country to respect and revere him. Similarly, it is obligatory for me to pray for his well-being, long life and safety.[42]

Ghulām ʿAlī ranked Mawlānā Khālid higher than Aḥmad Sirhindī and Ādam Banūrī in some of his attainments[43] and he urged his addressees to protect Mawlānā Khālid from those who were jealous of this.[44]

In Shāh Ghulām ʿAlī's *Malfūẓāt*, there are ample references to seekers of spiritual guidance from major cities in Afghanistan, Central Asia and India who came to his *khānqāh*.[45] In his words:

> From this inadequate (*nā-ahl*) person [i.e. Ghulām ʿAlī] immense blessings are emanating. How can I express my gratitude [to God] that people in their quest for Truth come here [Delhi] from places such as Baghdad, Samarqand, Bukhārā and Tashkent to receive the grace of the Naqshbandī Mujaddidī connection.[46]

However, Shāh Ghulām ʿAlī's master, Mīrzā Maẓhar Jān-i Jānān did not initiate many Central Asians. He was an accomplished Naqshbandī Sufi, heralded by his contemporary, Shāh Walī Allāh (d. 1762)[47] and he initiated thousands of people in India and some from Afghanistan, as recorded by his biographer and *khalīfa*, Shāh Ghulām ʿAlī, but none from Central Asia who remotely approached the stature of Muḥammad Murād and Mawlānā Khālid Rūmī.

An interesting letter in Maẓhar's *Maktūbāt* specifically refers to the dwindling traffic to and from Central Asia. It is addressed to Sayyid Mūsā Khan Dahbīdī[48] a disciple of Maẓhar's master, Muḥammad ʿĀbid Sunāmī (d. 1747). Maẓhar wrote from Pānīpat at the beginning of Ṣafar 1188/1774. He was delighted to receive greetings from Mūsā through a certain ʿAbd al-Qādir. It was Mūsa's first communication after a long time and rekindled fond memories of the past. But times had changed. Most of their contemporaries were dead, and Mīrzā himself was almost eighty years old, weak and fragile, but still holding four meetings a day. The important point for our purpose is that Maẓhar recognised that the movement of people from and to Samarqand had dried up, and a regular exchange of letters was therefore not possible. India was in turmoil. The chaotic conditions in Delhi forced him to move to Pānīpat.[49] In comparison with Maẓhar's turbulent times, as he himself described it, his successor, Shāh Ghulām ʿAlī, found some stability in Delhi after Lord Lake's takeover in 1803. This may have contributed to a rapid increase in individuals coming to his *khānqāh* from within India and from Central Asia.

## Concluding Remarks

Before concluding our discussion of the Mujaddidīs, it should be noted that the affinity of Northern Indian Muslims with Central Asia was not limited to the Mujaddidīs. The imprint of this affinity was so deep that even today, despite the intervening turbulent centuries, traditional etiquette, dress, cuisine and various fruits with their original names still exist which were introduced to the subcontinent by the Turkish sultans and the Mughal emperors. It is very much alive among intellectuals and ordinary people even today and is found in Urdu and Persian literature, in regional languages as well as in folk literature.[50] The most eminent philosopher-poet of the twentieth century, Muḥammad Iqbāl (d. 1938), referred to this strong bond:

> Although I was born in India, the brightness of my eyes
> is created by the pure soil of Bukhārā, Kābul and Tabrīz.[51]

In another verse, the poet saw no frontiers between South and Central Asia:

> I have generated a new enthusiasm, uproar
> in the hearts of people from Lahore to Bukhārā and Samarqand.[52]

The beauty of Balkh and Bukhārā still persists in a Punjabi villager's mind. Unaware of the ravages wrought on Central Asia in the last two centuries, he still hymns their beauty when he praises his own simple home:

> You will not find in Balkh and Bukhārā the pleasure/happiness
> you get in the upper level of Chajjū's house [in rural Punjāb].

In seeking to explain the success of the Mujaddidiyya in Central Asia, one inclines to Hamid Algar's view that it was 'an indication of the compatibility of its genius with the original Naqshbandī impulse that remained dominant in the area'.[53] Another reason often mentioned is the establishment of the Safawids in Iran, with Shiʿism as the state religion, producing a long period of religious uncertainty in Central Asia. The Mujaddidī order's uncompromising position on the primacy of the *sharīʿa* offered Sunni Muslims a sense of direction.[54] Above all, Sirhindī was preoccupied with this, reminding his disciples of the significance of the *ḥadīth*s as a source of guidance and providing a personal example by emulating the Sunna of the Prophet. Sirhindī's desire to eradicate *bidʿa*[55] increased the order's resolve to reject syncretic tendencies and to resist any stifling of their beliefs. More importantly perhaps, there was no shaykh in Central Asia of Sirhindī's stature as an *ʿālim* and a Sufi.

The credit for promoting the legacy of Sirhindī goes to Sirhindī's biological and spiritual descendants as well their disciples and *khalīfa*s. In recent scholarship and through publication of important primary sources (including the biography and the *Maktūbāt* of Maẓhar Jān-i Jānān, and the writings of his most prolific *khalīfa*,[56] Qāḍī Sanāʾ Allāh Pānīpatī, d. 1810, and of Shāh Faqīr Allāh ʿAlawī Shikārpurī, d. 1751), Sirhindī emerges as the restorer of a dynamic Islam whose message was amplified by the scholarship of his descendants and disciples[57] writing Manuals of the Rules of Conduct for Disciples, and compiling the *malfūẓāt* and *maktūbāt* of the Mujaddidī *shaykhs*. Sirhindī's spiritual descendant, Mawlānā Khālid wrote to his fellow *murīd*, Shāh Abū Sa'īd Mujaddidī, about the pan-Islamic sway of Shaykh Aḥmad Sirhindī. According to him, throughout Turkey, the Arab world, the Hijaz, Iraq, some regions of Iran ('Ajam) and in the whole of Kurdistān, people 'are intoxicated (*sar-shār*) with the passion for and sensation of the exalted Mujaddidī *ṭarīqa*. References to Ḥaẓrat Imām-i Rabbānī, the illuminator of the Second Millennium, and his laudable qualities (*maḥāmid*), are made day and night in social settings, in congregations, in mosques and madrasas by both the lowly and the exalted'.[58]

Even today the Mujaddidī tradition under various names is very much alive, from Dacca to Peshawar, from Kabul to Istanbul, from Baghdad to Bosnia, from West Java to Northern Sumatra, and from Europe to North America.

## Appendix: The Sources

The *Maktūbāt* was the main vehicle for the exchange of ideas and concerns on spiritual matters but also included references to mundane matters. I have given samples of letters by Shaykh Aḥmad Sirhindī, Mīrzā Maẓhar Jān-i Jānān, Shāh Ghulām 'Alī and Mawlānā Khālid to show their significance for the researcher. But in the absence of the letters written by disciples to their shaykhs across the Subcontinent and Central Asia, the picture remains incomplete.

During my trip to Tashkent in 1995, I made a concerted effort to look for the writings from Central Asian *khalīfas* to the Mujaddidī *shaykhs* in Sirhind and Delhi. The constraints of time and the ways of bureaucracy hampered my efforts. However, my search showed that several copies of the major writings of Sufi masters including Shaykh Aḥmad Sirhindī, his sons and Shāh Ghulām 'Alī were preserved in the Abū Rayḥān al-Birūnī Library at the Institute of Oriental Studies of the Academy of Sciences of Uzbekistan. The biographies of Aḥmad Sirhindī such as *Ḥaẓrāt al-quds* by Khwāja Badr al-Dīn Sirhindī, *Zubdat al-maqāmāt* by Hāshim Kishmī and Ra'ūf Aḥmad's writings on the life and teachings of his master Shāh Ghulām 'Alī, including *Risālat al-wuṣūl* and *Jawāhir-i 'alwīya'*, were also part of the collection. Their existence would indicate an interest in them in the region.

Of more appeal to me were the writings of the Central Asian *khalīfas* and disciples. There were two epistles numbered 2745 and 2747, both biographies of Shāh Ghulām 'Alī by anonymous authors. Manuscript No. 2745 is an incomplete manuscript containing four chapters (4–7). It contains the sayings of Ghulām 'Alī, the *mukāshafāt* of the author himself, and two chapters explaining the concept of revelation (*ilhām*) and the miracles (*karāmāt*) of the Sufis. *Risāla* No. 2748 by Darwīsh Muḥammad, also known as Mīrzā Raḥīm Beg, outlines the spiritual genealogy of Ghulām 'Alī ending with Shaykh Aḥmad Sirhindī.

Among the biographical dictionaries compiled in Samarqand and Bukhārā, I was able to consult the following: *Qawā'id al-mashā'ikh wa-ashjār al-khuld* (No.

498) by an unknown author outlining the genealogies of seven Sufi orders, including the Khwājagān-i Naqshbandiyya; *Tadhkirāt al-atqiyā' wa-musīrat al-aṣfiyā'* by Muḥammad Amīn b. Muḥammad 'Aẓīm Marghīnānī includes biographies of Shaykh Aḥmad Sirhindī, his son Muḥammad Sa'īd, his grandson, 'Abd al-Aḥad, and Shaykh Muḥammad 'Ābid, the master of Mīrzā Maẓhar and 'Isā Dahbīdī. The main sources given are Ghulām Sarwar's *Khazīnat al-aṣfiyā'* and *Rashḥāt-i jāmī*. *Khulaṣāt al-aḥwāl*, another very useful and interesting work, is the autobiography of Abū 'Ubayd-Allāh Muḥammad b. Sulṭān Khwāja, known as Ishān Khwāja Qārī Tashkandī. He was in the service of the governor of Tashkent, appointed by the Khāns of Kokand. It covers the period from 1835 to 1860 and discusses the adverse consequences of the Russian invasion. It contains a reference to a certain Miyān Khalīl Ṣaḥibzāda, a descendant of Sirhindī, who was appointed as a mediator in a local conflict, which shows that some of his family had emigrated there.

Of works published in Tashkent and Bukhārā and not available elsewhere as far as my search has shown, there are *Tuḥfat al-aḥbāb fi tadhkirāt al-aṣḥāb* (Tashkent, 1894) by Qāḍī Raḥmat Allāh, son of Muḥammad 'Āshūr Bukhārī, (*khalīfa* of Khwāja Ma'ṣūm, and compiler of the third volume of the *Maktūbāt-i Ma'ṣūmiyya*), Niẓām al-Dīn Balkhī's *Tuḥfat al-murshid* (Tashkent, 1910) and Nāṣir al-Dīn Bukhārī's *Tuḥfat al-zā'irīn* (Bukhārā, 1910).

This discussion would not be complete without mentioning *Jawāhir al-sarā'ir* written by Muḥammad 'Umar Chamkanī and finished in 1700–1701, which is to be used in a follow-up article. A biography of Shaykh Sa'dī Lāhawrī (d. 1108/1696), a leading *khalīfa* of Ādam Banūrī (d. 1053/1643, whom Emperor Shāhjahān banished to the Hijaz in 1052/1642) who in turn was the prominent *khalīfa* of Shaykh Aḥmad Sirhindī, it is a valuable source for the interaction of Mujaddidī *shaykhs* with their *murīds* in the relatively more conservative society of the Punjab and the Northwestern regions of India at the beginning of the eighteenth century.

## Notes

1. Shaykh Aḥmad Sirhindī, *Maktūbāt imām rabbānī*, Urdu tr. 'Ālim al-Dīn (Lahore, n.d.), vol. 3, Letter 99: 582–583. The remaining text of this letter is given below in the section, 'Samples of Shaykh Aḥmad Sirhindī's Correspondence'.

2. On the ethnic Chaghatay identity of the Timurids, see Beatrice Forbes Manz, 'The Development and Meaning of Chaghatay Identity', in Jo-Ann Gross, ed., *Muslims in Central Asia: Expressions of Identity and Change* (Durham and London, 1992), pp. 27–45. Re. Timurid influence, the Emperor Jahāngīr for instance is referred to as 'illuminator of the Gūrgān's lamp'. [Gūrgān was Tīmūr's title, meaning the royal (Chingīs Khān's) son-in-law because Tīmūr married a Chingissid princess.] Sajida S. Alvi, ed. and tr., *Advice on the Art of Governance: Mau'iẓa-i Jahāngīrī, An Indo-Islamic Mirror for Princes* (Albany, NY, 1989), p. 43, Persian text, p. 144. Jahāngīr's son, Shāhjahān (r. 1037–1068/1627–1657), who built the Tāj Maḥal, adopted Tīmūr's title, *Ṣāḥib-qirān*, and was referred to as *Ṣāḥib-qirān-i*

*Sānī* (the Second Lord of the Auspicious Planetary conjunction, i.e. pillar of the world and religion).

3. Arthur Buehler, 'The Naqshbandiyya in Tīmūrid India: The Central Asian Legacy', *JIS*, 7 (1996), pp. 208–228.

4. Richard Foltz, 'The Central Asian Naqshbandī Connections of the Mughal Emperors', *JIS*, 7 (1996), pp. 229–239.

5. See, for example, Muḥammad Iqbāl's poem, 'Panjab kē Pīrzādon sē', *Bāl-i jibrīl* in *Kulliyāt-i Iqbāl* (Lahore, 1973), pp. 450–451. For an English translation of the entire poem, see V. G. Kiernan, ed., 'To the Panjab Pirs', *Poems from Iqbal* (London, 1958), p. 58. I discuss this in my article, 'Islamic Renewal and Reform in the Seventeenth and Eighteenth Century-Northern India: Discourses of the Naqshbandī Mujaddidīs in Their Sociopolitical Context', in Bruce B. Lawrence, ed., *Pearls Beyond Measure: the Life and Legacy of Professor Khaliq Ahmad Nizami* (Gainesville, forthcoming).

6. Khwāja 'Abd al-Aḥad Waḥdat Sirhindī, *Sabīl al-rashād*, ed. Ghulām Muṣṭafā Khān (Hyderabad, Sind, 1978), pp. 5 and 7–8. For the content, see Sajida Alvi, 'The Mujaddid and Tajdid Traditions in the Indian Subcontinent: An Historical Overview', *JTS*, Special Issue, *Annemarie Schimmel Festschrift*, 18 (1994), pp. 4–5.

7. 'Abd al-'Azīz, *Surūr-i 'azīzī, al-ma'rūf, fatāwā-i 'azīzī* (Kanpur, n.d.), vol. 1, p. 395.

8. Muḥammad Nūr Bakhsh Tawakkulī, *Tadhkirat-i mashā'ikh-i naqshbandiyya* (Gujarat, n.d.), p. 225.

9. For a comparative study of these fundamental works see Sayyid Khurshīd Ḥusayn Bukhārī, '*Zubdat al-maqāmāt* aur *Haẓrāt al-quds* kā *taqābulī mutālā*', *Nūr-i Islām* (Ḥaẓrat Mujaddid Alf-i Thānī Number, part 2), 23, 2.1 (1988), pp. 83–101.

10. Hāshim came from Kishm, Badakhshān, and settled in India as an adult. He compiled the third volume of Sirhindī's *Maktūbāt*. His probable date of death is taken from Badr al-Dīn Sirhindī, *Haẓrāt al-quds* (Sialkot, 1403/1982), vol. 2, p. 415, n. 1.

11. Badr al-Dīn Sirhindī, *Haẓrāt al-quds*, Introduction, p. 12.

12. Khwāja Muḥammad Hāshim Kishmī Badakhshānī, *Zubdat al-maqāmāt* (Lahore, 1969), pp. 286–339. There are detailed accounts of only twenty-nine of the forty-three *khalīfas*; the rest are identified only by name for the sake of brevity, according to the author, *Zubdat al-maqāmāt*, p. 339. I have identified the non-Indian *khalīfas* by their place of origin: Badakhshī/ Badakhshānī, Samarqandī, Shādmānī, Rūmī, etc. Further research is needed to determine how many returned home and how many settled in India.

13. Badr al-Dīn Sirhindī, *Ḥaẓrāt al-quds*, vol. 2, pp. 320–447.

14. Muḥammad Iḥsān Mujaddidī, *Rawḍat al-qayyūmiyya*, ed. Iqbal Aḥmad Farūqī (Lahore, 1989), vol. 1, pp. 509–552.

15. In the sole letter to Abu'l-Makāram, Sirhindī praised him for his generosity and benevolence, and for being a 'refuge' for the needy. *Maktūbāt*, vol. 3, Letter 116: 634.

16. Aḥmad Sirhindī, *Maktūbāt*, vol. 3, Letter 99: 583–584.

17. Badr al-Dīn, *Ḥaẓrāt al-quds*, 2, pp. 64–65.

18. Sirhindī, *Maktūbāt*, vol. 1, Letter 131: 240.

19. Ibid., Letter 168: 285.

20. Ibid., Letter 221: 375.

21. Ibid., Letter 209: 346.

22. Ibid., Letter 33: 85–87; also see Letter 53: 125–126; and Letter 213: 356–357.

23. Badr al-Dīn says that Aḥmad Barkī was born in Vād, between Qandahār and Kabul. Later, his father moved to Kankrīt, alias Bark. *Ḥaẓrāt al-quds*, 2, 378. Muḥammad Yūsuf Mujaddidī says Bark lies between Kabul and Qandahār, *Jawāhir-i naqshbandiyya* (Faisalabād, 1990), p. 567.

24. Sirhindī, *Maktūbāt*, vol. 1, Letter 275: 569.

25 Ibid., vol. 2, Letter 61: 217–219.

26. Ibid., vol. 1, Letter 267: 538.

27. Badr al-Dīn, *Ḥaẓrāt al-quds*, 2, p. 283.

28. Muḥammad Iḥsān, *Rawḍat al-qayyūmiyya*, 2: 63; Zawwār Ḥusayn, *Anwār-i Maʿṣūmiyya* (Karachi, 1980), p. 39.

29. Khwāja Muḥammad Maʿṣūm, *Maktūbāt-i Maʿṣūmiyya*, Urdu tr. Zawwār Ḥusayn (Karachi, 1980), vol. 3, Letter 239: 323.

30. Sanāʾ Allāh Pānīpatī, *Irshād al-ṭālibīn*, ed. Maẓhar Ḥasan and Muḥammad Ḥasan (Murādābād, 1887), p. 20. Sanāʾ Allāh (d. 1810), spiritual descendant of Aḥmad Sirhindī, was a *qāḍī*, a prolific scholar and *khalīfa* of the major Naqshbandī Mujaddidī master, Mīrzā Maẓhar Jān-i Jānān. For more discussion on the institution of *shaykh*, see my forthcoming article, 'Islamic Renewal and Reform' in *Pearls Beyond Measure.*

31. Hamid Algar, 'A Brief History of the Naqshbandī Order', in *Naqshbandis: Historical Developments and Present Situation of a Muslim Mystical Order*, ed. Marc Gaborieu et al. (Istanbul, 1990), p. 24.

32. Khwāja Muḥammad Maʿṣūm, *Maktūbāt-i Maʿṣūmiyya*, Urdu tr. by Zawwār Ḥusayn (Karachi, 1986), vol. 1, Letter 178: 346–347.

33. Maʿṣūm, *Maktūbāt*, vol. 3, Letter 119: 186–187.

34. I discuss Khwāja Maʿṣūm in detail in my forthcoming article, 'Islamic Renewal and Reform' in *Pearls Beyond Measure.*

35. Algar, 'A Brief History', p. 27.

36. Ibid., p. 28.

37. Ibid., p. 29.

38. Ghulām Muḥyī al-Dīn Quṣūrī, *Malfūẓāt-i sharīfa*, tr. Iqbāl Aḥmad Fārūqī (Lahore, 1978), Persian text, pp. 132–133.

39. For the text of the three letters nos. 23, 38, 110, see Ghulām ʿAlī, *Makātīb-i sharīfa*, compiled by Raʾūf Aḥmad Rāʾfat Mujaddidī, ed. ʿAbd al-Majīd Aḥmad Sayfī (Lahore, 1371/1951–1952), pp. 27, 35 and 155–156.

40. For details, see *Makātīb-i sharīfa*, Letter 38: 35.

41. Ibid., Letter 32: 32.

42. Ibid., Letter 109: 153.

43. Ibid., p. 154.

44. Ibid.

45. Raʾūf Aḥmad Rāʾfat Mujaddidī, *Durr al-maʿarif: malfūẓāt-i ṭayyibāt-i haẓrat Shāh Ghulām ʿAlī Mujaddidī Dihlawī*, Urdu tr. by ʿAbd al-Ḥakīm Khān Akhtar (Lahore, 1983), 47: 159–160. This is a valuable work by an eye-witness who recorded the discourses of Shāh Ghulām ʿAlī, giving details of dates (*Durr al-maʿarif*, 37). In the Urdu translation, each discourse is also numbered. In my references I have included the session number as well.

46. *Durr al-maʿarif*, 82: 198. There are also examples of individuals who came with little

knowledge of Islam but received intensive training from Ghulām ʿAlī. For example see *Durr al-maʿarif*, 65: 178.

47. Shāh Ghulām ʿAlī, *Maqāmāt-i maẓharī*, ed. and tr. into Urdu by Muḥammad Iqbāl Mujaddidī (Lahore, 1983), p. 306.

48. Khwāja Mūsā Dahbīdī came from the town of Dahbīd, near Samarqand. He founded the Dahbīdī branch of the order.

49. Maẓhar Jān-i Jānān, *Makātīb-i mīrzā maẓhar*, ed. ʿAbd al-Razzāq Qurayshī (Bombay, 1966), Letter no. 147: 212–213.

50. For details, see Aḥmad Ḥasan Dani, *New Light on Central Asia* (Lahore, 1993), pp. 12–16.

51. Muḥammad Iqbal, *Payām-i mashriq* in *Kulliyāt-i Iqbāl: Farsī* (Lahore, 1973), p. 339.

52. Muḥammad Iqbal, *Ẓarb-i kalīm* in *Kulliyāt-i Iqbāl: Urdu* (Lahore, 1972), p. 485.

53. Algar, 'A Brief History', p. 24.

54. For a detailed study of this aspect of Sirhindī's thought, see Muḥammad ʿAbd al-Ḥaqq Anṣārī, *Sufism and Shari'ah: A Study of Shaykh Ahmad Sirhindi's Effort to Reform Sufism* (London, 1986), pp. 61–83.

55. Sirhindī is noted for his total rejection of *bidʿa* including good innovation *(bidʿa-i ḥasana)*. For example, see *Maktūbāt*, vol. 1, Letter 186: 83–86. He encouraged analogy (*qiyās*) and independent judgement (*ijtihād*) because these were not *bidaʿ*: *Maktūbāt*, vol. 1, p. 86. Distinguishing between acts of worship (*ʿibādāt*) and custom (*ʿādāt wa-ʿurf*), he held that only deviation from *ʿibādāt* was *bidʿa*. See Anṣārī, *Sufism and Shariʿah*, pp. 22–23. Also Muḥammad Farmān, *Radd-i bidʿat: Imām Rabbanī Ḥaẓrat Mujaddid Alf-i Thānī kī taʿlīmāt kī raushnī mēṇ* (Gujarāt, 1962).

56. See Sajida S. Alvi, 'Qazi Sanā' Allah Panipati, 'An Eighteenth-Century Sufi-ʿAlim: A Study of His Writings in Their Sociopolitical Context', in Wael B. Hallaq and D. P. Little, ed., *Islamic Studies Presented to Charles J. Adams* (Leiden, 1991), pp. 11–25.

57. As an example of a typical congregational meeting, see Ra'ūf Aḥmad, *Durr al-maʿārif*, 47: 158–159. For details of three Manuals for Disciples (*Ādāb-i murīdān*), see my forthcoming article, 'Islamic Renewal and Reform'.

58. Quoted without a reference by Tawakkulī in *Tadhkirat-i mashā'ikh-i Naqshbandiyya*, pp. 320–321. On the widespread popularity of Mawlānā Khālid, as testified by the British Resident, C. J. Rich, in Baghdad who was then travelling through Kurdistan, see Albert Hourani, 'Shaikh Khalid and the Naqshbandi Order', in S. M. Stern, Albert Hourani and Vivian Brown, ed., *Islamic Philosophy and Classical Tradition: Essays Presented by His Friends and Pupils to Richard Walzer on His Seventieth Birthday* (Columbia, 1972), p. 97. For his legacy in Kurdistan, see Ferhad Shakely, 'The Naqshbandī Sheikhs of Hawrāmān and the Heritage of Khāliddiyya-Mujaddidiyya in Kurdistan', in Elisabeth Özdalga, ed., *Naqshbandis in Western and Central Asia: Change and Continuity* (Istanbul, 1999), pp. 89–100.

# 31

# 'Le combattant du *ta'wīl*'. Un poème de Mollā Ṣadrā sur 'Alī (Aspects de l'imamologie duodécimaine IX)

*Mohammad Ali Amir-Moezzi*

Parmi les écrits de Mollā Ṣadrā (né en 979/1571 ou 980/1572 à Shiraz; mort en 1050/1640 à Bassorah), son œuvre en persan et plus particulièrement sa poésie ont peu retenu l'attention des chercheurs. En 1961, Seyyed Hossein Nasr publiait pour la première fois, à la suite du traité *Seh aṣl* du grand philosophe, le *Montakhab-e mathnavī* ainsi que huit *robā'īs*.[1] Beaucoup plus récemment, en 1997, Moḥammad Khājavī, l'infatigable éditeur et traducteur en persan de l'œuvre de Mollā Ṣadrā, a édité le 'Recueil des poèmes' de celui-ci comprenant, outre les textes déjà publiés par S. H. Nasr, une quarantaine d'autres poèmes.[2] Quelques mois avant la parution de l'édition Khājavī, la Bibliothèque de l'Ayatollah Mar'ashī Najafī avait publié une autre édition de l'œuvre poétique du philosophe, faite par le savant religieux, Moṣṭafā Fayḍī.[3] Cette édition, effectuée à partir d'un manuscrit unique, offre souvent des leçons fort différentes par rapport aux deux autres et contient de nombreux vers supplémentaires, inconnus des éditions Nasr et Khājavī; cependant leur authenticité reste à démontrer, étant donné que presque rien n'est dit au sujet du manuscrit utilisé.[4] En tous les cas, avec ces trois éditions, nous disposons sans doute maintenant de la quasi-totalité de l'œuvre poétique de Mollā Ṣadrā, à laquelle il faudrait penser ajouter ses quelques vers éparpillés dans son œuvre.[5]

La poésie de Mollā Ṣadrā illustre souvent quelques-unes de ses préoccupations théologiques et philosophiques et, peut-être encore de manière plus insistante, sa pensée eschatologique.[6] De valeur littéraire inégale, elle est cependant parcourue, de bout en bout, d'un puissant souffle mystique qui inspire aux vers une intensité toute particulière. Bien qu'aucun poème ne soit daté, les éditeurs s'accordent à penser que, comme tout lettré iranien digne de ce nom, Mollā Ṣadrā aurait composé des poèmes tout le long de sa vie d'adulte, tout en revenant très probablement sur des compositions anciennes pour les modifier ou les compléter selon son évolution intellectuelle et spirituelle.[7]

Les rapports entre le *Montakhab-e mathnavī* (littéralement 'extraits', 'fragments' ou 'morceaux choisis' du *mathnavī*) et les poèmes de la *majmū'e* qui forment, eux aussi, un *mathnavī* posent quelques problèmes pour le moment insolubles. Les deux sont présentés dans les manuscrits comme des recueils indépendants;[8] pourtant beaucoup de vers du *Montakhab* se retrouvent dans la *majmū'e* mais avec des variantes parfois considérables alors que d'autres vers ne s'y retrouvent pas du tout. Ces deux ensembles proviennent-ils chacun de sources différentes jusqu'ici inconnues? Le terme *montakhab* ne serait-il pas un ajout de copiste, le poème étant, comme le pense d'ailleurs M. Khājavī,[9] une composition indépendante et plus tardive par rapport à la *majmū'e*? Celle-ci constitue-t-elle un seul et même *mathnavī* ou bien un ensemble de poèmes plus ou moins indépendants consacrés à des thèmes différents mais composés tous sur le même mètre *ramal musaddas maḥdhūf*?[10]

Le poème sur 'Alī est le quatrième de la *majmū'e* et est intitulé (par l'auteur ou par le copiste?): 'De l'éloge du Prince des croyants et de la Famille de la Demeure (du Prophète)' (*dar manqabat-e ḥaḍrat-e amīr al-mo'menīn va ahl-e beyt*):[11]

1. *Shahsavār-e lā fatā shīr-e vaghā / az khodā vo moṣṭafā bar vey thanā*
   Chevalier de *lā fatā*, lion de la bataille / Celui que Dieu et le Pur Elu (Moḥammad) ont loué.

*Lā fatā*: allusion à la tradition: *lā sayfa illā dhu'l-faqār wa lā fatā illā 'Alī*, 'Pas de sabre hormis Dhu'l-Faqār et pas de héros chevaleresque hormis 'Alī'.[12]

L'éloge de 'Alī par Dieu figure, selon l'exégèse Imamite, dans le texte même du Qur'an. Mollā Ṣadrā va y revenir dans la suite de son poème.

2. *Sāqī-ye kowthar valī-ye kardegār / dāde tīghash dīn-e aḥmad rā qarār*
   L'échanson du (fleuve paradisiaque) Kowthar, l'ami de Dieu / Celui dont le sabre consolida la religion de Aḥmad (i.e. Moḥammad).

Dès le début du poème, deux caractéristiques de 'Alī sont fortement soulignées: le fait qu'il est l'ami de Dieu, *walī*, et qu'il est le guerrier de la foi par excellence. Comme on verra par la suite, pour Mollā Ṣadrā les deux attributs semblent inséparables et constituent ensemble le fondement de l'interprétation spirituelle (*ta'wīl*) qu'il offre de la figure de 'Alī.[13]

3. *Az zabān-e tīgh zang-e kofr o jowr / ḥakk namūd az ṣafḥe-ye 'ālam be-fowr*
   Par la langue de son sabre, la rouille de l'infidélité et de l'oppression / Fut vite grattée de la face du monde. (Voir *infra* le vers no 16.)[14]
4. *Az vojūdash 'aql īmān yāfte / az jabīnash nūr riḍvān yāfte*
   Grâce à son être, la raison découvrit la foi / Grâce à son front, le paradis eut la lumière.[15]

Plus loin, dans le 22^e poème de la *majmūʿe* dans l'édition Khājavī, Mollā Ṣadrā distingue entre une raison céleste, angélique (*ʿaql-e malakī*), illuminée par la foi, et une raison mondaine, coupée d'En-Haut, ruse ténébreuse et bestiale, celle des égarés (*ʿaql-e gomgashtegān*).[16] ʿAlī ou l'amitié divine (*walāya*) et l'imamat qu'ils représentent, sont identifiés ici à la lumière de la foi qui transforme la raison humaine en raison céleste.[17]

5. *ʿAql-e peyghambar co qorʾān āmadī / nafs-e vey mānand-e forqān āmadī*[18]
   Comme le Qurʾan, il (ʿAlī) manifeste l'intelligence du Prophète / Sa personne sert à distinguer le bien et le mal.

*Furqān* (prononciation persane *forqān*) désigne ce qui sert à distinguer le bien et le mal, le licite et l'illicite, d'où tout code ou recueil de loi sacré, plus particulièrement le Qurʾan. Ce vers, ainsi que les six qui suivent, posent les rapports entre l'imamologie et la prophétologie, entre le *walī*, messager de l'ésotérique de la religion, et le *nabī*, messager de l'exotérique mais qui cumule secrètement en lui la *walāya* et la *nubuwwa*. La *walāya / imāma* est le 'lieu' du secret de la *nubuwwa*, la révélation de l'essence de celle-ci.[19] Les deux fonctions sont évidemment symbolisées respectivement par ʿAlī Murtaḍā et Moḥammad Muṣṭafā.

6. *Farq joz ejmāl o joz tafṣīl nīst / īn do hamrah qābel-e tabdīl nīst*
   Leur différence c'est celle du résumé et du détaillé / Les deux sont unis mais on ne peut les confondre.
7. *Har ce dar ejmāl bod bā moṣṭafā / gasht ẓāher az vojūd-e mortaḍā*
   Ce qui, grâce à Muṣṭafā, est exposé en résumé / S'est manifesté (en détail) grâce à la personne de Murtaḍā.[20]

L'enseignement de l'Imam consiste essentiellement à expliciter le message du prophète qui est concentrée dans la Révélation. Ceci est rappelé par de nombreuses traditions selon lesquelles le hadith, c'est-à-dire principalement l'enseignement des Imams, explique en détail (*tafṣīl*) ce que le Qurʾan expose sous une forme condensée (*mujmal*).[21]

8. *Maʿnī-ye al-yawma akmalt īn bovad / gar to hastī mard-e dīn ey moʿtamad*
   C'est cela le sens profond de '*al-yawma akmaltu*' / (Sache-le) ô confident, si tu es homme de foi.

*Al-yawma akmaltu lakum dīnakum wa atmamtu ʿalaykum niʿmatī*: 'Aujourd'hui, J'ai rendu parfaite pour vous votre religion et parachevé pour vous Mon bienfait.' Ce morceau du troisième verset de la sourate 5, *al-māʾida*, concerne, selon l'exégèse Imamite la plus classique et la plus fréquente, la révélation divine de la *walāya* de ʿAlī à Moḥammad. Ce verset fait de la *walāya*, amitié fidèle à l'égard des Imams, un devoir cultuel (*farīḍa*) au même titre que la prière canonique ou le pèlerinage à la Mekke.[22] Pour Mollā Ṣadrā, l'enseignement des Imams, représenté ici par celui de

ʿAlī et consistant en l'explicitation du message prophétique, constitue le contenu essentiel de la *walāya*. C'est par cet enseignement que Dieu a rendu parfaite la religion.[23]

9. *Ūst bābā-ye nofūs-e owliyā / hamconān ke moṣṭafā bā anbiyā*
   C'est lui (ʿAlī) le Père des Amis (de Dieu) / Comme l'est (Moḥammad) Muṣṭafā pour les prophètes;
10. *Owliyā yek yek co farzandān-e ū / jīre khārān-e navāl-e khān-e ū*
   Les Amis sont, un par un, ses enfants / Se nourrissant aux portions posées sur sa nappe.

Moḥammad, dans sa réalité essentielle appelée 'lumière Moḥammadienne', constitue l'origine et la substance de la prophétie (*nubuwwa*); de même que la lumière de ʿAlī est l'origine et la substance même de l'Amitié ou l'Alliance divine (*walāya*).[24]

11. *Ānke pāyash dūsh-e peyghambar bodī / habbadhā shākhī ke īnash bar bodī*
   Celui qui eut son pied sur l'épaule du Prophète / Quel merveilleux arbre qui porte un tel fruit![25]
12. *Ānke nafsash būd dast-e kardegār / īn yadollā rā ke dānad kard khār?*
   Celui qui fut la main de Dieu en personne / Cette Main nul n'est capable de l'abaisser?

Lieu de manifestation et instrument de la volonté de Dieu, l'Imam est souvent dit être un 'organe' de Dieu: œil, langue, main, oreille, face, cœur, etc.[26] Le dernier hémistiche, faisant allusion aux adversaires de ʿAlī, sert d'introduction aux quinze vers suivants où Mollā Ṣadrā s'adonne à une véritable exégèse spirituelle de la dimension guerrière de la figure du premier Imam:

13. *Gar kasī rā būdī az qadrash khabar / key conān bā vey namūdandī ḍarar?*
   Si quelqu'un avait connu sa véritable valeur / Comment aurait-il pu chercher à lui porter préjudice?
14. *Kofr-hā-ye mokhtafī dar jāneshān / būd dā'em rahzan-e īmāneshān*
   Or, des infidélités cachées au fond d'eux (i.e. les adversaires de ʿAlī) / ravissaient constamment leur foi.
15. *Dhāt-e ū con būd tanzīl-e kalām / kard az shamshīr ta'vīl-e kalām*[27]
   Comme sa réalité essentielle (celle de ʿAlī) constituait la lettre de la Révélation/ Il fit du sabre l'exégèse spirituelle de celle-ci.
16. *Az zabān-e tīgh tafsīr-e sokhan / mīnamūd az baḥr-e aṣḥāb-e badan*[28]
   Le commentaire de la Parole, par le langage du glaive, / Il le fit pour les gens de l'extériorité.

Le *dhāt*, littéralement l'essence, de ʿAlī, que je traduis par 'réalité essentielle', c'est la *walāya* laquelle est présentée par de nombreuses traditions comme le but ultime de la Révélation, le message caché sous la lettre du Qur'an.[29] Ceux qui s'opposent à ʿAlī s'opposent donc à ce que le Qur'an porte de plus profond. Ce sont les adversaires de la *walāya*, dimension ésotérique de la *nubuwwa*. Il revient donc à ʿAlī de les combattre afin que la Révélation ne devienne pas une lettre sans esprit; ce qui évoque bien entendu la célèbre tradition attribuée au Prophète: 'Il y a parmi vous quelqu'un qui combat pour l'interprétation spirituelle du Qur'an comme moi-même j'ai combattu pour la lettre de sa révélation, et cette personne c'est ʿAlī b. Abī Ṭālib.'[30] Le sabre de ʿAlī est donc présenté comme l'instrument de l'intériorité du Qur'an, symbole d'une violence sacrée contre la violence profanatrice qui consiste à vider l'Islam de son contenu essentiel. Il est intéressant de noter que l'expression *aṣḥāb-e badan*, littéralement 'les gens du corps', que je traduis par 'les gens de l'extériorité', est utilisée telle quelle ou sous la forme de *tan parast*, littéralement 'adorateur du corps', dans *Seh aṣl*, pour désigner les puissants religieux officiels de l'époque que le philosophe dénonce justement comme 'les gens de l'apparence' ou 'de l'exotérique' (*ahl-e ẓāher*) qui ne cherchent qu'à satisfaire leur corps et leurs ambitions.[31]

17. *Qāriyān būdand ahl-e nahravān / līk kajrow dar nahān o dar ʿayān*
Les gens de Nahrawān étaient des lecteurs du Qur'an /Et cependant des égarés, secrètement et manifestement.
18. *Dar darūn-shān naqsh hā-ye por ghalaṭ / maʿnī-ye qor'ān nabāshad zīn namaṭ*
A l'intérieur d'eux, des impressions erronées / Qui n'avaient rien à voir avec le sens du Qur'an.
19. *Īn ghalaṭ-hā ḥakk namūd az tīgh-e tīz / kard az ta'vīl-e qor'ān rastkhīz*
Il (ʿAlī) effaça ces erreurs par le tranchant de son glaive / Faisant de l'herméneutique du Qur'an une résurrection.

Les 'gens de Nahrawān' désignent bien entendu les adversaires de ʿAlī,[32] tout comme les 'lecteurs du Qur'an' désignent des religieux 'égarés' aux idées fausses sur le vrai 'sens du Qur'an'. ʿAlī, symbole de la *walāya*, est lui-même ce vrai sens; ses adversaires sont les adversaires du sens et donc, selon le poète, les gens qui ne connaissent que la lettre seule, d'où l'expression 'lecteurs du Qur'an' (*qāriyān*). Revenant sur le thème évoqué plus haut, et de manière encore plus audacieuse, Mollā Ṣadrā répète que le sabre de ʿAlī est non seulement l'instrument de l'herméneutique spirituelle du Qur'an, mais que c'est en éliminant les gens de l'extériorité, et en quelque sorte la lettre qu'ils représentent, que ce *ta'wīl* devient à son tour instrument de résurrection du sens.

20. *Ṣeḥḥat-e qor'ān conīn bāyad namūd*[33] */ eqtedā bā shāh-e dīn bāyad namūd*
C'est ainsi qu'il faut montrer la véracité du Qur'an / Il faut ainsi suivre l'exemple du Roi de la religion (ʿAlī).
21. *Zang-e kofr az rūy-e dīn bestorde ast / Khāṣef on-naʿl īn ḥedāthat būde ast*[34]
Il gratta de cette manière la rouille recouvrant la religion / C'est pourquoi il fut appelé 'réparateur de sandale'.
22. *Ḥarb bar ta'vīl karde murtaḍā / hamco bar tanzīl*[35] *ṣadr-e anbiyā*

Murtaḍā ('Alī) s'est combattu pour 'l'esprit' (du Qur'an) / Tout comme le chef des prophètes (Moḥammad) s'est combattu pour sa 'lettre'.[36]

'Réparateur de sandale', *khāṣif al-na'l*: dans certaines versions du hadith du 'combattant du *ta'wīl*' (voir ci-dessus vers 15 et note 30), le Prophète appelle 'Alī par ce sobriquet, parce qu'à ce moment-là, dit-on, ce dernier était en train de recoudre une sandale.[37] La racine *KhṢF* signifie littéralement joindre deux morceaux détachées ou bien recoudre ce qui est déchiré. Mollā Ṣadrā semble vouloir indiquer que par son combat pour le *ta'wīl*, 'Alī, messager de l'ésotérique du Qur'an, rectifiait les erreurs, dues à un littéralisme violent, survenues dans la religion de Moḥammad; d'où ma traduction de *khāṣif* par 'réparateur'. De même dans l'expression *ṣeḥḥat-e qor'ān* que j'ai traduit par 'véracité du Qur'an' (vers 20), le terme *ṣeḥḥat* (*ṣiḥḥa* en arabe) signifie littéralement 'santé, état de ce qui est sans défaut', mais aussi en persan 'correction, rectification' (sens de la deuxième forme de la racine en arabe). Les guerres menées par 'Alī sont ainsi inséparables de sa vocation d'Imam, de *walī*, d'Ami de Dieu et d'interprète du sens caché de la Révélation. Les cinq vers suivants paraissent souligner cette double dimension du personnage, celle, apparente, symbolisée par 'le jour', du guerrier intrépide et joyeux du *ta'wīl* et celle, cachée, symbolisée par 'la nuit', du triste Ami et Allié de Dieu:

23. *Rūz-e hayjā cūn be-peydā āmadī / cūn khor az ṣobḥ-e dovom khande zadī*
    Lorsqu'il sortait le jour de la bataille / Il se mettait à sourire tel un second soleil.
24. *Shab co dar meḥrāb-e ṭā'at mīshodī / khūn ze gerye bar moṣallā mīzadī*
    La nuit, lorsqu'il se retirait dans le *miḥrāb* du culte / Il aspergeait le lieu de prière de ses larmes amères.
25. *Rūz tīghash āb-e ātash bār būd / ashk-e cashmash shab dar-e raḥmat goshūd*
    Le jour, son sabre était ravageur comme une eau faite de feu / La nuit, grâce à ses larmes, s'ouvraient les portes de la miséricorde.
26. *Dar waghā ḍaḥḥāk o shab bakkā bodī / bā khodā shab rūz bā a'dā bodī*
    Dans la clameur du combat, il riait, et la nuit, il pleurait / C'est que la nuit, il était avec Dieu et le jour avec les ennemis.
27. *Rūz kār-e doshmanān rā sākhtī / shab be kār-e dūstān pardākhtī*
    Le jour, il réglait le compte des adversaires / La nuit, il s'occupait des amis.

Les sept vers suivants forment une suite d'allusions aux versets qur'aniques et aux hadiths que la tradition duodécimaine rattache à la figure du premier Imam:

28. *Alladhīna yonfiqūn dar sha'n-e ū / qaddemū bayna yaday eḥsān-e ū*
    '*Alladhīna yunfiqūn*' (est révélé) pour son cas / '*Qaddimū bayna yaday*' (indique) sa bonté.

*Alladhīna yunfiqūn*: le Qur'an 3, *Āl 'Imrān*: 134: *Alladhīna yunfiqūna fi s-sarrā' wa ḍ-ḍarrā' wa l-kāẓimīna l-ghayẓ wa l-'āfīn 'ani n-nās wa'llāhu yuḥibbu l-muḥsinīn*;

'Ceux qui font don dans la prospérité comme dans la difficulté, qui maîtrisent leur colère et qui pardonnent aux gens; certes Dieu aime ceux qui font le bien.'[38]

*Qaddimū bayna yaday*: le Qur'an 58, *al-mujādala*: 12: *Yā ayyuhā lladhīna āmanū idhā nājaytumu r-rasūli fa-qaddimū bayna yaday najwākum ṣadaqatan*; 'Vous qui croyez, quand vous tenez un entretien privé avec l'Envoyé, préludez au moment de cet entretien par une aumône.'[39]

29. *Khel'at-e ennā hadaynā dar barash / mighfarī az lā fatā andar sarash*
La robe d'honneur de '*innā hadaynā*' sur lui / La coiffe de '*lā fatā*' couvrant sa tête.

*Innā hadaynā*: le Qur'an 76, *al-dahr*: 3: *Innā hadaynāhu s-sabīl*; 'Nous l'avons dirigé sur la voie droite'.[40]

30. *Dar kafash az o'ṭiyanna rāyatī / dar delash az ennamā khosh āyatī*
Dans sa main, l'étendard de '*u'ṭiyanna*' / Dans son cœur, le beau signe (ou 'verset') de '*innamā*'.

*U'ṭiyanna*: allusion au hadith remontant au Prophète, censé avoir été dit lors de la bataille de Khaybar: *la-u'ṭiyanna l-rāya ghadan rajulan yuḥibbu llāha wa rasūlahu wa yuḥibbuhu llāhu wa rasūluhu yaftahu llāhu 'alā yadayhi laysa bi-farrār*; 'Demain, je donnerai l'étendard à un homme (i.e. 'Alī) qui aime Dieu et Son Envoyé et que Dieu et Son Envoyé aiment; grâce à lui, Dieu accordera la victoire et il ne s'enfuira point.'[41] *Innamā*: le Qur'an 5, *al-mā'ida*: 55: *Innamā waliyyukumu llāhu wa rasūluhu wa lladhīna āmanū lladhīna yuqīmūna ṣ-ṣalāt wa yu'tūna z-zakāt wa hum rāki'ūn*; 'Votre allié-protecteur ce sont Dieu, Son Envoyé et ceux qui croient, qui effectuent la prière et offrent le don purificateur alors qu'ils sont en prostration.'[42]

31. *Anta mennī ma'nī-ye īmān-e ū / āyat-e taṭhīr andar sha'n-e ū*
'*Anta minnī*' est le sens de sa foi / le verset de 'la Purification' le concerne.

*Anta minnī*: tiré du hadith remontant au Prophète qui, rapporte-t-on, s'adressa ainsi à 'Alī: *Anta minnī bi-manzila hārūn min mūsā illā annahu lā nabiyya ba'dī*; 'Tu as à mon égard le même rapport que celui qu'avait Aaron à l'égard de Moïse, à la différence près qu'après moi, il n'y a pas d'autre prophète'; ce qui prouve, pour les Shi'a, que 'Alī était bien l'Imam et le successeur de Moḥammad.[43] Le verset de la Purification (*taṭhīr*): le Qur'an 33, *al-aḥzāb*: 33: *Innamā yurīdu llāhu li-yudhhiba 'ankumu r-rijsa ahl al-bayti wa yuṭahhirakum taṭhīrā*; 'Dieu ne veut qu'écarter de vous la souillure, ô famille de la demeure, et vous purifier totalement.'[44]

32. *Ū madīne-y 'elm rā bāb āmade / jān fedā dar jāme-ye khāb āmade*
Il est la porte de 'la cité de la connaissance' / S'offrant en sacrifice, il se mit au lit.

'Cité de la connaissance': tiré du hadith attribué au Prophète: *Anā madīnatu l-'ilm* (autre version: *madīnatu l-ḥikma*) *wa 'Alī bābuhā*'; 'Je suis la cité de la connaissance (ou 'de la sagesse') et 'Alī en est la porte'.[45] Le second hémistiche fait allusion au célèbre épisode connu sous le nom de *laylat al-mabīt* ('la nuit de l'abri'), où, selon la *sīra*, lorsque Moḥammad, menacé par ses adversaires, s'enfuit nuitamment de la Mekke vers Médine, 'Alī se mit dans le lit de celui-ci pour tromper les poursuivants de son cousin, risquant ainsi sa vie pour l'Islam naissant et son prophète.

33. *Ennamā anta bar ū nāzel shode / az salūnī 'elm-e dīn ḥāsel shode*
'*Innamā anta*' est révélé pour lui / Grâce à '*salūnī*' la science de la religion est acquise.

*Innamā anta*: le Qur'an 13, *al-ra'd*: 7: *Innamā anta mundhirun wa li-kulli qawmin hādin*; 'Tu es l'avertisseur et chaque peuple a un guide.' La tradition exégétique Imamite identifie 'l'avertisseur' avec le Prophète et 'le guide' avec 'Alī.[46] *Salūnī*: allusion à la formule *Salūnī* (ou *is'alūnī*) *qabla an tafqidūnī*, 'Interrogez-moi avant que vous ne me perdiez', formule par laquelle commencent de nombreux sermons remontant à 'Alī,[47] allusion directe au fait que le premier Imam est le sage initié par excellence et donc la source de toute connaissance.

34. *Būde nafsash 'endaho 'elmo l-ketāb / qol kafā be'llā govāh-e īn kheṭāb*
''*Indahu 'ilmu l-kitāb*' concerne sa personne / '*Qul kafā bi llāh*' en est témoin.

*'Indahu 'ilmu l-kitāb* et *Qul kafā bi llāh*: le Qur'an 13, *al-ra'd*: 43: *Wa yaqūlu lladhīna kafarū lasta mursalan qul kafā bi llāhi shahīdan baynī wa baynakum wa man 'indahu 'ilmu l-kitāb*; 'Et ceux qui dénient disent que tu n'es pas un Envoyé. Dis: Dieu suffit comme témoin entre vous et moi ainsi que celui qui détient la science de l'Ecriture'. Pour l'exégèse Imamite, Dieu et 'Alī, 'celui qui détient la science de l'Ecriture' ou 'du Livre', suffisent comme témoins pour prouver la véracité de la mission prophétique de Moḥammad.[48]

35. *Moṣḥaf-e āyāt-e īzad rūy-e ū / selsele-y ahl-e valāyat mūy-e ū*
Sa face est le Recueil des signes de Dieu / Les boucles de sa chevelure, la chaîne des gens de l'Amitié (divine).

Mollā Ṣadrā utilise ici deux termes du lexique technique du symbolisme érotique de la poésie mystique persane pour faire allusion aux fonctions théologiques et hagiologiques de l'Imam; 'la face' ou 'le visage' (*rū*) de 'Alī est le lieu de manifestation des signes divins. La personne de l'Imam est dite être la Face de Dieu dans de nombreuses traditions.[49] En outre, *moṣḥaf-e āyāt-e īzad* que j'ai traduit par 'le Recueil des signes de Dieu' peut tout aussi bien se traduire par 'le Livre des versets de Dieu' c'est-à-dire le Livre céleste, révélé. La Figure de 'Alī, l'Imam par excellence, constitue donc la véritable Parole révélée ou dans le sens inverse, la réalité de la Révélation c'est la Face de l'Imam. La chevelure (*mū*) de ʿAlī est ce qui relie entre eux les 'gens de l'Amitié divine', *ahl-e valāyat*. Cette expression désigne bien entendu les *awliyāʾ Allāh*, les amis ou les alliés de Dieu, les saints pour le dire plus simplement. La *walāya* de ʿAlī constitue la substance même de la sainteté, ce qui garantit la succession effective des hommes de Dieu.[50]

36. *Goft peyghambar ke ey yārān-e man / dūstān o peyrovān-e moʾtaman*[51]
Le Prophète déclara: 'O compagnons! / Amis et camarades de confiance,
37. *Mīgozāram baʿd-e khod nazd-e shomā / bahr-e peydā kardan-e rāh-e khodā*
Je laisse, après moi, auprès de vous / Afin que vous puissiez trouver le chemin de Dieu,
38. *Dō gerān qeymat co māh o āftāb / ahl-e beyt o īn ketāb-e mostaṭāb*
Deux (objets) précieux comme la lune et le soleil / La Famille de (ma) Demeure et ce Livre sublime.'

Il s'agit évidemment de la tradition prophétique des 'deux objets précieux' (*ḥadīth al-thaqalayn*): 'Je vous laisse, après moi, deux objets précieux, le Livre de Dieu et ma famille.'[52]

39. *ʿĀlemān-e ahl-e beyt-e moṣṭafā*[53] */ hamco qorʾān būde har yek bar shomā*
Les sages initiateurs (i.e. les Imams) parmi la Famille de la Demeure de Muṣṭafā / Sont, chacun pour vous, identiques au Qur'an

*ʿĀlim*, en persan *ʿālem*, ici au pluriel *ʿālemān*, littéralement 'savant', est un des titres les plus récurrents des Imams et signifie, plus particulièrement dans le corpus Imamite ancien et dans la 'tradition ésotérique non-rationnelle', le maître ou le sage qui initie surtout à un enseignement secret.[54] Selon le second hémistiche, Mollā Ṣadrā semble opter pour l'égalité entre les Deux Objets Précieux, le Qur'an et la Famille prophétique. C'est que dans certaines versions du *ḥadīth al-thaqalayn*, rapportées aussi bien par les sources Shiʿi que Sunni, il est explicitement dit que l'un des Deux Objets, que la majorité des exégètes identifie au Qur'an, est supérieur à l'autre (*al-thaqalayn aḥaduhumā akbar min al-ākhar*).[55] Cependant une version typiquement Shiʿi du hadith est: 'Je vous laisse, après moi, deux objets précieux: le Livre de Dieu et ʿAlī b. Abī Ṭālib et sachez que pour vous ʿAlī est supérieur au Livre de Dieu car, pour vous, il en est l'interprète',[56] c'est-à-dire que sans l'interprétation de l'Imam, le Qur'an reste incompréhensible; ce qui touche bien entendu la notion Shiʿi de la figure de l'Imam comme interprète par excellence du Qur'an, l'Imam comme langue du Qur'an ou comme 'le Qur'an parlant' (*kitāb Allāh al-nāṭiq, qurʾān nāṭiq*). Ce dont parle d'ailleurs le vers suivant:

40. *Har yekī zīshān kalām-e nāṭeqī / rāh-e ḥaqq rā nūr-e īsḥān sāʾeqī*
Chacun d'entre eux (i.e. les Imams) est un verbe parlant / Leur lumière est un guide sur le chemin du Réel.[57]
41. *Gar nadādī nūr-e shān dīn rā neẓām / montasher gashtī dayājīr-e ẓalām*

Si leur lumière (aux Imams) n'ordonnait pas la religion / La poussière des ténèbres (ou 'de l'injustice') se serait répandue partout.

42. *Gar nabūdī kashtī-ye anvār-e shān*[58] / *dar jahālat gharqe gashtī ens o jān*[59]
Si l'Arche de leurs lumières n'existait pas / Toutes les créatures (litt. les humains et les *djinns*) seraient noyées dans l'ignorance.

43. *Ahl-e beyt-e anbiyā zīnsān bodand / ke najāt-e ommat az nīrān bodand*[60]
Les Familles des Demeures des prophètes ont toutes été ainsi / Sauvant des feux leur communauté.

44. *Har ke bāshad 'ālem-e rāh-e khodā / īn safīne sāzad az bahr-e hodā*
Tout sage sur le chemin de Dieu / Se tient à cet Arche pour se faire guider.

Le mot persan *kashtī* (vers 42), comme le terme arabe *safīna* (vers 44) font allusion au célèbre hadith prophétique de l'Arche de Noé: 'Les Gens de ma Famille sont à l'exemple de l'Arche de Noé; quiconque y prend place est sauvé et quiconque s'en écarte est noyé.'[61] Ainsi, Mollā Ṣadrā passe de 'Alī aux autres Imams de la Famille du Prophète. Tout comme 'Alī, leur père à tous, les Imams sont les instruments de l'intériorité du Qur'an, les messagers de la dimension ésotérique de la religion de Moḥammad. C'est pourquoi dans ses quatre derniers vers, le poète revient à la charge contre 'les gens de l'extériorité', ceux qu'il avait appelé auparavant *aṣḥāb-e badan* (ci-dessus vers 16), les faux savants qui, ne connaissant pas 'les secrets et les intentions' des préceptes religieux et recherchant les plaisirs mondains, vendent leur religion et leur foi. Ces vers finaux semblent résumer le propos de Mollā Ṣadrā dans *Seh aṣl* (écrit comme on le sait contre une certaine catégorie de théologiens-juristes littéralistes) et encore plus précisément, ils résument les 'trois fondements' (qui ont donnée le titre de l'ouvrage) des obstacles à la gnose transformatrice: l'ignorance de la réalité et du but ultime de l'existence humaine qui ne doit être en fait qu'une étape préparatoire pour le voyage vers l'Autre Monde (*ākherat*),[62] l'amour du pouvoir, de la richesse, des passions basses et des plaisirs mondains qui tous, ternissant le cœur, empêchent la connaissance de soi,[63] et enfin les pièges et les ruses de l'égo à cause desquels les réalités se montrent à l'envers, le bien passe pour le mal et le mal pour le bien:[64]

45. *Kār-e jāhel nīst*[65] *gheyr az sokhriyat / nīst jān āgah ze*[66] *asrār o niyat*
L'ignorant ne fait que se moquer de tout / Certes, il ne connaît ni les secrets ni les intentions.

46. *Ṭab'-e jāhel hamco ṭeflān tā abad /'ākef āmad*[67] *sūy-e ladhdhāt-e jasad*
Comme des enfants, sa nature reste perpétuellement / Captive des plaisirs du corps mortel.

47. *Ṣan'at-e donyā safīne sākhtan / kār-e nādān*[68] *dīn be donyā bākhtan*
Le Grand Œuvre dans ce monde c'est de préparer son Arche / Alors que l'ignorant ne fait qu'échanger sa foi contre ce bas monde.

48. *Īn safīne sāzad az bahr-e najāt / ān hamī dar baḥr-e donyā gashte māt*[69]

L'un construit l'Arche pour le salut / L'autre reste ballotté au milieu de l'océan du monde.

Il est intéressant de noter comment Mollā Ṣadrā établit, dans les deux derniers vers et à travers les images de l'Arche (*safīna*) et du Grand Œuvre alchimique (*ṣanʿa*), une équivalence entre les Imams et leurs enseignements d'une part et le corps de résurrection de l'autre. Il semble que selon cette pensée, qui toucherait la notion sadrienne du 'mouvement substantiel' (*al-ḥaraka al-jawhariyya*), l'assimilation de l'enseignement sacré des Imams marque, par une alchimie intérieure, l'intensification de l'être et l'élaboration du corps de résurrection qui traverse le monde sensible pour atteindre le salut dans l'au-delà.[70] Nous y reviendrons.

Terminons notre propos avec quelques mots sur la forme et le contenu du poème. Celui-ci appartient au genre poétique qu'on appelle *ghadīriyya*, poème de célébration de la Figure et de la *walāya* de ʿAlī, puisque l'événement de Ghadīr Khumm, d'après la tradition Shiʿi, en fut l'occasion par excellence. Il semble que ce genre composé en persan était particulièrement prisé des penseurs et philosophes d'époque safawide. Nous ont en effet laissé des *ghadīriyya*: Fayyāḍ Lāhījī (m. 1072/1661),[71] Lāmiʿ Darmiyānī (m. 1076/1665),[72] Fayḍ Kāshānī (m. 1091/1680)[73] ou encore Ḥazīn Lāhījī (né en 1103/1691).[74] Mollā Ṣadrā y a constamment recours à deux procédés poétiques complémentaires: le *talmīḥ*, allusion furtive à un sujet que l'auditeur (ou le lecteur) est censé connaître, et le *iḍmār*, littéralement 'introduire dans la conscience', *ḍamīr*, qui consiste à ne prononcer que le début ou un fragment d'un énoncé célèbre, poussant ainsi l'auditeur (ou le lecteur) à en reconstituer mentalement le reste.[75] Le procédé est aussi ancien que constant dans les *ghadīriyya* persanes, puisqu'on le rencontre, du 4ᵉ/10ᵉ siècle, chez un Kasāʾī Marwazī (m. 341/952)[76] aux 8ᵉ et 9ᵉ/14ᵉ et 15ᵉ siècles, chez un Shāh Niʿmatullāh Walī (m. 834/1430).[77]

Sur le plan formel, le *mathnavī* de Mollā Ṣadrā ne présente donc rien d'original. L'apport personnel du penseur réside surtout dans la nature et le contenu de ses vers. D'abord, les procédés de *talmīḥ* et de *iḍmār* sont partout appliqués aux données relevant du Qur'an, du hadith et de la *sīra*. Le poème s'appuie donc exclusivement sur les disciplines traditionnelles (*naqlī*) et non sur les sciences spéculatives (*ʿaqlī*). Ensuite, le poème sur ʿAlī, on l'a vu, est écrit dans la même veine que les *Seh aṣl*. On peut y entendre résonner, entre les lignes, l'écho des souffrances et du long exil qu'a dû subir le philosophe de Shiraz à cause de certains *fuqahāʾ*.[78] Mollā Ṣadrā fut lui-même juriste et théologien, on le sait mais on l'oublie souvent.[79] Pourtant, en plus des *Seh aṣl*, épître monographique sur le sujet, dans de nombreux endroits de son œuvre, il n'a pas manqué d'attaquer les religieux fréquentant les cercles du pouvoir safawide ou encore ceux d'entre eux qui, selon lui, négligeaient la connaissance de la dimension ésotérique (*ʿilm al-bātin*) du Shiʿisme, soit par ignorance soit par hypocrisie.[80] Les mêmes religieux que son célèbre disciple et gendre Fayḍ Kāshānī appelle ironiquement 'les détenteurs des turbans' (*arbāb-e ʿamāʾem*) ou encore 'les enturbannés, savants mondains de la masse' (*ahl-e 'amāme va dastār ke dāneshmandān-e donyā va 'olamā-ye 'avāmmand*).[81] Dans le sens inverse, au sein des milieux religieux, Mollā Ṣadrā n'a jamais cessé d'être considéré par certains comme un hérétique notoire. Chose curieuse, il paraît qu'il n'est pas tant accusé à cause de sa pratique de la philosophie que parce qu'il est perçu et dénoncé comme un habile théoricien du Sufisme.[82] Il s'agit manifestement, chez ces détracteurs, d'une confusion (délibérée?) entre la gnose mystique (*'irfān*) à laquelle se rattache Mollā Ṣadrā, et le Sufisme contre une certaine forme duquel celui-ci a pourtant écrit son *Kasr aṣnām al-jāhiliyya*.[83] Dans un tel contexte historique de conflits des idées, la nature traditionaliste du poème prend un sens tout à fait particulier, celui d'affronter l'adversaire sur son propre terrain. Et ce d'autant plus que le véritable centre de gravité du poème se trouve incontestablement dans son insistance sur la présentation de 'Alī et les autres Imams de sa descendance comme les combattants du *ta'wīl* et par conséquent la présentation de leurs ennemis comme les adversaires du *ta'wīl*. Il est intéressant de noter que plus de la moitié des vers du poème, aussi bien dans l'édition Khājavī que dans celle de Fayḍī, ont directement trait à ces deux sujets. Quelques autres y sont indirectement liés. En fondant son discours sur des exégèses Imamites des plus traditionnelles du Qur'an et du Ḥadīth, et plus particulièrement sur la célèbre tradition du 'combattant du *ta'wīl*', Mollā Ṣadrā ne fait lui-même rien d'autre qu'une herméneutique spirituelle de la Figure de 'Alī, de ses combats et de ses adversaires. Ailleurs, il écrit explicitement que la science divine par excellence, la connaissance qui transforme l'être, puisqu'elle est fondée sur la contemplation (*mushāhada*) et le dévoilement (*mukāshafa*), n'est rien d'autre que la connaissance du sens caché du Qur'an et du Ḥadīth.[84] Autrement dit, le *ta'wīl*, en tant qu'herméneutique spirituelle débouchant sur le discernement du sens caché sous la lettre des textes sacrés, constitue la clé de la gnose transformatrice. Aucune autre science ne possède une telle vertu:

> Alors la noble science divine … quelle est-elle? Le droit, la rhétorique ou bien la théologie spéculative? La philologie, la grammaire, la médecine, l'astrologie ou la philosophie? La géométrie, l'arithmétique, l'astronomie ou la physique? Non, aucune de ces sciences, prise isolément (*hic yek az afrād-e īn 'ulūm*), ne possède ce rang sublime. Elle est exclusivement contenue dans la science des aspects ésotériques du Qur'an et du ḥadīth et non dans la lettre (de ces textes) à laquelle peut avoir accès n'importe qui (*īn 'elm monḥaṣer ast dar 'elm-e boṭūn-e qor'ān va ḥadīth na ẓāher-e ānce fahm-e hame kas bedān mīrasad*).[85]

Dans ses autres ouvrages également, plus précisément dans ses différents prologues (et/ou épilogues), Mollā Ṣadrā insiste, parfois lourdement, sur l'importance, dans le processus du perfectionnement de soi, de la conjugaison de la piété, du dévoilement spirituel et de la découverte du sens caché des textes sacrés du Shi'isme.[86] Dans ce sens, les autres sciences, y compris la philosophie, ne sont que des sciences préparatoires de *la* Science par excellence qu'est le *ta'wīl*. Les derniers vers du poème sur 'Alī semble indiquer que, selon notre philosophe, cette connaissance joue un rôle central dans le Grand Œuvre spirituel, la constitution du corps subtil de résurrection. Tout au long de son œuvre, et très explicitement dans *Seh aṣl*,[87] Mollā Ṣadrā présente ce qu'il appelle la véritable Science, *'ilm*, comme une connaissance intégrale où l'expérience intérieure, le dévoilement spirituel (*mokāshafa*) soutenue par l'inspiration divine (*ilhām*) et la science de la face cachée des réalités s'appellent, se déterminent et se complètent, faisant du fidèle un sage divin (*ḥakīm muta'allih*), un homme de vision intérieure (*baṣīr*) parmi les 'gens des cœurs' (*aṣḥāb al-qulūb*).[88] Le regretté Moḥammad Taqī Dāneshpažūh n'avait sans doute pas tort lorsqu'il écrivait que Mollā Ṣadrā, dans son insistance sur l'importance du *bāṭin* et du *ta'wīl*, semble aller plus loin que des théosophes mystiques tels que Ḥaydar Āmolī, Rajab Bursī ou encore Ibn Abī Jumhūr Aḥsā'ī.[89] Pour Mollā Ṣadrā, le véritable savant Shi'i, l'authentique continuateur de la voie des Imams, en l'occurrence lui-même, doit être par-dessus tout un combattant du *ta'wīl*.

## Notes

*Neuvième article de la série consacrée aux 'Aspects de l'imamologie duodécimaine' (abr. AID) I: 'Remarques sur la divinité de l'Imam', *SIr*, 25 (1996), pp. 193–216. II: 'Contribution à la typologie des rencontres avec l'imam caché', *JA*, 284 (1996), pp. 109–135. III: 'L'Imam dans le ciel. Ascension et initiation', dans M. A. Amir-Moezzi, éd., *Le voyage initiatique en terre d'Islam. Ascensions célestes et itinéraires spirituels* (Louvain-Paris, 1997), pp. 99–116. IV: 'Seul l'homme de Dieu est humain. Théologie et anthropologie mystique à travers l'exégèse imamite ancienne', *Arabica*, 45 (1998), pp. 193–214. V: 'Savoir c'est Pouvoir. Exégèses et implications du miracle dans l'Imamisme ancien', dans D. Aigle, éd., *Miracle et karāma. Hagiographies médiévales comparées* (Turnhout-Paris, 2000), pp. 251–286. VI: 'Fin du Temps et Retour à l'Origine', *Revue du Monde Musulman et de la Méditerranée*, no. spécial 91–94 (2001), 'Millénarisme et Messianisme en Islam', pp. 55–74. VII: 'Une absence remplie de présences. Herméneutiques de l'Occultation chez les Shaykhiyya', *BSOAS*, 64 (2001), pp. 1–18; (version anglaise dans éd. W. Ende and R. Brunner, *The Twelver Shia in Modern Times*, Leiden, 2001, pp. 38–57). VIII: 'Visions d'imams en mystique imamite moderne et contemporaine', dans éd. E. Chammont *et alii*, *Autour de regard: Mélanges islamologiques offerts à Daniel Gimaret* (Louvain et Paris, 2003), pp. 97–124.

Par ailleurs, étant donné le contexte iranien de cette étude ainsi que la langue du texte analysé, les transcriptions sont le plus souvent faites selon la prononciation persane.

1. Ṣadr al-Dīn Shīrāzī (Mullā Ṣadrā), *Seh aṣl*, éd. S. Ḥ. Naṣr (Téhéran 1340 Sh./1380/1961), *Montakhab-e mathnavī*, pp. 131–153 (d'après deux manuscrits: no 849 de la collection Meshkāt de la Bibliothèque Centrale de l'Université de Téhéran et le manuscrit personnel de Mr Lājevardī de Qomm); *robā'īyāt*, pp. 159–160 (d'après le manuscrit autographe de Mollā Ṣadrā, *Sharḥ al-hidāya*, collection Meshkāt no 254, ainsi que ses *rasā'il*, et encore *Riyāḍ al-'ārifīn* de Hedāyat, *Shams al-tawārīkh* de Golpāyegānī et *al-Dharī'a* de Āghā Bozorg Ṭehrānī).

2. Mollā Ṣadrā, *Majmū'e-ye ash'ār*, éd. M. Khājavī (Téhéran, 1376 Sh./1418/1997),

*Montakhab-e mathnavī*, pp. 79–100; *robā'īyāt*, p.78. Les autres poèmes, pp. 3–78, sont édités d'après deux manuscrits: no. 2992 de Majles de Téhéran et no. 322-D de la Faculté de Théologie de la Bibliothèque Centrale de l'Université de Téhéran. Auteur de *Lawāmi' al-'ārifīn fī aḥwāl Ṣadr al-muta'allihīn* (Téhéran, 1366 Sh./1987), M. Khājavī a édité et traduit en persan, pendant les deux dernières décennies à Téhéran, quelques ouvrages majeurs de Mollā Ṣadrā comme *Mafātīḥ al-ghayb*, *Asrār al-āyāt*, plusieurs *Tafsīrs* ou encore *Sharḥ al-Uṣūl min al-Kāfī*.

3. Moṣṭafā Fayḍī, éd., *Mathnavī-ye Mollā Ṣadrā* (Qomm, 1376 Sh./1417/1997); *Mathnavī*, pp. 102–205.

4. Dans sa (trop) courte préface, Dr Sayyid Maḥmūd Mar'ashī, actuel directeur de la Bibliothèque Mar'ashī, écrit rapidement que ce manuscrit provient de ce qui a survécu de la bibliothèque de Muḥsin Fayḍ Kāshānī (m. 1091/1680), disciple et gendre de Mollā Ṣadrā, ajoutant, sans aucun argument, qu'il s'agit sans doute d'un manuscrit autographe (*Mathnavī-ye Mollā Ṣadrā*, pp. 3–4). En plus d'une assez mauvaise reproduction d'un folio non numéroté (*Mathnavī-ye Mollā Ṣadrā*, p. 5), c'est tout ce qui nous est présenté au sujet de ce manuscrit. Dans son introduction de près d'une centaine de pages sur le philosophe, son milieu et son œuvre, l'éditeur n'en dit pas un mot non plus (*Mathnavī-ye Mollā Ṣadrā*, pp. 7–102).

5. C'est ce que fait par exemple M. Khājavī (*Majmū'e-ye ash'ār*, pp. 77–78) avec les sept vers en persan du commentaire du verset de la Lumière (Mollā Ṣadrā, *Tafsīr āyat al-nūr*, éd. M. Khājavī (Téhéran, 1362 Sh./1403/1993), p. 182 (texte arabe), p. 99 (trad. persane); mais il y en a d'autres, par exemple à la suite du commentaire du Qur'an 32, *al-Sajda*: 4 (Mollā Ṣadrā, *Tafsīr*, litho., Téhéran, s.d., p. 531) ou encore tout le long des *Seh aṣl*.

6. Sur l'eschatologie ṣadrienne voir maintenant Ch. Jambet, *Se rendre immortel,* suivi du *Traité de la résurrection* (traduction de la *Risālat al-ḥashr*) *de Mollā Ṣadrā Shīrāzī* (Paris, 2000).

7. *Seh aṣl*, pp. xxxiii–xxxiv; *Majmū'e-ye ash'ār*, pp. xii–xv. On aurait pu penser que les vers supplémentaires de l'édition Fayḍī dans *Mathnavī-ye Mollā Ṣadrā* seraient des ajouts ultérieurs du philosophe, mais, comme on le verra plus loin, la grande médiocrité de certains de ces vers semble affaiblir une telle hypothèse.

8. *Majmū'e-ye ash'ār*, p. xii. Seul le manuscrit unique utilisé par M. Fayḍī semble les présenter comme un seul ensemble.

9. *Majmū'e-ye ash'ār*, p. xiii.

10. Tous les poèmes de la *majmū'e* sont de mètre *ramal musaddas mahdhūf* (*fā'ilātun fā'ilātun fā'ilun*), mètre habituel des *mathnavīs* mystiques persans. Certains poèmes offrent une suite logique et constituent manifestement un ensemble cohérent (par exemple les 10 ou 11 derniers poèmes du Recueil consacrés à l'eschatologie); d'autres, touchant des thèmes religieux, philosophiques, mystiques etc. paraissent souvent comme des morceaux indépendants les uns des autres.

11. *Majmū'e-ye ash'ār*, pp. 7–11; *Mathnavīye Mollā Ṣadrā*, pp. 107–110 (titre: 'de l'éloge du prince des croyants'; comme on le verra plus tard, dans cette édition, les 13 derniers vers du poème sont présentés séparément, sous le titre de 'de l'éloge de la Famille de la Demeure'). Sur la traduction de *ahl al-bayt* (*ahl-e beyt* en persan) par 'Famille de la Demeure', voir M. A. Amir-Moezzi, 'Considérations sur l'expression *dīn 'Alī*. Aux origines de la foi shiite', *ZDMG*, 150 (2000), pp. 29–68, notes 36 et 55 et les textes afférents.

12. Ou bien *Lā fatā illā ʿAlī la sayfa illā dhu'l-faqār;* voir par exemple Furāt al-Kūfī, *Tafsīr*, éd. M. al-Kāẓim (Téhéran, 1410/1990), p. 95; Ibn Bābūye al-Ṣadūq, *Maʿānī'l-akhbār*, éd. ʿA. A. Ghaffārī (Téhéran, 1379/1959), pp. 63 et 119; id., *al-Khiṣāl*, même éditeur (Qomm, 1403/1983), pp. 550 et 557; id., *ʿIlal al-sharāʾiʿ* (Najaf, 1385/1966), pp. 7 et 160. Sur Dhu'l-faqār, littéralement '(sabre) à échine' (à double tranchant?), apporté selon la tradition par l'ange Gabriel à Moḥammad et transmis par celui-ci à ʿAlī, voir par ex. al-Ṣaffār al-Qommī, *Baṣāʾir al-darajāt*, éd. M. Kūtchebāghī (Tabriz, 2de éd., s.d. [vers 1960]), section 4 du chapitre 4; al-Kulaynī, *al-Uṣūl min al-Kāfī*, éd. J. Muṣṭafawī (Téhéran, s.d.), 4 vols., *'kitāb al-ḥujja'*, *bāb mā ʿinda l-aʾimma min silāḥ rasūli llāh*, vol. 1, pp. 337 sqq.; Ibn Bābūye al-Ṣadūq, *Amālī* (*al-Majālis*), éd., Ṭabāṭabāʾī Yazdī (Téhéran, 1404/1984), *'majlis'* 17, p. 71 et *'majlis'* 48, p. 289. Sur la prononciation *faqār* et non *fiqār*, plus conventionnelle, voir Abū ʿUbayd al-Bakrī, *Muʿjam mā staʿjam*, éd. M. al-Saqqā (Le Caire, 1364–1371/1945–1951), vol. 1, p. 156 et vol. 3, p. 1026.

13. Sur ʿAlī comme celui qui abreuve les croyants (i.e. les Shiʿa) le Jour de la Résurrection – *sāqī l-muʾminīn fī'l-qiyāma* – ou qui abreuve les habitants du paradis par l'eau du fleuve Kawthar – *sāqī min nahr al-kawthar* – voir al-Majlisī, *Biḥār al-anwār*, éd. sur la base de celle de Kumpānī (Téhéran-Qomm, 1376–1392/1956–1972), 90 tomes en 110 vols., vol. 39, p. 61, vol. 17, p. 324, vol. 26, p. 264. Pour le mystérieux terme qur'anique *kawthar*, voir le Qur'an, *al-kawthar* 108:1.

14. *Mathnavī-ye Mollā Ṣadrā* a ici *az zabān o tīgh* (par sa langue et son son sabre), ce qui ne correspond pas au contexte. Cette édition Fayḍī comporte en outre un quatrième vers qui ne figure pas dans l'édition Khājavī:

> *ennamā vo hal atā dar sha'n-e ū / qāʾed-e īmān-e mā īmān-e ū*
> '*innamā* et *hal atā* sont (révélés) à son sujet / le commandant de notre foi est sa foi à lui.

Sur *innamā* et *hal atā*, deux expressions qur'aniques, voir ci-après respectivement les vers 29 et 30 ainsi que les explications et notes afférentes.

15. Ce quatrième vers de l'édition Khājavī est le onzième de l'édition Fayḍī.

16. *Majmūʿe-ye ashʿār*, pp. 47–48.

17. Sur le *ʿaql* et ses différentes significations (raison, intelligence, hiéro-intelligence) dans la littérature Imamite ancienne, voir M. A. Amir-Moezzi, *Le Guide divin dans le shīʿisme originel* (Paris, 1992), pp. 15–33; voir aussi D. S. Crow, 'The Role of al-ʿAql in Early Islamic Wisdom, with Reference to Imām Jaʿfar al-Ṣādiq' (PhD, McGill University, 1996).

18. Dans l'édition Fayḍī, le second hémistiche est: *vīn khalīfe hamco forqān āmadī*; 'et ce calife (i.e. ʿAlī) sert à distinguer le bien et le mal.'

19. H. Corbin, *En Islam iranien* (Paris, 1971–1972), vol. 1, tout le Livre Premier, en particulier chapitre VI, id., *Histoire de la philosophie islamique* (Paris, 1986), partie II-A, surtout pp. 69–85; M. A. Amir-Moezzi, 'AID III'(cf. ci-dessus la note préliminaire), en particulier pp. 110–116. Pour la position de Mollā Ṣadrā sur les rapports entre la prophétie et la *walāya*, on consultera avec intérêt les pages magistralement synthétiques de ses *Mafātīḥ al-ghayb*, éd. M. Khājavī (Téhéran, 1363 Sh./1994), 'Miftāḥ' 14, '*Inna li'l-nubuwwa bāṭinan wa huwa'l-walāya*', pp. 483–495, trad. persane de M. Khājavī (Téhéran, 1363 Sh./1404/1994), pp. 810–825.

20. L'édition Fayḍī comporte ici un vers supplémentaire, poétiquement fort médiocre

et philosophiquement confus: *āncenān ke ʿaql-e kol bā nafs-e kol* (faut-il lire *kel* pour faire rimer avec *monfaṣel*?) / *hast ān yek mojmal o īn monfaṣel* (faut-il lire *monfaṣol* pour faire rimer avec *kol*?); 'Tout comme l'Intellect universel à l'égard de l'Ame universelle / le premier est condensé, la seconde est séparée (i.e. détaillée?).'

21. Par ex. al-Ṣaffār, *Baṣā'ir al-darajāt*, pp. 11–12; al-Kulaynī, *al-Uṣūl min al-Kāfī*, vol. 1, pp. 77 sqq. M. M. Bar-Asher a raison de présenter cette notion comme un fondement méthodologique de l'exégèse Imamite; voir son *Scripture and Exegesis in Early Imāmī Shiism* (Leiden et Jérusalem, 1999), pp. 92–93.

22. Furāt al-Kūfī, *Tafsīr*, pp. 117–120; ʿAlī b. Ibrāhīm al-Qommī, *Tafsīr*, éd., rééd. T. al-Mūsawī al-Jazā'irī (Beyrouth, 1411/1991), vol. 1, p. 190; Abu'l-Naḍr al-ʿAyyāshī, *Tafsīr*, éd. H. Rasūlī Maḥallātī (Qomm, 1380/1960), vol. 1, pp. 292–293 (selon le *ḥadīth* no 21 rapporté par al-ʿAyyāshī, la révélation qur'anique, faite par l'ange Gabriel, un vendredi et jour de *ʿarafāt*, contenait à l'origine l'expression 'par l'Amitié divine de ʿAlī fils d'Abū Ṭālib': *al-yawma akmaltu lakum dīnakum* bi-walāyat ʿAlī b. Abī Ṭālib *wa atmamtu ʿalaykum niʿmatī* ... .) Ceci touche bien entendu la croyance Shiʿi ancienne selon laquelle la vulgate ʿuthmānienne est une version falsifiée et censurée de la révélation qur'anique originelle; voir à cet égard E. Kohlberg, 'Some Notes on the Imamite Attitude to the Qur'an', dans éd. S. M. Stern et al., *Islamic Philosophy and the Classical Tradition: Essays Presented by his friends and pupils to Richard Walzer* (Oxford, 1972), pp. 209–224; T. Lawson, 'Note for the Study of the Shīʿī Qur'ān', *Journal of Semitic Studies*, 36 (1991), pp. 279–295; M. A. Amir-Moezzi, *Le Guide divin*, pp. 200–227; M. M. Bar-Asher, 'Variant Readings and Additions of the Imāmī-Shīʿa to the Quran', *Israel Oriental Studies*, 13 (1993), pp. 39–74; R. Brunner, *Die Schia und die Koranfälschung* (Würzburg, 2001); pour une vision différente des choses voir H. Modarressi, 'Early Debates on the Integrity of the Qur'ān', *SI*, 77 (1993), pp. 5–39. Sur les différents sens Shiʿi du terme *walāya*, voir *Le Guide divin*, p. 74, note 151.

23. L'édition Fayḍī comporte ici quinze vers supplémentaires:

> *Sāqī-ye kowthar shah-e rūz-e jazā / ebn-e ʿamm-e moṣṭafā serr-e khodā*
> 'L'échanson du Kawthar (voir ci-dessus vers 2), souverain du Jour de la Rétribution (allusion au rôle eschatologique de ʿAlī, appelé souvent *qasīm al-janna wa'l-nār* – celui qui partage (les gens) entre le Jardin (du paradis) et le Feu (de l'enfer)'; voir par ex. Furāt, *Tafsīr*, p. 178, al-ʿAyyāshī, *Tafsīr*, vol. 2, pp. 17–18) / le cousin germain de Moṣṭafā, le secret de Dieu'.
> Le vers suivant, onzième de l'édition Fayḍī, est le quatrième vers de l'édition Khājavī.
> *Man gedāyam āmade dar kū-ye to/mīzanam shay'un lelāhi* (sic. Le mètre est déficient) *az rū-ye to*
> Je suis un mendiant parvenu à ta ruelle (ô ʿAlī)/te suppliant de m'accorder la vision de ta face (littéralement: disant *shay'un li'llāh* – quelque chose pour (plaire à) Dieu (la supplication des mendiants) – au sujet de ta face).
> *Gar to khānī ommat-e khīsham yekī* (sic; très maladroitement dit)/*jān daham bar yād-e rūyat bī shakī*
> Si tu me considères comme un de tes fidèles (litt. communauté)/j'offrirai sans doute ma vie à la seule pensée de ton visage.

*Āftābī var bekhānī dharre-am/tāj-e raf'at bogzarad az sedre-am*
Tu es soleil, appelle-moi ton atome/et la couronne de ma gloire dépassera l'Arbre céleste (allusion à la *Sidrat al-muntahā* qur'anique, Qur'an, *al-Najm* 53 :14–16).
*Man kī am gomgashte-yī dar rāh-e to/khāk būs o bande-ye dargāh-e to*
Qui suis-je? Un égaré sur ton chemin (ô 'Alī)/baisant la poussière et serviteur de ton Seuil.
*Gar to khānī ommat-e 'āṣī-ye khad (= khod)/man fedā sāzam del o jān tā abad*
Si tu me considères comme un compagnon même pécheur/j'en sacrifierai éternellement cœur et âme.
*Ommat-e 'āṣī ṭalab kār-e to ast/gar bad ast ar nīk dar kār-e to ast*
Ton compagnon pécheur est ton créancier/méchant ou bon, il ne cherche que toi.
*Īn bas-am kaz bandegān bāsham torā/bande ce kāsh az sagān bāsham torā*
Il me suffit d'être parmi tes serviteurs/que dis-je? Il me suffit amplement d'être ton chien.
*Har ke rā con to shahanshāhī bovad/farq-e ū az haft gardūn bog zarad*
Celui qui t'a comme grand roi/aura la tête plus haute que les sept cieux.
*Gīsovānat hast ān ḥablo l-matīn/ke forū hesht-ast az carkh-e barīn*
Tes cheveux sont cette anse solide (Qur'an 3, *Āl 'Imrān*: 103 et 112)/descendue du plus haut du ciel.
*Tā biyāvīzand dar vey ommatān/az belā-ye īn jahān yāband amān.*
Afin que les compagnons s'y agrippent/pour être sauvés de l'épreuve de ce monde.
*Ey shafī' al-modhnibīn ey shāh-e dīn/cand bāsham īn conīn zār o ḥazīn?*
toi, intercesseur des pécheur (sur la *shafā'a* des Imams, voir maintenant M. M. Bar-Asher, *Scripture and Exegesis in Early Imāmī Shiism*, Leiden, 1999, pp. 180 sqq.), souverain de la foi/jusque quand dois-je rester si misérable, si triste?
*Rū-ye to hast āyatī az kardegār/mū-ye to bahr-e najāt-e jormkār*
Ta face est un signe de Dieu/ta chevelure, le salut du fautif (sur le couple 'face et chevelure', voir ci-après vers 35).
*Rū-ye to bāshad behesht o mū-ye to/gashte āvīzān be mā az rū-ye to*
Ton visage est le paradis et ta chevelure/descend de ton visage jusqu'à nous.
*Hamco lafẓ o ma'nī-ye qor'ān be mā/gashte nāzel bahr-e ḥājat az samā*
Tout comme le Qur'an, dans sa lettre et son contenu/descendu du ciel pour répondre à nos besoins.

24. Sur la relation métaphysique de Moḥammad avec les prophètes et de 'Alī avec les Imams/ *awliyā* voir U. Rubin, 'Pre-existence and light. Aspects of the concept of Nūr Muḥammad', *Israel Oriental Studies*, 5 (1975), pp. 62–112; *id.*, 'Prophets and Progenitors in the Early Shī'a Tradition', *Jerusalem Studies in Arabic and Islam*, 1 (1979), pp. 41–65; M. A. Amir-Moezzi, *Le Guide divin*, parties II–1 et II–2, pp. 73–112; *id.*, 'Cosmology and Cosmogony in Twelver Shī'ism', *EIr*, vol. 6, pp. 317–322, en particulier pp. 319–321.

25. Allusion soit à l'épisode de Ghadīr Khumm où, selon certaines versions, Moḥammad prit 'Alī sur son épaule (voir L. Veccia Vaglieri, 'Ghadīr Khumm', *EI2*), soit à l'épisode où, pour enlever les idoles qui se trouvaient sur le toit de la Ka'ba, Moḥammad fit monter 'Alī sur son épaule (épisode appelé *iṣ'ādu l-nabī 'aliyyan 'alā saṭḥi l-ka'ba*): voir al-Muwaffaq b. Aḥmad al-Khwārazmī, *al-Manāqib*, éd. M. al-Maḥmūdī (Qomm, 1411/1991), chapitre 11;

al-Majlisī, *Biḥār al-anwār*, vol. 35, p. 49 et vol. 38, p. 82. La scène évoque pour Mollā Ṣadrā l'image d'un arbre, Moḥammad, portant un fruit, 'Alī, à sa branche (*shākh* signifiant aussi bien 'arbre' que 'branche').

26. M. A. Amir-Moezzi, 'AID I' (cf. ci-dessus note préliminaire), en particulier p. 200 et note 27 pour les sources anciennes.

27. L'édition Fayḍī comporte ici *ta'bīr* et *tafsīr* au lieu de *tanzīl* et *ta'wīl* de l'édition Khājavī.

28. Edition Fayḍī: *az zabān-e tīgh tafsīr-e kalām/mīnamūd o dād dīn rā entezām*: traduction du second hémistiche: 'Il le fit et consolida ainsi la religion.'

29. Sur cette notion et les sources anciennes sur elle, voir M. A. Amir-Moezzi, 'AID III', en particulier pp. 113–116.

30. *'Inna fīkum man yuqātilu 'alā ta'wīli l-qur'ān kamā qātaltu 'alā tanzīlihi wa huwa 'Alī ibn abī ṭālib*', al-'Ayyāshī, *Tafsīr*, vol. 1, p. 15; al-Khazzāz al-Rāzī, *Kifāyat al-athar* (Qomm, 1401/1980), pp. 76, 88, 117, 135 (à la p. 66, dans une tradition prophétique, c'est le *qā'im* qui est présenté comme 'le combattant du *ta'wīl*'); al-Majlisī, *Biḥār*, vol. 19, pp. 25–26; Hāshim b. Sulaymān al-Baḥrānī, *al-Burhān fī tafsīr al-qur'ān* (Téhéran, s.d.), 5 vols., vol. 1, p. 17. D. Gimaret traduit *ta'wīl* par 'l'esprit' et *tanzīl* par 'la lettre' du Qur'an; V. Shahrastānī, *Livre des religions et des sectes*, vol. 1, trad. D. Gimaret et G. Monnot (Paris-Louvain, 1986), p. 543. Pour d'autres sources voir M. M. Bar-Asher, *Scripture and Exegesis*, p. 88, note 1.

31. *Seh aṣl*, par exemple pp. 10 et 66. D'une manière générale, cet écrit de Mollā Ṣadrā est rédigé contre une certaine catégorie parmi les *fuqahā'*, ceux qui gravitent dans les cercles de pouvoir safawide et/ou ceux qui refusent l'herméneutique spirituelle des textes scripturaires; il en est de même avec un autre de ses livres, *Kasr aṣnām al-jāhiliyya*, éd. M. T. Dānishpažūh (Téhéran, 1340 Sh./1962), principalement dirigé contre les Sufis mais aussi contre les juristes littéralistes. Je vais y revenir.

32. Pour les sources sur la bataille de Nahrawān qui opposa 'Alī à ses adversaires Khārijī, voir l'article de M. Morony dans *EI2*, vol. 7, p. 913.

33. L'édition Fayḍī a *ṣoḥbat* au lieu de *ṣeḥḥat*; ce qui n'a pas de sens.

34. Dans l'édition Fayḍī, au lieu de *ḥedāthat* il y a *conīn farmūde*, 'C'est pourquoi il (i.e. le Prophète) a dit "réparateur de sandale".'

35. Il faut certainement rectifier le *tafsīr* des textes édités en *tanzīl*, puisqu'il s'agit manifestement d'une évocation du hadith cité ci-dessus en note 30. En outre, dans le second hémistiche, l'édition Fayḍī a *shāh-e anbiyā* ('le roi des prophètes') et non *ṣadr-e anbiyā*.

36. Traductions de *ta'wīl* et de *tanzīl* faites selon celles de D. Gimaret, mentionnées ci-dessus en note 30.

37. Soit la sienne propre (Ibn al-Athīr, *al-Nihāya fī gharīb al-ḥadīth wa l-āthār*, éd. al-Zāwī et al-Ṭināḥī, Le Caire, 1963–1966, vol. 2, p. 38; al-Qundūzī, *Yanābī' al-mawadda*, Bombay, s.d., p. 59; al-Baḥrānī, *al-Burhān*, vol. 1, p. 17); soit celle du Prophète (Ibn Ḥanbal, *Musnad*, vol. 3, pp. 31 et 33; al-Muḥibb al-Ṭabarī, *al-Riyāḍ al-naḍira* (réimp. Téhéran, ca. 1985), vol. 2, pp. 52–53). Dans la littérature talmudique, c'est le prophète Enoch (Ukhnūkh / Idrīs en Islam) qui est appellé 'réparateur/couseur de sandales' (en hébreu: *tofer min 'alīm*). Le parallèle mérite une étude indépendante. Je dois l'information à mon collègue de l'Université Hébraîque de Jérusalem, M. M. Bar-Asher, que je remercie cordialement.

38. Pour le rattachement de ce verset à 'Alī voir par ex. al-Baḥrānī, *al-Burhān*, vol. 1, p. 315; al-Fayḍ al-Kāshānī, *al-Ṣāfī fī tafsīr al-Qur'ān*, s.l. (Téhéran?, s.d.), 3 vols., vol. 1, p. 152.

39. Sur le rapport de ce verset avec ʿAlī, voir Furāt al-Kūfī, *Tafsīr*, p. 469; al-Qommī, *Tafsīr*, vol. 2; p. 369, al-Ṭūsī, (*Tafsīr) al-Tibyān*, éd. A. H. Q. al-ʿĀmilī (Najaf, années 1380/1960), 10 vols., vol. 9 (1389/1969), pp. 549–550; al-Faḍl b. al-Ḥasan al-Ṭabrisī/Ṭabarsī, *Majmaʿ al-bayān*, éd. H. al-Rasūlī al-Maḥallātī (Beyrouth, 1379/1959–1960), 10 tomes en 5 vols., vol. 9, p. 253.

40. Al-Qommī, *Tafsīr*, vol. 2, p. 422; al-Ṭūsī, *al-Tibyān*, vol. 10, pp. 204 sqq.; al-Ṭabrisī, *Majmaʿ al-bayān*, vol. 10, pp. 402 sq. D'une manière générale, la sourate '*al-dahr*', dite encore 'al-insān' ou 'hal atā' (les deux premiers mots de la sourate), est rattachée par la tradition Imamite à ʿAlī. Pour '*lā fatā*' du second hémistiche, voir ci-dessus vers 1 et le texte afférent.

41. Voir Ibn Ḥanbal, *Musnad*, 3, 16, ʿAlī b. ʿĪsā al-Irbilī, *Kashf al-ghumma* (Qomm, 1381/1961), vol. 1, p. 212; al-Sayyid ʿAlī al-Hamadhānī, *al-Mawadda fi'l-qurbā*, en marge d'al-Qundūzī, *Yanābīʿ al-mawadda*, p. 48.

42. Sur le rattachement de ce verset à ʿAlī, voir par ex: Furāt al-Kūfī, *Tafsīr*, pp. 123–129; al-ʿAyyāshī, *Tafsīr*, vol. 1, pp. 327–329; al-Ṭūsī, *al-Tibyān*, vol. 3, pp. 549 sqq.; al-Ṭabrisī, *Majmaʿ al-bayān*, vol. 3, pp. 209 sqq.; al-Majlisī, *Biḥār*, vol. 9, pp. 34 sqq.; al-Ḥurr al-ʿĀmilī, *Ithbāt al-hudāt*, éd. H. Rasūlī Maḥallātī (Qomm, s.d.), vol. 3, pp. 542 sqq.; al-Baḥrānī, *al-Burhān*, vol. 1, pp. 482 sqq.

43. Par ex. Ibn Bābūye, *ʿIlal al-sharāʾiʿ*, p. 222; *id.*, *Kamāl al-dīn*, p. 278; *id.*, *ʿUyūn akhbār al-Riḍāʾ* (Téhéran, s.d. [vers 1980]), vol. 1, p. 232 et vol. 2, pp. 10, 59, 194; Ibn Shādhān al-Qommī, *Miʾa manqaba*, éd. N. R. ʿUlwān (Qomm, 1413/1994), '*manqaba*' 57, p. 112; al-Sharīf al-Murtaḍā, *al-Shāfī fi'l-imāma*, éd. litho. (Téhéran, 1301/1884), pp. 148 sqq.; Ibn Shahrāshūb, *Manāqib Āl Abī Ṭālib* (Najaf, 1956) vol. 2, pp. 219 sqq. et vol. 3, p. 46. Aussi M. M. Bar-Asher, *Scripture and Exegesis*, p. 156, note 122.

44. Bien entendu, pour les Imamites, 'la famille de la demeure' qurʾanique désigne ʿAlī, Fāṭima et leurs descendants; voir par ex. Furāt al-Kūfī, *Tafsīr*, pp. 331–342; al-Qommī, *Tafsīr*, vol. 2, pp. 193–194; al-Ṭūsī, *al-Tibyān* (1388/1968), vol. 8, pp. 307–308; al-Ṭabrisī, *Majmaʿ al-bayān*, vol. 8, p. 357. Pour les discussions au sujet de l'expression *ahl al-bayt*, voir M. Sharon, '*Ahl al-Bayt*. People of the House', *Jerusalem Studies in Arabic and Islam*, 8 (1986); *id.*, 'The Umayyads as *Ahl al-Bayt*', *Jerusalem Studies in Arabic and Islam*, 14 (1991); W. Madelung, 'The *Hāshimiyyāt* of al-Kumayt and Hāshimi Shiʿism', *SI*, 70 (1989); *id.*, *The Succession to Muhammad* (Cambridge, 1997), index, s.v.; M. A. Amir-Moezzi, 'Considérations sur l'expression *dīn ʿAlī* ...', voir ci-dessus note 11.

45. Voir par ex. Furāt, *Tafsīr*, pp. 63–64; Ibn Bābūye, *Kamāl al-dīn*, p. 241; *id.*, *Kitāb al-tawḥīd*, éd. al-Ḥusaynī al-Ṭihrānī (Téhéran, 1398/1978), p. 307; *id.*, *al-Khiṣāl*, p. 574; d'une manière générale, pour une bibliographie très riche sur ce hadith, voir *Ṣaḥīfat al-imām al-Riḍā*, éditeur(s) non indiqué(s) (Qomm, 1366 Sh./1408/1987), pp. 123–133.

46. Furāt, *Tafsīr*, p. 206; al-ʿAyyāshī, *Tafsīr*, vol. 2, pp. 203–204; ʿAlī b. al-Ḥusayn b. Bābūye, *al-Imāma wa al-tabṣira min al-ḥayra* (Qomm, 1404/1984), p. 132; Ibn Shādhān, *Miʾa manqaba*, '*manqaba*' 4, p. 44; al-Ṭūsī, *al-Tibyān*, vol. 6, p. 223; al-Ṭabrisī, *Majmaʿ al-bayān*, vol. 6, pp. 278–279; al-Ḥurr al-ʿĀmilī, *Ithbāt al-hudāt*, vol. 3, pp. 548 sqq.; al-Baḥrānī, *al-Burhān*, vol. 2, pp. 277 sqq.

47. Il suffit, pour s'en rendre compte, de feuilleter par exemple le *Nahj al-balāgha*.

48. Voir al-ʿAyyāshī, *Tafsīr*, vol. 2, pp. 220–221; al-Ṭūsī, *al-Tibyān*, vol. 6, pp. 267–268; al-Ṭabrisī, *Majmaʿ al-bayān*, vol. 6, p. 301; al-Majlisī, *Biḥār*, vol. 9, pp. 82–83; al-Baḥrānī, *al-Burhān*, vol. 2, p. 303; al-Kāshānī, *Tafsīr al-ṣāfī*, vol. 1, p. 880.

49. Voir M. A. Amir-Moezzi, *Le Guide divin*, index *s.v. wajh*; *id.*, 'AID I', en particulier pp. 199–202 et p. 211, note 69. Cf. aussi *supra* vers no 12.

50. Dans l'édition Fayḍī, le poème sur 'Alī semble se terminer avec ce vers. Ce qui est quelque peu abrupt. Les vers suivants y sont présentés comme ceux d'un poème consacré à l'éloge des *ahl al-bayt* et du Qur'an (*dar madḥ-e ahl al-bayt 'alayhim al-salām va qor'ān kalām-e elāhī*); *Mathnavī-ye Mollā Ṣadrā*, p. 110.

51. L'édition Fayḍī comporte: *peyrovān o dūstān-e mo'taman.*

52. ... *Innī tārikun fīkum al-thaqalayn kitāba llāh wa 'itratī* ... ; sur cette tradition et ses versions, voir maintenant M. M. Bar-Asher, *Scripture and Exegesis*, pp. 93–98. Pour compléter les sources, voir *Le Guide divin*, p. 215, n. 440 et surtout la riche bibliographie mentionnée par le ou les éditeur(s) de la *Ṣaḥīfat al-imām al-Riḍā*, pp. 135–150.

53. Pour des questions évidentes de sens que l'on va voir tout de suite, je préfère cette lecture *'ālemān-e ahl-e beyt*, 'les sages ... *parmi* la Famille de la Demeure', à la leçon du texte édité: *'ālemān o ahl-e beyt*, 'les sages ... *et* la Famille de la Demeure'. L'édition Fayḍī, quant à elle, comporte *'āmelān-e ahl-e beyt* ... ('les pratiquants parmi la Famille de la Demeure'), et dans le second hémistiche *dā'em rahnomā* ('guidant toujours') au lieu de *har yek bar shomā*.

54. Cf. *Le Guide divin*, partie 3. 2, 'la Science sacrée', pp. 174–199; pour les glissements sémantiques du terme voir M. A. Amir-Moezzi, 'Réflexions sur une évolution du shi'isme duodécimain: tradition et idéologisation', dans E. Patlagean et A. LeBoulluec, éds., *Les retours aux Ecritures. Fondamentalismes présents et passés*, Bibliothèque de l'École des Hautes Études (Louvain et Paris, 1993), vol. 99, pp. 63–82. Sur la 'tradition ésotérique non-rationnelle', voir *Le Guide divin*, pp. 33–48.

55. *Ṣaḥīfat al-imām al-Riḍā*, p. 135 et notes.

56. ... *Kitābu'llāh wa 'Alī b. abī tālib wa a'lamū anna 'aliyyan lakum afdal min kitābi'llāh li-annahu yutarjimu lakum kitāba llāhi ta'ālā*; voir par exemple Ibn Shādhān al-Qommī, *Mi'a manqaba*, '*manqaba*' 86, p. 140; al-Muwaffaq b. Ahmad al-Khwārazmī, *Maqtal al-Ḥusayn* (Najaf, 1367/1948), vol. 1, p. 114; al-Ḥasan b. Moḥammad al-Daylamī, *Irshād al-qulūb ilā l-ṣawāb* (Najaf, 1342/1923), p. 378.

57. Sur cette notion voir M. Ayoub, 'The Speaking Qur'ān and the Silent Qur'ān: A Study of the Principles and Development of Imāmī Tafsīr', dans A. Rippin, éd., *Approaches to the History of the Interpretation of the Qur'ān* (Oxford, 1988), pp. 177–198; M. M. Bar-Asher, *Scripture and Exegesis*, chapitre 3, parties 1 et 2. Ajoutons que le terme *kalām* du premier hémistiche rappelle immanquablement l'expression *kalām Allāh*, Parole ou Verbe de Dieu, c'est-à-dire le Qur'an.

58. L'édition Fayḍī a, au lieu de *anvār-e shān*, *a'lām-e shān* ('Si l'Arche de' 'leur signe' ou 'des plus célèbres parmi eux'(?) 'n'existait pas').

59. Ibid.

60. Edition Fayḍī: *pīrān* ('les vieillards'?) au lieu de *nīrān*; ce qui n'a pas de sens.

61. *Mathalu ahli baytī mathalu safīnati nūḥin man rakibahā najā wa man takhallafa 'anhā ghariqa* (ou bien *zukhkha fi'l-nār*, 'est poussé dans le feu', d'où peut-être 'les feux', *nīrān*, du vers 43). Pour les très nombreuses sources sur ce hadith, voir *Ṣaḥīfat al-imām al-Riḍā*, pp. 116–120.

62. *Seh aṣl*, pp. 13 sqq.

63. Ibid., pp. 28 sq.

64. Ibid., pp. 32 sqq.

65. Edition Faydī: *cīst* au lieu de *nīst*: 'Que fait l'ignorant si ce n'est se moquer de tout?'

66. Edition Fayḍī comporte au lieu de *jān āgah ze: con vāqef bar*; ce qui a la même signification.

67. Edition Fayḍī a *gashte 'ākef* au lieu de *'ākef āmad*; même signification.

68. Edition Fayḍī: *jāhel* au lieu de *nādān;* ce qui évidemment revient au même.

69. L'édition Fayḍī offre une leçon légèrement différente de ce vers: *īn hamī sāzad safīne dar najāt / ān yekī dar baḥr-e donyā gashte māt*. La phraséologie est maladroite mais le sens reste le même.

70. Voir par exemple H. Corbin, *Corps spirituel et Terre céleste* (Paris, 1979), pp. 194–200; *id.*, *La philosophie iranienne islamique aux XVIIe et XVIIIe siècles* (Paris, 1981), pp. 69 sqq.; Ch. Jambet, *Se rendre immortel*, pp. 78 sqq.

71. La *qaṣīda* qui commence ainsi: *Sezā-ye emāmat be ṣūrat be ma'nā / 'aliyye valī ān ke shāhast o mowlā; Dīvān-e Fayyāḍ-e Lāhījī*, A. B. Karīmī, éd. (Téhéran, 1372 Sh./1993), pp. 23–26.

72. '*Maqbūl-e* anta minnī *o mamdūḥ-e* hal atā/*qā'el be qowl-e* law kashaf *o dāfe'-e maḍārr*', *Dīvān-e Lāme'*, éd. M. Rafī'ī et Z. Moṣaffā (Téhéran, 1365 Sh./1986), p. 51.

73. '*Āmadam bar sar-e thanā-ye 'Alī/ey del o jān-e man fedā-ye 'Alī*', Mullā Moḥammad Muḥsin Fayḍ Kāshānī, *Dīvān*, éd. M. F. Kāshānī (Téhéran, 1371 Sh./1992), p. 423.

74. *Āmad saḥar ze kūy-e to dāman keshān ṣabā / ahda s-salāma minka 'alā tābi'i l-hudā*; *Dīvān-e Ḥazīn-e Lāhījī*, éd. B. Taraqqī (Téhéran, 1350 Sh./1971), p. 130.

75. Voir les chapitres consacrés à ces deux procédés (*talmīḥ* est également dit *tamlīḥ*) dans les ouvrages de *badī'* comme par exemple Ṣāḥib b. 'Abbād, *al-Iqnā'* (Qomm, s.d.); Taftāzānī, *Muṭawwal* (Téhéran, 1333 Sh./1955); *id.*, *Mukhtaṣar al-ma'ānī* (Qomm, 1386/1966); al-Qazwīnī al-Khaṭīb, *al-Talkhīṣ* (Le Caire, s.d.). Pour l'utilisation de *talmīḥ* en poésie persane, voir S. Shamīsā, *Farhang-e talmīḥāt* (Téhéran, 1366 Sh./1987), pour celle de *iḍmār*, voir M. Dhākerī, 'Shegerd hā-ye nā ma'lūf dar she'r-e Sa'dī', *Nashr-i Dānish*, 16e année, no 2 (été 1378 Sh./1999), pp. 16–24, en particulier pp. 21–23.

76. '*Fahm kon gar mo'menī faḍl-e amīr al-mo'menīn / faḍl-e ḥeydar shīr-e yazdān morteḍā-ye pākdīn*', M. A. Riyāḥī, *Kasā'ī-ye Marvazī* (Téhéran, 1367 Sh./1988), p. 93. L'authenticité de ce poème n'est cependant pas certaine.

77. '*Ān amīr al-mo'menīn ya'nī 'Alī / vān emām al-mottaqīn ya'nī 'Alī*', *Dīvān-e Shāh Ne'matollāh-e Valī*, éd. J. Nūrbakhsh (Téhéran, 1361 Sh./1982), p. 762; voir également ci-dessus note 72, le poème de Lāmi' Darmiyānī où les deux procédés sont utilisés.

78. Sur cette question et la retraite forcée de plusieurs années de Mollā Ṣadrā à Kahak, petit bourg à proximité de Qomm, voir par exemple S. H. Nasr, introduction à *Seh aṣl*, p. v., H. Corbin, *En Islam iranien*, vol. 4, pp. 60–61; introduction de A. Shafī'īhā à son édition de Mollā Ṣadrā, *al-Wāridāt al-qalbiyya fī ma'rifa al-rubūbiyya* (Téhéran, 1358 Sh./1979), pp. 4–5; M. Khājavī, *Lawāmi' al-'ārifīn*, pp. 23 sqq.

79. Cf. l'introduction de S. H. Nasr a *Seh aṣl*, pp. xi–xii.

80. Voir par exemple *al-Asfār al-arba'a*, éd. litho. (Téhéran, 1282/1865), p. 876; *Sharḥ al-Uṣūl min al-Kāfī*, p. 11; *Tafsīr sūrat al-baqara*, éd. litho. (Téhéran, s.d.), pp. 183 et 450; *Kasr aṣnām al-jāhiliyya*, pp. 32 sqq.

81. Mullā Muhsin Fayḍ Kāshānī, *Sharḥ-e ṣadr* dans *Risālāt* (Téhéran, 1321 Sh./1943), pp. 15–16.

82. C'est du moins ce que donnent à penser les critiques de Yūsuf al-Baḥrānī dans *Lu'lu'at*

*al-Baḥrayn* (Najaf, 1386/1966), *s.n.* Fayḍ Kāshānī (citant Sayyid Niʿmatallāh al-Shūshtarī qui dénonçait la philosophie et surtout le Sufisme de Mollā Ṣadrā) ou encore celles de Mīrzā Ḥusayn al-Nūrī al-Ṭabrisī/Ṭabarsī dans *Mustadrak al-wasā'il*, litho. (Téhéran, n.d.), vol. 3, pp. 422–424, qui reconnaît l'étendue de la science de Mollā Ṣadrā mais ajoute, sur un ton critique, qu'il propage les 'prétentions' des Sufis, attaque fréquemment les *fuqahā'* et admire Ibn ʿArabī. Attaquant le commentaire de Mollā Ṣadrā des *Uṣūl min al-Kāfī* d'al-Kulaynī, al-Nūrī le considère comme un écrit Sufi et cite à son propos le vers satirique d'un auteur qu'il ne nomme pas: 'les commentaires d'*al-Kāfī* sont nombreux et précieux / Or, le premier qui le commenta en infidèle fut Ṣadrā' (*Shurūḥ 'l-kāfī kathīra jalīlatu qadrā / wa awwalu man sharaḥahu bi 'l-kufri ṣadrā*).

83. Cependant, certains Sufis n'ont apparemment pas manqué de se rattacher au *taṣawwuf* de Mollā Ṣadrā, par exemple Moḥammad Karīm Sharīf Qommī dans sa *Tuḥfat al-ʿushshāq* (écrite en 1097/1685; cité par M. T. Dānishpažūh dans son introduction au *Kasr aṣnām al-jāhiliyya*, p. 4) ou Quṭb al-Dīn Moḥammad Nayrīzī Shīrāzī (m. 1173/1759) dans son *Faṣl al-khiṭāb* (cité par M. Istakhrī, *Oṣūl-e taṣavvof*, Téhéran, 1338 Sh./1960, p. 30). Il est vrai que Mollā Ṣadrā semble s'opposer à un Sufisme confrérique qu'il considère comme décadent par rapport au Sufisme originel authentique. Ses critiques n'ont donc rien de commun avec celles par exemple d'un Moḥammad Ṭāhir al-Qommī (m. 1098/1686), *Tuḥfat al-akhyār* (Qomm, 1393/1973) ou encore, bien avant lui, celles du sosie Imamite du Ḥanbalī Ibn al-Jawzī, Murtaḍā b. Dāʿī al-Ḥasanī al-Rāzī (auteur, au 7e/13e s., de la *Tabṣirat al-ʿawāmm fī maʿrifat maqāmāt al-anām*, éd., 2de éd. 'A. Eqbāl (Téhéran, 1364 Sh./1985); selon Āghā Bozorg al-Ṭihrānī le nom de l'auteur est: Jamāl al-Dīn Murtaḍā Moḥammad b. al-Ḥusayn al-Rāzī, voir *al-Dharīʿa ilā taṣānīf al-shīʿa*, Téhéran/Najaf, 1353–1398/1934–1978, 25 vols., vol. 24, p. 123), savants Imamites selon lesquels le Sufisme constitue en soi une déviation hérétique. Sur l'attitude très positive de Mollā Ṣadrā envers le Sufisme ancien voir maintenant N. Pūrjavādī (Pourjavady), 'Ḥallāj va Bāyazīdī az naẓar-e Mollā Ṣadrā', *Nashr-i dānish*, 16e année, no. 3 (été 1378 Sh./1999), pp. 14–24. Sur l'opposition au Sufisme au sein de l'Imamisme, voir *id.*, 'Opposition to Sufism in Twelver Shiism', dans F. de Jong et B. Radtke, éd., *Islamic Mysticism Contested: Thirteen Centuries of Controversies and Polemics* (Leiden, 1999), pp. 614–623.

84. *Seh aṣl*, pp. 74–75 et 83–84.

85. Ibid., p. 84.

86. Par exemple *al-Asfār*, p. 2; *al-Shawāhid al-rubūbiyya fi'l-manāhij al-sulūkiyya*, éd. S. J. Āshtiyānī (Téhéran, 2de éd., 1360 Sh./1981), p. 4; *al-Ḥikmat al-ʿarshiyya*, éd. litho. (Téhéran, 1315/1897), p. 1; (trad. persane de Gh. Ḥ. Āhanī, *ʿArshiyya*, Téhéran, 1341 Sh./1962, p. 2, trad. anglaise de J. W. Morris, *The Wisdom of the Throne*, Princeton, NJ, 1981, pp. 90–92); *Sharḥ al-Uṣūl min al-Kāfī*, tout le prologue; *Asrār al-āyāt*, M. Khājavī, éd. (Téhéran, 1362 Sh./1983), toute la *muqaddima* (trad. persane du même savant, Téhéran, 1363 Sh./1984, pp. 3–55), *al-Wāridāt al-qalbiyya*, pp. 120–121 (texte arabe), pp. 186–187 (trad. persane).

87. En particulier chapitres 8 et 9.

88. Sur la dimension mystique de la pensée de Molla Ṣadrā voir aussi maintenant P. Ballanfat, 'Considérations sur la conception du cœur chez Mullā Sadrā', (1) *Kār-nāmeh*, 5 (1999), pp. 33–46; (2), P. Ballanfat, 'Considérations', *Kār-nāmeh*, 6 (2000), pp. 67–84; J. Eshots, '*al-Wāridāt al-qalbiyya fī maʿrifat al-rubūbiyya*, resāle-yi ʿerfān az yek ḥakīm', *Kherad-nāmeh Ṣadrā*, 15 (1999), pp. 74–82; *id.*, 'Ṣadr al-Dīn Shīrāzī mobtaker-e ḥekmat-e ʿarshī', *Kherad-*

*nāmeh Ṣadrā*, 20 (2000), pp. 61–66; *id.*, 'Unification of Perceiver and Perceived and Unity of Being', *Transcendent Philosophy* 1 (2000), pp. 1–7.

89. Introduction au *Kasr aṣnām al-jāhiliyya*, p. 13. Ainsi, on comprend mal les points de vue de S. Rizvi dans sa recension de l'ouvrage de Ch. Jambet, 'Se rendre immortel', parue dans *Transcendent Philosophy*, 2 (2001), pp. 98–101, lorsqu'en croyant épingler le 'corbinisme' radical de Jambet, il refute le fait que Mollā Ṣadrā ait été un adepte de *ta'wīl* et de la supériorité du *bāṭin* sur le *ẓāhir*. Une telle méconnaissance des écrits sadriens de la part d'un recenseur est tout simplement inadmissible. Il est symptomatique que quelques pages plus tôt, le même chercheur ait publié un compte-rendu exagérément dithyrambique de l'ouvrage de Y. Ch. Bonaud sur la pensée mystique de l'ayatollah Khomeyni (Beyrouth, 1997). L'objectivité scientifique serait-elle ainsi repoussée au second plan par des considérations d'ordre idéologique.

# 32

# Fayḍ al-Kāshānī's *Walāya*: The Confluence of Shiʿi Imamology and Mysticism

*Shigeru Kamada*

With the death of Ḥasan al-ʿAskarī (d. 260/873–874), the eleventh Imam of Ithnāʿasharī Shiʿism in Sāmarrāʾ, his son Muḥammad, the twelfth and last Imam, hid himself too. Muḥammad al-Mahdī maintained contact with his followers through four agents (s., *safīr, nāʾib*) for about seventy years, the period known as the Minor Occultation (*al-ghayba al-ṣughrā*). In 329/941 al-Mahdī cut off all communication. This initiated the Major Occultation (*al-ghayba al-kubrā*) which has continued until the present day. The original concept of the Imam, that he should directly control various affairs of the Muslim community as its active leader, has been greatly modified by the *ghayba* of the Imam of the Time. The period without an absolute authority started then and will continue till the last Imam returns as the Messiah, who will bring justice (*qisṭ*) and righteousness (*ʿadl*) to the world. The orthodox dogma of *ghayba* in Ithnāʿasharī Shiʿism became established as a result of this process of modifying the idea of *imāma*.[1] After the crystallisation of the classical concept of *imāma*, further modifications were introduced into the arguments of certain thinkers, adding different features to the established concept.[2]

This paper deals with a Shiʿi thinker, Muḥsin Fayḍ al-Kāshānī (d. 1091/1680–1681), of Safawid Iran, and tries to understand how he approached and modified the idea of *imāma*. According to Corbin[3] the history of Shiʿi thought can be divided into four periods, the last of which covers the period from the 'Safawid Renaissance' (the first half of the seventeenth century CE) to the present day. With the penetration of the mystical thought of Ibn al-ʿArabī (d. 638/1240) and others into different aspects of Shiʿi thought, this period gave birth to Shiʿi mystical philosophy (*ḥikma, ʿirfān*). It was typically seen in the thought of Mullā Ṣadrā (d. 1050/1640), who created a rational framework to support his intuition based on the Peripatetic philosophy of Ibn Sīnā (d. 428/1037). This period is characterised as one during which the formation of novel features through the confluence of different trends of thought occurred.

## I. Muḥsin Fayḍ al-Kāshānī

Fayḍ al-Kāshānī was raised in Qumm and later moved to Iṣfahān, where he died in 1091/1680–1681. He left many works in Arabic and Persian, which cover a wide range of religious and philosophical topics. But he is especially celebrated as a *ḥadīth* scholar. Some 120 of al-Kāshānī's works are known to us, though some of them seem to be listed more than once under different titles.[4] He maintains that the present text of the Qur'an has suffered alteration by those antagonistic to the Imams and that it is not the same as that which God revealed to the Prophet Muḥammad.[5] In the field of jurisprudence he held opinions which do not conform to established regulations.[6] He was a *ḥadīth* scholar of the Akhbārī school, which does not accept the authority of the experts of Islamic law (*mujtahid*), and he is criticised as being too inclined towards philosophy and mysticism, which last must be a cardinal point when we consider his notion of *imāma*. Yūsuf al-Baḥrānī[7] (d. 1186/1772) in his *Lu'lu'at al-Baḥrayn* criticised his scholarship.[8]

Fayḍ al-Kāshānī was so committed an Akhbārī scholar that he denied the claim of *mujtahid*s that common believers had no right to judge on matters of law and that they must obey their judgements, saying that such a claim was disbelief (*kufr*). Like his master Mullā Ṣadrā, he accepted Ibn al-ʿArabī's insights and expounded and taught a point of view strongly coloured with mysticism and philosophy. Baḥrānī criticised Fayḍ al-Kāshānī because of the latter's inclination towards 'heretical' mysticism, rather than for his Akhbārī affiliation.[9]

Concerning Fayḍ al-Kāshānī, in his biographical dictionary of Shiʿi *ʿulamā'*, *Rawḍāt al-jannāt*, al-Khwānsārī (d. 1313/1895) quotes al-Baḥrānī's statement, but he does not take his side. In an entry on Fayḍ al-Kāshānī, al-Khwānsārī remarks that Baḥrānī's statement that al-Kāshānī and Mullā Ṣadrā were heretical mystics is wrong. On the reasons for al-Baḥrānī's misunderstanding al-Khwānsārī gives the following:

> He [al-Baḥrānī] is far removed from the way of those who have intelligence and he does not distinguish between the suprasensible unveiling (*mukāshafāt*) of those who have knowledge and understanding by following the Messenger and his Household and the vanities (*muzakhrafāt*) of those who are ignorant and stupid enough to fancy that they could reach [the Divine Presence] without grasping the rope made secure by them [the Imams].[10]

In al-Khwānsārī's words we are certainly able to assume that according to his classification Fayḍ al-Kāshānī is a gnostic who receives suprasensible unveiling with the assistance of the Imams, and is not a 'false mystic' who claims to have reached God without their assistance.[11] Many of the *'ulamā'* who did not distinguish such gnostics from 'false mystics', must have been suspicious of him. As for the causes of this, al-Khwānsārī mentions his imitation of 'false mystics' by association with an 'extreme and heretical' Shi'a (*ghulāt, mulḥidīn*), rejection of compliance with the rulings of *mujtahids*, ignoring dissent from established consensus (*ijmā'*), and his omission of certain religious obligations.[12] He was sometimes suspected of straying from orthodoxy by scholars of the later Safawid and the Qajar periods. During these times Ithnā'asharī Shi'ism tended more and more to so-called Uṣūlism, that is to say the position of the *mujtahids*, while the Akhbārī were pushed out of the mainstream, and there was also occasional suppression of mysticism and philosophy by such well-known figures as Muḥammad Bāqir al-Majlisī (d. 1110/1698).

## II. The Perfect Man and the Self-manifestation of the Absolute

Mystical thought presumes unification in a certain mode between the Absolute and man (or the world). Why and how does the Absolute, who by definition is transcendent beyond man and the world, become one with them? It is an eternal question, because it is a real fact experienced by mystics in spite of the definition of the Absolute. One of the central concepts of Islamic mysticism is that of the Perfect Man (*insān kāmil*). Some Muslim mystics try to overcome the gap between the Absolute and man through postulating the idea of the Perfect Man. Fayḍ al-Kāshānī was one of them, and he discussed the idea in the context of a wide range of the subjects under the general heading of mystical philosophy in his short work, 'The Hidden Discourses Concerning the Knowledge of Those Who Have Wisdom and Gnosis' (*Kalimāt maknūna min 'ulūm ahl al-ḥikma wa'l-ma'rifa*).[13] He understood the idea of the Perfect Man in the framework of the self-manifestation of the Absolute.

According to the framework of the self-manifestation of the Absolute, He is not the object of cognition and he is self-sufficient, without any need of others. The self-sufficient mode of the Absolute, which is beyond any opposition or conflict, is properly named the absolute oneness (*aḥadiyya*). On the contrary, our actual world, where everything has its own exclusive identity and cannot be another but itself, has manyness as its intrinsic nature. A cardinal point for those who perceive the oneness between the Absolute and the world is how they understand the relationship between the self-sufficient Absolute and the actual world. Islam presupposes that the world is created by God, by virtue of whom it has a certain reality. Therefore, the existence of the world cannot be explained away as unreal illusion in the way that the Hindu concept of *māyā* explains the unreality of the world. Rather, Islamic thinkers adopt the scheme of emanation (*fayḍ*) or self-manifestation (*tajallī*) to understand this relationship. The Absolute is the plenum of reality before 'His' self-determination into the actual world. In other words, the self-sufficient whole is determined into individual realities, which insist on their own independent exclusive identities. The actual world, whose intrinsic nature is manyness, emerges through this process. The world is one with the Absolute and participates in His reality insofar as the world is one of His determined forms. But, at the same time, the world remains far from the Absolute insofar as it is determined and is a limited existent. In order to explain the relationship between absolute oneness and manyness, a certain intermediate dimension between them is presupposed in the whole process of the divine manifestation or emanation.

This dimension is called that of 'relative oneness' (*wāḥidiyya*), which corresponds to the position of the divine Names discussed in detail in Islamic theology down the centuries. As the Qur'an shows, God has many names such as the Creator (*al-khāliq*), the Beneficent (*al-raḥmān*), the Provider (*al-razzāq*), the Avenger (*al-muntaqim*) and others. This means that while He keeps supreme oneness for himself, God has aspects that correspond to the manyness of the world.

> Those who have gnosis say: the presence of the Absolute, Glory be to Him, does not need the world and what exists in the world through His essence. But the infinite divine names need the world, for each of them has a locus of manifestation in order that a trace of that name may manifest itself in that particular locus of manifestation. The Named, who is the essence, His rank be the Most High, appears as splendid to the eyes of one who believes in the unity of God, just like the Beneficent (*raḥmān*), the Provider (*razzāq*) and the Subduer (*qahhār*). Every one of the above is one of the names of the Absolute, Glory be to Him the Most High. The manifestation of that is possible through [the pairing of] a beneficent (*raḥīmī*) and a beneficiary (*marḥūmī*), a provider and a provided, and a subduer and a subdued (*maqhūr*). This is possible because beneficence is not manifest as long as both a beneficent and a beneficiary are not present in the external world. Similarly, provision, subdual and all the other names must be like this. Therefore, on account of the manifestation of the Absolute in the entirety of particular existents, the names of the Absolute, His rank be glorified, are sought. All the names are comprehended under the name 'God' (*Allāh*), which includes the entirety of names and comprehends all existents. The name 'God' also demands a particular locus of manifestation of all, and that locus has correspondence to the comprehensive name by virtue of its comprehensiveness. Therefore, the locus may be a vicegerent of God (*khalīfat-i Allāh*) in his conveyance of [divine] emanation and perfection from the name 'God' to others. That comprehensive locus of manifestation is the Perfect Man (*al-insān al-kāmil*), who is a treasure house of the divine lights and a hidden treasury of the uncountable [divine] emanations, or rather a treasure house of all existence and the key to the entire treasuries of generosity.[14]

> The locus of manifestation that reflects the Absolute in His manifold forms is the world. The sphere of the divine names, which is the divine dimension corresponding to the manyness of the world, is included in the comprehensive name, Allāh. Each individual divine name is manifested by an individual thing in the created world as a locus of its manifestation. The comprehensive name, Allāh, is manifested in the Perfect Man as its locus of manifestation, who comprehends the entire world in himself, since he corresponds to Allāh in his comprehensiveness.

The process of the self-manifestation or emanation of the Absolute is divided into two steps. The first is the step of the manifestation of the divine names, and the second that of the manifestation of the actual world.

> Then, the Absolute wills that He manifest His essence in a perfect locus of manifestation. The locus includes all the other illuminated loci of manifestation as well as the shadowed loci of appearance. It also comprises the entire realities, both secret and open, and encompasses all the particles, both hidden and manifest. The ipseity (*huwiyya*) necessary for its own essence (*dhāt*) cognises its own essence without any addition to its essence. There is nothing distinguished from the ipseity either in intellection (*taʿaqqul*) or in concrete reality (*al-wāqiʿ*). In the same way, the attributes and names of the ipseity are cognised as suprasensible essential relations without their having to manifest their traces or to distinguish one from another in concrete forms.

The passage quoted above shows the first step of the self-manifestation, and there is no influence on the external world yet. In this step the Absolute is virtually determined towards the external world, but still in His oneness. Our author continues as follows:

> Then, the divine ipseity manifests itself in particularised forms of differentiated loci of manifestation, namely, the loci of manifestation of these worlds. The manifestation is done according to a specified will and various preparedness (*istiʿdādāt*), and through different means (*wasāʾiṭ*). Thus, the divine ipseity does not cognise its essence and its reality insofar as it comprehends in itself the entire concrete perfections and all the divine attributes and names.[15]

At this stage existents in this world individually appear as loci of manifestation of divine names, and the world of manyness establishes itself. After mentioning that any form which the Absolute assumes in His self-manifestation corresponds to the form of the loci of manifestation, Fayḍ al-Kāshānī continues as follows:

> The divine ipseity emanates voluntarily to the universal locus of manifestation and to the comprehensive universe of existents present to the divine order, which includes the meaning of the real perfect collective oneness, to which no

> increase is conceivable regarding its completeness and perfection. No increase is conceivable because the divine ipseity manifests itself according to the real perfect oneness and cognises its essence comprehensively. It is the Perfect Man (*al-insān al-kāmil*). He comprehends both, being locus of manifestation of the absolute essence, and that of the names, attributes and acts. His comprehension is done through the collectivity (*jamʿiyya*) and the moderation (*iʿtidāl*) of his universal mode of being and through the abundance and the perfection of his being a locus of manifestation. He also comprehends both the necessary realities, or the relations of divine names, and the possible realities, or the attributes of creation. He comprehends both the levels of collectivity, and of particularisation. He encompasses all the levels in the chains of existence.[16]

Just as the process of the self-manifestation of the Absolute being is divided into two steps, the Perfect Man seems to have two aspects. Namely, the first is one in which the unknowable essence of the Absolute comes into existence by His determining himself as a name. By reflecting himself in the form of the Perfect Man, the Absolute descends on the world of relativity and is manifested. The Perfect Man is an indispensable mirror for revealing the manifestation of the Absolute. The second aspect is one which mediates between the divine Names, which are of necessary existence, and the individual existents in the world of creation, and makes them manifest. The individual and limited forms of the Absolute in the forms of divine Names need their counterparts in the world of creation as loci of their manifestation. Each divine Name reflected in the Perfect Man continues to exist through its finding an individual existent in the world of creation as a locus of its manifestation, which corresponds to its counterpart among divine Names.

By virtue of divine love, that is to say the self-manifestation of the Absolute which is unknowable in itself, the world of creation comes into existence. In this cosmic scheme of divine self-manifestation, the Perfect Man is located in its focal point, which mediates between, and connects, the divine names and the world of creation. Fayḍ al-Kāshānī states in Persian as follows:

> In general the Absolute, Glory be to Him the Most High, manifests himself in the mirror of the heart of the Perfect Man, who is His vicegerent. The reflection of the lights of the self-manifestations emanates across the world from the mirror of his heart. With the arrival of this emanation the existence of the world continues. As long as this Perfect Man remains in the world, he draws from the Absolute the essential self-manifestations. They are the mercy of divine clemency and compassion made evident through the divine Names and Attributes, whose loci of manifestation are these worldly existents. Therefore, by this process of drawing and emanation, the self-manifestations are preserved as long as this Perfect Man is in the world. No meanings come to the outer from the inner without his judgement (*ḥukm*), and nothing comes to the inner from the outer without his order (*amr*).[17]

Fayḍ al-Kāshānī tries to understand the unitive state of the Absolute and man in this way. The Perfect Man is his key to understanding this relationship.

## III. Prophethood and Sainthood

By following Ḥaydar al-Āmulī's formulation,[18] Fayḍ al-Kāshānī can view historical prophets and Imams as different forms of the Perfect Man, whose manifestations are summed up in the following four categories: absolute prophethood (*nubūwwa*), absolute sainthood (*walāya*), limited prophethood, and limited sainthood:

> The Perfect Man is either a prophet (*nabī*) or a *walī*. Both prophethood and sainthood are to be considered from two points of view. One is that of absoluteness (*iṭlāq*), and the other is that of limitation (*taqyīd*). In other words, from the view of the general (*'āmm*) and the special (*khāṣṣ*).
>
> As for absolute prophethood, it is real prophethood actualised in pre-eternity (*azal*) and remaining in post-eternity (*abad*). It is knowledge of the prophet specific to absolute prophethood concerning the preparedness (*isti'dād*) of the entirety of existents according to their essences and quiddities. Absolute prophethood is also given to everyone who is qualified to have a right, his right, which he demands by the tongue of his preparedness insofar as it is the essential notification, the pre-eternal real instruction which is called the greatest lordship (*al-rubūbiyya al-'uẓmā*) and the mightiest authority (*al-salṭana al-kubrā*).
>
> The owner of this position is named the greatest vicegerent (*al-khalīfa al-a'ẓam*), the pole of poles (*quṭb al-aqṭāb*), the *macroanthropos* (*al-insān al-kabīr*), and the true Adam. He is also explained as the highest pen, the first intellect and the greatest spirit … Founded on him are all sorts of knowledge and works. To him at the end return all degrees and positions, whether prophet or *walī*, messenger (*rasūl*) or trustee (*waṣī*).[19]

First he mentions the Perfect Man as a concept which comprises both prophets and *walī*s, and further divides them into two kinds, absolute and limited. In the quotation above, absolute prophethood is identified as the 'first intellect' which is the first emanation from the Absolute in the cosmogonical scheme of 'emanational' Islamic philosophy, and also as the 'highest pen'[20] and the 'greatest spirit'. It refers to the initial stage of the formation of the actual world, encompassing virtually the entire world in itself. Absolute prophethood is, in other words, the eternal formative power which makes the existents exist as they are to exist in accordance with their preparedness (*isti'dād*) for their self-realisation.

In contrast to absolute prophethood, which can be called the principle of formation of the actual world, absolute sainthood is explained as follows:

> The inner dimension of this prophethood is absolute sainthood. Absolute sainthood means the actualisation (*ḥuṣūl*) of the totality of these perfections

according to the inner dimension in pre-eternity and their enduring in post-eternity. Absolute sainthood finally goes back to man's extinction (*fanā'*) in the Absolute and his enduring (*baqā'*) with Him.[21]

While absolute prophethood continues to have an effect on the actual world, absolute sainthood is a state in which all perfections are kept within, without manifestation. It may be characterised as a state in which man loses his human identity and is unified with the Absolute. This is because the state is described in the quotation above as 'extinction' and 'enduring', the terms used by Islamic mystics since early times to allude to the final goal of their quest for the Absolute. In this state man is unified with the Absolute in an unarticulated form with loss of external form in the unfathomable depth of the Absolute.

All the existents are to seek their own perfection in the actual world. All perfections realised in the actual world are due to absolute prophethood. On the other hand, absolute sainthood means the totality of perfections in an inner hidden dimension, which absolute prophethood actualises in an outer manifest dimension.

Next he mentions limited prophethood and limited sainthood in the following manner:

> Limited prophethood is communication (*ikhbār*) of the divine realities, that is, of knowledge of the essence of the Absolute and His names, attributes and judgements. If a prophet combines it with execution of judgements, giving moral education, instruction of wisdom, and carrying out government, it becomes legislative prophethood (*nubūwwa tashrī'iyya*) and is specifically called messengership (*risāla*).[22]

Limited prophethood is the characteristic or function of the individual prophets in history, who conveyed God's words to the people. Those prophets who established laws to prescribe how men should live (for example, the *sharī'a* of Islam) are called messengers (*rasūl*). As for limited sainthood, he does not define clearly what it is, saying only: '[You may] determine the meaning of limited sainthood, by analogy, with absolute sainthood.'[23]

However, we can assume that it is the realisation in the inner dimension of respective Imams of the divine perfections due to their unity with the Absolute. In this way both prophethood and sainthood are grouped into 'absolute' when it is a divine attribute not restricted to particular persons, and 'limited' when it is one connected to a certain individual prophet or Imam. The limited continues to exist by virtue of the Absolute, while the latter manifests himself through the former.[24] In other words, the prophethood of individual prophets is a specific form of absolute prophethood, as limited sainthood is of absolute sainthood.[25]

Each of the four groups has a seal (*khātam*), beyond which there is no stage in the scale of perfection.[26] The function of the prophet is to ensure that the order of the world of existence develops towards perfection in accordance with divine predestination. This order was developed step by step from the time of Adam until in the end it reached the stage of perfection at Muḥammad, the last and greatest Prophet. Therefore he is called the 'seal' of both absolute and limited prophethood.

On the other hand, 'Alī, who embodies the perfection of the invisible inner world, had already realised perfection of the highest degree even before the creation of this world, that is to say the outer visible world. In this sense he is given the epithet 'seal' just as Muḥammad is. However, 'Alī in history may be one of the limited saints (*walī*) as a manifest form of absolute sainthood, but he is not the seal of limited sainthood, namely the perfect embodiment of sainthood. The series of limited or specific saints, each of whom embodies a spiritual perfection in his time, starts from a saint who accompanied Adam, the first prophet (although this is not clearly mentioned in the text) and ends with the Mahdī, the last *walī* who is identified as the Twelfth Imam as understood in historical Shi'i Islam. The seal means the ultimate degree of the characteristic given by God. Muḥammad is identified as the seal of both limited and absolute prophethood, while the Mahdī is identified as the seal of limited sainthood and 'Alī only as that of absolute sainthood.[27]

## IV. Aspects of the Perfect Man

The Perfect Man is described with such different expressions as 'Muhammadan Light' and 'Reality of Realities'.

> The root, the place of origination, the place of return and the place of beginning of the entire creature are the presence (*ḥaḍra*) of the Reality of Realities. That is the Muhammadan Reality (*Ḥaqīqat-i Muḥammadī*), and the Muhammadan Light (*nūr-i Aḥmadī*). The form of the presence is one and unique, comprehending in it all divine perfections as well as those of the world, and setting the scale of all the degrees of moderation pertaining to angels, animals and human beings. The world and those in it are forms and parts of its elaboration. Adam and human beings are subjugated to its power to create perfection (*takmīl*).[28]

From this quotation we understand that the Muhammadan Reality is the reality of the entire created world, and the world created is the externally developed form of the Muhammadan Reality. Human beings in the actual world are subject to the Reality insofar as they are transformed from virtuality into actuality in accordance with their predetermined forms in the Muhammadan Reality.

Al-Kāshānī quotes a *ḥadīth* which may be interpreted in this context:

> I [the Prophet Muḥammad] and 'Alī are of one light. God created my spirit and 'Alī b. Abī Ṭālib's spirit two thousand years before He created humankind. He sent 'Alī secretly with every prophet and openly with me.[29]

'Alī, as the reality of the absolute sainthood, existed even before the creation of the world, while *walī*s in history are individual and specific manifestations of absolute sainthood, namely, "Alī sent secretly", accompanying all the prophets. 'Alī in history, namely, "Alī sent openly", is a specific manifestation at the time of the Prophet Muḥammad. The *ḥadīth* can be understood in this way. In another *ḥadīth* ascribed to 'Alī, 'I was a *walī* even while Adam was between water and clay',[30] 'I' ('Alī) alludes to his absolute sainthood. Similarly in a *ḥadīth* ascribed to the Prophet Muḥammad, 'The first of what God created is my light, and I was a prophet even while Adam was between water and clay',[31] 'I' (the Prophet Muḥammad) alludes to absolute prophethood. These *ḥadīth*s convey that the Prophet Muḥammad and the first Shi'i Imam existed even before the creation of the world. The expression of their existence before creation is interpreted as their existence in the form of realities or light beyond time and space. The aspect expressed here is completely different from that of limited prophethood and sainthood, which are embodied in historical figures like Muḥammad and 'Alī.

According to Imām Ja'far al-Ṣādiq the Imams are the different forms in which the same absolute sainthood manifests itself. He calls them gatekeepers between God and His creation meaning that God and His creation are mutually divided and concealed from each other, and they know each other only through the mediation between them of an existing Imam.[32]

They may also be considered manifestations of the reality of the Perfect Man or Perfect Men. From the intermediate position of the Perfect Man between God and men can be drawn the idea that the Perfect Man supports the existence of the world and that the world would cease to be without his existence. Fayḍ al-Kāshānī states as follows:

> Since the objective of the creation and continuation of the world is the Perfect Man, namely the just Imam who is the vicegerent (*khalīfa*) of God on the earth in the same way as the purpose of the body is the rational soul (*al-nafs al-nāṭiqa*), it must follow that the lowest world [this world] would perish with the removal of this man in the same way as the body would decay and perish with the departure of the rational soul. He, Praise be to Him, does not manifest himself in the lowest worlds without an intermediary. Therefore with his [Perfect Man's] absence (*inqiṭā'*) the assistance [of God] which is imperative for the continuation of [the world's] existence and perfections would cease. This world would pass away with his passing (*intiqāl*), and the meanings and the perfections that are in it would leave it for the other world. At this moment, the firmament would split, the sun would lose its radiance and the stars would be darkened and dispersed.[33]

We have seen various characteristics given to the Perfect Man. Here let us examine how al-Kāshānī interprets a *ḥadīth* attributed to the Prophet Muḥammad, a statement found in the Old Testament (Genesis, 1.27), 'God created Adam in

His form'.[34] He interprets it in the context of divine self-manifestation. It is clear that the pronoun in the phrase 'in His form' (*'alā ṣūrati-hi*) refers to God, since in another version of the *ḥadīth* [35] the text runs 'in the form of the Compassionate' (one of God's names).

Al-Kāshānī interprets the form of God in the following manner: 'The form is of invisible simple realities that are not rationally recognised and that do not appear except through [the form]. That is to say, the divine form is existence determined with all the self-determinations through which the source of all becomes perfect actions and active traces.'[36] Further he divides the divine form into two kinds: 'The world with all its parts, spiritual and bodily, substantial and accidental, is the form of the Divine Presence in detail (*tafṣīl*), while the Perfect Man is His form in integration (*jam'*).'[37] Thus both the world and the Perfect Man are different aspects of the same divine self-manifestation.

Adam, who is the first messenger and the first Perfect Man according to Islamic understanding, is a form in which the Absolute determines and manifests himself. He is a Divine Presence, a form which keeps its divine unity and at the same time has virtual multiplicity corresponding to the complex developed forms of the actual world. Based on the theory of divine self-manifestation which al-Kāshānī accepts, the *ḥadīth* is understood in such a way that God manifests himself in the form of Adam as the Perfect Man who comprehends all the world in himself in integrated form.

## V. Conclusion

We find in Fayḍ al-Kāshānī's understanding of *imāma*, (or rather *walāya*) the overwhelming influence of Ibn al-'Arabī's world view. The idea of the Imam in Shi'i Islam started with the believers' ardent veneration of their Master, and Shi'i thinkers developed an idea of the supranatural and semi-divine nature residing within the Imam. As the notion of Imam crystallised, Ibn al-'Arabī's world view, especially his idea of the Perfect Man, was adjusted to fit and incorporated into their speculations. The confluence of Shi'i Imamology and Ibn al-'Arabī's mysticism is typically seen in Safawid *'irfān*, and Fayḍ al-Kāshānī's exposition in his *Kalimāt-i maknūna* is a good example of this.[38] However, scholastic endeavour towards this confluence has its own history, and its first fruit is manifest in the work of Ḥaydar al-Āmulī. But to assess the role and influence of Ḥaydar al-Āmulī on the later development of Shi'i mystical thought would be the topic of another paper, though the present paper sheds a limited degree of light on how much Fayḍ al-Kāshānī owes to Ḥaydar al-Āmulī's work.

## Notes

1. See A. A. Sachedina, *Islamic Messianism. The Idea of the Mahdi in Twelver Shiʿism* (Albany, NY, 1981).

2. For example, Ḥaydar Āmulī in the latter half of the 14th century CE interprets the return of the 12th Imam in the context of an inner spiritual transformation. Sayyid Ḥaydar Āmulī, *Kitāb jāmiʿ al-asrār wa-manbaʿ al-anwār*, ed. H. Corbin and O. Yahia (Paris and Tehran, 1969), p. 102.

3. H. Corbin, *Histoire de la philosophie islamique* (Paris, 1964), pp. 54–57.

4. Muḥammad ʿAlī Mudarris, *Rayḥānat al-adab fī tarājim al-maʿrūfīn bi'l-kunya wa'l-laqab* (Tabrīz, n.d.), vol. 4, pp. 374–378. C. Brockelmann, *GAL*, Suppl. 2, pp. 584–585 lists 32 titles. His best-known work is the *Wāfī*, which collects and minutely classifies all *ḥadīths* found in the four canonical Shiʿi *Ḥadīth* collections. The work is counted as the first of the three collections compiled by three Muḥammads: Muḥammad Ḥurr al-ʿĀmilī (d. 1104/1692–1693), Muḥammad Bāqir al-Majlisī (d. 1110/1698) and Muḥammad Muḥsin Fayḍ al-Kāshānī himself. The last is regarded as the most inclined to philosophy. See Muḥammad Bāqir al-Khwānsārī, *Kitāb rawḍāt al-jannāt fī aḥwāl al-ʿulamāʾ wa'l-sādāt* (Qumm, 1351/1932–1933), vol. 6, p. 87; al-Khwānsārī, *Rawḍāt al-jannāt* (n.p., 1367, Repr. of 1287 lithograph edition), pp. 518–519 and Āqā Buzurg al-Ṭihrānī, *al-Dharīʿa ilā taṣānīf al-shīʿa* (Beirut, n.d.), vol. 25, pp. 13–14 (no. 73).

5. Mahmud Ayoub, 'The Speaking Qurʾān and the Silent Qurʾān: A Study of the Principles and Development of Imāmī Shiʿi *tafsīr*', in A. Rippin, ed., *Approaches to the History of the Interpretation of the Qurʾān* (Oxford, 1988), p. 190.

6. Hossein Modarresi Tabatabaʾi, *An Introduction to Shīʿī Law: A Bibliographical Study* (London, 1984), pp. 16, 51–52.

7. He is well known as the author of *al-Ḥadāʾiq al-nāḍira*, a book on *fiqh*. He was also counted among Akhbārīs for at least some time in the beginning of his carrier. See *al-Ḥadāʾiq al-nāḍira* (Beirut, 1406/1985), vol. 1, p. 167.

8. Yūsuf b. Aḥmad al-Baḥrānī, *Luʾluʾat al-Baḥrayn fī'l-ijāzāt wa-tarājim rijāl al-ḥadīth*, ed. al-Sayyid Muḥammad Ṣādiq Baḥr al-ʿUlūm (Beirut, 1406/1985), pp. 121–122.

9. The Akhbārī school was dominant in most centres of Shiʿi learning from the mid 11th/17th century to the middle of the following century. Fayḍ al-Kāshānī's Akhbārī affiliation was not a valid reason to criticise his scholarship. See Modarresi Tabatabaʾi, *An Introduction to Shīʿī Law*, pp. 54–55.

10. Al-Khwānsārī, *Kitāb rawḍāt al-jannāt*, vol. 6, p. 100; lithograph edition, p. 522. I read *muzakhrafāt* according to the text of the lithograph edition, not *min khuruqāt* of the printed edition.

11. The former group are gnostics (s., *al-ḥakīm al-rabbānī, al-walī al-īmānī*) while the latter group are Sufis (s., *al-faqīr al-ṣūfī*) in al-Khwānsārī, *Kitāb rawḍāt al-jannāt*, vol. 6, p. 100; [lithograph edition] p. 522. The expression 'false mysticism' (*al-taṣawwuf al-bāṭil*) is used in reference to Fayḍ al-Kāshānī in al-Khwānsārī, *Kitāb rawḍāt al-jannāt*, vol. 6, p. 94; [lithograph edition] p. 520. Mullā Ṣadrā, Fayḍ al-Kāshānī's teacher, criticises Sufism, namely the 'false mysticism' from the standpoint of *ḥikma* philosophy in his *Kasr aṣnām al-jāhilīya*, ed. M. T. Dānishpazhūh (Tehran, 1340 Sh./1961–62).

12. Al-Khwānsārī, *Kitāb rawḍāt al-jannāt*, vol. 6, p. 94; lithograph edition, p. 520.

13. This book deals with various subjects of mystical philosophy (*ʿirfān*). As the preface shows, the author quotes copiously from the Qurʾan, *ḥadīths* and works of other thinkers with occasional inclusions of poems. It is written in a mixture of Arabic and Persian, and even small sections often have paragraphs both in Arabic and in Persian. Fayḍ al-Kāshānī, *Kalimāt al-maknūna min ʿulūm ahl al-ḥikma waʾl-maʿrifa*, ed. ʿAzīz Allāh al-Qūchānī (Tehran, 1383/1963) (Abbreviated as *Kalimāt* in the following notes). For the text readings I also consulted the *Kitāb al-kalimāt al-maknūna*, Manuscript no. 2233 (Film no. 6274), Kitābkhāna-yi Markazī, Dānishgāh-i Tihrān. Unless otherwise stated, all translations are from the Arabic.

14. *Kalimāt*, p. 116 in Persian.

15. Ibid., p. 117.

16. Ibid., pp. 117–118.

17. Ibid., p. 121 in Persian.

18. These passages seem to be quoted from Ḥaydar al-Āmulī, *Jāmiʿ al-asrār*, pp. 380–382.

19. *Kalimāt*, p. 186.

20. A pen creates various letters or pictures by using ink from an inkwell, where ink is an indistinguishable black substance. The pen alludes to the principle of articulation.

21. *Kalimāt*, p. 186. This quotation is also found in Ḥaydar al-Āmulī, *Jāmiʿ al-asrār*, p. 382.

22. *Kalimāt*, p. 186.

23. Ibid., pp. 186–187.

24. Ibid., p. 187.

25. Ibid.

26. Ibid.

27. The idea of 'seal' (*khātam*) was fixed in Islam by the mystic Tirmidhī (d. ca. 320/932), and was later adopted as an important element in Islamic mysticism by Ibn al-ʿArabī (d. 638/1240), one of the greatest mystical thinkers. Fayḍ al-Kāshānī's discussions on the identity of the Seal of prophethood and sainthood seem to be based on Ḥaydar Āmulī's understanding who discusses in detail the identity of the seals of absolute sainthood and of limited sainthood in his *Jāmiʿ al-asrār wa-manbaʿ al-anwār*, where he argues against Ibn al-ʿArabī's identity of the seals from the three points of view: *naql*, *ʿaql* and *kashf*. For Ḥaydar al-Āmulī's thought, see his work quoted in note 2, pp. 395–448 (clearly summed up on pp. 384–385), H. Corbin, *En Islam iranien* (Paris, 1972), vol. 3, pp. 149–213, especially pp. 190–213; P. Antes, *Zur Theologie der Schiʿa Eine Untersuchung des Ǧāmiʿ al-asrār wa-manbaʿ al-anwār von Sayyid Ḥaydar Āmolī* (Freiburg im Breisgau, 1971), pp. 95–97, and H. Landolt, 'Walāyah', *ER*, vol. 15, p. 320.

28. *Kalimāt*, pp. 187–188, in Persian.

29. Ibid., p. 186.

30. Ibid.

31. Ibid.

32. Ibid. p. 192. I omitted *li* and read *faḍlu-nā min Allāh* instead of *li-faḍli-nā* according to the manuscript mentioned above in note 16, f. 107r. This *ḥadīth* is recorded in al-Majlisī, *Biḥār al-Anwār*, vol. 25, p. 363 (no. 23) as the words of Imām Jaʿfar al-Ṣādiq and confirms this reading.

33. *Kalimāt*, pp. 130–131.

34. Ibid., p. 125. This *ḥadīth* is found in both Shiʿi and Sunni collections. Amongst the Shiʿa it is quoted in the words of Imām Muḥammad Bāqir. Although it is judged weak by *ḥadīth* scholars this would mean nothing to Fayḍ al-Kāshānī since as an Akhbārī he refrains from judging *ḥadīth* altogether. Al-Kulaynī, *Uṣūl min al-kāfī* (Tehran, 1388/1968), vol. 1, p. 134; Muḥammad Bāqir al-Majlisī, *Mir'āt al-ʿuqūl fī sharḥ akhbār al-rasūl* (Tehran, 1404/1983), vol. 2, p. 84. As for other sources, see Badīʿ al-Zamān Furūzānfar, *Aḥādīth-i mathnawī* (Tehran, 1334 Sh./1955–56), pp. 114–115.

35. *Kalimāt*, p. 125.

36. Ibid.

37. Ibid.

38. Mullā Ṣadrā, one of Fayḍ al-Kāshānī's teachers, gives an exposition on the idea of the Perfect Man in his commentary on the *Āyat al-Nūr* (Qur'an, 24:35). However, it can be argued that he does not explicitly develop the Shiʿi Imamological aspect of the Perfect Man in his discussion as much as seen in that of Fayḍ al-Kāshānī. Ṣadr al-Muta'allihīn-i Shīrāzī, *Tafsīr-i āyat-i mubāraka-yi nūr*, ed. and tr. into Persian by Muḥammad Khājawī (Tehran, 1362 Sh./1983–84), pp. 171–190. See also Muhsen Mahmud Saleh, 'The Verse of Light: A Study of Mullā Ṣadrā's Philosophical Qur'an Exegesis' (Ph.D., Temple University, 1994).

# Part Four

# Modern Islam

# 33

# The Faith of Pharaoh: A Disputed Question in Islamic Theology

*Eric Ormsby*

## I

The question of the faith of Pharaoh is one of a number of disputed questions that occupied the learned in the later Islamic scholastic tradition.[1] Such questions were often sparked by a controversial passage, or even a single phrase, in the work of some eminent authority after which critics or defenders of the opinion lined up to deliver responses or put their arguments in brief treatises (*rasā'il*). These sometimes became set questions, repeated over generations; the dispute which I examine here extended, with gaps, over some five hundred years. Though at times the issue may appear to be minor, and the arguments undistinguished, reputations could be enhanced or damaged, depending upon the responses. One later chronicler of the dispute admonished potential disputants not to broach these questions for the wrong reasons; thus, the Ottoman polymath Ḥājjī Khalīfa (Kātib Chelebi, d. 1068/1657): 'Be not eager to recount the controversies described in this book, and similar subtleties, for the sake of obtaining a larger audience and becoming well known.'[2] But beyond ambition and personal prestige, other larger and still unresolved questions often underlay these seemingly lesser topics.

As with most of the other disputes, ours occurred over those long centuries which Gardet and Anawati have termed a period of 'congealed Ashʿarism' (*l'ashʿarisme figé*);[3] and yet, these were not always dead questions embedded in a barren curriculum (nor were all the participants Ashʿarī). In fact, they often led back to certain insoluble theological problems that had haunted discussion since at least the eighth century, e.g. the definition, and boundaries of faith, predestination and free will, the nature of God's goodness, and the like. No matter how settled such grand issues might have seemed, they kept springing back to life, sometimes covertly, at others with startling gusto. In any case, the ferocity of certain disputants towards their opponents indicates that these remained exasperating issues (though the intensity of the vituperation tends to rise as the arguments weaken). Terms of abuse such as 'ranting fanatic', 'feeble minded' and 'mentally unbalanced', as well as 'infidel' and 'heretic', are not uncommon and seem to exceed the usual level of *ad hominem* contumely. In the present debate, the Shaykhī master Aḥmad b. Zayn al-Dīn al-Aḥsā'ī (d. 1241/1826) lambasted Ibn al-ʿArabī with such epithets as 'Murderer of Religion' (*mumīt al-dīn*, a play on his honorific title 'Reviver of Religion' or *Muḥyī al-Dīn*) and 'The Supremely Moronic Shaykh' (*al-shaykh al-aḥmaq* instead of the usual *al-shaykh al-akbar*, 'The Greatest Shaykh').[4] But it could be more dangerous to attack Ibn al-ʿArabī than to defend him; in Aleppo, in 1535, one Muḥammad al-Falūjī was reportedly condemned to death for accusing the Shaykh al-Akbar of heresy.[5]

In the literature, as in Ḥājjī Khalīfa's aforementioned treatment, which offers an overview of the controversy, certain of these persistent debates are treated alongside such legal questions as the lawfulness of coffee and tobacco, the cursing of Yazīd, the practice of shaking hands, or pilgrimages to tombs, or the status of the supererogatory prayers in the month of Rajab. But the topics went beyond the legalistic into shadier matters: the status of the parents of the Prophet, for example, or the dilemmas engendered by the age-old problem of theodicy. The problem of the faith of Pharaoh offers a good instance of a dispute that seems to be centred upon lesser issues (e.g. the exact status of Ibn al-ʿArabī) and yet abruptly reveals unexpected intricacies.[6]

## II

In Islamic tradition, Pharaoh, the 'Pharaoh of Moses' (*Firʿawn Mūsā*), is the epitome of the arrogant despot; however, Pharaoh also embodies blasphemous pretensions to divinity, exclaiming in the Qur'an (79:24), 'I am your Lord most high' (*anā rabbukum al-aʿlā*).[7] If only for this, there clings about him a particular aura of abhorrence.[8] (For instance the prime assassin of Anwar al-Sadat, in 1981, the young Egyptian lieutenant Khalid Istanbuli declared, 'I shot the Pharaoh'.)[9] Even Ibn al-ʿArabī in his *Futūḥāt al-makkiyya* places Pharaoh among the 'four groups of the damned' who will remain eternally in hell, and not solely because Pharaoh was 'haughty' (*mutakabbir*) but because he entertained pretensions to divinity.[10] In keeping with his colossal hubris, Pharaoh also typifies intransigent unbelief. He remains the individual who will not believe, even if God Himself offers him belief. Of course, in a certain sense, belief is not possible for him and it would have entailed grave theological difficulties. As the theologian al-Māturīdī (d. 333/944) expressed it, 'If Pharaoh had been able to believe, he would have been able to invalidate God's [fore-]knowledge. This is so of Pharaoh and of everyone who in God's knowledge will not believe.'[11]

This is the first of the dilemmas: If God knows from all eternity that Pharaoh will not believe, then his change of heart becomes impossible, for it would impugn divine omniscience; but if his acceptance of belief is impossible, how can he be responsible for his unbelief?

If God does not know from all eternity that Pharaoh will not believe, then His knowledge is imperfect and, even worse, dependent somehow on a contingent thing: Pharaoh's human heart. If He knows, however, that Pharaoh will not believe, is His knowledge a factor in that unbelief? Is it God's foreknowledge that in fact necessitates and so causes it? This is of course the familiar problem of whether divine foreknowledge is itself causative. Underneath such logical and philosophical concerns lurks the more difficult, indeed excruciating, theological problem of why God singles out some for belief and salvation and others for unbelief and damnation. What kind of God condemns those whom He Himself has made as they are? But in fact, the dilemma is even more acute, for the scriptures make plain that God Himself hardens Pharaoh's heart. This is true in the Hebrew Bible, as well as in its translations into the Septuagint and Vulgate, and in the Qur'an itself.[12] In the Qur'an (10:88) Moses asks God to 'harden the hearts' (*wa'shdud ʿalā qulūbihim*) of the Egyptians:

> Our Lord, obliterate their possessions and harden their hearts so that they do not believe...

God answers obligingly, 'Your prayer is answered.' In the next verse occurs the much-disputed passage in question (10:89) which reads as follows:

> And We brought the Children of Israel over the sea; and Pharaoh and his hosts followed them insolently and impetuously till, when the drowning overtook him, he said, 'I believe that there is no god but He in whom the Children of Israel believe; I am of those that surrender'.[13]

The question prompted by these verses, for most commentators, is whether Pharaoh's apparent profession of faith is genuine; and if so, whether God accepted it and so saved him. The prevailing view, perhaps best epitomised by the Ashʿarī theologian and commentator Fakhr al-Dīn al-Rāzī (d. 606/1209) in his commentary on this verse, is that Pharaoh did not truly believe and was not saved, his last words notwithstanding. According to al-Rāzī, a man cannot articulate the profession of faith at the moment of drowning, if only for the 'technical' reason that his own death rattle in his throat prevents him; this is in keeping too with the Qur'anic censure of death-bed repentance.[14] Still another problem arises: Why then does God recount in the Qur'an what Pharaoh said? For al-Rāzī this is done, not to exculpate Pharaoh, but to affirm the validity of 'internal speech', (*al-kalām bi'l-nafs*) as opposed to 'voiced speech' (*al-kalām bi'l-lisān*); only internal speech is genuine (*ḥaqīqī*). In other words, God is merely illustrating the reality of mental discourse – articulate speech may not be possible at the moment of death, but mental discourse is, for it has been proved, and proved apodictically, that Pharaoh 'did not say this with his tongue'.[15]

For al-Rāzī, Pharaoh's words were invalid for a number of reasons. To profess belief in the face of impending punishment nullifies the profession. Worse, Pharaoh was only practising *taqlīd*, slavish adherence to imposed belief, and this, too, compromised his profession; did he not say, 'I believe that there is no God but He in whom the Children of Israel believe'? He is merely echoing what the Israelites say, not what he himself sincerely believes. Al-Rāzī notes further that 'in certain books' he has read that the Israelites after they traversed the Red Sea began worshipping 'a calf' (this is of course the golden calf of Exodus 32); thus, when Pharaoh mimes Israelite beliefs, he is only worshipping the calf. Moreover, the Israelites were much given to anthropomorphism (*tashbīh*) and corporealism (*tajsīm*) and believed that God was incarnate in the body of the calf and it is in this corporeal divinity that Pharaoh professes his belief. Another disqualifying reason is that Pharaoh says nothing about the Prophet Muḥammad in his *shahāda*, as is required, and this too demonstrates the invalidity of his belief.[16]

## III

It was disturbing, therefore, to traditional sensibilities when the great Andalusian Sufi Muḥyī al-Dīn Ibn al-ʿArabī (638/1240) stated in his *Fuṣūṣ al-ḥikam* that God had granted Pharaoh belief and that he had died as a believer, pure and cleansed of all his sins:

> Pharaoh's consolation was in the faith God endowed him with when he was drowned. God took him to Himself spotless, pure and untainted by any defilement, because He seized him at the moment of belief, before he could commit any sin, since submission [to God: *islām*] extirpates all that has occurred before. God made him a sign of His loving kindness [*ʿināya*] to whomever He wishes, so that no one may despair of the mercy of God, for indeed, no one but despairing folk despairs of the spirit of God (12:87). Had Pharaoh been despairing, he would not have hastened to believe.[17]

Ibn al-ʿArabī's views were, of course, controversial to many not simply because of what he said, but because it was he who said it. (Indeed, another concurrent late scholastic debate centred on Ibn al-ʿArabī's own status as believer or *kāfir*; Ḥājjī Khalīfa devotes a chapter to it in *Mizān al-ḥaqq* and others engaged hotly in it.)[18] To be sure, this is hardly the most outrageous of Ibn al-ʿArabī's opinions or scriptural interpretations, though Ibn Taymiyya, not surprisingly, thought so;[19] compared to other passages of the *Fuṣūṣ*, it is even rather tame.[20] Still, according to Ḥājjī Khalīfa, people 'swarmed about [Ibn al-ʿArabī's] head like ants and hornets' because of it.[21]

Perhaps the issue was of unusual interest because it concerned legitimacy of belief, an issue hotly debated from the earliest period.[22] If the blasphemous, despotic Pharaoh might be welcomed even *in extremis* into the community of believers, who could be excluded? Of course, it might be that the ostensible issue concealed another, even thornier problem; thus, one of Ibn al-ʿArabī's chief defenders, the philosopher Jalāl al-Dīn al-Dawwānī (d. 907/1501), would claim that the real issue was the breadth of the divine mercy. But the anti-nominalistic implications were clear. As ʿAlī b. Sulṭān Muḥammad al-Qāḍī al-Harawī (d. 1014/1605), al-Dawwānī's implacable critic, would object, belief has juridical conditions and obligations that must be observed; in addition, as al-Harawī notes in an access of legalistic indignation, Pharaoh's profession of faith was not merely insincere but even worse, he could not complete the full *shahāda* since he nowhere proclaims his belief in the prophethood of Muḥammad. Therefore, even if he might have been saved by a mere verbal profession, this incompleteness would have invalidated it.[23]

Traditionally, to be sure, Pharaoh's profession of faith in Qur'an 10:90, extracted under duress, was deemed invalid. Thus, according to Ibn ʿAbbās (d. 68/686), as reported by Ibn al-Jawzī (d. 597/1200), 'God did not accept his faith in the face of punishment'.[24] And in his *Kashshāf*, the Muʿtazilī commentator al-Zamakhsharī (d. 538/1144) interrogates Pharaoh harshly, 'Do you believe in the Last Judgement at the moment when you are compelled, when drowning has overtaken you and you despair for yourself?'[25] The consensus was that Pharaoh had simply wanted to save his skin at the last possible moment. His belief was the belief of desperation (*īmān al-ya's*) and as such, unacceptable.[26]

Perhaps there was even so a vague uneasiness in some traditional interpretations. To hear words of faith from the mouth of such a malefactor was disturbing. According to some traditions, the angel Gabriel himself stopped up Pharaoh's mouth with slime and mud from the seabed to prevent him from completing his profession of faith; for had he completed it, 'Four hundred years of sinful living and unbelief would have been forgiven him'.[27] According to other traditions, Gabriel is anxious to shut Pharaoh's mouth before God's compassion can 'overtake' him, as though a completed *shahāda* would irresistibly prompt divine mercy.

## IV

Ibn al-ʿArabī's view of Pharaoh was not without precedent. Sufi tradition had embellished the figure of Pharaoh with provocative complications. While most Sufis from the earliest period agreed that Pharaoh stood condemned, they also saw him as the embodiment of a profound paradox. Pharaoh was the unwitting enunciator of a secret truth, revealed only to him. In our later dispute this reappears and undergoes development. One of Ibn al-ʿArabī's defenders, whom we know only as 'Akmal al-Dīn', argued that Pharaoh's final acceptance of faith signified a reconciliation of the disparity between his outer illusory grandeur and his true inner lowliness and furthermore, that belief worked within him continually like 'a leaven' (*khamīra*) until he attained equilibrium at the instant of death.[28]

In certain Sufi traditions, to be sure, the figure of Pharaoh – in this like Iblīs – was considerably more nuanced. Yaḥyā b. Mu'ādh (d. 258/872) might berate those who lived too luxuriously by exclaiming, 'Your faces are pharaonic, your morals satanic!'[29] and view Pharaoh as only an object lesson: If God was patient and long-suffering with regard to Pharaoh, how much the more so will He be mild to those who recognise His lordship?[30] Other Sufis were subtler. Sahl al-Tustarī (d. 283/896) said: '... know that the soul (*nafs*) has a secret (*sirr*). That secret did not become manifest to any of His creatures save to Firʿawn when he said, "I am your Lord, the Most High."'[31] In this view, Pharaoh speaks a hidden truth but for the wrong reason; or, as G. Böwering puts it, 'Firʿaun ... confuses the human ego with the divine, and thus fails to realise the faith in God to which he is summoned by the prophetic speech and symbolic actions of Mūsā'.[32] For other later mystics, such as al-Ghazālī, Pharaoh is sometimes the epitome of the human self: prone to consider itself virtually autonomous, the self usurps God's prerogatives if it is not disciplined.[33] Ibn al-ʿArabī himself writes: 'God knows that when He creates man, he claims divinity and says, "I am your Lord the most high!" and yet, His creation of man must come to pass because of God's foreknowledge.'[34]

Of course Ibn al-ʿArabī's true precursor is Ḥusayn b. Manṣūr al-Ḥallāj (executed 309/922). For al-Ḥallāj, Pharaoh (like Iblīs) represents a particular form of *futuwwa*, or manly virtue, and his refusal to acknowledge the Prophet Muḥammad (like the refusal of Iblīs to bow down before Adam) is seen as its essence.[35] There is an obvious affinity between Pharaoh's declaration of divinity – 'I am your Lord most high' – and such Ḥallājian *shaṭḥiyyāt* as 'I am the Truth (i.e. God: *anā'l-ḥaqq*)'. This affinity was often noted and both admirers and detractors of al-Ḥallāj commented upon it.[36]

Among these were some who sought to defend Ibn al-ʿArabī by neutralising any objections. Thus, for the commentator and mystic ʿAbd al-Razzāq al-Kāshānī, or Qāshānī, (d. 730/1330), a follower of Ibn al-ʿArabī, there were only two issues: whether God accepted Pharaoh's faith and whether it was beneficial to Pharaoh to believe. Now Kāshānī clearly wishes to support Ibn al-ʿArabī while simultaneously blunting objections from critics. Scripture and logic prove, he says, that Pharaoh's last-minute belief was both sincere and accepted. But his profession saved him merely from 'doctrinal defilement' (*khubth iʿtiqādī*) and did not absolve him of the sins he had committed towards his fellow man.[37] As a result, his faith was acceptable but he was consigned to hell anyway. What was the advantage of his faith? Only the certain knowledge that he will not remain eternally in hell.

Others, to be sure, defended Ibn al-ʿArabī without attempting to compromise his position. Jalāl al-Dīn al-Dawwānī was willing to entertain bolder notions, arguing that repentance alone is the crucial element. God accepts repentance whenever it occurs, and Pharaoh both repented and believed. Al-Dawwānī goes so far as to restate Pharaoh's profession of faith in far more explicit terms, thus:

> I affirm and state as a certainty that there is not any true object of worship in existence other than the God in whom the Children of Israel believe ... He is truly to be worshipped.[38]

And he notes, perhaps with justice, that Pharaoh must be sincere as his are hardly words one might utter while drowning! Al-Dawwānī is even willing to attempt a radical reinterpretation of Qur'an 10:91, the verse immediately after Pharaoh's outcry and which is usually seen as sealing his condemnation. In it Gabriel replies to Pharaoh, 'What! Now? When before you rebelled and were among the evildoers?' By a complicated (and not very convincing) piece of grammatical legerdemain, al-Dawwānī tries to show that the verse should be read as though it meant, 'You have *not* sinned, O Pharaoh! *Now* your belief has uprooted your sin!'

Ḥājjī Khalīfa might praise al-Dawwānī's treatise as a logical proof of Ibn al-ʿArabī's position but others were not so easily impressed. Indeed, it was al-Dawwānī's misfortune to arouse the ire of the formidable above-mentioned seventeenth-century theologian ʿAlī al-Qāḍī al-Harawī. In his hostile commentary, which twines around al-Dawwānī's text with a python grip, al-Harawī lets no lapse of logic, doctrine, or grammar pass unnoticed; and he delights in gibes, sarcastic asides, and downright insults, calling al-Dawwānī both feeble-minded and ignorant. Though himself at times an admirer of Ibn al-ʿArabī, his position is radically opposed to al-Dawwānī's. While the latter stresses the efficacy of repentance and the breadth of the divine compassion, al-Harawī places unyielding insistence on the eternal decree of God. In his view, Moses and Aaron were blessed with felicity while still in their father's loins while Pharaoh even in his mother's womb had already been predestined to misery. Pharaoh's repentance was false, his apparent belief coerced. God saves Pharaoh's drowned body as a physical sign of his condemnation (Qur'an 10:92). This is a mock deliverance, a sort of bitter parody of genuine divine redemption; as al-Harawī puts it, 'fictitious deliverance is conformable with compelled belief'.[39]

Al-Dawwānī begins his treatise on the question with a frank admission that his purpose is to refute those who accuse Ibn al-ʿArabī of *kufr*.[40] He notes further that even among scholars there is a divergence of opinion on the faith of Pharaoh. There are, first, those who consider him an unbeliever. At the opposite extreme are those who consider him a believer. For al-Dawwānī, however 'the truth is that the illustrious verse clearly states belief without any hindrance either explicitly or implicitly.'[41] Here he attempts the unequivocal rewording already noted above. And he goes further to assert that 'whoever has a healthy nature and a sound mind knows that [Pharaoh] made this statement [of belief] only in the soundness of his mind, and not because he was at the moment of drowning ... .'[42] According to theologians, says al-Dawwānī, 'Belief is assent with the heart (*al-īmān huwa al-taṣdīq bi'l-qalb*) while recitation with the tongue is to fulfil the juridical precepts'. This being so, i.e. that Pharaoh believed with his heart and accomplished the prescribed declaration, the meaning of the Shaykh's statement is that death 'seized him at the instant of belief before any of his sins had been written down, for he lived no more after that [moment]. Submission (*islām*) cancels whatever preceded it in regard to the Creator, though not in regard to creatures'.[43] Moreover, God did this to make of Pharaoh 'a sign of His providence to whomsoever He will, so that no one might despair of the mercy of God'.[44]

For al-Dawwānī the fact that Pharaoh is cursed (*mal'ūn*) does not in itself exclude him from the community of belief; indeed, he comes under the heading provided by the verse 'except for him who repents and believes (*illā man tāba wa-amana*: Qur'an 19:60 and 25:70)'. Furthermore, it was drowning itself that was the 'most painful torment' promised to Pharaoh, (*ashaddu al-'adhāb huwa al-gharaq*); after all, Pharaoh was actually hostile not to God but to Moses.[45]

In conclusion, al-Dawwānī turns to a brief defence of Ibn al-'Arabī against the charge of *ilḥād*. Those who so accuse him are ignorant, for 'whoever does not know something denies it'. These ignorant accusers do not understand the technical terminology (*iṣṭilāḥ*) of the Shaykh, and they miss the obvious point of his comments. For Ibn al-'Arabī meant to uphold the 'vastness of God's mercy (*ya'nī bi-dhālika sa'at raḥmat Allāh*)'. In fact, the critics of the Shaykh, by denying this, 'vex believers and frighten them into despair in God's spirit'.[46]

The hostile al-Qāḍī al-Harawī, writing almost a century later, begins with the unequivocal affirmation of predestination in the very *ḥamdala* of his treatise: 'Praise be to Him who grants felicity to him who is fortunate, even while still in the loins of his father such as Moses and Aaron, and [praise be to Him] who inflicts misery on him who is miserable, even while still in his mother's belly, such as Pharaoh and Qārūn.'[47] He goes on to deny both that there is a wide divergence of opinion on the question and that anyone but Ibn al-'Arabī has ventured to declare Pharaoh a believer; in fact, he is not only isolated in this opinion but even denies it himself in the *Futūḥāt*, thus contradicting himself.[48] Moreover, al-Dawwānī defames the *'ulamā'* and claims for the disagreement a dignity that it does not deserve. As for the 'belief of desperation' which al-Dawwānī is so ready to approve, al-Harawī is adamant: Belief of this contemptible sort will be available to every *kāfir* on Judgement Day. Indeed, as Abū Ḥanīfa pointed out with grim wit, there will be no unbelievers in hell. By Judgement Day all will have resorted to the same despairing faith.[49]

Al-Harawī's sharpest indignation is reserved, however, for two points. First, he considers it a form of defamation that al-Dawwānī should make the scope of the divine mercy the focus of the debate. In doing so, he casts aspersions on the integrity of the *'ulamā'*. It is 'a stupendous slander' (*buhtān 'aẓīm*) and tantamount to accusing respectable savants of denying the divine compassion. In such accusations al-Dawwānī in fact commits *kufr* himself; never mind that in the vexed passage itself, as al-Harawī conveniently ignores, Ibn al-'Arabī explains God's action under the rubrics of 'providence' (*'ināya*) and 'mercy' (*raḥma*). Al-Dawwānī is merely following his master's lead; and yet, it must be said that throughout the treatise, al-Dawwānī seems to be a handy target for abuse al-Harawī does not dare direct at Ibn al-'Arabī himself. In any case, the attacker continues, the controversial opinion is Ibn al-'Arabī's alone; it has no basis in tradition. Worse, an ignorant person hearing of this controversy 'thinks that this is the kind of disputed question that took place between the *Ahl al-sunna wa'l-jamā'a* and the Mu'tazila and those like them, or between the Ḥanafīs and the Shāfi'īs'.[50] Al-Qāḍī al-Harawī thus wishes to treat the dispute as a grotesque anomaly, and nothing more. But this is a debater's trick. Indeed, it is partly because the topics, both tacit and expressed, had long roots in the past that the controversy assumed such vehemence on both sides.

Early on in his rebuttal, al-Qāḍī al-Harawī attempts to refute al-Dawwānī without, however, seeming to limit the divine mercy. Had God intended to demonstrate mercy by His treatment of Pharaoh, and had Pharaoh's faith been sincere, God would have preserved him alive and not flung his naked body, perishing and alone, on the sea shore; but instead, God manifested the counterfeit (*tazwīr*) nature of his profession of faith.[51] Against al-Dawwānī's claim that Pharaoh's faith is proved by the fact that he alone of all his host was washed up on the shore, al-Qāḍī al-Harawī counters with his dictum, that this is merely 'fictitious deliverance' (*al-khalāṣ al-ṣūrī*) as is appropriate for 'compelled belief' (*al-īmān al-iḍṭirārī*). God does not waste the rewards He reserves for those who perform good works on such as Pharaoh; true, sometimes the actions of unbelievers take the form of the actions of believers, such as feeding the poor and helping the weak, but this does not entitle unbelievers to rewards.[52]

To the claim that Pharaoh believed 'with his heart', al-Qāḍī al-Harawī responds that this too must be rejected 'since what is in the heart is not knowable except to the Knower of the Invisible (*amr al-qalb ghayr ma'lūm illā li-'ālim al-ghayb*)', i.e. God Himself.[53] Had Pharaoh been saved from drowning, this would have proved that his faith was genuine. Instead his body washed up so that his followers would not think that he had somehow escaped God's judgement. For both sides the drowned corpse of Pharaoh is a sign, but a sign that accommodates contraries: for al-Dawwānī it signifies God's mercy, for al-Qāḍī al-Harawī God's wrath and retribution.

## V

The best defender of Ibn al-ʿArabī is, not surprisingly, Ibn al-ʿArabī himself; indeed, his chapter on Moses represents both an affirmation of Pharaoh's faith as well as an anticipation of the arguments against it together with a persuasive defence of his position within the confines of his system. By and large his defenders will draw on the arguments he devised, though often in considerably weakened form. It is interesting to note that Ibn al-ʿArabī's main arguments here rest on a close and rather literal reading of the Qur'anic text. Pharaoh was taken despite his faith but he had no certainty that he was perishing; his belief then is not based on desperation. Moreover, his drowned body is itself a sign of his salvation; indeed, 'salvation encompassed him both physically and spiritually' (*ḥiss*$^{an}$ *wa-maʿn*$^{an}$).[54] But on the most fundamental level, 'though it is deeply implanted in the common people's minds that [Pharaoh] is lost, they have no explicit text (*naṣṣ*) on which they can lean to prove it'.[55] It is thus on the Qur'anic text itself that Ibn al-ʿArabī rests and it says nothing explicitly about the authenticity or not of Pharaoh's faith or his ultimate destiny. This is true enough; the very fact that the text is open to more than one interpretation made debate over its implications unavoidable. Ibn al-ʿArabī's reading of the passage is consistent with his larger view. In the exordium of the *Fuṣūṣ al-ḥikam* Ibn al-ʿArabī makes it plain that the book with its title was given to him by the Prophet Muḥammad with his own hands in a 'visitation' (or 'annunciation' *mubashshara*): 'I saw the Emissary of God (may God bless him and grant him peace) in a visitation that I was given to see in the last part of the month Muḥarram in the year 627 [1229] in Damascus … '.[56] The book thus comes with a singular authority as a final statement of Ibn al-ʿArabī's vision.[57] It seems safe to assume that his position on Pharaoh represents a deepening of his view rather than a contradiction. And it is possible, however imperfectly, to attempt to understand Ibn al-ʿArabī's position within the context of his mystical system.

Ultimately, Moses and Pharaoh are one; they represent 'a single essence' (*ʿayn wāḥid*).[58] In a monistic world view as radical as Ibn al-ʿArabī's, no genuine opposition or disharmony can endure in the final analysis; some reconciliation of contending contraries must take place for the unicity of being to remain intact. If the universe, if indeed, all being, represents the incessant self-disclosure of God in the process that Ibn al-ʿArabī (here following al-Ghazālī and others) names *tajallī*, then even Pharaoh must in some way participate in this divine epiphany. First, like Moses, Pharaoh is a locus of manifestation (*maẓhar*)[59] of the Divine Names, especially those linked with power, authority and wrath; indeed, there is some analogue, however pallid, with God's authority in the regal authority Pharaoh enjoyed.[60] Juridically, yes, Pharaoh is reprehensible but as a manifestation of God's own nature he is not merely redeemable but good (though in the final analysis, 'good' and 'bad' are irrelevant).[61] He must act as he does for this is his appointed role; he is part of that intrinsic polarity of the cosmos which is its very nature as the arena of God's self-disclosure.[62] Moreover, Pharaoh is merely the transitory figment of that 'fixed essence' (*'ayn thābit*) or, to use Izutsu's formulation,[63] that 'permanent archetype' known as Pharaoh and which exists in the supra-sensible, transcendent realm.

From this perspective, concerns over Pharaoh's ultimate status become meaningless for no malefactor, no matter how grave a sinner, will remain forever in hell. To posit an enduring hell is to compromise the 'oneness of being' (*waḥdat al-wujūd*) that is the *raison d'être* of Ibn al-ʿArabī's system, though, as Landolt himself pointed out many years ago, he nowhere employs that particular phrase.[64] Even more pertinently, it is pointless to quarrel over whether Pharaoh acted on his own volition or was impelled by God; the question of free will becomes irrelevant in such a monism. Only God possesses genuine existence; all else is fictive, however real it seems. And everything that appears to exist exists as a revelation of God's nature. Indeed, creation betokens not the fashioning of distinct and autonomous entities but the gradual coming to consciousness of all things as prompted by love; God Himself acts out of love and it is their nascent love that draws things from non-being into being.[65] Being is itself a form of self-realisation. From the divine perspective nothing changes when creatures assume existence. Neither Pharaoh nor anyone else can truly rebel against God; the very notion is ludicrous for all that is exists only insofar as it manifests God Himself and is a part of Him. For an Ashʿarī or other 'orthodox' theologian, rebellion against God is meaningless because of God's unimaginable omnipotence; for Ibn al-ʿArabī and his followers, rebellion is meaningful enough and may indeed be necessary (so that the divine attributes may be given full play), but is ultimately harmonised within the utter oneness of God which encompasses all polarities.

The divine mercy which Ibn al-ʿArabī's champions espouse in their defences of him reveals itself most fully in the conferral of existence on creatures. Indeed, the Divine Name 'the Merciful' is the most comprehensive of God's names and subsumes all the others.[66] Compassion is the very 'breath of the Merciful' and it not only pities and absolves creation but is the instrumentality by which creatures are accorded the self-actualisation that is being. When Ibn al-ʿArabī's defenders such as al-Dawwānī resort to the vast extent of the divine mercy they are not simply saying that God's 'mercy outstrips His wrath', as in the famous *ḥadith qudsī*.[67] Rather, they are upholding a *Weltanschauung* drastically at odds with 'orthodox' doctrine. 'Mercy' is, as it were, a code word for a system in which (from the viewpoint of 'the orthodox') the ineffable transcendence of God is fatally compromised; if everything that exists, however fictive its existence, is somehow ultimately part and parcel of God's self-manifestation, the distinction between God and creature is blurred, if not effaced. Moreover, all our distinctions, such as that between good and evil, are ultimately illusory; neither Pharaoh nor anyone else can be adjudged wicked in the end.[68]

ʿAbd al-Qādir al-Jazāʾirī (d. 1300/1883), the last participant known to me in the present debate, was a lifelong disciple of Ibn al-ʿArabī, though (as Chodkiewicz in particular has pointed out) he was no mere imitator of his master but an original mind who elaborated his own mystical insights in an impressive body of work. (Until 1966, in fact, when his remains were returned to Algeria, ʿAbd al-Qādir lay alongside Ibn al-ʿArabī in the latter's tomb on the slopes of Mt. Qāsiyūn in Damascus which symbolised vividly the close connection of ʿAbd al-Qādir and his master.) In the present context, ʿAbd al-Qādir furnishes several distinctive replies to certain objections raised by al-Harawī and others, and so it is fitting to close with him. In his brief consideration of the question of Pharaoh, ʿAbd al-Qādir claims that his own instruction comes directly from God. 'God taught me,' he says (*la-qad aʿlamanī al-Ḥaqq taʿālā*), 'for example, that He intended the drowning of Pharaoh as an example (*nakāl*) to others but only in this world, and not the next'.[69]

On two other crucial points ʿAbd al-Qādir sides with, and defends, Ibn al-ʿArabī and such defenders of his as al-Dawwānī: These are the genuineness of Pharaoh's belief *in extremis* and the equal validity of his *shahāda*. Pharaoh's recognition of God's oneness, his declaration of *tawḥīd*, is authentic because he implicitly accepts the prophecy of Moses and Aaron (and so, by extension, that of the Prophet Muḥammad); this acceptance occurs when Pharaoh says, 'I believe that there is no God but He in whom the children of Israel believe' (Qur'an 10:89). By 'children of Israel' Pharaoh actually means Moses and Aaron; his acceptance of their belief betokens his acceptance of their prophetic role. Therefore his apparently truncated *shahāda* is complete, and legally valid as well. Moreover, his belief was not the 'belief of despair' (*īmān al-yaʾs*); if anything, it bore witness to God's miracles and testified to His omnipotence to Moses himself.[70]

In a sense the debate over the faith of Pharaoh is yet another chapter in an ongoing attempt by orthodox thinkers, from Ibn Taymiyya on, to check the dangerous advance of 'incarnationism' (*ḥulūl*).[71] That is in any case the ostensible issue. It seems probable though that the persistence of the debate reflects another, more tacit matter; namely, the continuing spread and influence of Ibn al-ʿArabī's teachings which by the fifteenth century appeared virtually unstoppable. Of course it is not really a question of stopping Ibn al-ʿArabī or his followers; only the most stridently quixotic, like al-Biqāʿī, thought to achieve that. Rather, it is a question of how to interpret and control a speculative mysticism as profoundly conceived as it is beautifully articulated. The gingerly way in which most of the disputants treat the person of Ibn al-ʿArabī indicates his growing, and eventually well-nigh unassailable, status. (Thus, al-Qāḍī al-Harawī is remarks dryly that 'it is safer to pass over him in silence'.)[72] But in Islamic theology, the skirmishes and sometimes the decisive battles are often fought out in the commentaries, glosses, super-commentaries and super-glosses rather than in the text, the *matn*, itself. In this sense, interpretation, especially of thought as esoteric and difficult as Ibn al-ʿArabī's, can be as much stratagem and power-play as it is hermeneutic.

It is hardly possible to do justice to either the complexity or the extent of the debate over the faith of Pharaoh in a brief article. Suffice it to say that the interest in Pharaoh was neither historical nor antiquarian. He represented the extreme instance. For some, like al-Dawwānī and his followers, he signified the utmost reach of God's mercy and so, the farthest acceptable limit of the community of believers; for others, more traditionalistic, more precise, and perhaps even more beleaguered, Pharaoh remained the prototype of the irredeemable unbeliever, a kind of negative examplar. For certain of these more circumspect and more legalistic participants, there may have lurked as well the fear that if Pharaoh might be saved in the end, then even Ibn al-ʿArabī himself together with his disciples could be forgiven too.

## Appendix

### The Participants in the Debate: A Provisional Listing[73]

1. Muḥyī al-Dīn Ibn al-ʿArabī (d. 638/1240)[74]
2. Ibn Taymiyya (d. 721/1328)[75] *contra*
3. ʿAbd al-Razzāq al-Kāshānī (d. 730/1330) *pro*
4. Dā'ūd al-Qayṣarī (d. 751/1350)[76] *pro*
5. Masʿūd b. ʿUmar al-Taftāzānī (d. 792/1390)[77] *contra*
6. Walī al-Dīn Aḥmad al-ʿIrāqī (d. 826/1422)[78]
7. Quṭb al-Dīn al-Iznīqī (d. 885/1480)[79] *contra*
8. Ibrāhīm b. ʿUmar al-Biqāʿī (d. 885/1480)[80] *contra*
9. ʿAbd al-Raḥmān b. Aḥmad Jāmī (d. 898/1492)[81] *pro*
10. Jalāl al-Dīn al-Dawwānī (d. 907/1501) *pro*
11. Muḥammad b. ʿAlī al-Qarabāghī (d. 942/1535)[82]
12. Muḥammad b. Muḥammad al-Ghumrī, Ṣibṭ al-Marsafī (d. 970/1562)[83]
13. ʿAbd al-Wahhāb al-Shaʿrānī (d. 973/1565)[84] *pro*
14. ʿAlī al-Qāḍī al-Harawī (d. 1014/1605) *contra*
15. ʿAbd Allāh al-Rūmī al-Busnawī (d. 1054/1644)[85]
16. Ḥājjī Khalīfa (d. 1068/1657) *pro*
17. Muḥammad b. ʿAbd al-Rasūl al-Barzanjī (d. 1103/1691)[86]
18. Badrān b. Aḥmad al-Khalīlī (d. ca. 1103/1691)[87] *contra*
19. Aḥmad b. Zayn al-Dīn al-Aḥsā'ī (d. 1241/1826)[88] *contra*
20. Abū Muḥyī al-Dīn ʿAbd al-Qādir b. Muḥyī al-Dīn al-Jazā'irī (d. 1300/1883)[89] *pro*

## Notes

1. An earlier, briefer version of this article was delivered at the Annual Meeting of the American Oriental Society, Ann Arbor, April 1985. I thank colleagues who were present for their valuable comments, and especially Professor Eleazar Birnbaum.

2. Ḥājjī Khalīfa, *The Balance of Truth*, tr. G. L. Lewis (London, 1957), p. 149. This is a translation from the Ottoman Turkish of *Mīzān al-ḥaqq fī ikhtiyār al-aḥaqq* (Istanbul, 1306/1888). Ḥājjī Khalīfa devotes a brief section of his monumental *Kashf al-ẓunūn ʿan asāmī al-kutub wa'l-funūn* (Beirut, 1994 ed.) to the commentaries on Ibn al-ʿArabī's *Fuṣūṣ al-ḥikam*; see vol. 4, pp. 133–134.

3. L. Gardet and M.-M. Anawati, *Introduction à la théologie musulmane* (Paris, 1948), p. 169.

4. See his *Jawāmiʿ al-kalim* (Tabriz, 1276/1859), vol. 2, pp. 113 ff. The dispute is mentioned in the bibliography of al-Aḥsā'ī's *responsa* and *fatāwā*; see Abu al-Qāsim Ibrāhīmī, *Fihrist-i kutub-i shaykh-i ajall-i awḥad-i marḥūm-i Aḥmad-i Aḥsā'ī va-sā'ir-i mashāyikh-i ʿiẓam* (Kirmān, n.d.), vol. 2, p. 307. For al-Aḥsā'ī, see *GALS*, vol. 1, pp. 844–845, the pioneering studies of Nicolas, the work of Henry Corbin and most recently studies by Juan Cole and M. A. Amir-Moezzi. See also the important but unpublished Ph.D. dissertation by Hamid Samawi (Buffalo, NY, 1998).

5. Eric Geoffroy, *Le soufisme en Egypte et en Syrie* (Damascus, 1995), cited in Michel Chodkiewicz, 'Le procès posthume d'Ibn ʿArabī' in Frederick de Jong and Bernd Radtke, ed., *Islamic Mysticism Contested: Thirteen Centuries of Controversies and Polemics* (Leiden, 1999), p. 115, n. 76.

6. For earlier treatments of the question, see Denis Gril, 'Le personnage coranique de Pharaon d'après l'interprétation d'Ibn ʿArabī', *Annales Islamologiques*, 14 (1978), pp. 37–57; and the shorter study by Carl W. Ernst, 'Controversies over Ibn al-ʿArabī's *Fuṣūṣ*: The Faith of Pharaoh', *Islamic Culture*, 59 (1985), pp. 259–266. (For a useful overview of several manuscripts devoted to the question in hand, see Ernst, p. 260, n. 5.) A more recent discussion of the dispute is in Alexander D. Knysh, *Ibn ʿArabī in the Later Islamic Tradition* (Albany, NY, 1999), pp. 158–165. (On the figure of Pharaoh, see A. J. Wensinck and G. Vajda, 'Firʿawn', *EI2*, vol. 2, pp. 917–918.) I have drawn here largely on the manuscripts held in the Princeton University Library; for which see Rudolf Mach, *Catalogue of Arabic Manuscripts (Yahuda Section) in the Garrett Collection* ... (Princeton, NJ, 1977), p. 186.

7. Not all theologians understood the verse this way. The early theologian al-Qāsim b. Ibrāhīm (169–246/785–860), later claimed as a Zaydī imam, in his *Kitāb al-dalīl al-kabīr* denies that the offending statement involves a pretension to divinity on Pharaoh's part, see Binyamin Abrahamov, *al-Qāsim B. Ibrāhīm on the Proof of God's Existence:* Kitāb al-Dalīl al-Kabīr (Leiden, 1990), pp. 174–177. (For the question of al-Qāsim's Zaydī status, see pp. 7 and 11ff.)

8. Pharaoh is 'the chief villain of the Koran', as William C. Chittick nicely puts it in his *The Self-Disclosure of God: Principles of Ibn al-ʿArabī's Cosmology* (Albany, NY, 1998), p. 53.

9. See Fouad Ajami, *The Dream Palace of the Arabs* (New York, 1998), pp. xiv and 193 ff.

10. *Al-Futūḥāt al-makkiyya*, ed. O. Yahya (Cairo, 1975–1990), vol. 4, p. 393. The word *mutakabbir* has a dual denotation: when it applies to God (as in Qur'an 59:23 and elsewhere),

it means 'sublime, mighty, great', but if applied to creatures, denotes 'conceited' or ' haughty', as in Qur'an 7:13, where God applies it to Iblīs for refusing to prostrate himself before Adam; see Manfred Ullmann, *Wörterbuch der klassischen arabischen Sprache* (Wiesbaden, 1970—), vol. 1, p. 23.

11. Abū Manṣūr Muḥammad b. Muḥammad al-Māturīdī, *Kitāb al-tawhid*, ed. F. Kholeif (Beirut, 1970), p. 274.

12. See Exodus 14:8: *wa-yekhazzeq Adonai et-lev Far'oh*: the Vulgate renders this *induravitque Dominus cor Pharaonis …*

13. The final phrase – *wa-anā min al-muslimīn* – 'And I am among those that surrender,' literally, *the muslims*, – is in some ways the crux of the passage. For the translation see A. J. Arberry, *The Koran Interpreted* (New York, 1967), p. 235.

14. See Qur'an 4:18 (tr. Dawood): 'But He will not forgive those who do evil and, when death comes to them, say: "Now we repent!"'

15. Fakhr al-Dīn al-Rāzī, *Mafātīḥ al-ghayb* (Cairo, 1357/1938), vol. 17, pp. 153 ff.

16. Ibid., p. 155.

17. *Fuṣūṣ al-ḥikam*, ed. A. 'Afifi (Cairo, 1946) vol. 1, p. 201; translation (somewhat modified) by R. W. J. Austin, *The Bezels of Wisdom* (New York, 1980), p. 255. See also Ibn al-'Arabī's *al-Futūḥāt al-makkiyya*, esp. vol. 3, p. 251; vol. 4, pp. 245, 393, 424; vol. 5, pp. 324–325; vol. 6, pp. 359–360, 362; vol. 7, p. 122; vol. 13, pp. 243–244, 575. For a brief comment in the earlier work *Kitāb 'anqa' mughrib*, see now Gerald T. Elmore, *Islamic Sainthood in the Fullness of Time* (Leiden, 1999), pp. 487–488 and 560. In his *Kitāb al-isfār 'an natā'ij al-asfār*, Ibn al-'Arabī makes two veiled references to Pharaoh which are clearly condemnatory; See the text and translation in *Le dévoilement des effets du voyage*, ed. Denis Gril (Paris, 1994), pp. 2 and 73–74. In the latter passage Pharaoh is termed 'the enemy of religion' (*'adūw al-dīn).*

18. See, among several possible examples, *Jalāl al-Dīn al-Suyūṭī*, ed. and tr. E. M. Sartain (Cambridge, 1975), vol. 1, p. 55. Al-Suyūṭī defended Ibn al-'Arabī as a saint, even though, like Ibn Taymiyya, he condemned the practitioners of *ḥulul* and *ittiḥād* uncompromisingly. I suspect that in his treatise entitled *Tanbi'at al-ghabi bi-tabri'a Ibn 'Arabī* al-Suyūṭī discusses our question, but I have not had access to this manuscript which is in the Egyptian National Library (*Majāmi'* 182). Note that a comparable debate involved the reputation of the great mystical poet Ibn al-Fāriḍ and involved a number of the same disputants.

19. As paraphrased in Chodkiewicz, 'Le procès posthume d'Ibn 'Arabī', pp. 102–103: 'Ni musulman, ni juif, ni chrétien n'avait jamais osé proférer une erreur aussi scandaleuse, déclare Ibn Taymiyya', citing the latter's *Majmū'at al-rasā'il wa'l-masā'il* (Cairo, n.d.), vol. 4, pp. 91–92 and 98–101 (I have used the Beirut 1992, edition where the passage occurs in vol. 4, pp. 110 ff.). Al-Biqā'ī parrots Ibn Taymiyya on this point; See the former's *Maṣra' al-taṣawwuf* (Cairo, 1953), p. 130. For Ibn Taymiyya's venomous tirades against Ibn al-'Arabī, see also M. Chodkiewicz, *Le sceau des saints: prophétie et sainteté dans la doctrine d'Ibn Arabi* (Paris, 1986), pp. 31 f.

20. As Claude Addas has pointed out, Ibn al-'Arabī has been generally known since the 8th century AH as the 'author of the *Fuṣūṣ*', despite his voluminous *œuvre*. Addas speculates that this may be due to 'la paresse intellectuelle des *fuqahā*'' since this work was briefer and more compact than certain others; See Addas, *Ibn 'Arabī ou la qûete du Soufre Rouge* (Paris, 1989), p. 326.

21. Khalifa, *The Balance of Truth*, pp. 76–77.

22. See, among others, A. J. Wensinck, *The Muslim Creed* (Cambridge, 1932), p. 37; also Josef van Ess, *Theologie und Gesellschaft im 2. und 3. Jahrhundert Hidschra* (Berlin and New York, 1991), vol. 1, pp. 20–23.

23. Al-Harawī, *Farr al-ʿawn min muddaʿī īmān Firʿawn*, Arabic ms. 5386 (Mach #2181), Yahuda Collection, Princeton University, f. 307a. For al-Harawī, see *GAL*, vol. 2, p. 517; *GALS*, vol. 2, p. 539.

24. Ibn al-Jawzī, *Zād al-masīr fī ʿilm al-tafsīr* (Damascus and Beirut, 1965), vol. 4, p. 59.

25. Al-Zamakhsharī, *Kashshāf*, ed. W. N. Lees (Calcutta, 1856), vol. 1, p. 596.

26. *Īmān al-yaʾs* is the form of belief that unbelievers will strive for on the Day of Judgement and is unacceptable; al-Dawwānī, *Risāla īmān Firʿawn*, Yahuda Arabic ms. 2180/3, f. 57b. Earlier the great historian and commentator al-Ṭabarī had considered Pharaoh's *shahāda* a statement made under duress (*iljāʾ*) and so invalid. Cited in al-Ṭabarī, *Majmaʿ al-bayān fī tafsīr al-Qurʾan* (Qumm, 1403/1983), vol. 3, p. 131.

27. H. Ritter, *Das Meer der Seele* (Leiden, 1955), p. 74, citing ʿAṭṭār, *Muṣībat-nāma*; (see also, p. 272); and Ibn al-Jawzī, *Zād al-masīr fī ʿilm al-tafsīr*, vol. 4, p. 60. Jalāl al-Dīn al-Suyūṭī gives a number of variants on this motif in his *tafsīr*; See *al-Durr al-manthūr fī tafsīr al-maʾthūr* (Beirut, 1411/1990), vol. 3, pp. 568–569.

28. Akmal al-Dīn, *Risālat īmān Firʿawn*, (Yahuda Arabic ms., Mach 2184), f. 54a. The notion of a leaven comes from Ibn al-ʿArabī, see Toshihiko Izutsu, *A Comparative Study of the Key Philosophical Concepts in Sufism and Taoism* (Tokyo, 1966), vol. 1, p. 142.

29. Cited in Ritter, *Das Meer der Seele*, p. 98. Also the opinion of al-Muḥāsibī (d. 243/857); See Josef van Ess, *Die Gedankenwelt des Ḥāriṯ al-Muḥāsibī* (Bonn, 1961), p. 51 (with reference to *Riʿāya*, p. 236).

30. See Fritz Meier, *Abū Saʿīd-i Abu-l'Ḫayr (357–440/967–1049): Wirklichkeit und Legende* (Leiden, 1976), p. 176.

31. Cited in G. Böwering, *The Mystical Vision of Existence in Classical Islam* (Berlin, 1980), p. 190. See also Izutsu, *A Comparative Study*, vol. 1, pp. 105–106; and Louis Massignon, *La passion de Ḥusayn Ibn Manṣûr Ḥallâj* (Paris, 1975) vol. 1, p. 111, n. 5.

32. Ibid. See also Böwering's article 'Sahl al-Tustarī', *EI2*, vol. 8, pp. 840–841.

33. See al-Ghazālī, *Iḥyāʾ ʿulūm al-dīn* (Beirut, 1417/1996), vol. 4, p. 73.

34. *Al-Futūḥāt al-makkiyya*, vol. 13, p. 575.

35. So in Rūzbihān Baqlī, *Sharḥ shaṭḥīyāt*, ed. Henry Corbin (Tehran and Paris, 1966), p. 373. In the same passage Rūzbihān ascribes to al-Ḥallāj the statement, 'My master and my teacher is Iblīs as well as Pharaoh (*ṣāḥib-i man wa-ustadh-i man Iblīs wa-Firʿawn ast*)'. (Elsewhere in the same work he refers to Pharaoh as the 'Pharaoh of Nature' (*Firʾawn-i ṭabīʿa*), e.g. pp. 87, 144, and 237). These are probably not to be taken as actual dicta of al-Ḥallāj but epitomise an attitude of which he was considered the main exemplar by later Sufis.

36. See Louis Massignon, *La passion*, vol. 2, pp. 46 and 189, for examples.

37. ʿAbd al-Razzāq al-Qāshānī, *Sharḥ Fuṣūṣ al-ḥikam* (Cairo, 1321/1903–1904), p. 254. See *GAL*, vol. 2, p. 262; *GALS*, vol. 2, p. 280, and for this work, *GALS*, vol. 1, p. 793(c). For an extensive overview of Ibn al-ʿArabī's followers and commentators, see James W. Morris, 'Ibn ʿArabī and his Interpreters', *JAOS*, 106 (1986), Part 1, pp. 539–551 and Part 2, pp. 733–756; for al-Qāshānī, see pp. 751 f. Osman Yahya (='Uthmān Yaḥyā), *Histoire et classification de l'œuvre d'Ibn ʿArabī* (Damascus, 1964), vol. 1, pp. 241–256, lists some 108 commentaries on the *Fuṣūṣ*; for al-Qāshānī, see p. 243 (#9).

38. Al-Dawwānī, *Risāla īmān Firʿawn*, Yahuda ms. 2180, f. 138b, ll. 16 ff.

39. *Al-khalāṣ al-ṣūri kāna fī muṭabaqāt al-īmān al-iḍṭirārī* in al-Qāḍī al-Harawī, *Farr al-ʿawn*, Yahuda Arabic ms. 2181, f. 308a, l. 11. According to Michel Chodkiewicz in his selection and translation of the Amir ʿAbd al-Qādir's works entitled *Ecrits spirituels* (Paris, 1982), p. 190, n. 61, both al-Dawwānī's and al-Qāḍī al-Harawī's treatises have been published in M. ʿAbd al-Laṭīf b. al-Khāṭib, *Īmān Firʿawn* (Cairo, 1963), a work to which I have not had access.

40. *Risāla fī īmān Firʿawn*, Yahuda Arabic ms #2180/1, f. 138b, l. 8: *al-radd ʿalā man qāla bi-takfīr mawlā al-ʿulamā'*. (I have used this manuscript as well as Yahuda #2180/3. There is another manuscript in the Garrett Collection, Princeton University Library, Garrett #464H, Hitti no. 2197.)

41. *Risāla fī īmān Firʿawn*, Yahuda Arabic ms #2180/1, f. 138b, l. 12.

42. *Risāla fī īmān Firʿawn*, f. 139a, l. 2.

43. Ibid., f. 139a, l. 5.

44. Ibid., f. 139a, l. 8.

45. *Risāla fī īmān Firʿawn*, Yahuda Arabic ms. #2184, f. 57b.

46. *Risāla fī īmān Firʿawn*, f. 58b.

47. *Farr al-ʿawn min muddaʿī īmān Firʿawn*, Yahuda Arabic ms.#2181, f. 305a.

48. *Farr al-ʿawn*, f. 306b. For the *Futūḥāt*, see vol. 4, p. 393, and vol. 6, pp. 359–360, for two examples of apparent contradiction.

49. *Farr al-ʿawn*, f. 310b.

50. Ibid., f. 306b. This is hardly true, as we have already seen; See footnote 7 supra.

51. Ibid., f. 308a, l. 6 ff.

52. Ibid., l. 12 ff.

53. Ibid., f. 307b, l. 2.

54. See William C. Chittick, *Imaginal Worlds: Ibn al-ʿArabī and the Problem of Religious Diversity* (Albany, NY, 1994), p. 74.

55. *Fuṣūṣ*, vol. 1, p. 212.

56. Ibid., p. 47 (tr. Austin, modified, p. 45).

57. Ibid., p. 197 (tr. Austin, p. 252).

58. Ibid., p. 209: *wa'l-ʿayn wāḥid fa-kayfa furriqa*? See also the pertinent comments in Tilman Nagel, *Geschichte der islamischen Theologie* (Munich, 1994), p. 196.

59. For this rendering of *maẓhar* see Chittick, *Imaginal Worlds*, p. 17 f.

60. *Fuṣūṣ*, vol. 1, p. 211.

61. According to ʿAfīfī in his commentary on the *Fuṣūṣ*, the question rests on the distinction (for which it is difficult to find exact equivalents in English) between a 'command [or matter] of constituent existence' (*amr takwīnī*) and a 'command of juridical obligation' (*amr taklīfī*), 'between which there is a significant gulf'. Thus Ibn al-ʿArabī saw Pharaoh as 'obedient in an *amr takwīnī* even if he had been disobedient in an *amr taklīfī*', *Fuṣūṣ*, vol. 2, p. 65.

62. *Fuṣūṣ*, vol. 1, p. 200; tr. Austin, p. 254.

63. Izutsu, *A Comparative Study*, vol. 1, p. 163.

64. Hermann Landolt, 'Simnani on *Waḥdat al-Wujūd*', in M. Mohaghegh and H. Landolt, ed., *Collected Papers on Islamic Philosophy and Mysticism* (Tehran, 1971), (pp. 91–112), p. 100.

65. See *Fuṣūṣ*, vol. 1, p. 203, and Izutsu, *A Comparative Study*, vol. 1, p. 131.

66. See Izutsu, *A Comparative Study*, vol. 1, p. 101. Izutsu's discussion of the Divine Mercy in Ibn al-ʿArabī remains unsurpassed; see especially pp. 109–132 of the above-cited work.

67. See Muslim, *Ṣaḥīḥ* (Cairo, 1955–1956), vol. 4, pp. 2107 ff. For a wider discussion, see my *Theodicy in Islamic Thought* (Princeton, NJ, 1984), pp. 252–253 and 257.

68. Izutsu puts it succinctly as usual: 'All events that occur in this world, all actions that are done, are, without even a single exception, due to the Divine Will. In this sense, there can be no distinction between good and bad, or right and wrong. Every phenomenon, as it actually is, is a direct effect of the Will of God', in *A Comparative Study*, p. 120.

69. *Mawāqif* (n.p., 1329/1911), vol. 1, p. 54. On ʿAbd al-Qādir's instruction by God (as well as his human masters), see M. Chodkiewicz's remarks in the introduction to his selection and translation of the *Mawāqif* under the title *Ecrits spirituels* (Paris, 1982), pp. 24–25.

70. *Mawāqif*, vol. 1, p. 54.

71. For Ibn Taymiyya's campaign for a 'pure Sunni belief', see the summary by Nagel, *Geschichte der islamischen Theologie*, pp. 232–233.

72. *Farr al-ʿawn*, f. 315b.

73. These are the participants I have been able to identify to date; I have no doubt that there are others. The indications *pro* and *contra* given here are meant only as general designations of the disputants' positions since some opposed Ibn al-ʿArabī's view of Pharaoh while supporting him; for others, the debate merged with the larger issue of whether hell was eternal or not. Still others, like al-Ṭabarī, believed that Pharaoh's faith was sincere but that he was damned anyway for his misdeeds.

74. Ibn al-ʿArabī commented on his own *Fuṣūṣ al-ḥikam* in a work entitled *Naqsh al-fuṣūṣ*. I have used the Arabic text in Jāmī's *Naqd al-nuṣūṣ fī sharḥ Naqsh al-Fuṣūṣ*, ed. William C. Chittick (Tehran, 1977), pp. 3–13. See Chittick's remarks in his Persian introduction to this edition, p. 25 (#39).

75. See Ernst, 'Controversies over Ibn al-ʿArabī's *Fuṣūṣ*', p. 260, n. 5; *GAL*, vol. 2, pp. 125–127 and *GALS*, vol. 2, pp. 119–126.

76. See Yaḥyā, *Histoire et classification de l'œuvre d'Ibn ʿArabī*, vol. 1, pp. 244–245.

77. See the useful discussion in Knysh, *Ibn ʿArabī*, pp. 158–165.

78. His condemnation of Ibn al-ʿArabī for his opinion on Pharaoh is cited in al-Biqāʿī, *Maṣraʿ al-taṣawwuf*, p. 135. (This seems to be the al-ʿIrāqī listed among *ḥadīth* experts in *GALS*, vol. 2, p. 946)

79. See his *Maṣraʿ al-taṣawwuf aw Tanbīh al-ghabī ilā takfīr Ibn ʿArabī* (*s.l.*, 1953), pp. 127–141. On al-Biqāʿī, see my *Theodicy in Islamic Thought* (Princeton, NJ, 1984), pp. 113–117 and 135–148.

80. See Bursalī Meḥmed Ṭāhir, *Osmanlī müellifleri* (Istanbul, 1334–1343/1915–1925), vol. 1, p. 160 (cited in R. Mach, *Catalogue of Arabic Manuscripts*, p. 186 [#2179]). Al-Iznīqī takes the position that Pharaoh's belief was coerced, and not voluntary; hence, it is invalid. Al-Iznīqī is listed as a commentator on the *Fuṣūṣ* in Osman Yaḥyā, *Histoire et classification de l'œuvre d'Ibn ʿArabī*, vol. 1, p. 247 (23a).

81. Jāmī wrote a commentary on *Fuṣūṣ al-ḥikam* entitled *Sharḥ Fuṣūṣ al-ḥikam*, as well as a super-commentary (in Persian) on Ibn al-ʿArabī's own commentary, entitled *Naqd al-nuṣūṣ fī sharḥ Naqsh al-Fuṣūṣ*, ed. William C. Chittick (Tehran, 1977). See also Osman Yaḥyā, *Histoire et classification de l'œuvre d'Ibn ʿArabī*, vol. 1, p. 247 (#24).

82. See Mach, *Catalogue of Arabic Manuscripts*, p. 186 (#2182).

83. See Ernst, 'Controversies over Ibn al-'Arabī's *Fuṣūṣ*', p. 260, n. 5; his work is entitled *Tanzīh al-kawn 'an i'tiqād islām Fir'awn*, see Osman Yahya, *Histoire et classification*, vol. 1, p. 117.

84. See his *al-Yawāqit wa'l-jawāhir* (Cairo, 1312/1894–1895), vol. 1, p. 12. Al-Sha'rānī, a fervent follower of Ibn al-'Arabī, defends him against the charge of *kufr* and denies that he attributed faith to Pharaoh; such attributions, he argues, have been interpolated (*madsūs*) by adversaries into his work and he cites *al-Futūḥāt al-makkiyya* in support.

85. See Ernst, 'Controversies over Ibn al-'Arabī's *Fuṣūṣ*', p. 260, n. 5. His work is entitled *Risālat al-Busnawī fī īmān Fir'awn* and is in the Azhar library (2794 [*ḥalam*] 33397/27–28); see also Osman Yahya, *Histoire et classification de l'œuvre d'Ibn 'Arabī*, vol. 1, p. 250 (#44) and *GALS*, vol. 1, 793/12.

86. Mach, *Catalogue of Arabic Manuscripts*, p. 186 (#2183); this manuscript consists of selections from al-Barzanjī's *al-Ta'yīd wa'l-'awn lil-qā'ilīn bi īmān Fir'awn* made by Naṣrī b. Aḥmad al-Ḥusrī.

87. See Ernst, 'Controversies over Ibn al-'Arabī's *Fuṣūṣ*', p. 260, n. 5. His work is entitled *Natījat al-tawfīq wa'l-'awn fi al-radd 'alā al-qā'ilin bi-ṣiḥḥat īmān Fir'awn* and is in the India Office Library, London (ms. 4644).

88. See endnote 4 supra.

89. See his *Mawāqif* (n.p., 1329/1911), vol. 1, pp. 53–55 (*Mawqif* #21); see also *Ecrits spirituels*, ed. and tr. Michel Chodkiewicz (Paris, 1982), pp. 32–33 and 190, n. 61; this has now been translated into English as *The Spiritual Writings of Amir 'Abd al-Kader* (Albany, NY, 1995), see pp. 17–18.

# 34

# The Eight Rules of Junayd: A General Overview of the Genesis and Development of Islamic Dervish Orders*

*Bernd Radtke*

In the region of the present-day states of Senegal, Mali and Nigeria, there arose in the first half of the nineteenth century a government organisation which was set up through the activities of 'Umar b. Sa'īd al-Fūtī (1793–1864), usually known as al-Ḥājj 'Umar.[1] He was a member of the Tijāniyya, an Islamic Sufi or dervish order which had been founded at the end of the eighteenth century by the Algerian Aḥmad al-Tijānī.[2] This order today has a membership of millions and exerts a powerful political influence, particularly in West Africa.[3]

The state which al-Ḥājj 'Umar established may be designated a Tijāniyya state, that is one whose 'ideological' foundations consisted of the teachings of the Tijāniyya order. The establishment of a state in conjunction with the organisation and teachings of a dervish order is in no way an unusual phenomenon in the course of Islamic history and civilisation. To name only a few examples: the Republic of Iran has roots which go back to the activity of the Ṣafawiyya order whose adherents conquered the present-day territory of Iran around 900/1500.[4] Libya owes its existence to the Sanūsiyya order, which was organised among the tribes of the Sahara in the 1840s by Muḥammad b. 'Alī al-Sanūsī.[5] In 'Asīr, the region in Saudi Arabia to the south of Mecca, a state existed until 1934 which had arisen due to the activities of the leader of the Idrīsiyya order in the second half of the nineteenth century.[6] Thus, it would seem perfectly natural and worthwhile to pose the question as to what it was in dervish orders that provided the bases for this state-building power.

To return to al-Ḥājj 'Umar. He has presented his teachings in a book entitled *Rimāḥ ḥizb al-raḥīm 'alā nuḥūr ḥizb al-rajīm – The Lances of the Party of the Compassionate (God) against the Throats of the Party of the Lapidated One (Satan).*

The work contains fifty-five chapters of widely varying length. The subjects dealt with can be conveniently divided into three categories: 1. Juridical questions – in particular, concerning the relationship of the Tijāniyya brotherhood with the outside world. 2. The internal organisation of the brotherhood, its own particular understanding of itself, and the special role of al-Ḥājj ʿUmar. 3. Mystical themes: travelling the mystic path, spiritual withdrawal (*khalwa*), and the recollection of God (*dhikr*).

The subject matter is presented in the actual words of al-Ḥājj ʿUmar and by means of numerous quotations from other sources. I have counted approximately 125 such sources.[7] The name of one of these authors in particular caught my attention: Jibrīl al-Khurramābādhī.[8] *Khurramābādhī* is a *gentilicium*, a *nisba* in Arabic, formed from the West-Iranian city of Khurramābādh.[9]

How did the book of this Iranian author – the title of the work is not mentioned by al-Ḥājj ʿUmar – manage to become known in West Africa? The identification of this person was made possible for me through Hermann Landolt's study on the Persian mystic Nūr al-Dīn al-Isfarāyīnī who died in Iran in 717–718/1317–1318. Jibrīl al-Khurramābādhī, in Persian Jibrīl-i Khurramābādhī, was al-Isfarāyīnī's student.[10] However, the quotations from al-Khurramābādhī found in al-Ḥājj ʿUmar's *Rimāḥ* are not cited directly from a work by al-Khurramābādhī but are taken from a fifteenth-century intermediary source. The source which al-Ḥājj ʿUmar drew on directly is a treatise by the Egyptian mystic Shams al-Dīn al-Madyanī who died in Cairo in 880/1476.[11] To sum up, a West African author of the first half of the nineteenth century quotes from a ninth/fifteenth-century Egyptian work passages which go back to an Iranian author of the first half of the eighth/fourteenth century.

In fact, a Persian treatise by Jibrīl al-Khurramābādhī has survived in manuscript without its title[12] and it deals with the rules governing the mystic path. Al-Ḥājj ʿUmar's Arabic quotations, via Shams al-Dīn al-Madyanī, can for the most part be identified in this Persian text.[13] It is unclear whether al-Khurramābādhī composed his work in Arabic as well as in Persian, or only in Persian so that the Arabic adaptation or translation stems from another, later hand.

Al-Khurramābādhī and his teacher, al-Isfarāyīnī, were members of the Kubrawiyya order whose founder is considered to be Najm al-Dīn Kubrā who was active in Khīwa in the Āmū Daryā delta south of the Aral Sea and who lost his life in 617/1220 or 618/1221 during the Mongol invasion.[14] The Sufi order which is traced back to him spread throughout Central Asia, Iran and India.[15]

How al-Khurramābādhī's work reached Egypt from Iran remains unclear. It is easy enough to demonstrate that in the eighth/fourteenth and ninth/fifteenth centuries there were lively contacts between Sufis from Iran and Egypt.[16] Al-Ḥājj ʿUmar, for his part, most probably acquired a manuscript of Shams al-Dīn al-Madyanī's work when he went on pilgrimage to Mecca – a journey which he undertook via Cairo some time in the 1820s or 1830s.[17] The chief section of the surviving Persian treatise of al-Khurramābādhī offers a commentary on the so-called *Eight Rules of Junayd* for travelling the mystic path, which will be engaging our attention in what follows. The eight rules of Junayd were formulated initially by Najm al-Dīn Kubrā.[18] They were transmitted in his school and in his order. But not only in those particular circles as, for instance, al-Ḥājj ʿUmar's work the *Rimāḥ* testifies. In the *Rimāḥ* we also find quotations from the Arabic work *al-Waṣāyā al-qudsiyya*[19] by the Persian Sufi Zayn al-Dīn al-Khwāfī. Al-Khwāfī originated from Eastern Iran where he also died, after having resided in Syria, Egypt and the Ḥijāz. Originally a member of the Suhrawardiyya order, he eventually founded his own order, the Zayniyya, which then spread throughout the Ottoman Empire, amongst other places.[20] He also refers to the eight rules of Junayd in his *Waṣāyā* and comments on them in detail.[21]

It is now time to look at what these eight rules entail. In fact, they consist of eight requirements which the novice (*murīd*) is obliged to fulfil and which are usually presented in the following sequence: 1. *dawām al-wuḍūʾ* (ritual purity); 2. *dawām al-khalwa* (spiritual withdrawal); 3. *dawām al-ṣawm* (fasting); 4. *dawām al-sukūt* (silence); 5. *dawām al-dhikr* (recollecting God); 6. *dawām nafy al-khawāṭir* (rejecting stray thoughts); 7. *dawām rabṭ al-qalb biʾl-shaykh* (binding the heart to the shaykh, the master); 8. *dawām tark al-iʿtirāḍ ʿalāʾ allāh wa-ʿalāʾ al-shaykh* (non-opposition to God and the shaykh).[22] The sequence of the rules may vary. Occasionally, a ninth and a tenth condition are added. (More about this below.)

Junayd – or more precisely al-Junayd b. Muḥammad – to whom these rules are first attributed by Najm al-Dīn Kubrā, died in 297/910 or 298/911 in Baghdad.[23] He is held to be *the* great Sufi authority of his own, as well as of subsequent, times, and numerous later orders claim affiliation with him. That the eight rules do stem from Junayd himself cannot be proven and is highly improbable. It is also unclear whether the formulation of the eight rules originated with Najm al-Dīn Kubrā himself or whether he is repeating already available materials.[24] In any case, they are not to be found in the writings of his teacher ʿAmmār al-Bidlīsī.[25] What is without any doubt, however, is that by the time of Najm al-Dīn Kubrā the attitudes, behaviour and practices required in the eight rules could already look back on a long tradition in Sufism. One is reminded in some ways of the emergence of the *regula* of the Benedictines. In that case as well a long period of incubation had preceded the final formulation.[26]

A few brief remarks concerning the development of Sufism seem to be appropriate at this point.[27] Sufism emerged during the first centuries of Islamic history. Its earliest manifestations were ascetic endeavours that can be traced back to certain aspects of the doctrine and practice of the Prophet Muḥammad and various of his followers. In the second/eighth and third/ninth centuries, in association with asceticism a science of the soul is developed, a psychological discipline known in Arabic as *ʿilm al-bāṭin*, the science of the interior.[28] Knowledge of the exterior (*ʿilm al-ẓāhir*) Islamic mystics take to be knowledge of the law whose area of jurisdiction and application is the world accessible to the external senses. The mystics do not consider their science of the interior to be in contradiction to the law or the legal sciences, but rather as what in their eyes is a necessary supplement, an *interpretatio ab intra*, of the law and the sacred tradition of the Qur'an and Sunna.[29] The content of this science of the soul is a psychagogia: both guidance in disciplining the soul, as well as an explanatory system of psychic phenomena which the mystic may encounter. The goal of disciplining the soul is to train the soul or the lower self, in Arabic the *nafs*, in such a way that all activities associated with it become completely extinguished. The extinction of the ego and its activities is experienced by the mystic as being drawn upwards, as a passing away (*fanā'*) in God.

Sufism's further development, to be dated approximately from the third/ninth to the fifth/eleventh centuries, witnessed the appropriation of various theological, cosmological and theosophical concepts and systems, and their incorporation into the individual experiences of the mystics.[30] This is illustrated by the so-called handbooks of Sufism which were chiefly composed in the fourth/tenth century, and not least by the work of the great philosopher, theologian and mystic Muḥammad al-Ghazālī in the second half of the fifth/eleventh century.[31]

Roughly from the fifth/eleventh century on new developments are noticeable. On the one hand, mystical experience and the life of mystics become more and more organised. There eventually emerges from this trend what we commonly call orders, using the terminology of Western Christianity. The Arabic word for a Sufi order is *ṭarīqa* or *ṭarīq*, i.e. path – in Persian-speaking areas this is often referred to as a *silsila*, an affiliation.[32]

On the other hand, the visionary element now comes to play an increasingly important role, at least in the case of certain personalities and orders. This in turn leads to the emergence of a literature concerned with interpreting visions and shaping one's relation to them.[33] What then, one may ask, are the distinguishing peculiarities, the defining characteristics, of a dervish order? Further, in which period and which place are these typical features first to be identified? It has been rightly remarked that varying possible answers can be given to this question.[34] In any case, if one considers the present-day situation, the following broad features may be singled out:

1. An order possesses a chain of affiliation, a *silsila*, which is traced back, in an uninterrupted sequence, from the present-day head of the order to the Prophet Muḥammad. The Prophet is thus considered to be the actual founder of the order. Nowadays such a *silsila* may consist of more than forty links. The authenticity of the *silsila* very often cannot, however, stand up to critical historical examination.[35] That the Prophet – or in the case of the Shiʿa, the son-in-law of the Prophet, ʿAlī b. Abī Ṭālib – is meant to have founded the order in question, is no more than pious projection.

Increasingly since the eleventh/seventeenth century, founders of orders no longer base themselves only on a chronological succession originating with the Prophet. Many make the claim that they have been authorised to lead an order, or to found a new one through a direct encounter with the Prophet.[36] How the claim that one is able to have a personal meeting with the Prophet is justified cannot be entered into here. This subject belongs to the complex of ideas associated with the *Ṭarīqa Muḥammadiyya*.[37]

2. A Sufi order exhibits a hierarchical structure. At the top stands the leader of the entire order, the pivot (*quṭb*). Under him stands the shaykh who is often the leader of a branch order. Under the shaykh is the representative, the *khalīfa*. And finally there are the ordinary members of the order.[38]

3. The orders often make use of handbooks – of varying size – in which the order's affiliation, as well as its rules and doctrines, are presented. These *shurūṭ*-collections, i.e. handbooks of regulations as one might call them, often adopt the eight rules of Junayd as their structural framework.[39]

In which period we date the emergence of orders will depend on how we define an order. One indication of the time the orders formed is the fixed canon of regulations itself, the eight rules of Junayd, which go back to Najm al-Dīn Kubrā in the second half of the sixth/twelfth and the first half of the seventh/thirteenth centuries. Associations similar to orders certainly existed earlier in the form of groups centred around imposing individual personalities. Social institutions maintained by Sufi communities also contributed to shaping the emergence of orders. For instance, during the fifth/eleventh century in Kāzarūn in south-western Iran a form of hospice was set up which, among other functions, provided food for the poor. The initiative for the undertaking came from the Sufi shaykh, Abū Isḥāq al-Kāzarūnī.[40] ʿAlī Hujwīrī Jullābī, the author of the *Kashf al-maḥjūb*, the oldest Persian handbook on Sufism, talks in the fifth/eleventh century about ten Sufi schools of traditions which in his day and age were to be found in Iran.[41]

Similarly, the grave of an important master could become the centre of activities like those of an order. The direct family descendants, as well as the master's students, were frequently involved in such activities. One clear early example of such an environment is the sepulchral shrine of the Sufi master of Mīhana in present-day Turkmenistan, Abū Saʿīd Abu'l-Khayr, whose biography documents for us fifth/eleventh- and sixth/twelfth-century practices at his shrine.[42]

One particular development, which began towards the end of the third/ninth century in Eastern Iran, almost certainly played a decisive role in the formation of the organisational structure of orders – namely, the transition from the lecture-giving shaykh to the shaykh of training, from the *shaykh al-taʿlīm* to the *shaykh al-tarbiya*.[43] The relationship between master and student was rather casual in the early period of Sufism. The student often frequented different masters, received instruction and exhortation without, however, entering into a more binding relationship with the master. This situation changed, it seems, for the first time in Eastern Iran. Now the shaykh, along with his function as teacher and transmitter of knowledge, assumed more and more the function of a spiritual trainer. The pupil was subjected to a rigorous routine of discipline. He had to surrender himself to the shaykh and become completely submissive. Increasingly, quasi-divine characteristics were attributed to the shaykh so that for the novice obedience to the shaykh came to be equated with obedience to God. He owed the shaykh unconditional allegiance. He was obliged to obey the shaykh even if he saw him do things which to all appearances were contrary to the religious law. He was to place his worldly goods at the disposition of the shaykh. He must never walk in front of the shaykh. He ought never to ask him 'why?' and he should not speak in the shaykh's presence without having been invited to do so. He was not allowed to marry or to travel without permission from his shaykh – and, especially, he was not allowed to visit other shaykhs without his own shaykh's consent.[44]

It is perfectly obvious how rules of behaviour like these could be used to further the formation of strictly organised social groups. Let us take a closer look at the eight rules themselves. To reiterate: 1. ritual purity; 2. spiritual withdrawal; 3. fasting; 4. silence; 5. recollection of God; 6. rejecting stray thoughts; 7. binding the heart to the shaykh; 8. surrender to God and the master.

If we rearrange the sequence of these requirements, perhaps it will help to form a clearer picture of what they aim at. The most general of the rules is the eighth requirement, surrender to God and to His representative, the master. This corresponds to the fundamental Islamic duty incumbent on human beings: *islām* means surrender to the will of God who is the only ontologically real subject behind all actions. The special Sufi endeavour to discipline and to extinguish the ego is understood by Sufis as the actual realisation of Islam. Benedikt Reinert has dealt with this subject exhaustively in his study on trust in God (*tawakkul*).[45]

The first requirement, ritual purity, aims in general terms at strict conformity to the external prescriptions of the law. Sufism is never in opposition to the law – at least not in the eyes of its own adherents. On the contrary, true fulfilment of the law is only possible through a realisation of Islam which mystical practices alone can achieve. Thus, actively carrying out the prescriptions of law is given a prominent position alongside passive surrender to the will of God.[46]

Fasting and silence, rules three and four, can be located in the area of asceticism, abandonment of the world, which from earliest times has been considered one of the fundamental pre-conditions of the mystic path.[47]

With the sixth rule, the rejection of stray thoughts, attention is turned to the soul itself. The novice should achieve complete control over his inner self so that he rejects all thoughts which distract him from his goal, God. Sufism distinguishes different forms of stray thoughts, depending on their origin. They can arise from the soul. They can be inspired by Satan. They can stem from an angel or also come from God.

To reject a sudden thought which comes from God, however, is virtually impossible. But the mystic must learn to recognise the kind of stray thoughts he receives.[48]

Spiritual withdrawal and recollection of God, rules two and five, belong to the standard means which the Sufi employs in progressing on the mystic path. Spiritual withdrawal entails separating oneself from the surrounding world for varying lengths of time. The ideal period of time involved is forty days.[49] During this time the mystic is meant chiefly to be engaged in recollection of God, *dhikr* in Arabic, i.e. the repetition of words or short phrases containing the Arabic names of God such as *Allāh*, and which in later times were often associated with the request to bless the Prophet Muḥammad. This repetition is carried out in fixed rhythms with control of the breathing and specific body movements.[50] The ultimate goal of spiritual withdrawal is illumination (*fatḥ*).[51] This may be preceded by visions which the novice must report to the shaykh for him to interpret. The same holds true for dreams. In no case must he dare to interpret his visions and dreams by himself.[52] It is particularly in *dhikr*-practices that considerable differences occur between the various orders. These are described, as far as Iran is concerned, in the second volume of Richard Gramlich's work, *Die schiitischen Derwischorden Persiens.*

As our last rule we have binding the heart to the master (*rabṭ al-qalb bi'l-shaykh*). Here, besides the unconditional obedience to the shaykh which we have already discussed, something further is understood: at the beginning of his novitiate the novice will have an imaginary image of his shaykh implanted in his heart – the sources mostly refer to it with the Arabic word *khayāl*, sometimes *ṣūra* – by means of a procedure that I would designate as occult.[53] Thereafter the master is continually present before the novice's inner eye. In this way an inextinguishable bond is established between the heart of the shaykh and that of the novice.[54]

This rule in particular provides for the internal cohesion of the community. The requirement regarding binding the heart to the master, as far as I can see, is made by all orders. At present, we possess more precise knowledge on this practice as carried out in the Naqshbandiyya order which, like the Kubrawiyya, arose in Central Asia and from there spread across the whole Islamic world, with the exception of the Islamic west.[55]

It is rather striking – to consider briefly the question of where the formation of orders began – that almost all Sufi orders arose in the Islamic east, i.e. in the region of present-day Iraq and in the Iranian world. The Kubrawiyya and the Naqshbandiyya emerged in Central Asia. The Chishtiyya, which chiefly played a role in India, emerged in Afghanistan.[56] The Khalwatiyya, which spread throughout the whole Ottoman Empire, originated in Western Iran,[57] as did the Ṣafawiyya.[58] The Qādiriyya,[59] the Suhrawardiyya[60] and the Rifāʿiyya[61] come from Iraq. The exception in this respect is the Shādhiliyya, which arose and was chiefly active in North Africa.[62] Nonetheless, this order also practices the technique of binding the heart to the shaykh.[63]

Frequently the eight rules are not cited as general pre-conditions for membership in an order but are applied in connection with spiritual withdrawal and recollection of God. Then, as was already the case with Najm al-Dīn Kubrā himself, further conditions are added: 1. Sleeping only when overcome by fatigue. 2. Avoiding excessive eating and drinking.[64] In the *Rimāḥ* of al-Ḥājj 'Umar, these additional rules are increased to more than twenty. Thus, for instance, the posture of the body to be adopted during recollection of God is prescribed, and instructions concerning the location and the furnishing of the cell of seclusion are given.[65]

Research into the history of the influence of the eight rules is only in its initial stages. As noted above, after Kubrā we find the rules referred to among his students and his students' students. Likewise, they were also taken up by the historically more recent Persian dervish orders, as Gramlich has shown.[66] They were disseminated throughout the Arabic-speaking world and then spread from Egypt to West Africa.[67] In the twelfth/eighteenth century one finds the rules in the work of Muṣṭafā al-Bakrī, who played an important role in the development of the Khalwatiyya order. Moreover, in Bakrī they appear in a formulation different from that of Kubrā's original.[68] Al-Bakrī's student 'Abd al-Karīm al-Sammān, who died in 1189/1775 in Mecca,[69] is the founder of the Sammāniyya which not only spread as far as Indonesia but is especially significant in the region of the present-day Republic of Sudan. Indeed, one of al-Sammān's second-generation students was the famous Mahdī, Muḥammad Aḥmad.[70]

It is perfectly plausible that groups which are held together by strong 'ideological' ties such as our eight rules, especially binding the heart to the master, should also be capable of developing strong social and political allegiances. A shaykh who was perceived as a charismatic personality often received rich endowments from contemporary rulers which he might use to expand the worldly influence of his order.[71] He could win the loyalty of entire tribes if, as was often the case, he came forward in tribal society as a peacemaker[72] comparable in this respect to Nicholas von Flüe.[73] A society sworn to loyalty could take form around his person. Such is the case with al-Ḥājj 'Umar, for instance, who was able in this way to found a state in West Africa which only fell victim to French imperialism as late as 1892.[74] Likewise, thanks to its ability, among other things, to intervene as a peacemaker, the Sanūsiyya state was established in Libya, as was the Idrīsid state in 'Asīr. If an order's power in military undertakings was directed outwards, as was the case with the Ṣafawiyya at the end of the ninth/fifteenth century in Iran, then it was even possible to found an empire.

The phenomenon of such strong group cohesion also impressed European observers in the nineteenth century, in particular colonial functionaries whose job it was to watch over Islamic movements.[75] They noted that behind resistance to European colonialisation there often stood Sufi shaykhs and Sufi brotherhoods. A famous example of this is Shāmil who organised resistance in Dāghistān against the

Russian conquest.[76] For similar resistance in Africa, one may cite the Sanūsiyya[77] and the amir 'Abd al-Qādir, who was a member of the Qādiriyya order.[78] Thus, in the so-called *littérature de surveillance* produced by the colonial functionaries an image emerged of a sinister, clandestine Sufi shaykh who controlled an immense international network and stood at the head of a fanatical conspiracy against European civilisation. This literature, which was often based on dubious and misinterpreted sources, is still capable of exerting a considerable influence on European scholarship today.[79]

Regarding the present position of dervish orders in the Islamic world today, I will only add some brief remarks. All in all they do not have an easy time of it. Many western-oriented Muslim reformers see in the orders one of the causes of the weakness and decadence of the Islamic world. The prime example of this attitude is the Republic of Turkey where orders have actually been forbidden since 1925.[80]

For so-called fundamentalists such as the Wahhābīs, for instance, who are ideologically dominant in Saudi Arabia, Sufism is an aberration from what they hold to be the true form of Islam. The reverence accorded to shaykhs, which is so essential a concept within the orders, the Wahhābīs take to be a variety of idolatry which God wishes to be rooted out by every possible means.[81] Consequently, the Sufi orders are also forbidden in Saudi Arabia and the Saudi state spends sizeable sums of money everywhere in the Muslim world in an effort to suppress the influence of Sufi orders. In Iran as well the orders function under certain constraints.[82] Many orders have moved their headquarters to Western countries, particularly to England and America. As for discussion within the Sufi orders themselves concerning the best way to confront this double challenge of Western rationalism and Islamic fundamentalism, as far as I can see, the subject has scarcely been broached.[83]

In the scholarly field of Islamic Studies attention has begun to be focused on social networks, especially in research dealing with the history of the eighteenth and nineteenth centuries. The rich biographical literature, particularly in Arabic, makes this task that much easier, and abundant factual information of interest has been transmitted. However, it must be stated that to date there remains a glaring lack of competent investigation of the intellectual context of these networks which can only be remedied by means of applied philology and the mapping out of a cultural and intellectual overview.[84]

## Notes

*I wish to express my warmest thanks to John O'Kane for having translated the present article.

1. B. Radtke, 'Von Iran nach Westafrika: zwei Quellen für al-Ḥaǧǧ 'Umars *Kitāb rimāḥ ḥizb ar-rahīm*: Zaynaddin al-Ḫwāfī und Šamsaddīn al-Maydānī', *Die Welt des Islams*, 35 (1995), pp. 37–69, pp. 39–41.

2. Radtke, 'Von Iran', pp. 38 f.

3. A. Popovic and G. Veinstein, *Les ordres mystiques dans L'Islam: Cheminements et situation actuelle* (Paris, 1986), pp. 282–291; A. Popovic and G. Veinstein, *Les voies d'Allah: les ordres mystiques dans le monde musulman des origins à aujourd'hui* (Paris, 1996), pp. 475 f.

4. M. Gronke describes the preparatory stages of this process in *Derwische im Vorhof der Macht* (Stuttgart, 1993).

5. See K. S. Vikør, *Sufi and Scholar on the Desert Edge: Muḥammad b. ʿAlī al-Sanūsī and his brotherhood* (London, 1995) especially chap. 6 (pp. 132–160) and chap. 8 (pp. 181–217).

6. R. S. O'Fahey, *Enigmatic Saint: Ahmad ibn Idris and the Idrisi tradition* (Evanston, 1990), pp. 122 ff.; and especially A. K. Bang, *The Idrīsī State in ʿAsīr 1906–1934* (Bergen, 1996).

7. B. Radtke, '*Studies on the Sources of the Kitāb Rimāḥ Ḥizb al-Raḥīm* of al-Hajj 'Umar', *Sudanic Africa*, 6 (1995), especially pp. 109–112.

8. Radtke, 'Von Iran', pp. 50 f.

9. On the *nisba* see 'Izz al-Dīn ibn al-Athīr, *al-Lubāb fī tahdhīb al-ansāb* (Beirut, n.d.), 3 vols., vol. 1, p. 436; Samʿānī, Abd al-Karīm, *al-Ansāb*, ed. (facs.) D. S. Margoliouth (Leiden and London, 1912), f. 1965b.

10. H. Landolt, *Le Révélateur des Mystères* (Lagrasse, ca.1986), p. 30.

11. Radtke, 'Von Iran', p. 49.

12. Ibid., p. 51.

13. Ibid., pp. 51–64, *passim*.

14. F. Meier, *Die Fawā'iḥ al-ğamāl wa-fawātiḥ al-ğalāl des Nağm ad-dīn al-Kubrā* (Wiesbaden, 1957), pp. 58–60.

15. Popovic and Veinstein, *Les ordres mystiques*, p. 31; Popovic and Veinstein, *Les voies d'Allah*, pp. 311–313.

16. Cf. the affiliations which are given in Radtke, 'Von Iran', pp. 56–59.

17. Radtke, 'Von Iran,' p. 65 and 'Studies on the Sources of the *Kitāb Rimāḥ*', p. 111.

18. Landolt, *Révélateur*, pp. 39 ff.; p. 99, n. 113; F. Meier, 'Der unbekannte Schriftsteller al-Muwaffaq al-Ḥāṣī', *Der Islam*, 66 (1989), p. 325 in E. Glassen and G. Chubert ed., *Bausteine: Ausgewählte Aufsätze zur Islamwissenschaft* (Istanbul and Stuttgart, ca.1992), 3 vols., vol. 1, p. 488; Meier, *Fawā'iḥ*, tr. pp. 48 f.

19. Radtke, 'Von Iran', pp. 44–47.

20. Ibid., pp. 43 f.

21. Ibid., p. 46.

22. Meier, '*Ḥāṣī*', p. 325; in *Bausteine*, vol. 1, p. 488; *Fawā'iḥ*, introduction, pp. 48 f.

23. 'Al-Dj̱unayd, Abu'l-Ḳāsim b. Muḥammad', *EI2*.

24. See, for instance, the ten rules which Abū Sa'īd-i Abu'l-Khayr is portrayed as formulating for residents in a *khānqāh*. F. Meier, *Abū Sa'īd-i Abu'l-Ḫayr*, pp. 310 f.; Muḥammad b. Munawwar, *Asrār al-tawḥīd fī maqāmāt al-Shaykh Abī Sa'īd*, ed. Muḥammad R. Shafīʿī Kadkanī (Tehran, 1371 Sh./1992), 2 vols., vol. 1, pp. 316, 24 ff.; J. O'Kane, *The Secrets of God's Mystical Oneness* (Costa Mesa, CA, 1992), pp. 493 f. They bear hardly any similarity to Kubrā's rules.

25. On Bidlīsī see E. Badeen, *Zwei mystische Schriften des ʿAmmār al-Bidlīsī* (Beirut and Stuttgart, 1999).

26. 'Benediktsregel', *Die Religion in Geschichte und Gegenwart; Handwörterbuch für*

*Theologie und Religionswissenschaft*, ed. Kurt Galling (Tübingen, 1965).

27. Other overview: '*Taṣawwuf* (General)', *EI1*; F. Meier, 'The Mystic Path', in *The World of Islam*, ed. B. Lewis (London, 1976), pp. 117–128.

28. 'Bāṭen', *EIr.*

29. Meier, 'Ein wichtiger handschriftenfund zur Sufik,' *Oriens*, 20 (1967), pp. 103 f.; in *Bausteine*, vol. 1, p. 320; *Essays on Islamic Piety and Mysticism by F. Meier*, tr. J. O'Kane, ed. B. Radtke (Leiden, 1999), p. 184.

30. The earliest known example of incorporating cosmological and theosophical conceptions into a mystical system appears in the work of Ḥakīm Tirmidhī; see B. Radtke and J. O'Kane, *The Concept of Sainthood in Early Islamic Mysticism, Two Works by Hakim al-Tirmidh. An Annotated Translation with an Introduction* (Richmond, Surrey, 1996), pp. 4–7; B. Radtke, *Drei Schriften des Theosophen von Tirmidh* (Beirut and Stuttgart, 1996), 2 vols., vol. 2, p. 4 f.

31. Abū Bakr al-Kalābādhī (d. 379–380/990), the author of the Sufi handbook *al-Taʿarruf li-madhhab ahl al-taṣawwuf*, is already completely under the influence of Ashʿari theology; see H. Ritter, *Das Meer der Seele: Mensch, Welt und Gott in den Geschichten des Farīduddīn ʿAttār* (Leiden, 1978), pp. 66–70; tr. J. O'Kane, ed. B. Radtke, *The Ocean of the Soul* (Leiden, 2003), pp. 68–72.

32. On the formation of orders see Popovic and Veinstein, *Les voies d'Allah*, pp. 44 ff.; J. S. Trimingham, *The Sufi Orders of Islam* (Oxford, 1971), pp. 1–30. There is no satisfactory treatment of this subject.

33. See Meier, *Fawā'iḥ*, tr. pp. 240 f.

34. R. Gramlich, *Die schiitischen Derwischorden Persiens* (Wiesbaden, 1965–1981), 3 vols., vol. 2, pp. 141 f.

35. Cf. the examples in B. Radtke, R. S. O'Fahey and J. O'Kane, 'Two Sufi Treatises of Aḥmad b. Idrīs', *Oriens*, 35 (1996), pp. 149–153.

36. This claim is made, for instance, by Aḥmad b. Idrīs, Aḥmad al-Tijānī, Muḥammad ʿUthmān al-Mīrghanī and Ismāʿīl al-Walī; more information in B. Radtke, 'De betekenis van de Ṭarīqa muḥammadiyya in de Islamitische mystiek van de 18e en 19e eeuw', in Marjo Buitellar and Johan ter Haar, ed., *Mystiek, het andere gezicht van de islam* (Bussum, 1999), pp. 43 f.

37. A bibliography on this subject can be found in B. Radtke, J. O'Kane, K. S. Vikør and R. S. O'Fahey, *The Exoteric Aḥmad Ibn Idrīs* (Leiden, 2000), p. 18 and p. 58 n.

38. R. Gramlich, *Derwischorden*, vol. 2, pp. 160 ff.; F. Meier, *Abū Saʿīd-i Abu al-Ḫayr 357–440/967–1049: Wirklichkeit und Legende* (Leiden, 1976), pp. 438 ff. Meier's treatment of the subject has not been generally taken into account, let alone become accepted. This is made shockingly clear in Popovic and Veinstein, *Les voies d'Allah*.

39. A list of such handbooks is found in Radtke et al., 'Two Sufi Treatises', pp. 146 f.

40. F. Meier, *Die Vita des Scheich Abū Isḥāq al-Kāzarūnī in der persischen Bearbeitung von Maḥmūd b. ʿUthmān* (Leipzig, 1948), tr. pp. 47 ff.

41. Meier, Abū Saʿīd, pp. 10 f. and 441 f.

42. Ibid., especially pp. 455 ff.; and see O'Kane, *The Secrets*, Introduction, pp. 45–50, where information to be found in the text about the shrine in Mīhana is conveniently collected and examined.

43. Meier, 'Qušayrī's *Tartīb as-sulūk*,' *Oriens*, 16 (1963), p. 2; in *Bausteine*, vol. 2, p. 237;

*Essays*, p. 94; F. Meier, 'Ḫurāsān und das ende der klassischen ṣūfik,' in *Atti del convegno internazionale sul tema: La Persia nel Medioevo* (Rome, 31 March–5 April), Accademia Nazionale dei Lincei (Rome, 1971), pp. 546 f.; in *Bausteine*, vol. 2, pp. 132 f.; *Essays*, pp. 190 f.

44. B. Radtke, 'Sufism in the 18th Century: An Attempt at a Provisional Appraisal', *Die Welt des Islams*, 36 (1996), pp. 326–364, pp. 344 f.

45. B. Reinert, *Die Lehre vom tawakkul in der klassischen Sufik* (Berlin, 1968).

46. F. Meier, 'Das sauberste über die vorbestimmung. Ein stück Ibn Taymiyya', *Saeculum*, 32 (1981), pp. 88 f. in *Bausteine*, vol. 2, p. 710; *Essays*, pp. 333 f.; B. Radtke, 'Die Stellung der islamischen Theologie und Philosophie zur Astrologie', *Saeculum*, 39 (1988), pp. 259–267, pp. 264 f.

47. The fundamental treatment of the subject is R. Gramlich, *Weltverzicht. Grundlagen und Weisen islamischer Askese* (Wiesbaden, 1997).

48. Radtke et al., 'Two Sufi Treatises', p. 158.

49. 'Khalwa', *EI2*; cf. as well the information in B. Radtke, 'Lehrer-Schüler-Enkel. Aḥmad b. Idrīs. Muḥammad 'Uṯmān al-Mīrġanī, Ismā'īl al-Walī', *Oriens*, 33 (1992), pp. 98–103, 129 f.; R. Gramlich, *Derwischorden*, vol. 2, p. 365, n. 2041.

50. Descriptions of different techniques are found in R. Gramlich, *Derwischorden*, vol. 2, pp. 370–408.

51. Radtke, 'Sufism in the 18th Century', p. 358 and 'Lehrer', pp. 129 f.; 'Der Ibrīz Lamaṭīs', in Holger Preissler and Heidi Stein, ed., *XXVI Deutscher Orientalistentag. Annäherung an das Fremde* (Stuttgart, 1998), p. 330.

52. Radtke et al., 'Two Sufi Treatises', pp. 158 f.

53. Ibid., pp. 157 f.; B. Radtke, 'Sufism in the 18th Century', p. 345; for the Naqshbandiyya see F. Meier, *Zwei Abhandlungen uber die Naqshbandiyya* (Stuttgart, 1994), pp. 117 ff.

54. Meier, *Zwei Abhandlungen*, pp. 129 ff.

55. The fundamental study of this subject is Ibid., pp. 15–241.

56. Popovic and Veinstein, *Les voies d'Allah*, pp. 288 ff.

57. Radtke, 'Von Iran', pp. 37 f.

58. See Gronke, *Derwische im Vorhof der Macht.*

59. Popovic and Veinstein, *Les voies d'Allah*, pp. 461 ff.; Meier, F., 'Die Ṣumādiyya ein zweigorden der qādiriyya in Damaskus', in Ulrich Haarmann and Peter Bachmann, ed., *Die islamische Welt zwischen Mittelalter und Neuzeit. Festschrift für Hans Robert Roemer zum 65. Geburtstag*, (Beirut, 1979), pp. 445 f. in *Bausteine*, vol. 1, pp. 370 f.; *Essays*, pp. 283 f.

60. 'Suhrawardiyya', *EI2*.

61. Popovic and Veinstein, *Les voies d'Allah*, pp. 492 ff.

62. Ibid., pp. 509 ff.

63. B. Radtke, '*Zwischen Traditionalismus und Intellektualismus: Geistesgeschichtliche und historiografische Bemerkungen zum Ibrīz* des Aḥmad b. al-Mubārak al-Lamaṭī', in *Built on a Solid Rock, Festschrift für Ebbe Knudsen* (Oslo, 1997), pp. 240–267, p. 251; 'Ibrīziana: Themes and Sources of a Seminal Sufi Work', *Sudanic Africa*, 7 (1996), pp. 113–158, p. 123.

64. Meier, 'Ḫāṣī', p. 488.

65. Radtke, 'Sufism in the 18th Century', p. 343.

66. Gramlich, *Derwischorden*, vol. 2, pp. 251 f.

67. The example of al-Ḥājj 'Umar dealt with here.

68. Radtke, 'Sufism in the 18th Century', p. 343.

69. R. S. O'Fahey et al., *Arabic Literature of Africa I: The Writings of Eastern Sudanic Africa to ca.1900* (Leiden, 1994), pp. 91–94.

70. Radtke, 'De betekenis', pp. 35 f.

71. Examples in Gronke, *Derwische im Vorhof der Macht*, pp. 294 ff.

72. Examples: Muḥammad al-Sanūsī's activities in Cyrenaica, see above n. 5; and those of Aḥmad Idrīs's grandson, Muḥammad b. ʿAlī al-Idrīsī, in ʿAsīr.

73. *Lexikon des Mittelalters* (Munich, 2002), 12 vols., vol. 6, pp. 1179–1180.

74. Radtke, 'Von Iran', p. 41.

75. O'Fahey and Radtke, 'Neo-Sufism Reconsidered', pp. 61 ff.

76. 'Shāmil', *EI*.

77. See above n. 5.

78. See M. Chodkiewicz, *The Spiritual Writings of Amir ʿAbd al-Kader*, tr. J. Chrestensen, T. Manning et al. (Albany, NY, 1995), Introduction, pp. 1–6.

79. See above n. 75.

80. Popovic and Veinstein, *Les voies d'Allah*, pp. 372 ff.

81. An example of the Wahhābī attitude towards Sufism is vividly illustrated in the dispute (*munāẓara*) which took place in 1832 between Aḥmad b. Idrīs and Wahhābī theologians in Ṣabyā ('Asīr): see Radtke, O'Kane, Vikør and O'Fahey, *The Exoteric Aḥmad Ibn Idrıs*, especially pp. 145 ff.

82. M. van den Bos, *Mystical Regimes: Sufi and the State in Iran: from the Late Qajar Era to the Islamic Republic* (Leiden, 2002).

83. Radtke, 'Zwischen Traditionalismus und Intellektualismus', pp. 256 f.

84. An outstanding example of how not to proceed in such an undertaking is criticised in B. Radtke, *Autochthone islamische Aufklärung im achtzehnten Jahrhundert: theoretische und filologische Bemerkungen: Fortführung einer Debatte* (Utrecht, 2000).

# 35

# Symphony of Gnosis: A Self-Definition of the Ismaili Ginān Tradition

*Shafique N. Virani*

The True Guide proclaims:
Upon arrival I take my seat within the heart's abode
And all seventy-two chambers resound with divine music.
The darkness of night is dispelled by the vigil
As the Symphony of Gnosis begins ...[1]

This fascinating verse is found in a medieval South Asian Ismaili mystical text. The stanza is particularly revealing because the term translated here as gnosis, ginān, in a usage apparently unique to the Ismailis, refers also to a corpus of esoteric literature revered by them.[2] Hence, to the Ismailis, the Symphony of Gnosis depicted in this verse is nothing other than a symphony of their sacred literature, the gināns.

According to the Ismaili texts, the prefatory overture of this 'symphony' commenced at a time before the dawn of creation. A fifteenth-century work tells us that in the abysmal darkness of pre-eternity (*dhandhukār*), when the misty stars that compose the galaxies had not yet formed, the Incomprehensible One was rapt in profound contemplation. Before the curtains of the cosmos were raised, he revealed his eternal gnosis (*amar ginān*) to the True Guide. A celestial concert thus unfolded in which the True Guide became the conductor of a Symphony of Gnosis and commenced his convocation to the Path of Truth (*satpanth*), summoning all souls to salvation through ginān.[3]

The belief in a pre-eternal esoteric or gnostic wisdom in the possession of the Prophet's family (*ahl al-bayt*) has been a characteristic feature of Shiʿi Islam since its earliest days.[4] The Ismaili branch of Shiʿism, in particular, was well known for its proselytising activities (*daʿwa*) and call to recognise the inherited knowledge (*ʿilm*) of its line of Imams. Ismaili tradition maintains that from at least the time of the

Fatimid empire in Egypt,[5] the Ismaili Imams dispatched their proponents, the *dāʿīs*, to the Indian subcontinent for the propagation and exposition of the *Satpanth*, the Path of Truth. These *dāʿīs* sought to summon humankind to a recognition of the spiritual supremacy of the Prophet's family. This activity continued when the Nizārī branch of the Imams moved to the fort of Alamūt in 1094 and was maintained even after the Mongol onslaught wiped out this Ismaili state in 1256. Among the *dāʿīs* dispatched were several figures whose names appear in the traditional list of *pīrs*, or chief representatives of the Imams. They were second only to the Imam himself in the Ismaili hierarchy. The Ismailis attribute to certain of these *pīrs*, along with a few of their family members and descendants, works that are styled 'ginān's'. This corpus of esoteric literature, written in both prose and poetry, numbers some 1,000 extant compositions. The ginān range in length from three verses to literally hundreds of pages and deal with a wide array of subjects including divine love, cosmology, meditation, ritual practice, eschatology and ethical behaviour.[6]

While earlier scholars have noted the dual significance of the term ginān among the Ismailis as referring both to their sacred literature as well as to gnosis, a comprehensive study of the purport and use of this expression in the ginān tradition itself has yet to be carried out. It is this void that the present article hopes to fill.

For the most part, the gināns will be allowed to tell their own tale, either in direct translation or in paraphrases of selected passages. Virtually the entire extant ginānic corpus has been analysed for this study. All references to the over fifty original compositions cited are to be found in the notes. By studying the use of the term ginān in the gināns themselves, an attempt will be made to understand how the tradition defines itself.

The word ginān and its variants *gyān* and *gnān* are ultimately derived from the Sanskrit root *jñāna*, which Seyyed Hossein Nasr has tellingly translated as 'supreme knowledge'. Nasr further notes that the 'term *jnāna* implies principial knowledge which leads to deliverance and is related etymologically to gnosis, the root *gn* or *kn* meaning knowledge in various Indo-European languages including English'.[7] Wladimir Ivanow, generally considered the father of modern Ismaili studies, comments on the particular employment of this term by the Ismailis of the subcontinent: 'It is used in the sense of *the* knowledge, i.e. the real and true, as the Arabic Ismaili term *haqā'iq*'.[8] In view of both the conceptual and etymological relationship between the words ginān and gnosis, they will be used interchangeably in this article; though the term ginān will be used exclusively when the poetic compositions themselves are referred to, for to use the other term would require the invention of an expression such as 'gnosis-text'. On the whole, however, wherever one of the terms is used, the other is equally implied.

As the traditional symphony is often divided into four movements, so is this study of the Symphony of Gnosis composed of four sections. The *sonata* is an exploration of the soul's emergence from the womb of gnosis. The Ismaili texts hold that in this state, the as yet unborn souls possess supreme knowledge. After being touched by ginān in the womb and pledging a sacred covenant to the True Guide, the soul enters the physical world. Here, it becomes bewildered by its entrancing surroundings and falls into a profound slumber of ignorance. The temptations of earthly existence make it forget its lofty status, its covenant and the ginān with which it was endowed. However, from its deepest recesses is heard celestial music that emanates from the Great Gnostic. This enchanting melody within it arouses a deep nostalgia for its lost origin and the soul seeks out the True Guide. In the following movement, the *andante*, the soul encounters the Perfect Guide, the supreme embodiment of the Great Gnostic. He demands the soul's absolute and unconditional submission and devotion. This provokes rebellion in the deluded soul, which has now acquired a sense of ego. Only when this ego submits to the Guide can the soul once again be led by ginān. The *scherzo* brings the symphony to a crescendo as the soul discovers in the gināns a hidden meaning and eternal life. The gināns claim to contain immeasurable depths of esoteric knowledge. Nothing is to be gained without probing beyond their apparent import. Just as the fabled philosopher's stone has the power to transmute base metals into gold, realisation of the sempiternal heart of the gināns resurrects the receptive soul to everlasting life. Indeed, the Lord himself dwells within ginān. Hence, once the soul has achieved this gnosis, it experiences the untold joy of Divine Light (*nūr*) and the beatific vision (*dīdār*) of its beloved Master. The symphony concludes in the *finale*, a consummation of gnosis in which the instruments are laid down and there is only silence, yet the mystical music plays on.

## *Sonata*: Emergence from the Womb of Gnosis

> O dear creature, at the time when you dwelt in the womb,
> You were imbued with gnosis ... [9]

The gināns hold the soul's sojourn in the womb to be of profound import, for at this time the soul is endowed with supreme knowledge, with ginān. While in this state of gnosis, a momentous event takes place in the life of the unborn soul. It is approached by the Lord of the Resurrection (*kāyam*, Ar. *qā'im*)[10] who asks it to proffer its sacred vow (*kol*, Ar. *qaul*; Sk. *vachan*). The covenant is then consecrated, forever binding the gnostic-soul with its Lord.[11]

This dramatic encounter derives inspiration from the mystical understanding of a parallel passage in the Qur'an, 7:172, where the Almighty summons the hitherto uncreated descendants of Adam into his presence and asks, 'Am I not your Lord?' (*alastu bi rabbikum*). The unborn souls seal the covenant by replying in the affirmative, 'Yes, we witness it!' (*balā shahidnā*). The Islamic revelation draws attention to the holy pact lest the children of Adam 'should say on the Day of the Resurrection, "Lo! We were unaware of this!"'

But, the gināns tell us, despite being thus bound, upon entering this bewitching world, the soul is deluded into forgetting its primordial covenant and the gnosis with which it was entrusted.[12] The enchantment of the corporeal world, dubbed the wine of Satan (*sharāb shaytānī*) by the gināns, intoxicates the soul and drives gnosis from the heart.[13] Whilst people repent of drinking wine made from grapes, they have no inhibitions about quaffing the even more destructive wine of Satan. Thus deluded, ginān having been driven away, the soul loses consciousness of its lofty status. Like a mighty lion whose lifelong association with a herd of goats has made it forget its own nature, association with the physical world makes the soul fall into a state of ignorance and egoism because of which the divine Beloved is lost.[14] The fall from gnosis is compared to a profound slumber from which the heedless souls must arise. Only contemplation of the gināns can awaken them from this sleep by rekindling in them a longing for the gnosis with which they had been endowed.[15]

Repeatedly, the gināns prevail upon the believers not to forsake the ancient promise given while in the womb.[16] Pīr Tāj al-Dīn bewails the soul's failure to fulfil this promise and its even more dismal refusal to heed the gināns, which would make it remember the gnosis with which it was once entrusted:

Speak not to those who waver in the promise they give to the Guide.
If they rejoice not in the gināns, fulfill not their covenant with the Guide,
What is the point of their existence?
Though we have composed in the diapason of sounds and musical modes,
The deaf will not listen![17]

When the lotus of the heart does not produce gnosis, the soul is cast into chaos and the faith of the believers spins like a potter's wheel.[18] However, within the deepest recesses of the soul resides the Great Gnostic (*baḍā ginānī)*, a reflection of the Guide, from whom a divine and enchanting melody resonates within the heart, yet whose lofty status remains unknown to the heedless.[19] If the soul hears the call of the Great Gnostic, it experiences a nostalgia and longs for the ginān that it once possessed while in the womb. However, having emerged from its former abode, it can only reacquaint itself with that gnosis by submitting itself to the True Guide, without whom the treacherous ocean of ignorance can never be crossed.[20]

In a charming allegory, a ginān compares the situation of the deluded souls to a group of birds whose capacity for flight has been snatched away in a trap set by the manifest non-reality, i.e. the illusory world.

The manifest non-reality cast its net
And the birds went there to sit.
One bird, seeing the others, became curious
And because of this, he too became entangled.
The fruit of liberation will only be obtained

When you become a disciple of the Guide.
You will only escape from this cage that entraps you
If you fulfil your covenant with the True Guide.
This illusion will be destroyed, this hapless wandering will cease
If you go and enquire of the True Guide about gnosis![21]

The world is a manifest non-reality. It is nothing more than an illusion, a mirage. But its delights are cast as a net in which human souls become entangled. The alluring pleasures of physical existence attract human beings, just as the delicacies placed in a net by a hunter attract unsuspecting birds. Despite the soul's birthright of gnosis, it disregards its higher knowledge because it becomes fascinated by the gathering of souls that have already been caught. Ginān is forgotten as the soul ceases to fly and alights in the middle of the trap.

In order to escape from this ensnarement, the soul must fulfil its covenant with the True Guide. Its master is the Lord of the Resurrection, not the dictates of its passions. If the soul wishes to fly once again, to escape from its cage and to be released from its illusion, it must receive the True Guide's ginān.

## *Andante*: The True Guide and Gnosis

Offer everything – body, self and possessions – to the Guide,
So that by gnosis and through gnosis there will remain nothing but gnosis.[22]

Absolute and utter submission to the Perfect Guide (*murshid kāmil*), according to the gināns, is the only recourse for the soul plunged in ignorance and darkness.[23] Gnosis is unobtainable without him.[24] Though one may have studied all fourteen branches of learning, art and science, the path cannot be found without the Guide.[25]

In a captivating text cast as a colloquy between the great Ismaili sage, Pīr Ḥasan Kabīr al-Dīn, and the renowned yogic master, Kānīpā, the Pīr chastises Kānīpā for failing to recognise the Ismaili Imam as the Guide of the Age. Kānīpā is taught to seek out the Imam, described as the Man of Gnosis (*ginān purush*), and is told:

O ascetic, when you encounter the Guide
He shall reveal to you mysteries.
All your misgivings will be dispelled.
Certainly, a lotus cannot flourish without water … [26]

The symbolism in the verse is striking. The splendid lotus flower (*kamal*), with its delicate white petals, blooms in vile and putrid swamps. Despite its sordid habitat, it is the epiphany of purity and unsullied beauty, majestically rising above the murky quagmire. It refuses to feed on the repulsive bog and instead awaits the nourishment of crystal-clear rain from the heavens. The gnostic's circumstances are similar. He lives in the world but is not of the world. Uninterested in the mundane temptations of his environs, he remains undefiled by the surroundings. Rather, he longs for the life-giving water of ginān (*ginān jal*) which the True Guide brings from the heavens. As the lotus would rather die than drink from its fetid swamp, the pure soul cannot survive without the water of gnosis from the True Guide. Without this precious source of nourishment, the lotus-soul would wither and ultimately die. The composition continues:

O ascetic, the night is dark, your companions treacherous,
You must traverse the perilous mountain path ahead.
Without a Leader how will you negotiate the way?
So take heed while you can …

O ascetic, within your heart are the earth's nine continents,
Within your heart is Paradise itself.
The seven seas dwell within your heart,
But without the Guide you will die thirsty![27]

The seductive temptations of the world thus represent a menacing danger through which the soul cannot pass alone. Only with a Leader can the soul traverse the mountain pass safely and reach the other side. But, as the next verse informs us, the purpose of the Guide is not only to lead the way; he must help the soul realise and benefit from the source of salvation that lies within it. Though the seven seas of knowledge dwell within the heart, the soul may die thirsty. While in the womb, the soul has been invested with ginān, but only the True Guide can lead it back to that state of gnosis which lies within. It must be rediscovered, for 'without ginān the faithful are in utter darkness, a total darkness from which there is no liberation after death.'[28] The mission of the Guide is thus to 'bring back to the Path by means of the gināns those who have forgotten.'[29]

The soul's greatest deterrent to heeding the Guide and following the gināns, however, is the sense of ego (*huṃ khudī, ahuṅkār;* Sk. *ahamkāra*), the capricious self or mind (*man*), that stubbornly asserts its independence. It is the ginānic counterpart to the *nafs al-ammāra* (Qur'an 12:53) or carnal instincts of Arabic mystical literature. While the ego still holds sway, it is impossible to attain ginān.[30] If, despite holding the lamp of ginān, the intrigues of the capricious self cause the believer to tumble into a dark well, what can the Guide do about it?[31] Thus, absolute and unconditional love for the Lord must conquer the self. Only this can render it submissive and amenable to receive gnosis.

Love the Beloved in such a way
That divine gnosis arises from within.
Slay the self and make it your prayer carpet.
Brother, remain steadfast in contemplation.[32]

And again in the ginān 'Awake! For the True Guide has Arrived', in a verse that displays an ingenious play on words:

The Guide says:
Slay the self (*man ne māro*) that you may meet me (*mane maro*).
I shall hold you close,
For indeed, a precious diamond has come into your grasp.
Behold it, O chivalrous one – contemplate this ginān.[33]

Only when the self's inane excuses are cast away can the Guide exercise his transforming effect and the soul acquire ginān.[34] This effect is picturesquely compared to that of a fragrant sandalwood tree in a forest filled with *nimb* trees. Just as the presence of the sandalwood makes the surrounding *nimb* trees scented, so does the perfume of the Guide's knowledge transform the disciples.[35] However, contact with the Guide does not ensure the absorption of ginān. Unless the self has first been subdued, the believer is no better than the neighbouring bamboo trees which are next to the sandalwood tree but not affected in the least by its scent.[36] The True Guide, represented by the sandalwood tree, has his antitheses in the teachers of the six schools of philosophy who, like gourds, contaminate all the adherents who surround them with their bitter smell.[37] The Ismaili texts thus admonish the believers to disregard the teachings of the six schools of philosophy. Indeed, they are replete with cautions that though teachers abound, true ginān is only obtainable from the Ismaili Imam or his appointed agent. In a verse addressed to King Lotus, that is to say, the pure lotus-soul, Sayyid Quṭb al-Dīn says:

O King! Truth is unassailable,
For if it could be assailed, how could it be the Truth?
How can there be ginān without the Guide?
It would be like the advice of a butcher who nonchalantly says:
'O bullock, turn not your head;
Bear your burden and you will attain salvation.'
Assuredly, O King, I see a difficult road before you, a difficult road indeed.
Though the clouds may burst forth with torrential rains,
Do not drink the unfiltered water.[38]

True ginān is unobtainable without the Guide. The counsel of those who pretend to possess gnosis is like that of a butcher whose advice to a bullock ultimately leads to the animal's destruction. The bullock carries the burden of the yoke that binds it to the oil mill around which it turns constantly. As it is blindfolded, it believes that it is travelling to some destination. However, when the blindfold is removed it discovers, to its dismay, that it has been travelling in circles and has made no progress whatsoever. The butcher wishes it to come along blindly, without turning its head, assuring it that it will attain salvation. Utlimately, after years of futile travelling, when the bullock is old and can no longer bear its burden, its owner will take it for slaughter. The situation of those who accept pseudo-ginān from false teachers is similar. They are blinded by ignorance and continue travelling along the same route, unaware of the fact that they are travelling nowhere. Their hypocritical teachers assure them that if they continue to bear their burdens without turning their heads to see what is really going on, they will ultimately achieve salvation. In reality, these mercenary teachers expectantly await the day when their protégés will be taken for slaughter. Hence, Sayyid Quṭb al-Dīn advises his disciples that though water-like teachings may abound, only that which is filtered, given by the True Guide, is fit for consumption. If it is not uttered by the Guide, how can it be considered ginān? Just as sandalwood does not grow in every forest nor does a lotus flower bloom in every pond, the flawless wisdom of the Ismaili teachers are not available from any ordinary guide.[39]

Here we come to a crucial question: who is this 'True Guide' who has the authority to dispense ginān? The texts themselves are very explicit on this point – nobody but the Shah (Imam) and the Pīr (his supreme representative) have the authority to instruct the believers. According to the gināns, the Shah occupies the throne of 'Alī (Alī ke takhat, Ar. 'Alī, P. takht) and the Pīr occupies the prayer carpet of Muḥammad (nabī ke musale, Ar. muṣallā).[40] Muḥammad is the Seal of the Prophets (khātam al-nabiyyīn, Qur'an 33:40), after whom there can be no other prophets; but he is also the first Pīr (aval pīr). He thus initiates the cycle of pīratan, the function of which is to reveal the esoteric teaching of the Prophet's family and to lead humankind to the recognition of the manifest Imam (paratak, Sk. pratyakṣ shāhā).[41] So, as Pīr Shams explains, while Ḥasan, the elder son of 'Alī, was the Pīr, the younger son, Ḥusayn, was the Imam.[42] The names of both the designated Imams and appointed Pīrs were formerly recited daily in the prayer composed by Pīr Ṣadr al-Dīn. The emphasis on seeking guidance only from this specifically favoured lineage is based, among other things, on a Qur'anic passage, oft quoted in Shiʻi literature, that asserts: 'Indeed, God chose Adam, Noah, the family of Abraham and the family of 'Imrān above the worlds; offspring, one of the other. And God is the All-Seeing, the All-Knowing' (3:33–34). Nevertheless, certain other figures, always from among the descendants of the Prophet and 'Alī but not necessarily appointed as Pīrs, were permitted, according to community tradition, to compose gināns as they preached in the name and with the permission of the Ismaili Imam and were therefore considered authorised guides.

The gināns thus vehemently oppose those who are not of the divinely invested family and yet who falsely aspire to the position of Guide.[43] In fact, such people spread agnosticism (aginān) because of their own failure to recognise the True Guide, who alone can bestow ginān.[44] If the believers contemplate the gināns, they will see that these false guides are groping about in ignorance that resembles the darkness caused by a total solar eclipse when the demon Rāhu swallows the sun.[45]

## *Scherzo*: A Meaning that is Hidden, a Life that is Eternal

Understand the essence of this composition.
How can it be grasped without understanding?
For the ginān of the Guide is impenetrable and beyond ordinary perception.[46]

The gināns are insistent in their emphasis that the apparent words of their compositions contain depths of meaning hidden from unperceiving readers. Without attempting to understand this esoteric meaning, they will gain nothing. Part of the reason for the expulsion of ʿAzāzīl (Satan) from Paradise when he refused to bow before Adam was because of his failure to perceive the essence of what he had studied. As one ginān tells us, despite acquiring the knowledge equivalent to having read 360 million books, he did not fathom the inner meaning.[47] Being unable to comprehend the mystery of the True Guide, he was banished into impenetrable darkness (*goḍ andhār*).[48]

Similarly, the *Man Samajāṇī* ('Edification of the Self') criticises pundits who pore over their books, but are unable to penetrate beyond the literal meaning:

They read the scriptures
But recognise not the inner meaning,
Relying on but a word or two.
The great pundit reads everything,
Just like an ass carrying a load of fragrant sandalwood.
What can he know of the precious cargo
Hoisted upon him?
The donkey gains nothing from their value,
The load is removed,
The animal eventually returns to dust.
Whoever has edified the self
Attains all knowledge.
The True Guide himself has explained the inner meaning.
You have received the remembrance (*jikar*, Ar. *dhikr*),
You have received the Word (*jap)*
Now, a true pundit
Is the one who finds all the inner meanings hidden within.[49]

It is not only the pundits who are admonished for failing to capture the inner meaning, but the followers of the Ismaili Pīrs themselves:

Reading and reading their books, the pundits have wearied,
Yet they have been unable to grasp the inner meaning of God
Composing and composing these gināns, we have wearied,
Yet you have neglected God and Muḥammad.[50]

The *Vāek Moṭo nī Vel* laments that:

All call themselves believers,
Every one of them hears the gināns,
But though the Guide has explained each and every letter,
They have not come to their senses![51]

Once again, it is the fickle mind that prevents the believers from understanding the esoteric import of the gināns. Thus, Pīr Shams insists in the closing lines of one of his Punjabi compositions that he is addressing his ginān to the world of spirits (*arawāh*ʿ Ar. *arwāḥ*, sing. *rūḥ*) and commands his listeners to subjugate their capricious minds so that their spirits may be edified by his teachings.[52] If the fickle mind prevents a believer from understanding the hidden meaning of the gināns, 'the entire life of that heedless one is lost.'[53]

This tremendous emphasis on plunging to the depths of inner meaning and not being satisfied simply with the superficial spans all periods and encompasses all geographical areas of Ismaili presence. Hence, the early Muslim heresiographers dubbed the Ismailis *bāṭiniyya*, the Esotericists or 'people of inner meaning'. The Qur'an and other sacred texts are attributed with profound and enthralling worlds of understanding beyond their literal forms. However, such perceptions are not the fortune of the masses who make no attempt to probe into the celestial archetypes that are symbolised by earthly forms and texts. Only by probing beyond the *ẓāhir*, the exoteric, into the *bāṭin*, the esoteric, can the believers enter into a spiritual realm of all-encompassing supreme knowledge. Thus, a composition such as *Hamadhil khālak allāh soī vasejī* asserts:

Within the gināns is to be found knowledge of everything.
Search, search and you will find it![54]

In the gināns we thus find verses that rank the perspicacity of different individuals on a scale ranging from egoism to gnosis. He who is overwhelmed by the physical world due to his preoccupation with himself is manifestly blind; the eyes of his heart remain unopened and he gropes about in the dark. Most people have two eyes, while learning grants a third eye and virtue has seven eyes. Still, none of these can compare with gnosis, which has a hundred thousand eyes 'that are beyond time and space'. By these eyes, the gnostic recognises the essence of the soul and attains a rank of the highest status. But above all of these is the Gnostic of the Essence, the True Guide himself, who is recognised but by a few: 'His sight encompasses everything, for he has infinite eyes.'[55] The *Sat Veṇī Moṭī* ('Tales of Truth, the Larger') also mentions the power of perception associated with ginān:

Listen, O saints, to this proof of Truth,
For these are the 'Tales of Truth' to meet the Beloved.

Obey the true words of the Guide,
Open within you the eyes of Gnosis.[56]

He who does not open 'the eyes of gnosis' and remains oblivious to the hidden meaning of the gināns is compared to a stone. Though a stone may be placed in the ocean for a year, not a drop of water will be absorbed. Similarly, a fool may listen to the gināns constantly, but if he fails to understand them and they do not penetrate his heart, he is no better than a stone.[57] However, in the case of a true believer, gnosis enters and permeates his heart, 'as water is absorbed by the earth'.[58]

The primordial time alluded to in the text cited at the beginning of this article when the Guide was entrusted with gnosis is once again invoked in the *Vāek Moṭo*. Here, this gnosis is symbolised by the key to Paradise which was bestowed upon the Guide after his constant worship for 800,000 æons (*karaṇ*).[59] The progeny of knowledge (*elam āl*, Ar. *'ilm*) then confers this holy key upon the worthy believers. It is by this means that they are able to open the lock that seals their hearts.[60] For indeed, within the heart lie immeasurable riches,[61] but only the key of ginān can unlock it.[62]

The gināns themselves are a precious treasure, their esoteric meaning being compared to diamonds, emeralds, rubies and especially pearls; but these gems are of value only to those who recognise them as such. Thus, in the last canto of the *Sat Varaṇī Moṭī* ('Account of Truth, the Larger'), the composer writes:

Sayyid Muḥammad Shāh has related this tale,
The volume of the 'Account of Truth' has been completed.
Whoever, male or female, shall heed its admonitions
Will cease haplessly wandering through the world of earthly phenomena.
Its secret is so profound
That only the elect can fathom its mystery.
Every path has been expounded upon,
For I have written everything about them in this work.
Only the sage will comprehend its mystery,
Just as only the jeweller recognises the value of a diamond.
O you, my Beloved, the True Master is none other than you!
How can the ignorant understand
That this 'Account of Truth' is like a precious gem?
Only the elect shall recognise it,
Few will fathom its value.[63]

A touching story in the *Man Samajāṇī* tells the tale of a precious jewel that was found by a fool one day as he was strolling on the road.[64] The fool picked it up, thinking it was a pretty pebble, perhaps worth a penny or so. In his stupidity he bored a hole right through it. He then strung the ruined stone around his neck. How was the fool any different from those who listen to the gināns but do not take them to heart, as if they were listening to a bunch of drums? 'They understand nothing of the inner meaning, and without understanding they create a racket and cacophony, being no better than the fool who pierced the gem.' The broken-hearted jewel, contemplating its terrible plight, longed to return to the mine from which it had been extracted; but the real tragedy was yet to occur. Someone who recognised the fool's bauble to be a jewel purchased it from him for a trifle and then left it sitting in a box. In the darkness of the box the precious jewel wept at having been sold for a piddling sum at the hands of a fool and, even worse, at being mistreated by someone who realised its worth. While a fool may be forgiven for his actions, it is inexcusable for someone who recognises the value of the gināns not to seek out their inner meaning. As the author of the story concludes, 'If a Gnostic contemplates the gināns, he will find a treasure in each and every letter ... but if a buffoon sings the gināns as if they were common songs and makes no attempt to probe their inner meaning, he is no better than the fool who found a jewel and strung it like a pebble.'

The believers are cautioned to distinguish between authentic jewels, available only from the True Guide, and the worthless glass baubles of imitators. His caravan laden with precious gems, the Imam is depicted as having come from a distant land to conduct trade with his priceless cargo. Those who deal with him will gain abundant wealth, while those who patronise the glass-dealers will be swindled.[65] He scatters his priceless gems everywhere by relating the gināns, but only the souls that are swan-like will recognise these jewels.[66] Indeed, in the Indian poetic imagination, the swan, a symbol of the purified soul, selects only pearls for its repast, whereas the deceiving stork feasts on the mire.[67] Unfortunately, most human beings are like storks, ignorant of the value of the pearls of gnosis:

> For glass baubles wear a shiny garment, while pearls may seem soiled at first sight. Thus, when gems and glass baubles were once gathered together, everyone pushed and shoved, trying to grab the glass. The pearls remained where they were until finally someone who recognised them came along. He picked them up and treasured them as they deserved to be.[68]

But these precious pearls are not to be revealed to all and sundry. They are to be disclosed only to those who can esteem them as is their due.[69]

Thus we find a ginān on meditation addressed directly to the swan-soul, in the hopes that it will recognise the valuable pearls of gnosis:

> O my swan, in the musket of intellect filled with the gunpowder of concentration,
> load the bullet of gnosis.
> O my swan, light the priming wick of love with the fire of your heart,
> and commence the attack with the blast of the Word.[70]

The essential role played by ginān in the spiritual search outlined above is noteworthy. Gnosis is essential for the mystic word to have its effect. This is emphasised in the *Jog Vāṇī* of Sayyid Imām Shāh:

A true *jogī* is he who knows the method of meditation,
Who applies gnosis to the Word.
When gnosis is achieved
The orbit blazes forth with brilliant light,
So remain focused on your absorption in the Word.[71]

Within the mystical orbit of gnosis (*ginān maṇḍal*) is the shining splendour of esoteric mystery, a light to be seen only when ginān is applied to the Word. But this brilliance must be achieved through the practice ordained by the True Guide (*jugat*, Sk. *yukti*). As Pīr Ḥasan Kabīr al-Dīn explains to the yogic master, Kānīpā:

O ascetic, when you meet the Guide, you must recognise him, my sage,
For without the Guide the path cannot be found.
In the mystical orbit of gnosis lies a shimmering lamp,
But without the Guide it will never enter your grasp!

The Guide's lamp radiates ginān, without which there is nothing but unfathomable darkness.[72] How can the believers fall into the depths of a dark well when they hold in their hands the blazing light of the lamp of gnosis?[73] By treading the path with this lamp in hand, the believers will attain the beatific vision of the Lord.[74] However, the gināns do not claim to shed just any ordinary type of light, they claim to be Divine Light (*nūr*) itself, as in the ecstatic verse of Pīr Ṣadr al-Dīn:

Perpetually recite the gināns, for they are filled with Divine Light,
Your heart will be unable to contain such rapturous joy![75]

But as the Almighty Lord is the Light of the heavens and the earth (*nūr al-samāwāt wa'l-arḍ*, Qur'an 24:35), the gināns are the repositories of this Light.[76] As the introduction to Nūr Muḥammad Shāh's *Sat Veṇī Moṭī* ('Tales of Truth, Larger?')promises:

An effulgence of light lies ahead
For all those souls who immerse themselves in love
This composition has been named 'The Tales of Truth'
In it, you will find the residence of the Beloved.[77]

The Beloved is to be found in ginān because gnosis makes that which is beyond any earthly knowledge knowable.

O ascetic, the Unapproachable, the Imperceptible, the Indescribable has been described!
The gināns have comprehended He who is Incomprehensible![78]

Once the ginān̄s completely penetrate the soul, they have the power to transform it. Thus, one ginān describes the fruits of gnosis as being a body and raiment of Divine Light as the 'Guide of infinite millions' leads the soul to the City of Eternity.[79] The transforming power of ginān is no less than that of the legendary philosopher's stone that transmutes base metal into gold: 'How can there be darkness where the Guide has given the philosopher's stone to the believers? If you are my saints, you will contemplate these ginān̄s.'[80] Just as a sword gleams after contact with a running stream and silken garments gleam by being exposed to water, so a believer gleams by understanding the inner meaning of the ginān̄s;[81] for listening to and understanding these words of gnosis destroys sins in the manner that the universe is destroyed at the end of every cosmic cycle.[82] Indeed, contemplating the ginān̄s with full concentration liberates human souls.[83]

Ginān is the nectar of eternity, the most commonly recurring symbol for gnosis in the Ismaili texts. Like celestial ambrosia, it has the power to resurrect receptive souls to an eternal life of gnosis. The signature verses (*bhāṇitā* or *chhāp*) of many ginān̄s end with lines such as, 'O beloved ones, Pīr Ṣadr al-Dīn utters this ginān of supreme bliss. My dear believers, come and drink this celestial ambrosia!'[84] But it is only by penetrating the inner meaning that the soul is granted eternal life, as in this verse that addresses the lotus-soul in the following words:

> If you discover the elixir hidden within the ginān̄s,
> Taste it with love, taste it![85]

This elixir fills the heart with the luminous splendour of gnosis so that death cannot touch it,[86] for:

> The whole world dies the false death,
> But no one dies the death of Truth.
> He who dies in the ginān of the Guide
> Will never die again![87]

The reference here is clearly to the Prophet Muḥammad's celebrated tradition, *ḥadīth qudsī*, 'Die before you die'. When the self passes away and the True Guide takes his seat in the heart, there remains nothing but gnosis, for by dying unto Truth, the soul is resurrected to eternal life and light.

## *Finale*: Consummation of the Symphony of Gnosis

> There is no flute, yet there is melody. There is no sound, yet there is music![88]

The ginān̄s' definition of themselves commences in the utter silence and stillness of pre-eternity. Before the curtains of creation are drawn, the True Guide is entrusted with ginān and commissioned with the task of summoning all souls to a recognition of this supernal knowledge. As it passes through the womb, the soul is touched by that ginān and, in this state of perfect awareness, swears a sacred covenant with its Lord, recognising him as supreme. But after birth, dazed by the enchanting world about it, it forgets both its covenant and the gnosis with which it was endowed. However, if it is receptive, in the most profound depths of its existence it hears the Great Gnostic's celestial music. It then becomes nostalgic for its home and longs to return. Thus, it seeks the company of the True Guide, the possessor of ginān.

The Guide commands utter and total obedience. However, the soul's ego becomes defiant and blinds it to the Truth. Eventually, love conquers this sense of self and it becomes the soul's prayer carpet. The Guide teaches the soul to seek the ginān hidden within itself. His company transforms the soul as it absorbs the perfume of his ginān, just as the *nimb* trees become fragrant in the presence of the sandalwood tree.

The soul then discovers that just as pearls are hidden in the depths of the sea, true gnosis is concealed within the depths of the gināns. This is where the treasures of esoteric knowledge are to be found. If the esoteric meaning of the gināns, their *bāṭin*, is penetrated, they will be found to contain a boundless ocean of knowledge. Those who read without probing the inner meaning are like donkeys carrying loads of fragrant sandalwood – what do they know about the precious cargo that they bear? Hence, the gināns are addressed to the world of spirits, for these inspired compositions originate in that noble world.

Ginān is essential for the spiritual search. When it is applied to the mystical Word the lamp within the orbit of gnosis blazes forth with a brilliant light. But the light within the gināns is no ordinary light, it is the Divine Light. The Beloved himself dwells in the gināns. As an expression of supreme gnosis, the gināns enable one to comprehend the One who is beyond all comprehension. This is not a product of their apparent words, but of the depths of esoteric meaning contained within them. Such a quality enables them to transform the receptive soul, much as the legendary philosopher's stone transmutes base metal into gold. They are thus celestial ambrosia, the mystical nectar that resurrects the dead to an eternal life. Indeed, to die the death of Truth and be resurrected into the life of ginān means never to taste death again.

This is how the gināns define themselves. Once their inner meaning is understood, the True Guide establishes his seat in the heart's abode. Though the curtains are drawn on the concert and only silence remains, the whispering strains of celestial music continue to be heard and the eternal Symphony of Gnosis plays on … .

## Notes

It is an immense privilege to write an article for this Festschrift in honour of my former professor and thesis supervisor, Dr Hermann Landolt. I know Dr Landolt to be an exacting scholar, a brilliant academic and a wonderful human being. It was under his tutelage that I learned about the bewitching world of Islamic mysticism and philosophy. Dr Landolt has always been a constant source of inspiration, advice and enlightenment.

I would also like to thank al-Wāʿiz Amirali Amlani and Dr Neelima Shukla-Bhatt for reading through a draft of this paper and making many invaluable suggestions. Any mistakes that remain are, of course, my own.

All the ginān cited in this study are from the Khojkī editions based on the original texts first established by Mukhī Lāljībhāī Devrāj and his associates in the early 1900s. A slightly modified version of the ALA-LC Romanization Table for Gujarati was used to transliterate the Khojkī text. Virtually all subsequent publications of ginān by the Ismaili community in Gujarati, Urdu, English, French and Spanish transliteration are based primarily on these texts. Among the volumes produced were six books of approximately 100 ginān each. Reference to the compositions contained in these collections will include the incipit as a title equivalent, followed by the book number, the page on which the ginān begins and the specific verse (v.) or verses (vv.) alluded to. Frequently occurring formulae at the beginning of many ginān, such as the expressions *ejī* and *jīrebhāi*, are omitted in the titles, while less common expressions such as *abadhu* are retained. Thus, a citation such as *Sarave jīvuṃnā jāre lekhāṃ lese*, vol. 2, p. 34, vv. 173–175 would refer to verses 173 to 175 of the ginān *Eji sarave jīvuṃnā jāre lekhāṃ lese* which begins on page 34 of the second collection of 100 ginān. Longer ginān with individual titles, known as *granths*, are cited simply by name and verse, canto (c., cc.) or, in the case of those that contain prose, page number. Thus, *Man Samajāṇī*, c. 303 refers to canto 303 of the *granth Man Samajāṇī.*

Bibliographical information for the Khojkī texts cited in this study follows. Dates are in the Christian era unless labelled VS, in which case they are in the Vikramāditya Saṃvat era. Attributions of the authorship of the ginān cited in this work are recorded as they appear in the received texts.

*100 Ginānanī Chopaḍī*. Book 1., 5th ed., 1990 VS/1934; Book 2., 5th ed., 1993 VS/1936; Book 3., 5th ed. Mumbai, 1991 VS/1935; Book 5., 4th ed. Mumbai, 1990 VS/1934; Book 6., 4th ed. Mumbai, 1989 VS/1933.

*102 Ginānajī Chopaḍī*. Book 4., 3rd ed. Mumbai, 1968 VS/[ca. 1912].

*Brahm Prakāsh*, in *Bujanirījanabaramaparakāsh*. Mumbai, 1905.

*Man Samajāṇī*. No publication information available.

*Muman Chit Varaṇī* [a.k.a. *To Munīvar Bhāi Nānī*]. [Mumbai], 1904.

*Muman Chit Veṇī* [a.k.a. *To Munīvar Bhāi Moṭī*]. [Mumbai], 1905.

*Pīr Hasan Kabīradīn ne Kānipāno Samvād*. Mumbai, 1905.

*Sat Varaṇī Moṭī*. No publication information available.

*Sat Varaṇī Moṭī nī Vel* [a.k.a. *Sat Veṇī jī Vel*]. Mumbai, 1962 VS/1905.

*Sat Veṇī Moṭī*, in *Sataveṇī vadī tathā niṇḍhī tathā sī harafī*. Mumbai, 1959 VS/[ca. 1903].

*Sat Veṇī Nānī*, in *Sataveṇī vadī tathā niṇḍhī tathā sī harafī*. Mumbai, 1959 VS/[ca. 1903].

*Saloko Moṭo* in *Saloko moṭo tathā nāno*. Mumbai, 1904.
*Saloko Nāno*, in *Saloko moṭo tathā nāno*. Mumbai, 1904.
*Surabhāṇ nī Vel*, in *5) Girathane Ginān: 100*, vol. 1. Mumbai, 1966 VS/[c.1910].

1. *Saloko Moṭo*, v. 105.

2. In this connection see Christopher Shackle and Zawahir Moir, *Ismaili Hymns from South Asia: An Introduction to the Ginans* (London, 1992), p. 17. Of course, the word ginān is also used in this sense by certain other groups such as the Imām Shāhīs. However, these are splinter groups that have split off from the parent Ismaili movement and so the usage of the term ginān in this specific sense can still be considered to be uniquely Ismaili.

3. *Sat Veṇī Nānī*, c. 3.

4. Shafique N. Virani, 'Ahl al-Bayt', *Encyclopedia of Religion* (2nd ed.). ed. Lindsay Jones (Detroit, 2005), vol. 1, pp. 198–199.

5. Some Indic Ismaili sources, such as the *Ghaṭ Pāṭ Duā* of Pīr Ṣadr al-Dīn, date the period of this propagation activity even earlier, to the time of Imām Ismāʿīl b. Jaʿfar. There is some support for this assertion in the testimony of the 13th-century author, ʿAlāʾ al-Dīn ʿAṭā-Malik b. Muḥammad al-Juwaynī. See S. M. Stern, 'The Early Ismāʿīlī Missionaries in North-West Persia and in Khurasan and Transoxiana', *BSOAS*, 23 (1960), pp. 85–87. Stern, however, has expressed suspicion about this information. Nevertheless, we do know reliably from the Fatimid jurist al-Qāḍī al-Nuʿmān's *Iftitāḥ al-daʿwa*, ed. W. al-Qāḍī (Beirut, 1970), pp. 45, 47, that immediately upon establishing an Ismaili base in Yemen in 883, Abu'l-Qāsim b. Ḥawshab 'Manṣūr al-Yaman' dispatched his nephew, al-Haytham, to spread Ismailism in Sindh.

6. The best introduction to the history of *Satpanth* Ismailism remains Azim Nanji's *The Nizārī Ismāʿīlī Tradition in the Indo-Pakistan Subcontinent* (Delmar, NY, 1978). The later history should be supplemented by the present author's 'The Voice of Truth: Life and Works of Nūr Muḥammad Shāh, a 15th/16th Century Ismāʿīlī Mystic' (M.A. thesis, McGill University, 1995). The earlier period has been studied in Tazim Kassam, *Songs of Wisdom and Circles of Dance: Hymns of the Satpanth Ismāʿīlī Muslim Saint, Pīr Shams* (Albany, NY, 1995). Aziz Esmail's *A Scent of Sandalwood* (London, 2002) and the collection of Ali Asani's previously published articles, entitled *Ecstasy and Enlightenment* (London, 2002), are two recent contributions to the field that contain up-to-date bibliographies.

7. Seyyed Hossein Nasr, *Knowledge and the Sacred* (Edinburgh, 1981), pp. 7, 50 n. 14.

8. Wladmir Ivanow, 'Satpanth' in *Collectanea* (Leiden, 1948), vol. 1, p. 2, n. 1.

9. *Hojīre parāṇī jāre tuṃ gīrabhā thān vasanto*, vol. 5, p. 117, v. 1.

10. In this study, ginānic words whose origin may not be immediately apparent are followed by a gloss containing the classical Arabic, Persian or Sanskrit form, as the case may be.

11. *Juṭhīre dunīyā tame kāṃi bhulo*, vol. 1, p. 118, v. 2; *Gurajīe rachanā rachāveā*, vol. 2, p. 118, v. 4.

12. *Satane mārage chālīe*, vol. 6, p. 42, v. 6; *Man Samajāṇī*, c. 5.

13. *Sat Veṇī Moṭī*, c. 20.

14. *Kesarīsiṃh sarup bhulāyo*, vol. 6, p. 35, vv. 1–3.

15. *Ṭāḍhuṃ ṭāḍhuṃ mīṭhaḍuṃ bolīe*, vol. 4, p. 95, v. 1.

16. *Dharam murat paelā gur bharamā pichhāṇo*, vol. 1, p. 143, vv. 8–9; *Sum nahī tuṃ jāg saverā*, vol. 2, p. 141, v. 2.

17. *Dehī gurake vāchā heje thir na rehṇāṃ*, vol. 4, p. 21, vv. 1–3.

18. *Sācho jāṇo ne pīr pīchhāṇo*, vol. 3, p. 7, v. 3.

19. *Ātamā rām tame baḍā ginānī*, vol. 1, p. 121, v. 1.

20. *Hojīre parāṇī jāre tuṃ gīrabhā thān vasanto*, vol. 5, p. 117, *passim*.

21. *Paratak viloḍīne phāṃs māṇḍī*, vol. 2, p. 110, v. 1.

22. *Āe rahem rahemān ab to rahem karoṃge*, vol. 3, p. 121, v. 1.

23. *Kesarīsīṃh sarup bhulāyo*, vol. 6, p. 35, v. 4.

24. *Sācho dhiāvo ne ginān vichāro*, vol. 2, p. 19, v. 1.

25. *Man Samajāṇī*, c. 158; *Sat Veṇī Moṭī*, c. 154.

26. *Pīr Hasan Kabīradīn ne Kānīpāno Samvād*, p. 20. Selection reproduced in *Abadhu man jīte man ichhā fal upaje*, vol. 5, p. 141, v. 7.

27. *Pīr Hasan Kabīradīn ne Kānīpāno Samvād*, p. 20. Selection reproduced in *Abadhu man jīte man ichhā phal upaje*, vol. 5, p. 141, vv. 9, 20.

28. *Huṃ balahārī gur āpaṇe*, vol. 4, p. 91, v. 11.

29. *Sāheb kero bhed na bujere koe*, vol. 3, p. 129, v. 5.

30. *Man Samajāṇī*, c. 7.

31. *Vāek Moṭo*, v. 52.

32. *Pīr vinā pār na pāmīe*, vol. 3, p. 17, v. 12; cf. *Pīyu pīyu kījīe*, vol. 3, p. 15, v. 1 and *Sīrīe salāmashāhā amane malīyā*, vol. 5, p. 36, v. 3.

33. *Satagur padhāreā tame jāgajo*, vol. 3, p. 161, v. 4.

34. *Sāmī tamārī vāḍī māṃhe*, vol. 3, p. 45, v.7; cf. *Imāmapurī nagarī ne kuṃvārakā khetara*, vol. 6, p. 69 (section 2), v. 6.

35. *Satagur bheṭeā kem jāṇīe*, vol. 2, p. 137, v. 1.

36. *Āj te amar āveā*, vol. 2, p. 127, v. 2.

37. *Muman Chit Varaṇī*, vv. 187–191.

38. *Jīre rājā sat taṇe mukh mār na hove*, vol. 3, p. 94, v. 1.

39. *Ṭāḍhuṃ ṭāḍhuṃ mīṭhaḍuṃ bolie*, vol. 4, p. 95, v. 1.

40. *Man Samajāṇī*, c. 397; *Surabhāṇ nī Vel*, c. 11.

41. *Jāgo rīkhīsar morā bhāī*, vol. 3, p. 127, v. 22.

42. *Man Samajāṇī*, c. 144; cf. *Jāgat keṃv nahīre*, vol. 6, p. 21, v. 2.

43. *Sarave jīvuṃnā jāre lekhāṃ lese*, vol. 2, p. 34, v. 130 and *Muman Chit Varaṇī*, v. 64.

44. *Muman Chit Varaṇī*, vv. 359–360, 422.

45. *Sate chālo mārā munīvaro*, vol. 1, p. 23, vv. 3–4.

46. *Man Samajāṇī*, c. 336.

47. *Allah ek khasam sabhukā*, vol. 4, p. 110, v. 6.

48. *Het guranarasuṃ kījīe*, vol. 3, p. 36.

49. *Man Samajāṇī*, c. 301.

50. *Pusatak paḍī paḍī paṇḍat thākā*, vol. 1, p. 184, vv. 1, 9.

51. *Vāek Moṭo nī Vel*, v. 14; cf. vv. 8–9 and *Sat Varaṇī Moṭī*, c. 295.

52. *Ek tīrath vedhaḍā pīr shamas gājī sadhaṇā*, vol. 2, p. 83, v. 4.

53. *Chet chet bānā man chañchal karī cheto*, vol. 1, p. 65, v. 1.

54. *Hamadhil khālak allāh soī vasejī*, vol. 4, p. 74, v. 10; cf. *Sarave jīvuṃnā jāre lekhām lese*, vol. 2, p. 34, v. 14 and *Jītuṃ lāl sirīa e sārang dhar āshā trībhovar vado sāmi*, vol. 4, p. 10, v. 18.

55. *Bhāio bharame na bhulīe*, vol. 1, p. 163, vv. 10–13.

56. *Sat Veṇī Moṭī*, c. 220; cf. *Sāchāre sāhīāṃku nisadhin sirevo*, vol. 4, p. 86, v. 1.

57. *Satane mārage chālīe*, vol. 6, p. 42, vv. 1–5.

58. *Vāek Moṭo nī Vel*, vv. 26–28.

59. Either from Ar. *qarn*, century or, more likely, from Sk. *karaṇ*, which can refer either to a period of thirty *ghaḍīs* or to an astronomical division of time of which there are eleven, seven movable and four fixed, two of which are equal to a lunar day.

60. *Vaek Moṭo*, vv. 15, 57.

61. *Sācho dhīāvo ne ginān vīchāro*, vol. 2, p. 19, v. 10.

62. *Mānā mānā mānā māṃhe raheṇā*, vol. 6, p. 26, v. 3.

63. *Sat Varaṇī Moṭī*, c. 316.

64. *Man Samajāṇī*, c. 364–365.

65. *Dur deshathī āyo vaṇajāro*, vol. 5, p. 56, passim.

66. *Sat ho sukarīt guranar gatasuṃ ārādho*, vol. 1, p. 70, v. 7.

67. *Saṃsār sāgar madhe vāṇ āpaṇā satagure norīyāṃre*, vol. 1, p. 117, vv. 3–4.

68. *Man Samajāṇī*, c. 331.

69. *Jīre rājā sat taṇe mukh mār na hove*, vol. 3, p. 94, v. 2.

70. *Ho jīre mārā haṃsa karaṇī kamāvo to rabajīsuṃ rācho*, vol. 5, p. 32, vv. 2–3.

71. *Ād uṇāde ahuṅkār upanā*, vol. 5, p. 155, v. 2, reprinted in vol. 6, p. 15 (section 2).

72. *Sarave jīvuṃnā jāre lekhāṃ lese*, vol. 2, p. 34, v. 167.

73. *Kalajug goḍ andhāre upanā*, vol. 2, p. 59, vv. 2, 7.

74. *Man Samajāṇī*, c. 324.

75. *Ginān bolore nit nure bhareā*, vol. 4, p. 135, v. 1; cf. *Sarave jīvuṃnā jāre lekhāṃ lese*, vol. 2, p. 34, v. 181 and *Jītun lāl sirīa e sārang dhar āshā trībhovar vado sāmī*, vol. 4, p. 10, v. 18.

76. *Sāchāre sāhīāṃku nisadhin sirevo*, vol. 4, p. 86, v. 7.

77. *Sat Veṇī Moṭī*, c. 3.

78. *E abadhu jamīn na hotī āsamān na hotā re abadhu*, vol. 5, p. 151, v. 6.

79. *Valī valī nar māṃhī māṃhī ramase ke ho jīrebhāī*, vol. 2, p. 176, vv. 7–10.

80. *Kalajug āvīyo utāvalo*, vol. 5, p. 34, v. 9.

81. *Das bandhī yārā sir bandhī*, vol. 2, p. 135, v. 7.

82. *Dehīnā dhandhā kāraṇ tame jugamāṃhe phīro*, vol. 3, p. 176.

83. *Navarojanā: dhin: sohāmaṇāṃ*, vol. 4, p 43, v. 5 and *Sāchāre sāhīāṃku nisadhin sirevo*, vol. 4, p 86, v. 5.

84. *Jīrevālā pāṭ maṇḍhāvī ne chok purāvo*, vol. 4, p. 38, v. 6.

85. *Jīre rājā sat taṇe mukh mār na hove*, vol. 3, p. 94, v. 6.

86. *Velā potīne vilamb na kījīe*, vol. 2, p. 13, v. 6.

87. *Saloko Nāno*, v. 17.

88. *Brahm Prakāsh*, v. 71.

36

# The Attitude of the ʿUlamāʾ towards the Government in Nineteenth-Century Iran

*Ahmad Kazemi Moussavi*

*ʿUlamāʾ*-government relations in nineteenth-century Iran entered a new phase when the Shiʿi *ʿulamāʾ* became the source of the government's legitimacy. After centuries of a reserved and sceptical attitude towards temporal authority, often imbued with a denial of the legitimacy of any government but that of the awaited Imam, most of the *ʿulamāʾ* began to function as an *ad hoc* legitimiser for the Qajar government on behalf of the Imam of the Age. This change of position was due to the circumstances of the post-Safawid Shiʿi community. These include firstly the rise of popular Shiʿism and its impact on the expansion of the *ʿulamāʾ*'s financial and teaching networks. Secondly, the enhancement of the role of the supreme jurist so that it was converted into the institution of *marjaʿ-i taqlīd*, in which position were combined the vicegerency of the Imam and the Uṣūlī conception of *ijtihād* (an intellectual power to articulate and interpret the law). Finally, the crisis of legitimacy facing the post-Safawid dynasties drove Qājār rulers to regard the authority of the religious leaders as the natural support, and often as the very source, of the government's legitimacy.

Popular Shiʿism in this period was based on devotional attachment to the Shiʿi Imams. Such attachment produced mourning rites (*ʿazādārī*) especially that of the Muḥarram processions, and pilgrimages to shrines (*ziyāra*). Both of these practices had been legally institutionalised in the late Safawid period. Before the Safawid period, we have evidence of the practice of mourning rites by the Shiʿa, and even some Sunnis, in certain cities during Muḥarram;[1] but as a community-wide and legally sanctioned practice, it was a late Safawid phenomenon. The Persian and Arabic writings of Majlisī the Younger (d. 1111/1699) *inter alia* seem to aim at incorporating elements of devotional folk Shiʿism into formal *fiqh* so as to enable the *ʿulamāʾ* to control all the ritualistic performances of Shiʿi life.[2] Before the Safawid period, folk Sufism and its associated *futuwwa* rites shared with the *ʿulamāʾ* a mandate over formal rituals, particularly among the bazaar classes. This can be witnessed in the semi-Sufi codes of ethics such as the 'Futuwwa Nāma-yi of the Chintz-makers'.[3] Majlisī's hostile attitude towards Sufism on the one hand, and his enthusiastic efforts to popularise *fiqh* on the other, clearly indicate his intention to divert popular attention to his proposed folk rituals. Majlisī's outstanding place in contemporary Shiʿi biographical works shows how successful he was.[4]

The efforts of the Safawid jurists to popularise Shiʿism bore fruit during the Qājār period when the shrine cities of Iraq (*ʿatabāt*) emerged as the foci of Shiʿi ritual and catharsis. *ʿAtabāt* seminaries[5] had already attained prominence through the immigration of the Iranian *ʿulamāʾ* following the breakdown of Iṣfahān as a centre of learning during the Afghan invasion of 1722; nevertheless, a new socio-economic life was introduced to these cities as they became the centres of Shiʿi pilgrimage and emotional recourse. The mourning rites turned into a set of processions and festivals which involved almost all businesses particularly during the month of Muḥarram. The shrine cities became the focus for ritual gatherings, devotional prayers, pleas for intercession, spiritual recourse and even political refuge, in addition to housing the Shiʿi seminaries. This, as we can see, increased the scope of charities, alms and the pious endowments allocated to these seminaries and to the *ʿulamāʾ*.

The *ʿulamāʾ*'s source of income was increased in two ways. First doctrinally, by extension of the fifth (*khums*) to include all income earned from trade, mineral and agricultural produce as well as spoils of war. Second practically, by the expansion of the mourning rituals of Muḥarram. *Khums* was originally applicable to booty only, as understood from the Qurʾan (8:41) and the Tradition of the Prophet.[6] But the Shiʿi authors of the fourth/tenth century, by relating certain traditions on the authority of Imām Jaʿfar al-Ṣādiq, gave a new character to *khums*. That is, *khums* came to mean the fifth of all kinds of income earned on a personal, natural and commercial basis.[7] *Khums* being freed from item limitation, in contrast to *zakāt*, includes six shares: three belonging to the Hidden Imam and the rest to orphans, the homeless and the poor. All these shares should be spent by, or under supervision of, a qualified jurist. The Shiʿi jurists of the following centuries again expanded the scope of the *khums* to include appropriation of the properties earned from dubious sources.[8] Majlisī the Younger, among other things, worked hard to popularise *khums* by emphasising its other-worldly rewards.[9] For almost a thousand years of the absence of the Imams, the Shiʿi *ʿulamāʾ* enjoyed several other sources of income such as pious endowments, government donations, charities, a third portion of bequests (*thulth*) and *zakāt*; but none of them constituted a stable source of income in the way that *khums* did during the Qājār period. The flow of *khums* to the ʿAtabāt in this period was due to the popularity of undertaking pilgrimages to shrines, a state of affairs that Majlisī worked his hardest to encourage.[10]

The *ʿulamāʾ* of the nineteenth century took full advantage of their expanded roles in the performance of ritual and in the collection of money on the authority of the Hidden Imam. They increased their ties with the bazaar classes so that they controlled virtually all aspects of ritual life while they made the collection of *khums* a sanction for most dubious transactions. These two factors established the basis for an independent income (beyond the domain of the government) and enabled them to develop a financial network. This growth of income in its turn contributed to an increase in the number of seminaries and students. In the cities of Iran students would gather round a given *mujtahid* who taught them Islamic law and on occasion sent them to nearby villages as propagandists for his authority. The *mujtahid* would determine the time and limits of ritual processions and direct the payer of alms to the most eminent *mujtahid* in the ʿAtabāt who in turn would reimburse the local *mujtahid* generously. This kind of hierarchical (albeit informal) relationship between the *ʿulamāʾ* demonstrates the last stage in the institutionalisation of the so-called *marjaʿiyya* to which we now turn.

*Marjaʿiyya-yi taqlīd*, as the highest clerical position, played a significant role in representing the attitude of the *ʿulamāʾ* towards both the government and social movements. The notion of *marjaʿ* in the sense of a source of reference in religious matters had existed in Shiʿism since the fourth/tenth century when Imāmī *ḥadīth*s were being collected.[11] Such references to the *ʿulamāʾ*, however, were limited to specific cases, mainly on administering justice among the Shiʿa. The emergence of the *marjaʿ* as a referential model who could set an example for the whole community is peculiar to the nineteenth century when this same concept evolved into an institution. The appearance of this institution at this particular juncture was due to a number of theoretical developments, in addition to the financial and practical elements described above. The origins of this enhancement of the authority of the *ʿulamāʾ* and their general attitude towards the government can best be explained through the study of these theoretical developments.

The factor that most contributed to the public prestige of the *ʿulamāʾ* was the status of viceregent of the Imam. During the nineteenth century, the *ʿulamāʾ* managed both to enhance the scope of and to single themselves out for this charismatic position by outwitting their traditional opponents such as the Sufis, the Akhbārīs and Shaykhīs. The notion that the *ʿulamāʾ* should represent some of the practical authority of the Twelfth Imam had existed for centuries, but there was no precedent for seeking legitimacy for the government from the *mujtahid*s who were viceregents of the Imam – as became the case during the early Qājār period. The idea of viceregency originated from Imāmī *ḥadīth*s in which the Shiʿa are advised to take cases to the transmitters of *ḥadīth*s (i.e. the *ʿulamāʾ*) for the administration of justice. The *ʿulamāʾ* of the following centuries gradually extended the scope of this administration to include the collection of alms and organising certain public duties such as *ḥisba* and *jihād*, while at the same time assuming the designation of general agency. Enjoying the favourable conditions of the early Qājār period, some of the *ʿulamāʾ* turned this latter notion into a fully-fledged doctrine of juristic mandate (*al-wilāya al-ʿāmma*), in addition to the special cases.[12]

The doctrine of a fully-fledged mandate for the *ʿulamāʾ* was not, during the nineteenth century, taken as seriously as the status of viceregent of the Imam. A considerable number of pious *ʿulamāʾ* in this period either opposed it[13] or did not take it into serious consideration.[14] The doctrine, however, did not affect public concern as much as did the designation 'viceregent of the Imam', because almost all scholars who spoke for the all-embracing juristic mandate maintained the best possible relations with the sovereign, Fatḥ ʿAlī Shāh. Besides, the shah did not appear wholly sincere in his so-called 'game of legitimacy'. We will have a chance to examine these dual approaches from the points of view of both sides later on. The question at hand is why the *ʿulamāʾ* struggled so hard to represent the charismatic authority of the Hidden Imam despite the fact that their knowledge of the *sharīʿa* had already provided them with a sufficiency of authoritative roles in public affairs and rituals.

Charismatic representation of authority, which had never lost its appeal in Iran, had gained new momentum with the rise of Shaykhism at the turn of the century. Shaykh Aḥmad al-Aḥsāʾī (1245/1826), the founder of the Shaykhī school of thought, proposed that a new genre of scholar, *al-ʿulamāʾ al-rabbāniyyūn* (theosophers), should represent the authority of the Imams, relegating the regular *ʿulamāʾ* to the category of mediators between the people and their rulers.[15] The successors of Aḥsāʾī proposed a different set of hierarchies for the representation of the Imam's authority. These alternative approaches to Shiʿi doctrine alarmed the *ʿulamāʾ*, particularly when the actual reappearance of the Imam was claimed by the Bābī movement in 1260/1844. These events indicate the degree of messianic expectancy in the milieu of nineteenth-century Shiʿism. The *ʿulamāʾ* met this need in a timely fashion by extending the scope of their viceregency and rationally reformulating the doctrine of juristic mandate.

The victory of the Uṣūlī school over the Akhbārī traditionists at the turn of the century not only upheld the principle of *ijtihād* theoretically, but furnished the office of *mujtahid* with a much wider command, and occasionally with executive power. The importance of *ijtihād*, which had been an outstanding characteristic of Shiʿi jurisprudence since the seventh/thirteenth century, diminished to some extent during the prevalence of the Akhbārīs in the Safawid period. The triumph of the Uṣūlī restorer Muḥammad Bāqir Bihbahānī (d. 1205/1791) not only equipped the *mujtahids*' pronouncements with speculative and general knowledge,[16] but also provided them with a new structure of authority. Bihbahānī's students (including his son) developed a peripheral network of *mullās* in the shrine and other major cities to collect alms and administer justice, using their own executive body if the occasion allowed.[17] With such a broad scope of authority, *mujtahids* were not to be regarded as mere *muftī*s any more, but rather as popular figures who could share governing power.

As a by-product of the elevation of the doctrine of *ijtihād*, the principle of superiority in learning (*aʿlamiyya*) was brought forward in this period in order to distinguish between different categories of the *ʿulamāʾ* and, more importantly, to distinguish the most learned individuals. Arguments over the legitimacy of a superior (in knowledge and piety) has a long and problematic history in both Shiʿi and Sunni jurisprudence. Whereas the question of *aʿlamiyya* was treated within the discussion of the qualifications for *qāḍī* and *muftī* in Shiʿi law, it involves the problem of the Imamate in Sunni law at a fundamental level. Although no standard method of establishing the most learned *ʿālim* has ever been practised, it helped the newly-born institution of *marjaʿiyya* to lay out its hierarchy more distinctively. The nineteenth-century Shiʿi *ʿulamāʾ*, however, laid more emphasis on the rights of the superior *mujtahid* to issue *fatwā*s on public affairs.[18] This marks the introduction of *taqlīd* in a new compulsory form on which the authority of *marjaʿ* must rest.

The idea of adopting the words of a learned individual (*ʿālim*) as authoritative in matters of faith arose in the Muslim community in the second/eighth century. This is evident in the writings of some Shiʿi authors who, on the authority of the Fifth and Sixth Imams, rejected the common practice of the Companions of the Prophet as an illegal *taqlīd*. In his introduction to *Uṣūl al-kāfī*, Kulaynī refuted *taqlīd* on an equal basis with *istiḥsān*: juristic preference.[19] Later, on the authority of Imām Jaʿfar al-Ṣādiq, he criticised Jewish and Christian communities for their unquestioned following of rabbis and priests.[20] This kind of rejection of *taqlīd*, however, should be read in the light of a general Shiʿi denial of the authority of common Sunni practices;[21] otherwise the bulk of the same *al-Kāfī* implies nothing but strict following of the infallible Imams and the learned reporters of their traditions.

In early periods, nevertheless, the practice of following the learned in matters of sacred law was optional, as was the choice of *muftī* for obtaining an opinion. *Taqlīd* had generally been categorised as permissible by pre-Safawid Shiʿi sources.[22] As a by-product of folk Shiʿism, the spirit of the popular religious following received serious attention from the Safawid *ʿulamāʾ*. For example, Astarābādī (d. 1635), the Akhbārī leader of the time, although categorically rejecting the notion of the office of *mujtahid*, proposed that it was incumbent to follow a *marjaʿ* who transmits the traditions of the Imams.[23] Majlisī the Younger, too, despite his leanings towards Akhbārism, ruled in favour of following *mujtahid*s during the absence of the Imam.[24] From the Uṣūlī camp Mullā Aḥmad Ardabīlī al-Muqaddas (d. 993/1585) pronounced in favour of the necessity of following the most learned jurist.[25] Nevertheless, it was left to the Uṣūlī *ʿulamāʾ* of the Qājār period to elaborate fully the principle of *taqlīd*.

*Taqlīd* as an individual obligation of every Shiʿi towards the learned *mujtahid* of the time appeared sporadically in the writings of leading authorities of the nineteenth century such as the above-mentioned Mīrzā Abu'l-Qāsim Qummī and Narāqī.[26] It was the most Uṣūlī-minded jurist of the time, Shaykh Murtaḍā Anṣārī, who explicitly pronounced on it. In the opening of his Persian religio-legal discourse, Anṣārī set *taqlīd* as a binding principle for all lay Shiʿi who wished their religious observances to be acceptable to God.[27] Nevertheless, in this work, Anṣārī does not seem mindful of the consequences he was encouraging by setting *taqlīd* as the prime obligation of common Muslims. This can be understood by his pious rejection of the doctrine of a juristic mandate which invests the *ʿulamāʾ* with the authority of the Imam. Anṣārī seems rather to be taking it as a matter of piety to instruct the Shiʿa that, to ensure the acceptability of their religious observances, they should follow the teaching and example of a learned jurist.

After Anṣārī, however, there appeared jurists who had no doubts about the compulsory nature of *taqlīd*. Obviously, this affected their attitude towards both the people and the government. Among these *ʿulamāʾ* the anti-Constitutionalist ayatollah Sayyid Muḥammad Kāẓim Yazdī (d. 1337/1919) appears to have elaborated *taqlīd* more than his contemporaries. In his *al-ʿUrwah al-wuthqā*, which is still the most celebrated framework for the writing of Shiʿi law, Ayatollah Yazdī opened his discourse with the problem of *taqlīd* versus *ijtihād*, an Uṣūlī topic not directly relevant to the subject of law. He defined *taqlīd* as the commitment to follow the utterances of a certain *mujtahid* even though (those utterances) were in practice not implemented.[28] Nevertheless, without this commitment the actions and prayers of all Muslims were void even though in reality they were correct and in conformity with *sharīʿa*. Besides *taqlīd*, he proposed the alternatives of practising *ijtihād* and precaution (*iḥtiyāṭ*); but none of these possibilities could actually help a Muslim, whether ordinary or learned. Because to qualify for the status of *mujtahid*, one must be in full command of jurisprudence, and to observe prudence, too, one must follow a *mujtahid* in order to be able to discern those cases requiring precaution.[29] In this manner, by ranking *taqlīd* as a prerequisite for all Muslim observances, Yazdī had actually given new scope to the authority of *mujtahid*s whose following secures the validity of the practices of all Muslims.

Having surveyed the popular and doctrinal bases of the evolution of the *ʿulamāʾ*'s position during the Qājār period, we now turn to the historical developments in which their enhanced status functioned as a source of the government's legitimacy. In this regard, we will examine the circumstances in which the government used religious authority to insure its legitimacy on the one hand, and on the other, how the *ʿulamāʾ* tried to subordinate political matters to their rulings.

After the collapse of the Safawids in 1722/1135, the *ʿulamāʾ* suffered a temporary setback due to the unfavourable attitude of the Afghan, Afshār and Zand regimes. Their influence, nevertheless, increased at the popular level and at the beginning of the Qājār period they were moving towards a position of autonomy. The reign of the Qājārs did not of itself bring about change in the structure of kingship or religious authority in Iran. The old Persian tradition which considered the state and religion as twin brothers continued to form the principle of legitimacy for both government and religious classes. What is more, the political instability of post-Safawid Iran impelled the early Qājār monarchs to look for support amongst popular religious elements. At this point, the Uṣūlī *'ulamā'*, who had managed to gain control of almost all the judiciary, ritual and educational structures of the community, appeared to be the government's natural ally. By successfully removing the Sufis, Sunnis, Akhbārīs and (later on) the Shaykhīs from the religious scene, the Uṣūlīs often emerged as representatives of orthodoxy and almost as if singled out to reciprocate recognition with support for the government. Amir Arjomand explains this need for legitimacy by reference to Max Weber's pronouncement that 'if the legitimacy of the ruler is not clearly identifiable through hereditary charisma, another charismatic power is needed; normally this can be hierocracy'.[30]

In the case of the Qājārs it seems that both Āghā Muḥammad Khān, the founder of the dynasty, and his successor Fatḥ 'Alī Shāh tried to acquire religious legitimacy for their governments by having the *'ulamā'* acknowledge their qualifications, i.e. religious knowledge and piety. Both shahs had some religious training[31] which, in sharp contrast to preceding rulers, would appear to distinguish them from the typical tribal khan. Āghā Muḥammad Khān, because of his knowledge and piety, was marked out as the most respected hostage at the court of Karīm Khān Zand.[32] It seems both shahs wanted to be regarded as highly learned individuals, if not *mujtahids* in Shi'i jurisprudence. In fact, Āghā Muḥammad Khān was addressed as the *mujtahid* of kings by at least one contemporary writer, Rustam al-Ḥukamā'.[33]

Not only the historical sources, but also the writings of the *'ulamā'* of the time testified to the desire of these rulers to be equally acknowledged as scholars of religion. The above-mentioned Qummī in his *Irshād-nāma* addressed to the reigning shah (Āghā Muḥammad Khān) echoes this desire:

> I am not preaching to you as a learned man does to an ignorant one, nor am I guiding the one who supposedly is perplexed … rather I am engaging with you in scholarly negotiation as two erudite scholars are wont to do, or as if in the sort of secret consultation which is undertaken between two referential sources [*marja'*].[34]

Given this, Qummī who was one of the leading *mujtahids* of the period, seems well prepared to identify the shah as scholar, and even *marja'* (in a general sense), with whom the *'ulamā'* may negotiate on an equal basis. In the same letter, Qummī stated that *'ulamā'* were needed for the protection of religion as rulers were needed for the state.[35] It is evident that unless he had regarded his authority as independent of the state, Qummī would never have dared to deem the *'ulamā'* as equal to and worthy of consultation by such a powerful monarch. This degree of independence is peculiar to the Qājār period.

The foundations of the independent authority of the *'ulamā'* were laid down under the prevalence of the new kind of folk rites and rituals – i.e. pilgrimages to shrines and Muḥarram processions – which, as seen earlier, the *'ulamā'* of the late Safawid period had worked so extensively to control (see above). When Āghā Muḥammad Khān ascended the throne in Tehran (1200/1785), the *'ulamā'* appeared to be the most respected legitimate authority after Qājār tribal legitimacy. Only *mujtahids* could voice a different view to that of the shah during the eleven years of his despotic rule. Besides his own personal piety, the prestige that the *'ulamā'* enjoyed was the main reason compelling the shah to treat them differently from the rest of the population. The British observer, Sir John Malcolm, gives a good description of the *'ulamā'*'s informal influence:

> [They] fill no office, receive no appointment, have no specific duties, but are called, from their superior learning, piety and virtue by the silent but unanimous suffrage of their countrymen, to be their guides in religion, and their protectors against their rulers; and they receive a respect and duty which lead the proudest kings to join the popular voice, and to pretend, if they do not feel, a veneration for them.[36]

This kind of popular but informal position within Shi'i society in the Qājār era was peculiar to the Uṣūlī *'ulamā'* at the beginning of the period. Before this, Sufi saints, Akhbārī scholars and philosophic theosophers had shared this position with them. Āghā Muḥammad Khān was the first Shi'i ruler after Safawids who tried to incorporate the authority of the *'ulamā'* into government. He invited Āghā Muḥammad 'Alī the *mujtahid* of Kirmānshāh to Tehran for consultation in 1205/1791[37] the year his celebrated father, the founder of the new Uṣūlī trend, died. Āghā Muḥammad 'Alī's visit to Tehran, although short, was in line with the kind of consultation to which Mīrzā-yi Qummī had referred. This type of association with the *'ulamā'*, without having been formally appointed by the monarch, marks the beginning of the *'ulamā'*'s autonomous authority. Amir Arjomand regards this invitation as 'the beginning of rapprochement between the Qājār state and the Shi'i hierocracy'.[38]

During the reign of Fatḥ 'Alī Shāh, the *'ulamā'* not only consolidated their authority, but gave it a definitive form. They based religious authority on a new hierarchical order, i.e. *marja'iyya*. The shah repeatedly acknowledged the political rights of the *'ulamā'* and tried to share in their legitimacy by both confirming his own qualification as learned and representing the authority of high-ranking *mujtahids*. He asked the chief jurisconsult, Shaykh Ja'far Najafī, to appoint him as his deputy to reign.[39] 'Permission to reign' (*idhn-i salṭanat*) was the context which the shah used to reformulate his right to rule. This clearly delineates the new status of the *'ulamā'* as a source of the government's legitimacy during this time. Nevertheless, it must be noted that the shah's interest in associating with Shi'i spiritual leaders was not confined to the Uṣūlī *'ulamā'* although they maintained the most stable relations with the government. Except for the popular Sufi masters, the shah welcomed the blessings of other Shi'i spiritual leaders including, for instance, Akhbārīs and Shaykhīs. However, despite his good relations with these leaders, both trends were eventually stigmatised by the Uṣūlī *'ulamā'* without any objection from the shah.

What Fatḥ 'Alī Shāh actually gained from the support of and alliance with the *'ulamā'* should be read in the light of the general expectant mood of the time which the shah must have shared. Nineteenth-century Iran was the era of messianic expectations. Any kind of spiritual performance would draw the public's attention if it could meet a moral or ritual need of the community. The Uṣūlī *mujtahid*s managed to rank first, magnetising public attention by both representing the charismatic authority of the Hidden Imam and controlling a string of mourning and pilgrimage rites. Moreover, their works on applying a rational (Uṣūlī) methodology for the expansion of Shi'i law contributed to their popularity in another way. The *mujtahids*' achievement in the details of applied law was so significant that even other contemporary Shi'i trends such as the Sufis and Shaykhīs often referred their followers to local *mujtahid*s for settlement of judicial disputes.[40] Evidently, Fatḥ 'Alī Shāh wanted to participate with the *'ulamā'* in this public call for reciprocal support and recognition, if not to include himself amongst them.

Unlike Fatḥ 'Alī Shāh, his successor Muḥammad Shāh was a Sufi sympathiser and appointed his Sufi master Ḥājjī Mīrzā Āqāsī as prime minister. Despite the inauspicious attitudes of this shah and his prime minister, the *'ulamā'*'s authority reached another peak thanks to control of the popular rite and rational Uṣūlī argumentation. During the reign of this shah, the office of *marja'* was singled out in the person of Shaykh Muḥammad Ḥasan Najafī (d. 1266/1849) who turned the Najaf seminary into the centre of Shi'i spiritual, educational, ritual and devotional activities. Najafī began to delegate his authority to the local (but often 'Atabāt-graduated) *'ulamā'* in such numbers that the shah criticised him for turning Najaf into a factory for the production of *mujtahid*s.[41] Muḥammad Shāh tried in vain to put an end to the way that the powerful local *mujtahid*s had (since the time of Fatḥ 'Alī Shāh) checked the authority of the governors and expelled them if they were not considered to be in line with the thinking of the Uṣūlī *mujtahid*s.[42] The inevitable clash of the government with the *'ulamā'* is best demonstrated by Ḥujjat al-Islām Shaftī's takeover of Iṣfahān.

Ḥujjat al-Islām Shaftī began his juridical career as a local judge and the imam of a mosque in Iṣfahān. His competence in settling cases earned him a great reputation not only for the administration of justice but also for accumulating wealth and business interests. However, he did not content himself with judicial and commercial matters. He developed close ties with the bazaar and ruffian classes and with their help took control of the city expelling the governor from his office.

With his authority unchallenged, Ḥujjat al-Islām Shaftī, as grand *mujtahid* of Iṣfahān, began to harbour critics of the government, rebels and criminals, and to make contact with foreign emissaries. In the end he recruited his own police force and, eventually, an army in preparation for a conflict with central government.[43] In 1254/1839 when Muḥammad Shāh, after a long but covert military campaign recaptured Iṣfahān, he treated the grand *mujtahid* with due respect, and contented himself with only banishing Shaftī's son and punishing some of the ruffian leaders. The sanctity of the grand *mujtahid* remained so unaffected by all this that official historians and chroniclers were not allowed to say that the purpose of the expedition was to break his power.

These events point to the fact that the new body of Uṣūlī *ʿulamāʾ* was so well established that an antipathetic, albeit victorious, king was not able to punish an insurgent grand *mujtahid* nor to challenge his religious authority. This clearly shows that Shaftī's authority did not lie in the military and economic power he had established in Iṣfahān; rather, it was due to his connection to the new structure of Shiʿi hierarchy supported by the Najafī centre of *marjaʿiyya* which could de-legitimise any public figure, even a king. Moreover, the way this incident was recorded indicates that public opinion was not accustomed to witnessing the government challenging the authority of high-ranking clerics. For this reason, the return of Ḥujjat al-Islām Shaftī to his position of authority may be considered the best evidence for the configuration of what is now called a 'dual structure of authority'[44] in the Qājār period. Shaftī's case set an example for other influential *ʿulamāʾ* such as Sayyid Muḥammad Bāqir the *mujtahid* of Qazwīn,[45] and more significantly the well-known Āghā Najafī in Iṣfahān during the reign of Muḥammad Shāh's successor.

The reign of Nāṣir al-Dīn Shāh witnessed another round of *ʿulamāʾ* involvement in public affairs. Unlike Fatḥ ʿAlī Shāh, this shah did not call himself a deputy of the *mujtahids*, nor did he invite their participation in politics. Nevertheless, he frequently exchanged signs of recognition with the *ʿulamāʾ* and asked them to give support to his government. In tandem with the prevalence of mourning rites, the influence of the *ʿulamāʾ* penetrated most aspects of social life. In addition to the administration of justice, education, rituals and alms, the *ʿulamāʾ* more or less dominated public opinion and emotion so that following their rulings became the prime responsibility of every Shiʿa. This evolving process eventually included the political sphere despite the efforts of the shah and his ministers to keep the *ʿulamāʾ* out of politics. The rise of powerful *mujtahids* in Tabrīz, Iṣfahān, Tehran and Shīrāz, who constantly challenged temporal authority, had become a matter for serious government concern by the end of the century. The clash between the government and the *mujtahids* was sparked by the protests against the Tobacco monopoly in 1309/1891.

This crisis over the Tobacco monopoly demonstrates the long-standing power struggle between the traditional *ʿulamāʾ* and the government which was intensified after the Perso-Russian wars by the government's growing preoccupation with seeking economic support from Europe. This latter point was particularly brought to the attention of the *'ulamā'* by the famous Sayyid Jamāl al-Dīn al-Afghānī. The granting of a monopoly on the sale of tobacco to a British company in 1891, combined with marked disrespect towards the *mujtahid* of Shīrāz, led the *mujtahid* networks of Iṣfahān and Tehran to check the government's absolutism with the help of the Shiʿi hierarchy of the ʿAtabāt. The result was the publication of the now-famous *fatwā* banning the use of tobacco on the authority of the Imam of the Age. Universal acceptance of the *fatwā* by the people and the subsequent demonstrations left the government no choice but to cancel the contract and to renew its allegiance with religious dignitaries. This was the first organic demonstration of a public voice in national politics and it forced the government to change its policy in accordance with the rulings of the Shiʿi hierarchy.

The *'ulamā'*'s political role increased during the following decades. Shīrāzī's successor, Ayatollah Khurāsānī (d. 1329/1911), not only defended and on occasion led the Constitutional movement of 1906–1909, but also took responsibility for legitimising elements of modern institutions in areas such as banking, military and educational reform. Khurāsānī issued a number of rulings and outlines for guidance to the people of Iran and the government of Muḥammad ʿAlī Shāh (r. 1907–1909) which indicate the supreme role of the *marjaʿ* in counterbalancing the power of the reigning monarch. When the same monarch, by use of force, closed the newly created Iranian parliament, Khurāsānī ruled in favour of rebellion against the shah and prohibited the payment of taxes to this oppressive government.[46] It is generally considered that Khurāsānī's *fatwā*s played a pivotal role in the uprising in Tabrīz and the subsequent collapse of the shah's administration. It should be noted that all the pro-Constitution *mujtahid*s in Tehran were closely connected to Khurāsānī. When they divided into two opposing groups, Khurāsānī, while supporting the pro-Constitution party paid special attention to the fate of those *mujtahid*s such as Sayyid ʿAbd Allāh Bihbahānī and Shaykh Faḍl Allāh Nūrī who opposed reform. The latter was hanged by the new Constitutional government in 1329/1911 and the former was mysteriously assassinated in the following year. The impact of the execution of a *mujtahid* upon Khurāsānī, amongst other things, was so great that he decided to move from Iraq to Iran. Because of his own sudden death, this journey never took place, but the setback which the *'ulamā'* suffered in the following decade proved that Khurāsānī's earlier assessment of the threat had been accurate.

As can be seen from the above, there were many roles for the *'ulamā'* in public affairs. To characterise these roles, Qājār historians and authors presented various views. The contemporary writer Yaḥyā Dawlatābādī, who also played a role in late Qājār politics, assessed the Shiʿi clergy as the second ruling power, parallel to the government. 'The *'Atabāt*', he said, 'was the centre of the *'ulamā'*'s hierarchy, whose following by the masses was considered obligatory.'[47]

A. K. S. Lambton, one the first Western scholars to evaluate the attitude of the Qājār monarchs towards the *ʿulamāʾ*, says that:

> The Qājārs had no real or pretended claim to descent from the Imams as had the Ṣafawids. Like others before them, they had usurped power, but having done so they were recognised, as had been dynasties before them, as exercising power as 'the shadow of God upon Earth'. The religious institution was no longer subordinate to the political to the extent it had been under the Ṣafawids: it stood over against the state, not wholly incorporated in it. Neither was absolute. The Shah could not dispense with the *ʿulamāʾ* because he required their co-operation for the performance of certain public functions, and in any case could not afford to alienate them because of the support they enjoyed from the common people.[48]

The theory of legitimacy, as presented here by Lambton, was widely held and elaborated on by contemporary authors. Nevertheless, it is only applicable to the attitudes of the first two Qājār rulers. After the Second Perso-Russian War (1803–1813), the element of foreign support,[49] was to some extent, a substitute for the backing of the *ʿulamāʾ*. The *ʿulamāʾ*'s influence continued to increase, but, after the reign of Fatḥ ʿAlī Shāh, it was not the problem of legitimacy – in the above sense of the term – that dictated the attitudes of government towards the *ʿulamāʾ*. Rather, the Qājārs having the endorsement of the Russian and British governments for their rule, were now concerned only with the judicial, ritual and educational functions of the *ʿulamāʾ*.

In her studies on the recent history of Iran, Nikki Keddie holds that 'the Twelver Shiʿi doctrine of the illegitimacy of any state, even a Twelver one, pending the return of the Hidden Imam, [was] a basis of the Iranian *ʿulamāʾ*'s effective and growing hostility towards the Qājār dynasty in the nineteenth and early twentieth centuries'.[50] '[T]he *ʿulamāʾ* resisted Qājār encroachments on their power.' Keddie quotes Wilferd Madelung's fine argument that 'according to some major Imāmī writers, "In the absence of the Imam … any ruler or government acting in his name and in accordance with the Imāmī law acquires a derivative, functional legitimacy."' However, Keddie reacts to this argument saying that 'The recent vogue for criticising Western scholars for views not sanctioned by early Shiʿi doctrines, even though such views have been widely held among educated Shiʿa, ignores the fact that in Shiʿism, as in most religions, doctrine in large degree is what educated clerics say it is, whether or not they are interpreting correctly.'[51] Obviously, Keddie is not including Ayatollah Khomeinī's words on Islamic government,[52] nor those of like-minded models such as Shaykh Faḍl Allāh Nūrī and Mullā Aḥmad Narāqī amongst the sayings of those educated clerics. Shiʿi jurists in general, as Madelung alluded to, provided enough formulae (such as consideration of necessity, expediency and establishing order and justice) to legitimise the functions of government while retaining their original expectation of the establishment of the just and legitimate rule of the Twelfth Imam.

Like Keddie, Hamid Algar maintains that the Shiʿi *ʿulamāʾ* categorically denied the legitimacy of any government pending the return of the Twelfth Imam. However, Algar considers the reassertion of Shiʿi theological technique as a significant factor that 'placed heavy emphasis on the functions and duties of the *ʿulamāʾ*'. This 'theological technique' would be the same Uṣūlī methodology which was extensively elaborated during the Qājār period. This development adapted Shiʿi jurisprudence to the requirements of the time though it often aimed at the expansion of *taqlīd*, mass following, rather than *ijtihād* in the sense of independent reasoning. On the other hand, Algar claims that the Qājār shahs 'motivated both by personal piety and considerations of policy, sought an accommodation with clerical power'.[53] 'Consideration of policy', as Algar makes clear throughout his book, is an indication the prestige of the Uṣūlī *ʿulamāʾ* which was based on the newly established position of the viceregent of the Imam and the popularity of the rituals associated in this period with the mourning for Imām Ḥusayn.

Said Amir Arjomand, who has studied the rise of the Shiʿi polity and its hierocracy in the light of Weberian theorems, maintains that a dual structure of authority was consolidated in Shiʿi Iran during the reign of Fatḥ ʿAlī Shāh.[54] He considers the support of the Shiʿi *ʿulamāʾ* specifically during the First Perso-Russian War as 'an instance of cooperation between the state and the hierocracy as two organs of the reconstituted Shiʿi polity'.[55] He also maintains that the statement of the *marjaʿ* of the time, Mīrzā Ḥasan Shīrāzī, upheld 'the theory of dual power (*dawla wa-milla* [government and community]) during the occultation of the Imam'.[56] The formula of a 'dual structure of authority', however, seems a suitable context for looking at the complex relationship between the *ʿulamāʾ* and state under the Qājārs. Nevertheless, this formula, in my reading of Iranian history, is only applicable after the reign of Fatḥ ʿAlī Shāh Qājār, although the old principle of 'state and religion are twin brothers' is more or less a constant throughout Persian history. The cause for the rise of such an exceptionally strong body of *ʿulamāʾ* at this time lies in the prevalence of popular Shiʿism, especially the mourning rites which, as mentioned above, gave a new scope and energy to the phenomenon of mass allegiance and the payment of the *khums* to individual clerics through a network of religious officials.

For this reason, the character of *ʿulamāʾ*-government relations in the nineteenth century was often determined by the power that the *ʿulamāʾ* obtained from a mass following created by responses to the mourning ceremonies during Muḥarram. The mourning processions and the example of the Shiʿi Imams required a degree of piety and submissiveness characterised by the *ʿulamāʾ*'s pious withdrawal from temporal power. However, they never surrendered their right to power since they believed that they were the true representatives of the authority of the saviour Imam, and as such were required to instruct the community on his behalf. This attitude served a dual purpose for the *ʿulamāʾ*, subordinating the state to their instructions while disassociating themselves from any direct responsibility. These objectives were achieved by the fact that they had been a source of the government's legitimacy since the reign of Fatḥ ʿAlī Shāh. Subsequent shahs had to acknowledge the high status of the Uṣūlī *ʿulamāʾ* as the community's custodians of morality and orthodoxy with a restraining role in politics. The crisis over the Tobacco monopoly proved the *ʿulamāʾ*'s ability to mobilise the masses when the occasion required. Politically, the *ʿulamāʾ*'s role as the guardians of the legislation was eventually incorporated by the Iranian parliament into the Constitution of 1907. This demonstrates the compromise that was worked out between modernist and traditional forces at the turn of the century. A disregard for the spirit and content of the Constitution by Qājār and Pahlavi rulers *inter alia* encouraged the ambivalent and even rejectionist attitude of the *ʿulamāʾ* towards government which was characteristic of the next period of Iranian history.

## Notes

1. ʿAbd al-Jalīl Qazwīnī al-Rāzī, *Kitāb al-naqḍ* (Tehran, 1331 Sh./1952), pp. 402–406. Also Muḥammad Jaʿfar Maḥjūb, '*Az faḍāʾil khwānī wa-manāqib khwānī tā rawḍa khwānī*', *Iran-nāma*, 2 (1984), p. 402.

2. Muḥammad Bāqir al-Majlisī, *Biḥār al-anwār* (Beirut, 1403/1983), 110 vols.; *Jawāhir al-ʿuqūl* (Tehran: lithograph, 1303/1885); *Tadhkirat al-aʾimma* (Tehran: lithograph, n.d.); *Tuḥfat al-zāʾir* (Tehran, 1312/1894); *Zād al-maʿād* (Tehran: lithograph, 1306/1888).

3. Murtaẓā Ṣarrāf, *Rasāʾil-i jawānmardān* (Tehran, 1352 Sh./1973), pp. 226–239.

4. E.g. Muḥammad ʿAlī Mudarris al-Khiyābānī, *Rayḥānat al-adab* (Tehran, 1369 Sh./1990), vol. 5, p. 194.

5. The *ʿAtabāt* include the tombs of six Shiʿi Imams in Najaf, Karbalā, Kaẓimayn and Samarrāʾ in modern Iraq. Najaf had been a centre of learning for Imāmīs since the immigration there of Shaykh Muḥammad b. al-Ḥasan al-Ṭūsī in 449/1057–1058. See H. Algar, "ʿAtabāt', *EIr*, vol. 2, pp. 902–904.

6. Early Muslim authors such as Abū Yūsuf al-Qāḍī (182/798) leave no doubt that by *khums al-ghanīma* they meant booty exclusively. See his *Kitāb al-kharāj*, ed. Iḥsān ʿAbbās (Cairo, 1983), p. 101.

7. Muḥammad b. Yaʿqūb al-Kulaynī, *Uṣūl al-kāfī*, ed. Muḥammad Jawād al-Faqīh (Beirut, 1413/1992), vol. 1, p. 605; Ibn Bābūya al-Ṣadūq, *Man lā yaḥḍuruhu al-faqīh*, ed. ʿAlī Akhbar al-Ghaffārī (Tehran, 1988–1990), vol. 2, p. 347.

8. Al-Majlisī, *Biḥār*, vol. 72, p. 382 and vol. 93, p. 236. These passages should be read in the light of Majlisī's Persian writings in which the role of the *ʿulamāʾ* is precisely defined. E.g. see his *Zād al-maʿād* (Tehran: lithograph, 1306/1888), chapter on *khums*; see also *ʿAyn al-ḥayāt* (Tehran, 1404/1984), pp. 126–128.

9. Al-Majlisī, *Zād al-maʿād*, chapter on *khums*; *Naẓm al-laʾālī* known as *Suʾāl wa Jawāb* (Qumm, 1411/1990–1991), pp. 225–228.

10. Al-Majlisī, *Biḥār*, vol. 93, pp. 184–203.

11. E.g. Ibn Bābūya, *Kamāl*, p. 484; al-Kulaynī, *Uṣūl al-kāfī*, vol. 1, p. 119.

12. Mullā Aḥmad al-Narāqī, *'Awā'id al-ayyām* (Qumm, 1321/1903), pp. 185–205; Shaykh Ja'far Kāshif al-Ghiṭā, *al-Ḥaqq al-mubīn* (Iran: lithograph, 1316/1898), p. 146.

13. Shaykh Murtaḍā al-Anṣārī, *al-Makāsib* (Tabrīz, 1334 Sh./1955), p. 153.

14. Shaykh Muḥammad Ḥasan al-Najafī, *Jawāhir al-kalām* (Najaf, 1378/1958), vol. 21, pp. 386–399.

15. Shaykh Aḥmad al-Aḥsā'ī, *Jawāhir al-kalim* (Tabrīz: lithograph, 1273/1856), vol. 1, p. 37.

16. Muḥammad Bāqir Bihbahānī, *Risālat al-ijtihād wa'l-akhbār* (Tehran: lithograph, 1313/1895), p. 16. For more details, see Ahmad Kazemi Moussavi, *Religious Authority in Shi'ite Islam* (Kuala Lumpur, 1996), pp. 171–174.

17. Muḥammad b. Sulaymān Tunakābunī, *Qiṣaṣ al-'ulamā'* (Tehran, n.d.), p. 119.

18. E.g. Shaykh Ja'far Najafī, *Kashf al-Ghiṭā'* (Tehran: lithograph, 1316/1898), p. 394. See also Ann K. S. Lambton, 'A Nineteenth Century View of Jihād', *SI*, 32 (1970), p. 188.

19. Al-Kulaynī, *Usūl al-kāfī*, p. 25.

20. Ibid., pp. 157–158.

21. Ibid., p. 198.

22. E.g., Najm al-Dīn Ja'far b. Ḥasan al-Muḥaqqiq al-Ḥillī, *Ma'ārij al-uṣūl* (Qumm, 1404/1984), p. 181; Jamāl al-Dīn Ḥasan b. Yūsuf al-'Allāma al-Ḥillī, *Mabādi' al-uṣūl ilā 'ilm al-uṣūl* (Beirut, 1406/1986), p. 247. Among the Sunni authors see Fakhr al-Dīn al-Rāzī, *al-Maḥṣūl fī uṣūl al-fiqh* (Beirut, 1413/1992), vol. 6, p. 73. 'Allāma al-Ḥillī, *Tahdīb al-wuṣūl* cited in Said Amir Arjomand, *The Shadow of God and the Hidden Imam: Religion, Political Order, and Societal Change in Shi'ite Iran from the Beginning to 1890* (Chicago, IL, 1984), p. 139. It should be noted that on the question of incumbency, authors such as al-Sharīf al-Murtaḍā and Abū Ḥāmid al-Ghazālī (*al-Mustaṣfā min 'ilm al-uṣūl*, Cairo, n.d., vol. 2, p. 389) ruled in favour of optional obligation (*al-wājib al-mukhayyar*) rather than obligatory as the *'ulamā'* of the late Qājār period proposed.

23. Al-Astarābādī, *al-Fawā'id al-madaniyya* ([Iran], 1405/1985), p. 153. It should be borne in mind that al-Astarābādī used the term *marja'* in two senses: one referring to the actual traditions of the Imams, and one to the transmitters of these traditions. With regard to the title of this chapter (*fi'l-ittabā' al-ruwāt*), *marja'* has been translated in the latter sense.

24. *Naẓm al-la'ālī*, pp. 225–228.

25. Arjomand, *The Shadow of God*, p. 141.

26. *Qiṣaṣ*, p. 161 and *'Awā'id*, p. 191, respectively.

27. Al-Anṣārī, *Ṣirāṭ al-najāt* (Tehran: lithograph, 1290/1873), p. 1.

28. Sayyid Muḥammad Kāẓim Ṭabāṭabā'ī al-Yazdī, *al-'Urwa al-wuthqā* (Qumm, 1400/1980), pp. 2–3: *'al-taqlīd huwa al-iltizām bi'l-'amal bi qawl al-mujtahid al-mu'ayyan wa-in lam ya'mal ba'd, bal wa-law lam ya'khudh fatwā'*. By making *taqlīd* subject to the condition of 'even though not implemented practically', Ayatollah Yazdī means that the *mujtahid* will not be responsible for the proper implementation of his *fatwās*. See also Ayatollah R. Khomeinī, *Taḥrīr al-wasīla* (Beirut, 1408/1987), p. 7.

29. Ibid.

30. Arjomand, *The Shadow of God*, p. 222.

31. Riḍā Qulī Khān Hidāyat, *Rawḍat al-ṣafā-yi Nāṣirī* (Tehran, 1339 Sh./1960), vol. 9, pp. 240–241; 'Abd Allāh Mustawfī, *Zindigānī-yi man yā tārīkh-i ijtimā'ī wa idārī-yi dawra-yi*

*Qājār* (Tehran, 1326 Sh./1947), vol. 1, p. 49.

32. Hidāyat, *Rawḍa*, vol. 9, pp. 116 and 280.

33. Muḥammad Hāshim Āṣif, *Rustam al-Ḥukamāʾ*, *Rustam al-tawārīkh* (Tehran, 1352 Sh./1973), pp. 449 and 451.

34. Ḥasan Qāḍī Ṭabāṭabāʾī, '*Irshād-nāma-yi* Mīrzā-yi Qummī', *Majalla-yi Dānishkada-yi Adabīyāt-i Tabrīz*, 87 (Autumn, 1347/1968), p. 370; ʿAbd al-Hādī Ḥāʾirī, *Nakhustīn rūyārūʾīhā-yi andīshagarān* (Tehran, 1367 Sh./1988), pp. 327–328.

35. Ṭabāṭabāʾī, '*Irshād-nāma-yi* Mīrzā-yi Qummī', p. 382.

36. Lambton, 'A Nineteenth Century View of Jihād', p. 186

37. Hidāyat, *Rawḍa*, vol. 9, p. 241.

38. Arjomand, *The Shadow of God*, p. 230.

39. Al-Tunakābunī, *Qiṣaṣ*, p. 191.

40. Ibid., p. 137.

41. Shaykh Āghā Buzurg Tihrānī, *Ṭabaqāt aʿlām al-Shīʿa* (Mashhad, 1404/1984), vol. 2, p. 1205.

42. Hamid Algar, *Religion and State in Iran 1785–1906* (Berkeley, CA, 1969), p. 117.

43. Homa Nateq, *Iran dar rāhyābī-yi farhangī 1834–1848* (London, 1988), p. 57.

44. Ibid., p. 7.

45. Algar, *Religion and State*, p. 117.

46. ʿAbd al-Ḥusayn Majid Kafāʾī, *Margi dar nūr* (Tehran, 1359 Sh./1980), pp. 179–182.

47. Yaḥyā Dawlatābādī, *Tārīkh-i muʿāṣir: Ḥayāt-i Yaḥyā* (Tehran, 1371 Sh./1992), vol. 1, p, 50.

48. Lambton, 'A Nineteenth Century View of Jihād', p. 186.

49. In the Treaty of Turkaman Chāy (1243/1828), Article 7. See Saʿīd Nafīsī, *Tārīkh-i siyāsī wa-ijtimāʿī-yi Īrān dar dawra-yi muʿāṣir* (Tehran, 1362 Sh./1983), vol. 2, pp. 81 and 182.

50. Nikki Keddie, 'The Roots of the *ulamā*''s Power in Modern Iran', *SI*, 29 (1969), p. 32.

51. Nikki Keddie, *Iran and the Muslim World* (Houndmills, 1995), pp. 98, 277 and 279.

52. Ayatollah R. Khomeinī, *Wilāyat-i faqīh: ḥukūmat-i islāmī* (Tehran, 1398/1978).

53. Algar, *Religion and State*, pp. 257–258.

54. Arjomand, *The Shadow of God*, p. 7.

55. Ibid., p. 224.

56. Ibid., p. 228.

37

# Traditional Philosophy in Iran with Reference to Modern Trends

*Mehdi Mohaghegh*

From earliest times the people of Iran were interested in rational argumentation and philosophical discussion. In Zoroastrian literature there are frequent instances of the discussion of religious problems through philosophical reasoning. Jundi Shapur, founded in the third century AD, was an important academic centre not only for the study of medicine and mathematics, but also for philosophy. It is known, for example, that in 526 AD, when the Academy of Athens was closed by the emperor Justinian, six Greek scholars took refuge in Iran at Jundi Shapur, including the Neoplatonist Simplicius.

After the coming of Islam, philosophical studies continued to flourish, and philosophical argumentation became an important tool for the exegesis of the Qur'an. Although in the Qur'an there are no philosophical allusions, the commentators, most of whom were Iranians, read philosophical meanings into parts of it. For example, the verse (16:125) which reads 'Call to the way of thy Lord with wisdom (*ḥikma*) and goodly exhortation (*maw'iẓa*) and argue with them (*jādilhum*) in the best manner' has been interpreted as meaning that the Prophet was ordered to use first demonstration, then rhetoric and finally dialectic argumentation. The word 'philosophy' is not found in the Qur'an, but the word *ḥikma* occurs often and has been interpreted as meaning philosophical reasoning.

Islamic philosophy developed more fully in Iran than elsewhere because Shi'ism, unlike other Islamic communities and traditions, relies more on speculative reasoning than on simply following tradition. Whenever speculation and tradition contradict each other, the Shi'a interpret tradition in the light of reason. When the writings of the Greek philosophers were translated into Arabic, Iranian scholars were among the first to pay close attention to the Greek philosophical tradition.

Not only did they consider philosophy an independent discipline but they also applied philosophical argumentation to other disciplines. The grammarians of Basra employed Greek logic in their disputations; the Muʿtazilī commentators depended on philosophical reasoning for their rigorous interpretation of the Qurʾan; and underlying the principles of Islamic jurisprudence, employed by legal scholars, is a careful philosophical reasoning.

It is generally assumed that Islamic philosophy ended with the death of Ibn Rushd (Averroes). What died with Ibn Rushd, however, was the predominance of the Hellenistic Aristotelian system in Islamic thought. What lived on and flourished in Iran was philosophy in a new form – the philosophy of *ḥikmat*.

*Ḥikmat* is a uniquely structured combination of rational thinking and gnostic intuition, or, we might say, rationalist philosophy and mystical experience. It is a special type of rationalist philosophy based on the existential intuition of Reality, a result of turning the gnostic ideas and visions obtained through intellectual contemplation in philosophical speculation. Historically speaking, this tendency towards the spiritualisation of philosophy finds its origin in the metaphysical visions of Ibn ʿArabī and Suhrawardī. In making this observation, however, we must not lose sight of the fact that *ḥikmat* is also, at least in its formal make-up, a rationalist philosophy with a solid and strictly logical structure. And in this it goes beyond Ibn ʿArabī and Suhrawardī back to Avicenna and the first phase of the history of Islamic philosophy.

The most famous representatives of this school are Mīr Dāmād, Ṣadrā al-Dīn Shīrāzī and Sabzawārī. Although these philosophers became well known for their special interest in particular aspects of *ḥikmat* (e.g. substantial motion, perpetual duration, mental existence), each one dealt seriously with all aspects of philosophy. The last great master of this tradition was Mullā Hādī Sabzawārī, who lived in the nineteenth century. The followers of Sabzawārī are still engaged in teaching philosophy in Iran.

Sabzawārī's most important work is his *Sharḥ manẓūma*, a popular philosophical text which is still taught in traditional schools (*madrasa*s) and universities. A part of it was translated from Arabic into English by the present writer and T. Izutsu of Keio University and published in New York in 1977 under the title *The Metaphysics of Sabzawārī.*

In the first part of his book Sabzawārī deals with several problems regarding the notion of existence which may be summarised as follows:

1. Existence is self-evident and the so-called defining terms can neither be a definition nor a description, because existence is absolutely simple, having neither specific difference nor genus. Moreover, a defining term must always be more immediately known and clearer than the defined term. But nothing is more evident than existence. Sabzawārī states that although the notion of existence

is one of the best-known concepts, its deepest reality is in the extremity of hiddeness. So he harmonises the theses of those who assert that the notion of existence is self-evident with the theses of those who hold that the fundamental reality of existence is absolutely inconceivable. Finally, he concludes that all so-called defining terms of existence like, for example, 'self-subsistent' or 'that which allows of predication' etc. are only explanations of the word.

2. Existence is analogically predicated because the notion of existence is capable of being the source of division, that is to say, by the fact that existence is divided into the existence of the necessary and possible beings, and into substance and accident. Sabzawārī supports by this argument his theological view of understanding God, the Most High, through the following explanation:

   When we say that God is Existent we understand thereby the self-evident concept which remains the same in anything of which 'existence' can rightly be predicated; otherwise we have to understand it as meaning 'non-existent' or deprive our intellect of all knowledge of God. The same is true of His Attributes, because when we say, for example, 'He is Knowing' we mean by the word 'Knowing' one to whom things are disclosed, in which case we would have used the term in the same way in which we use it for human beings, so that the 'analogicity' of the word has been proved. Otherwise we would have to confess that either we mean by the word 'Knowing' the exact opposite of 'knowing', or we do not understand anything at all, in which case all prayers and acts of worship remain meaningless.

3. Existence is a single reality having various degrees of richness and poverty, intensity and weakness, priority and posteriority. It is comparable to light that can be perceived with the sense of sight, because the characteristics of light are those which are self-apparent and which make others apparent. Light is an analogical entity having various degrees. Since various lights are not different in terms of species – rather, they are different in terms of intensity and weakness – he considers existence as the real light, analogically predicated to the strongest and fullest luminosity which is the Light of lights and to the weakest which is darkness. Sabzawārī attributes this idea to the old Persian philosophers whom he calls al-Fahlawīyūn.
4. On the relation between existence and essence Sabzawārī states that whatever is found in the world is duality composed of 'quiddity' and 'existence', the former being that by which each thing is differentiated from all others, and the latter being a factor in which all things equally and without exception participate. This fundamental fact about the two ontological factors is what Sabzawārī refers to when he says that 'existence' is the principle of unity, while 'quiddities' raise only the dust of multiplicity.

Having shown some aspects of Sabzawārī's philosophical thinking, we conclude that *ḥikmat* is not an outcome of mere intellectual labour on the level of reason. It is rather an original product of the activity of keen analytical reason combined with, and backed by, a profound intuitive grasp of reality, or even of something beyond that kind of reality which is accessible to human consciousness. It represents logical thinking based on something grasped by what we might call supra-consciousness.

Finally, we have to state that since the Islamic Revolution of Iran Sabzawārī's philosophy has become more popular amongst the new generation. The first edition of the Persian translation of *The Metaphysics of Sabzawārī* by the late Murtaḍā Mutahharī has been one of the best-sellers of the last ten years. This is mainly due to the fact that his philosophy is a combination of the rational thinking of Avicenna, the illuminationist philosophy of Suhrawardī and the mysticism of Ibn ʿArabī, all under the light of traditional Shiʿi interpretation.

# 38

# Traces of Modernisation and Westernisation Some Comparative Considerations concerning Late Bukhāran Chronicles

*Bert G. Fragner*

The subject of this paper is to present the first results of an attempt to analyse a number of late chronicles referring to the Amirate of Bukhārā, all of them having been written between 1890 and 1930.[1] Some preliminary remarks should make clear my intentions.

1. Bukhāran amirs belonging to the so-called Mang'it dynasty ruled throughout a period of roughly 170 years, until 1920. On the one hand, they saw themselves as legitimate successors to the Shayboniy and Ashtarxoniy lines of late Chinggisid-Juchid *khāns* (uzb.: *xon*) of Transoxiana (arab.: *mā warā' al-nahr*) but on the other hand they stopped the centuries-long tradition of Chinggisid rule in Central Asia, replacing the Chinggisid rulers with members of a tribal aristocracy – in their case of the Mang'it tribe – and in this respect were comparable to the tribal Qunggirat rulers in Khīwa (uzb.: *Xeva*). These Mang'it rulers, instead of *khan* (*xon*) used to bear the title *amir*, as their primary semantic indication of rulership. There were various reasons for this choice of a new title for the rulers: Originally, the title *khan* (*xon*) was reserved for rulers of Chinggisid descent. It was for this reason that, in the fourteenth century, Amir Temur preferred the title amir to *khan* (*xon*), despite his personal title *gurakon* ('son-in-law', which referred to his kinship to the contemporary officially ruling *khans* from the Chaghatay affiliation of the Chinggisids). His descendants, the Temurid rulers, used therefore the title *mirzo* (derived from Persian *amīrzāda*). To the Mang'its, passing over from *khan* (*xon*) to amir meant on the one hand that they refrained from using a title connoting Chinggisid noblesse but on the other hand, it meant

that they presented themselves as rulers of Amir Temur's rank. But there might have been even more reasons: it was roughly around the same time that the ruler of neighbouring Afghanistan, Do'st Muḥammad Xon, decided also to adopt the title amir, in this case explicitly as an elliptical form for *amīr al-mu'minīn*, the 'Commander of the Believers' – a decision which made it clear that this ruler should no longer be understood as a primarily Pashtoon ruler but as the ruler of all Muslim inhabitants of his realm. The intention of the Mang'it rulers was obviously a similar one, but in their case it was against the background of the fact that until then rulers in Transoxiana had been of Chinggisid origin – and therefore bore the title *xon*. In this connection it deserves to be pointed out that members of another Uzbek dynasty of the eighteenth and nineteenth century, the 'Ming' rulers from Khokand (uzb.: *Qo'kon*) in the Farg'ona valley[2] had in mind to combine Chinggisid, and also Temurid legitimacy, with tribal legitimacy: for this reason they continued to use the title *xon* but added to it the invented but allusive title *amīr al-muslimīn*; in this way, they allowed themselves to use the titles *xon* and *amir* at an equal level.

2. During the heyday of the Mang'it dynasty, their Amirate lost a war against the conquering Russian army. As a consequence of the disaster of 14 May 1868 (the Russian conquest of Samarqand), the Amirate of Bukhārā lost, in the long run, its independence, and the amirs became protected vassals of the Russian Tzar.[3] Until the middle of the nineteenth century, the Central Asian principalities (Bukhārā, Khīwa, Khokand) represented, in a world-wide perspective, what Immanuel Wallerstein calls 'external areas', not yet really touched by the hegemonic intentions of colonial powers, either Russian or British.
3. During the following decades, the Amirate of Bukhārā became gradually subject to the various constraints of externally centred modernisation, whether technical (e.g. railway construction, new – westernised – architectural styles as, for instance, the *Imorati Sitorai Mohi Xossa* palace), or administrative, or intellectual. The last aspect used to attract more attention among researchers than the others.[4] In Soviet scholarship, influences passed to Bukhārā directly from Russia formed an important subject of scholarly study but the connections between Bukhāran intellectual life and the outside world were obviously more complicated than a simple one-way process. The Russian connection allowed contacts to be established not only with Tatar and other Russian Muslim modernists (the so-called Jadids) but also indirectly with the Ottoman empire, maybe even with Iran and, much too neglected until recently, with the British dominated Indian subcontinent.
4. All these influences from abroad caused reactions within the intellectual circles in the Amirate of Bukhārā. Some of these were reflex reactions to externally centred aspects of modernisation as can be seen in the confessions of originally reformist Jadid thinkers like Abdurrauf Fitrat[5] or Mahmud Xo'ja Behbudiy[6] who

reacted very sensitively towards what they experienced outside the Amirate. But there were also aspects of the transformation towards modernity which were only indirectly caused by such external events and elements. To put this into a more precise wording: I am looking for indications pointing towards the development of internal perceptions of modernity, not directly caused by external challenges but developed within the frame of indigenous tradition and, nevertheless, dealing with new, 'modern' aspects of the colonial age, and the early Soviet period. Let me go into some detail concerning the concepts of modernity and modernisation.

## Modernity and Modernisation

It is widely accepted that the concept of modernity is closely related to the phenomenon of 'enlightenment', and it seems also to be more or less accepted among historians, philosophers, and intellectuals that the origins of enlightenment are usually centred historically in post-medieval Europe, mainly in western Europe. Nevertheless, as early as the second part of the nineteenth century, a critical debate arose about the question of what the consequences of this 'Eurocentric' concept of modernity for non-European civilisations could be. This debate, from its very beginning, was stamped by the fact that it took place under worldwide conditions of imperialist colonialism. The central question in the debate was whether or not non-European civilisations had any possible means of finding a way to modernise without European guidance, that is to say *de facto* colonialist coercion? Some otherwise allegedly 'progressive' and evolutionary European thinkers were very explicit on this subject: Hegel, for instance, was convinced that Asian cultures were doomed to decline, and he saw the only way out of their ultimate crisis in modernisation, which according to him was nothing other than coerced westernisation. In some respects, Karl Marx followed Hegel's view: thinking about his concept of the 'Asiatic Mode of Production' as being a possible formative factor for a further so-called 'social formation' (in the Marxist sense, therefore on the same level as slave-holding society, Feudalism, Capitalism and Socialism), he also accepted the historically progressive role of colonialism, as for instance in his contributions to the daily press concerning British India after the Mutiny. According to this point of view, colonial rule would help to forcibly draw non-European civilisations (like India or China) into the turmoil of the progressive dynamics of modern world history – civilisations which Marx himself characterised as stagnant and ahistorical entities. On this point, Hegel and Marx shared the conservative perceptions of colonialism, interpreting worldwide imperialism as 'the white man's burden'.

Within leftist and anti-colonialist discourses, positions were developed step by step that severely criticised concepts like those just mentioned. We are accustomed to the term 'Third-Worldism' (*tièrsmondisme*) being used to denote such critical positions. It is interesting that early roots of Third-Worldism are to be traced back to the so-called Muslim regions of Russian colonialism and, later on, of the early Soviet realm: the Tatar revolutionary Sultangaliev was clearly one of the first Third-Worldists in the twentieth century, and it was in Tashkent that the Indian communist Manabendra Nath Roy tried, in vain, to transform the Comintern into an international Third-Worldist movement. As we all know, early Soviet dogmatic Marxism-Leninism did not follow Third-Worldism but tried to take a somewhat neutral position between Hegel's theoretical apotheosis of colonialism on the one side and consequent anti-colonialism, notwithstanding strong verbal confessions championing the victims of colonial rule.[7] This lame theoretical position meant that later, under Stalin's guidance, it was possible to celebrate officially Central Asia's 'unification with the Russian Empire' – meaning the Tzarist colonialisation – as an important progressive step in World History that served the aims of so-called Soviet Patriotism.

Yet, the question to be raised does not so much concern politics but the problem of whether modernity and modernisation outside the realm of Western civilisation can only be conceived of externally as deriving from Western initiative or, at least potentially, also as an indigenous phenomenon. A recent contribution to this on-going discussion was given by Reinhard Schulze (Bern, Switzerland), postulating a worldwide process of enlightenment during the eighteenth century, encompassing all cultures at the same level. This idea of simultaneous and also indigenous enlightenment all over the world, and particularly in the lands of Islamic civilisation, is absolutely fascinating, above all in terms of morality: this model offers a possibility of perceiving all human cultures as having been equal on the eve of modernity.

But there are some more considerations: For a great number of historians it might be difficult to follow Reinhard Schulze's concept of a worldwide, temporarily coincident, process of 'enlightenment' in his *Geschichte der Islamischen Welt im 20 Jahrhundert*. This coincidence forms a strong element in Schulze's argument, since otherwise the pretensions of equally enlightened societies would lose their validity. Moreover, might it not have been possible for some elements or modules, usually conceived of as constituent parts of 'modernity', to have existed in non-Western cultures much earlier than in the West, but without having caused a complex phenomenon like 'enlightenment'? The unique meeting and merging of such modules in Western modernity are, in that case, a process which must not be transferred forcibly from the Western model to the rest of mankind. But specific aspects of current modernity might have existed much earlier in various civilisations, and contemporary 'modernity' of the Western type might therefore also refer to indigenous traditions without being derived from them.

It is not the purpose of this paper to give a conclusive answer to this controversial question which is being vigorously discussed all over the world; but this consideration offers me a macro-theoretical frame within which I am going to discuss problems concerning the literary genre of historical chronicle-writing in Central Asia.

Within the so-called Islamic civilisation,[8] it was the Perso-Arabic historian al-Ṭabarī who established firm traditions of chronicle writing with his multi-volume *Ta'rīkh al-rusūl wa'l-mulūk*. But throughout centuries these traditions experienced different destinies when they turned out to be differentiated by linguistic criteria. While Arabic chronicle writing followed, for a long period, the annalistic scheme of al-Ṭabarī, chronicles written in Persian appear to be far more literary in their style, approach and outlook, thus giving greater space to the individual intentions of their authors. We encounter this point as early as the so-called *Ta'rīkh-i Balʿamī* an early Persian selective adaptation of al-Ṭabarī's œuvre, which concentrates much more on elements of story-telling than its great model and which was conceived in Samanid (*somoniy*) Bukhārā (tenth century CE). It was Central Asia and the so-called Islamic East, including the Iranian plateau from Azerbaijan to Khurasān and today's Afghanistan, which turned out to be the home of this new type of historiography. According to my hypothesis this kind of historical writing, which for a long period developed mainly in Persian and later passed into the Turkic languages – particularly Central Asian Chaghatay Turkic, was more closely associated with *adab*, i.e. literary structures than with *ʿilm al-ta'rīkh* (historiography) in the more narrow sense employed by al-Ṭabarī. This led to interesting consequences: Persophone chronicle writing soon developed into a specific literary genre in eastern Islamic civilisation, demanding from its authors a greater individuality than did the writing of other scholarly disciplines, including the Arabophone historiography of *ʿilm al-ta'rīkh*, i.e. history as a scholarly discipline. As a consequence, this genre displayed a wider range of themes, perceptions, stylistic varieties and possibilities for the selection and arrangement of material than the tradition of al-Ṭabarī could have foreseen. Therefore political criticism and, even more, the personal criticism of rulers and important individuals in public and political life are far from uncommon in the texts belonging to this tradition. The widespread prejudice that authors of this genre are to be castigated as sycophants and lickspittles favouring their rulers and protectors is therefore the result of revisionism. If we compare this originally mainly Persian medieval chronicle writing to the writings of Arab authors of the same age we may notice that the literary component in the latter case was usually far weaker. It is interesting to note that in late medieval Egypt and Syria, then ruled by the Turkic Mamluk sultans and their Turkic military elite, Arab historiography also began to develop literary or belletrist forms and elements.[9]

Notably during Mongol rule in the thirteenth and fourteenth centuries CE, this literary kind of Persian historical writing became extremely popular and, by the way, creative! Allow me just a short glimpse: Juwaynī's report on the history of the early Mongols (based on original Mongol sources and traditions) and Chinggis

Khan's rise to power – the so-called *Ta'rīkh-i jahān-gushāy* is a fascinating piece of literature comprising the ethnographic description of a culture hitherto unknown to the author's expected audience, comparable only to Central Asia's great scientist Abū Rayhān al-Birūnī's unique description of India (albeit written in Arabic) which, by the way, is not to be subsumed under the heading of 'historiography' proper. Another example is Rashīd al-Dīn's almost modernist *Jāmiʿ al-tawārīkh* which presents extremely sober, not to say naturalistic, reports on his personal experiences with the Mongol rulers and occupiers of Iran, combining these with a totally new concept of World History (including Europe, China, India and so on). Being a contemporary of Rashīd al-Dīn, Waṣāf composed a history on somewhat similar topics which is one of the most precious examples of this stylistically highly-refined Persian prose. We may therefore conclude that the expression and representation of the author's 'self', and even of a collective 'self' – something usually judged as a constituent element of modernity or modernisation – is in fact an important element of this specific tradition of writing history in what is known as the 'Islamic East'.

In post-Mongol Central Asia, mainly during Temurid rule, the linguistic criteria of this kind of 'historiographic literature' or 'literary historiography' gradually ceased being exclusively Persian: Chaghatay Turki started to develop as an additional medium for this genre: Ẓahiruddin Bobur's memoirs prove that the Chaghatay language could be effectively used within the general principles and scheme of our genre, and, at that period, seemed to be particularly useful for describing individual and personal intentions, at least for Turkophone authors. This applies particularly to works from Xorazm: The Turkic *Shajarat-ul-atrok* is much more in line with Persian texts like the Temurid *Mu'izz al-ansāb* or the late Mongol *Majmaʿ al-ansāb* than, for example, Sam'oniy's older classical Arabic genealogy the *Kitāb al-ansāb*. The Xorazmian Ogahiy's Turkic chronicle *Firdaus-ul-iqbol* also fits perfectly with Persophone traditions as described above.

After the fourteenth century, the basic principles of this genre transferred to the Indo-Pakistani Subcontinent. The genre even influenced the rise of Ottoman historiography, at least in its initial phase, but under the Ottomans a special historiographic genre – Ottoman imperial chronicle writing – gradually arose, distinguishing itself clearly from the 'Eastern Islamic tradition'. As an example: specialists in early modern Indian history frequently refer to a chronicle from the beginning of the eighteenth century which was written in Persian by the Hindu official Bhimsen as a remarkable milestone in the development of self-reflection and self-consciousness, thus indicating an awakening modernisation in Indian societal and political thinking. If we regard this Hindu author as part of a trend like the 'Persianate' tradition which includes Ẓahiruddin Bobur and Zaynuddin Vosifiy then the representation of Bhimsen's 'self' is no longer surprising. It is, at the very least, not so much an indication of change as of continuity.

Up to now, I have insisted firmly on the hypothesis that this historiographic genre, by virtue of its primarily literary character, gave a wide range of freedom to chronicle writers. These freedoms were eventually limited by concrete political conditions but not – and this is the essence of my message – by the constricting limitations of the genre's intrinsic traditions. The most striking example – excellent in terms of literary value, but by no means exceptional with regard to the genre's basic characteristics – is the great Central Asian writer Vosifiy's highly individualised and 'self-reflecting' chronicle *Badoyi'-ul-vaqoyi'* describing the politics and public and private life of late Temurid Samarqand and Transoxiana. This text is, in my view, nothing less than a piece of great world literature deserving to be translated into all major languages.

Why have I dealt at length with these rather abstract considerations? I am aiming at some kind of revisionism in evaluating a series of historiographic texts from Central Asia, or, more precisely, from the last phase of authochtonous statehood in Bukhārā, the period from 1890 to 1930.[10]

Chronicle writing from the period of Amir Muzaffar Mang'it (1860–1885) down to the end of the 1920s seems to me to be a genre of particular interest in terms of my quest for 'aspects of internal modernisation' in Bukhārā. I am just working on a detailed comparison of – at the time being – six historiographic texts from Bukhārā (some more may be added in future) dealing with the rule of the Mang'it amirs. All these six texts were written in Persian (or in Tajik). A major consideration in the selection of these texts was the fact that they are published and readily available for study. The oldest of my selected texts is Ahmad-i Maxdum 'Donish''s *Risola, yo muxtasare az ta'rixi saltanati xonidoni mang'itiya*[11] written in the 1890s. The next is Mirzo Abd-ul-Azim Somiy's *Ta'rixi salotini mang'itiyai Dorussaltanai Buxoroi sharif* from 1906/1907.[12] In the year 1920/1921, Sadriddin Ayni published the first version of his *Ta'rixi amironi mang'itiyai Buxoro* in the early Soviet journal *Shu'lai inqilob*; his text was republished as an enlarged version a year later by the State Publishing House of the Republic of Bukhārā.[13] Between 1923 and 1927 Muḥammad 'Alī Baljuvoniy wrote his commentary on the Bukhāran revolution under the title *Ta'rixi Nofe'iy*.[14] In 1928 a short Persian text was published in Paris bearing the title *Ta'rīxi Huzn-ul-milal-i-Buxoro*. Its author was Amir Olim-Xon himself, the last ruler of the Mang'it dynasty.[15] Only a year later (1929), Abdurrauf Fitrat conceived another essay on the late phase of the Bukhāran Amirate entitled *Davrai hukmronii Amir Olimxon*.[16] This list should at least be complemented by Mirzo Muḥammad Salim Bek 'Salimiy''s famous chronicle *Ta'rixi Salimiy*, written between 1917 and 1920, describing the history of Bukhārā from Chinggis Khan until the year 1920(!). About 70 per cent of Salimiy's text deals with the period between 1860 and 1920, thus representing something like the personal memoirs of its author.[17] I regret that I have had no chance of obtaining a copy of this hitherto unpublished but extremely important text, a manuscript of which is kept at the Beruniy Institute of Oriental Studies (Uzbek Academy of Sciences; *Aburayhon Beruniy nomidagi sharqshunoslik ilmgohi*), Tashkent. Until now, this lack of accessibility has prohibited me from using any other chronicles of the same period.

My intention is not so much to evaluate these texts according to their factual reliability but rather to trace the impact of the characteristics of traditional chronicle writing to be found in these texts, and to discover to what degree their authors transformed their historiographic traditions into a new type of history writing through extending their scope of subjects and themes – perhaps under the direct influence of external Western ideas or models, or through developing new trends within the given standards of their indigenous literary traditions.

Some ten or fifteen years ago, analysing these texts would have been thought a somewhat strange if not bizarre task for Western scholarship on the Islamic world. The Central Asian Amirates and Khanates, especially their history during the last two or three centuries, were perceived as being remote from mainstream research, just as Central Asia as a geographical concept was also regarded as remote in Western public consciousness. It is only a few years ago that things started to change: Bukhāran historiography from the Mang'it period is receiving more and more attention. While preparing the present paper, I found an extremely inspiring article by Jo-Ann Gross[18] dealing with one of the six texts being presented here and also concentrating on the author's report of the Russian conquest of the Amirate, just as I did myself. On the occasion of the twenty-seventh *Deutscher Orientalistentag* in Bonn (Germany) in September 1998, Anke von Kügelgen presented a paper on the historiography of the Mang'it dynasty, starting from the late eighteenth century but also treating – amongst other generally more ancient sources – Donish, Somiy and Ayniy (see note 10).

Dealing with the first and the oldest of 'my' six authors, Ahmadi Maxdum 'Donish', leads me to a revisionist judgement as far as a widespread prejudice found in Western orientalist scholarly literature, and particularly Soviet scholarly writing, is concerned. Donish used to be (and still is) celebrated as an important forerunner of the modernist Jadidi movement and, until recently, as the most eminent enlightened thinker of late nineteenth-century Bukhārā. In Soviet scholarship he was depicted as a critical and brave intellectual who, influenced by his encounter with Russian culture on the occasion of certain Bukhāran diplomatic missions to St Petersburg, developed open-minded political ideas.[19]

In contrast to this and looking at him through the perspective of my concept of traditional chronicle writing, it can be seen that Donish did not abandon any of the traditions of this genre, neither in the 'History of the Mang'it Dynasty', nor in his famous treatise, *Navodir-ul-vaqoyi'*, which as its title indicates was an open analogy of Zaynuddin Vosifiy's sixteenth-century *Badoyi'-ul-vaqoyi'*. Criticising the personal and individual characteristics of rulers, even despots, was not at all alien to the traditions of chronicle writing, as already explained above. We have striking examples of the fact that, like other pre-modern societies, the highest respect was rendered to the ruling institution as such but much less to the actual individuals representing this institution – the rulers themselves. The identification of the individual with the institution might even be rather more typical of contemporary historiography than of earlier periods! We find good examples of this hypothesis as early as in *Ta'rīkh-ī Bayhāqī* (eleventh century CE), in Rāwandī's *Rāḥat al-ṣudūr* (early thirteenth century CE), in Rashīd al-Dīn's writings, and in Zaynoddin Vosifiy's *Badoyi'-ul-vaqoyi'*, already mentioned as Donish's model for his *Navodir-ul-vaqoyi'*. Let me refer to a report by Vosifiy on an unusually harsh winter in Samarqand, which brought starvation to the inhabitants of the city: The writer and his friends decided to present a *qaṣida* to the Temurid ruler Abu Sa'id, in return for which they expected generous remuneration. They discussed at length the problem that the ruler did not have enough Persian to be able to understand such a *qaṣida*, and they themselves had no idea of Turki so that Vosifiy could not conceive of his poem in Abu Sa'id's language. Ultimately, they played a trick by using a courtier who knew both languages and was one of the ruler's confidantes. Vosifiy does not refrain from recounting bluntly his ruler's inability to understand the most important literary language of the age.[20] And he makes it clear that he well knew how to differentiate between the position of the ruler and his personality, the latter not having been subject to any substantial taboos, following the traditions of Eastern-Islamic chronicle writing.

So it seems plausible that Donish did not need to receive any specific Russian or Western 'enlightenment' in order to criticise the individual rulers of the Mang'it Dynasty as this criticism is found in his *risola*; and there is no reason to interpret this text as anything other than a traditional chronicle, including all its passages of criticism although they contain no specific indications of a concealed – but not approved – modernity on Donish's part. This applies also to his *Navodir-ul-vaqoyi'*.

According to L. M. Epifanova, Mirzo Abd-ul-Azim Somiy's chronicle was the private and much more critical version of another, earlier chronicle (*Tuhfati shohiy*) which was written for official purposes.[21] Disregarding Somiy's strong criticism of the Mang'it rulers, to be found in the unofficial *Tarixi salotini mang'itiya*, this author was far less esteemed a 'critical intellectual' and 'early indigenous modernist' than Donish was. I examined in detail his reports of the Russian conquest of the city of Samarqand. To me, it was interesting to notice that he paid no attention whatsoever to any Russian observations or to whether they might have been accessible to him or not. In his account of the loss of Samarqand, Russians simply do not feature! Instead of referring to Russian warfare, he severely criticises Amir Muzaffaruddin and his army. But even this kind of criticism is not alien to the Perso-Turkic traditions of chronicle writing. Jo-Ann Gross[22] tried painstakingly to trace any indications of modernity in Somiy's political ideas, but eventually she too ended by defining this author as somebody who was obviously untouched by 'modern' influences.

There can be no doubt that, immediately after the Bukhāran revolution and the establishment of the People's Republic of Bukhārā in 1920, Sadriddin Ayniy was an outspoken enemy not only of the individual rulers who held onto the institution of the amirate of Bukhārā but first and foremost, of the institution itself.[23] Around 1920 he was surely one of the most outstanding intellectual representatives of what had formerly been the Young Bukhārans and who had just started establishing the Bukhāran Communist Party, and one would expect to discover echoes of this attitude in his *Ta'rixi amironi Mang'itiyai Buxoro*. Alas! Despite his obvious revolutionary and anti-monarchical intentions, he would not abandon the limitations of traditional chronicle writing; it turns out that the 'rules of the genre', if I may use such an expression, allowed him to include all kinds of hostile and sarcastic criticism of the Mang'it amirs without casting aside the qualities of the traditional chronicle. An interesting but illustrative detail: Ayniy did not even acknowledge the existence of Ahmadi Donish's chronicle devoted to the same theme. Referring to his sources, Ayniy stresses, first of all, the importance he paid to Somiy's chronicle! Repeatedly, Ayniy includes long quotations from Somiy. Ayniy's description of the fall of Samarqand may serve as a good example in that he exactly follows Somiy's account, citing his source clearly. Moreover, there is a particularly interesting point in Ayniy's reference to his sources: he allegedly relied on the nineteenth-century Hungarian orientalist Arminius Vámbéry's accounts and studies of Central Asia[24] and particularly those on the so-called 'khanates', but this circumstance did not affect the character of his deliberately progressive chronicle: the text remained at least as traditional as Somiy's *Ta'rix* or Donish's *risola*.

This makes clear that, in the case of Ayniy, in order to import modernist or even revolutionary content a change in the traditional genre was not required. The individualist and critical potential inherent in Perso-Turkic chronicle writing could even allow for Ayniy's radical intentions without breaking the 'rules of the genre'.

A comparison with the late amir's *Ta'rixi Huzn-ul-milali Buxoro* offers some reason for surprise: leaving aside the traditional wording of its title, this is not a traditional chronicle but in many respects a Western-style 'modern' essay, corresponding rather to aspects of contemporary international journalism. The text was lithographed in the beautiful *nasta'liq ductus* of the Arabic script but it was promoted by exiled representatives of the amir's political interests in Paris. Its author tried, at the very least, to offer a sober survey of what the vanished Amirate had once been in terms of a Central Asian political entity. In content far more nostalgic and counter-revolutionary than Ayniy's chronicle, the *Huzn-ul-milal* turns out to be much more profoundly transformed in its literary structure in the sense of being an 'externally centred' (i.e. Westernised) modernity than other examples given.

A similar statement can be made with regard to Baljuvoniy's short chronicle *Ta'rixi Nofe'iy* from the late 1920s. Being also rather conservative in content, it clearly goes beyond the literary limits of traditional chronicle writing and appears to be somewhat like a journalist's report on contemporary political and administrative affairs.

Of the six texts referring to the history of the later Mang'it rulers in the Amirate of Bukhārā that I have tried to compare, there is just one to be found in which modernist and critical thinking is perfectly married to subsuming the centuries-old literary traditions of chronicle writing. This is Abdurrauf Fitrat's *Davrai hukmronii Amir Olimxon*. Fitrat wrote this essay at the order of The State Publishing House of Tajikistan ('*Nashritoj*') in 1929, at a time when he was already exposed to official Soviet criticism because of his 'nationalist' attitudes. It might be worth analysing Fitrat's philosophical, literary and political attitudes in the context of the 'Third-Worldism' I referred to earlier. For him, the creation of specific stylistic measures and methods, albeit also in terms of literature and language, was an important theme. He strove enthusiastically in the 1920s for an appropriate and modernised literisation of Chaghatay Turki and (by no means a contradiction), for the dethroning of classical Persian as the generally accepted literary language, seeking to replace it with a popular and more vernacular standardised 'Tajik' which would have, according to Fitrat and similar thinkers, opened the linguistic structures of Persian to modern usage. This was clearly due to the impact of international debates on modernity and modernisation that he had become acquainted with during his stay in Constantinople about the year 1910. These discussions were not invented by the Young Turks but had been taken over from the Panslavist and other national movements that were basically established along the lines of the German philosopher and writer Herder's romantic nationalism. Fitrat, amongst other modernists, introduced these debates to Central Asia, and he made a serious attempt to develop specific guidelines for modernity and modernisation in and of his home region. In his treatise on the Bukhāran amirs, especially when writing about the last one, he makes an ostentatious break with all the literary traditions of chronicle writing. No trace of formal or stylistic respect for past rulers and, above all, the ruling institution, can be found. He curses the Mang'it '*hukmrons*' – the rulers – when he finds cursing them appropriate, he uses a polemical, semi-vernacular style of language far removed from the requirements of traditional chronicle writing. And, above all, Fitrat uses his pamphlet for promoting and trying out his ideas on language structure and modernisation.

Fitrat's contributions to policies on language remained hidden for more than fifty years from the peoples of Central Asia, Uzbeks and Tajiks as well. When his report *Davrai hukmronii Amir Olimxon* was published, he had already been imprisoned. Eight years later he perished in a prison camp.

Let me return to my initial considerations: Donish and Ayniy provide evidence that political criticism was far from alien to the basic requirements of the conventional genre of chronicle writing. To develop this kind of criticism there was no need to leave the path of tradition in favour of any new, so-called 'modern', patterns created by the West. In contradistinction to prejudices found among many Western (and Westernised) orientalists the tradition of chronicle writing in the Islamic East did not require a stagnant and dogmatic self-discipline by authors towards the political conditions and powerful individuals of their age. Therefore the 'enlightened' Donish did not respond to Russian coercion or influence – he was in a situation in which he could develop his intellectual criticism on the basis of the indigenous traditions of eastern Islamic and Central Asian political writing, i.e. historiography. This suited a revolutionary like Ayniy who could thus write a traditional chronicle in order to convey all the revolutionary messages he wanted to promote.

In contrast, Baljuvoniy and, even more so, Amir Olim-Xon, did not hesitate to adopt alien, that is to say rather Westernised and 'modern' patterns when writing the anti-revolutionary texts mentioned above.

And it was the sworn progressive and emancipating nationalist Fitrat who, at least in terms of literary criteria, turns out to have behaved like a real internationalist following discourses and patterns of argument from all over the world, whenever he felt their employment was useful for, or indispensable to, his intellectual goals. Of 'my' six authors he was the only one who tried consciously to strive for modern content and modern stylistic requirements, thus modernising Central Asian traditions of history writing along lines that were internationally accepted during his lifetime.

What is the 'message' to be drawn from these considerations? Through thorough analysis, many aspects and elements apparently 'modern' or 'new' may turn out to be part of long-established pre-modern traditions. A modernised appearance does not necessarily indicate new content, and even radical new ideas may appear in the guise of traditional literary forms. And even in the case of a convergence of both aspects of modernist innovation – content and form – there is certainly yet no sound guarantee for its permanent success, as the tragic fate of Abdurrauf Fitrat can illustrate.

This leads me to a final theoretical consideration: it seems that theoretical arguments on modernisation as indicated by whatever given parameters, for instance evidence of aspects of individualism or social criticism, is somewhat ill suited to the context of the cultural and historical area of Bukhārā – and also to contemporary Central Asia.

Recently, there has appeared a perhaps better suited and more useful theoretical model that can be applied to explain some of the seemingly paradoxical elements dealt with in this article: the German cultural anthropologist Andreas Hartmann (University of Münster) offered a tool that was ideal for researching cultural problems, particularly when studying apparently contradictory aspects of modernisation. In his article '*Transformation und Wiederkehr*' ('Transformation and Return'),[25] he points out that cultural change usually has two aspects – systemic and individual. As regards the systemic, he sees the phenomenon 'change' mainly under the aspect of transformation. This systemic transformation is, according to Hartmann, accompanied by an individual and personal aspect of tradition, which he calls '*Wiederkehr*' (return). This means that systemic transformation – in our case thematic modernisation – may be often accompanied (even unconsciously) by personal aspects of traditional attitudes, the unforeseen and unexpected 'return' of traditional ideas and structures, notwithstanding intended modernisation. Moreover, according to Hartmann's reasoning systemic change – transformation – relies dialectically and permanently on another element of tradition, which is called '*Rekurrenz*' by Hartmann. According to Hartmann, *Rekurrenz* denominates the phenomenon that every case of transformation needs to define its starting point, and bears therefore an element of immanent tradition in itself.

The concise and limited examples I give in my paper fit more or less with this theoretical model of change contrasted with tradition. Over a long period of modernisation, *Rekurrenz* cannot be avoided in a system, because any change can only be marked by defining its starting point. On the other hand, the individuals – in our case, the authors – will always be endangered by unexpected cases of '*Wiederkehr*' (return) caused by random systemic '*Rekurrenz*'. If we take this model into consideration, apparently paradoxical and contradictory phenomena suddenly appear to fit together. Following this model, we may easily see that the example of Fitrat is the only one that does not fit with these interrelated elements. So it might have been not only by mere chance and for external reasons that his initially promising concept of modernisation failed when confronted by reality and moreover, we can see that this phenomenon is corroborated by theoretical evidence as well.

## Notes

1. I aplogise for not having quoted a recently published, excellent study on Bukhāran chronicle writing by Anke von Kügelen, *Die Legitimierung der mittelasiatischen Mangitendynastie in der Werken ihrer Historiker (18 und 19 Jahrhundert)* (Istanbul, 2002). With certain exceptions, all Arabo-Perso-Turkic terms and names are given in a latinised transcription close to the recent latinised alphabet of Uzbek. This implies that certain Perso-Tajik words will also appear in this Latino-Uzbek scriptural version which is basically very close to the Latin representation of standard Cyrillic Tajik orthography, disregarding some minor deviations. To me, this seems to be a rather practical way to optimise Jirī Beckas latinisation of Tajik-Cyrillic script, as found in Jan Rypka's *History of Iranian Literature* (Dordrecht, 1968). This also goes for geographical terms, with the exception of some generally used Europeanised expressions like Bukhārā instead of Buxoro, Khīva instead of Xeva, or Tashkent instead of Toshkent. As for Samarqand, I decided to use 'q' instead of 'k'. Given the fact that standard Uzbek orthography does not represent the Turkic synharmonic vowel system, I prefer the use

of 'I' to 'i' or 'I' in words like 'Mang'it' (instead of 'Manghit' or 'Manghıt'). For the standard latinised Uzbek 'o' I use the 'o'' widely in practical use in present-day Uzbekistan. According to this newly implemented orthographic system, 'g'' represents the 'ghayn' of Arabic script (see also: 'Mang'it').

2. The Uzbek word '*ming*' which means literally 'thousand' must not be confused with the famous Chinese dynasty of that name. It refers to an Uzbek tribal federation.

3. According to the treaty of 18 July 1868, the Bukhāran amir had, among other concessions, to submit control of the cities and *viloyat*s of Samarqand and Katta-Qurg'on to Russia. A detailed account of the conquest and its consequences is to be found in Seymour Becker, *Russia's Protectorates in Central Asia: Bukhara and Khiva 1865–1924* (Cambridge, MA, 1968), pp. 25–43.

4. As a typical Western study, Hélène Carrère d'Encausse's *Reforme et revolution chèz les musulmans de l'empire russe* (Paris, 1966), English translation: *Islam and the Russian Empire: Reform and Revolution in Central Asia* (Berkeley and Los Angeles, CA, 1988) can be mentioned.

5. As for Fitrat, there are a number of recent studies referring to this outstanding character in Central Asia's modern history, among them some passages within the already mentioned work by Hélène Carrère d'Encausse (Paris, 1966; Berkeley and Los Angeles, CA, 1988); further, Alexandre A. Bennigsen and S. Enders Wimbush, *Muslim National Communism in the Soviet Union. A Revolutionary Strategy for the Colonial World* (Chicago, IL, 1979), p. 197; Hisao Komatsu, 'The Evolution of Group Identity among Bukharan Intellectuals in 1911–1928: An Overview', in *The Memoirs of the Toyo Bunko* (Nr. 47) (Tokyo, 1989), pp. 115–144; a study about Fitrat was recently published in Turkey: Yusuf Avci, *Fıtrat ve Eserleri* (Ankara, 1997); moreover, see Ingeborg Baldauf, 'Abdurauf Fitrat', in *Kindlers Literatur Lexikon* (Munich, 1998). Already in various earlier writings by Baymirza Hayit, Fitrat is usually referred to as an Uzbek or Turkic nationalist. At his presentation at the Third European Conference of Iranian Studies (Cambridge, 1995), Mikhail Zand (Jerusalem) examined Fitrat's early efforts at reforming and modernising the Persian/Tajik language in writing his *Munozirai mudarrisi Buxoroiy bo yak nafar farangiy dar Hindiston dar borai makotibi jadida* (Istanbul, 1327/1911); also Komatsu interprets Fitrat more as a Bukhāran patriotic intellectual than as exclusively bound to Turkism or Uzbekism. Ingeborg Baldauf, *'Kraevedenie' and Uzbek National Consciousness* (Bloomington, IN, 1992) points to the ideological and programmatic changes in Fitrat's thinking on language politics. One should not forget Fitrat's efforts in the latinisation of Tajik, when he was accused of 'Panturkism' because of his intention to make Tajik and Uzbek orthography as compatible as possible. Already, when Fitrat was temporarily imprisoned, this intention was quietly made reality. So that by standardising Uzbek along the phonetic structure of the so-called 'Iranised' urban dialects of Samarqand and Tashkent and also, after Fitrat's death, by cyrillising both scripts, despite some minor deviations, Uzbek and Tajik orthographies became practically interchangeable. Amongst others, Komatsu, Zand and also Avci, refer to the fact, that Sadriddin Ayniy, in his *Namunai adabiyoti tojik* (Moscow, 1926) stresses Fitrat's contribution to the emergence of the contemporary Tajik literary language.

6. Mahmudxo, ja Behbudiy, *Tanlangan asarlar*, ed. Begali Qosimov (Tashkent, 1997). 'Bixbudi, Maxmud-Xvadzha', in *Islam na territorii bïvshey Rossiyskoy imperii. Entsiklopedicheskiy slovar*' (Moscow, 1998), vïpusk I, pp. 18–19. Ingeborg Baldauf, 'Maḥmūd-Xvadzha

Behbūdī and his journal *ojna* (Samarkand, 1913–1915): Pragmatic pluralism versus ethnicist monism', in Bert G. Fragner, Christa Fragner and Roxanne Haag-Higuchi, ed., *Mehrsprachigkeit und Sprachkontakt in iranischen Kulturen,* not yet published.

7. Carrère-d'Encausse gives a beautiful example of this, quoting a letter written by Lenin at the end of 1921 to a certain Adolph Joffe, fighting against what he calls Great-Russian chauvinism: 'It is terribly important for all our Weltpolitik to win the confidence of the natives; to win it over and over again; to prove that we are not imperialists, that we will not tolerate any deviation in that direction. It is a worldwide issue, and that is no exaggeration. There you must be especially strict. It will have an effect on India and the East; it is no joke, it calls for exceptional caution.' *Islam and the Russian Empire*, p. 188, following Lenin, *Collected Works* (Moscow, 1970), vol. 45, pp. 197–198.

8. This is not the place to discuss the validity of the concept of a World of Islam, Islamic Civilisation etc. as an 'international system'. I confine myself to mentioning a recent contribution to the debate on this subject by Stefan Reichmuth: 'The Interplay of Local Developments and Transnational Relations in the Islamic World: Perceptions and Perspectives', in Anke von Kügelgen, Michael Kemper and Allan J. Frank, ed., *Muslim Culture in Russia and Central Asia from the 18th to the Early 20th Centuries*, vol. 2, *Inter-Regional and Inter-Ethnic Relations* (Berlin, 1998), pp. 5–38. In the following passages, I adhere rather to a modified model: the idea of an 'Islamic communicative and cultural sub-system in the Eastern Islamic World' stamped by the Perso-Turkic linguistic and cultural element and to be seen apart from the Mediterranean regions of Islam. In the 'Middle Period' (according to Richard Bulliet) the Ottomans represented, to a limited extent, a somewhat intermediary position between these two areas.

9. I have dealt in more detail with the phenomenon of the markedly narrative character of Persian (and 'Persianate') historiography in my *Die 'Persophonie': Regionalität, Identität und Sprachkontakt in der Geschichte Asiens* (Halle and Berlin, 1999), pp. 51–58.

10. The most recent intrinsic and detailed study of Bukhāran chronicle writing from the Mang'it period will be published soon by Anke von Kügelgen, who devoted her *Habilitationsschrift* at the University of Bochum ('Ruhr-Universität-Bochum') to this theme.

11. Ahmad Maxdumi Donish, *Risola, yo muxtasare az ta'rixi xonadoni Mang'itiya*, ed. Abdulghaniy Mirzoev (Stalinobod, 1960).

12. Mīrzā 'Abdal'ẓīm Sāmī, *Ta'rīx-i salāṭīn-i mangītīya (istoriya mangïtskix gosudarey)*, ed. L. M. Epifanova (Moscow, 1962) (facsimile, introduction and Russian translation by Epifanova).

13. This text was published again in Sadriddin Ayni, *Kulliyot, jildi 10* (Dushanbe, 1966), pp. 7–191.

14. Muḥammad 'Alī ibn-i Muḥammad Sayyid Baljuwānī, *Ta'rīkh-i Nāfi'ī*, ed. Ahror Muxtorov (Dushanbe, 1994) in the Arabic script.

15. A'lā-Ḥaẓrat Amīr 'Ālim Xān, *Ta'rīx-i ḥuzn al-milal-i Buxārā*, ed. General Ḥajjī Yūsuf Muqīm-Bay (Paris, 1928) in *nasta'līq*; further editions were published in Peshawar, Kabul and Tehran: A'lā-Ḥaẓrat Amīr 'Ālim Xān, '*Ta'rīx-i ḥuzn al-milal-i Buxārā*', ed. Abu Xalid, in *Mī–āq-i xūn*, second year (Peshawar, 1365 Sh./1986–1987); A'lā-Ḥaẓrat Amīr 'Ālim Xān, *Ta'rīx-i ḥuzn al-milal-i Buxārā, ḫaṭirat-i A'lā-Ḥaẓrat Amīr 'Ālim Xān 1910–1920 mīlādī*, ed. Muḥammad Akbar 'Aḵiq-Kābulī (Kabul, 1370 Sh./1991–1992); Amīr 'Ālim Xān, *Xāṭirahā-yi Amīr 'Ālim Xān* [*Ta'rīx-i ḥuzn al-milal-i Buxārā*], ed. Aḥrār Muxtāruf (=Ahror Muxtorov)

(Tehran, 1373 Sh./1994–1995). Moreover, an Uzbek translation was published in Tashkent: Amir Sayyid Olimxon, *Buxoro halqining hasrati tarixi*, tr. Abdusodiq Irisov (Tashkent, 1991).

16. ʻAbd ar-Raʼūf Fiṭrat, *Daura-yi ḥukmrānī-yi Amīr ʻĀlim-Xān* (Tashkent and Stalinobod, 1930) in the Arabic script. Tajik republication in the Cyrillic script: Fitrat, *Davrai hukmronii Amir Olimxon*, ed. Asomuddin Nasriddinov, with an introduction by A. Muhiddinov (Dushanbe, 1991).

17. See Ch. A. Stori, *Persidskaya literatura. Bio-bibliograficheskiy obzor. Pererabotal i dopolnil Yu. E. Bregel* (Moscow, 1972), vol. 2, pp. 1174–1177 (nr. 1035).

18. Jo-Ann Gross, 'Historical Memory, Cultural Identity, and Change: Mirza ʻAbd al-ʻAziz [*sic*!] Sami's Representation of the Russian Conquest of Bukhara', in Daniel R. Brower and Edward J. Lazzerini, ed., *Russia's Orient. Imperial Borderlands and Peoples, 1700–1917* (Bloomington and Indianapolis, IN, 1997), pp. 203–226.

19. This attitude towards Donish is a commonplace in Soviet scholarly writing. As for Western views, Becker, *Russia's Protectorates in Central Asia*, p. 202, Carrère d'Encausse, *Islam and the Russian Empire*, pp. 62–64, and more recently, Turaj Atabaki, 'A study in the history of Bukhāran modernism. The journey of Aḥmad Dānish to St Petersburg', in Ingeborg Baldauf and Michael Friederich, ed., *Bamberger Zentralasienstudien* (Berlin, 1993), pp. 263–269. Here, Atabaki makes the observation that Donish offered precise and vivid descriptions of strange places, following a model which he – Atabaki – ascribes to, amongst others, Balzac, as an indication of modernity in writing. I must confess that I have not yet dealt with this aspect of '*chronotopos*' ('time-space', according to Mikhail Bakhtin) as a possible element of modernity in narrative texts. The phenomenon, however, occurs frequently in 19th- and 20th-century prose, not only written in French but in English, German, and Russian too. As a recent intercultural contribution to this intriguing theme see Roxane Haag-Higuchi, 'Schreckliches Teheran – der Roman als Vermittler moderner Weltsicht?' (forthcoming).

20. Zayn al-Dīn Wāṣifī, *Badāyiʼ al-waqāyiʼ*, ed. Aleksander Boldïrev (Tehran, 1349 Sh./ 1970–1971), vol. 1, pp. 62–72. As for Vosifiy's unveiled and sarcastic criticism on the orgiastic sexual debauchery among prominent members of the political and social elite see Lutz Rzehak, 'Ungleichheit in der Gleichheit: Materialien zu männlich-männlicher Erotik in iranischsprachigen Kulturen Mittelasiens', in Michaela Ofitsch, ed., *Eros, Liebe und Zuneigung in der Indogermania* (Graz, 1997), pp. 37–64.

21. See Epifanova's discussion of this subject (pp. 14–21) in the facsimile edition of Somiy's chronicle.

22. See her article mentioned above in note 15; according to her, 'given the scholarly emphasis that has been placed on … reformist movements in the study of the "Russian Orient", Sami's text provides a contrasting perspective, rooted in the cultural history of Central Asia, from which to view local sentiment regarding the conquest period and the changes that were to follow'. (p. 221)

23. Sadriddin Ayniy (d. 1954) was celebrated as the founder and *spiritus rector* of Tajik Soviet literature, and also as an important contributor to early Soviet literature in Uzbek. A biographical monograph on Ayniy, based mainly on Soviet sources and evaluation but with an overall critical view, was written by Jirī Becka, *Sadriddin Ayni – Father of Modern Tajik Culture* (Naples, 1980). On Ayniy's political opinions and ideas in the 1920s see Gero Fedtke, 'Jadids, Young Bukharans, Communists and the Bukharan Revolution: From an

Ideological Debate in the Early Soviet Union', in Anke von Kügelgen, Michael Kemper and Allen J. Frank, ed., *Muslim Culture in Russia and Central Asia from the 18th to the Early 20th Centuries* (Berlin, 1998), vol. 2, pp. 483–512.

24. Vámbéry's reports were unusually popular in the second half of the 19th century, in Hungary and the German-speaking countries, and particularly in England. There are numerous editions and variants of his travelogues on Central Asia. I confine myself to mentioning Hermann Vámbéry, *Geschichte Bochara's oder Transoxaniens von den frühesten Zeiten bis auf die Gegenwart. Nach orientalischen benützten und unbenützten handschriftlichen Geschichtsquellen* (Stuttgart, 1872), 2 vols., and *Reise in Mittelasien von Teheran durch die Turkmanische Wüste an der Ostküste des Kaspischen Meeres nach Chiwa, Bochara und Samarkand, ausgeführt im Jahr 1863* (Leipzig, 1865).

25. Andreas Hartmann, 'Transformation und Wiederkehr', in Heidrun Alzheimer-Haller, ed., *Bayerische Blätter für Volkskunde 1997* (Würzburg, 1997), pp. 76–87.